Chevrolet & GMC Pick-ups Automotive Repair Manual

by Ken Freund and John H Haynes
Member of the Guild of Motoring Writers

Models covered:
Chevrolet and GMC pick-ups
1988 through 2000

Suburban, Blazer, Jimmy, Tahoe and Yukon
1992 through 2000

Two- and four-wheel drive versions
Does not include diesel or heavy-duty (C3HD) model information

(4H4 - 24065)

ABCDE
FGH

Haynes Publishing Group
Sparkford Nr Yeovil
Somerset BA22 7JJ England

Haynes North America, Inc
861 Lawrence Drive
Newbury Park
California 91320 USA

Acknowledgements

We are grateful to Dominik Scharding for providing the 454 SS pick-up seen in certain photos. Wiring diagrams and certain illustrations originated exclusively for Haynes North America, Inc. by Valley Forge Technical Information Services. Technical writers who contributed to this project include Mike Stubblefield, Jon LaCourse, Jeff Killingsworth and Robert Maddox.

A book in the Haynes Automotive Repair Manual Series

Printed in the U.S.A.

ISBN 1 56392 426 9

Library of Congress Control Number: 2001089936

01-304

Contents

Haynes mechanic, author and photographer with Chevrolet 1500 pick-up

About this manual

Its purpose

The purpose of this manual is to help you get the best value from your vehicle. It can do so in several ways. It can help you decide what work must be done, even if you choose to have it done by a dealer service department or a repair shop; it provides information and procedures for routine maintenance and servicing; and it offers diagnostic and repair procedures to follow when trouble occurs.

We hope you use the manual to tackle the work yourself. For many simpler jobs, doing it yourself may be quicker than arranging an appointment to get the vehicle into a shop and making the trips to leave it and pick it up. More importantly, a lot of money can be saved by avoiding the expense the shop must pass on to you to cover its labor and overhead costs. An added benefit is the sense of satisfaction and accomplishment that you feel after doing the job yourself.

Using the manual

The manual is divided into Chapters. Each Chapter is divided into numbered Sections, which are headed in bold type between horizontal lines. Each Section consists of consecutively numbered paragraphs.

At the beginning of each numbered Section you will be referred to any illustrations which apply to the procedures in that Section. The reference numbers used in illustration captions pinpoint the pertinent Section and the Step within that Section. That is, illustration 3.2 means the illustration refers to Section 3 and Step (or paragraph) 2 within that Section.

Procedures, once described in the text, are not normally repeated. When it's necessary to refer to another Chapter, the reference will be given as Chapter and Section number. Cross references given without use of the word "Chapter" apply to Sections and/or paragraphs in the same Chapter. For example, "see Section 8" means in the same Chapter.

References to the left or right side of the vehicle assume you are sitting in the driver's seat, facing forward.

Even though we have prepared this manual with extreme care, neither the publisher nor the author can accept responsibility for any errors in, or omissions from, the information given.

NOTE

A **Note** provides information necessary to properly complete a procedure or information which will make the procedure easier to understand.

CAUTION

A **Caution** provides a special procedure or special steps which must be taken while completing the procedure where the Caution is found. Not heeding a Caution can result in damage to the assembly being worked on.

WARNING

A **Warning** provides a special procedure or special steps which must be taken while completing the procedure where the Warning is found. Not heeding a Warning can result in personal injury.

Introduction to the full-size Chevrolet and GMC pick-ups

The 1988 and later full-size (C and K model) Chevrolet and GMC pick-up trucks have a conventional front engine/rear wheel drive layout. Four-wheel drive (4WD) is available on some models.

The V6 and V8 engines equipped in these vehicles use Throttle Body Injection (TBI) on early models (1988 through 1995) or Central Sequential Fuel Injection (Central SFI) on late models (1996 through 2000). Power from the engine is transferred to either a four or five-speed manual or three or four-speed automatic transmission. A transfer case and driveshaft are used to drive the front driveaxles on 4WD models.

The suspension is independent at the front. On 2WD models, coil springs are used at the front. On 4WD models, torsion bars are used instead of coil springs. The solid rear axle is suspended by leaf springs on all models. Conventional shock absorbers are used at both the front and rear.

The steering box is mounted to the left of the engine and is connected to the steering arms through a series of rods. Power assist is standard on all models.

The brakes are disc at the front and drums at the rear, with power assist standard. Most models are equipped with an Antilock Braking System (ABS).

Vehicle identification numbers

Modifications are a continuing and unpublicized process in vehicle manufacturing. Since spare parts manuals and lists are compiled on a numerical basis, the individual vehicle numbers are essential to correctly identify the component required.

Vehicle Identification Number (VIN)

This very important identification number is stamped on a plate attached to the left side of the dashboard, just inside the windshield on the driver's side of the vehicle **(see illustration)**. The VIN also appears on the Vehicle Certificate of Title and Registration. It contains information such as where and when the vehicle was manufactured, the model year and the body style.

Certification label

The Certification label is attached to the rear edge of the left door. The label contains the name of the manufacturer, the month and year of production, the Gross Vehicle Weight Rating (GVWR) and the certification statement.

Service parts identification label

This label is located inside the glove compartment door. It lists the VIN number, wheelbase, paint number, options and other information specific to the vehicle to which it's attached. Always refer to this label when ordering parts

Engine identification number

The engine ID number is normally located on a machined surface at the front edge of the block, under the right cylinder head. It may also be located at the left rear edge of the block, above the oil filter **(see illustration)**.

Automatic transmission identification number

The ID number on automatic transmissions is located on the right side, either

The vehicle identification number (VIN) is visible from outside the vehicle through the driver's side of the windshield

V8 engine number locations (arrow)

V6 engine number locations (arrow)

Location of the ID number on the four-speed
automatic transmission

stamped into a machined surface above the pan or on a metal tag **(see illustrations)**.

Transfer case identification number (4WD models)

This number is on a metal tag attached to the rear case half or the extension housing.

Rear axle identification number

The rear axle identification number is normally stamped into the top surface of the right axle tube.

Vehicle Emissions Control Information (VECI) label

This label is normally located on top of the radiator fan shroud. It contains information on the emissions control equipment installed on the vehicle as well as tune-up specifications.

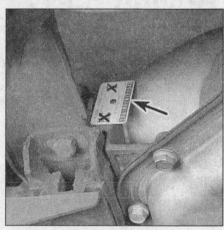

Location of the automatic transmission
identification number

Buying parts

Replacement parts are available from many sources, which generally fall into one of two categories - authorized dealer parts departments and independent retail auto parts stores. Our advice concerning these parts is as follows:

Retail auto parts stores: Good auto parts stores will stock frequently needed components which wear out relatively fast, such as clutch components, exhaust systems, brake parts, tune-up parts, etc. These stores often supply new or reconditioned parts on an exchange basis, which can save a considerable amount of money. Discount auto parts stores are often very good places to buy materials and parts needed for general vehicle maintenance such as oil, grease, filters, spark plugs, belts, touch-up paint, bulbs, etc. They also usually sell tools and general accessories, have convenient hours, charge lower prices and can often be found not far from home.

Authorized dealer parts department: This is the best source for parts which are unique to the vehicle and not generally available elsewhere (such as major engine parts, transmission parts, trim pieces, etc.).

Warranty information: If the vehicle is still covered under warranty, be sure that any replacement parts purchased - regardless of the source - do not invalidate the warranty!

To be sure of obtaining the correct parts, have engine and chassis numbers available and, if possible, take the old parts along for positive identification.

Maintenance techniques, tools and working facilities

Maintenance techniques

There are a number of techniques involved in maintenance and repair that will be referred to throughout this manual. Application of these techniques will enable the home mechanic to be more efficient, better organized and capable of performing the various tasks properly, which will ensure that the repair job is thorough and complete.

Fasteners

Fasteners are nuts, bolts, studs and screws used to hold two or more parts together. There are a few things to keep in mind when working with fasteners. Almost all of them use a locking device of some type, either a lockwasher, locknut, locking tab or thread adhesive. All threaded fasteners should be clean and straight, with undamaged threads and undamaged corners on the hex head where the wrench fits. Develop the habit of replacing all damaged nuts and bolts with new ones. Special locknuts with nylon or fiber inserts can only be used once. If they are removed, they lose their locking ability and must be replaced with new ones.

Rusted nuts and bolts should be treated with a penetrating fluid to ease removal and prevent breakage. Some mechanics use turpentine in a spout-type oil can, which works quite well. After applying the rust penetrant, let it work for a few minutes before trying to loosen the nut or bolt. Badly rusted fasteners may have to be chiseled or sawed off or removed with a special nut breaker, available at tool stores.

If a bolt or stud breaks off in an assembly, it can be drilled and removed with a special tool commonly available for this purpose. Most automotive machine shops can perform this task, as well as other repair procedures, such as the repair of threaded holes that have been stripped out.

Flat washers and lockwashers, when removed from an assembly, should always be replaced exactly as removed. Replace any damaged washers with new ones. Never use a lockwasher on any soft metal surface (such as aluminum), thin sheet metal or plastic.

Fastener sizes

For a number of reasons, automobile manufacturers are making wider and wider use of metric fasteners. Therefore, it is important to be able to tell the difference between standard (sometimes called U.S. or SAE) and metric hardware, since they cannot be interchanged.

All bolts, whether standard or metric, are sized according to diameter, thread pitch and length. For example, a standard 1/2 - 13 x 1 bolt is 1/2 inch in diameter, has 13 threads per inch and is 1 inch long. An M12 - 1.75 x 25 metric bolt is 12 mm in diameter, has a thread pitch of 1.75 mm (the distance between threads) and is 25 mm long. The two bolts are nearly identical, and easily confused, but they are not interchangeable.

In addition to the differences in diameter, thread pitch and length, metric and standard bolts can also be distinguished by examining the bolt heads. To begin with, the distance across the flats on a standard bolt head is measured in inches, while the same dimension on a metric bolt is sized in millimeters (the same is true for nuts). As a result, a standard wrench should not be used on a metric bolt and a metric wrench should not be used on a standard bolt. Also, most standard bolts have slashes radiating out from the center of the head to denote the grade or strength of the bolt, which is an indication of the amount of torque that can be applied to it. The greater the number of slashes, the greater the strength of the bolt. Grades 0 through 5 are commonly used on automobiles. Metric bolts have a property class (grade) number, rather than a slash, molded into their heads to indicate bolt strength. In this case, the higher the number, the stronger the bolt. Property class numbers 8.8, 9.8 and 10.9 are commonly used on automobiles.

Strength markings can also be used to distinguish standard hex nuts from metric hex nuts. Many standard nuts have dots stamped into one side, while metric nuts are marked with a number. The greater the number of dots, or the higher the number, the greater the strength of the nut.

Metric studs are also marked on their ends according to property class (grade). Larger studs are numbered (the same as metric bolts), while smaller studs carry a geometric code to denote grade.

It should be noted that many fasteners, especially Grades 0 through 2, have no distinguishing marks on them. When such is the case, the only way to determine whether it is standard or metric is to measure the thread pitch or compare it to a known fastener of the same size.

Standard fasteners are often referred to as SAE, as opposed to metric. However, it should be noted that SAE technically refers to a non-metric fine thread fastener only. Coarse thread non-metric fasteners are referred to as USS sizes.

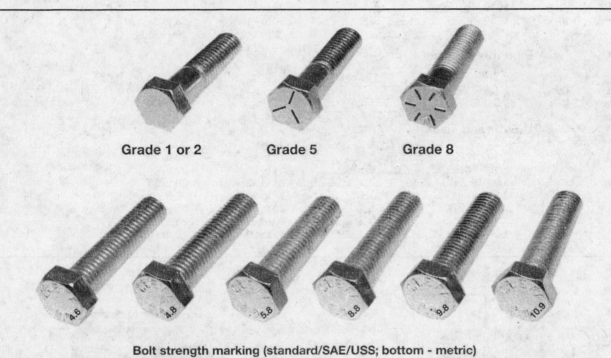

Grade 1 or 2   Grade 5   Grade 8

Bolt strength marking (standard/SAE/USS; bottom - metric)

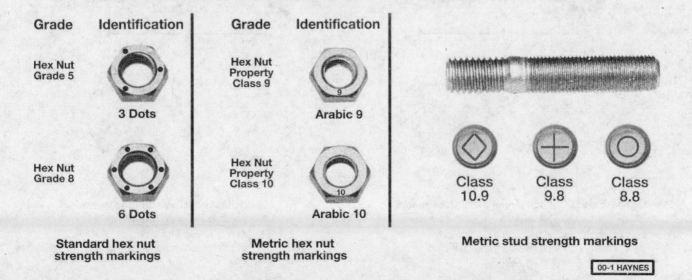

Grade	Identification
Hex Nut Grade 5	3 Dots
Hex Nut Grade 8	6 Dots

Grade	Identification
Hex Nut Property Class 9	Arabic 9
Hex Nut Property Class 10	Arabic 10

Class 10.9   Class 9.8   Class 8.8

Standard hex nut strength markings

Metric hex nut strength markings

Metric stud strength markings

Since fasteners of the same size (both standard and metric) may have different strength ratings, be sure to reinstall any bolts, studs or nuts removed from your vehicle in their original locations. Also, when replacing a fastener with a new one, make sure that the new one has a strength rating equal to or greater than the original.

Tightening sequences and procedures

Most threaded fasteners should be tightened to a specific torque value (torque is the twisting force applied to a threaded component such as a nut or bolt). Overtightening the fastener can weaken it and cause it to break, while undertightening can cause it to eventually come loose. Bolts, screws and studs, depending on the material they are made of and their thread diameters, have specific torque values, many of which are noted in the Specifications at the beginning of each Chapter. Be sure to follow the torque recommendations closely. For fasteners not assigned a specific torque, a general torque value chart is presented here as a guide. These torque values are for dry (unlubricated) fasteners threaded into steel or cast iron (not aluminum). As was previously mentioned, the size and grade of a fastener determine the amount of torque that can safely be applied to it. The figures listed here are approximate for Grade 2 and Grade 3 fasteners. Higher grades can tolerate higher torque values.

Fasteners laid out in a pattern, such as cylinder head bolts, oil pan bolts, differential cover bolts, etc., must be loosened or tightened in sequence to avoid warping the component. This sequence will normally be shown in the appropriate Chapter. If a specific pattern is not given, the following procedures can be used to prevent warping.

Metric thread sizes	Ft-lbs	Nm
M-6	6 to 9	9 to 12
M-8	14 to 21	19 to 28
M-10	28 to 40	38 to 54
M-12	50 to 71	68 to 96
M-14	80 to 140	109 to 154
Pipe thread sizes		
1/8	5 to 8	7 to 10
1/4	12 to 18	17 to 24
3/8	22 to 33	30 to 44
1/2	25 to 35	34 to 47
U.S. thread sizes		
1/4 - 20	6 to 9	9 to 12
5/16 - 18	12 to 18	17 to 24
5/16 - 24	14 to 20	19 to 27
3/8 - 16	22 to 32	30 to 43
3/8 - 24	27 to 38	37 to 51
7/16 - 14	40 to 55	55 to 74
7/16 - 20	40 to 60	55 to 81
1/2 - 13	55 to 80	75 to 108

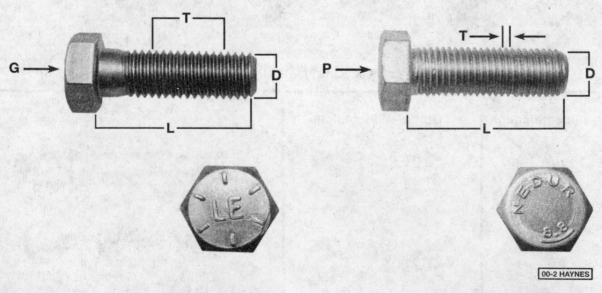

00-2 HAYNES

Standard (SAE and USS) bolt dimensions/grade marks

- G Grade marks (bolt strength)
- L Length (in inches)
- T Thread pitch (number of threads per inch)
- D Nominal diameter (in inches)

Metric bolt dimensions/grade marks

- P Property class (bolt strength)
- L Length (in millimeters)
- T Thread pitch (distance between threads in millimeters)
- D Diameter

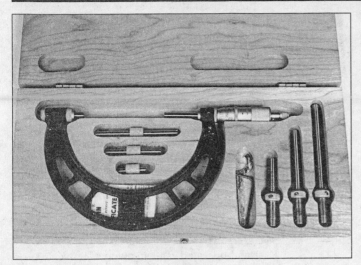

Micrometer set

Dial indicator set

Initially, the bolts or nuts should be assembled finger-tight only. Next, they should be tightened one full turn each, in a criss-cross or diagonal pattern. After each one has been tightened one full turn, return to the first one and tighten them all one-half turn, following the same pattern. Finally, tighten each of them one-quarter turn at a time until each fastener has been tightened to the proper torque. To loosen and remove the fasteners, the procedure would be reversed.

Component disassembly

Component disassembly should be done with care and purpose to help ensure that the parts go back together properly. Always keep track of the sequence in which parts are removed. Make note of special characteristics or marks on parts that can be installed more than one way, such as a grooved thrust washer on a shaft. It is a good idea to lay the disassembled parts out on a clean surface in the order that they were removed. It may also be helpful to make sketches or take instant photos of components before removal.

When removing fasteners from a component, keep track of their locations. Sometimes threading a bolt back in a part, or putting the washers and nut back on a stud, can prevent mix-ups later. If nuts and bolts cannot be returned to their original locations, they should be kept in a compartmented box or a series of small boxes. A cupcake or muffin tin is ideal for this purpose, since each cavity can hold the bolts and nuts from a particular area (i.e. oil pan bolts, valve cover bolts, engine mount bolts, etc.). A pan of this type is especially helpful when working on assemblies with very small parts, such as the carburetor, alternator, valve train or interior dash and trim pieces. The cavities can be marked with paint or tape to identify the contents.

Whenever wiring looms, harnesses or connectors are separated, it is a good idea to identify the two halves with numbered pieces of masking tape so they can be easily reconnected.

Gasket sealing surfaces

Throughout any vehicle, gaskets are used to seal the mating surfaces between two parts and keep lubricants, fluids, vacuum or pressure contained in an assembly.

Many times these gaskets are coated with a liquid or paste-type gasket sealing compound before assembly. Age, heat and pressure can sometimes cause the two parts to stick together so tightly that they are very difficult to separate. Often, the assembly can be loosened by striking it with a soft-face hammer near the mating surfaces. A regular hammer can be used if a block of wood is placed between the hammer and the part. Do not hammer on cast parts or parts that could be easily damaged. With any particularly stubborn part, always recheck to make sure that every fastener has been removed.

Avoid using a screwdriver or bar to pry apart an assembly, as they can easily mar the gasket sealing surfaces of the parts, which must remain smooth. If prying is absolutely necessary, use an old broom handle, but keep in mind that extra clean up will be necessary if the wood splinters.

After the parts are separated, the old gasket must be carefully scraped off and the gasket surfaces cleaned. Stubborn gasket material can be soaked with rust penetrant or treated with a special chemical to soften it so it can be easily scraped off. A scraper can be fashioned from a piece of copper tubing by flattening and sharpening one end. Copper is recommended because it is usually softer than the surfaces to be scraped, which reduces the chance of gouging the part. Some gaskets can be removed with a wire brush, but regardless of the method used, the mating surfaces must be left clean and smooth. If for some reason the gasket surface is gouged, then a gasket sealer thick enough to fill scratches will have to be used during reassembly of the components. For most applications, a non-drying (or semi-drying) gasket sealer should be used.

Hose removal tips

Warning: *If the vehicle is equipped with air conditioning, do not disconnect any of the A/C hoses without first having the system depressurized by a dealer service department or a service station.*

Hose removal precautions closely parallel gasket removal precautions. Avoid scratching or gouging the surface that the hose mates against or the connection may leak. This is especially true for radiator hoses. Because of various chemical reactions, the rubber in hoses can bond itself to the metal spigot that the hose fits over. To remove a hose, first loosen the hose clamps that secure it to the spigot. Then, with slip-joint pliers, grab the hose at the clamp and rotate it around the spigot. Work it back and forth until it is completely free, then pull it off. Silicone or other lubricants will ease removal if they can be applied between the hose and the outside of the spigot. Apply the same lubricant to the inside of the hose and the outside of the spigot to simplify installation.

As a last resort (and if the hose is to be replaced with a new one anyway), the rubber can be slit with a knife and the hose peeled from the spigot. If this must be done, be careful that the metal connection is not damaged.

If a hose clamp is broken or damaged, do not reuse it. Wire-type clamps usually weaken with age, so it is a good idea to replace them with screw-type clamps whenever a hose is removed.

Tools

A selection of good tools is a basic requirement for anyone who plans to maintain and repair his or her own vehicle. For the owner who has few tools, the initial investment might seem high, but when compared to the spiraling costs of professional auto maintenance and repair, it is a wise one.

To help the owner decide which tools are needed to perform the tasks detailed in this manual, the following tool lists are offered: *Maintenance and minor repair,*

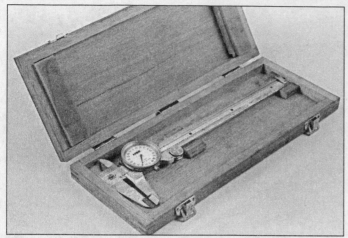

Dial caliper

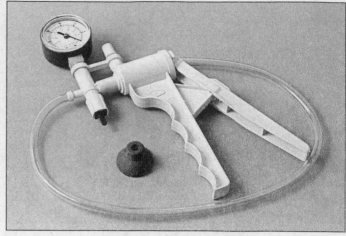

Hand-operated vacuum pump

Timing light

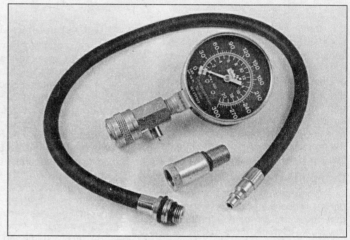

Compression gauge with spark plug hole adapter

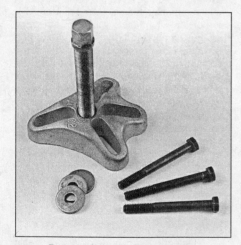

Damper/steering wheel puller

General purpose puller

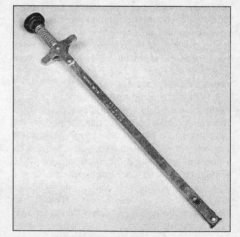

Hydraulic lifter removal tool

Repair/overhaul and *Special*.

The newcomer to practical mechanics should start off with the *maintenance and minor repair* tool kit, which is adequate for the simpler jobs performed on a vehicle. Then, as confidence and experience grow, the owner can tackle more difficult tasks, buying additional tools as they are needed.

Eventually the basic kit will be expanded into the *repair and overhaul* tool set. Over a period of time, the experienced do-it-yourselfer will assemble a tool set complete enough for most repair and overhaul procedures and will add tools from the special category when it is felt that the expense is justified by the frequency of use.

Maintenance and minor repair tool kit

The tools in this list should be considered the minimum required for performance of routine maintenance, servicing and minor repair work. We recommend the purchase of combination wrenches (box-end and open-

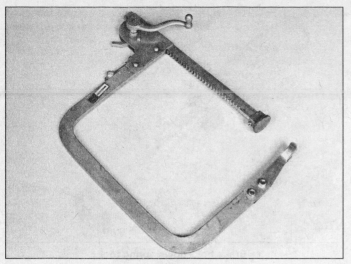

Valve spring compressor

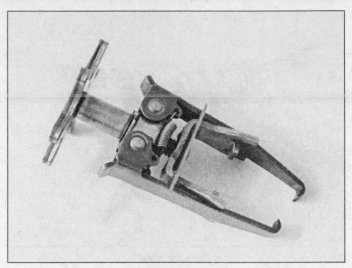

Valve spring compressor

Ridge reamer

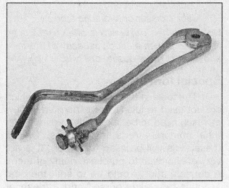

Piston ring groove cleaning tool

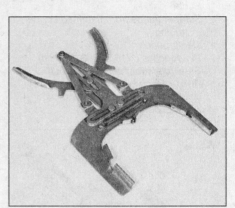

Ring removal/installation tool

end combined in one wrench). While more expensive than open end wrenches, they offer the advantages of both types of wrench.

> Combination wrench set (1/4-inch to
>   1 inch or 6 mm to 19 mm)
> Adjustable wrench, 8 inch
> Spark plug wrench with rubber insert
> Spark plug gap adjusting tool
> Feeler gauge set
> Brake bleeder wrench
> Standard screwdriver (5/16-inch x
>   6 inch)
> Phillips screwdriver (No. 2 x 6 inch)
> Combination pliers - 6 inch
> Hacksaw and assortment of blades
> Tire pressure gauge
> Grease gun
> Oil can
> Fine emery cloth
> Wire brush
> Battery post and cable cleaning tool
> Oil filter wrench
> Funnel (medium size)
> Safety goggles
> Jackstands (2)
> Drain pan

Note: *If basic tune-ups are going to be part of routine maintenance, it will be necessary to purchase a good quality stroboscopic timing*

light and combination tachometer/dwell meter. Although they are included in the list of special tools, it is mentioned here because they are absolutely necessary for tuning most vehicles properly.

Repair and overhaul tool set

These tools are essential for anyone who plans to perform major repairs and are in addition to those in the maintenance and minor repair tool kit. Included is a comprehensive set of sockets which, though expensive, are invaluable because of their versatility, especially when various extensions and drives are available. We recommend the 1/2-inch drive over the 3/8-inch drive. Although the larger drive is bulky and more expensive, it has the capacity of accepting a very wide range of large sockets. Ideally, however, the mechanic should have a 3/8-inch drive set and a 1/2-inch drive set.

> Socket set(s)
> Reversible ratchet
> Extension - 10 inch
> Universal joint
> Torque wrench (same size drive as
>   sockets)
> Ball peen hammer - 8 ounce
> Soft-face hammer (plastic/rubber)

Ring compressor

> Standard screwdriver (1/4-inch x 6 inch)
> Standard screwdriver (stubby -
>   5/16-inch)
> Phillips screwdriver (No. 3 x 8 inch)
> Phillips screwdriver (stubby - No. 2)
> Pliers - vise grip
> Pliers - lineman's
> Pliers - needle nose
> Pliers - snap-ring (internal and external)
> Cold chisel - 1/2-inch

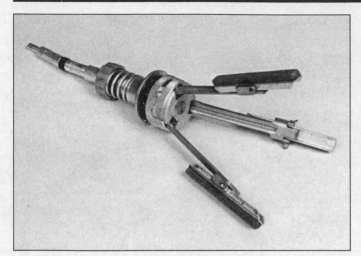

Cylinder hone

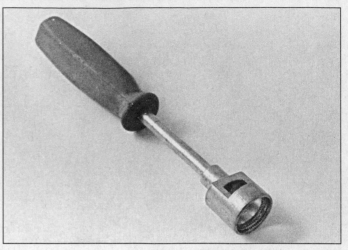

Brake hold-down spring tool

Scribe
Scraper (made from flattened copper tubing)
Centerpunch
Pin punches (1/16, 1/8, 3/16-inch)
Steel rule/straightedge - 12 inch
Allen wrench set (1/8 to 3/8-inch or 4 mm to 10 mm)
A selection of files

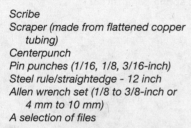

Brake cylinder hone

Wire brush (large)
Jackstands (second set)
Jack (scissor or hydraulic type)
Note: *Another tool which is often useful is an electric drill with a chuck capacity of 3/8-inch and a set of good quality drill bits.*

Special tools

The tools in this list include those which are not used regularly, are expensive to buy, or which need to be used in accordance with their manufacturer's instructions. Unless these tools will be used frequently, it is not very economical to purchase many of them. A consideration would be to split the cost and use between yourself and a friend or friends. In addition, most of these tools can be obtained from a tool rental shop on a temporary basis.

This list primarily contains only those tools and instruments widely available to the public, and not those special tools produced by the vehicle manufacturer for distribution to dealer service departments. Occasionally, references to the manufacturer's special tools are included in the text of this manual. Generally, an alternative method of doing the job without the special tool is offered. How-

ever, sometimes there is no alternative to their use. Where this is the case, and the tool cannot be purchased or borrowed, the work should be turned over to the dealer service department or an automotive repair shop.

Valve spring compressor
Piston ring groove cleaning tool
Piston ring compressor
Piston ring installation tool
Cylinder compression gauge
Cylinder ridge reamer
Cylinder surfacing hone
Cylinder bore gauge
Micrometers and/or dial calipers
Hydraulic lifter removal tool
Balljoint separator
Universal-type puller
Impact screwdriver
Dial indicator set
Stroboscopic timing light (inductive pick-up)
Hand operated vacuum/pressure pump
Tachometer/dwell meter
Universal electrical multimeter
Cable hoist
Brake spring removal and installation tools
Floor jack

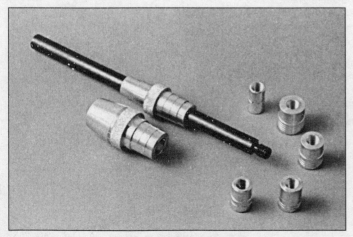

Clutch plate alignment tool

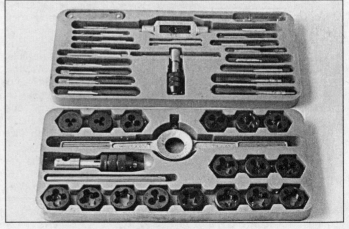

Tap and die set

Buying tools

For the do-it-yourselfer who is just starting to get involved in vehicle maintenance and repair, there are a number of options available when purchasing tools. If maintenance and minor repair is the extent of the work to be done, the purchase of individual tools is satisfactory. If, on the other hand, extensive work is planned, it would be a good idea to purchase a modest tool set from one of the large retail chain stores. A set can usually be bought at a substantial savings over the individual tool prices, and they often come with a tool box. As additional tools are needed, add-on sets, individual tools and a larger tool box can be purchased to expand the tool selection. Building a tool set gradually allows the cost of the tools to be spread over a longer period of time and gives the mechanic the freedom to choose only those tools that will actually be used.

Tool stores will often be the only source of some of the special tools that are needed, but regardless of where tools are bought, try to avoid cheap ones, especially when buying screwdrivers and sockets, because they won't last very long. The expense involved in replacing cheap tools will eventually be greater than the initial cost of quality tools.

Care and maintenance of tools

Good tools are expensive, so it makes sense to treat them with respect. Keep them clean and in usable condition and store them properly when not in use. Always wipe off any dirt, grease or metal chips before putting them away. Never leave tools lying around in the work area. Upon completion of a job, always check closely under the hood for tools that may have been left there so they won't get lost during a test drive.

Some tools, such as screwdrivers, pliers, wrenches and sockets, can be hung on a panel mounted on the garage or workshop wall, while others should be kept in a tool box or tray. Measuring instruments, gauges, meters, etc. must be carefully stored where they cannot be damaged by weather or impact from other tools.

When tools are used with care and stored properly, they will last a very long time. Even with the best of care, though, tools will wear out if used frequently. When a tool is damaged or worn out, replace it. Subsequent jobs will be safer and more enjoyable if you do.

How to repair damaged threads

Sometimes, the internal threads of a nut or bolt hole can become stripped, usually from overtightening. Stripping threads is an all-too-common occurrence, especially when working with aluminum parts, because aluminum is so soft that it easily strips out.

Usually, external or internal threads are only partially stripped. After they've been cleaned up with a tap or die, they'll still work. Sometimes, however, threads are badly damaged. When this happens, you've got three choices:

1) *Drill and tap the hole to the next suitable oversize and install a larger diameter bolt, screw or stud.*

2) *Drill and tap the hole to accept a threaded plug, then drill and tap the plug to the original screw size. You can also buy a plug already threaded to the original size. Then you simply drill a hole to the specified size, then run the threaded plug into the hole with a bolt and jam nut. Once the plug is fully seated, remove the jam nut and bolt.*

3) *The third method uses a patented thread repair kit like Heli-Coil or Slimsert. These easy-to-use kits are designed to repair damaged threads in straight-through holes and blind holes. Both are available as kits which can handle a variety of sizes and thread patterns. Drill the hole, then tap it with the special included tap. Install the Heli-Coil and the hole is back to its original diameter and thread pitch.*

Regardless of which method you use, be sure to proceed calmly and carefully. A little impatience or carelessness during one of these relatively simple procedures can ruin your whole day's work and cost you a bundle if you wreck an expensive part.

Working facilities

Not to be overlooked when discussing tools is the workshop. If anything more than routine maintenance is to be carried out, some sort of suitable work area is essential.

It is understood, and appreciated, that many home mechanics do not have a good workshop or garage available, and end up removing an engine or doing major repairs outside. It is recommended, however, that the overhaul or repair be completed under the cover of a roof.

A clean, flat workbench or table of comfortable working height is an absolute necessity. The workbench should be equipped with a vise that has a jaw opening of at least four inches.

As mentioned previously, some clean, dry storage space is also required for tools, as well as the lubricants, fluids, cleaning solvents, etc. which soon become necessary.

Sometimes waste oil and fluids, drained from the engine or cooling system during normal maintenance or repairs, present a disposal problem. To avoid pouring them on the ground or into a sewage system, pour the used fluids into large containers, seal them with caps and take them to an authorized disposal site or recycling center. Plastic jugs, such as old antifreeze containers, are ideal for this purpose.

Always keep a supply of old newspapers and clean rags available. Old towels are excellent for mopping up spills. Many mechanics use rolls of paper towels for most work because they are readily available and disposable. To help keep the area under the vehicle clean, a large cardboard box can be cut open and flattened to protect the garage or shop floor.

Whenever working over a painted surface, such as when leaning over a fender to service something under the hood, always cover it with an old blanket or bedspread to protect the finish. Vinyl covered pads, made especially for this purpose, are available at auto parts stores.

Booster battery (jump) starting

Observe the following precautions when using a booster battery to start a vehicle:

a) *Before connecting the booster battery, make sure the ignition switch is in the Off position.*

b) *Turn off the lights, heater and other electrical loads.*

c) *Your eyes should be shielded. Safety goggles are a good idea.*

d) *Make sure the booster battery is the same voltage as the dead one in the vehicle.*

e) *The two vehicles MUST NOT TOUCH each other.*

f) *Make sure the transmission is in Neutral (manual transaxle) or Park (automatic transaxle).*

g) *If the booster battery is not a maintenance-free type, remove the vent caps and lay a cloth over the vent holes.*

Connect the red jumper cable to the positive (+) terminals of each battery.

Connect one end of the black cable to the negative (-) terminal of the booster battery. The other end of this cable should be connected to a good ground on the engine block **(see illustration)**. Make sure the cable will not come into contact with the fan, drivebelts or other moving parts of the engine.

Start the engine using the booster battery, then, with the engine running at idle speed, disconnect the jumper cables in the reverse order of connection.

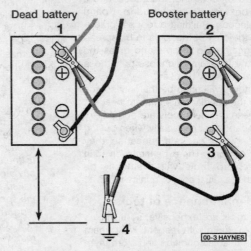

Make the booster battery cable connections in the numerical order shown (note that the negative cable of the booster battery is NOT attached to the negative terminal of the dead battery)

Anti-theft audio system

General information

1   Some of these models are equipped with THEFTLOCK audio systems, which include an anti-theft feature that will render the stereo inoperative if stolen. If the power source to the stereo is cut with the anti-theft feature activated, the stereo will be inoperative. Even if the power source is immediately re-connected, the stereo will not function.

2   If your vehicle is equipped with this anti-theft system, do not disconnect the battery, remove the stereo or disconnect related components unless you have either turned off the feature or have the individual ID (code) number for the stereo.

Disabling the anti-theft feature

3   Press the stereo's 1 and 4 buttons at the same time for five seconds with the ignition on and the radio power off. The display will show SEC, indicating the unit is in the secure mode (anti-theft feature enabled).

4   Press the MIN button. The display will show "000".

5   Press the MIN button until the last two numbers are the same as your secret code.

6   Press HR until the first one or two numbers displayed match your code. The numbers will be displayed as entered.

7   Press AM/FM. If the display shows "_ _ _" you have successfully disabled the anti-theft feature. If SEC is displayed, the code you entered was incorrect and the anti-theft feature is still enabled.

Unlocking the stereo after a power loss

8   When the power is restored to the stereo, the stereo won't turn on and LOC will appear on the display. Enter your ID code as follows, without pausing more than 15 seconds between Steps.

9   Turn the ignition switch to ON, but leave the stereo off.

10   Press the MIN button. "000" should display.

11   Press the HR button to make the last two numbers match your code, then release the button.

12   Press the HR button until the first one or two numbers match your code.

13   Press AM/FM. SEC should appear, indicating the stereo is unlocked. If LOC appears, the numbers you entered were not correct and the stereo is still inoperative.

14   You should have the code written down in a secure place, for use in unlocking the THEFTLOCK feature. **Note:** *When performing the above procedures, you are allowed only eight tries. After that, the system shuts down for an hour, with the radio displaying "INOP." At the end of that period, you have another three tries, after which you will have to bring the vehicle to your dealer for activation.*

Jacking and towing

Jacking

The jack supplied with the vehicle should only be used for raising the vehicle when changing a tire or placing jackstands under the frame. **Warning:** *Never work under the vehicle or start the engine while the jack is being used as the only means of support.*

The vehicle should be on level ground with the hazard flashers on, the wheels blocked, the parking brake applied and the transmission in Park (automatic) or Reverse (manual). If a tire is being changed, loosen the lug nuts one-half turn and leave them in place until the wheel is raised off the ground. Make sure no one is in the vehicle as it's being raised with the jack.

Place the jack under the vehicle suspension in the indicated position **(see illustrations)**. Operate the jack with a slow, smooth motion until the wheel is raised off the ground. Remove the lug nuts, pull off the wheel, install the spare and thread the lug nuts back on with the beveled sides facing in. Tighten them snugly, but wait until the vehicle is lowered to tighten them completely.

Lower the vehicle, remove the jack and tighten the nuts (if loosened or removed) in a criss-cross pattern. If possible, tighten them with a torque wrench (see Chapter 1 for the torque figures). If you don't have access to a torque wrench, have the nuts checked by a service station or repair shop as soon as possible.

Towing

These vehicles can be towed with all four wheels on the ground, provided speeds don't exceed 35 mph and the distance is less than 50 miles.

Equipment specifically designed for towing should be used and must be attached to the main structural members of the vehicle, not the bumper or brackets.

Safety is a major consideration when towing and all applicable state and local laws must be obeyed. A safety chain must be used at all times.

While towing, the parking brake should be released and the transmission and transfer case (if equipped) must be in Neutral. The steering must be unlocked (ignition switch in the Off position). Remember that power steering and power brakes will not work with the engine off.

Front jack location

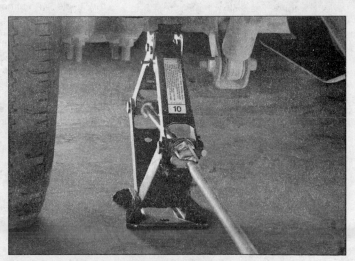

Rear jack location

Automotive chemicals and lubricants

A number of automotive chemicals and lubricants are available for use during vehicle maintenance and repair. They include a wide variety of products ranging from cleaning solvents and degreasers to lubricants and protective sprays for rubber, plastic and vinyl.

Cleaners

Carburetor cleaner and choke cleaner is a strong solvent for gum, varnish and carbon. Most carburetor cleaners leave a dry-type lubricant film which will not harden or gum up. Because of this film it is not recommended for use on electrical components.

Brake system cleaner is used to remove grease and brake fluid from the brake system, where clean surfaces are absolutely necessary. It leaves no residue and often eliminates brake squeal caused by contaminants.

Electrical cleaner removes oxidation, corrosion and carbon deposits from electrical contacts, restoring full current flow. It can also be used to clean spark plugs, carburetor jets, voltage regulators and other parts where an oil-free surface is desired.

Demoisturants remove water and moisture from electrical components such as alternators, voltage regulators, electrical connectors and fuse blocks. They are non-conductive, non-corrosive and non-flammable.

Degreasers are heavy-duty solvents used to remove grease from the outside of the engine and from chassis components. They can be sprayed or brushed on and, depending on the type, are rinsed off either with water or solvent.

Lubricants

Motor oil is the lubricant formulated for use in engines. It normally contains a wide variety of additives to prevent corrosion and reduce foaming and wear. Motor oil comes in various weights (viscosity ratings) from 0 to 50. The recommended weight of the oil depends on the season, temperature and the demands on the engine. Light oil is used in cold climates and under light load conditions. Heavy oil is used in hot climates and where high loads are encountered. Multi-viscosity oils are designed to have characteristics of both light and heavy oils and are available in a number of weights from 5W-20 to 20W-50.

Gear oil is designed to be used in differentials, manual transmissions and other areas where high-temperature lubrication is required.

Chassis and wheel bearing grease is a heavy grease used where increased loads and friction are encountered, such as for wheel bearings, balljoints, tie-rod ends and universal joints.

High-temperature wheel bearing grease is designed to withstand the extreme temperatures encountered by wheel bearings in disc brake equipped vehicles. It usually contains molybdenum disulfide (moly), which is a dry-type lubricant.

White grease is a heavy grease for metal-to-metal applications where water is a problem. White grease stays soft under both low and high temperatures (usually from -100 to +190-degrees F), and will not wash off or dilute in the presence of water.

Assembly lube is a special extreme pressure lubricant, usually containing moly, used to lubricate high-load parts (such as main and rod bearings and cam lobes) for initial start-up of a new engine. The assembly lube lubricates the parts without being squeezed out or washed away until the engine oiling system begins to function.

Silicone lubricants are used to protect rubber, plastic, vinyl and nylon parts.

Graphite lubricants are used where oils cannot be used due to contamination problems, such as in locks. The dry graphite will lubricate metal parts while remaining uncontaminated by dirt, water, oil or acids. It is electrically conductive and will not foul electrical contacts in locks such as the ignition switch.

Moly penetrants loosen and lubricate frozen, rusted and corroded fasteners and prevent future rusting or freezing.

Heat-sink grease is a special electrically non-conductive grease that is used for mounting electronic ignition modules where it is essential that heat is transferred away from the module.

Sealants

RTV sealant is one of the most widely used gasket compounds. Made from silicone, RTV is air curing, it seals, bonds, waterproofs, fills surface irregularities, remains flexible, doesn't shrink, is relatively easy to remove, and is used as a supplementary sealer with almost all low and medium temperature gaskets.

Anaerobic sealant is much like RTV in that it can be used either to seal gaskets or to form gaskets by itself. It remains flexible, is solvent resistant and fills surface imperfections. The difference between an anaerobic sealant and an RTV-type sealant is in the curing. RTV cures when exposed to air, while an anaerobic sealant cures only in the absence of air. This means that an anaerobic sealant cures only after the assembly of parts, sealing them together.

Thread and pipe sealant is used for sealing hydraulic and pneumatic fittings and vacuum lines. It is usually made from a Teflon compound, and comes in a spray, a paint-on liquid and as a wrap-around tape.

Chemicals

Anti-seize compound prevents seizing, galling, cold welding, rust and corrosion in fasteners. High-temperature anti-seize, usually made with copper and graphite lubricants, is used for exhaust system and exhaust manifold bolts.

Anaerobic locking compounds are used to keep fasteners from vibrating or working loose and cure only after installation, in the absence of air. Medium strength locking compound is used for small nuts, bolts and screws that may be removed later. High-strength locking compound is for large nuts, bolts and studs which aren't removed on a regular basis.

Oil additives range from viscosity index improvers to chemical treatments that claim to reduce internal engine friction. It should be noted that most oil manufacturers caution against using additives with their oils.

Gas additives perform several functions, depending on their chemical makeup. They usually contain solvents that help dissolve gum and varnish that build up on carburetor, fuel injection and intake parts. They also serve to break down carbon deposits that form on the inside surfaces of the combustion chambers. Some additives contain upper cylinder lubricants for valves and piston rings, and others contain chemicals to remove condensation from the gas tank.

Miscellaneous

Brake fluid is specially formulated hydraulic fluid that can withstand the heat and pressure encountered in brake systems. Care must be taken so this fluid does not come in contact with painted surfaces or plastics. An opened container should always be resealed to prevent contamination by water or dirt.

Weatherstrip adhesive is used to bond weatherstripping around doors, windows and trunk lids. It is sometimes used to attach trim pieces.

Undercoating is a petroleum-based, tar-like substance that is designed to protect metal surfaces on the underside of the vehicle from corrosion. It also acts as a sound-deadening agent by insulating the bottom of the vehicle.

Waxes and polishes are used to help protect painted and plated surfaces from the weather. Different types of paint may require the use of different types of wax and polish. Some polishes utilize a chemical or abrasive cleaner to help remove the top layer of oxidized (dull) paint on older vehicles. In recent years many non-wax polishes that contain a wide variety of chemicals such as polymers and silicones have been introduced. These non-wax polishes are usually easier to apply and last longer than conventional waxes and polishes.

Conversion factors

Length (distance)
Inches (in)	X 25.4	= Millimetres (mm)	X 0.0394	= Inches (in)
Feet (ft)	X 0.305	= Metres (m)	X 3.281	= Feet (ft)
Miles	X 1.609	= Kilometres (km)	X 0.621	= Miles

Volume (capacity)
Cubic inches (cu in; in^3)	X 16.387	= Cubic centimetres (cc; cm^3)	X 0.061	= Cubic inches (cu in; in^3)
Imperial pints (Imp pt)	X 0.568	= Litres (l)	X 1.76	= Imperial pints (Imp pt)
Imperial quarts (Imp qt)	X 1.137	= Litres (l)	X 0.88	= Imperial quarts (Imp qt)
Imperial quarts (Imp qt)	X 1.201	= US quarts (US qt)	X 0.833	= Imperial quarts (Imp qt)
US quarts (US qt)	X 0.946	= Litres (l)	X 1.057	= US quarts (US qt)
Imperial gallons (Imp gal)	X 4.546	= Litres (l)	X 0.22	= Imperial gallons (Imp gal)
Imperial gallons (Imp gal)	X 1.201	= US gallons (US gal)	X 0.833	= Imperial gallons (Imp gal)
US gallons (US gal)	X 3.785	= Litres (l)	X 0.264	= US gallons (US gal)

Mass (weight)
Ounces (oz)	X 28.35	= Grams (g)	X 0.035	= Ounces (oz)
Pounds (lb)	X 0.454	= Kilograms (kg)	X 2.205	= Pounds (lb)

Force
Ounces-force (ozf; oz)	X 0.278	= Newtons (N)	X 3.6	= Ounces-force (ozf; oz)
Pounds-force (lbf; lb)	X 4.448	= Newtons (N)	X 0.225	= Pounds-force (lbf; lb)
Newtons (N)	X 0.1	= Kilograms-force (kgf; kg)	X 9.81	= Newtons (N)

Pressure
Pounds-force per square inch (psi; lbf/in^2; lb/in^2)	X 0.070	= Kilograms-force per square centimetre (kgf/cm^2; kg/cm^2)	X 14.223	= Pounds-force per square inch (psi; lbf/in^2; lb/in^2)
Pounds-force per square inch (psi; lbf/in^2; lb/in^2)	X 0.068	= Atmospheres (atm)	X 14.696	= Pounds-force per square inch (psi; lbf/in^2; lb/in^2)
Pounds-force per square inch (psi; lbf/in^2; lb/in^2)	X 0.069	= Bars	X 14.5	= Pounds-force per square inch (psi; lbf/in^2; lb/in^2)
Pounds-force per square inch (psi; lbf/in^2; lb/in^2)	X 6.895	= Kilopascals (kPa)	X 0.145	= Pounds-force per square inch (psi; lbf/in^2; lb/in^2)
Kilopascals (kPa)	X 0.01	= Kilograms-force per square centimetre (kgf/cm^2; kg/cm^2)	X 98.1	= Kilopascals (kPa)

Torque (moment of force)
Pounds-force inches (lbf in; lb in)	X 1.152	= Kilograms-force centimetre (kgf cm; kg cm)	X 0.868	= Pounds-force inches (lbf in; lb in)
Pounds-force inches (lbf in; lb in)	X 0.113	= Newton metres (Nm)	X 8.85	= Pounds-force inches (lbf in; lb in)
Pounds-force inches (lbf in; lb in)	X 0.083	= Pounds-force feet (lbf ft; lb ft)	X 12	= Pounds-force inches (lbf in; lb in)
Pounds-force feet (lbf ft; lb ft)	X 0.138	= Kilograms-force metres (kgf m; kg m)	X 7.233	= Pounds-force feet (lbf ft; lb ft)
Pounds-force feet (lbf ft; lb ft)	X 1.356	= Newton metres (Nm)	X 0.738	= Pounds-force feet (lbf ft; lb ft)
Newton metres (Nm)	X 0.102	= Kilograms-force metres (kgf m; kg m)	X 9.804	= Newton metres (Nm)

Vacuum
Inches mercury (in. Hg)	X 3.377	= Kilopascals (kPa)	X 0.2961	= Inches mercury
Inches mercury (in. Hg)	X 25.4	= Millimeters mercury (mm Hg)	X 0.0394	= Inches mercury

Power
Horsepower (hp)	X 745.7	= Watts (W)	X 0.0013	= Horsepower (hp)

Velocity (speed)
Miles per hour (miles/hr; mph)	X 1.609	= Kilometres per hour (km/hr; kph)	X 0.621	= Miles per hour (miles/hr; mph)

Fuel consumption*
Miles per gallon, Imperial (mpg)	X 0.354	= Kilometres per litre (km/l)	X 2.825	= Miles per gallon, Imperial (mpg)
Miles per gallon, US (mpg)	X 0.425	= Kilometres per litre (km/l)	X 2.352	= Miles per gallon, US (mpg)

Temperature

Degrees Fahrenheit = ($^\circ$C x 1.8) + 32

Degrees Celsius (Degrees Centigrade; $^\circ$C) = ($^\circ$F - 32) x 0.56

*It is common practice to convert from miles per gallon (mpg) to litres/100 kilometres (l/100km), where mpg (Imperial) x l/100 km = 282 and mpg (US) x l/100 km = 235

Safety first!

Regardless of how enthusiastic you may be about getting on with the job at hand, take the time to ensure that your safety is not jeopardized. A moment's lack of attention can result in an accident, as can failure to observe certain simple safety precautions. The possibility of an accident will always exist, and the following points should not be considered a comprehensive list of all dangers. Rather, they are intended to make you aware of the risks and to encourage a safety conscious approach to all work you carry out on your vehicle.

Essential DOs and DON'Ts

DON'T rely on a jack when working under the vehicle. Always use approved jackstands to support the weight of the vehicle and place them under the recommended lift or support points.

DON'T attempt to loosen extremely tight fasteners (i.e. wheel lug nuts) while the vehicle is on a jack - it may fall.

DON'T start the engine without first making sure that the transmission is in Neutral (or Park where applicable) and the parking brake is set.

DON'T remove the radiator cap from a hot cooling system - let it cool or cover it with a cloth and release the pressure gradually.

DON'T attempt to drain the engine oil until you are sure it has cooled to the point that it will not burn you.

DON'T touch any part of the engine or exhaust system until it has cooled sufficiently to avoid burns.

DON'T siphon toxic liquids such as gasoline, antifreeze and brake fluid by mouth, or allow them to remain on your skin.

DON'T inhale brake lining dust - it is potentially hazardous (see *Asbestos* below).

DON'T allow spilled oil or grease to remain on the floor - wipe it up before someone slips on it.

DON'T use loose fitting wrenches or other tools which may slip and cause injury.

DON'T push on wrenches when loosening or tightening nuts or bolts. Always try to pull the wrench toward you. If the situation calls for pushing the wrench away, push with an open hand to avoid scraped knuckles if the wrench should slip.

DON'T attempt to lift a heavy component alone - get someone to help you.

DON'T rush or take unsafe shortcuts to finish a job.

DON'T allow children or animals in or around the vehicle while you are working on it.

DO wear eye protection when using power tools such as a drill, sander, bench grinder, etc. and when working under a vehicle.

DO keep loose clothing and long hair well out of the way of moving parts.

DO make sure that any hoist used has a safe working load rating adequate for the job.

DO get someone to check on you periodically when working alone on a vehicle.

DO carry out work in a logical sequence and make sure that everything is correctly assembled and tightened.

DO keep chemicals and fluids tightly capped and out of the reach of children and pets.

DO remember that your vehicle's safety affects that of yourself and others. If in doubt on any point, get professional advice.

Asbestos

Certain friction, insulating, sealing, and other products - such as brake linings, brake bands, clutch linings, torque converters, gaskets, etc. - may contain asbestos. Extreme care must be taken to avoid inhalation of dust from such products, since it is hazardous to health. If in doubt, assume that they do contain asbestos.

Fire

Remember at all times that gasoline is highly flammable. Never smoke or have any kind of open flame around when working on a vehicle. But the risk does not end there. A spark caused by an electrical short circuit, by two metal surfaces contacting each other, or even by static electricity built up in your body under certain conditions, can ignite gasoline vapors, which in a confined space are highly explosive. Do not, under any circumstances, use gasoline for cleaning parts. Use an approved safety solvent.

Always disconnect the battery ground (-) cable at the battery before working on any part of the fuel system or electrical system. Never risk spilling fuel on a hot engine or exhaust component. It is strongly recommended that a fire extinguisher suitable for use on fuel and electrical fires be kept handy in the garage or workshop at all times. Never try to extinguish a fuel or electrical fire with water.

Fumes

Certain fumes are highly toxic and can quickly cause unconsciousness and even death if inhaled to any extent. Gasoline vapor falls into this category, as do the vapors from some cleaning solvents. Any draining or pouring of such volatile fluids should be done in a well ventilated area.

When using cleaning fluids and solvents, read the instructions on the container carefully. Never use materials from unmarked containers.

Never run the engine in an enclosed space, such as a garage. Exhaust fumes contain carbon monoxide, which is extremely poisonous. If you need to run the engine, always do so in the open air, or at least have the rear of the vehicle outside the work area.

If you are fortunate enough to have the use of an inspection pit, never drain or pour gasoline and never run the engine while the vehicle is over the pit. The fumes, being heavier than air, will concentrate in the pit with possibly lethal results.

The battery

Never create a spark or allow a bare light bulb near a battery. They normally give off a certain amount of hydrogen gas, which is highly explosive.

Always disconnect the battery ground (-) cable at the battery before working on the fuel or electrical systems.

If possible, loosen the filler caps or cover when charging the battery from an external source (this does not apply to sealed or maintenance-free batteries). Do not charge at an excessive rate or the battery may burst.

Take care when adding water to a non maintenance-free battery and when carrying a battery. The electrolyte, even when diluted, is very corrosive and should not be allowed to contact clothing or skin.

Always wear eye protection when cleaning the battery to prevent the caustic deposits from entering your eyes.

Household current

When using an electric power tool, inspection light, etc., which operates on household current, always make sure that the tool is correctly connected to its plug and that, where necessary, it is properly grounded. Do not use such items in damp conditions and, again, do not create a spark or apply excessive heat in the vicinity of fuel or fuel vapor.

Secondary ignition system voltage

A severe electric shock can result from touching certain parts of the ignition system (such as the spark plug wires) when the engine is running or being cranked, particularly if components are damp or the insulation is defective. In the case of an electronic ignition system, the secondary system voltage is much higher and could prove fatal.

Troubleshooting

Contents

This section is an easy reference guide to the more common problems which may occur during the operation of your vehicle. The problems and their possible causes are grouped under headings denoting various components or systems, such as Engine, Cooling system, etc. They also refer you to the chapter and/or section which deals with the problem.

Remember, successful troubleshooting isn't a mysterious "black art" practiced only by professional mechanics. It's simply the result of the right knowledge combined with an intelligent, systematic approach to a problem. Always follow a logical approach, starting with the simplest solution and working through to the most complex - and never overlook the obvious. Anyone can run the gas tank dry or leave the lights on overnight, so don't assume that it can't happen to you.

Finally, always try to establish a clear idea why a problem has occurred and take steps to ensure it doesn't happen again. For example, if the electrical system fails because of a poor connection, check all other connections in the system to make sure they don't fail as well. If a particular fuse continues to blow, find out why - don't just replace one fuse after another. Remember, failure of a small component often indicates potential failure or malfunction of a more important component or system.

Engine and performance

1 Engine will not rotate when attempting to start

1 Battery terminal connections loose or corroded. Check the cable terminals at the battery; tighten cable clamp and/or clean off corrosion as necessary (see Chapter 1).
2 Battery discharged or faulty. If the cable ends are clean and tight on the battery posts, turn the key to the On position and switch on the headlights or windshield wipers. If they won't run, the battery is discharged.
3 Automatic transmission not engaged in park (P) or Neutral (N).
4 Broken, loose or disconnected wires in the starting circuit. Inspect all wires and connectors at the battery, starter solenoid and ignition switch (on steering column).
5 Starter motor pinion jammed in flywheel ring gear. If manual transmission, place transmission in gear and rock the vehicle to manually turn the engine. Remove starter (Chapter 5) and inspect pinion and flywheel (Chapter 2) at earliest convenience.
6 Starter solenoid faulty (Chapter 5).
7 Starter motor faulty (Chapter 5).
8 Ignition switch faulty (Chapter 12).
9 Engine seized. Try to turn the crankshaft with a large socket and breaker bar on the pulley bolt.

2 Engine rotates but will not start

1 Fuel tank empty.
2 Battery discharged (engine rotates slowly). Check the operation of electrical components as described in previous Section.
3 Battery terminal connections loose or corroded. See previous Section.
4 Fuel not reaching the fuel injection unit. Check for clogged fuel filter or lines and defective fuel pump. Also make sure the tank vent lines aren't clogged (Chapter 4).
5 Faulty distributor components. Check the cap and rotor (Chapter 1).
6 Defective oil pressure/fuel pump switch (Chapters 2B and 4).
7 Low cylinder compression. Check as described in Chapter 2.
8 Valve clearances not properly adjusted (Chapter 2A).
9 Water in fuel. Drain tank and fill with new fuel.
10 Defective ignition coil (Chapter 5).
11 Dirty or clogged fuel injector (Chapter 4).
12 Wet or damaged ignition components (Chapters 1 and 5).
13 Worn, faulty or incorrectly gapped spark plugs (Chapter 1).
14 Broken, loose or disconnected wires in the starting circuit (see previous Section).
15 Loose distributor (changing ignition timing). Turn the distributor body as necessary to start the engine, then adjust the ignition timing as soon as possible (Chapter 1).
16 Broken, loose or disconnected wires at the ignition coil or faulty coil (Chapter 5).
17 Timing chain failure or wear affecting valve timing (Chapter 2).

3 Starter motor operates without turning engine

1 Starter pinion sticking. Remove the starter (Chapter 5) and inspect.
2 Starter pinion or flywheel/driveplate teeth worn or broken. Remove the inspection cover and inspect.

4 Engine hard to start when cold

1 Battery discharged or low. Check as described in Chapter 1.
2 Fuel not reaching the fuel injectors. Check the fuel filter, lines and fuel pump (Chapters 1 and 4).
3 Problem with the fuel injection system (see Chapter 4).
4 Defective spark plugs (Chapter 1).

5 Engine hard to start when hot

1 Air filter dirty (Chapter 1).
2 Fuel not reaching the fuel injectors (see Section 4). Check for a vapor lock situation, brought about by clogged fuel tank vent lines.
3 Bad engine ground connection.
4 Defective pick-up coil in distributor (Chapter 5).

6 Starter motor noisy or engages roughly

1 Pinion or flywheel/driveplate teeth worn or broken. Remove the inspection cover on the left side of the engine and inspect.
2 Starter motor mounting bolts loose or missing.

7 Engine starts but stops immediately

1 Loose or damaged wire harness connections at distributor, coil or alternator.
2 Intake manifold vacuum leaks. Make sure all mounting bolts/nuts are tight and all vacuum hoses connected to the manifold are attached properly and in good condition.
3 Insufficient fuel flow (see Chapter 4).

8 Engine "lopes" while idling or idles erratically

1 Vacuum leaks. Check mounting bolts at the intake manifold for tightness. Make sure that all vacuum hoses are connected and in good condition. Use a stethoscope or a length of fuel hose held against your ear to listen for vacuum leaks while the engine is running. A hissing sound will be heard. A soapy water solution will also detect leaks. Check the intake manifold gasket surfaces.
2 Leaking EGR valve or plugged PCV valve (see Chapters 1 and 6).
3 Air filter clogged (Chapter 1).
4 Fuel pump not delivering sufficient fuel (Chapter 4).
5 Leaking head gasket. Perform a cylinder compression check (Chapter 2).
6 Timing chain worn (Chapter 2).
7 Camshaft lobes worn (Chapter 2).
8 Valve clearance out of adjustment (Chapter 2A). Valves burned or otherwise leaking (Chapter 2).
9 Ignition timing out of adjustment (Chapter 1).
10 Ignition system not operating properly (Chapters 1 and 5).
11 Thermostatic air cleaner not operating properly (Chapter 1).
12 Dirty or clogged injectors.

9 Engine misses at idle speed

1 Spark plugs faulty or not gapped properly (Chapter 1).
2 Faulty spark plug wires (Chapter 1).

3   Wet or damaged distributor components (Chapter 1).
4   Short circuits in ignition, coil or spark plug wires.
5   Sticking or faulty emissions systems (see Chapter 6).
6   Clogged fuel filter and/or foreign matter in fuel. Remove the fuel filter (Chapter 1) and inspect.
7   Vacuum leaks at intake manifold or hose connections. Check as described in Section 8.
8   Incorrect idle speed or idle mixture. Have the vehicle checked by a dealer service department.
9   Incorrect ignition timing (Chapter 1).
10   Low or uneven cylinder compression. Check as described in Chapter 2.
11   Clogged or dirty fuel injectors (Chapter 4).

10   Excessively high idle speed

1   Sticking throttle linkage (Chapter 4).
2   Idle speed incorrectly adjusted (Chapter 1).
3   Valve clearances incorrectly adjusted (Chapter 2A).

11   Battery will not hold a charge

1   Alternator drivebelt defective or not adjusted properly (Chapter 1).
2   Battery cables loose or corroded (Chapter 1).
3   Alternator not charging properly (Chapter 5).
4   Loose, broken or faulty wires in the charging circuit (Chapter 5).
5   Short circuit causing a continuous drain on the battery.
6   Battery defective internally.

12   Alternator light stays on

1   Fault in alternator or charging circuit (Chapter 5).
2   Alternator drivebelt defective or not properly adjusted (Chapter 1).

13   Alternator light fails to come on when key is turned on

1   Faulty bulb (Chapter 12).
2   Defective alternator (Chapter 5).
3   Fault in the printed circuit, dash wiring or bulb holder (Chapter 12).

14   Engine misses throughout driving speed range

1   Fuel filter clogged and/or impurities in the fuel system. Check fuel filter (Chapter 1) or clean system (Chapter 4).
2   Faulty or incorrectly gapped spark plugs (Chapter 1).
3   Incorrect ignition timing (Chapter 1).
4   Cracked distributor cap, disconnected distributor wires or damaged distributor components (Chapter 1).
5   Defective spark plug wires (Chapter 1).
6   Emissions system components faulty (Chapter 6).
7   Low or uneven cylinder compression pressures. Check as described in Chapter 2.
8   Weak or faulty ignition coil (Chapter 5).
9   Weak or faulty ignition system (Chapter 5).
10   Vacuum leaks at intake manifold or vacuum hoses (see Section 8).
11   Dirty or clogged fuel injector(s) (Chapter 4).
12   Leaky EGR valve (Chapter 6).

15   Hesitation or stumble during acceleration

1   Ignition timing incorrect (Chapter 1).
2   Ignition system not operating properly (Chapter 5).
3   Dirty or clogged fuel injector(s) (Chapter 4).
4   Low fuel pressure. Check for proper operation of the fuel pump and for restrictions in the fuel filter and lines (Chapter 4).

16   Engine stalls

1   Idle speed incorrect. Have it checked by a dealer service department.
2   Fuel filter clogged and/or water and impurities in the fuel system (Chapter 1).
3   Damaged or wet distributor cap and wires.
4   Emissions system components faulty (Chapter 6).
5   Faulty or incorrectly gapped spark plugs (Chapter 1). Also check the spark plug wires (Chapter 1).
6   Vacuum leak at the throttle body, intake manifold or vacuum hoses. Check as described in Section 8.

17   Engine lacks power

1   Incorrect ignition timing (Chapter 1).
2   Excessive play in distributor shaft. At the same time check for faulty distributor cap, wires, etc. (Chapter 1).
3   Faulty or incorrectly gapped spark plugs (Chapter 1).
4   Air filter dirty (Chapter 1).
5   Faulty ignition coil (Chapter 5).
6   Brakes binding (Chapters 1 and 9).
7   Automatic transmission fluid level incorrect, causing slippage (Chapter 1).
8   Clutch slipping (Chapter 8).

9   Fuel filter clogged and/or impurities in the fuel system (Chapters 1 and 4).
10   EGR system not functioning properly (Chapter 6).
11   Use of sub-standard fuel. Fill tank with proper octane fuel.
12   Low or uneven cylinder compression pressures. Check as described in Chapter 2.
13   Air leak at throttle body or intake manifold (check as described in Section 8).

18   Engine backfires

1   EGR system not functioning properly (Chapter 6).
2   Ignition timing incorrect (Chapter 1).
3   Thermostatic air cleaner system not operating properly (Chapter 6).
4   Vacuum leak (refer to Section 8).
5   Valve clearances incorrect (Chapter 2A).
6   Damaged valve springs or sticking valves (Chapter 2).
7   Intake air leak (see Section 8).

19   Engine surges while holding accelerator steady

1   Intake air leak (see Section 8).
2   Fuel pump not working properly (Chapter 4).

20   Pinging or knocking engine sounds when engine is under load

1   Incorrect grade of fuel. Fill tank with fuel of the proper octane rating.
2   Ignition timing incorrect (Chapter 1).
3   Carbon build-up in combustion chambers. Remove cylinder head(s) and clean combustion chambers (Chapter 2).
4   Incorrect spark plugs (Chapter 1).

21   Engine diesels (continues to run) after being turned off

1   Idle speed too high. Have it checked by a dealer service department.
2   Ignition timing incorrect (Chapter 1).
3   Incorrect spark plug heat range (Chapter 1).
4   Intake air leak (see Section 8).
5   Carbon build-up in combustion chambers. Remove the cylinder head(s) and clean the combustion chambers (Chapter 2).
6   Valves sticking (Chapter 2).
7   Valve clearance incorrect (Chapter 2A).
8   EGR system not operating properly (Chapter 6).
9   Fuel shut-off system not operating properly (Chapter 6).
10   Check for causes of overheating (Section 27).

22 Low oil pressure

1   Improper grade of oil.
2   Oil pump worn or damaged (Chapter 2).
3   Engine overheating (refer to Section 27).
4   Clogged oil filter (Chapter 1).
5   Clogged oil strainer (Chapter 2).
6   Oil pressure gauge not working properly (Chapter 2).

23 Excessive oil consumption

1   Loose oil drain plug.
2   Loose bolts or damaged oil pan gasket (Chapter 2).
3   Loose bolts or damaged front cover gasket (Chapter 2).
4   Front or rear crankshaft oil seal leaking (Chapter 2).
5   Loose bolts or damaged rocker arm cover gasket (Chapter 2).
6   Loose oil filter (Chapter 1).
7   Loose or damaged oil pressure switch (Chapter 2).
8   Pistons and cylinders excessively worn (Chapter 2).
9   Piston rings not installed correctly on pistons (Chapter 2).
10   Worn or damaged piston rings (Chapter 2).
11   Intake and/or exhaust valve oil seals worn or damaged (Chapter 2).
12   Worn valve stems.
13   Worn or damaged valves/guides (Chapter 2).

24 Excessive fuel consumption

1   Dirty or clogged air filter element (Chapter 1).
2   Incorrect ignition timing (Chapter 1).
3   Incorrect idle speed. Have it checked by a dealer service department.
4   Low tire pressure or incorrect tire size (Chapter 10).
5   Fuel leakage. Check all connections, lines and components in the fuel system (Chapter 4).
6   Dirty or clogged fuel injectors (Chapter 4).

25 Fuel odor

1   Fuel leakage. Check all connections, lines and components in the fuel system (Chapter 4).
2   Fuel tank overfilled. Fill only to automatic shut-off.
3   Charcoal canister filter in Evaporative Emissions Control system clogged (Chapter 1).
4   Vapor leaks from Evaporative Emissions Control system lines (Chapter 6).

26 Miscellaneous engine noises

1   A strong dull noise that becomes more rapid as the engine accelerates indicates worn or damaged crankshaft bearings or an unevenly worn crankshaft. To pinpoint the trouble spot, remove the spark plug wire from one plug at a time and crank the engine over. If the noise stops, the cylinder with the removed plug wire indicates the problem area. Replace the bearing and/or service or replace the crankshaft (Chapter 2).
2   A similar (yet slightly higher pitched) noise to the crankshaft knocking described in the previous paragraph, that becomes more rapid as the engine accelerates, indicates worn or damaged connecting rod bearings (Chapter 2). The procedure for locating the problem cylinder is the same as described in Paragraph 1.
3   An overlapping metallic noise that increases in intensity as the engine speed increases, yet diminishes as the engine warms up indicates abnormal piston and cylinder wear (Chapter 2).To locate the problem cylinder, use the procedure described in Paragraph 1.
4   A rapid clicking noise that becomes faster as the engine accelerates indicates a worn piston pin or piston pin hole. This sound will happen each time the piston hits the highest and lowest points in the stroke (Chapter 2). The procedure for locating the problem piston is described in Paragraph 1.
5   A metallic clicking noise coming from the water pump indicates worn or damaged water pump bearings or pump. Replace the water pump with a new one (Chapter 3).
6   A rapid tapping sound or clicking sound that becomes faster as the engine speed increases indicates "valve tapping" or improperly adjusted valve clearances. This can be identified by holding one end of a section of hose to your ear and placing the other end at different spots along the rocker arm cover. The point where the sound is loudest indicates the problem valve. Adjust the valve clearances (Chapter 2A). If the problem persists, you likely have a collapsed valve lifter or other damaged valve train component. Changing the engine oil and adding a high viscosity oil treatment will sometimes cure a stuck lifter problem. If the problem still persists, the lifters, pushrods and rocker arms must be removed for inspection (see Chapter 2).
7   A steady metallic rattling or rapping sound coming from the area of the timing chain cover indicates a worn, damaged or out-of-adjustment timing chain. Service or replace the chain and related components (Chapter 2).

Cooling system

27 Overheating

1   Insufficient coolant in system (Chapter 1).
2   Drivebelt defective or not adjusted properly (Chapter 1).
3   Radiator core blocked or radiator grille dirty and restricted (Chapter 3).
4   Thermostat faulty (Chapter 3).
5   Fan not functioning properly (Chapter 3).
6   Radiator cap not maintaining proper pressure. Have cap pressure tested by gas station or repair shop.
7   Ignition timing incorrect (Chapter 1).
8   Defective water pump (Chapter 3).
9   Improper grade of engine oil.
10   Inaccurate temperature gauge (Chapter 12).

28 Overcooling

1   Thermostat faulty (Chapter 3).
2   Inaccurate temperature gauge (Chapter 12).

29 External coolant leakage

1   Deteriorated or damaged hoses. Loose clamps at hose connections (Chapter 1).
2   Water pump seals defective. If this is the case, water will drip from the weep hole in the water pump body (Chapter 3).
3   Leakage from radiator core or header tank. This will require the radiator to be professionally repaired (see Chapter 3 for removal procedures).
4   Engine drain plugs or water jacket freeze plugs leaking (see Chapters 1 and 2).
5   Leak from coolant temperature switch (Chapter 3).
6   Leak from damaged gaskets or small cracks (Chapter 2).
7   Damaged head gasket. This can be verified by checking the condition of the engine oil as noted in Section 30.

30 Internal coolant leakage

Note: *Internal coolant leaks can usually be detected by examining the oil. Check the dipstick and inside the rocker arm cover for water deposits and an oil consistency like that of a milkshake.*
1   Leaking cylinder head gasket. Have the system pressure tested or remove the cylinder head (Chapter 2) and inspect.
2   Cracked cylinder bore or cylinder head. Dismantle engine and inspect (Chapter 2).
3   Loose cylinder head bolts (tighten as described in Chapter 2).

31 Abnormal coolant loss

1   Overfilling system (Chapter 1).
2   Coolant boiling away due to overheating (see causes in Section 27).
3   Internal or external leakage (see Sec-

tions 29 and 30).
4　Faulty radiator cap. Have the cap pressure tested.
5　Cooling system being pressurized by engine compression. This could be due to a cracked head or block or leaking head gasket(s).

32　Poor coolant circulation

1　Inoperative water pump. A quick test is to pinch the top radiator hose closed with your hand while the engine is idling, then release it. You should feel a surge of coolant if the pump is working properly (Chapter 3).
2　Restriction in cooling system. Drain, flush and refill the system (Chapter 1). If necessary, remove the radiator (Chapter 3) and have it reverse flushed or professionally cleaned.
3　Loose water pump drivebelt (Chapter 1).
4　Thermostat sticking (Chapter 3).
5　Insufficient coolant (Chapter 1).

33　Corrosion

1　Excessive impurities in the water. Soft, clean water is recommended. Distilled or rainwater is satisfactory.
2　Insufficient antifreeze solution (refer to Chapter 1 for the proper ratio of water to antifreeze).
3　Infrequent flushing and draining of system. Regular flushing of the cooling system should be carried out at the specified intervals as described in (Chapter 1).

Clutch

Note: *All clutch related service information is located in Chapter 8, unless otherwise noted.*

34　Fails to release (pedal pressed to the floor - shift lever does not move freely in and out of Reverse)

1　Clutch contaminated with oil. Remove clutch plate and inspect.
2　Clutch plate warped, distorted or otherwise damaged.
3　Diaphragm spring fatigued. Remove clutch cover/pressure plate assembly and inspect.
4　Leakage of fluid from clutch hydraulic system. Inspect master cylinder, operating cylinder and connecting lines.
5　Air in clutch hydraulic system. Bleed the system.
6　Insufficient pedal stroke. Check and adjust as necessary.
7　Piston seal in operating cylinder deformed or damaged.
8　Lack of grease on pilot bushing.

35　Clutch slips (engine speed increases with no increase in vehicle speed)

1　Worn or oil soaked clutch plate.
2　Clutch plate not broken in. It may take 30 or 40 normal starts for a new clutch to seat.
3　Diaphragm spring weak or damaged. Remove clutch cover/pressure plate assembly and inspect.
4　Flywheel warped (Chapter 2).
5　Debris in master cylinder preventing the piston from returning to its normal position.
6　Clutch hydraulic line damaged.

36　Grabbing (chattering) as clutch is engaged

1　Oil on clutch plate. Remove and inspect. Repair any leaks.
2　Worn or loose engine or transmission mounts. They may move slightly when clutch is released. Inspect mounts and bolts.
3　Worn splines on transmission input shaft. Remove clutch components and inspect.
4　Warped pressure plate or flywheel. Remove clutch components and inspect.
5　Diaphragm spring fatigued. Remove clutch cover/pressure plate assembly and inspect.
6　Clutch linings hardened or warped.
7　Clutch lining rivets loose.

37　Squeal or rumble with clutch engaged (pedal released)

1　Improper pedal adjustment. Adjust pedal free play.
2　Release bearing binding on transmission shaft. Remove clutch components and check bearing. Remove any burrs or nicks, clean and relubricate before reinstallation.
3　Pilot bushing worn or damaged.
4　Clutch rivets loose.
5　Clutch plate cracked.
6　Fatigued clutch plate torsion springs. Replace clutch plate.

38　Squeal or rumble with clutch disengaged (pedal depressed)

1　Worn or damaged release bearing.
2　Worn or broken pressure plate diaphragm fingers.

39　Clutch pedal stays on floor when disengaged

Binding linkage or release bearing. Inspect linkage or remove clutch components as necessary.

Manual transmission

Note: *All manual transmission service information is located in Chapter 7, unless otherwise noted.*

40　Noisy in Neutral with engine running

1　Input shaft bearing worn.
2　Damaged main drive gear bearing.
3　Insufficient transmission oil (Chapter 1).
4　Transmission oil in poor condition. Drain and fill with proper grade oil. Check old oil for water and debris (Chapter 1).
5　Noise can be caused by variations in engine torque. Using the accelerator pedal, change the idle speed and see if noise disappears.

41　Noisy in all gears

1　Any of the above causes, and/or:
2　Worn or damaged output gear bearings or shaft.

42　Noisy in one particular gear

1　Worn, damaged or chipped gear teeth.
2　Worn or damaged synchronizer.

43　Slips out of gear

1　Transmission loose on clutch housing.
2　Stiff shift lever seal.
3　Shift linkage binding.
4　Broken or loose input gear bearing retainer.
5　Dirt between clutch lever and engine housing.
6　Worn linkage.
7　Damaged or worn check balls, fork rod ball grooves or check springs.
8　Worn mainshaft or countershaft bearings.
9　Loose engine mounts (Chapter 2).
10　Excessive gear end play.
11　Worn synchronizers.

44　Oil leaks

1　Excessive amount of lubricant in transmission (see Chapter 1 for correct checking procedures). Drain lubricant as required.
2　Rear oil seal or speedometer oil seal damaged.
3　To pinpoint a leak, first remove all built-up dirt and grime from the transmission. Degreasing agents and/or steam cleaning will achieve this. With the underside clean, drive the vehicle at low speeds so the air flow will not blow the leak far from its source. Raise the vehicle and determine where the leak is located.

45 Difficulty engaging gears

1   Clutch not releasing completely.
2   Loose or damaged shift linkage. Make a thorough inspection, replacing parts as necessary.
3   Insufficient transmission oil (Chapter 1).
4   Transmission oil in poor condition. Drain and fill with proper grade oil. Check oil for water and debris (Chapter 1).
5   Worn or damaged striking rod.
6   Sticking or jamming gears.

46 Noise occurs while shifting gears

1   Check for proper operation of the clutch (Chapter 8).
2   Faulty synchronizer assemblies. Measure baulk ring-to-gear clearance. Also, check for wear or damage to baulk rings or any parts of the synchromesh assemblies.

Automatic transmission

Note: *Due to the complexity of the automatic transmission, it's difficult for the home mechanic to properly diagnose and service. For problems other than the following, the vehicle should be taken to a reputable mechanic.*

47 Fluid leakage

1   Automatic transmission fluid is a deep red color, and fluid leaks should not be confused with engine oil which can easily be blown by air flow to the transmission.
2   To pinpoint a leak, first remove all built-up dirt and grime from the transmission. Degreasing agents and/or steam cleaning will achieve this. With the underside clean, drive the vehicle at low speeds so the air flow will not blow the leak far from its source. Raise the vehicle and determine where the leak is located. Common areas of leakage are:
a) *Fluid pan: tighten mounting bolts and/or replace pan gasket as necessary (Chapter 1).*
b) *Rear extension: tighten bolts and/or replace oil seal as necessary.*
c) *Filler pipe: replace the rubber oil seal where pipe enters transmission case.*
d) *Transmission oil lines: tighten fittings where lines enter transmission case and/or replace lines.*
e) *Vent pipe: transmission overfilled and/or water in fluid (see checking procedures, Chapter 1).*
f) *Speedometer connector: replace the O-ring where speedometer cable enters transmission case.*

48 General shift mechanism problems

Chapter 7 deals with checking and adjusting the shift linkage on automatic transmissions. Common problems which may be caused by out of adjustment linkage are:
a) *Engine starting in gears other than P (park) or N (Neutral).*
b) *Indicator pointing to a gear other than the one actually engaged.*
c) *Vehicle moves with transmission in P (Park) position.*

49 Transmission will not downshift with the accelerator pedal pressed to the floor

Chapter 7 deals with adjusting the TV linkage to enable the four-speed transmission to downshift properly.

50 Engine will start in gears other than Park or Neutral

Chapter 7 deals with adjusting the Neutral start switch installed on automatic transmissions.

51 Transmission slips, shifts rough, is noisy or has no drive in Forward or Reverse gears

1   There are many probable causes for the above problems, but the home mechanic should concern himself only with one possibility; fluid level.
2   Before taking the vehicle to a shop, check the fluid level and condition as described in Chapter 1. Add fluid, if necessary, or change the fluid and filter if needed. If problems persist, have a professional diagnose the transmission.

Driveshaft

Note: *Refer to Chapter 8, unless otherwise specified, for service information.*

52 Leaks at front of driveshaft

Defective transmission rear seal. See Chapter 7 for replacement procedure. As this is done, check the splined yoke for burrs or roughness that could damage the new seal. Remove burrs with a fine file or whetstone.

53 Knock or clunk when transmission is under initial load (just after transmission is put into gear)

1   Loose or disconnected rear suspension components. Check all mounting bolts and bushings (Chapters 7 and 10).
2   Loose driveshaft bolts. Inspect all bolts and nuts and tighten them securely.
3   Worn or damaged universal joint bearings. Replace driveshaft (Chapter 8).
4   Worn sleeve yoke and mainshaft spline.

54 Metallic grating sound consistent with vehicle speed

Pronounced wear in the universal joint bearings. Replace U-joints or driveshafts, as necessary.

55 Vibration

Note: *Before blaming the driveshaft, make sure the tires are perfectly balanced and perform the following test.*
1   Install a tachometer inside the vehicle to monitor engine speed as the vehicle is driven. Drive the vehicle and note the engine speed at which the vibration (roughness) is most pronounced. Now shift the transmission to a different gear and bring the engine speed to the same point.
2   If the vibration occurs at the same engine speed (rpm) regardless of which gear the transmission is in, the driveshaft is NOT at fault since the driveshaft speed varies.
3   If the vibration decreases or is eliminated when the transmission is in a different gear at the same engine speed, refer to the following probable causes.
4   Bent or dented driveshaft. Inspect and replace as necessary.
5   Undercoating or built-up dirt, etc. on the driveshaft. Clean the shaft thoroughly.
6   Worn universal joint bearings. Replace the U-joints or driveshaft as necessary.
7   Driveshaft and/or companion flange out of balance. Check for missing weights on the shaft. Remove driveshaft and reinstall 180-degrees from original position, then recheck. Have the driveshaft balanced if problem persists.
8   Loose driveshaft mounting bolts/nuts.
9   Defective center bearing, if so equipped.
10   Worn transmission rear bushing (Chapter 7).

56 Scraping noise

Make sure the dust cover on the sleeve yoke isn't rubbing on the transmission extension housing.

57 Whining or whistling noise

Defective center bearing, if so equipped.

Rear axle and differential

Note: *For differential servicing information, refer to Chapter 8, unless otherwise specified.*

58 Noise - same when in drive as when vehicle is coasting

1 Road noise. No corrective action available.
2 Tire noise. Inspect tires and check tire pressures (Chapter 1).
3 Front wheel bearings loose, worn or damaged (Chapter 1).
4 Insufficient differential oil (Chapter 1).
5 Defective differential.

59 Knocking sound when starting or shifting gears

Defective or incorrectly adjusted differential.

60 Noise when turning

Defective differential.

61 Vibration

See probable causes under Driveshaft. Proceed under the guidelines listed for the driveshaft. If the problem persists, check the rear wheel bearings by raising the rear of the vehicle and spinning the wheels by hand. Listen for evidence of rough (noisy) bearings. Remove and inspect (Chapter 8).

62 Oil leaks

1 Pinion oil seal damaged (Chapter 8).
2 Axleshaft oil seals damaged (Chapter 8).
3 Differential cover leaking. Tighten mounting bolts or replace the gasket as required.
4 Loose filler or drain plug on differential (Chapter 1).
5 Clogged or damaged breather on differential.

Transfer case (4WD models)

63 Gear jumping out of mesh

1 Incorrect shift linkage adjustment (Chapter 7C).

2 Interference between the control lever and the console.
3 Play or fatigue in the transfer case mounts.
4 Internal wear or incorrect adjustments.

64 Difficult shifting

1 Lack of oil.
2 Internal wear, damage or incorrect adjustment.

65 Noise

1 Lack of oil in transfer case.
2 Noise in 4H and 4L, but not in 2H indicates cause is in the front differential or front axle.
3 Noise in 2H, 4H and 4L indicates cause is in rear differential or rear axle.
4 Noise in 2H and 4H but not in 4L, or in 4L only, indicates internal wear or damage in transfer case.

Brakes

Note: *Before assuming a brake problem exists, make sure the tires are in good condition and inflated properly, the front end alignment is correct and the vehicle is not loaded with weight in an unequal manner. All service procedures for the brakes are included in Chapter 9, unless otherwise noted.*

66 Vehicle pulls to one side during braking

1 Defective, damaged or oil contaminated brake pad on one side. Inspect as described in Chapter 1. Refer to Chapter 9 if replacement is required.
2 Excessive wear of brake pad material or disc on one side. Inspect and repair as necessary.
3 Loose or disconnected front suspension components. Inspect and tighten all bolts securely (Chapters 1 and 10).
4 Defective caliper assembly. Remove caliper and inspect for stuck piston or damage.
5 Brake pad to rotor adjustment needed. Inspect automatic adjusting mechanism for proper operation.
6 Scored or out-of-round rotor.
7 Loose caliper mounting bolts.
8 Incorrect wheel bearing adjustment.

67 Noise (high-pitched squeal)

1 Front brake pads worn out. This noise comes from the wear sensor rubbing against the disc. Replace pads with new ones immediately!

2 Glazed or contaminated pads.
3 Dirty or scored rotor.
4 Bent support plate.

68 Excessive brake pedal travel

1 Partial brake system failure. Inspect entire system (Chapter 1) and correct as required.
2 Insufficient fluid in master cylinder. Check (Chapter 1) and add fluid - bleed system if necessary.
3 Air in system. Bleed system.
4 Excessive lateral rotor play.
5 Brakes out of adjustment. Check the operation of the automatic adjusters.
6 Defective proportioning valve. Replace valve and bleed system.

69 Brake pedal feels spongy when depressed

1 Air in brake lines. Bleed the brake system.
2 Deteriorated rubber brake hoses. Inspect all system hoses and lines. Replace parts as necessary.
3 Master cylinder mounting nuts loose. Inspect master cylinder bolts (nuts) and tighten them securely.
4 Master cylinder faulty.
5 Incorrect shoe or pad clearance.
6 Defective check valve. Replace valve and bleed system.
7 Clogged reservoir cap vent hole.
8 Deformed rubber brake lines.
9 Soft or swollen caliper seals.
10 Poor quality brake fluid. Bleed entire system and fill with new approved fluid.

70 Excessive effort required to stop vehicle

1 Power brake booster not operating properly.
2 Excessively worn linings or pads. Check and replace if necessary.
3 One or more caliper pistons seized or sticking. Inspect and rebuild as required.
4 Brake pads or linings contaminated with oil or grease. Inspect and replace as required.
5 New pads or linings installed and not yet seated. It'll take a while for the new material to seat against the rotor or drum.
6 Worn or damaged master cylinder or caliper assemblies. Check particularly for frozen pistons.
7 Also see causes listed under Section 69.

71 Pedal travels to the floor with little resistance

Little or no fluid in the master cylinder

reservoir caused by leaking caliper piston(s) or loose, damaged or disconnected brake lines. Inspect entire system and repair as necessary.

72 Brake pedal pulsates during brake application

1   Wheel bearings damaged, worn or out of adjustment (Chapter 1).
2   Caliper not sliding properly due to improper installation or obstructions. Remove and inspect.
3   Rotor not within specifications. Remove the rotor and check for excessive lateral runout and parallelism. Have the rotors resurfaced or replace them with new ones. Also make sure that all rotors are the same thickness.
4   Out-of-round rear brake drums. Remove the drums and have them turned or replace them with new ones.

73 Brakes drag (indicated by sluggish engine performance or wheels being very hot after driving)

1   Output rod adjustment incorrect at the brake pedal.
2   Obstructed master cylinder compensator. Disassemble master cylinder and clean.
3   Master cylinder piston seized in bore. Overhaul master cylinder.
4   Caliper assembly in need of overhaul.
5   Brake pads or shoes worn out.
6   Piston cups in master cylinder or caliper assembly deformed. Overhaul master cylinder.
7   Rotor not within specifications (Section 72).
8   Parking brake assembly will not release.
9   Clogged brake lines.
10 Wheel bearings out of adjustment (Chapter 1).
11 Brake pedal height improperly adjusted.
12 Wheel cylinder needs overhaul.
13 Improper shoe to drum clearance. Adjust as necessary.

74 Rear brakes lock up under light brake application

1   Tire pressures too high.
2   Faulty ABS system. Have the vehicle checked by a dealer service department.

75 Rear brakes lock up under heavy brake application

1   Tire pressures too high.
2   Tires excessively worn (Chapter 1).

3   Front brake pads contaminated with oil, mud or water. Clean or replace the pads.
4   Front brake pads excessively worn.
5   Defective ABS system. Have the vehicle checked by a dealer service department.

Suspension and steering

Note: *All service procedures for the suspension and steering systems are included in Chapter 10, unless otherwise noted.*

76 Vehicle pulls to one side

1   Tire pressures uneven (Chapter 1).
2   Defective tire (Chapter 1).
3   Excessive wear in suspension or steering components (Chapter 1).
4   Front end alignment incorrect.
5   Front brakes dragging. Inspect as described in Section 73.
6   Wheel bearings improperly adjusted (Chapter 1).
7   Wheel lug nuts loose.

77 Shimmy, shake or vibration

1   Tire or wheel out of balance or out-of-round. Have them balanced on the vehicle.
2   Loose, worn or out of adjustment wheel bearings (Chapter 1).
3   Shock absorbers and/or suspension components worn or damaged. Check for worn bushings in the upper and lower links.
4   Wheel lug nuts loose.
5   Incorrect tire pressures.
6   Excessively worn or damaged tire.
7   Loosely mounted steering gear housing.
8   Steering gear improperly adjusted.
9   Loose, worn or damaged steering components.
10 Damaged idler arm.
11 Worn balljoint.

78 Excessive pitching and/or rolling around corners or during braking

1   Defective shock absorbers. Replace as a set.
2   Broken or weak leaf springs and/or suspension components.
3   Worn or damaged stabilizer bar or bushings.

79 Wandering or general instability

1   Improper tire pressures.
2   Worn or damaged upper and lower link or tension rod bushings.
3   Incorrect front end alignment.
4   Worn or damaged steering linkage or suspension components.

5   Defective steering gear.
6   Out of balance wheels.
7   Loose wheel lug nuts.
8   Worn rear shock absorbers.
9   Fatigued or damaged rear leaf springs.

80 Excessively stiff steering

1   Lack of lubricant in power steering fluid reservoir, where appropriate (Chapter 1).
2   Incorrect tire pressures (Chapter 1).
3   Lack of lubrication at balljoints (Chapter 1).
4   Front end out of alignment.
5   Improperly adjusted wheel bearings.
6   Worn or damaged steering gear.
7   Interference of steering column with turn signal switch.
8   Low tire pressures.
9   Worn or damaged balljoints.
10 Worn or damaged steering linkage.
11 See also Section 79.

81 Excessive play in steering

1   Loose wheel bearings (Chapter 1).
2   Excessive wear in suspension bushings (Chapter 1).
3   Steering gear defective.
4   Incorrect front end alignment.
5   Steering gear mounting bolts loose.
6   Worn steering linkage.

82 Lack of power assistance

1   Steering pump drivebelt faulty or not adjusted properly (Chapter 1).
2   Fluid level low (Chapter 1).
3   Hoses or pipes restricting the flow. Inspect and replace parts as necessary.
4   Air in power steering system. Bleed system.
5   Defective power steering pump.

83 Steering wheel fails to return to straight-ahead position

1   Incorrect front end alignment.
2   Tire pressures low.
3   Steering gears improperly engaged.
4   Steering column out of alignment.
5   Worn or damaged balljoint.
6   Worn or damaged steering linkage.
7   Improperly lubricated idler arm.
8   Insufficient oil in steering gear.
9   Lack of fluid in power steering pump.

84 Steering effort not the same in both directions (power system)

1   Leaks in steering gear.
2   Clogged fluid passage in steering gear.

85 Noisy power steering pump

1 Insufficient oil in pump.
2 Clogged hoses or oil filter in pump.
3 Loose pulley.
4 Improperly adjusted drivebelt (Chapter 1).
5 Defective pump.

86 Miscellaneous noises

1 Improper tire pressures.
2 Insufficiently lubricated balljoint or steering linkage.
3 Loose or worn steering gear, steering linkage or suspension components.
4 Defective shock absorber.
5 Defective wheel bearing.
6 Worn or damaged suspension bushings.
7 Damaged leaf spring.
8 Loose wheel lug nuts.
9 Worn or damaged rear axleshaft spline.

10 Worn or damaged rear shock absorber mounting bushing.
11 Incorrect rear axle endplay.
12 See also causes of noises at the rear axle and driveshaft.

87 Excessive tire wear (not specific to one area)

1 Incorrect tire pressures.
2 Tires out of balance. Have them balanced on the vehicle.
3 Wheels damaged. Inspect and replace as necessary.
4 Suspension or steering components worn (Chapter 1).

88 Excessive tire wear on outside edge

1 Incorrect tire pressure.

2 Excessive speed in turns.
3 Front end alignment incorrect (excessive toe-in).

89 Excessive tire wear on inside edge

1 Incorrect tire pressure.
2 Front end alignment incorrect (toe-out).
3 Loose or damaged steering components (Chapter 1).

90 Tire tread worn in one place

1 Tires out of balance. Have them balanced on the vehicle.
2 Damaged or buckled wheel. Inspect and replace if necessary.
3 Defective tire.

Notes

Chapter 1
Tune-up and routine maintenance

Contents

Specifications

Recommended lubricants and fluids

Engine oil
    Type .... SG, SF/CC or SF/CD
    Viscosity .... See accompanying chart

Note: *Listed here are manufacturer recommendations at the time this manual was printed. Manufacturers occasionally upgrade their fluid lubricant specifications so check with your local auto parts store for the most current fluid and lubricant recommendations.*

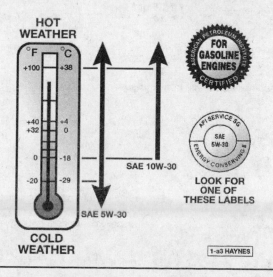

Engine oil viscosity chart

For best fuel economy and cold starting, select the lowest SAE viscosity grade oil for the expected temperature range

1-a3 HAYNES

Recommended lubricants and fluids

Automatic transmission fluid	Dexron II, IIE or III ATF
Manual transmission lubricant	
Normal-duty* transmissions	GM 1052931 manual transmission fluid or equivalent
Heavy-duty* four-speed	API 80W-90 GL-5 gear lubricant
Heavy-duty* five-speed	Castrol Syntorq GL4 transmission fluid or equivalent
Differential lubricant..	API 80W-90 GL-5 gear lubricant
Transfer case lubricant	Dexron II, IIE or III ATF
Chassis grease	NLGI no. 2 chassis grease
Engine coolant	Mixture of water and ethylene glycol-base antifreeze
Brake fluid...	Delco Supreme 11 or DOT-3 brake fluid
Clutch fluid..	Delco Supreme 11 or DOT-3 brake fluid
Power steering fluid	GM power steering fluid or equivalent
Front wheel bearing grease (2WD models)............................	NLGI no. 2 moly-base wheel bearing grease

Capacities

Note: *All capacities approximate. Add as necessary to bring to the appropriate level.*

Engine oil (with filter change)	
4.3L V6 engine	
1988 through 1991...	5 qts
1992 and later	4.5 qts
5.0L and 5.7L V8 engines	5 qts
7.4L V8 engine..	7 qts
Cooling system (approximate)	
4.3L V6 engine	
1988 through 1995...	11 qts
1996 and later	13 qts
5.0L V8 engine (all)	18 qts
5.7L V8 engine	
1988 through 1995...	18 qts
1996 and later	
Without A/C	18 qts
With A/C	20 qts
7.4L V8 engine	
1988 through 1995	
Without A/C	23 qts
With A/C	25 qts
1996 and later	
Without A/C	25 qts
With A/C	28 qts
Automatic transmission (when draining oil pan and replacing filter)	
Three speed	4.2 qts
Four speed	
1988 through 1994...	5 qts
1995 and later	
4L60-E transmission	5 qts
4L80-E transmission	7.7 qts
Manual transmission	
1988 through 1991	
Normal-duty* transmissions	1.8 qts
Heavy-duty four-speed*.......................................	4.2
Heavy-duty five-speed*	4.0 qts
1992 and later	
New Venture 3500 transmission	2.2 qts
New Venture 4500 transmission	4 qts

* See Chapter 7, Part A, for information on identifying normal and heavy-duty four-speed transmissions.

Brakes

Brake pad wear limit..	1/8 in
Brake shoe wear limit	1/16 in

Ignition system

Ignition timing*	
4.3L V6	
1988 and 1989	Electronically controlled, not adjustable
1990 through 1995	TDC
1995 and later	Electronically controlled, not adjustable
5.0L, 5.7L V8	
1988 through 1995	TDC
1996 and later	Electronically controlled, not adjustable

7.4L V8
   1988 through 1995 .... 4 degrees BTDC
   1996 and later .... Electronically controlled, not adjustable
Spark plug type and gap*
   1988 through 1995 .... AC CR43TS or equivalent @ 0.035 in
   1996 and later .... AC 41-932 or equivalent @ 0.060 in
* Refer to the Vehicle Emission Control Information label. If different from what is listed, use the information on the label.
Firing order
   V6 engine... 1-6-5-4-3-2
   V8 engine... 1-8-4-3-6-5-7-2

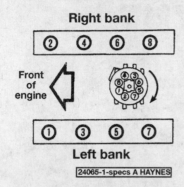

Cylinder location and distributor rotation
(1988 through 1995 TBI V8 engines)

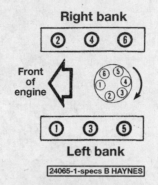

Cylinder location and distributor rotation
(1988 through 1995 TBI V6 engines)

Cylinder location and distributor rotation
(1996 and later SFI V8 engines)

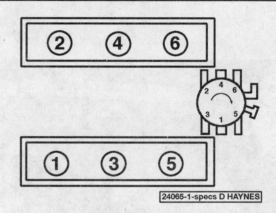

Cylinder location and distributor rotation
(1996 and later SFI V6 engines)

Torque specifications

	Ft-lbs (unless otherwise indicated)
Differential (axle) fill plug	10 to 20
Engine oil drain plug	
1991 and later V8 models	16
All others	20
Manual transmission check/fill plug	15 to 25
Manual transmission drain plug	15 to 25
Automatic transmission pan bolts	120 in-lbs
Throttle body mounting bolts	
1995 and earlier	144 in-lbs
1996 and later	18
Spark plugs	120 to 180 in-lbs
Wheel lug nuts	
1990 and earlier	
With dual rear wheels	125
With single rear wheels	105
1991 and later	
With dual rear wheels	140
With single rear wheels	120

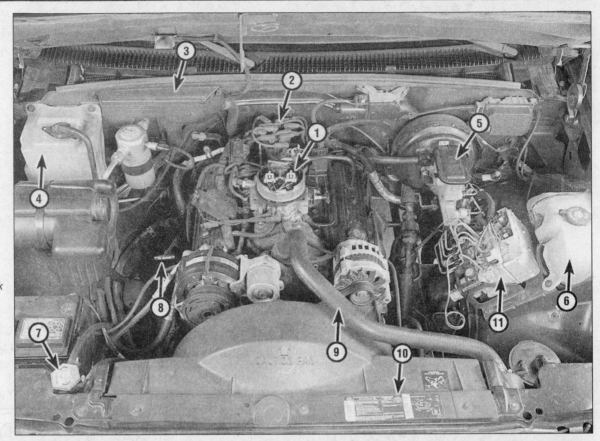

Typical engine compartment layout (5.0L engine shown)

1   TBI unit
2   Distributor cap
3   Relay cover
4   Coolant reservoir
5   Brake fluid reservoir
6   Windshield washer fluid reservoir
7   Radiator cap
8   Engine oil dipstick
9   Upper radiator hose
10 VECI label
11 4WAL Electronic Hydraulic Control Unit

Typical engine compartment component layout (1995 and earlier models) (7.4L V8 shown)

1	Air cleaner assembly	5	Engine oil dipstick
2	Brake fluid reservoir	6	Alternator
3	Battery	7	Engine oil filler cap
4	Upper radiator hose	8	Coolant reservoir

9	Windshield washer fluid reservoir
10	Relay cover
11	Radiator cap

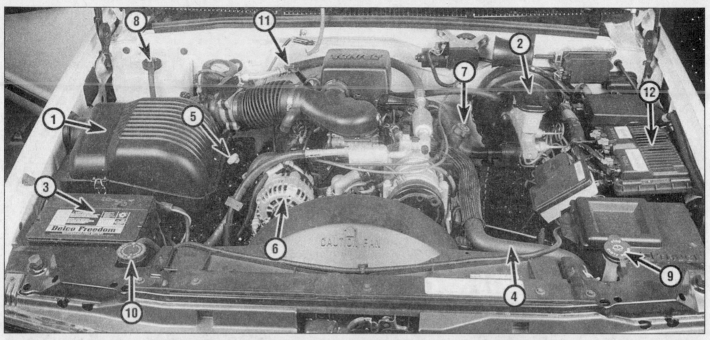

Typical engine compartment component layout, SFI models (5.7L engine shown)

1	Air filter housing	5	Engine oil dipstick	9	Windshield washer reservoir
2	Brake fluid reservoir	6	Alternator	10	Radiator cap
3	Battery	7	Engine oil filler cap	11	Transmission fluid dipstick
4	Upper radiator hose	8	Coolant reservoir	12	Powertrain Control Module (computer)

Typical under side view of engine/ transmission on 2WD models

1   Radiator hose
2   Drivebelt
3   Steering linkage
4   Balljoint grease fitting
5   Automatic transmission pan
6   Exhaust pipe
7   Shock absorber
8   Oil filter

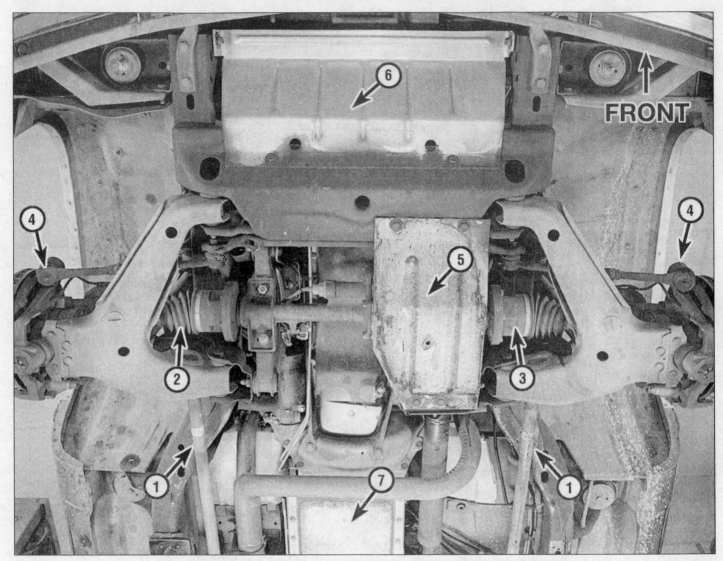

FRONT

Typical under side view of engine/transmission on 4WD models

1	Torsion bars	5	Differential skid plate
2	Right side driveaxle	6	Front skid plate
3	Left side driveaxle	7	Automatic transmission pan
4	Outer tie rod grease fitting		

Typical rear under side component layout on 2WD models

1	Spring	4	Driveshaft U-joint	7	Brake line
2	Shock absorber	5	Rear axle/differential	8	Parking brake cable
3	Muffler	6	Exhaust pipe		

Typical rear under side component layout on 4WD models

1	Spring	4	Rear driveshaft	7	Parking brake cables
2	Shock absorber	5	Rear axle/differential	8	Gas tank shield
3	Muffler	6	Exhaust pipe		

1   Introduction

This Chapter is designed to help the home mechanic maintain the Chevrolet\GMC Pick-up with the goals of maximum performance, economy, safety and reliability in mind.

Included is a master maintenance schedule (page 1-9), followed by procedures dealing specifically with each item on the schedule. Visual checks, adjustments, component replacement and other helpful items are included. Refer to the **accompanying illustrations** of the engine compartment and the underside of the vehicle for the locations of various components.

Servicing your vehicle in accordance with the mileage/time maintenance schedule and the step-by-step procedures will result in a planned maintenance program that should produce a long and reliable service life. Keep in mind that it's a comprehensive plan, so maintaining some items but not others at the specified intervals will not produce the same results.

As you service your vehicle, you will discover that many of the procedures can - and should - be grouped together because of the nature of the particular procedure you're performing or because of the close proximity of two otherwise unrelated components to one another.

For example, if the vehicle is raised for chassis lubrication, you should inspect the exhaust, suspension, steering and fuel systems while you're under the vehicle. When you're rotating the tires, it makes good sense to check the brakes since the wheels are already removed. Finally, let's suppose you have to borrow or rent a torque wrench. Even if you only need it to tighten the spark plugs, you might as well check the torque of as many critical fasteners as time allows.

The first step in this maintenance program is to prepare yourself before the actual work begins. Read through all the procedures you're planning to do, then gather up all the parts and tools needed. If it looks like you might run into problems during a particular job, seek advice from a mechanic or an experienced do-it-yourselfer.

2 Full-size Chevrolet and GMC Pick-ups Maintenance schedule

The following maintenance intervals are based on the assumption the vehicle owner will be doing the maintenance or service work, as opposed to having a dealer service department do the work. Although the time/mileage intervals are loosely based on factory recommendations, most have been shortened to ensure, for example, that such items as lubricants and fluids are checked/changed at intervals that promote maximum engine/driveline service life. Also, subject to the preference of the individual owner interested in keeping the vehicle in peak condition at all times, and with the vehicle's ultimate resale in mind, many of the maintenance procedures may be performed more often than recommended in the following schedule. We encourage such owner initiative.

When the vehicle is new it should be serviced initially by a factory authorized dealer service department to protect the factory warranty. In many cases the initial maintenance check is done at no cost to the owner (check with your dealer service department for additional information).

Every 250 miles or weekly, whichever comes first

Check the engine oil level (Section 4)
Check the engine coolant level (Section 4)
Check the windshield washer fluid level (Section 4)
Check the brake and clutch fluid levels (Section 4)
Check the tires and tire pressures (Section 5)

Every 3000 miles or 3 months, whichever comes first

All items listed above, plus . . .
Check the automatic transmission fluid level (Section 6)
Check the power steering fluid level (Section 7)
Check and service the battery (Section 8)
Check the cooling system (Section 9)
Inspect and replace, if necessary, all underhood hoses (Section 10)
Inspect and replace, if necessary, the windshield wiper blades (Section 11)
Change the engine oil and filter (Section 12)
Lubricate the chassis components (Section 13)
Inspect the suspension and steering components (Section 14)
Inspect the exhaust system (Section 15)
Check the manual transmission lubricant level (Section 17)
Check the differential lubricant level (Section 19)

Every 7500 miles or 12 months, whichever comes first

All items listed above, plus . . .
Check the hydraulic clutch (Section 16)
Rotate the tires (Section 20)
Check the brakes (Section 21)
Inspect the fuel system (Section 22)
Replace the air filter (Section 23)
Replace the fuel filter (Section 24)
Check the throttle body mounting bolt torque (Section 25)
Check the throttle linkage (Section 26)
Check the engine drivebelt (Section 27)
Check the seatbelts (Section 28)
Check the starter safety switch (Section 30)
Check the thermostatically-controlled air cleaner (Section 39)

Every 30,000 miles or 24 months, whichever comes first

All items listed above, plus . . .
Change the automatic transmission fluid (Section 31)**
Change the differential lubricant (Section 33)
Check and repack the front wheel bearings (Section 34)*
Service the cooling system (drain, flush and refill) (Section 35)
Check the EGR system (Section 38)
Replace the spark plugs (Section 40)
Inspect the spark plug wires, distributor cap and rotor (Sections 41 and 42)
Check and adjust, if necessary, the ignition timing (Section 43)

Every 60,000 miles or 36 months, whichever comes first

All items listed above, plus . . .
Change the manual transmission lubricant (Section 32)
Inspect and replace, if necessary, the PCV valve (Section 36)
Inspect the evaporative emissions control system (Section 37)
Inspect the electronic vacuum regulator valve, if equipped (Section 38)

* This item is affected by "severe" operating conditions as described below. If the vehicle is operated under severe conditions, perform all maintenance indicated with an asterisk (*) at 3000 mile/3 month intervals. Severe conditions exist if you mainly operate the vehicle . . .

in dusty areas
towing a trailer
idling for extended periods and/or driving at low speeds
when outside temperatures remain below freezing and most trips are less than four miles long

** If operated under one or more of the following conditions, change the automatic transmission fluid every 15,000 miles:

In heavy city traffic where the outside temperature regularly reaches 90-degrees F or higher
In hilly or mountainous terrain
Frequent trailer pulling

4.4 The engine oil level must be maintained between the marks at all times - it takes one quart of oil to raise the level from the ADD mark to the FULL mark

4.6 Oil is added to the engine after unscrewing the cap from the rocker arm cover

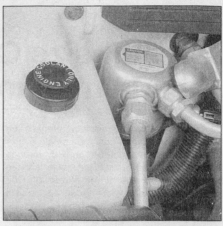

4.8 Be aware of the engine temperature when checking the coolant level

3   Tune-up general information

The term tune-up is used in this manual to represent a combination of individual operations rather than one specific procedure.

If, from the time the vehicle is new, the routine maintenance schedule is followed closely and frequent checks are made of fluid levels and high wear items, as suggested throughout this manual, the engine will be kept in relatively good running condition and the need for additional work will be minimized.

More likely than not, however, there will be times when the engine is running poorly due to lack of regular maintenance. This is even more likely if a used vehicle, which has not received regular and frequent maintenance checks, is purchased. In such cases, an engine tune-up will be needed outside of the regular routine maintenance intervals.

The first step in any tune-up or diagnostic procedure to help correct a poor running engine is a cylinder compression check. A compression check (see Chapter 2, Part B) will help determine the condition of internal engine components and should be used as a guide for tune-up and repair procedures. If, for instance, the compression check indicates serious internal engine wear, a conventional tune-up won't improve the performance of the engine and would be a waste of time and money. Because of its importance, the compression check should be done by someone with the right equipment and the knowledge to use it properly.

The following procedures are those most often needed to bring a generally poor running engine back into a proper state of tune.

Minor tune-up

Check all engine related fluids (Section 4)
Clean, inspect and test the battery
*   (Section 8)*
Check the cooling system (Section 9)
Check all underhood hoses (Section 10)
Check the air filter (Section 23)
Check and adjust the drivebelts
*   (Section 27)*
Check the PCV valve (Section 36)
Replace the spark plugs (Section 40)
Inspect the spark plug and coil wires
*   (Section 41)*
Inspect the distributor cap and rotor
*   (Section 42)*
Check and adjust the ignition timing
*   (Section 43)*

Major tune-up

All items listed under Minor tune-up,
*   plus . . .*
Check the fuel system (Section 22)
Replace the air filter (Section 23)
Check the EGR system (Section 38)
Replace the spark plug wires (Section 41)
Replace the distributor cap and rotor
*   (Section 42)*
Check the ignition system (Chapter 5)
Check the charging system (Chapter 5)

4   Fluid level checks

Refer to illustrations 4.4, 4.6, 4.8, 4.14 and 4.19

Note: *The following are fluid level checks to be done on a 250 mile or weekly basis. Additional fluid level checks can be found in specific maintenance procedures which follow. Regardless of intervals, be alert to fluid leaks under the vehicle which would indicate a fault to be corrected immediately.*

1   Fluids are an essential part of the lubrication, cooling, brake, clutch and windshield washer systems. Because the fluids gradually become depleted and/or contaminated during normal operation of the vehicle, they must be periodically replenished. See *Recommended lubricants and fluids* at the beginning of this Chapter before adding fluid to any of the following components. **Note:** *The vehicle must be on level ground when fluid levels are checked.*

Engine oil

2   The engine oil level is checked with a dipstick that extends through a tube and into the oil pan at the bottom of the engine.

3   The oil level should be checked before the vehicle has been driven, or about 15 minutes after the engine has been shut off. If the oil is checked immediately after driving the vehicle, some of the oil will remain in the upper engine components, resulting in an inaccurate reading on the dipstick.

4   Pull the dipstick out of the tube and wipe all the oil from the end with a clean rag or paper towel. Insert the clean dipstick all the way back into the tube, then pull it out again. Note the oil at the end of the dipstick. Add oil as necessary to keep the level between the ADD and FULL marks on the dipstick **(see illustration)**.

5   Do not overfill the engine by adding too much oil since this may result in oil fouled spark plugs, oil leaks or oil seal failures.

6   Oil is added to the engine after unscrewing a cap from the rocker arm cover **(see illustration)**. A funnel may help to reduce spills.

7   Checking the oil level is an important preventive maintenance step. A consistently low oil level indicates oil leakage through damaged seals, defective gaskets or past worn rings or valve guides. If the oil looks milky or has water droplets in it, the cylinder head gasket(s) may be blown or the head(s) or block may be cracked. The engine should be checked immediately. The condition of the oil should also be checked. Whenever you check the oil level, slide your thumb and index finger up the dipstick before wiping off the oil. If you see small dirt or metal particles clinging to the dipstick, the oil should be changed (Section 12).

Engine coolant

Warning: *Do not allow antifreeze to come in contact with your skin or painted surfaces of the vehicle. Flush contaminated areas immediately with plenty of water. Don't store new coolant or leave old coolant lying around*

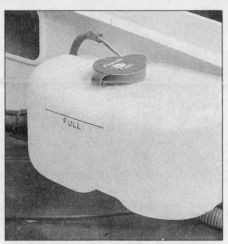

4.14 The windshield washer fluid level can be checked visually through the translucent plastic reservoir- do not fill it above the on the side

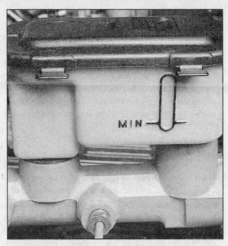

4.19 the brake fluid level is easily checked by looking through the translucent reservoir - when adding fluid, grasp the tabs and rotate the cover up

where it's accessible to children or pets - they're attracted by its sweet taste. Ingestion of even a small amount of coolant can be fatal! Wipe up garage floor and drip pan coolant spills immediately. Keep antifreeze containers covered and repair leaks in the cooling system as soon as they are noted.

8   All vehicles covered by this manual are equipped with a pressurized coolant recovery system. A white plastic coolant reservoir located in the engine compartment is connected by a hose to the radiator filler neck **(see illustration)**. If the engine overheats, coolant escapes through a valve in the radiator cap and travels through the hose into the reservoir. As the engine cools, the coolant is automatically drawn back into the cooling system to maintain the correct level. **Warning:** *Do not remove the radiator cap to check the coolant level when the engine is warm.*

9   The coolant level in the reservoir should be checked regularly. The level in the reservoir varies with the temperature of the engine. When the engine is cold, the coolant level should be at or slightly above the FULL COLD mark on the reservoir. Once the engine has warmed up, the level should be at or near the FULL HOT mark. If it isn't, allow the engine to cool, then remove the cap from the reservoir and add a 50/50 mixture of ethylene glycol-based antifreeze and water.

10   Drive the vehicle and recheck the coolant level. If only a small amount of coolant is required to bring the system up to the proper level, water can be used. However, repeated additions of water will dilute the antifreeze and water solution. In order to maintain the proper ratio of antifreeze and water, always top up the coolant level with the correct mixture. An empty plastic milk jug or bleach bottle makes an excellent container for mixing coolant. Do not use rust inhibitors or additives.

11   If the coolant level drops consistently, there may be a leak in the system. Inspect the radiator, hoses, filler cap, drain plugs and

water pump (see Section 9). If no leaks are noted, have the radiator cap pressure tested by a service station.

12   If you have to remove the radiator cap, wait until the engine has cooled, then wrap a thick cloth around the cap and turn it to the first stop. If coolant or steam escapes, let the engine cool down longer, then remove the cap.

13   Check the condition of the coolant as well. It should be relatively clear. If it's brown or rust colored, the system should be drained, flushed and refilled. Even if the coolant appears to be normal, the corrosion inhibitors wear out, so it must be replaced at the specified intervals.

Windshield washer fluid

14   Fluid for the windshield washer system is located in a plastic reservoir in the engine compartment **(see illustration).**

15   In milder climates, plain water can be used in the reservoir, but it should be kept no more than 2/3 full to allow for expansion if the water freezes. In colder climates, use windshield washer system antifreeze, available at any auto parts store, to lower the freezing point of the fluid. Mix the antifreeze with water in accordance with the manufacturer's directions on the container. **Caution:** *Don't use cooling system antifreeze - it will damage the vehicle's paint.*

16   To help prevent icing in cold weather, warm the windshield with the defroster before using the washer.

Battery electrolyte

17   All vehicles with which this manual is concerned are equipped with a battery which is permanently sealed (except for vent holes) and has no filler caps. Water doesn't have to be added to these batteries at any time. If a maintenance-type battery is installed, the caps on the top of the battery should be removed periodically to check for a low water

level. This check is most critical during the warm summer months.

Brake and clutch fluid

18   The brake master cylinder is mounted on the front of the power booster unit in the engine compartment. The clutch cylinder used on manual transmission-equipped vehicles is mounted adjacent to it on the firewall.

19   The fluid inside is readily visible. The level should be above the MIN marks on the reservoirs **(see illustration)**. If a low level is indicated, be sure to wipe the top of the reservoir cover with a clean rag to prevent contamination of the brake and/or clutch system before removing the cover.

20   When adding fluid, pour it carefully into the reservoir to avoid spilling it on surrounding painted surfaces. Be sure the specified fluid is used, since mixing different types of brake fluid can cause damage to the system. See *Recommended lubricants and fluids* at the front of this Chapter or your owner's manual. **Warning:** *Brake fluid can harm your eyes and damage painted surfaces, so use extreme caution when handling or pouring it. Do not use brake fluid that has been standing open or is more than one year old. Brake fluid absorbs moisture from the air. Excess moisture can cause a dangerous loss of brake performance.*

21   At this time the fluid and master cylinder can be inspected for contamination. The system should be drained and refilled if deposits, dirt particles or water droplets are seen in the fluid.

22   After filling the reservoir to the proper level, make sure the cover is on tight to prevent fluid leakage.

23   The brake fluid level in the master cylinder will drop slightly as the pads and the brake shoes at each wheel wear down during normal operation. If the master cylinder requires repeated additions to keep it at the proper level, it's an indication of leakage in the brake system, which should be corrected immediately. Check all brake lines and connections (see Section 21 for more information).

24   If, upon checking the master cylinder fluid level, you discover one or both reservoirs empty or nearly empty, the brake system should be bled (Chapter 9).

5   Tire and tire pressure checks

Refer to illustrations 5.2, 5.3, 5.4a, 5.4b and 5.8

1   Periodic inspection of the tires may spare you the inconvenience of being stranded with a flat tire. It can also provide you with vital information regarding possible problems in the steering and suspension systems before major damage occurs.

2   The original tires on this vehicle are equipped with 1/2-inch wear bands that will appear when tread depth reaches 1/16-inch, but they don't appear until the tires are worn

out. Tread wear can be monitored with a simple, inexpensive device known as a tread depth indicator **(see illustration)**.

3   Note any abnormal tread wear **(see illustration)**. Tread pattern irregularities such as cupping, flat spots and more wear on one side than the other are indications of front end alignment and/or balance problems. If any of these conditions are noted, take the vehicle to a tire shop or service station to correct the problem.

4   Look closely for cuts, punctures and embedded nails or tacks. Sometimes a tire will hold air pressure for a short time or leak down very slowly after a nail has embedded itself in the tread. If a slow leak persists, check the valve stem core to make sure it's tight **(see illustration)**. Examine the tread for an object that may have embedded itself in the tire or for a "plug" that may have begun to leak (radial tire punctures are repaired with a plug that's installed in a puncture). If a puncture is suspected, it can be easily verified by spraying a solution of soapy water onto the puncture area **(see illustration)**. The soapy solution will bubble if there's a leak. Unless the puncture is unusually large, a tire shop or service station can usually repair the tire.

5   Carefully inspect the inner sidewall of each tire for evidence of brake fluid leakage. If

you see any, inspect the brakes immediately.

6   Correct air pressure adds miles to the lifespan of the tires, improves mileage and enhances overall ride quality. Tire pressure cannot be accurately estimated by looking at a tire, especially if it's a radial. A tire pressure gauge is essential. Keep an accurate gauge in the vehicle. The pressure gauges attached to the nozzles of air hoses at gas stations are often inaccurate.

7   Always check tire pressure when the tires are cold. Cold, in this case, means the vehicle has not been driven over a mile in the three hours preceding a tire pressure check. A pressure rise of four to eight pounds is not uncommon once the tires are warm.

8   Unscrew the valve cap protruding from the wheel or hubcap and push the gauge firmly onto the valve stem **(see illustration)**. Note the reading on the gauge and compare the figure to the recommended tire pressure shown on the placard on the driver's side door pillar. Be sure to reinstall the valve cap to keep dirt and moisture out of the valve stem mechanism. Check all four tires and, if necessary, add enough air to bring them up to the recommended pressure.

9   Don't forget to keep the spare tire inflated to the specified pressure (refer to your owner's manual or the tire sidewall).

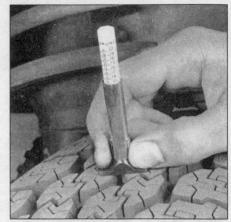

5.2 Use a tire tread depth indicator to monitor tire wear - they are available at auto parts stores and service stations and cost very little

6   Automatic transmission fluid level check

Refer to illustration 6.6

1   The automatic transmission fluid level should be carefully maintained. Low fluid level can lead to slipping or loss of drive,

UNDERINFLATION

CUPPING

Cupping may be caused by:
- Underinflation and/or mechanical irregularities such as out-of-balance condition of wheel and/or tire, and bent or damaged wheel.
- Loose or worn steering tie-rod or steering idler arm.
- Loose, damaged or worn front suspension parts.

OVERINFLATION

INCORRECT TOE-IN OR EXTREME CAMBER

FEATHERING DUE TO MISALIGNMENT

5.3 This chart will help you determine the condition of the tires, the probable cause(s) of abnormal wear and the corrective action necessary

5.4a If a tire loses air on a steady basis, check the valve core first to make sure it's snug (special inexpensive wrenches are commonly available at auto parts stores)

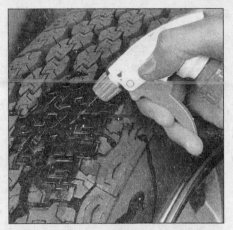

5.4b If the valve core is tight, raise the corner of the vehicle with the low tire and spray a soapy water solution onto the tread as the tire is turned slowly - leaks will cause small bubbles to appear

5.8 To extend the life of the tires, check the air pressure at least once a week with an accurate gauge (don't forget the spare!)

while overfilling can cause foaming and loss of fluid.

2   With the parking brake set, start the engine, then move the shift lever through all the gear ranges, ending in Park. The fluid level must be checked with the vehicle level and the engine running at idle. **Note:** *Incorrect fluid level readings will result if the vehicle has just been driven at high speeds for an extended period, in hot weather in city traffic, or if it has been pulling a trailer. If any of these conditions apply, wait until the fluid has cooled (about 30 minutes).*

3   With the transmission at normal operating temperature, remove the dipstick from the filler tube. The dipstick is located at the rear of the engine compartment on the passenger's side.

4   Carefully touch the fluid at the end of the dipstick to determine if it's cool, warm or hot. Wipe the fluid from the dipstick with a clean rag and push it back into the filler tube until the cap seats.

5   Pull the dipstick out again and note the fluid level.

6   If the fluid felt cool, the level should be in the COLD FULL range **(see illustration)**. If it

felt warm, the level should be near the lower part of the operating range. If the fluid was hot, the level should be near the HOT FULL mark. If additional fluid is required, add it directly into the tube using a funnel. It takes about one pint to raise the level from the bottom of the operating range to the HOT FULL mark with a hot transmission, so add the fluid a little at a time and keep checking the level until it's correct.

7   The condition of the fluid should also be checked along with the level. If the fluid at the end of the dipstick is a dark reddish-brown color, or if it smells burned, it should be changed. If you are in doubt about the condition of the fluid, purchase some new fluid and compare the two for color and smell.

7   Power steering fluid level check

Refer to illustrations 7.2 and 7.6

1   Unlike manual steering, the power steering system relies on fluid which may, over a period of time, require replenishing.

2   The fluid reservoir for the power steering pump is located on the pump body at the front of the engine **(see illustration)**.

3   For the check, the front wheels should be pointed straight ahead and the engine should be off.

4   Use a clean rag to wipe off the reservoir cap and the area around the cap. This will help prevent any foreign matter from entering the reservoir during the check.

5   Twist off the cap and check the temperature of the fluid at the end of the dipstick with your finger.

6   Wipe off the fluid with a clean rag, reinsert the dipstick, then withdraw it and read the fluid level. The level should be at the HOT mark if the fluid was hot to the touch **(see illustration)**. It should be at the COLD mark if the fluid was cool to the touch. Never allow the fluid level to drop below the ADD mark.

7   If additional fluid is required, pour the specified type directly into the reservoir, using a funnel to prevent spills.

8   If the reservoir requires frequent fluid additions, all power steering hoses, hose connections and the power steering pump should be carefully checked for leaks.

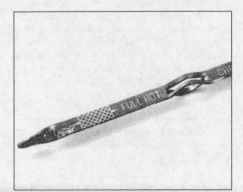

6.6 When checking the automatic transmission fluid level, be sure to note the fluid temperature- the operating range is indicated by the crosshatched area

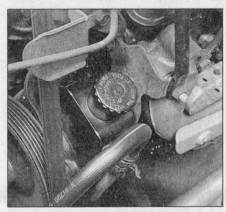

7.2 The power steering fluid reservoir is located near the front of the engine - turn the cap counterclockwise to remove it

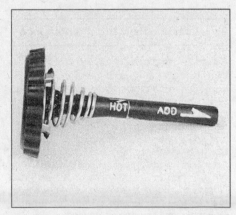

7.6 The marks on the power steering fluid dipstick indicate the safe range

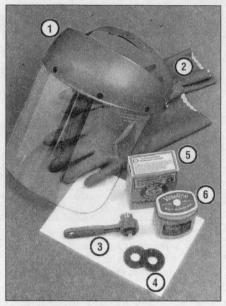

8.6a Make sure the battery terminal bolts are tight

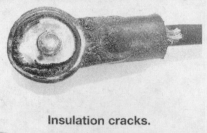

Terminal end corrosion or damage.

Insulation cracks.

Chafed insulation or exposed wires.

Burned or melted insulation.

8.6b Typical battery cable problems

8.1 Tools and materials required for battery maintenance

1 *Face shield/safety goggles* - When removing corrosion with a brush, the acidic particles can easily fly up into your eyes
2 *Rubber gloves* - Another safety item to consider when servicing the battery - remember that's acid inside the battery!
3 *Battery terminal/cable cleaner* - This wire brush cleaning tool will remove all traces of corrosion from the battery and cable
4 *Treated felt washers* - Placing one of these on each terminal, directly under the cable end, will help prevent corrosion (be sure to get the correct type for side-terminal batteries)
5 *Baking soda* - A solution of baking soda and water can be used to neutralize corrosion
6 *Petroleum jelly* - A layer of this on the battery terminal bolts will help prevent corrosion

8   Battery check and maintenance

Refer to illustrations 8.1, 8.6a and 8.6b
Warning: *Certain precautions must be followed when checking and servicing the battery. Hydrogen gas, which is highly flammable, is always present in the battery cells, so don't smoke and keep open flames and sparks away from the battery. The electrolyte inside the battery is actually dilute sulfuric acid, which will cause injury if splashed on your skin or in your eyes. It will also ruin clothes and painted surfaces. When removing the battery cables, always detach the negative cable first and hook it up last!*
1 Battery maintenance is an important procedure which will help ensure that you are not stranded because of a dead battery. Several tools are required for this procedure **(see illustration)**.
2 When checking/servicing the battery, always turn the engine and all accessories off.
3 A sealed (sometimes called maintenance-free), side-terminal battery is standard equipment on these vehicles. The cell caps cannot be removed, no electrolyte checks are required and water cannot be added to the cells. However, if a maintenance-type aftermarket battery has been installed, the following maintenance procedure can be used.
4 Remove the caps and check the electrolyte level in each of the battery cells. It must be above the plates. There's usually a split-ring indicator in each cell to indicate the correct level. If the level is low, add distilled water only, then reinstall the cell caps. **Caution:** *Overfilling the cells may cause electrolyte to spill over during periods of heavy charging, causing corrosion and damage to nearby components.*
5 The external condition of the battery should be checked periodically. Look for damage such as a cracked case.
6 Check the tightness of the battery cable bolts **(see illustration)** to ensure good electrical connections. Inspect the entire length of each cable, looking for cracked or abraded insulation and frayed conductors **(see illustration)**.
7 If corrosion (visible as white, fluffy deposits) is evident, remove the cables from the terminals, clean them with a battery brush and reinstall them. Corrosion can be kept to a minimum by applying a layer of petroleum jelly or grease to the bolt threads.
8 Make sure the battery carrier is in good condition and the hold-down clamp is tight. If the battery is removed (see Chapter 5 for the removal and installation procedure), make sure that no parts remain in the bottom of the carrier when it's reinstalled. When reinstalling the hold-down clamp, don't overtighten the bolt.
9 Corrosion on the carrier, battery case and surrounding areas can be removed with a solution of water and baking soda. Apply the mixture with a small brush, let it work, then rinse it off with plenty of clean water.
10 Any metal parts of the vehicle damaged by corrosion should be coated with a zinc-based primer, then painted.
11 Additional information on the battery, charging and jump starting can be found in the front of this manual and Chapter 5.

9   Cooling system check

Refer to illustration 9.4
1 Many major engine failures can be attributed to a faulty cooling system. If the vehicle is equipped with an automatic transmission, the cooling system also cools the transmission fluid and thus plays an important role in prolonging transmission life.

Check for a chafed area that could fail prematurely.

Check for a soft area indicating the hose has deteriorated inside.

Overtightening the clamp on a hardened hose will damage the hose and cause a leak.

Check each hose for swelling and oil-soaked ends. Cracks and breaks can be located by squeezing the hose.

9.4 Hoses, like drivebelts, have a habit of failing at the worst possible time - to prevent the inconvenience of a blown radiator or heater hose, inspect them carefully as shown here

2   The cooling system should be checked with the engine cold. Do this before the vehicle is driven for the day or after it has been shut off for at least three hours.

3   Remove the radiator cap by turning it to the left until it reaches a stop. If you hear a hissing sound (indicating there is still pressure in the system), wait until this stops. Now press down on the cap with the palm of your hand and continue turning to the left until the cap can be removed. Thoroughly clean the cap, inside and out, with clean water. Also clean the filler neck on the radiator. All traces of corrosion should be removed. The coolant inside the radiator should be relatively transparent. If it is rust colored, the system should be drained and refilled (Section 35). If the coolant level is not up to the top, add additional antifreeze/coolant mixture (see Section 4).

4   Carefully check the large upper and lower radiator hoses along with the smaller diameter heater hoses which run from the engine to the firewall. Inspect each hose along its entire length, replacing any hose which is cracked, swollen or shows signs of deterioration. Cracks may become more apparent if the hose is squeezed **(see illustration)**. Regardless of condition, it's a good idea to replace hoses with new ones every two years.

5   Make sure all hose connections are tight. A leak in the cooling system will usually show up as white or rust colored deposits on the areas adjoining the leak. If wire-type clamps are used at the ends of the hoses, it may be a good idea to replace them with more secure screw-type clamps.

6   Use compressed air or a soft brush to remove bugs, leaves, etc. from the front of the radiator or air conditioning condenser. Be careful not to damage the delicate cooling fins or cut yourself on them.

7   Every other inspection, or at the first indication of cooling system problems, have the cap and system pressure tested. If you don't have a pressure tester, most gas stations and repair shops will do this for a minimal charge.

10   Underhood hose check and replacement

Refer to illustration 10.1

General

1   **Caution:** *Replacement of air conditioning hoses must be left to a dealer service department or air conditioning shop that has the equipment to depressurize the system safely. Never remove air conditioning components or hoses* **(see illustration)** *until the system has been depressurized.*

2   High temperatures in the engine compartment can cause the deterioration of the rubber and plastic hoses used for engine, accessory and emission systems operation. Periodic inspection should be made for cracks, loose clamps, material hardening and leaks. Information specific to the cooling system hoses can be found in Section 9.

3   Some, but not all, hoses are secured to the fittings with clamps. Where clamps are used, check to be sure they haven't lost their tension, allowing the hose to leak. If clamps aren't used, make sure the hose has not expanded and/or hardened where it slips over the fitting, allowing it to leak.

Vacuum hoses

4   It's quite common for vacuum hoses, especially those in the emissions system, to be color coded or identified by colored stripes molded into them. Various systems require hoses with different wall thicknesses, collapse resistance and temperature resistance. When replacing hoses, be sure the new ones are made of the same material.

5   Often the only effective way to check a hose is to remove it completely from the vehicle. If more than one hose is removed, be sure to label the hoses and fittings to ensure correct installation.

6   When checking vacuum hoses, be sure to include any plastic T-fittings in the check. Inspect the fittings for cracks and the hose where it fits over the fitting for distortion, which could cause leakage.

7   A small piece of vacuum hose (1/4-inch inside diameter) can be used as a stethoscope to detect vacuum leaks. Hold one end of the hose to your ear and probe around vacuum hoses and fittings, listening for the "hissing" sound characteristic of a vacuum leak. **Warning:** *When probing with the vacuum hose stethoscope, be very careful not to come into contact with moving engine components such as the drivebelt, cooling fan, etc.*

Fuel hose

Warning: *There are certain precautions which must be taken when inspecting or servicing fuel system components. Work in a well ventilated area and do not allow open flames (cigarettes, appliance pilot lights, etc.) or bare light bulbs near the work area. Mop up any spills immediately and do not store fuel soaked rags where they could ignite. The fuel system is under pressure, so if any fuel lines are to be disconnected, the pressure in the system must be relieved first (see Chapter 4 for more information).*

8   Check all rubber fuel lines for deterioration and chafing. Check especially for cracks in areas where the hose bends and just before fittings, such as where a hose attaches to the fuel filter.

9   High quality fuel line, usually identified by the word Fluroelastomer printed on the hose, should be used for fuel line replacement. Never, under any circumstances, use unreinforced vacuum line, clear plastic tubing or water hose for fuel lines.

10.1 Air conditioning hoses are identified by the metal tubes used at all bends (arrow) - do not disconnect or accidentally damage the air conditioning hoses (the system is under high pressure)

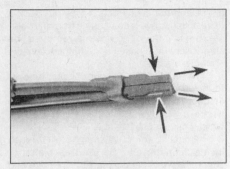

11.6 Use needle-nose pliers to push in and pull out the two metal clip, then slide the old element out - slide the new element in and lock in place with the metal clip

10   Spring-type clamps are commonly used on fuel lines. These clamps often lose their tension over a period of time, and can be "sprung" during removal. Replace all spring-type clamps with screw clamps whenever a hose is replaced.

Metal lines

11   Sections of metal line are often used for fuel line between the fuel pump and fuel injection unit. Check carefully to be sure the line has not been bent or crimped and that cracks have not started in the line.
12   If a section of metal fuel line must be replaced, only seamless steel tubing should be used, since copper and aluminum tubing don't have the strength necessary to withstand normal engine vibration.
13   Check the metal brake lines where they enter the master cylinder and brake proportioning unit (if used) for cracks in the lines or loose fittings. Any sign of brake fluid leakage calls for an immediate thorough inspection of the brake system.

11   Wiper blade inspection and replacement

Refer to illustration 11.6
1   The windshield and rear window (models so equipped) wiper and blade assembly should be inspected periodically for damage, loose components and cracked or worn blade elements.
2   Road film can build up on the wiper blades and affect their efficiency, so they should be washed regularly with a mild detergent solution.
3   The action of the wiping mechanism can loosen the bolts, nuts and fasteners, so they should be checked and tightened, as necessary, at the same time the wiper blades are checked.
4   If the wiper blade elements (sometimes called inserts) are cracked, worn or warped, they should be replaced with new ones.
5   Pull the wiper blade/arm assembly away from the glass.
6   Depress the blade-to-arm connector

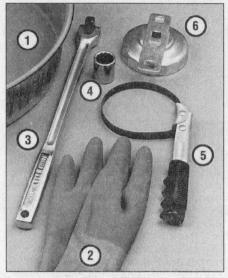

12.3 These tools are required when changing the engine oil and filter

1   *Drain pan - It should be fairly shallow in depth, but wide to prevent spills*
2   *Rubber gloves - When removing the drain plug and filter, you will get oil on your hands (the gloves will prevent burns)*
3   *Breaker bar - Sometimes the oil drain plug is tight, and a long breaker bar is needed to loosen it*
4   *Socket - To be used with the breaker bar or a ratchet (must be the correct size to fit the drain plug - six-point preferred)*
5   *Filter wrench - This is a metal band-type wrench, which requires clearance around the filter to be effective*
6   *Filter wrench - This type fits on the bottom of the filter and can be turned with a ratchet or breaker bar (different-size wrenches are available for different types of filters)*

and slide the blade assembly off the wiper arm and over the retaining stud **(see illustration)**.
7   Pinch the tabs at the end, then slide the element out of the blade assembly.
8   Compare the new element with the old for length, design, etc.
9   Slide the new element into place. It will automatically lock at the correct location.
10   Reinstall the blade assembly on the arm, wet the windshield or rear window and check for proper operation.

12   Engine oil and filter change

Refer to illustrations 12.3, 12.9, 12.14 and 12.18
1   Frequent oil changes are the most important preventive maintenance procedures that can be done by the home mechanic. As engine oil ages, it becomes diluted and contaminated, which leads to

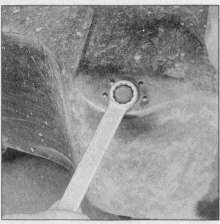

12.9 The oil drain plug is located at the bottom of the pan and should be removed with a socket or box-end-wrench- Do Not use an open-end wrench (the corners on the hex can be easily rounded off)

premature engine wear.
2   Although some sources recommend oil filter changes every other oil change, we feel that the minimal cost of an oil filter and the relative ease with which it is installed dictate that a new filter be installed every time the oil is changed.
3   Gather together all necessary tools and materials before beginning this procedure **(see illustration)**.
4   You should have plenty of clean rags and newspapers handy to mop up any spills. Access to the under side of the vehicle may be improved if the vehicle can be lifted on a hoist, driven onto ramps or supported by jackstands. **Warning:** *Do not work under a vehicle which is supported only by a bumper, hydraulic or scissors-type jack.*
5   If this is your first oil change, get under the vehicle and familiarize yourself with the locations of the oil drain plug and the oil filter. The engine and exhaust components will be warm during the actual work, so note how they are situated to avoid touching them when working under the vehicle.
6   Warm the engine to normal operating temperature. If the new oil or any tools are needed, use this warm-up time to gather everything necessary for the job. The correct type of oil for your application can be found in Recommended lubricants and fluids at the beginning of this Chapter.
7   With the engine oil warm (warm engine oil will drain better and more built-up sludge will be removed with it), raise and support the vehicle. Make sure it's safely supported!
8   Move all necessary tools, rags and newspapers under the vehicle. Set the drain pan under the drain plug. Keep in mind that the oil will initially flow from the pan with some force; position the pan accordingly.
9   Being careful not to touch any of the hot exhaust components, use a wrench to remove the drain plug near the bottom of the oil pan **(see illustration)**. Depending on how hot the oil is, you may want to wear gloves

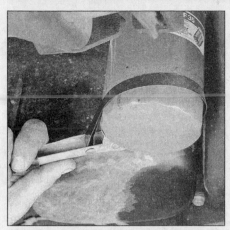

12.14 Use a strap-type oil filter wrench to loosen the filter- if access makes removal difficult , other types of filter wrenches are available

12.18 Lubricate the gasket with clean oil before installing the filter on the engine

13.1 Materials required for chassis and body lubrication

1   **Engine oil** - *Light engine oil in a can like this can be used for door and hood hinges*

2   **Graphite spray** - *Used to lubricate lock cylinders*

3   **Grease** - *Grease, in a variety of types and weights, is available for use in a grease gun. Check the Specifications for your requirements*

4   **Grease gun** - *A common grease gun, shown here with a detachable hose and nozzle, is needed for chassis lubrication. After use, clean it thoroughly*

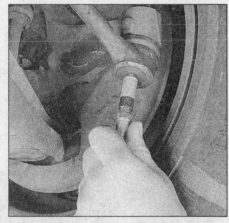

13.6 After cleaning the fitting, push the nozzle firmly into place and pump grease into the component - usually about two pumps of the gun will be sufficient

while unscrewing the plug the final few turns.

10   Allow the old oil to drain into the pan. It may be necessary to move the pan as the oil flow slows to a trickle.

11   After all the oil has drained, wipe off the drain plug with a clean rag. Small metal particles may cling to the plug and would immediately contaminate the new oil.

12   Clean the area around the drain plug opening and reinstall the plug. Tighten the plug securely with the wrench. If a torque wrench is available, use it to tighten the plug.

13   Move the drain pan into position under the oil filter.

14   Use the filter wrench to loosen the oil filter **(see illustration)**. Chain or metal band filter wrenches may distort the filter canister, but it doesn't matter since the filter will be discarded anyway.

15   Completely unscrew the old filter. Be careful; it's full of oil. Empty the oil inside the filter into the drain pan.

16   Compare the old filter with the new one to make sure they're the same type.

17   Use a clean rag to remove all oil, dirt and sludge from the area where the oil filter mounts to the engine. Check the old filter to make sure the rubber gasket isn't stuck to the engine. If the gasket is stuck to the engine (use a flashlight if necessary), remove it.

18   Apply a light coat of clean oil to the rubber gasket on the new oil filter **(see illustration)**.

19   Attach the new filter to the engine, following the tightening directions printed on the filter canister or packing box. Most filter manufacturers recommend against using a filter wrench due to the possibility of overtightening and damage to the seal.

20   Remove all tools, rags, etc. from under the vehicle, being careful not to spill the oil in the drain pan, then lower the vehicle.

21   Move to the engine compartment and locate the oil filler cap.

22   Pour the fresh oil through the filler opening. A funnel may be helpful.

23   Pour four quarts of fresh oil into the

engine. Wait a few minutes to allow the oil to drain into the pan, then check the level on the oil dipstick (see Section 4 if necessary). If the oil level is above the ADD mark, start the engine and allow the new oil to circulate.

24   Run the engine for only about a minute and then shut it off. Immediately look under the vehicle and check for leaks at the oil pan drain plug and around the oil filter. If either is leaking, tighten with a bit more force.

25   With the new oil circulated and the filter now completely full, recheck the level on the dipstick and add more oil as necessary.

26   During the first few trips after an oil change, make it a point to check frequently for leaks and proper oil level.

27   The old oil drained from the engine cannot be reused in its present state and should be disposed of. Oil reclamation centers, auto repair shops and gas stations will normally accept the oil, which can be refined and used again. After the oil has cooled it can be drained into a container (capped plastic jugs, topped bottles, milk cartons, etc.) for transport to one of these disposal sites. Don't dispose of the oil by pouring it on the ground or down a drain!

13   Chassis lubrication

Refer to illustrations 13.1 and 13.6

1   Refer to *Recommended lubricants and fluids* at the front of this Chapter to obtain the necessary grease, etc. You'll also need a grease gun **(see illustration)**. Occasionally plugs will be installed rather than grease fittings. If so, grease fittings will have to be purchased and installed.

2   Look under the vehicle and see if grease fittings or plugs are installed. If there are plugs, remove them and buy grease fittings, which will thread into the component. A dealer or auto parts store will be able to supply the correct fittings. Straight, as well as angled, fittings are available.

3   For easier access under the vehicle, raise it with a jack and place jackstands under the frame. Make sure it's safely supported by the stands. If the wheels are to be removed at this interval for tire rotation or brake inspection, loosen the lug nuts slightly while the vehicle is still on the ground.

4   Before beginning, force a little grease out of the nozzle to remove any dirt from the end of the gun. Wipe the nozzle clean with a rag.

5   With the grease gun and plenty of clean rags, crawl under the vehicle and begin lubricating the components.

6   Wipe one of the grease fitting nipples clean and push the nozzle firmly over it **(see**

illustration). Pump the gun until the component is completely lubricated. On balljoints, stop pumping when the rubber seal is firm to the touch. Do not pump too much grease into the fitting as it could rupture the seal. For all other suspension and steering components, continue pumping grease into the fitting until it oozes out of the joint between the two components. If it escapes around the grease gun nozzle, the nipple is clogged or the nozzle is not completely seated on the fitting. Resecure the gun nozzle to the fitting and try again. If necessary, replace the fitting with a new one.

7   Wipe the excess grease from the components and the grease fitting. Repeat the procedure for the remaining fittings.

8   On some four-speed manual transmissions, there's also a grease fitting for the shift linkage. Don't forget to lubricate it, also.

9   On manual transmission-equipped models, lubricate the clutch linkage pivot points with clean engine oil. Lubricate the pushrod-to-fork contact points with chassis grease.

10   On manual transmission-equipped models, lubricate the clutch fork ball stud. The fitting is located on the clutch housing. Do not over-lubricate this mechanism as this may cause the clutch assembly to malfunction. Also clean and lubricate the parking brake cable, along with the cable guides and levers. This can be done by smearing some of the chassis grease onto the cable and its related parts with your fingers.

11   Lube the driveshaft slip-yoke. On models with a one piece driveshaft, remove the driveshaft (see Chapter 8). Coat the slip-yoke splines with grease. Reinstall the driveshaft. On models with two piece driveshafts, a grease fitting is provided at the center slip-yoke. Pump several strokes into the slip-yoke.

12   The steering gear seldom requires the addition of lubricant, but if there is obvious leakage of grease at the seals, remove the plug or cover and check the lubricant level. If the level is low, add the specified lubricant.

14.3 With the steering wheel locked and the vehicle raised, grasp the front tire as shown and try to move it back-and-forth - if any play is noted, check the idler arm and tie-rod ends for looseness

13   Open the hood and smear a little chassis grease on the hood latch mechanism. Have an assistant pull the hood release lever from inside the vehicle as you lubricate the cable at the latch.

14   Lubricate all the hinges (door, hood, etc.) with engine oil to keep them in proper working order.

15   The key lock cylinders can be lubricated with spray graphite or silicone lubricant, which is available at auto parts stores.

16   Lubricate the door weatherstripping with silicone spray. This will reduce chafing and retard wear.

14   Suspension and steering check

Refer to illustrations 14.3 and 14.4

1   Indications of a fault in these systems are excessive play in the steering wheel before the front wheels react, excessive sway around corners, body movement over rough roads or binding at some point as the steering wheel is turned.

2   Raise the front of the vehicle periodically and visually check the suspension and steering components for wear. Because of the work to be done, make sure the vehicle cannot fall from the stands.

3   Check the wheel bearings. Do this by spinning the front wheels. Listen for any abnormal noises and watch to make sure the wheel spins true (doesn't wobble). Grab the top and bottom of the tire and pull in-and-out on it **(see illustration)**. Notice any movement which would indicate a loose wheel bearing assembly. If the bearings are suspect, refer to Section 34 and Chapter 10 for more information.

4   From under the vehicle check for loose bolts, broken or disconnected parts and deteriorated rubber bushings on all suspension and steering components. Look for fluid leaking from the steering assembly. Check the power steering hoses and connections for leaks **(see illustration)**.

5   Have an assistant turn the steering wheel from side-to-side and check the steering components for free movement, chafing and binding. If the steering doesn't react with the movement of the steering wheel, try to determine where the slack is located.

6   Check the driveaxle boots on 4WD models. The driveaxle boots are very important because they prevent dirt, water and foreign material from entering and damaging the constant velocity joints. Oil and grease can cause the boot material to deteriorate prematurely, so it's a good idea to wash the boots with soap and water. Inspect the boots for tears and cracks as well as loose clamps. If there is any evidence of cracks or leaking lubricant, they must be replaced as described in Chapter 8.

15   Exhaust system check

Refer to illustration 15.2

1   With the engine cold (at least three hours after the vehicle has been driven),

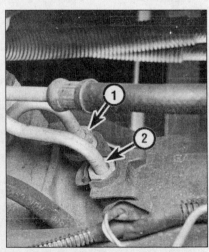

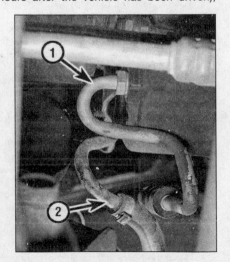

14.4 Typical power steering hose routing

1   Feed line   2   Return line

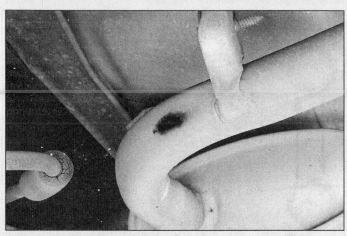

15.2 On light-colored exhaust pipes, leaks usually show up easily as brown or black stains - this stain around a small hole is indicative of a tailpipe needing replacement

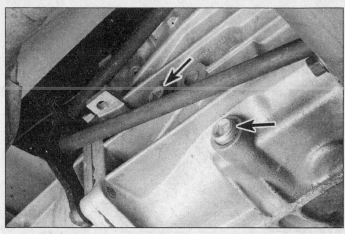

17.1 Typical locations of the manual transmission check and drain plugs (arrow)

check the complete exhaust system from the manifold to the end of the tailpipe. Be careful around the catalytic converter, which may be hot even after three hours. The inspection should be done with the vehicle on a hoist to permit unrestricted access. If a hoist isn't available, raise the vehicle and support it securely on jackstands.

2   Check the exhaust pipes and connections for signs of leakage and/or corrosion indicating a potential failure **(see illustration)**. Make sure that all brackets and hangers are in good condition and tight.

3   Inspect the underside of the body for holes, corrosion, open seams, etc. which may allow exhaust gasses to enter the passenger compartment. Seal all body openings with silicone or body putty.

4   Rattles and other noises can often be traced to the exhaust system, especially the hangers, mounts and heat shields. Try to move the pipes, mufflers and catalytic converter. If the components can come in contact with the body or suspension parts, secure the exhaust system with new brackets and hangers.

16   Hydraulic clutch check

1   Check all hoses for cracks and distortion.

2   Check the clutch master cylinder and slave cylinder for loose mounting screws and leaks.

3   Check for smooth operation of the clutch pedal with no binding, looseness or sponginess.

4   While an assistant depresses the clutch pedal, check the operation of the slave cylinder pushrod. You may need to remove a plug in the clutch housing first. The pushrod should move in and out of the slave cylinder about an inch as the pedal is depressed and released.

5   Replace any damaged or leaking components. Bleed the system if the pedal is

spongy, the pushrod travel is not sufficient, or the slave cylinder, master cylinder or any lines were disconnected (see Chapter 8).

17   Manual transmission lubricant level check

Refer to illustration 17.1

1   The manual transmission has a fill plug which must be removed to check the lubricant level **(see illustration)**. If the vehicle is raised to gain access to the plug, be sure to support it safely on jackstands - DO NOT crawl under a vehicle which is supported only by a jack!

2   Remove the plug from the transmission and use your little finger to reach inside the housing to feel the lubricant level. The level should be at or near the bottom of the plug hole.

3   If it isn't, add the recommended lubricant through the plug hole with a syringe or squeeze bottle.

4   Install and tighten the plug and check for leaks after the first few miles of driving.

18   Transfer case lubricant level check (4WD models only)

Refer to illustration 18.1

1   The transfer case lubricant is checked by removing the fill plug located in the side of the case **(see illustration)**.

2   After removing the plug, reach inside the hole. The lubricant level should be just at the bottom of the hole. If it isn't, add the recommended lubricant through the hole with a syringe or squeeze bottle.

19   Differential lubricant level check

Refer to illustrations 19.2a and 19.2b

1   The differential has a filler plug which must be removed to check the lubricant level. If the vehicle is raised to gain access to the plug, be sure to support it safely on jackstands - DO NOT crawl under the vehicle when it's supported only by the jack.

2   Remove the filler plug from the side of the differential **(see illustrations)**.

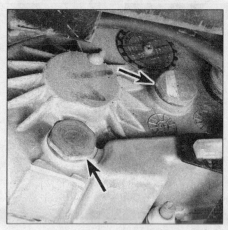

18.1 Locations of the transfer case drain and fill plugs (4WD models only)

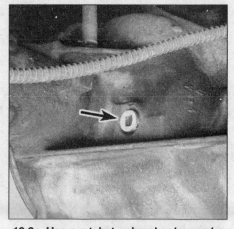

19.2a Use a ratchet or breaker bar and a 3/8-inch drive extension to remove the rear differential check/fill plug

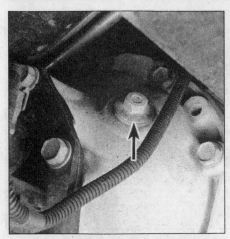

19.2b On 4WD models, you must also check the lubricant level in the front differential - remove the filler plug

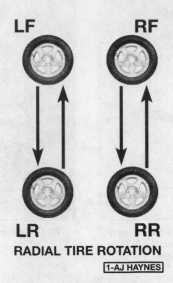

RADIAL TIRE ROTATION

1-AJ HAYNES

20.2 Tire rotation diagram

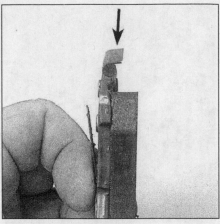

21.4 The brake pad wear sensors will contact the rotors and make a squealing noise when the pad is worn out

3   The lubricant level should be at the bottom of the plug opening. If not, use a syringe to add the recommended lubricant until it just starts to run out of the opening. On some models a tag is located in the area of the plug which gives information regarding lubricant type, particularly on models equipped with a limited slip differential.

4   Install the plug and tighten it securely.

20   Tire rotation

Refer to illustration 20.2

1   The tires should be rotated at the specified intervals and whenever uneven wear is noticed.

2   Refer to the **accompanying illustration** for the preferred tire rotation pattern.

3   Refer to the information in *Jacking and towing* at the front of this manual for the proper procedures to follow when raising the vehicle and changing a tire. If the brakes are to be checked, don't apply the parking brake as stated. Make sure the tires are blocked to prevent the vehicle from rolling as it's raised.

4   Preferably, the entire vehicle should be raised at the same time. This can be done on a hoist or by jacking up each corner and then lowering the vehicle onto jackstands placed under the frame rails. Always use four jackstands and make sure the vehicle is safely supported.

5   After rotation, check and adjust the tire pressures as necessary and be sure to check the lug nut tightness.

21   Brake check

Refer to illustrations 21.4, 21.6, 21.12, 21.14 and 21.16
Note: *For detailed photographs of the brake system, refer to Chapter 9.*
Warning: *Brake system dust may contain asbestos, which is hazardous to your health. DO NOT blow it out with compressed air, inhale it or use gasoline or solvents to remove*

it. *Use brake system cleaner or denatured alcohol only.*

1   In addition to the specified intervals, the brakes should be inspected every time the wheels are removed or whenever a defect is suspected.

2   To check the brakes, raise the vehicle and place it securely on jackstands. Remove the wheels (see *Jacking and towing* at the front of the manual, if necessary).

Disc brakes

3   Disc brakes are used on the front wheels. Extensive rotor damage can occur if the pads are not replaced when needed.

4   Some vehicles are equipped with a wear sensor attached to the inner pad. This is a small, bent piece of metal which is visible from the inner side of the brake caliper. When the pad wears to the specified limit, the metal sensor rubs against the rotor and makes a squealing sound **(see illustration)**.

5   The disc brake calipers, which contain the pads, are visible with the wheels removed. There is an outer pad and an inner pad in each caliper. All pads should be inspected.

21.6 The front disc brake pads can be easily by looking through the inspection window in each caliper

21.12 Moving the parking brake lever off its stop

21.14 The brake shoe lining thickness is measured from the outer surface of the lining to the metal shoe

21.16 To check for wheel cylinder leakage, use a small screwdriver to pry the boot away from the cylinder

6 Each caliper has a "window" to inspect the pads. Check the thickness of the pad lining by looking into the caliper at each end and down through the inspection window at the top of the housing **(see illustration)**. If the wear sensor is very close to the rotor or the pad material has worn to about 1/8-inch or less, the pads should be replaced.

7 If you're unsure about the exact thickness of the remaining lining material, remove the pads for further inspection or replacement (refer to Chapter 9).

8 Before installing the wheels, check for leakage and/or damage (cracks, splitting, etc.) around the brake hose connections. Replace the hose or fittings as necessary, referring to Chapter 9.

9 Check the condition of the rotor. Look for score marks, deep scratches and burned spots. If these conditions exist, the hub/rotor assembly should be removed for servicing (Section 35).

Drum brakes

10 On rear brakes, remove the drum by pulling it off the axle and brake assembly. If this proves difficult, make sure the parking brake is released, then squirt penetrating oil around the center hub areas. Allow the oil to soak in and try to pull the drum off again.

11 If the drum still cannot be pulled off, the parking brake lever will have to be lifted slightly off its stop. This is done by first removing the small round plug from the backing plate (leading/trailing type brake) or brake drum (duo-servo type brake).

12 With the plug removed, push the lever off of its stop using a phillips head screwdriver (leading/trailing type brake) **(see illustration)**. This will move the brake shoes away from the drum. If your vehicle has duo-servo drum brakes, refer to Chapter 9, **illustration 5.4** for the shoe retracting procedure. If the drum still won't pull off, tap around its inner circumference with a soft-face hammer.

13 With the drum removed, do not touch any brake dust (see the **Warning** at the beginning of this Section).

14 Note the thickness of the lining material on both the front and rear brake shoes. If the material has worn away to within 1/16-inch of the recessed rivets or metal backing, the shoes should be replaced **(see illustration)**. The shoes should also be replaced if they're cracked, glazed (shiny surface) or contaminated with brake fluid.

15 Make sure that all the brake assembly springs are connected and in good condition.

16 Check the brake components for any signs of fluid leakage. Carefully pry back the rubber cups on the wheel cylinders located at the top of the brake shoes **(see illustration)**. Any leakage is an indication that the wheel cylinders should be overhauled immediately (Chapter 9). Also check brake hoses and connections for signs of leakage.

17 Wipe the inside of the drum with a clean rag and brake cleaner or denatured alcohol. Again, be careful not to breathe the dangerous asbestos dust.

18 Check the inside of the drum for cracks, score marks, deep scratches and hard spots, which will appear as small discolorations. If these imperfections cannot be removed with fine emery cloth, the drum must be taken to a machine shop equipped to turn the drums.

19 If after the inspection process all parts are in good working condition, reinstall the brake drum.

20 Install the wheels and lower the vehicle.

Parking brake

21 The parking brake operates from a foot pedal and locks the rear brake system. The easiest, and perhaps most obvious method of periodically checking the operation of the parking brake assembly is to stop the vehicle on a steep hill with the parking brake set and the transmission in Neutral. If the parking brake cannot prevent the vehicle from rolling, adjust it (see Chapter 9).

22 Fuel system check

Warning: *Gasoline is extremely flammable,* *so take extra precautions when working on any part of the fuel system. Don't smoke or allow open flames or bare light bulbs in or near the work area, and don't work in a garage where a natural gas-type appliance (such as a water heater or clothes dryer) with a pilot light is present. If you spill fuel on your skin, rinse it off immediately with soap and water. Have a Class B fire extinguisher on hand. No components should be disconnected until the pressure has been relieved (see Chapter 4).*

1 On most models the main fuel tank is located under the left side of the vehicle.

2 The fuel system is most easily checked with the vehicle raised on a hoist so the components underneath the vehicle are readily visible and accessible.

3 If the smell of gasoline is noticed while driving or after the vehicle has been in the sun, the system should be thoroughly inspected immediately.

4 Remove the gas tank cap and check for damage, corrosion and an unbroken sealing imprint on the gasket. Replace the cap with a new one if necessary.

5 With the vehicle raised, check the gas tank and filler neck for punctures, cracks and other damage. The connection between the filler neck and the tank is especially critical. Sometimes a rubber filler neck will leak due to loose clamps or deteriorated rubber, problems a home mechanic can usually rectify. **Warning:** *Do not, under any circumstances, try to repair a fuel tank yourself (except rubber components). A welding torch or any open flame can easily cause the fuel vapors to explode if the proper precautions are not taken!*

6 Carefully check all rubber hoses and metal lines leading away from the fuel tank. Look for loose connections, deteriorated hoses, crimped lines and other damage. Follow the lines to the front of the vehicle, carefully inspecting them all the way. Repair or replace damaged sections as necessary.

7 If a fuel odor is still evident after the inspection, refer to Section 37.

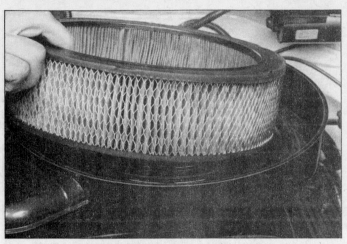

23.4a Lift the air cleaner out of the housing
(1995 and earlier models)

23.4b On SFI models, lift and hold the duct while pulling out the
filter (heavy-duty filter option shown). The arrow indicates the air
cleaner restriction indicator

23 Air filter replacement

Refer to illustrations 23.4a and 23.4b
Note: *1996 and later models are equipped with an air cleaner restriction indicator. It's located in the duct between the mass air flow sensor and the air cleaner. The normally green indicator will turn orange and "CHANGE AIR FILTER" will appear if the filter requires replacement. There is a reset button on top of the unit. Press the button after changing the filter.*

1   At the specified intervals, the air filter should be renewed.
2   On 1988 through 1995 TBI models, the air filter is located in a conventional filter housing mounted on top of the throttle body. Unscrew the wing nut and lift off the cover.
3   On 1996 and later SFI models, the air filter is located in a plastic filter housing mounted to the right inner fender well. Unsnap the lid retaining clips and pull off the cover.
4   On TBI models, lift out the filter **(see illustration)**. On SFI models, remove the filter by lifting up the duct and pulling and twisting the filter off the duct **(see illustration)**.
5   Place the new filter in the housing. Make sure the filter is properly seated and install the housing cover.

24 Fuel filter replacement

Refer to illustration 24.3
Warning: *Gasoline is extremely flammable, so take extra precautions when working on any part of the fuel system. Don't smoke or allow open flames or bare light bulbs in or near the work area, and don't work in a garage where a natural gas-type appliance (such as a water heater or clothes dryer) with a pilot light is present. If you spill fuel on your skin, rinse it off immediately with soap and water. Have a Class B fire extinguisher on hand.* Refer to Chapter 4 *and relieve the fuel system pressure before proceeding.*

1   All models employ an in-line fuel filter. The filter is located on the left side frame rail, under the bed.
2   Relieve the fuel system pressure (see Chapter 4). Place a drain pan under the filter area.
3   On most models, the fuel filter is an inline type mounted inside the frame rail **(see illustration)**. Use a flare-nut wrench to disconnect the fuel lines from the filter. Be sure to use a back-up wrench to hold the filter. **Note:** *The fuel filter will contain residual fuel, be prepared to deal with it when loosening the fittings.* On some later utility models, the fuel filter is in a cartridge type housing. Unscrew the housing and let the fuel drain. Clean the inside of the housing.
4   Install the filter as it was removed. On cartridge type systems, lightly oil the cartridge gasket and put a new filter into the housing. Tighten the housing 2/3 of a turn after the gasket makes contact.
5   Check the area carefully for fuel leaks after completing the work. **Note:** *If the fuel filter was plugged, the fuel tank may have dirt in it and you may need to clean it.*

24.3 Use back-up wrenches when loosening the fuel line fittings
at the filter (arrows)

25.4 Tighten the TBI mounting bolts to the torque listed in this
Chapter's Specifications

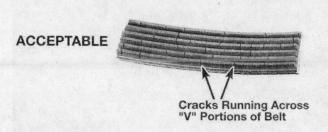

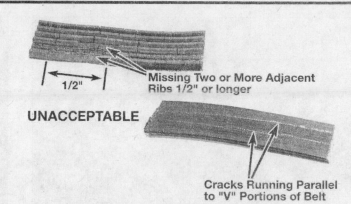

ACCEPTABLE

Cracks Running Across
"V" Portions of Belt

1/2"

Missing Two or More Adjacent
Ribs 1/2" or longer

UNACCEPTABLE

Cracks Running Parallel
to "V" Portions of Belt

27.2 Check the drivebelt for signs of wear like these - if the belt looks worn, replace it

25   Throttle body mounting bolt torque check

Refer to illustration 25.4

1   The TBI unit is attached to the top of the intake manifold by several bolts. These fasteners can sometimes work loose from vibration and temperature changes during normal engine operation and cause a vacuum leak.

2   If you suspect that a vacuum leak exists at the bottom of the throttle body, obtain a length of hose. Start the engine and place one end of the hose next to your ear as you probe around the base with the other end. You will hear a hissing sound if a leak exists (be careful of hot or moving engine components).

3   Remove the air cleaner assembly, tagging each hose to be disconnected with a piece of numbered tape to make reassembly easier.

4   Locate the mounting bolts at the top of the throttle body. Decide what special tools or adapters will be necessary, if any, to tighten the fasteners **(see illustration)**.

5   Tighten the bolts to the torque listed in this Chapter's specifications. Don't overtighten them, as the threads could strip.

6   If, after the bolts are properly tightened, a vacuum leak still exists, the throttle body

must be removed and a new gasket installed. See Chapter 4 for more information.

7   After tightening the fasteners, reinstall the air cleaner and return all hoses to their original positions.

26   Throttle linkage inspection

1   Inspect the throttle linkage for damage and missing parts and for binding and interference when the accelerator pedal is depressed.

2   Lubricate the various linkage pivot points with engine oil.

27   Drivebelt check, adjustment and replacement

Refer to illustrations 27.2, 27.5 and 27.7

1   A single serpentine drivebelt is located at the front of the engine and plays an important role in the overall operation of the engine and accessories. Due to its function and material makeup, the belt is prone to failure after a period of time and should be inspected periodically.

2   With the engine off, locate the drivebelt

at the front of the engine. Using your fingers (and a flashlight, if necessary), move along the belt, checking for cracks and separation of the belt plies **(see illustration)**. Also check for fraying and glazing, which gives the belt a shiny appearance.

Both sides of the belt should be inspected, which means you will have to twist the belt to check the underside. Check the pulleys for nicks, cracks, distortion and corrosion.

3   Check the ribs on the underside of the belt. They should be all the same depth, with none of the surface uneven.

4   The tension of the belt is automatically controlled by a tensioner, so the tension does not need to be adjusted.

5   To replace the belt, use a breaker bar and socket to rotate the tensioner counterclockwise **(see illustration)**. This will release the tension so the belt can be removed. When the belt is out of the way, release the tensioner slowly so you don't damage it.

6   Take the old belt with you when purchasing a new one to make a direct comparison for length, width and design.

7   When installing the new belt, make sure it is routed correctly (refer to the label in the engine compartment and **accompanying illustration**). Also, the belt must completely engage the grooves in the pulleys.

27.5 Rotate the tensioner counterclockwise to release the tension of the drivebelt

ACCESSORY
DRIVE BELT ROUTING

WITHOUT
A/C

PRINTED IN THE U.S.A.   PT. NO. 10065701

27.7 Typical drivebelt routing for small-block V8 engines. A specific routing diagram label should be located under the hood of your vehicle.

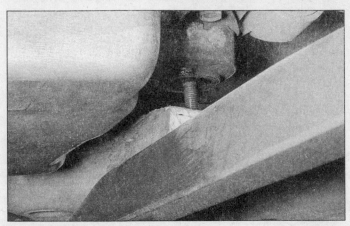

31.5 To gain clearance for removal of the pan, insert a block of wood between the mount and center support beam

31.7 With the rear bolts in place but loose, pull the front of the pan down to drain the transmission fluid

28 Seatbelt check

1   Check the seatbelts, buckles, latch plates and guide loops for any obvious damage or signs of wear.

2   Make sure the seatbelt reminder light comes on when the key is turned on.

3   The seatbelts are designed to lock up during a sudden stop or impact, yet allow free movement during normal driving. The retractors should hold the belt against your chest while driving and rewind the belt when the buckle is unlatched.

4   If any of the above checks reveal problems with the seatbelt system, replace parts as necessary.

29 Seat back latch check

1   It's important to periodically check the seat back latch mechanism to prevent the seat back from pivoting forward during a sudden stop or an accident.

2   Grasping the top of the seat, attempt to tilt the seat back forward. It should tilt only when the latch mechanism is released.

3   When returned to the upright position, the seat back should latch securely.

30 Starter safety switch check

Warning: *During the following checks there is a chance the vehicle could lunge forward, possibly causing damage or injuries. Allow plenty of room around the vehicle, apply the parking brake firmly and hold down the regular brake pedal during the checks.*

1   The starter safety switch used on these models is either a clutch interlock switch (manual transmission-equipped models) or a neutral start switch (automatic transmission-equipped models). The clutch interlock switch prevents the engine from being cranked unless the clutch is depressed. The neutral start switch prevents the engine from

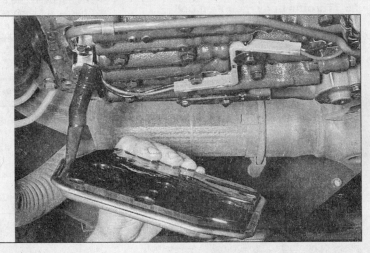

31.10 Rotate the filter out of the retaining clip, then lower it from the transmission

being cranked unless the gear selector is in Park or Neutral.

2   If the vehicle is equipped with an automatic transmission, try to start the vehicle in each gear. The engine should crank only in Park or Neutral. If it cranks in any other gear, the neutral start switch is faulty or in need of adjustment (see Chapter 7 Part B).

3   If the vehicle is equipped with a manual transmission, place the shift lever in Neutral. The engine should crank only when the clutch pedal is depressed. If it cranks without the pedal being depressed, the switch, located near the top of the clutch pedal arm, is probably faulty.

4   If the vehicle is equipped with an automatic transmission, make sure the steering column lock allows the key to go into the Lock position only when the shift lever is in Park.

5   The ignition key should come out only in the Lock position.

31 Automatic transmission fluid and filter change

Refer to illustrations 31.5, 31.7, 31.10 and 31.11

1   At the specified intervals, the transmis-

sion fluid should be drained and replaced. Since the fluid will remain hot long after driving, perform this procedure only after the engine has cooled down completely.

2   Before beginning work, purchase the specified transmission fluid (see *Recommended lubricants and fluids* at the front of this Chapter) and a new filter.

3   Other tools necessary for this job include a floor jack, jackstands to support the vehicle in a raised position, a drain pan capable of holding at least eight pints, newspapers and clean rags.

4   Raise the vehicle and support it securely on jackstands.

5   Remove the center transmission mount nut. Use a floor jack positioned under the transmission pan to raise the transmission slightly. Place a block of wood between the pan and jack head to prevent damage to the pan. Once the transmission is raised, insert a small wood block between the mount and crossmember **(see illustration). Warning:** *Do not put your hands between the crossmember and the transmission when it's supported in this way.*

6   Place the drain pan underneath the transmission pan. Remove the front and side pan mounting bolts, but only loosen the rear pan bolts approximately four turns.

7   Carefully pry the transmission pan loose

31.11 Use a screwdriver to remove the seal from the transmission - be careful not to gouge the aluminum housing

33.6a Remove the bolts from the lower edge of the cover . . .

with a screwdriver, allowing the fluid to drain **(see illustration)**.

8   Remove the remaining bolts, pan and gasket. Carefully clean the gasket surface of the transmission to remove all traces of the old gasket and sealant.

9   Drain the fluid from the transmission pan, clean it with solvent and dry it with compressed air.

10   Remove the filter from the mount inside the transmission **(see illustration)**.

11   If the seal did not come out with the filter, remove it from the transmission **(see illustration)**. Install a new filter and seal.

12   Make sure the gasket surface on the transmission pan is clean, then install a new gasket on the pan. Put the pan in place against the transmission and, working around the pan, tighten each bolt a little at a time until the final torque figure is reached.

13   Lower the vehicle and add approximately seven pints of the specified type of automatic transmission fluid through the filler tube (Section 6).

14   With the transmission in Park and the parking brake set, run the engine at a fast idle, but don't race it.

15   Move the gear selector through each range and back to Park. Check the fluid level. It will probably be low. Add enough fluid to bring the level up to the COLD FULL range on the dipstick.

16   Check under the vehicle for leaks during the first few trips.

32   Manual transmission lubricant change

1   Raise the vehicle and support it securely on jackstands.

2   Move a drain pan, rags, newspapers and wrenches under the transmission.

3   Remove the transmission drain plug at the bottom of the case **(see illustration 17.1)** and allow the lubricant to drain into the pan.

4   After the lubricant has drained com-

pletely, reinstall the plug and tighten it securely.

5   Remove the fill plug from the side of the transmission case. Using a hand pump, syringe or funnel, fill the transmission with the specified lubricant until it begins to leak out through the hole. Reinstall the fill plug and tighten it securely.

6   Lower the vehicle.

7   Drive the vehicle for a short distance, then check the drain and fill plugs for leakage.

33   Differential lubricant change

Refer to illustrations 33.6a, 33.6b, 33.6c and 33.8

1   Some differentials can be drained by removing the drain plug, while on others it's necessary to remove the cover plate on the differential housing. As an alternative, a hand suction pump can be used to remove the differential lubricant through the filler hole. If there is no drain plug and a suction pump isn't available, be sure to obtain a new gasket

at the same time the gear lubricant is purchased.

2   Raise the vehicle and support it securely on jackstands. Move a drain pan, rags, newspapers and wrenches under the vehicle.

3   Remove the fill plug from the differential.

4   If equipped with a drain plug, remove the plug and allow the differential lubricant to drain completely. After the lubricant has drained, install the plug and tighten it securely.

5   If a suction pump is being used, insert the flexible hose. Work the hose down to the bottom of the differential housing and pump the oil out.

6   If the differential is being drained by removing the cover plate, remove the bolts on the lower half of the plate **(see illustration)**. Loosen the bolts on the upper half and use them to keep the cover loosely attached **(see illustration)**. Allow the oil to drain into the pan, then completely remove the cover **(see illustration)**.

7   Using a lint-free rag, clean the inside of the cover and the accessible areas of the differential housing. As this is done, check for chipped gears and metal particles in the

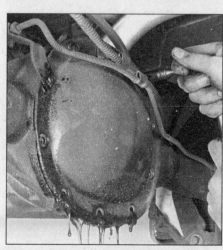

33.6b . . . then loosen the top bolts and let the lubricant drain

33.6c After the lubrication has drained, remove the cover

33.8 Carefully scrape the old gasket material off to ensure a leak-free seal with the new gasket

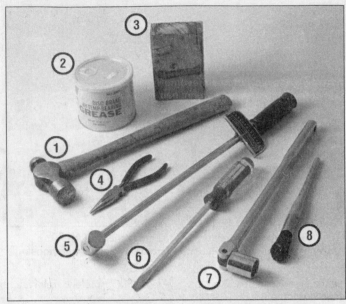

34.1 Tools and materials needed for front wheel bearing maintenance

1　**Hammer** - A common hammer will do just fine
2　**Grease** - High-temperature grease that is formulated specially for front wheel bearings should be used
3　**Wood block** - If you have a scrap piece of 2x4, it can be used to drive the new seal into the hub
4　**Needle-nose pliers** - Used to straighten and remove the cotter pin in the spindle
5　**Torque wrench** - This is very important in this procedure; if the bearing is too tight, the wheel won't turn freely - if it's too loose, the wheel will "wobble" on the spindle. Either way, it could mean extensive damage
6　**Screwdriver** - Used to remove the seal from the hub (a long screwdriver is preferred)
7　**Socket/breaker bar** - Needed to loosen the nut on the spindle if it's extremely tight
8　**Brush** - Together with some clean solvent, this will be used to remove old grease from the hub and spindle

34.6 Dislodge the dust cap by working around the outer edge with a hammer and chisel

lubricant, indicating that the differential should be more thoroughly inspected and/or repaired.
8　Thoroughly clean the gasket mating surfaces of the differential housing and the cover plate. Use a gasket scraper or putty knife to remove all traces of the old gasket **(see illustration)**.
9　If a gasket is used, apply a thin coating of gasket sealer to the cover flange and press a new gasket into place. If RTV sealant is used instead of a gasket, make sure that the mating surfaces are oil free by cleaning them with lacquer thinner or acetone. Apply a bead of RTV to one surface and install the cover while the RTV is still wet.
10　Place the cover on the differential housing and install the bolts. Tighten the bolts securely.
11　On all models, use a hand pump, syringe or funnel to fill the differential housing with the specified lubricant until it's level with the bottom of the plug hole.
12　Install the filler plug and tighten it securely.

34　Front wheel bearing check, repack and adjustment (2WD models only)

Refer to illustrations 34.1, 34.6, 34.7, 34.8, 34.11 and 34.15
1　In most cases the front wheel bearings will not need servicing until the brake pads are changed. However, the bearings should be checked whenever the front of the vehicle is raised for any reason. Several items, including a torque wrench and special grease, are required for this procedure **(see illustration)**.
2　With the vehicle securely supported on jackstands, spin each wheel and check for noise, rolling resistance and freeplay.
3　Grasp the top of each tire with one hand and the bottom with the other. Move the wheel in-and-out on the spindle. If there's any noticeable movement, the bearings should be checked and then repacked with grease or replaced if necessary.
4　Remove the wheel.

5　Fabricate a wood block (1-1/16 inch by 1/2-inch by 2-inches long) which can be slid between the brake pads to keep them separated. Remove the brake caliper (Chapter 9) and hang it out of the way on a piece of wire.

34.7 Remove the cotter pin and discard it - use a new one when the hub is reinstalled

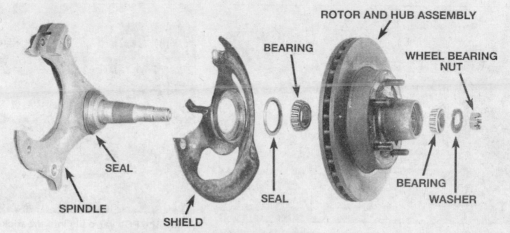

34.8 Typical 2WD front wheel hub and bearing components

ROTOR AND HUB ASSEMBLY
BEARING
WHEEL BEARING NUT
SEAL
SPINDLE
SHIELD
SEAL
BEARING
WASHER

6   Pry the dust cap out of the hub using a screwdriver or hammer and chisel (see illustration).
7   Straighten the bent ends of the cotter pin, then pull the cotter pin out of the nut (see illustration). Discard the cotter pin and use a new one during reassembly.
8   Remove the spindle nut and washer from the end of the spindle (see illustration).
9   Pull the hub/disc assembly out slightly, then push it back into its original position. This should force the outer bearing off the spindle enough so it can be removed.
10   Pull the hub/disc assembly off the spindle.
11   Use a screwdriver to pry the seal out of the rear of the hub (see illustration). As this is done, note how the seal is installed.
12   Remove the inner wheel bearing from the hub.
13   Use solvent to remove all traces of the old grease from the bearings, hub and spindle. A small brush may prove helpful; however make sure no bristles from the brush embed themselves inside the bearing rollers. Allow the parts to air dry.
14   Carefully inspect the bearings for cracks, heat discoloration, worn rollers, etc. Check the bearing races inside the hub for wear and damage. If the bearing races are defective, the hubs should be taken to a machine shop with the facilities to remove the old races and press new ones in. Note that the bearings and races come as matched sets and old bearings should never be installed on new races.
15   Use high-temperature front wheel bearing grease to pack the bearings. Work the grease completely into the bearings, forcing it between the rollers, cone and cage from the back side (see illustration).
16   Apply a thin coat of grease to the spindle at the outer bearing seat, inner bearing seat, shoulder and seal seat.
17   Put a small quantity of grease inboard of each bearing race inside the hub. Using your finger, form a dam at these points to provide extra grease availability and to keep thinned grease from flowing out of the bearing.
18   Place the grease-packed inner bearing

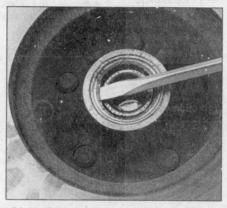

34.11 Use a large screwdriver to pry the grease seal out of the rear of the hub

into the rear of the hub and put a little more grease outboard of the bearing.
19   Place a new seal over the inner bearing and tap the seal evenly into place with a hammer and block of wood until it's flush with the hub.
20   Carefully place the hub assembly onto the spindle and push the grease-packed outer bearing into position.
21   Install the washer and spindle nut. Tighten the nut only slightly (no more than 12 ft-lbs of torque).
22   Spin the hub in a forward direction to seat the bearings and remove any grease or burrs which could cause excessive bearing play later.
23   Check to see that the tightness of the spindle nut is still approximately 12 ft-lbs.
24   Loosen the spindle nut until it's just loose, no more.
25   Using your hand (not a wrench of any kind), tighten the nut until it's snug. Install a new cotter pin through the hole in the spindle and spindle nut. If the nut slots don't line up, loosen the nut slightly until they do. From the hand-tight position, the nut should not be loosened more than one-half flat to install the cotter pin.
26   Bend the ends of the cotter pin until they're flat against the nut. Cut off any extra length which could interfere with the dust cap.
27   Install the dust cap, tapping it into place

34.15 Work grease into the bearing rollers by pressing it against the palm of your hand

with a hammer.
28   Place the brake caliper near the rotor and carefully remove the wood spacer. Install the caliper (Chapter 9).
29   Install the tire/wheel assembly on the hub and tighten the lug nuts.
30   Grasp the top and bottom of the tire and check the bearings in the manner described earlier in this Section.
31   Lower the vehicle.

35   Cooling system servicing (draining, flushing and refilling)

Refer to illustration 35.4
Warning: *Antifreeze is a corrosive and poisonous solution, so be careful not to spill any of the coolant mixture on the vehicle's paint or your skin. If this happens, rinse immediately with plenty of clean water. Consult local authorities regarding proper disposal procedures for antifreeze before draining the cooling system. In many areas, reclamation centers have been established to collect used oil and coolant.*
1   Periodically, the cooling system should be drained, flushed and refilled to replenish the antifreeze mixture and prevent formation of rust and corrosion, which can impair the performance of the cooling system and cause

35.4 The drain fitting is located at the lower corner of the radiator

36.2 The PCV valve fits into the rocker arm cover (arrow) - after removing the valve, place you finger over the opening to feel for suction and shake the valve, listening for a rattling sound

engine damage. When the cooling system is serviced, all hoses and the radiator cap should be checked and replaced if necessary.

2   Apply the parking brake and block the wheels. If the vehicle has just been driven, wait several hours to allow the engine to cool down before beginning this procedure.

3   Once the engine is completely cool, remove the radiator cap.

4   Move a large container under the radiator drain to catch the coolant. Attach a 3/8-inch diameter hose to the drain fitting to direct the coolant into the container, then open the drain fitting **(see illustration)** (a pair of pliers may be required to turn it).

5   After the coolant stops flowing out of the radiator, move the container under the engine block drain plugs - there's one on each side of the block. Remove the plugs and allow the coolant in the block to drain.

6   While the coolant is draining, check the condition of the radiator hoses, heater hoses and clamps (refer to Section 9 if necessary).

7   Replace any damaged clamps or hoses.

8   Once the system is completely drained, flush the radiator with fresh water from a garden hose until it runs clear at the drain. The flushing action of the water will remove sediments from the radiator but will not remove rust and scale from the engine and cooling tube surfaces.

9   These deposits can be removed with a chemical cleaner. Follow the procedure outlined in the manufacturer's instructions. If the radiator is severely corroded, damaged or leaking, it should be removed (Chapter 3) and taken to a radiator repair shop.

10   Remove the overflow hose from the coolant recovery reservoir. Drain the reservoir and flush it with clean water, then reconnect the hose.

11   Close and tighten the radiator drain. Install and tighten the block drain plugs.

12   Place the heater temperature control in the maximum heat position.

13   Slowly add new coolant (a 50/50 mixture of water and antifreeze) to the radiator until it's full. Add coolant to the reservoir up to the lower mark.

14   Leave the radiator cap off and run the engine in a well-ventilated area until the thermostat opens (coolant will begin flowing through the radiator and the upper radiator hose will become hot).

15   Turn the engine off and let it cool. Add more coolant mixture to bring the level back up to the lip on the radiator filler neck.

16   Squeeze the upper radiator hose to expel air, then add more coolant mixture if necessary. Replace the radiator cap.

17   Start the engine, allow it to reach normal operating temperature and check for leaks.

36   Positive Crankcase Ventilation (PCV) valve check and replacement

Refer to illustration 36.2

1   The PCV valve is usually located in the rocker arm cover.

2   With the engine idling at normal operating temperature, pull the valve (with hose attached) from the rubber grommet in the cover **(see illustration).**

3   Place your finger over the valve opening. If there's no vacuum at the valve, check for a plugged hose, manifold port, or the valve itself. Replace any plugged or deteriorated hoses.

4   Turn off the engine and shake the PCV valve, listening for a rattle. If the valve doesn't rattle, replace it with a new one.

5   To replace the valve, pull it from the end of the hose, noting its installed position.

6   When purchasing a replacement PCV valve, make sure it's for your particular vehicle and engine size. Compare the old valve with the new one to make sure they're the same.

7   Push the valve into the end of the hose until it's seated.

8   Inspect the rubber grommet for damage and replace it with a new one if necessary.

9   Push the PCV valve and hose securely into position.

37   Evaporative emissions control system check

Refer to illustration 37.2

1   The function of the evaporative emissions control system is to draw fuel vapors from the gas tank and fuel system, store them in a charcoal canister and route them to the intake manifold during normal engine operation.

2   The most common symptom of a fault in the evaporative emissions system is a strong fuel odor in the engine compartment. If a fuel odor is detected, inspect the charcoal canister, located in the engine compartment **(see illustration)**. Check the canister and all hoses for damage and deterioration.

3   The evaporative emissions control system is explained in more detail in Chapter 6.

38   Exhaust Gas Recirculation (EGR) system check and servicing

Refer to illustration 38.2
Note: *1996 and later models use an electron-*

37.2 The evaporative emissions control system canister is located at the left front corner of the engine compartment - inspect the hoses and the canister for damage

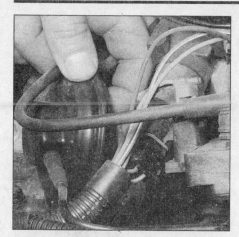

38.2 The EGR valve diaphragm should move easily with finger pressure

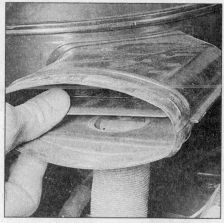

39.3 The damper door is located in the air cleaner snorkel

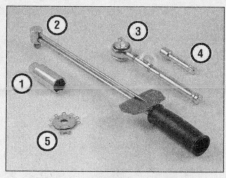

40.2 Tools required for changing spark plugs

1 **Spark plug socket** - This will have special padding inside to protect the spark plug's porcelain insulator
2 **Torque wrench** - Although not mandatory, using this tool is the best way to ensure the plugs are tightened properly
3 **Ratchet** - Standard hand tool to fit the spark plug socket
4 **Extension** - Depending on model and accessories, you may need special extensions and universal joints to reach one or more of the plugs
5 **Spark plug gap gauge** - This gauge for checking the gap comes in a variety of styles. Make sure the gap for your engine is included

ically operated EGR valve. *You must have these units checked by a dealer service department or other shop with the proper type scan tool that can operate the EGR valve electronically for testing.*

1 The EGR valve is usually located on the intake manifold, adjacent to the TBI unit. Most of the time when a problem develops in this emissions system, it's due to a stuck or corroded EGR valve.
2 With the engine cold to prevent burns, push on the EGR valve diaphragm. Using moderate pressure, you should be able to press the diaphragm in-and-out within the housing **(see illustration)**.
3 If the diaphragm doesn't move or moves only with much effort, replace the EGR valve with a new one. If in doubt about the condition of the valve, compare the free movement of your EGR valve with a new valve.
4 Some vehicles are equipped with an electronic Vacuum Regulator Valve (VRV). The filter in this valve should be cleaned at regular intervals. The valve is located on a bracket near the EGR valve.
5 Locate the valve and remove the old filter.
6 Clean the filter with a soapy solution and reinstall it.
7 Refer to Chapter 6 for more information on the EGR system.

39 Thermostatic air cleaner check

Refer to illustration 39.3
1 Later model engines are equipped with a thermostatically controlled air cleaner which draws air to the TBI unit from different locations, depending upon engine temperature.
2 This is a visual check. If access is limited, a small mirror may have to be used.
3 Open the hood and locate the damper door inside the air cleaner assembly **(see illustration)**. It's inside the long snorkel of the metal air cleaner housing.
4 If there is a flexible air duct attached to the end of the snorkel, leading to an area

behind the grille, disconnect it at the snorkel. This will enable you to look through the end of the snorkel and see the damper inside.
5 The check should be done when the engine is cold. Start the engine and look through the snorkel at the damper, which should move to a closed position. With the damper closed, air cannot enter through the end of the snorkel, but instead enters the air cleaner through the flexible duct attached to the exhaust manifold and the heat stove passage.
6 As the engine warms up to operating temperature, the damper should open to allow air through the snorkel end. Depending on outside temperature, this may take 10 to 15 minutes. To speed up this check you can reconnect the snorkel air duct, drive the vehicle, then check to see if the damper is completely open.
7 If the thermo-controlled air cleaner is not operating properly see Chapter 6 for more information.

40 Spark plug replacement

Refer to illustrations 40.2, 40.5a, 40.5b, 40.6 and 40.10
1 Open the hood and label each spark plug wire to ensure proper installation.
2 In most cases, the tools necessary for spark plug replacement include a spark plug socket which fits onto a ratchet (spark plug sockets are padded inside to prevent damage to the porcelain insulators on the new plugs), various extensions and a gap gauge to check and adjust the gaps on the new plugs **(see illustration)**. A special plug wire removal tool is available for separating the wire boots from the spark plugs, but it isn't absolutely necessary. A torque wrench should be used to tighten the new plugs.
3 The best approach when replacing the spark plugs is to purchase the new ones in advance, adjust them to the proper gap and replace them one at a time. When buying the new spark plugs, be sure to obtain the correct plug type for your particular engine. This

information can be found on the Emission Control Information label located under the hood and in the factory owner's manual. If differences exist between the plug specified on the emissions label and in the owner's manual, assume that the emissions label is correct.
4 Allow the engine to cool completely before attempting to remove any of the plugs. While you're waiting for the engine to cool, check the new plugs for defects and adjust the gaps.
5 The gap is checked by inserting the

40.5a Spark plug manufacturers recommend using a wire-type gauge when checking the gap - if the wire does not slide between the electrodes with a slight drag, adjustment is required

40.5b To change the gap, bend the side electrode only, as indicated by the arrows, and be very careful not to crack or chip the porcelain insulator surrounding the center electrode

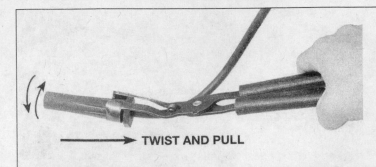

TWIST AND PULL

40.6 When removing spark plug wires, grasp the boot and use a twisting/pulling motion

40.10 A length of 3/16-inch ID rubber hose will save time and prevent damaged threads when installing the spark plugs

proper thickness gauge between the electrodes at the tip of the plug (see illustration). The gap between the electrodes should be the same as the one specified on the Emissions Control Information label. The wire should just slide between the electrodes with a slight amount of drag. If the gap is incorrect, use the adjuster on the gauge body to bend the curved side electrode slightly until the proper gap is obtained (see illustration). If the side electrode is not exactly over the center electrode, bend it with the adjuster until it is. Check for cracks in the porcelain insulator (if any are found, the plug should not be used).

6   With the engine cool, remove the spark plug wire from one spark plug. Pull only on the boot at the end of the wire - do not pull on the wire. A plug wire removal tool should be used if available (see illustration).

7   If compressed air is available, use it to blow any dirt or foreign material away from the spark plug hole. A common bicycle pump will also work. The idea here is to eliminate the possibility of debris falling into the cylinder as the spark plug is removed.

8   Place the spark plug socket over the plug and remove it from the engine by turning it in a counterclockwise direction.

9   Compare the spark plug to those shown in the photos on the inside back cover to get an indication of the general running condition of the engine.

10   Thread one of the new plugs into the hole until you can no longer turn it with your fingers, then tighten it with a torque wrench (if available) or the ratchet. It might be a good idea to slip a short length of rubber hose over the end of the plug to use as a tool to thread it into place (see illustration). The hose will grip the plug well enough to turn it, but will start to slip if the plug begins to cross-thread in the hole - this will prevent damaged threads and the accompanying repair costs.

11   Before pushing the spark plug wire onto the end of the plug, inspect it following the procedures outlined in Section 41.

12   Attach the plug wire to the new spark plug, again using a twisting motion on the boot until it's seated on the spark plug.

13   Repeat the procedure for the remaining spark plugs, replacing them one at a time to prevent mixing up the spark plug wires.

41   Spark plug wire check and replacement

1   The spark plug wires should be checked at the recommended intervals and whenever new spark plugs are installed in the engine.

2   The wires should be inspected one at a time to prevent mixing up the order, which is essential for proper engine operation.

3   Disconnect the plug wire from one spark plug. To do this, grab the rubber boot, twist slightly and pull the wire free. Do not pull on the wire itself, only on the rubber boot (see illustration 40.6).

4   Check inside the boot for corrosion, which will look like a white crusty powder. Push the wire and boot back onto the end of the spark plug. It should be a tight fit on the plug. If it isn't, remove the wire and use a pair of pliers to carefully crimp the metal connector inside the boot until it fits securely on the end of the spark plug.

5   Using a clean rag, wipe the entire length of the wire to remove any built-up dirt and grease. Once the wire is clean, check for holes, burned areas, cracks and other damage. Don't bend the wire excessively or the conductor inside might break.

6   Disconnect the wire from the distributor cap. A retaining ring at the top of the distributor may have to be removed to free the wires.

Again, pull only on the rubber boot. Check for corrosion and a tight fit in the same manner as the spark plug end. Reattach the wire to the distributor cap.

7   Check the remaining spark plug wires one at a time, making sure they are securely fastened at the distributor and the spark plug when the check is complete.

8   If new spark plug wires are required, purchase a new set for your specific engine model. Wire sets are available pre-cut, with the rubber boots already installed. Remove and replace the wires one at a time to avoid mix-ups in the firing order. The wire routing is extremely important, so be sure to note exactly how each wire is situated before removing it.

42   Distributor cap and rotor check and replacement

Refer to illustrations 42.4, 42.7a, and 42.7b

Note: *It's common practice to install a new distributor cap and rotor whenever new spark plug wires are installed.*

1   To gain access to the distributor cap, it may be necessary to remove the air cleaner assembly.

Check

2   Loosen the distributor cap mounting screws.

3   On some models, the cap is held in place with latches that look like screws - to release them, push down with a screwdriver and turn them about 1/2-turn. Pull up on the cap, with the wires attached, to separate it from the distributor, then position it to one side.

4   The rotor is now visible on the end of the distributor shaft. Check it carefully for cracks

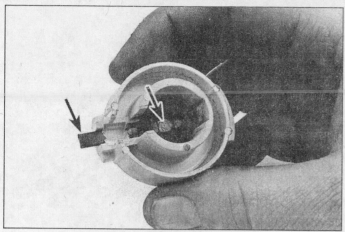

42.4 Check the rotor terminals (arrows) for wear
and burn marks

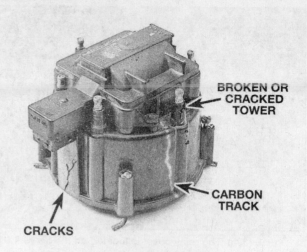

BROKEN OR
CRACKED
TOWER

CARBON
TRACK

CRACKS

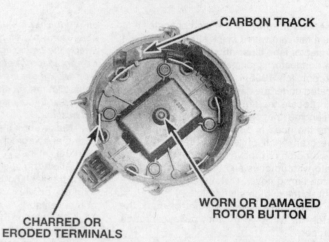

CARBON TRACK

WORN OR DAMAGED
ROTOR BUTTON

CHARRED OR
ERODED TERMINALS

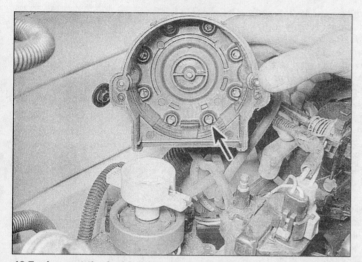

42.7a Inspect the inside of the cap, especially the metal terminals
(arrow), for corrosion, carbon tracks and wear

42.7b Shown here are some of the common defects to look for
when inspecting the distributor cap (if in doubt about its
condition, install a new one)

and carbon tracks. Make sure the center terminal spring tension is adequate and look for corrosion and wear on the rotor tip (see illustration). If in doubt about its condition, replace it with a new one.

5   If replacement is required, detach the rotor from the shaft and install a new one. On some models, the rotor is press fit on the shaft and can be pried or pulled off.

6   The rotor is indexed to the shaft so it can only be installed one way. Press fit rotors have an internal key that must line up with a slot in the end of the shaft (or vice versa). Rotors held in place with screws have one square and one round peg on the underside that must fit into holes with the same shape.

7   Check the distributor cap for carbon tracks, cracks and other damage. Closely examine the terminals on the inside of the cap for excessive corrosion and damage (see illustrations). Slight deposits are normal. Again, if in doubt about the condition of the cap, replace it with a new one. Be sure to apply a small dab of silicone lubricant to each terminal before installing the cap. Also, make sure the carbon brush (center terminal) is cor-

rectly installed in the cap - a wide gap between the brush and rotor will result in rotor burn-through and/or damage to the distributor cap.

Replacement

8   Simply separate the cap from the distributor and transfer the spark plug wires, one at a time, to the new cap. Be very careful not to mix up the wires!

9   Reattach the cap to the distributor, then tighten the screws or reposition the latches to hold it in place.

43   Ignition timing check and adjustment

Refer to illustrations 43.4a, 43.4b and 43.5

Note 1: If the information in this Section differs from the Vehicle Emission Control Information label in the engine compartment of your vehicle, the label should be considered correct.

Note 2: Ignition timing cannot be adjusted on 1996 and later SFI engines. On 4.3L V6 engines, the distributor cannot be rotated, and if it could be, it would not affect ignition timing. On SFI V8 engines the timing cannot be adjusted; however, if the distributor has been removed, it may need to be turned slightly in order to prevent cross-fire (cross-fire occurs when the ignition fires while the rotor is between two terminals on the distributor cap). A scan tool is necessary to test for cross-fire, so this operation must be performed by a dealer or qualified repair shop.

1   The engine must be at normal operating temperature and the air conditioner must be Off.

2   Apply the parking brake and block the wheels to prevent movement of the vehicle. The transmission must be in Park (automatic) or Neutral (manual).

3   If the SERVICE ENGINE SOON light is on, don't proceed with the ignition timing check (see Chapter 6 for more information).

4   The Electronic Spark Timing (EST) system must be bypassed prior to checking the ignition timing. Remove the relay cover

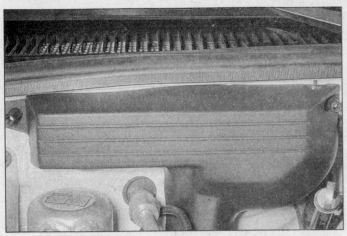

43.4a The relay cover is located on the firewall

43.4b Locate the connector (arrow) and unplug it

(see illustration). Locate the connector that has a tan wire with a black stripe. Unplug the connector (see illustration). On later models, the connector is located near the distributor (except for 1995 models; on these, it's located under the dash, below the glove box).

5 Locate the timing marks at the front of the engine (they should be visible from above after the hood is opened) (see illustration). The crankshaft pulley or vibration damper has a notch or groove in it and a small metal plate with notches and numbers is attached to the timing cover. Clean the plate with solvent so the numbers are visible.

6 Use chalk or white paint to mark the notch or groove in the pulley/vibration damper.

7 Highlight the notch or point on the timing plate that corresponds to the ignition timing specification on the Emission Control Information label.

8 Hook up the timing light by following the manufacturer's instructions (an inductive pick-up timing light is preferred). Generally, the power leads are attached to the battery terminals and the pick-up lead is attached to the number one spark plug wire. **Caution:** *If*

an inductive pick-up timing light isn't available, don't puncture the spark plug wire to attach the timing light pick-up lead. Instead, use an adapter between the spark plug and plug wire. If the insulation on the plug wire is damaged, the secondary voltage will jump to ground at the damaged point and the engine will misfire.

9 Make sure the timing light wires are routed away from the drivebelts and fan, then start the engine.

10 Allow the idle speed to stabilize, then point the flashing timing light at the timing marks - be very careful of moving engine components!

11 The mark on the pulley/vibration damper will appear stationary. If it's aligned with the specified point on the timing plate, the ignition timing is correct.

12 If the marks aren't aligned, adjustment is required. Loosen the distributor hold-down bolt and turn the distributor very slowly until the marks are aligned. Since access to the bolt is tight, a special distributor wrench may be needed.

13 Tighten the bolt and recheck the timing.

14 Turn off the engine and remove the tim-

43.5 The ignition timing marks are located at the front of the engine

ing light (and adapter, if used).

15 Reconnect the EST wire harness connector, then clear any ECM trouble codes set during the ignition timing procedure (see Chapter 6).

Chapter 2 Part A
Engines

Contents

Specifications

General

Cylinder numbers (front-to-rear)
   4.3L V6 engine
      Left (driver's) side 1-3-5
      Right side 2-4-6
   5.0L, 5.7L and 7.4L V8 engines
      Left (driver's) side 1-3-5-7
      Right side 2-4-6-8
Firing order
   V6 engine 1-6-5-4-3-2
   V8 engines 1-8-4-3-6-5-7-2

Camshaft

Bearing journal diameter
   4.3L engine .... 1.8682 to 1.8692 in
   5.0L and 5.7L engines
      1988 through 1995 .... 1.8682 to 1.8692 in
      1996 through 2000 .... 1.8677 to 1.8697 in
   7.4L engine
      1988 through 1994 .... 1.9482 to 1.9492 in
      1995 through 2000 .... 1.9477 to 1.9497 in

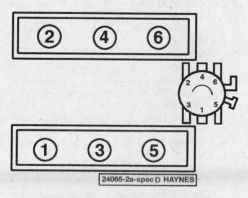

Cylinder location and distributor rotation
(1988 through 1995 TBI V6 engines)

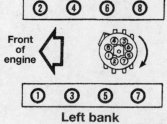

Cylinder location and distributor rotation (1988 through 1995 TBI V8 engines)

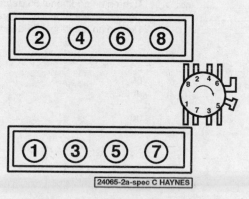

Cylinder location and distributor rotation
(1996 and later SFI V8 engines)

Cylinder location and distributor rotation
(1996 and later SFI V6 engines)

Camshaft (continued)
Lobe lift
Intake
4.3L engine
1988 through 1990 .... 0.238 in
1991 through 1995 .... 0.234 in
1996 .... 0.2763 in
1997 through 2000 .... 0.288 in
5.0L engine
1988 through 1995 .... 0.2336 in
1996 through 2000 .... 0.276 in
5.7L engine
1988 through1995 .... 0.2565 in
1996 through 2000 .... 0.276 in
7.4L engine
1988 through 1994 .... 0.2343 in
1995 .... 0.2487 in
1996 through 2000 .... 0.2821 in
Exhaust
4.3L engine
1988 through 1990 .... 0.260 in
1991 through 1995 .... 0.257 in
1996 .... 0.2855 in
1997 through 2000 .... 0.294 in
5.0L engine
1988 through 1995 .... 0.2565 in
1996 through 2000 .... 0.285 in
5.7L engine
1988 through 1995 .... 0.2690 in
1996 through 2000 .... 0.285 in
7.4L engine
1988 through 1994 .... 0.2530 in
1995 .... 0.2537 in
1996 through 2000 .... 0.2843 in
Balance shaft (4.3L engine only, 1994 and later)
Rear bearing journal diameter .... 1.4994 to 1.500 in

Torque specifications   **Ft-lbs (unless otherwise indicated)**
Balancer shaft (1994 and later 4.3L V6 engine)
Retainer bolts .... 120 in-lbs
Driven gear bolt .... 15 plus an additional 35-degrees rotation
Drive gear retaining stud .... 144 in-lbs
Camshaft sprocket bolts/nuts 20
Cylinder head bolts
4.3L, 5.0L and 5.7L engines
1988 through 1995
Step 1 25
Step 2 45
Step 3 65
1996 through 2000
Step 1 22
Step 2
Short bolts .... Tighten an additional 55 degrees
Medium bolts .... Tighten an additional 65 degrees
Long bolts .... Tighten an additional 75 degrees
7.4L engine
1988 through 1997
Step 1 30
Step 2 60
Step 3 85
1998 only
Step 1 30
Step 2 60
Step 3
Short bolts 89
Long bolts 92
1999 and 2000
Step 1 37
Step 2
Short bolts .... 90 degrees
Long bolts .... 150 degrees

Exhaust manifold nuts/bolts
    4.3L, 5.0L and 5.7L engines
        1988 through 1995
            Center bolts.. 26
            Outer bolts.. 20
        1996 through 2000
            Step 1.. 11
            Step 2.. 22
    7.4L engine
        1988 through 1995... 40
        1996 through 2000
            Bolts... 40
            Nuts.. 22
            Stud.. 22
            Adapter (if equipped)... 118
Flywheel bolts
    4.3L, 5.0L and 5.7L engines.. 75
    7.4L engine.. 65
Intake manifold bolts
    Lower intake manifold bolts
        4.3L, 5.0L and 5.7L engines
            1988 through 1995... 35
            1996 through 2000
                 Step 1.. 27 in-lbs
                Step 2.. 106 in-lbs
                Step 3.. 11
        7.4L engine
            1988 through 1991... 30
            1992 and 1993.. 40
            1994 and 1995.. 35
            1996 through 2000... 30
    Upper intake manifold bolts (1996 through 2000)
        4.3L, 5.0L and 5.7L engines
            Step 1.. 44 in-lbs
            Step 2.. 88 in-lbs
        7.4L engine
            1996 and 1997.. 10
            1998 through 2000
                 Step 1.. 71 in-lbs
                Step 2.. 13
Oil pan baffle nuts... 26
Oil pan-to-crankcase nuts/bolts
    4.3L, 5.0L and 5.7L engines
         1988 through 1995
             Nuts.. 17
             Bolts... 97 in-lbs
         1996 through 2000... 18
    7.4L engine
         1988 through 1994... 13
         1995 through 2000... 17
Oil pan-to-timing cover bolts.. 70 in-lbs
Oil pump bolt.. 65
Rear oil seal housing-to-block bolts... 135 in-lbs
Rocker arm cover nuts/bolts
    4.3L, 5.0L and 5.7L engines.. 106 in-lbs
    7.4L engine
        1988 through 1991... 60 in-lbs
        1992 through 1998... 72 in-lbs
        1999 and 2000.. 106 in-lbs
Rocker arm studs
    4.3L engines (1995 and later)... 35
    7.4L engine (1988 through 1990).. 50
Rocker arm nuts/bolts
    4.3L engine (1995 and later)... 20
    7.4L engine
        1991 through 1995... 40
        1996 and 1997.. 45
        1998 through 2000... 40

Torque specifications (continued)

	Ft-lbs (unless otherwise indicated)
Timing cover bolts	
4.3L engine	
1988 through 1995	124 in-lbs
1996 and later	106 in-lbs
5.0L and 5.7L engines	
1988 through 1995	100 in-lbs
1996 through 2000	106 in-lbs
7.4L engine	
1988 through 1995	96 in-lbs
1996 through 1998	106 in-lbs
1999 and 2000	30
Vibration damper bolt	
4.3L, 5.0L and 5.7L engines	
1988 through 1995	70
1996 through 2000	74
7.4L engine	
1988 through 1995	85
1996 through 2000	110

1 General information

This Part of Chapter 2 is devoted to in-vehicle repair procedures for the engines. All information concerning engine removal and installation and engine block and cylinder head overhaul can be found in Part B of this Chapter.

Since the repair procedures included in this Part are based on the assumption the engine is still installed in the vehicle, if they are being used during a complete engine overhaul (with the engine already out of the vehicle and on a stand) many of the Steps included here will not apply.

The Specifications included in this Part of Chapter 2 apply only to the procedures found here. The specifications necessary for rebuilding the block and cylinder heads are included in Part B.

The V8 engines used in Chevrolet and GMC trucks vary in displacement from 5.0 liters to 7.4 liters. The 5.0 liter (305 cubic inch) and 5.7 liter (350 cubic inch) engines are known as "small blocks". The 7.4 liter (454 cubic inch) engine is known as the Mark IV or "big block" engine.

The V6 engine displaces 4.3 liters (262 cubic inches) and is nearly identical to the small block V8 engine. Almost all procedures for the V6 engine are the same as the small block V8, with the exceptions noted within this Chapter.

2 Repair operations possible with the engine in the vehicle

Many major repair operations can be accomplished without removing the engine from the vehicle.

Clean the engine compartment and the exterior of the engine with some type of pressure washer before any work is done. A clean engine will make the job easier and will help keep dirt out of the internal areas of the engine.

Depending on the components involved, it may be a good idea to remove the hood to improve access to the engine as repairs are performed (refer to Chapter 11 if necessary).

If oil or coolant leaks develop, indicating a need for gasket or seal replacement, the repairs can generally be made with the engine in the vehicle. The oil pan gasket, the cylinder head gaskets, intake and exhaust manifold gaskets, timing cover gaskets and the crankshaft oil seals are accessible with the engine in place.

Exterior engine components, such as the water pump, the starter motor, the alternator, the distributor and the fuel injection unit, as well as the intake and exhaust manifolds, can be removed for repair with the engine in place.

Since the cylinder heads can be removed without pulling the engine, valve component servicing can also be accomplished with the engine in the vehicle.

Replacement of, repairs to or inspection of the timing chain and sprockets and the oil pump are all possible with the engine in place.

In extreme cases caused by a lack of necessary equipment, repair or replacement of piston rings, pistons, connecting rods and rod bearings is possible with the engine in the vehicle. However, this practice is not recommended because of the cleaning and preparation work that must be done to the components involved.

3 Rocker arm covers - removal and installation

Refer to illustrations 3.4a, 3.4b, 3.5a and 3.5b

Removal

1 Disconnect the negative cable from the battery.

2 Remove the air cleaner assembly.

3 Refer to Chapter 6 and detach any air management components that are in the way, if equipped.

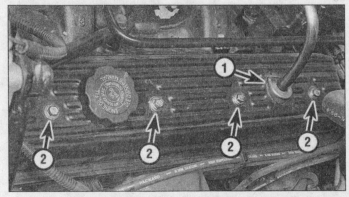
3.4a Left side rocker arm cover details - small block V8

1	*Breather tube*	*2*	*Bolts*

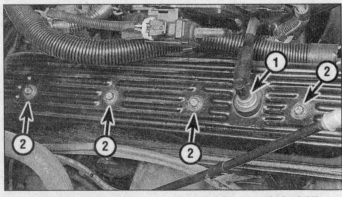
3.4b Right side rocker arm cover details - small block V8

1	*PVC valve*	*2*	*Bolts*

3.5 Remove the three cover mounting bolts - V6 engine

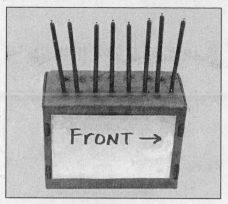

4.4 A perforated cardboard box can be used to store the pushrods to ensure they're reinstalled in their original locations - note the label indicating the front of the engine

4.10 The ends of the pushrods and the valve stems should be lubricated with moly-base grease prior to installation of the rocker arms

4 Remove the breather tube or PCV valve **(see illustrations)**.
5 Remove the rocker arm cover mounting bolts/nuts **(see illustrations)**. If equipped, slip the spark plug wire clip brackets and washers off the lower rocker arm cover studs and position the brackets/wires out of the way.
6 Remove the rocker arm cover. **Note:** *If the cover is stuck to the head, bump the cover with a block of wood and a hammer to release it. If it still won't come loose, try to slip a flexible putty knife between the head and cover to break the seal. Do not pry at the cover-to-head joint or damage to the sealing surface and cover flange will result and oil leaks will develop.*

Installation

7 The mating surfaces of each cylinder head and rocker arm cover must be perfectly clean when the covers are installed. Use a gasket scraper to remove all traces of sealant or old gasket, then clean the mating surfaces with lacquer thinner or acetone. If there's sealant or oil on the mating surfaces when the cover is installed, oil leaks may develop. Later model 7.4L V8 engines have a reusable gasket. Don't discard the old one unless it is damaged.
8 Make sure the threaded holes are clean. Run a tap into them to remove corrosion and restore damaged threads.
9 Mate the new gaskets to the covers before the covers are installed. Apply a thin coat of RTV sealant to the cover flange, then position the gasket inside the cover lip and allow the sealant to set up so the gasket adheres to the cover (if the sealant isn't allowed to set, the gasket may fall out of the cover as it's installed on the engine).
10 Carefully position the cover on the head and install the bolts.
11 Tighten the nuts/bolts in three steps to the torque listed in this Chapter's Specifications.
12 The remaining installation steps are the reverse of removal.
13 Start the engine and check carefully for oil leaks as the engine warms up.

4 Rocker arms and pushrods - removal, inspection and installation

Refer to illustrations 4.4, 4.10, 4.11 and 4.13

Removal

1 Refer to Section 3 and detach the rocker arm covers from the cylinder heads.
2 Beginning at the front of one cylinder head, loosen and remove the rocker arm stud nuts. Store them separately in marked containers to ensure they'll be reinstalled in their original locations. **Note:** *If the pushrods are the only items being removed, loosen each nut just enough to allow the rocker arms to be rotated to the side so the pushrods can be lifted out.*
3 Lift off the rocker arms and pivot balls and store them in the marked containers with the nuts (they must be reinstalled in their original locations).
4 Remove the pushrods and store them in order to make sure they don't get mixed up during installation **(see illustration)**. **Note:** *On 7.4 liter (big block) engines, the exhaust pushrods are longer than the intake pushrods.*

Inspection

5 Check each rocker arm for wear, cracks and other damage, especially where the pushrods and valve stems contact the rocker arm faces.
6 Make sure the hole at the pushrod end of each rocker arm is open.
7 Check each rocker arm pivot area for wear, cracks and galling. If the rocker arms are worn or damaged, replace them with new ones and use new pivot balls as well.
8 Inspect the pushrods for cracks and excessive wear at the ends. Roll each pushrod across a piece of plate glass to see if it's bent (if it wobbles, it's bent).

Installation

9 Lubricate the lower end of each pushrod with clean engine oil or moly-base grease

and install them in their original locations. Make sure each pushrod seats completely in the lifter socket.
10 Apply moly-base grease to the ends of the valve stems and the upper ends of the pushrods before positioning the rocker arms over the studs **(see illustration)**.
11 Set the rocker arms in place, then install the pivot balls and nuts. Apply moly-base grease to the pivot balls to prevent damage to the mating surfaces before engine oil pressure builds up. Be sure to install each nut with the flat side against the pivot ball **(see illustration)**.

Valve adjustment (all except 1991 and later 7.4L V8 and 1995 and later V6 engines)

Note: *On 1991 and later 7.4L V8 and 1995 and later V6 engines, there are no provisions for valve adjustment. The rocker arm studs/bolts have a positive stop shoulder for the rocker arm. After valve service, tighten the rocker arm nuts/bolts to the specified torque listed in this Chapter's Specifications. Unless there have been machining operations that significantly altered the valve lash, the adjustment should be correct.*

4.11 Moly-base grease applied to the pivot balls will ensure adequate lubrication until oil pressure builds up when the engine is started

12 Refer to Section 9 and bring the number one piston to top dead center on the compression stroke.

13 Tighten the rocker arm nuts (number one cylinder only) until all play is removed at the pushrods. This can be determined by rotating each pushrod between your thumb and index finger as the nut is tightened **(see illustration)**. You will be able to feel the point at which all play is eliminated because a slight drag will be felt as you turn the pushrod.

14 Tighten each nut an additional 3/4-turn (270-degrees) to center the lifters. Valve adjustment for cylinder number one is now complete. A cylinder number illustration and the firing order is included in the Specifications.

V6 engine only

15 If the vehicle is equipped with a V6 engine, you can also adjust the number two and three intake valves and number five and six exhaust valves at this time. When these valves have been adjusted, turn the crankshaft one full revolution (360-degrees) and adjust the number four, five and six intake valves and the number two, three and four exhaust valves.

V8 engines only

16 If the vehicle is equipped with a V8 engine, you can also adjust the number two, five and seven intake valves and the number three, four and eight exhaust valves at this time. After adjusting these valves, turn the crankshaft one complete revolution (360-degrees) and adjust the number three, four, six and eight intake valves and the number two, five, six and seven exhaust valves.

All engines

17 Refer to Section 3 and install the rocker arm covers. Start the engine, listen for unusual valve train noises and check for oil leaks at the rocker arm cover joints.

---

5   Valve springs, retainers and seals - replacement

Refer to illustrations 5.4, 5.8a, 5.8b, 5.9a, 5.9b and 5.18

Note: *Broken valve springs and defective valve stem seals can be replaced without removing the cylinder head. Two special tools and a compressed air source are normally required to perform this operation, so read through this Section carefully and rent or buy the tools before beginning the job. If compressed air isn't available, a length of nylon rope can be used to keep the valves from falling into the cylinder during this procedure.*

1 Refer to Section 3 and remove the rocker arm cover from the affected cylinder head. If all of the valve stem seals are being replaced, remove both rocker arm covers.

2 Remove the spark plug from the cylinder which has the defective component. If all of the valve stem seals are being replaced, all of the spark plugs should be removed.

3 Turn the crankshaft until the piston in the

4.13 Rotate each pushrod as the rocker arm nut is tightened to determine the point at which al play is removed, then tighten each nut an additional 3/4-turn

affected cylinder is at top dead center on the compression stroke (refer to Section 9 for instructions). If you're replacing all of the valve stem seals, begin with cylinder number one and work on the valves for one cylinder at a time. Move from cylinder-to-cylinder following the firing order sequence (see the specifications).

4 Thread an adapter (GM no. J-23590 or equivalent) into the spark plug hole and connect an air hose from a compressed air source to it **(see illustration)**. Most auto parts stores can supply an air hose adapter. **Note:** *Many cylinder compression gauges utilize a screw-in fitting that may work with your air hose quick-disconnect fitting.*

5 Remove the nut, pivot ball and rocker arm for the valve with the defective part and pull out the pushrod. If all of the valve stem seals are being replaced, all of the rocker arms and pushrods should be removed (refer to Section 4).

6 Apply compressed air to the cylinder. The valves should be held in place by the air pressure. If the valve faces or seats are in poor condition, leaks may prevent the air pressure from retaining the valves - refer to the alternative procedure below.

7 If you do not have access to compressed air, an alternative method can be used. Position the piston at a point just before TDC on the

5.8a You can use either a screw-type spring compressor . . .

5.4 Use compressed air, if available, to hold the valves closed when the springs are removed - the air hose adapter (arrow) threads into the spark plug hole and accepts the hose from the compressor

compression stroke, then feed a long piece of nylon rope through the spark plug hole until it fills the combustion chamber. Be sure to leave the end of the rope hanging out of the engine so it can be removed easily. Use a large breaker bar and socket to rotate the crankshaft in the normal direction of rotation until slight resistance is felt as the piston comes up against the rope in the combustion chamber.

8 Stuff shop rags into the cylinder head holes above and below the valves to prevent parts and tools from falling into the engine, then use a valve spring compressor to compress the spring/damper assembly. Remove the keepers with a pair of small needle-nose pliers or a magnet **(see illustrations)**. **Note:** *A couple of different types of tools are available for compressing the valve springs with the head in place. One type grips the lower spring coils and presses on the retainer as the knob is turned, while the other type utilizes the rocker arm stud and nut for leverage. Both types work very well, although the lever type is usually less expensive.*

9 Remove the spring retainer or rotator, oil shield and valve spring assembly, then remove the valve stem O-ring seal. Three different types of valve stem oil seals are used on these engines, depending on year, engine size and horsepower rating. The most com-

5.8b . . . or a lever-type as shown here

5.9a Make sure the O-ring under the retainer is seated in the groove and not twisted before installing the keepers

5.9b Some engines have an umbrella-type oil seal which fits over the valve guide boss

5.18 Keepers don't always stay in place, so apply a small dab of grease to each keeper as shown here before installation - it'll hold them in place on the valve stem as the spring is released

mon is a small O-ring which simply fits around the valve stem just above the guide boss. A second type is a flat O-ring which fits into a groove in the valve stem just below the valve stem keeper groove **(see illustration)**. On some applications, an umbrella type seal which extends down over the valve guide boss is used over the valve stem **(see illustration)**. In most cases the umbrella type seal is used in conjunction with the flat O-ring type seal. The O-ring type seals will most likely be hardened and will probably break when removed, so plan on installing a new one each time the original is removed. **Note:** *If air pressure fails to hold the valve in the closed position during this operation, the valve face or seat is probably damaged. If so, the cylinder head will have to be removed for additional repair operations.*

10 Wrap a rubber band or tape around the top of the valve stem so the valve will not fall into the combustion chamber, then release the air pressure. **Note:** *If a rope was used instead of air pressure, turn the crankshaft slightly in the direction opposite normal rotation.*

11 Inspect the valve stem for damage. Rotate the valve in the guide and check the end for eccentric movement, which would indicate that the valve is bent.

12 Move the valve up-and-down in the guide and make sure it doesn't bind. If the valve stem binds, either the valve is bent or the guide is damaged. In either case, the head will have to be removed for repair.

13 Inspect the rocker arm studs for wear. Worn studs on most small block engines can only be replaced by an automotive machine shop, since they must be pressed into place a precise depth. On some big block engines, however, and some high performance versions of the small block (not normally found in trucks), the studs are threaded into the head and can be replaced if worn. In addition, in some applications of screw-in studs, a guide plate is installed between the stud and head to aid in locating pushrod position in relation to the rocker arm. Be sure to replace the guide plate if the studs are removed and reinstalled, and use gasket sealer on the studs when threading them into the head.

6.3 Remove the alternator brace (arrow)

14 Reapply air pressure to the cylinder to retain the valve in the closed position, then remove the tape or rubber band from the valve stem. If a rope was used instead of air pressure, rotate the crankshaft in the normal direction of rotation until slight resistance is felt.

15 Lubricate the valve stem with engine oil and install a new oil seal of the type originally used on the engine (see Step 9).

16 Install the spring/damper assembly and shield in position over the valve.

17 Install the valve spring retainer or rotator and compress the valve spring assembly.

18 Position the keepers in the upper groove. Apply a small dab of grease to the inside of each keeper to hold it in place if necessary **(see illustration)**. Remove the pressure from the spring tool and make sure the keepers are seated.

19 Disconnect the air hose and remove the adapter from the spark plug hole. If a rope was used in place of air pressure, pull it out of the cylinder.

20 Refer to Section 4 and install the rocker arms and pushrods.

21 Install the spark plugs and hook up the wires.

22 Refer to Section 3 and install the rocker arm covers.

23 Start and run the engine, then check for oil leaks and unusual sounds coming from the rocker arm cover area.

6.4 Remove the ESC module bracket from the side of the manifold (arrows)

6 Intake manifold - removal and installation

Removal

Refer to illustrations 6.3, 6.4 and 6.6
Note: *A separate upper intake manifold is used on all 1996 and later models. On all except the 7.4L V8 engine, the entire assembly (upper and lower intake manifold together) can be removed together using the following procedure. On the 7.4L V8 engine, the upper intake manifold must be removed first.*

1 Disconnect the negative cable from the battery, then refer to Chapter 1 and drain the cooling system. On 1996 and later models with the 7.4L V8 engine, remove the upper intake manifold first (beginning with Step 18).

2 Remove the air cleaner assembly. If you intend to resurface or replace the manifold, remove the throttle body (see Chapter 4).

3 Remove the alternator rear brace, if equipped **(see illustration)**. On air conditioned models, move the compressor out of the way by removing the brackets.

4 Detach the ESC (Electronic Spark Control) module bracket on the side of the manifold **(see illustration)**. Remove the idler pulley rear bracket.

6.6 To detach this type of coolant fitting, pinch the ears together and pull up

6.9 After covering the lifter valley, use a gasket scraper to remove all traces of sealant and old gasket material from the head and manifold mating surfaces

6.10a The bolt hole threads must be cleaned and dry to ensure accurate torque readings when the manifold mounting bolts are reinstalled

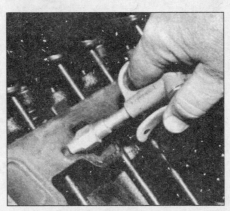

6.10b Clean the bolt holes with compressed air, but be careful - wear safety goggles!

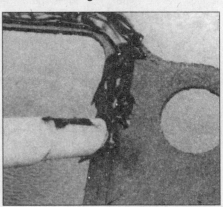

6.11 RTV sealant should be used around the coolant passage holes in the new intake manifold gaskets

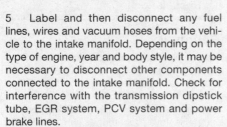

5   Label and then disconnect any fuel lines, wires and vacuum hoses from the vehicle to the intake manifold. Depending on the type of engine, year and body style, it may be necessary to disconnect other components connected to the intake manifold. Check for interference with the transmission dipstick tube, EGR system, PCV system and power brake lines.

6   Detach the upper radiator hose from the thermostat housing cover. If there is a heater fitting in the intake manifold, disconnect it (see illustration).

7   Refer to Chapter 5 and remove the distributor and the ignition coil wires.

8   Loosen the manifold mounting bolts in 1/4-turn increments until they can be removed by hand. The manifold will probably be stuck to the cylinder heads and force may be required to break the gasket seal. A large prybar can be positioned under the cast-in lug near the thermostat housing to pry up the front of the manifold. Caution: Do not pry between the block and manifold or the heads and manifold or damage to the gasket sealing surfaces may result and vacuum leaks could develop.

Installation

Refer to illustrations 6.9, 6.10a, 6.10b, 6.11, 6.12a, 6.12b, 6.14, 6.16a, 6.16b, 6.16c, 6.16d, 6.16e and 6.16f
Note: The mating surfaces of the cylinder heads, block and manifold must be perfectly clean when the manifold is installed. Gasket removal solvents in aerosol cans are available at most auto parts stores and may be helpful when removing old gasket material that is stuck to the heads and manifold. Be sure to follow the directions printed on the container.

9   Use a gasket scraper to remove all traces of sealant and old gasket material, then wipe the mating surfaces with a cloth saturated with lacquer thinner or acetone. If there is old sealant or oil on the mating surfaces when the manifold is installed, oil or vacuum leaks may develop. Cover the lifter valley with shop rags to keep debris out of the engine (see illustration). Use a vacuum cleaner to remove any gasket material that falls into the intake ports in the heads.

10   Use a tap of the correct size to chase the threads in the bolt holes, then use compressed air (if available) to remove the debris from the holes (see illustrations). Warning: Wear safety glasses or a face shield to pro-

tect your eyes when using compressed air.

11   Apply a thin coat of RTV sealant (see illustration) around the coolant passage holes on the cylinder head side of the new intake manifold gaskets (there is normally one hole at each end).

12   Position the gaskets on the cylinder heads. Make sure all intake port openings, coolant passage holes and bolt holes are aligned correctly and THIS SIDE UP is visible (see illustrations).

13   On 7.4L V8 engines, install the front and rear end seals on the block (see illustrations). Note that most seals have either rubber spikes which fit into matching holes in the block or rubber tabs which fit over the edge of the block to locate the seals. Apply a 3/16 inch bead of RTV sealant to each corner of the end seals where they meet the gaskets. Run the silicone 1/2 inch up each cylinder head. Note: The 1996 and later 7.4L lower intake manifold gasket and seals are reusable. Replace them only if they are damaged.

14   V6 and small-block V8 engines require a bead of RTV sealant at the ends of the block. Apply a 3/16-inch bead of RTV sealant to the front and rear of the block as shown (see illustrations). Extend the bead 1/2-inch up each cylinder head and retain the gaskets.

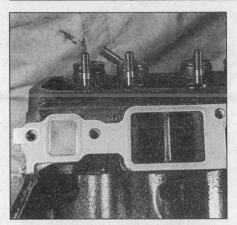

6.12a The rear coolant passages on some models are blocked off - make sure the gasket is installed with the blocked off hole at the rear!

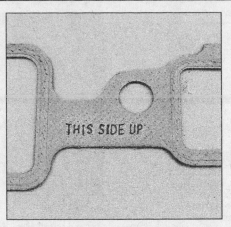

6.12b Be sure to install the gaskets with the marks UP!

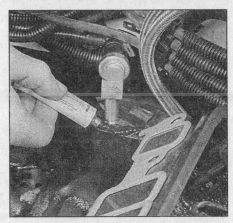

6.14 Apply a bead of sealant to the ends (ridges) of the block

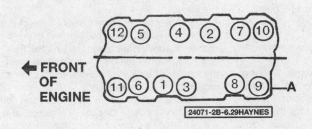

6.16a Intake manifold bolt tightening sequence - 1988 through 1995 V6 engine

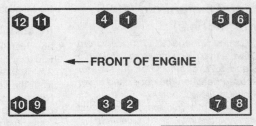

6.16b Intake manifold bolt tightening sequence - 1988 through 1995 small-block V8 engines

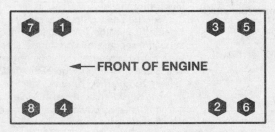

6.16c Intake manifold bolt tightening sequence - 1996 and later V6 and small-block V8 engines

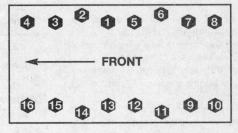

6.16d Intake manifold bolt tightening sequence 1988 through 1990 7.4L V8 engines

Refer to the instructions with the gasket set for further information.

15 Carefully set the manifold in place. Do not disturb the gaskets and do not move the manifold fore-and-aft after it contacts the front and rear seals.

16 Apply a thin coat of Loctite 242 or its equivalent to the manifold bolt threads, then install the bolts. While the sealant is still wet, tighten the bolts to the torque listed in this Chapter's Specifications, working from the center out in a criss-cross pattern (see illustrations). Work up to the final torque in three steps.

17 The remaining installation steps are the

6.16e Intake manifold bolt tightening sequence - 1991 through 1995 7.4L V8 engine

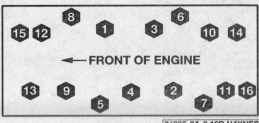

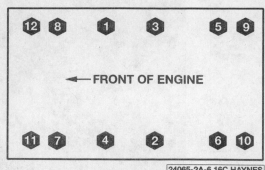

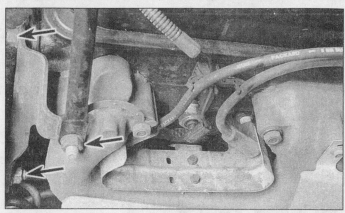

6.16f Intake manifold bolt tightening sequence - 1996 and later 7.4L V8 engine

7.5 Unbolt the alternator and power steering braces (arrows)

reverse of removal. Start the engine and check carefully for oil, vacuum and coolant leaks at the intake manifold joints.

Upper intake manifold (1996 and later models)

Note: *All Central SFI and MPFI models from 1996-on have a two piece intake manifold. On the 5.0L and 5.7L engines, the fuel meter body is housed between the upper and lower intake manifolds (see Chapter 4). On the 7.4L engine, the upper manifold must be removed before removing the lower intake manifold.*

Removal

18   Disconnect the negative battery cable, then refer to Chapter 1 and drain the cooling system.
19   Remove the air cleaner assembly and the duct.
20   Remove any wiring that would interfere with upper intake manifold removal.
21   Remove the throttle and cruise control cables and brackets (see Chapter 4).
22   Remove the fuel lines from the intake to the rear of the engine block on V6 and small block V8 engines.
23   Remove the coil and bracket.
24   On 7.4L V8 models, remove the PCV

hose, the EGR inlet tube, the purge solenoid with connectors and any spark plug wires that interfere.
25   Remove the upper intake manifold. Mark the locations of the various studs and bolts.

Installation

26   Install the gasket and the upper manifold.
27   Tighten the bolts in two steps, working from the center out in a criss-cross pattern. Refer to the torque specifications in this chapter. On the 7.4L models, coat the bolts with thread locking compound such as Loctite 242.
28   The remainder of installation is the reverse of removal.

7   Exhaust manifolds - removal and installation

Refer to illustrations 7.5, 7.8, 7.10a and 7.10b
Warning: *Allow the engine to cool completely before following this procedure.*

Removal

1   Disconnect the negative cable from the battery.

2   Remove the air cleaner assembly for access to the right manifold.
3   If you are removing the manifold with the oxygen sensor in it, disconnect the wire to the sensor.
4   Remove the air management tube at the check valve and the pipe bracket from the manifold stud, if equipped (see Chapter 6).
5   Remove the alternator and power steering braces (if equipped) from the left exhaust manifold **(see illustration)**.
6   Disconnect the spark plug wires and the spark plugs (refer to Chapter 1 if necessary). If there is any danger of mixing the plug wires up, we recommend labeling them with small pieces of tape.
7   If you are removing the right manifold on V8 models, unbolt the dipstick tube.
8   Remove the spark plug heat shields **(see illustration)**.
9   Set the parking brake and block the rear wheels. Raise the front of the vehicle and support it securely on jackstands. Disconnect the exhaust crossover pipe from the manifold outlet (see Chapter 4). **Note:** *Penetrating oil is usually required to remove frozen exhaust pipe nuts. Don't apply excessive force to frozen nuts - you could shear off the exhaust manifold studs.*

7.8 The spark plug heat shields are attached with bolts (arrows)

7.10a Small block V8 engine exhaust manifold fasteners

7.10b Remove the exhaust manifold retaining bolts (arrows) - 7.4 liter engine shown

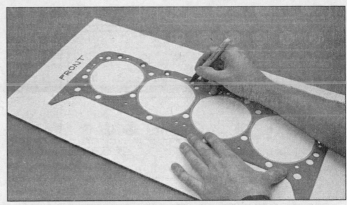

8.5 To avoid mixing up the head bolts, use a new gasket to transfer the bolt hole pattern to a piece of cardboard, then punch holes to accept the bolts

10   Remove the two front and two rear manifold mounting bolts first, then the center bolts (see illustrations) to separate the manifold from the head. Some models use locking tabs under the manifold bolts to keep the bolts from vibrating loose. On these models the tabs will have to be flattened before the bolts can be removed.

Installation

11   Installation is basically the reverse of the removal procedure. Clean the manifold and head gasket surfaces to remove old gasket material, then install new gaskets. Do not use any gasket cement or sealer on exhaust system gaskets.
12   Install all the manifold bolts and tighten them to the specified torque. Work from the center out and approach the final torque in three steps.
13   Apply anti-seize compound to the exhaust manifold-to-exhaust pipe studs and use a new exhaust "doughnut" gasket, if equipped.

8   Cylinder heads - removal and installation

Refer to illustrations 8.5, 8.12, 8.16a, 8.16b and 8.16c

Removal

1   Refer to Section 3 and remove the rocker arm covers.
2   Refer to Section 6 and remove the intake manifold. Note that the cooling system must be drained (see Chapter 1) to prevent coolant from getting into internal areas of the engine when the manifold and heads are removed.
3   Refer to Section 7 and detach both exhaust manifolds.
4   Refer to Section 4 and remove the rocker arms and pushrods.
5   Using a new head gasket, outline the cylinders and bolt pattern on a piece of cardboard (see illustration). Be sure to indicate the front of the engine for reference. Punch holes at the bolt locations.

6   Loosen the head bolts in 1/4-turn increments until they can be removed by hand. Work from bolt-to-bolt in a pattern that's the reverse of the tightening sequence. **Note:** *Don't overlook the row of bolts on the lower edge of each head, near the spark plug holes. Store the bolts in the cardboard holder as they're removed. This will ensure the bolts are reinstalled in their original holes.*
7   Lift the heads off the engine. If resistance is felt, do not pry between the head and block as damage to the mating surfaces will result. To dislodge the head, place a block of wood against the end of it and strike the wood block with a hammer. Store the heads on blocks of wood to prevent damage to the gasket sealing surfaces.
8   Cylinder head disassembly and inspection procedures are covered in detail in Chapter 2, Part B.

Installation

9   The mating surfaces of the cylinder heads and block must be perfectly clean when the heads are installed.
10   Use a gasket scraper to remove all traces of carbon and old gasket material, then clean the mating surfaces with lacquer thinner or acetone. If there's oil on the mating surfaces when the heads are installed, the gaskets may not seal correctly and leaks could develop. When working on the block, cover the lifter valley with shop rags to keep debris out of the engine. Use a vacuum cleaner to remove any debris that falls into the cylinders.
11   Check the block and head mating surfaces for nicks, deep scratches and other damage. If damage is slight, it can be removed with a file. If it's excessive, machining may be the only alternative.
12   Use a tap of the correct size to chase the threads in the head bolt holes in the block. Mount each bolt in a vise and run a die down the threads to remove corrosion and restore the threads (see illustration). Dirt, corrosion, sealant and damaged threads will affect torque readings.
13   Position the new gaskets over the dowel pins in the block. **Note:** *If a steel gasket is*

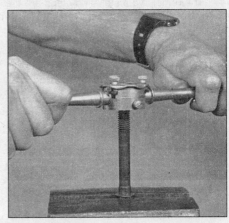

8.12 A die should be used to remove sealant and corrosion from the head bolt threads prior to installation

used (shim-type gasket), apply a thin, even coat of sealant such as K&W Copper Coat to both sides prior to installation. Steel gaskets must be installed with the raised bead UP. Composition gaskets must be installed dry; do not use sealant.
14   Carefully position the heads on the block without disturbing the gaskets.
15   Before installing the head bolts, coat the threads with a non-hardening sealant such as Permatex no. 2.
16   Install the bolts in their original locations and tighten them finger-tight. Following the recommended sequence, tighten the bolts in

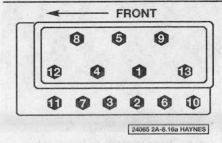

8.16a Cylinder head bolt tightening sequence - 4.3L V6 engine

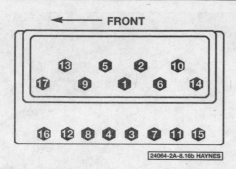

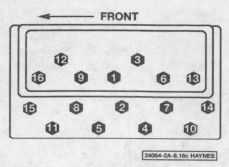

8.16b Cylinder head bolt tightening sequence - small block V8 engines

8.16c Cylinder head bolt tightening sequence for big block V8 engines

several steps to the specified torque **(see illustrations)**.

17 The remaining installation steps are the reverse of removal.

9   Top Dead Center (TDC) for number one piston - locating

Refer to illustrations 9.6 and 9.7

1   Top Dead Center (TDC) is the highest point in the cylinder that each piston reaches as it travels up-and-down when the crankshaft turns. Each piston reaches TDC on the compression stroke and again on the exhaust stroke, but TDC generally refers to piston position on the compression stroke. The timing marks on the vibration damper installed on the front of the crankshaft are referenced to the number one piston at TDC on the compression stroke.

2   Positioning the pistons at TDC is an essential part of many procedures such as rocker arm removal, valve adjustment, timing chain and sprocket replacement and distributor removal.

3   In order to bring any piston to TDC, the crankshaft must be turned using one of the methods outlined below. When looking at the front of the engine, normal crankshaft rotation is clockwise. **Warning:** *Before beginning this procedure, be sure to place the transmission in Neutral and disable the ignition system*

by disconnecting the primary wires from the coil.

a) *The preferred method is to turn the crankshaft with a large socket and breaker bar attached to the vibration damper bolt that is threaded into the front of the crankshaft.*

b) *A remote starter switch, which may save some time, can also be used. Attach the switch leads to the S (switch) and B (battery) terminals on the starter solenoid. Once the piston is close to TDC, use a socket and breaker bar as described in the previous paragraph.*

c) *If an assistant is available to turn the ignition switch to the Start position in short bursts, you can get the piston close to TDC without a remote starter switch. Use a socket and breaker bar as described in Paragraph a) to complete the procedure.*

4   Scribe or paint a small mark on the distributor body directly below the number one spark plug wire terminal in the distributor cap.

5   Remove the distributor cap as described in Chapter 1.

6   Turn the crankshaft (see Step 3 above) until the line on the vibration damper is aligned with the zero mark on the timing plate **(see illustration)**. The timing plate and vibration damper are located low on the front of the engine, behind the pulley that turns the drivebelt.

7   The rotor should now be pointing directly at the mark on the distributor base **(see illustration)**. If it isn't, the piston is at TDC on the exhaust stroke.

8   If the rotor is 180-degrees off, turn the crankshaft one complete turn (360-degrees) clockwise. The rotor should now be pointing at the mark. When the rotor is pointing at the number one spark plug wire terminal in the distributor cap (which is indicated by the mark on the distributor body or intake manifold) and the timing marks are aligned, the number one piston is at TDC on the compression stroke.

9   After the number one piston has been positioned at TDC on the compression stroke, TDC for any of the remaining cylinders can be located by turning the crankshaft 90-degrees at a time and following the firing order (refer to the Specifications).

10 Timing cover, chain and sprockets - removal and installation

Note: *1995 and later V6 and small block V8 models are equipped with a non-reusable plastic front cover. Once it is removed it must be discarded or oil leaks could develop. 1996 and later 7.4L V8 engines have a reusable front cover gasket as well as having a*

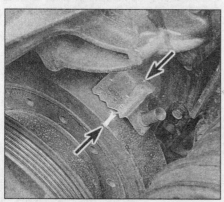

9.6 Align the mark on the vibration damper with the zero mark on the timing plate (arrows)

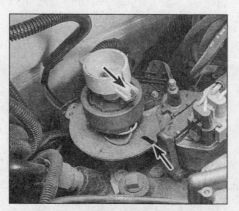

9.7 The rotor aligns with the mark on the distributor base (arrows) below the number one terminal on the cap

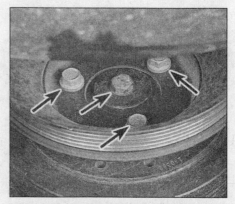

10.2 The crankshaft pulley is attached to the vibration damper by four bolts (arrows) - viewed from below

reusable front cover. Replace the gasket on 7.4L engines only if the original gasket is damaged.

Removal

Refer to illustrations 10.2, 10.4 and 10.6

1   Refer to Chapter 3 and remove the water pump.

2   Remove the bolts **(see illustration)** and separate the crankshaft drivebelt pulley from the vibration damper.

3   Refer to Section 9 and position the number one piston at TDC on the compression stroke. Rotate the crankshaft an additional 360-degrees. **Caution:** *Once this has been done, do not turn the crankshaft until the timing chain and sprockets have been reinstalled.*

4   Most engines use a large bolt threaded into the nose of the crankshaft to secure the vibration damper in position. If your engine has a bolt, remove it from the front of the crankshaft, then use a puller to detach the vibration damper **(see illustration)**. **Caution:** *Do not use a puller with jaws that grip the outer edge of the damper. The puller must be the type that utilizes bolts to apply force to the damper hub only.*

5   On most V6 and small block V8 engines, the timing cover cannot be removed with the oil pan in place. The pan bolts will have to be loosened and the pan lowered slightly for the timing cover to be removed. If the pan has been in place for an extended period of time it's likely the pan gasket will break when the pan is lowered. In this case the pan should be removed and a new gasket installed.

6   Detach any accessories such as the power steering pump, alternator and air conditioning compressor that block access to the timing chain cover. Leave the hoses/wires connected and tie the components aside. Refer to Chapters 3, 5 and 10 for additional information. Unbolt the accessory bracket from the front of the engine **(see illustration)**.

7   After the accessories are moved aside, remove the bolts and separate the timing chain cover from the block. **Note:** *Some engines have a bolt-on timing scale - note the location and be sure to reinstall it in the same way.* The cover may be stuck; if so, use a putty knife to break the gasket seal. The cover is easily distorted, so don't attempt to pry it off.

8   On big block engines, pull the cover forward far enough to insert a knife between the cover and the block, cut the forward portion of the oil pan gasket on each side, then remove the cover.

9   On 1995 and later models, remove the crankshaft position sensor reluctor ring. **Note:** *On 7.4L engines, a special tool will be required to remove the ring. Once the ring has been removed from the 7.4L engine with a puller, it must be discarded and replaced with a new one.*

10   Measure the timing chain free play. If it is more than 5/8 inch, it should be replaced along with the gears.

11   Remove the three bolts (all except 1994

10.4 Use a bolt-type like this - a jaw-type puller will damage the vibration damper

and later 4.3L V6 engines) or two bolts and one nut (1994 and later 4.3L V6 from the end of the camshaft, then detach the camshaft sprocket and chain as an assembly. **Note:** *On 1994 and later 4.3L V6 engines, the balancer shaft drive gear will stay attached to the camshaft and the driven gear will stay attached to the balancer shaft. The sprocket on the crankshaft can be removed with a two- or three- jaw puller, but be careful not to damage the threads in the end of the crankshaft.* **Note:** *If the timing chain cover oil seal has been leaking, refer to Section 15 and install a new one.*

Installation

Refer to illustration 10.15

12   Use a gasket scraper to remove all traces of old gasket material and sealant from the cover and engine block. Stuff a shop rag into the opening at the front of the oil pan to keep debris out of the engine. Clean the cover and block sealing surfaces with lacquer thinner or acetone.

13   Check the cover flange for distortion, particularly around the bolt holes. If necessary, place the cover on a block of wood and use a hammer to flatten and restore the gasket surface.

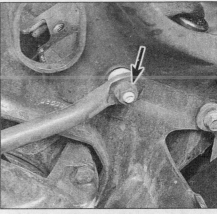

10.6 Remove the accessories and unbolt the bracket (arrows) from the front of the engine

14   If new parts are being installed, be sure to align the keyway in the crankshaft sprocket with the Woodruff key in the end of the crankshaft. **Note:** *Timing chains must be replaced as a set with the camshaft and crankshaft gears. Never put a new chain on old gears. Align the sprocket with the Woodruff key and press the sprocket onto the crankshaft with the vibration damper bolt, a large socket and some washers or tap it gently into place until it is completely seated.* **Caution:** *If resistance is encountered, do not hammer the sprocket onto the crankshaft. It may eventually move onto the shaft, but it may be cracked in the process and fail later, causing extensive engine damage.*

15   Loop the new chain over the camshaft sprocket, then turn the sprocket until the timing mark is in the 6 o'clock position **(see illustration)**. Mesh the chain with the crankshaft sprocket and position the camshaft sprocket on the end of the cam. If necessary, turn the camshaft so the dowel pin fits into the sprocket hole with the timing mark in the 6 o'clock position. **Note:** *The number four piston (V6) or number six piston (V8) must be at TDC on the compression stroke as the chain and sprockets are installed (see Step 3 above).*

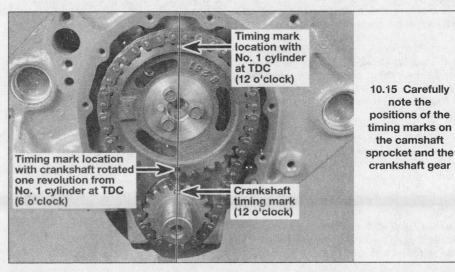

Timing mark location with No. 1 cylinder at TDC (12 o'clock)

Timing mark location with crankshaft rotated one revolution from No. 1 cylinder at TDC (6 o'clock)

Crankshaft timing mark (12 o'clock)

10.15 Carefully note the positions of the timing marks on the camshaft sprocket and the crankshaft gear

11.3 When checking the camshaft lobe lift, the dial indicator plunger must be positioned directly above and in-line with the pushrod (use a short length of vacuum hose to hold the plunger over the pushrod end if you have difficulty keeping the plunger on the pushrod)

11.11 The lifters in an engine that has accumulated many miles may have to be removed with a special tool (arrow) - store them in an organized manner to make sure they're reinstalled in their original locations

11.13a On the V6 engine, the camshaft is retained by the thrust plate

11.13b Thread three long bolts into the end of the camshaft to use as a handle

16   Apply thread locking compound to the camshaft sprocket bolt threads, then install and tighten them to the specified torque. Lubricate the chain with clean engine oil.

17   On V6 and small block V8 engines, apply a small amount of RTV sealant to the U-shaped channel in the bottom of the cover.

18   On big block V8 engines, cut the tabs from a new front oil pan seal and use gasket sealer to hold the seal in the bottom of the front cover. Apply a 1/8-inch bead of RTV-type gasket sealer to the junction of the oil pan and front face of the block on each side.

19   V6 and small block V8 engines use one-piece oil pan gaskets, which should be checked for cracks and deformation before installing the timing cover. If the gasket has deteriorated it must be replaced before rein-stalling the timing cover.

20   Apply a thin layer of RTV sealant to both sides of the new cover gasket, then position it on the engine block. The dowel pins and sealant will hold it in place.

21   Install the timing chain cover on the block, tightening the bolts finger-tight.

22   If the oil pan was removed on a V6 or small block V8 engine, reinstall it (see Section 12). If it was only loosened, tighten the oil pan bolts, bringing the oil pan up against the tim-ing chain cover.

23   Tighten the timing chain cover bolts to the specified torque.

24   Lubricate the oil seal contact surface of the vibration damper hub with moly-base grease or clean engine oil, then install the damper on the end of the crankshaft. The keyway in the damper must be aligned with the Woodruff key in the crankshaft nose. If the damper cannot be seated by hand, slip a large washer over the bolt, install the bolt and tighten it to push the damper into place. Remove the large washer and tighten the bolt to the specified torque.

25   The remaining installation steps are the reverse of removal.

---

11   Camshaft, bearings and lifters - removal, inspection and installation

Camshaft lobe lift check

Refer to illustration 11.3

1   To determine the extent of cam lobe wear, the lobe lift should be checked prior to camshaft removal. Refer to Section 3 and remove the rocker arm covers.

2   Position the number one piston at TDC on the compression stroke (see Section 9).

3   Beginning with the number one cylinder, loosen the rocker arm nuts and pivot the rocker arms sideways. Mount a dial indicator on the engine and position the plunger against the top of the first pushrod **(see illustration)**.

4   Zero the dial indicator, then very slowly turn the crankshaft in the normal direction of rotation until the indicator needle stops and begins to move in the opposite direction. The point at which it stops indicates maximum cam lobe lift.

5   Record this figure for future reference, then reposition the piston at TDC on the compression stroke.

6   Move the dial indicator to the other num-ber one cylinder pushrod and repeat the check. Be sure to record the results for each valve.

7   Repeat the check for the remaining valves. Since each piston must be at TDC on the compression stroke for this procedure, work from cylinder-to-cylinder following the firing order sequence.

8   After the check is complete, compare the results to the Specifications. If camshaft lobe lift is less than specified, cam lobe wear has occurred and a new camshaft should be installed.

Removal

Refer to illustrations 11.11, 11.13a and 11.13b

9   Refer to the appropriate Sections and remove the intake manifold, the rocker arms, the pushrods and the timing chain and camshaft sprocket. The radiator should be removed as well (Chapter 4). **Note:** *If the vehicle is equipped with air conditioning it may be necessary to remove the air condi-tioning condenser to remove the camshaft. If the condenser must be removed the system must first be depressurized by a dealer ser-vice department or service station. Do not disconnect any air conditioning lines until the system has been properly depressurized.*

10   There are several ways to extract the lifters from the bores. A special tool designed to grip and remove lifters is manufactured by many tool companies and is widely available, but it may not be required in every case. On newer engines without a lot of varnish buildup, the lifters can often be removed with a small magnet or even with your fingers. A machinist's scribe with a bent end can be used to pull the lifters out by positioning the point under the retainer ring inside the top of

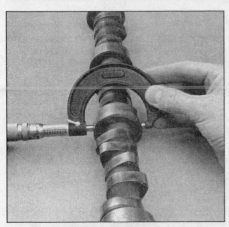

11.16 Check the diameter of each camshaft bearing journal to pinpoint excessive wear and out-of-round conditions

11.19a If the bottom of any lifter is worn concave, scratched or galled, replace the entire set with new lifters

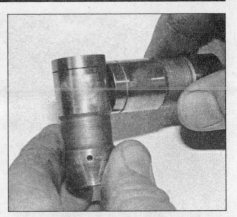

11.19b The foot of each lifter should be slightly convex - the side of another lifter can be used as a straightedge to check it; if it appears flat, it is worn and must not be reused

11.19c If the lifters are pitted or rough, they shouldn't be reused

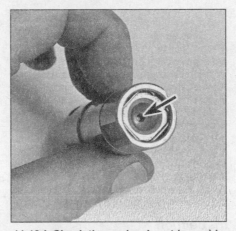

11.19d Check the pushrod seat (arrow) in the top of each lifter for wear

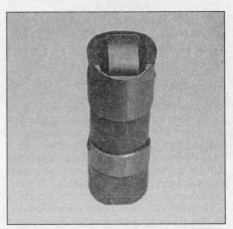

11.21 The roller on roller lifters must turn freely - check for wear and excessive play as well

each lifter. **Caution:** *Do not use pliers to remove the lifters unless you intend to replace them with new ones (along with the camshaft). The pliers will damage the precision machined and hardened lifters, rendering them useless.*

11　Before removing the lifters, arrange to store them in a clearly labeled box to ensure that they are reinstalled in their original locations. **Note:** *On engines equipped with roller lifters, the retainer must be removed before the lifters are withdrawn).* Remove the lifters and store them where they will not get dirty **(see illustration)**. Do not attempt to withdraw the camshaft with the lifters in place.

12　On 1994 4.3L V6 engines, remove the balancer shaft drive and driven gears (see Section 12).

13　On V6 engines, remove the camshaft thrust plate (if equipped) **(see illustration)**. Thread 6-inch long 5/16 - 18 bolts into the camshaft sprocket bolt holes to use as a handle when removing the camshaft from the block **(see illustration)**.

14　Carefully pull the camshaft out. Support the cam near the block so the lobes do not nick or gouge the bearings as it is withdrawn.

Inspection

Refer to illustrations 11.16, 11.19a, 11.19b, 11.19c, 11.19d and 11.21

Camshaft and bearings

15　After the camshaft has been removed from the engine, cleaned with solvent and dried, inspect the bearing journals for uneven wear, pitting and evidence of seizure. If the journals are damaged, the bearing inserts in the block are probably damaged as well. Both the camshaft and bearings will have to be replaced. Replacement of the camshaft bearings requires special tools and techniques which place it beyond the scope of the home mechanic. The block will have to be removed from the vehicle and taken to an automotive machine shop for this procedure.

16　Measure the bearing journals with a micrometer to determine if they are excessively worn or out-of-round **(see illustration)**.

17　Check the camshaft lobes for heat discoloration, score marks, chipped areas, pitting and uneven wear. If the lobes are in good condition and if the lobe lift measurements are as specified, the camshaft can be reused.

Conventional lifters

18　Clean the lifters with solvent and dry them thoroughly without mixing them up.

19　Check each lifter wall, pushrod seat and foot for scuffing, score marks and uneven wear. Each lifter foot (the surface that rides on the cam lobe) must be slightly convex, although this can be difficult to determine by eye. If the base of the lifter is concave **(see illustrations)**, the lifters and camshaft must be replaced. If the lifter walls are damaged or worn (which is not very likely), inspect the lifter bores in the engine block as well. If the pushrod seats are worn, check the pushrod ends.

20　If new lifters are being installed, a new camshaft must also be installed. If a new camshaft is installed, then use new lifters as well. Never install used lifters unless the original camshaft is used and the lifters can be installed in their original locations.

Roller lifters

21　Check the rollers carefully for wear and damage and make sure they turn freely without excessive play **(see illustration)**. The inspection procedure for conventional lifters

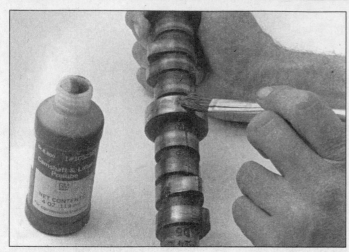

11.23 Coat the lobes and journals with special camshaft lube

11.25 After the camshaft is in place, turn it until the dowel pin (arrow) is in the 9 o'clock position as shown here

also applies to roller lifters.

22 Used roller lifters can be reinstalled with a new camshaft and the original camshaft can be used if new lifters are installed.

Installation

Refer to illustrations 11.23 and 11.25

23 Lubricate the camshaft bearing journals and cam lobes with moly-base grease or engine assembly lube **(see illustration)**.

24 Slide the camshaft into the engine. Support the cam near the block and be careful not to scrape or nick the bearings.

25 Turn the camshaft until the dowel pin is in the 9 o'clock position **(see illustration)**.

26 On 1994 and later 4.3L V6 engines, install the balancer shaft drive and driven gears (see Section 12).

27 Refer to Section 10 and install the timing chain and sprockets.

28 Lubricate the lifters with clean engine oil and install them in the block. If the original lifters are being reinstalled, be sure to return them to their original locations. If a new camshaft was installed, be sure to install new lifters as well.

29 The remaining installation steps are the reverse of removal.

30 Before starting and running the engine, change the oil and install a new oil filter (see Chapter 1).

---

12   Balancer shaft - removal and installation (1994 and later V6 engines)

Removal

1 Remove the air cleaner assembly and air intake duct.

2 Remove the timing cover, chains and sprockets (see Section 10).

3 Remove the hood latch (see Chapter 11).

4 Remove the intake manifold (see Section 5).

5 Remove the radiator grille and headlight

bezels (see Chapter 11).

6 Remove the radiator and its support braces, then remove the air conditioning condenser - if equipped - (see Chapter 3).

7 Remove the radiator support crossover.

8 Remove the retaining stud and the balancer shaft drive gear from the camshaft.

9 Remove the retaining bolt and the balancer shaft driven gear.

10 Remove the two bolts securing the balancer shaft retainer and remove the retainer.

11 Unbolt and remove the lifter retainer **(see illustration 11.11a)**.

12 Using a soft-faced mallet, carefully tap the balancer shaft out of the block.

Inspection

13 After the balancer shaft has been removed from the engine, cleaned with solvent and dried, inspect the rear bearing journal for uneven wear, pitting and evidence of seizure. If the journal is damaged, the rear bearing in the block is probably damaged as well. The bearing will have to be replaced.

14 Check the balancer drive and driven

12.22 Make sure the balancer shaft timing marks on both the drive and driven gears are aligned

gears for cracks, missing teeth and excessive wear. If the teeth are highly polished, pitted or galled, or if the outer hardened surface of the teeth is flaking off, new parts will be required. If one gear is worn or damaged, replace both gears as a set. Never install one new gear and one used gear.

Bearing replacement

Note: *The balance shaft and it's front bearing are an assembly. Don't try to disassemble the front bearing or remove it from the shaft.*

15 Balancer shaft bearing replacement requires special tools and expertise that place it outside the scope of the home mechanic. Take the engine block to a dealer service department or an automotive machine shop to ensure that the job is done correctly.

Installation

Refer to illustration 12.22

16 Lubricate the balancer shaft bearing journals with moly-base grease or engine assembly lube.

17 Slide the balancer shaft into the engine. Support the balancer near the block and be careful not to scrape or nick the bearing. It may be necessary to gently tap on the shaft with a soft-face mallet.

18 Install the balance shaft retainer and two bolts and tighten them to the torque listed in this Chapter's Specifications.

19 Install the lifter retainer and bolts, then tighten the bolts securely.

20 Rotate the balancer shaft by hand to make sure there is sufficient clearance between the balancer shaft and the lifter retainer. Replace the lifter retainer if necessary.

21 Install the balancer shaft driven gear and tighten the bolt to the torque listed in this Chapter's Specifications.

22 Rotate the camshaft so that, with the drive gear temporarily installed, the timing mark is straight up at the 12 o'clock position **(see illustration)**. Remove the drive gear.

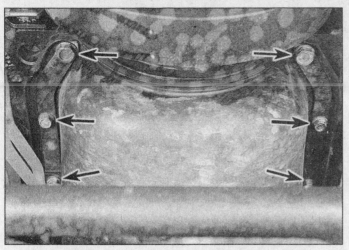

13.19a Working at the front of the engine, remove the oil pan bolts (arrows)

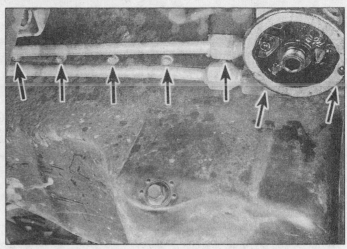

13.19b On the driver's side of the engine, the oil cooler lines and filter housing obscure the bolts (arrows)

23 Rotate the balancer shaft until the timing mark is facing straight down at the 6 o'clock position **(see illustration 12.22).**

24 Install the balancer drive gear onto the camshaft and install the retaining stud, then tighten it to the torque listed in this Chapter's Specifications.

25 Install the timing chain, sprockets and cover (see Section 10).

13 Oil pan - removal and installation

Refer to illustrations 13.19a and 13.19b

Removal

1 Disconnect the negative cable from the battery.

2 Raise the vehicle and support it securely on jackstands.

3 Drain the engine oil and remove the oil filter (see Chapter 1).

4 Unbolt the crossover pipe at the exhaust manifolds.

5 If equipped with strut rods, remove the strut rods at the bellhousing cover and the strut rod brackets at the front engine mounts. Disconnect the engine oil cooler and/or transmission cooler lines from the oil pan, as necessary.

6 Remove the lower bellhousing cover.

7 Remove the starter, if necessary for clearance (see Chapter 5).

Four-wheel drive vehicles only

8 Remove the skid plate.

9 Remove the front driveshaft.

10 Remove the two right side bolts and nuts of the front driveaxle. Remove the one upper left bolt and nut.

11 Remove the front axle shaft by rotating the drive axle forward after you turn the wheels to the left.

Big block V8 engine only

12 Disconnect the oil pressure gauge line

from the side of the block.

13 Remove the distributor cap to prevent breakage against the firewall as the engine is lifted.

14 Unbolt the fan shroud and move it back over the fan (see Chapter 3). If clearance is tight, insert a piece of heavy cardboard between the fan and radiator to protect the radiator fins from the fan when the engine is raised.

15 Remove the engine mount through-bolts.

16 Use an engine hoist to lift the engine approximately three inches. **Caution:** *On most engines the oil pump pickup is very close to the bottom of the oil pan, and it can be damaged easily if concentrated pressure from a jack is applied to the pan. When lifting the engine, check to make sure the distributor isn't hitting the firewall and the fan isn't hitting the radiator.*

17 Place blocks of wood between the crossmember and the engine block in the area of the motor mounts to hold the engine in the raised position, then remove the engine hoist.

All engines

18 Turn the crankshaft until the timing mark on the vibration damper is at the bottom.

19 Remove the oil pan bolts **(see illustrations)** and reinforcements. Note that some models use studs and nuts in some positions.

20 Remove the pan by tilting the rear down and working it away from the crankshaft throws, oil pump pick-up and front crossmember.

Installation

21 Use a scraper to remove all traces of old gasket material and sealant from the pan and block (this doesn't apply to engines with one-piece rubber gaskets).

22 Clean the sealing surfaces with lacquer thinner or acetone. Make sure the bolt holes in the block are clean.

23 Check the oil pan flange for distortion, particularly around the bolt holes. If necessary, place the pan on a block of wood and use a hammer to flatten and restore the gasket surface.

24 Remove the old rubber seals from the rear main bearing cap and timing chain cover, then clean the grooves and install new seals (this doesn't apply to engines with one-piece rubber gaskets). Use RTV sealant or gasket adhesive to hold the new seals in place, then apply a bead of RTV sealant to the block-to-seal junctions. Use the same sealant to attach the new side gaskets to the oil pan.

25 The one-piece rubber gasket used on some models should be checked carefully and replaced with a new one if damage is noted. **Note:** *The oil pan gasket on 1997 7.4L engines is reusable. Discard it only if it is damaged.* Apply a bead of RTV silicone to the four corners of the pan gasket. The sealant should extend one inch in each direction from each corner. Attach the gasket to the oil pan.

26 Carefully position the pan against the block and install the bolts/nuts finger-tight (don't forget the reinforcement strips, if used). Make sure the seals and gaskets haven't shifted, then tighten the bolts/nuts in three steps to the specified torque. Start at the center of the pan and work out toward the ends in a spiral pattern.

27 The remaining steps are the reverse of removal. **Caution:** *Don't forget to refill the engine with oil before starting it (see Chapter 1).*

14 Oil pump - removal and installation

Refer to illustrations 14.2 and 14.3

1 Remove the oil pan as described in Section 12.

2 While supporting the oil pump, remove

14.2 Remove the single bolt holding the oil pump to the rear main cap and remove the oil pump

14.3 Make sure the nylon sleeve is in place between the oil pump and driveshaft

15.2 The crankshaft front oil seal can be removed with the engine in the vehicle with a seal removal tool (shown here) or a large screwdriver

15.4 Installing the crankshaft front oil seal using a socket

the pump-to-rear main bearing cap bolt **(see illustration)**.

3   Lower the pump and remove it along with the pump driveshaft. Note that on most models a hard nylon sleeve is used to align the oil pump driveshaft and the oil pump shaft. Make sure this sleeve is in place on the oil pump driveshaft **(see illustration)**. If it is not there, check the oil pan for the pieces of the sleeve, clean them out of the pan, then get a new sleeve for the oil pump driveshaft.

4   Check the screen and the pickup tube for any damage or looseness. It must fit very tight onto the oil pump.

5   If a new oil pump is installed, make sure the pump driveshaft is mated with the shaft inside the pump.

6   Position the pump on the engine and make sure the slot in the upper end of the driveshaft is aligned with the tang on the lower end of the distributor shaft. The distributor drives the oil pump, so it is absolutely essential that the components mate properly.

7   Install the mounting bolt and tighten it to the specified torque.

8   Install the oil pan.

15 Crankshaft oil seals - replacement

Front seal

Note: *On models equipped with a plastic composite front cover, the front cover and seal are replaced as a unit. Any time the front cover is removed from these models it should be discarded and replaced or leaks could develop.*

Timing cover in place

Refer to illustrations 15.2 and 15.4

1   Remove the vibration damper as described in Section 10.

2   Carefully pry the seal out of the cover with a seal removal tool or a large screwdriver **(see illustration)**. Be careful not to distort the cover or scratch the wall of the seal bore.

3   Clean the bore to remove any old seal material and corrosion. Position the new seal in the bore with the open end of the seal facing IN. A small amount of oil applied to the outer edge of the new seal will make installa-

15.6 While supporting the cover near the seal bore, drive the old seal out from the inside with a hammer and punch or screwdriver

tion easier - don't overdo it!

4   Drive the seal into the bore with a large socket and hammer until it's completely seated **(see illustration)**. Select a socket that's the same outside diameter as the seal.

5   Lubricate the seal lips with engine oil and reinstall the vibration damper.

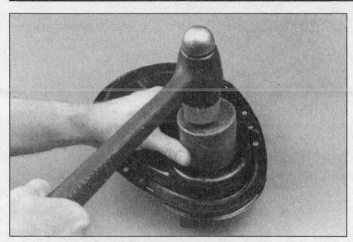

15.8 Clean the bore, then apply a small amount of oil to the outer edge of the seal and drive it squarely into the opening with a large socket and hammer - DO NOT damage the seal in the process!

15.13 Tap the seal end with a brass punch or wood dowel and hammer until it can be gripped with a pair of pliers and pulled out

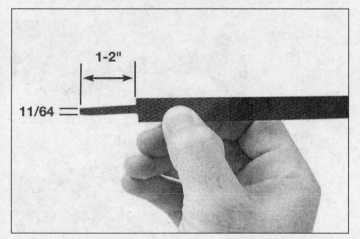

15.15 If a new seal did not include an installation tool, make one from a piece of brass shim stock 0.004-inch thick

15.16a Using the tool like a "shoehorn", attach the seal section to the bearing cap . . .

Timing cover removed

Refer to illustrations 15.6 and 15.8

6   Use a punch or screwdriver and hammer to drive the seal out of the cover from the back side. Support the cover as close to the seal bore as possible **(see illustration)**. Be careful not to distort the cover or scratch the wall of the seal bore. If the engine has accumulated a lot of miles, apply penetrating oil to the seal-to-cover joint on each side and allow it to soak in before attempting to drive the seal out.

7   Clean the bore to remove any old seal material and corrosion. Support the cover on blocks of wood and position the new seal in the bore with the open end of the seal facing in. A small amount of oil applied to the outer edge of the new seal will make installation easier.

8   Drive the seal into the bore with a large socket and hammer until it's completely seated **(see illustration)**. Select a socket with the same outside diameter as the seal (a section of pipe can be used if a socket isn't available).

9   Reinstall the timing chain cover.

Rear seal

1990 and earlier 7.4 liter (big block) V8 engine

Refer to illustrations 15.13, 15.15, 15.16a, 15.16b, 15.17 and 15.18

10   The rear main seal can be replaced with the engine in the vehicle. Refer to the appropriate Sections and remove the oil pan and oil pump.

11   Remove the bolts and detach the rear main bearing cap from the engine.

12   The seal section in the bearing cap can be pried out with a screwdriver.

13   To remove the seal section in the block, tap on one end with a hammer and brass punch or wood dowel until the other end protrudes far enough to grip it with a pair of pliers and pull it out **(see illustration)**. Be very careful not to nick or scratch the crankshaft journal or seal surface as this is done.

14   Inspect the bearing cap and engine block mating surfaces, as well as the cap seal grooves, for nicks, burrs and scratches. Remove any defects with a fine file or deburring tool.

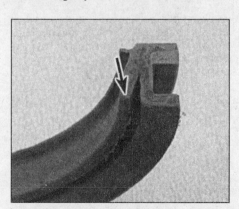

15.16b . . . with the oil seal lip pointing toward the front of the engine

15   A small seal installation tool is usually included when a new seal is purchased. If you didn't receive one, they can also be purchased separately at most auto parts stores or you can make one from an old feeler gauge or a piece of brass shim stock **(see illustration)**.

16   Using the tool, install one seal section in the cap with the lip facing the front of the

15.17 Position the tool to protect the back side of the seal as it passes over the sharp edge of the ridge - note that the seal straddles the ridge

15.18 Make sure the lip faces the front of the engine and hold the tool in place to protect the seal as it is installed

15.24 Notches (arrows) are provided in the housing to pry the oil seal out

15.28 Use a hammer and a block of wood to seat the seal

engine (if the seal has two lips, the one with the helix must face the front) **(see illustrations)**. The ends should be flush with the mating surface of the cap. Make sure it is completely seated.

17 Position the narrow end of the tool so that it will protect the backside of the seal as it passes over the sharp edge of the ridge in the block **(see illustration)**.

18 Lubricate the seal lips and the groove in the backside with moly-base grease or clean engine oil - do not get any lubricant on the seal ends. Insert the seal into the block, over the tool **(see illustration)**. **Caution:** *Make sure the lip points toward the front of the engine when the seal is installed.*

19 Push the seal into place, using the tool like a "shoehorn". Turning the crankshaft may help to draw the seal into place. When both ends of the seal are flush with the block surface, remove the tool.

20 Lubricate the cap seal lips with moly-base grease or clean engine oil.

21 Carefully position the bearing cap on the block, install the bolts and tighten them to 10-to-12 ft-lbs only. Tap the crankshaft forward-and-backward with a lead or brass

hammer to line up the main bearing and crankshaft thrust surfaces, then tighten the rear bearing cap bolts to the specified torque.

22 Install the oil pump and oil pan.

V6 and small block V8 engines

Refer to illustrations 15.24 and 15.28

23 All V6 and small block V8 engines use a one-piece rear main oil seal which is installed in a bolt-on housing. Replacing this seal requires removal of the transmission, clutch assembly and flywheel (manual transmission) or torque converter and driveplate (automatic transmission). Refer to Chapter 7 for the transmission removal procedures.

24 Although the seal can be removed by prying it out of the housing by inserting a screwdriver into the notches provided **(see illustration)**, installation with the housing still mounted on the block requires the use of a special tool, which attaches to the threaded holes in the crankshaft flange and then presses the new seal into place.

25 If the special installation tool is not available, remove the oil pan (see Section 12) and the bolts securing the housing to the block, then detach the housing and gasket. When-

ever the housing is removed from the block a new seal and gasket must be installed.

26 Remove the oil pan (see Section 13).

27 Insert a screwdriver blade into the notches in the seal housing and pry out the old seal. Be sure to note how far it's recessed into the housing bore before removal so the new seal can be installed to the same depth.

28 Clean the housing thoroughly, then apply a thin coat of engine oil to the new seal. Set the seal squarely into the recess in the housing, then, using two pieces of wood, one on each side of the housing, use a hammer to press the seal into place **(see illustration)**.

29 Carefully slide the seal over the crankshaft and bolt the seal housing to the block. Be sure to use a new gasket, but don't use any gasket sealant.

30 The remainder of installation is the reverse of the removal procedure.

1991 and later 7.4 liter (big block) V8 engine

Note: *We recommend using a special seal installation tool for this procedure. If the tool is not available, you may be able to install the seal using a piece of pipe with a diameter*

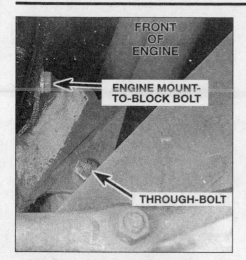

16.7a Front view of a V6 and small block
V8 engine mount shown - big block
V8 similar

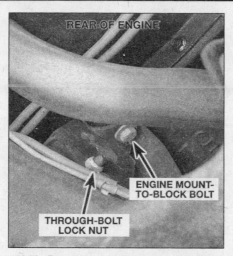

16.7b Rear view of a V6 and small block
V8 engine mount shown - big block
V8 similar

17.2 Hold the crankshaft to keep it from
turning while you loosen/tighten the bolts

*slightly smaller than the outer diameter of the
seal or a blunt punch and a hammer.*

31 This engine uses a one-piece rear main
oil seal, but, unlike the V6 and small block V8
engines, there is no bolt-on housing for the
seal. The seal is pressed into a bore
machined into the rear main bearing cap and
engine block. Remove the transmission,
clutch components (if equipped) and flywheel
or driveplate (see Section 17).

32 Pry out the old seal with a hooked tool or
a large screwdriver. **Caution:** *To prevent an
oil leak after the new seal is installed, be very
careful not to scratch or otherwise damage
the crankshaft sealing surface or the bore in
the bearing cap/engine block.*

33 Clean the crankshaft and seal bore in the
block/bearing cap thoroughly and de-grease
these areas by wiping them with a rag
soaked in lacquer thinner or acetone. Lubricate the lip and outer diameter of the new
seal with engine oil. **Note:** *When installing the
new seal, the lip of the seal must face the
front of the engine.*

34 If a special tool is available, install the
new seal on the tool and position the tool
against the crankshaft. Thread the attaching
screws into the crankshaft, then tighten the
screws securely with a screwdriver. Turn the
tool handle until it bottoms, then remove the
tool.

35 If a special tool is not available, tap the
new seal into place using a hammer and a
piece of pipe or a blunt punch. Work around
the seal, tapping it evenly into place until it
bottoms.

36 The remainder of installation is the
reverse of removal.

16 Engine mounts - check and replacement

Refer to illustrations 16.7a and 16.7b

1 Engine mounts seldom require attention,
but broken or deteriorated mounts should be
replaced immediately or the added strain
placed on the driveline components may
cause damage.

Check

2 During the check, the engine must be
raised slightly to remove the weight from the
mounts. Refer to Chapter 1 and remove the
distributor cap before raising the engine.

3 Raise the vehicle and support it securely
on jackstands, then position the jack under
the engine oil pan. Place a large block of
wood between the jack head and the oil pan,
then carefully raise the engine just enough to
take the weight off the mounts.

4 Check the mounts to see if the rubber is
cracked, hardened or separated from the
metal plates. Sometimes the rubber will split
right down the center. Rubber preservative
may be applied to the mounts to slow deterioration.

5 Check for relative movement between
the mount plates and the engine or frame
(use a large screwdriver or pry bar to attempt
to move the mounts). If movement is noted,
lower the engine and tighten the mount fasteners.

Replacement

6 Disconnect the negative cable from the
battery, then raise the vehicle and support it

securely on jackstands.

7 Remove the nut and withdraw the mount
through-bolt from the bracket **(see illustrations)**.

8 Raise the engine slightly, then remove
the mount-to-engine block bolts (V6 and
small block V8) or mount-to-frame bolts (big
block V8) and detach the mount.

9 Installation is the reverse of removal. Use
thread locking compound on the mount bolts
and be sure to tighten them securely.

17 Flywheel/driveplate - removal and installation

Refer to illustration 17.2

1 Refer to Chapter 7 and remove the transmission. If your vehicle has a manual transmission, the pressure plate and clutch will
also have to be removed (see Chapter 8).

2 Jam a large screwdriver through the
driveplate (on automatic transmission models) or in the starter ring gear (on manual
transmission models) to keep the crankshaft
from turning, then remove the mounting bolts
(see illustration). Since it's fairly heavy, support the flywheel as the last bolt is removed.

3 Pull straight back on the flywheel/drive-
plate to detach it from the crankshaft.

4 Installation is the reverse of removal. The
driveplate must be mounted with the torque
converter pads facing the transmission. Be
sure to align the hole in the flywheel/driveplate
with the dowel pin or untapped hole in the
crankshaft. Use thread locking compound on
the bolt threads and tighten them to the specified torque in a criss-cross pattern.

Notes

Chapter 2 Part B
General engine overhaul procedures

Contents

Specifications

General

Compression pressure (all engines)	150 psi
Maximum variation between cylinders	20 psi
Oil pressure (minimum)	
4.3L, 5.0L and 5.7L engines	
At 1000 rpm	6 psi
At 2000 rpm	18 psi
7.4L engine	
At 500 rpm	10 psi
At 2000 rpm	25 psi
Displacement	
V6 engine	262 cu in
V8 engines	
5.0L	305 cu in
5.7L	350 cu in
7.4L	454 cu in

Cylinder bore

Diameter	
4.3L V6 engine	
1988-1990	3.9995 to 4.0025 in
1991 and later	4.0007 to 4.0017 in
V8 engines	
5.0 liter	
1988 through 1998	3.7350 to 3.7385 in
1999 and 2000	3.7360 to 3.7381 in
5.7 liter	
1995 and earlier	3.9995 to 4.0025 in
1995 through 2000	4.0007 to 4.0017 in
7.4 liter	
1990 and earlier	4.2495 to 4.2525 in
1991 through 2000	4.2500 to 4.2507 in
Taper limit	0.001 in
Out-of-round limit	0.002 in

Cylinder heads and valve train

Warpage limit	0.004 in
Minimum valve margin width	1/32 in
Valve stem-to-guide clearance	
Intake valves	
Standard	0.0010 to 0.0027 in
Service limit	0.0037 in
Exhaust valves	
4.3L, 5.0L and 5.7L engines	
Standard	0.0010 to 0.0027 in
Service limit	0.0047 in
7.4L engine	
Standard	0.0012 to 0.0029 in
Service limit	0.0049 in
Valve spring free length	
4.3L, 5.0L and 5.7L engines	
1988 through 1996	2.03 in
1997 through 2000	2.02 in
7.4L engine	2.12 in
Valve spring installed height	
4.3L, 5.0L and 5.7L engines	
1988 through 1995	1-23/32 in
1996 through 2000	1.67 to 1.71 in
7.4L engine	
1988 through 1994	1-51/64 in
1995 through 2000	1.838 to 1.869 in

Crankshaft and connecting rods

Main journal diameter	
4.3L, 5.0L and 5.7L engines	
1988 through 1996	
1	2.4484 to 2.4493 in
2, 3 and 4	2.4481 to 2.4490 in
5	2.4479 to 2.4488 in
1997 through 2000	
1	2.4484 to 2.4493 in
2, 3 and 4	2.4481 to 2.4491 in
5	2.4479 to 2.4491 in
7.4L engine	
1988 through 1990	
1, 2, 3 and 4	2.7481 to 2.7490 in
5	2.7476 to 2.7486 in
1991 through 2000	2.7482 to 2.7489 in
Taper limit	0.001 in
Out-of-round limit	0.001 in
Main bearing oil clearance	
4.3L engine	
1988 through 1995	
Standard	
1	0.0008 to 0.0020 in
2 and 3	0.0011 to 0.0023 in
4	0.0017 to 0.0032 in
Service limit	
1	0.0010 to 0.0015 in
2 and 3	0.0010 to 0.0025 in
4	0.0025 to 0.0035 in
1996 through 2000	
Standard	
1	0.0008 to 0.0020 in
2, 3 and 4	0.0011 to 0.0023 in
Service limit	
1	0.0010 to 0.0020 in
2,3 and 4	0.0010 to 0.0024 in
5.0L and 5.7L engines	
1988 through 1995	
Standard	
1	0.0008 to 0.0020 in
2, 3 and 4	0.0011 to 0.0023 in
5	0.0017 to 0.0032 in

Service limit
  1 .... 0.0010 to 0.0015 in
  2, 3 and 4 .... 0.0010 to 0.0025 in
  5 .... 0.0025 to 0.0035 in
  1996 through 1998
    Standard
      1 .... 0.0007 to 0.0021 in
      2, 3 and 4 .... 0.0009 to 0.0024 in
      5 .... 0.0010 to 0.0027 in
    Service limit
      1 .... 0.0010 to 0.0020 in
      2, 3 and 4 .... 0.0010 to 0.0025 in
      5 .... 0.0015 to 0.0030 in
  1999 and 2000
    Standard
      1 .... 0.0007 to 0.0021 in
      2, 3 and 4 .... 0.0012 to 0.0027 in
      5 .... 0.0008 to 0.0024 in
    Service limit
      1 .... 0.0010 to 0.0020 in
      2, 3 and 4 .... 0.0010 to 0.0025 in
      5 .... 0.0015 to 0.0025 in
7.4L engine
  1988 through 1995
    Standard
      1 through 4 .... 0.0017 to 0.0030 in
      5 .... 0.0025 to 0.0038 in
    Service limit
      1 through 4 .... 0.0010 to 0.0030 in
      5 .... 0.0010 to 0.0040 in
  1996 through 2000
    Standard
      1 .... 0.0017 to 0.0030 in
      2, 3 and 4 .... 0.0011 to 0.0024 in
      5 .... 0.0025 to 0.0038 in
    Service limit
      1 through 4 .... 0.0010 to 0.0030 in
      5 .... 0.0025 to 0.0040 in
Connecting rod journal
  Diameter
    4.3L engine .... 2.2487 to 2.2497 in
    5.0L and 5.7L engines
      1988 through 1995 .... 2.0988 to 2.0998 in
      1996 through 1998 .... 2.0978 to 2.0998 in
      1999 and 2000 .... 2.0986 to 2.0998 in
    7.4L engine
      1988 through 1990 .... 2.1990 to 2.2000 in
      1991 through 2000 .... 2.1990 to 2.1996 in
  Taper limit .... 0.001 in
  Out-of-round limit .... 0.001 in
Connecting rod bearing oil clearance
  4.3L engine
    Standard .... 0.0013 to 0.0035 in
    Service limit .... 0.003 in max
  5.0L and 5.7L engines
    1988 through 1998
      Standard .... 0.0013 to 0.0035 in
      Service limit .... 0.003 in max
    1999 and 2000
      Standard .... 0.0013 to 0.0031 in
      Service limit .... 0.0025 in max
  7.4L engine
    1988 through 1990
      Standard .... 0.009 to 0.0025 in
      Service limit .... 0.003 in max
    1991 through 2000
      Standard .... 0.0011 to 0.0029 in
      Service limit .... 0.0039 in max

Crankshaft and connecting rods (continued)

Connecting rod sideplay
    4.3L engine
        1988 through 1995... 0.006 to 0.014 in
        1996 through 2000... 0.006 to 0.017 in
    5.0L and 5.7L engines
        1988 through 1990... 0.008 to 0.014 in
        1991 through 1997... 0.006 to 0.014 in
        1998 through 2000... 0.006 to 0.024 in
    7.4L engine... 0.013 to 0.023 in
Crankshaft endplay
    4.3L, 5.0L and 5.7L engines
        1988 through 1995... 0.002 to 0.006 in
        1996 through 2000... 0.002 to 0.008 in
    7.4L engine
        1988 through 1991... 0.006 to 0.010 in
        1992 through 2000... 0.005 to 0.011 in

Pistons and rings

Piston-to-bore clearance
    4.3L engine
        Standard
            1988 through 1995 .... 0.0007 to 0.0017 in
            1996 through 2000 .... 0.0007 to 0.0020 in
        Service limit... 0.0007 to 0.0024 in
    5.0L and 5.7L engines
        Standard .... 0.0007 to 0.0021 in
        Service limit... 0.0007 to 0.0027 in
    7.4L engine
        Standard
            1988 through 1993 .... 0.0030 to 0.0042 in
            1994 through 2000 .... 0.0018 to 0.0030 in
        Service limit
            1988 through 1993 .... 0.0030 to 0.0050 in
            1994... 0.0018 to 0.0050 in
            1995... 0.0018 to 0.0036 in
            1996 through 2000 .... 0.0018 to 0.0048 in
Piston ring side clearance
    4.3L, 5.0L and 5.7L engines
        Compression rings (both)
            1988 through 1997
                 Standard... 0.0012 to 0.0032 in
                Service limit .... 0.0042 in
            1998 through 2000
                 Top ring .... 0.0012 to 0.0027 in
                Second ring .... 0.0015 to 0.0030 in
                Service limit .... 0.0035 to 0.0040 in
        Oil control ring
            Standard.. 0.0020 to 0.0070
            Service limit .... 0.0080 in
    7.4L engine
        Compression rings (both)
            1988 through 1990 .... 0.0017 to 0.0032 in
            1991 through 2000
                 Standard... 0.0012 to 0.0029 in
                Service limit .... 0.0039 in
        Oil control ring
            Standard.. 0.0050 to 0.0065 in
            Service limit .... 0.0075 in
Piston ring end gap
    4.3L engine
        1988 through 1995
            Top compression ring
                Standard... 0.010 to 0.020 in
               Service limit .... 0.035 in
            Second compression ring
               Standard... 0.010 to 0.025 in
               Service limit .... 0.035 in

Oil control ring	
Standard	0.015 to 0.055 in
Service limit	0.065 in
1996 through 2000	
Top compression ring	
Standard	0.010 to 0.016 in
Service limit	0.035 in
Second compression ring	
Standard	0.018 to 0.026 in
Service limit	0.035 in
Oil control ring	
Standard	0.0115 to 0.055 in
Service limit	0.065 in
5.0L and 5.7L engines	
1988 through 1991	
Top compression ring	
Standard	0.010 to 0.020 in
Service limit	0.035 in
Second compression ring	
Standard	0.010 to 0.025 in
Service limit	0.035 in
Oil control ring	
Standard	0.015 to 0.055 in
Service limit	0.065 in
1992 through 1996	
Top compression ring	
Standard	0.010 to 0.020 in
Service limit	0.030 in
Second compression ring	
Standard	0.018 to 0.026 in
Service limit	0.036 in
Oil control ring	
Standard	0.010 to 0.030 in
Service limit	0.040 in
1997 and 1998	
Top compression ring	
Standard	0.010 to 0.020 in
Service limit	0.025 in
Second compression ring	
Standard	0.018 to 0.026 in
Service limit	0.035 in
Oil control ring	
Standard	0.010 to 0.030 in
Service limit	0.035 in
1999 and 2000	
Top compression ring	
Standard	0.009 to 0.015 in
Service limit	0.019 in
Second compression ring	
Standard	0.018 to 0.025 in
Service limit	0.031 in
Oil control ring	
Standard	0.009 to 0.029 in
Service limit	0.035 in
7.4L engines	
Top compression ring	
Standard	0.010 to 0.018 in
Service limit	0.028 in
Second compression ring	
Standard	0.016 to 0.024 in
Service limit	0.034 in
Oil control ring	
Standard	0.010 to 0.030 in
Service limit	0.040 in

Torque specifications*

	Ft-lbs
Connecting rod-cap nuts	
4.3L engine	
1988 through 1990	45

Torque specifications* (continued)

	Ft-lbs
1991 and 1992	
Step 1	20
Step 2	Tighten an additional 60 degrees
1993 through 2000	
Step 1	20
Step 2	Tighten an additional 70 degrees
5.0L and 5.7L engines	
1988 through 1995	45
1996 through 2000	
Step 1	20
Step 2	Tighten an additional 55 degrees
7.4L engine	
1988 through 1995	48
1996 and 1997	45
1998 through 2000	47
Main bearing cap bolts	
4.3L engine	
1988 through 1994	75
1995	81
1996 and later	77
5.0L and 5.7L engines	
Four bolt mains	
Outer bolts	
1988 through 1995	70
1996 through 2000	67
Inner bolts	
1988 through 1995	80
1996 through 2000	77
Two bolt mains	
1988 through 1995	70
1996 through 2000	77
7.4L engine	
1988 through 1990	110
1991 through 2000	102

***Note:** *Refer to Part A for additional torque specifications.*

1 General information

Included in this portion of Chapter 2 are the general overhaul procedures for cylinder heads and internal engine components. The information ranges from advice concerning preparation for an overhaul and the purchase of replacement parts to detailed, step-by-step procedures covering removal and installation of internal engine components and the inspection of parts.

The following Sections have been written based on the assumption the engine has been removed from the vehicle. For information concerning in-vehicle engine repair, as well as removal and installation of the external components necessary for the overhaul, see Part A of this Chapter and Section 7 of this Part.

The Specifications included here in Part B are only those necessary for the inspection and overhaul procedures which follow. Refer to Part A for additional Specifications.

2 Oil Pressure check

Refer to illustrations 2.2 and 2.3

1   Low engine oil pressure can be a sign of an engine in need of rebuilding. A "low oil pressure" indicator (often called an "idiot light") is not a test of the oiling system. Such indicators only come on when the oil pressure is dangerously low. Even a factory oil pressure gauge in the instrument panel is only a relative indication, although much better for driver information than a warning light. A better test is with a mechanical (not electrical) oil pressure gauge. When used in conjunction with an accurate tachometer, an engine's oil pressure performance can be compared to factory Specifications for that year and model.

2   Locate the oil pressure indicator sending unit **(see illustration)**.

3   Remove the oil pressure sending unit and install a fitting which will allow you to directly connect your hand-held, mechanical oil pressure gauge **(see illustration)**. Use Teflon tape or sealant on the threads of the adapter and the fitting on the end of your gauge's hose.

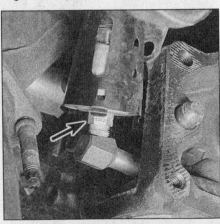

2.2 Remove the oil pressure sending unit (arrow) - on V6 and small block V8 engines, it's located above the oil filter

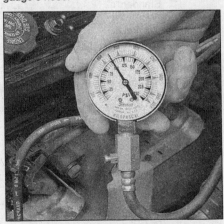

2.3 Connect a gauge to check the oil pressure

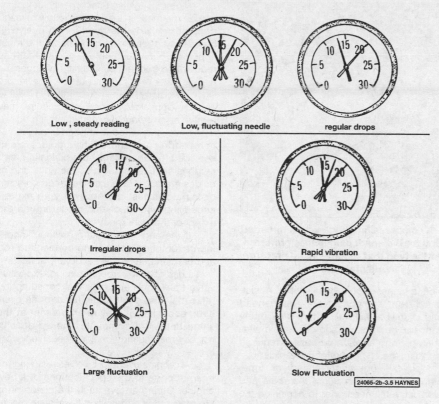

Low, steady reading   Low, fluctuating needle   regular drops

Irregular drops   Rapid vibration

Large fluctuation   Slow Fluctuation

24065-2b-3.5 HAYNES

3.5 Typical vacuum gauge diagnostic readings

uum hose or incorrect camshaft timing.

7   If the reading is 3 to 8 inches below normal and it fluctuates at that low reading, suspect an intake manifold gasket leak at an intake port or a faulty fuel injector.

8   If the needle regularly drops about two to four inches at a steady rate, the valves are probably leaking. Perform a compression check or leakdown test to confirm this.

9   An irregular drop or downward flicker of the needle can be caused by a sticking valve or an ignition misfire. Perform a compression check or leakdown test and inspect the spark plugs to identify the faulty cylinder.

10   A rapid needle vibration of about four inches at idle combined with exhaust smoke indicates worn valve guides. Perform a leakdown test to confirm this. If the rapid vibration occurs with an increase in engine speed, check for a leaking intake manifold gasket or head gasket, weak valve springs, burned valves, or ignition misfire.

11   A slight fluctuation - one inch up and down - may mean ignition problems. Check all the usual tune-up items and, if necessary, run the engine on an ignition analyzer.

12   If there is a large fluctuation, perform a compression or leakdown test to look for a weak or dead cylinder or a blown head gasket.

13   If the needle moves slowly through a wide range, check for a clogged PCV system or intake manifold gasket leaks.

14   Check for a slow return of the gauge to a normal idle reading after revving the engine by quickly snapping the throttle open until the engine reaches about 2,500 rpm and let it shut. Normally the reading should drop to near zero, rise about 5 inches above normal idle reading, and then return to the previous idle reading. If the vacuum returns slowly and doesn't peak when the throttle is snapped shut, the rings may be worn. If there is a long delay, look for a restricted exhaust system (often the muffler or catalytic converter). One way to check this is to temporarily disconnect the exhaust ahead of the suspected part and repeat the test.

3   Vacuum gauge diagnostic checks

Refer to illustration 3.5

1   A vacuum gauge provides valuable information about what is going on in the engine at a low cost. You can check for worn rings or cylinder walls, leaking head or intake manifold gaskets, vacuum leaks in the intake manifold, restricted exhaust, stuck or burned valves, weak valve springs, improper valve timing, and ignition problems. Vacuum gauge readings are easy to misinterpret, however, so they should be used in conjunction with other tests to confirm the diagnosis.

2   Both the absolute readings and the rate of needle movement are important for accurate interpretation. Most gauges measure vacuum in inches of mercury (in-Hg). The following references to vacuum assume the diagnosis is being performed at sea level. As elevation increases (or atmospheric pressure decreases), the reading will decrease. For

4   Connect an accurate tachometer to the engine, according to the tachometer manufacturer's instructions.

5   Check the oil pressure with the engine running (full operating temperature) at the specified engine speed, and compare it to this Chapter's Specifications. If it's extremely low, the bearings and/or oil pump are probably worn out.

every 1,000 foot increase in elevation above approximately 2000 feet, the gauge readings will decrease about one inch of mercury.

3   Connect the vacuum gauge directly to intake manifold vacuum, not to ported (throttle body) vacuum. Be sure no hoses are left disconnected during the test or false readings will result. **Note:** *Do not disconnect engine sensors or vacuum solenoids to connect the vacuum gauge. Disconnected engine control components can affect engine operation and produce abnormal vacuum gauge readings.*

4   Before you begin the test, warm the engine up completely. Block the wheels and set the parking brake. With the transmission in Park, start the engine and allow it to run at normal idle speed. **Warning:** *Carefully inspect the fan blades for cracks or damage before starting the engine. Keep your hands and the vacuum gauge clear of the fan and do not stand in front of the vehicle or in line with the fan when the engine is running.*

5   Read the vacuum gauge; an average, healthy engine should normally produce about 17 to 22 inches of vacuum with a fairly steady gauge needle at idle. Refer to the following vacuum gauge readings and what they indicate about the engine's condition **(see illustration):**

6   A low steady reading usually indicates a leaking intake manifold gasket. this could be at one of the cylinder heads, between the upper and lower manifolds, or at the throttle body. Other possible causes are a leaky vac-

4   Compression check

Refer to illustration 4.4

1   A compression check will tell you what mechanical condition the upper end (pistons, rings, valves, head gaskets) of your engine is in. Specifically, it can tell you if the compression is down due to leakage caused by worn piston rings, defective valves and seats or a blown head gasket. **Note:** *The engine must be at normal operating temperature for this check and the battery must be fully charged.*

2   Begin by cleaning the area around the spark plugs before you remove them (compressed air works best for this). This will prevent dirt from getting into the cylinders as the compression check is being done. Remove all of the spark plugs from the engine.

3   Block the throttle wide open and disconnect the primary wires from the coil.

4   With the compression gauge in the

number one spark plug hole, crank the engine over at least four compression strokes and watch the gauge (see illustration). The compression should build up quickly in a healthy engine. Low compression on the first stroke, followed by gradually increasing pressure on successive strokes, indicates worn piston rings. A low compression reading on the first stroke, which does not build up during successive strokes, indicates leaking valves or a blown head gasket (a cracked head could also be the cause). Record the highest gauge reading obtained.

5   Repeat the procedure for the remaining cylinders and compare the results to the Specifications.

6   Add some engine oil (about three squirts from a plunger-type oil can) to each cylinder, through the spark plug hole, and repeat the test.

7   If the compression increases after the oil is added, the piston rings are definitely worn. If the compression does not increase significantly, the leakage is occurring at the valves or head gasket. Leakage past the valves may be caused by burned valve seats and/or faces or warped, cracked or bent valves.

8   If two adjacent cylinders have equally low compression, there's a strong possibility the head gasket between them is blown. The appearance of coolant in the combustion chambers or the crankcase would verify this condition.

9   If the compression is unusually high, the combustion chambers are probably coated with carbon deposits. If that's the case, the cylinder heads should be removed and decarbonized.

10   If compression is way down or varies greatly between cylinders, it would be a good idea to have a leakdown test performed by an automotive repair shop. This test will pinpoint exactly where the leakage is occurring and how severe it is.

5   Engine removal - methods and precautions

If you have decided an engine must be removed for overhaul or major repair work, several preliminary steps should be taken.

Locating a work area is extremely important. A shop is, of course, the most desirable place to work. Adequate work space, along with storage space for the vehicle, will be needed. If a shop or garage isn't available, at the very least a flat, level, clean work surface made of concrete or asphalt is required.

Cleaning the engine compartment and engine before beginning the removal procedure will help keep tools clean and organized.

An engine hoist or A-frame will be needed. Make sure the equipment is rated in excess of the combined weight of the engine and accessories. Safety is of primary importance, considering the potential hazards involved in lifting the engine out of the vehicle.

If the engine is being removed by a

4.4 A compression gauge with a threaded fitting for the spark plug hole is preferred over the type that requires hand pressure to maintain the seal

novice, a helper should be available. Advice and aid from someone more experienced would also be helpful. There are many instances when one person cannot simultaneously perform all of the operations required when lifting the engine out of the vehicle.

Plan the operation ahead of time. Arrange for or obtain all of the tools and equipment you'll need prior to beginning the job. Some of the equipment necessary to perform engine removal and installation safely and with relative ease are (in addition to an engine hoist) a heavy duty floor jack, complete sets of wrenches and sockets as described in the front of this manual, wooden blocks and plenty of rags and cleaning solvent for mopping up spilled oil, coolant and gasoline. If the hoist must be rented, make sure you arrange for it and perform all of the operations possible without it in advance. This will save you money and time.

Plan for the vehicle to be out of use for a considerable amount of time. A machine shop will be required to perform some of the work which the do-it-yourselfer cannot accomplish due to a lack of special equipment. These shops often have a busy schedule, so it would be a good idea to consult them before removing the engine in order to accurately estimate the amount of time required to rebuild or repair components that may need work.

Always use extreme caution when removing and installing the engine. Serious injury can result from careless actions. Plan ahead, take your time and a job of this nature, although major, can be accomplished successfully.

6   Engine overhaul - general information

Refer to illustrations 6.4a, 6.4b and 6.4c

It's not always easy to determine when, or if, an engine should be completely overhauled, as a number of factors must be considered.

High mileage isn't necessarily an indication an overhaul is needed, while low mileage doesn't preclude the need for an overhaul. Frequency of servicing is probably the most important consideration. An engine that has regular and frequent oil and filter changes, as well as other required maintenance, will most likely give many thousands of miles of reliable service. Conversely, a neglected engine may require an overhaul very early in its life.

Excessive oil consumption is an indication piston rings and/or valve guides are in need of attention. Make sure oil leaks aren't responsible before deciding the rings and/or guides are bad. Have a cylinder compression or leakdown test performed by an experienced tune-up mechanic to determine the extent of the work required.

If the engine is making obvious knocking or rumbling noises, the connecting rod and/or main bearings are probably at fault.

Loss of power, rough running, excessive valve train noise and high fuel consumption rates may also point to the need for an overhaul, especially if they're all present at the same time. If a complete tune-up doesn't remedy the situation, major mechanical work is the only solution.

An engine overhaul involves restoring the internal parts to the specifications of a new engine. During an overhaul, the piston rings are replaced and the cylinder walls are reconditioned (rebored and/or honed). If a rebore is done, new pistons are required. The main bearings, connecting rod bearings and camshaft bearings are generally replaced with new ones and, if necessary, the crankshaft may be reground to restore the journals. Generally, the valves are serviced as well, since they're usually in less-than-perfect condition at this point. While the engine is being overhauled, other components, such as the distributor, starter and alternator, can be rebuilt as well. The end result should be a like new engine that will give many trouble free miles. **Note:** *Critical cooling system components such as the hoses, the drivebelts, the thermostat and the water pump MUST be replaced with new parts when an engine is overhauled. The radiator should be checked carefully to ensure it isn't clogged or leaking. If in doubt, replace it with a new one. Also, we do not recommend overhauling the oil pump - always install a new one when an engine is rebuilt.*

Before beginning the engine overhaul, read through the entire procedure to familiarize yourself with the scope and requirements of the job. Overhauling an engine isn't particularly difficult, but it is time consuming. Plan on the vehicle being tied up for a minimum of two weeks, especially if parts must be taken to an automotive machine shop for repair or reconditioning. Check on availability of parts and make sure any necessary special tools and equipment are obtained in advance. Most work can be done with typical hand tools, although a number of precision measuring tools are required for inspecting parts to determine if they must be replaced. Often an automotive machine shop will handle the inspection of parts and offer advice concerning reconditioning and replacement. **Note:** *Always wait until the engine has been completely disassembled and all components, especially the engine block, have been inspected before deciding what service and repair operations must be performed by an automotive machine shop. Since the block's condition will be the major factor to consider when determining whether to overhaul the original engine or buy a rebuilt one, never purchase parts or have machine work done on other components until the block has been thoroughly inspected. As a general rule, time is the primary cost of an overhaul, so it doesn't pay to install worn or substandard parts.*

As a final note, to ensure maximum life and minimum trouble from a rebuilt engine, everything must be assembled with care in a spotlessly clean environment.

7 Engine - removal and installation

Refer to illustrations 7.12, 7.14 and 7.24
1 Remove the hood (see Chapter 11).
2 Disconnect the negative cable from the battery.
3 Drain the cooling system (see Chapter 1).
4 Remove the air cleaner assembly.
5 Remove the drivebelts (see Chapter 1).
6 Remove the radiator, shroud, fan and water pump pulley (see Chapter 3).
7 Detach the radiator and heater hoses from the engine.
8 Remove the accelerator cable and kickdown linkage (if used) from the throttle body.
9 Remove the air conditioning compressor (if equipped) without disconnecting the lines and hang it out of the way.
10 Remove the power steering pump (if equipped) without disconnecting the hoses and tie it out of the way (see Chapter 10).
11 Remove the alternator (see Chapter 5).
12 Label and disconnect all wires from the engine **(see illustration)**.
13 Disconnect the fuel lines at the engine (see Chapter 4) and plug the lines to prevent fuel loss.
14 Label and remove all vacuum lines from the intake manifold **(see illustration)**.
15 Raise the vehicle and support it securely on jackstands.
16 Drain the engine oil (see Chapter 1).
17 Disconnect the exhaust pipes from the exhaust manifolds.
18 On four-wheel drive models with an automatic transmission, disconnect the strut rods at the engine mounts.
19 Remove the flywheel or torque converter inspection cover.
20 Remove the wiring harness from the clips along the oil pan rail.
21 Remove the starter (see Chapter 5).
22 If equipped with an automatic transmission, remove the torque converter-to-driveplate bolts.
23 Support the transmission with a floor jack.

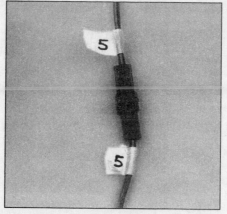

7.12 Label both ends of each wire before unplugging the connector

24 Attach an engine hoist to the engine and take the weight off the mounts **(see illustration)**.
25 Remove the bellhousing-to-engine bolts.
26 Remove the engine mount-to-frame bolts.
27 Lift the engine slightly, check to make sure everything is disconnected, then lift the engine out of the vehicle.
28 Installation is the reverse of the removal procedure.

8 Engine rebuilding alternatives

The do-it-yourselfer is faced with a number of options when performing an engine overhaul. The decision to replace the engine block, piston/connecting rod assemblies and crankshaft depends on a number of factors, with the number one consideration being the condition of the block. Other considerations are cost, access to machine shop facilities, parts availability, time required to complete the project and the extent of prior mechanical experience on the part of the do-it-yourselfer.

Some of the rebuilding alternatives include:
Individual parts - If the inspection procedures reveal the engine block and most engine components are in reusable condition, purchasing individual parts may be the most

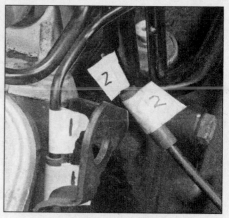

7.14 Label all vacuum lines and connecting points before removing the lines, this will save allot of time when the engine is reinstalled

economical alternative. The block, crankshaft and piston/connecting rod assemblies should all be inspected carefully. Even if the block shows little wear, the cylinder bores should be surface honed.
Crankshaft kit - This rebuild package consists of a reground crankshaft and a matched set of pistons and connecting rods. The pistons will already be installed on the connecting rods. Piston rings and the necessary bearings will be included in the kit. These kits are commonly available for standard cylinder bores, as well as for engine blocks which have been bored to a regular oversize.
Short block - A short block consists of an engine block with a crankshaft and piston/connecting rod assemblies already installed. All new bearings are incorporated and all clearances will be correct. The existing camshaft, valve train components, cylinder heads and external parts can be bolted to the short block with little or no machine shop work necessary.
Long block - A long block consists of a short block plus an oil pump, oil pan, cylinder heads, rocker arm covers, camshaft and valve train components, timing sprockets and chain and timing cover. All components are installed with new bearings, seals and gaskets incorporated throughout. The installation of manifolds and external parts is all that's necessary.

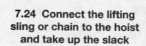

7.24 Connect the lifting sling or chain to the hoist and take up the slack

10.2 Have several plastic bags ready (one for each valve) before disassembling the head - label each bag and put the entire contents of each valve assembly in one bag as shown

10.3a Use a valve spring compressor to compress the springs, then remove the keepers from the valve stem with a magnet or small needle-nose pliers

10.3b If you can't pull the valve through the guide, deburr the edge of the stem end and the area around the top of the keeper groove with a file or whetstone

Give careful thought to which alternative is best for you and discuss the situation with local automotive machine shops, auto parts dealers and experienced do-it-yourselfers before ordering or purchasing replacement parts.

9   Engine overhaul - disassembly sequence

1   It's much easier to disassemble and work on the engine if it's mounted on a portable engine stand. These stands can often be rented quite cheaply from an equipment rental yard. Before the engine is mounted on a stand, the flywheel/driveplate should be removed from the engine (refer to Chapter 2A).

2   If a stand isn't available, it is possible to disassemble the engine with it blocked up on a workbench or on the floor. Be extra careful not to tip or drop the engine when working without a stand.

3   If you're going to obtain a rebuilt engine, all external components must come off first, to be transferred to the replacement engine, just as they will if you're doing a complete engine overhaul yourself. These include:

Alternator and brackets
Emissions control components
Distributor, spark plug wires and spark
    plugs
Thermostat and housing cover
Water pump
EFI components
Intake/exhaust manifolds
Oil filter
Engine mounts
Clutch and flywheel/driveplate

Note: *When removing the external components from the engine, pay close attention to details that may be helpful or important during installation. Note the installed position of gaskets, seals, spacers, pins, washers, bolts and other small items.*

4   If you're obtaining a short block, which consists of the engine block, crankshaft, pis-

tons and connecting rods all assembled, then the cylinder heads, oil pan and oil pump will have to be removed as well. See Engine rebuilding alternatives for additional information regarding the different possibilities to be considered.

5   If you're planning a complete overhaul, the engine must be disassembled and the internal components removed in the following general order:

Rocker arm covers
Intake and exhaust manifolds
Rocker arms and pushrods
Valve lifters
Cylinder heads
Timing chain cover
Timing chain and sprockets
Camshaft
Oil pan
Oil pump
Piston/connecting rod assemblies
Crankshaft and main bearings

6   Critical cooling system components such as the hoses, the drivebelts, the thermostat and the water pump MUST be replaced with new parts when an engine is overhauled. Also, we do not recommend overhauling the oil pump - always install a new one when an engine is rebuilt.

7   Before beginning the disassembly and overhaul procedures, make sure the following items are available:

Common hand tools
Small cardboard boxes or plastic bags for
    storing parts
Gasket scraper
Ridge reamer
Vibration damper puller
Micrometers
Telescoping gauges
Dial indicator set
Valve spring compressor
Cylinder surfacing hone
Piston ring groove cleaning tool
Electric drill
Tap and die set
Wire brushes
Oil gallery brushes
Cleaning solvent

10   Cylinder head - disassembly

Refer to illustrations 10.2, 10.3a and 10.3b

Note: *New and rebuilt cylinder heads are commonly available for most engines at dealerships and auto parts stores. Due to the fact that some specialized tools are necessary for the disassembly and inspection procedures, and replacement parts may not be readily available, it may be more practical and economical for the home mechanic to purchase replacement heads rather than taking the time to disassemble, inspect and recondition the originals.*

Caution: *On 7.4 liter (454 cubic inch) engines, two head designs are generally available - "open chamber" and "closed chamber." While these heads will interchange as far as bolt patterns, accessory mounting, etc. is concerned, the different combustion chamber designs require different piston dome shapes. If you're purchasing a set of reconditioned cylinder heads, make sure the new heads match the combustion chamber design of the originals.*

1   Cylinder head disassembly involves removal of the intake and exhaust valves and related components. If they're still in place, remove the rocker arm nuts, pivot balls and rocker arms from the cylinder head studs. Label the parts or store them separately so they can be reinstalled in their original locations.

2   Before the valves are removed, arrange to label and store them, along with their related components, so they can be kept separate and reinstalled in the same valve guides they are removed from **(see illustration)**.

3   Compress the springs on the first valve with a spring compressor and remove the keepers **(see illustration)**. Carefully release the valve spring compressor and remove the retainer or (if used) rotator, the shield, the springs and the spring seat or shims (if used). Remove the oil seal(s) from the valve stem and the umbrella-type seal from the guide (if used), then pull the valve out of the head. If the valve binds in the guide (won't pull

11.12 Check the cylinder head gasket surface for warpage by trying to slip a feeler gauge under the straightedge (see this Chapter's Specifications for the maximum warpage allowed and use a feeler gauge of that thickness)

11.14 A dial indicator can be used to determine the valve stem-to-guide clearance - move the valve stem as indicated by the arrows

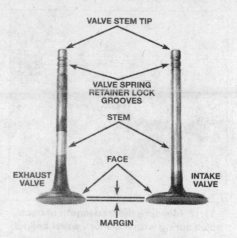

11.15 Check for valve wear at the points shown here

through), push it back into the head and deburr the area around the keeper groove with a fine file or whetstone **(see illustration)**.

4 Repeat the procedure for the remaining valves. Remember to keep all the parts for each valve together so they can be reinstalled in the same locations.

5 Once the valves and related components have been removed and stored in an organized manner, the head should be thoroughly cleaned and inspected. If a complete engine overhaul is being done, finish the engine disassembly procedures before beginning the cylinder head cleaning and inspection process.

11 Cylinder head - cleaning and inspection

Refer to illustrations 11.12, 11.14, 11.15, 11.16, 11.17, 11.18 and 11.19

1 Thorough cleaning of the cylinder heads and related valve train components, followed by a detailed inspection, will enable you to decide how much valve service work must be done during the engine overhaul.

Cleaning

2 Scrape away all traces of old gasket material and sealing compound from the head gasket, intake manifold and exhaust manifold sealing surfaces. Be very careful not to gouge the cylinder head. Special gasket removal solvents, which soften gaskets and make removal much easier, are available at auto parts stores.

3 Remove any built up scale from the coolant passages.

4 Run a stiff wire brush through the various holes to remove any deposits that may have formed in them.

5 Run an appropriate size tap into each of the threaded holes to remove corrosion and thread sealant that may be present. If compressed air is available, use it to clear the holes of debris produced by this operation.

6 Clean the rocker arm pivot stud threads with a wire brush.

7 Clean the cylinder head with solvent and dry it thoroughly. Compressed air will speed the drying process and ensure that all holes and recessed areas are clean. **Note:** *Decarbonizing chemicals are available and may prove very useful when cleaning cylinder heads and valve train components. They are very caustic and should be used with caution. Be sure to follow the instructions on the container.*

8 Clean the rocker arms, pivot balls, nuts and pushrods with solvent and dry them thoroughly (don't mix them up during the cleaning process). Compressed air will speed the drying process and can be used to clean out the oil passages.

9 Clean all the valve springs, shields, keepers and retainers (or rotators) with solvent and dry them thoroughly. Do the components from one valve at a time to avoid mixing up the parts.

10 Scrape off any heavy deposits that may have formed on the valves, then use a motorized wire brush to remove deposits from the valve heads and stems. Again, make sure the valves don't get mixed up.

Inspection

Cylinder head

11 Inspect the head very carefully for cracks, evidence of coolant leakage and other damage. If cracks are found, a new cylinder head should be obtained.

12 Using a straightedge and feeler gauge, check the head gasket mating surface for warpage **(see illustration)**. If the warpage exceeds the specified limit, it can be resurfaced at an automotive machine shop. **Note:** *If the heads are resurfaced, the intake manifold flanges will also require machining.*

13 Examine the valve seats in each of the combustion chambers. If they're pitted, cracked or burned, the head will require valve service that's beyond the scope of the home mechanic.

14 Check the valve stem-to-guide clearance by measuring the lateral movement of the valve stem with a dial indicator attached securely to

the head **(see illustration)**. The valve must be in the guide and approximately 1/16-inch off the seat. The total valve stem movement indicated by the gauge needle must be divided by two to obtain the actual clearance. After this is done, if there's still some doubt regarding the condition of the valve guides they should be checked by an automotive machine shop (the cost should be minimal).

Valves

15 Carefully inspect each valve face for uneven wear **(see illustration)**, deformation, cracks, pits and burned spots. Check the valve stem for scuffing and galling and the neck for cracks. Rotate the valve and check for any obvious indication that it's bent. Look for pits and excessive wear on the end of the stem. The presence of any of these conditions indicates the need for valve service by an automotive machine shop.

16 Measure the margin width on each valve. Any valve with a margin narrower than 1/32-inch will have to be replaced with a new one **(see illustration)**.

Valve components

17 Check each valve spring for wear (on the ends) and pits. Measure the free length

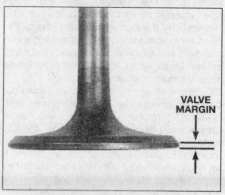

11.16 The margin width on each valve must be as specified (if no margin exists, the valve cannot be reused)

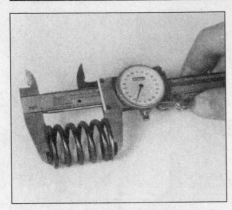

11.17 Measure the free length of each valve spring with a dial or vernier caliper

11.18 Check each valve spring for squareness

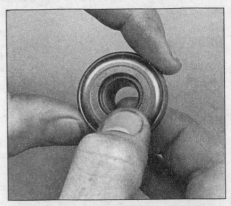

11.19 The exhaust valve rotators can be checked by turning the inner and outer sections in opposite directions to feel for smooth movement and excessive play

and compare it to the Specifications **(see illustration)**. Any springs that are shorter than specified have sagged and should not be reused. The tension of all springs should be checked with a special fixture before deciding they can be used in the rebuilt engine (take the springs to an automotive machine shop for this check).

18   Stand each spring on a flat surface and check it for squareness **(see illustration)**. If any of the springs are distorted or sagged, replace all of them with new parts.

19   Check the spring retainers (or rotators) and keepers for obvious wear and cracks **(see illustration)**. Any questionable parts should be replaced with new ones, as extensive damage will occur if they fail during engine operation.

Rocker arm components

20   Check the rocker arm faces (the areas that contact the pushrod ends and valve stems) for pits, wear, galling, score marks and rough spots. Check the rocker arm pivot contact areas and pivot balls as well. Look for cracks in each rocker arm and nut.

21   Inspect the pushrod ends for scuffing and excessive wear. Roll each pushrod on a flat surface, such as a piece of plate glass, to determine if it's bent.

22   Check the rocker arm studs in the cylinder heads for damaged threads and secure installation. The press-in rocker arm studs used in most small block engines can't be replaced by the home mechanic due to the need for precision reaming equipment and a press. If any studs are damaged, the head should be taken to an automotive machine shop for stud replacement.

23   Some small block engines and most big block engines have threaded rather than pressed-in rocker arm studs. Also, most engines with threaded studs have a guide plate, attached to the head by the studs, to maintain pushrod-to-rocker arm alignment. If an engine equipped with threaded studs has worn, bent or otherwise damaged studs, the studs can be removed individually and replaced. Be sure to replace the guide plates under the studs and apply RTV sealant to the stud threads.

24   Any damaged or excessively worn parts must be replaced with new ones.

25   If the inspection process indicates the valve components are in generally poor condition and worn beyond the limits specified, which is usually the case in an engine that's being overhauled, reassemble the valves in the cylinder head and refer to Section 12 for valve servicing recommendations.

26   If the inspection turns up no excessively worn parts, and if the valve faces and seats are in good condition, the valve train components can be reinstalled in the cylinder head without major servicing. Refer to the appropriate Section for the cylinder head reassembly procedure.

12   Valves - servicing

1   Because of the complex nature of the job and the special tools and equipment needed, servicing of the valves, the valve seats and the valve guides, commonly known as a valve job, is best left to a professional.

2   The home mechanic can remove and disassemble the heads, do the initial cleaning and inspection, then reassemble and deliver the heads to a dealer service department or an automotive machine shop for the actual valve servicing.

3   The dealer service department, or automotive machine shop, will remove the valves and springs, recondition or replace the valves and valve seats, recondition the valve guides, check and replace the valve springs, spring retainers or rotators and keepers (as necessary), replace the valve seals with new ones, reassemble the valve components and make sure the installed spring height is correct. The cylinder head gasket surface will also be resurfaced if it's warped.

4   After the valve job has been performed by a professional, the head will be in like new condition. When the head is returned, be sure to clean it again before installation on the engine to remove any metal particles and abrasive grit that may still be present from the valve service or head resurfacing operations. Use compressed air, if available, to blow out all the oil holes and passages.

13   Cylinder head - reassembly

Refer to illustrations 13.4, 13.5a, 13.5b, 13.6, 13.7 and 13.8

1   Regardless of whether or not the heads were sent to an automotive machine shop for valve servicing, make sure they're clean before beginning reassembly.

2   If the heads were sent out for valve servicing, the valves and related components will already be in place. Begin the reassembly procedure with Step 8.

3   Beginning at one end of the head, lubricate and install the first valve. Apply moly-base grease or clean engine oil to the valve stem.

4   Three different types of valve stem oil seals are used on these engines, depending on year, engine size and model. The most common is a small O-ring which simply fits around the valve stem just above the guide boss. A second type is a flat O-ring which fits into a groove in the valve stem just below the valve stem keeper groove. On some applications, an umbrella type seal which extends down over the valve guide is used **(see illustration)**. In most cases the umbrella type seal is used in conjunction with the flat O-ring type seal. If round O-ring or umbrella type seals are used, install them at this time.

13.4 Make sure the new valve stem seals are seated against the tops of the valve guides

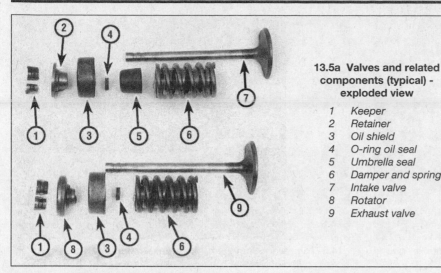

13.5a Valves and related components (typical) - exploded view

1   Keeper
2   Retainer
3   Oil shield
4   O-ring oil seal
5   Umbrella seal
6   Damper and spring
7   Intake valve
8   Rotator
9   Exhaust valve

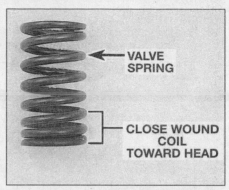

13.5b If the valve springs are wound closer at one end, install them as shown

13.6 Apply a small dab of grease to each keeper as shown here before installation - it'll hold them in place on the valve stem as the spring is released

5   Drop the spring seat or shim(s) over the valve guide and set the valve spring(s), shield and retainer (or rotator) in place (see illustrations).

6   Compress the springs with a valve spring compressor and if the flat O-ring type seal is used, carefully install it in the lower groove of the valve stem. Make sure the seal is not twisted - it must lie perfectly flat in the groove. Position the keepers in the upper groove, then slowly release the compressor and make sure the keepers seat properly. Apply a small dab of grease to each keeper to hold it in place if necessary (see illustration).

7   Repeat the procedure for the remaining valves. Be sure to return the components to their original locations - do not mix them up! Once all the valves are in place in both heads, the valve stem O-ring seals must be checked to make sure they don't leak. This procedure requires a vacuum pump and a special adapter, so it may be a good idea to have it done by a dealer service department, repair shop or automotive machine shop. The adapter is positioned on each valve retainer or rotator and vacuum is applied with the hand pump (see illustration). If the vacuum can't be maintained, the seal is leaking and

must be checked/replaced before the head is installed on the engine.

8   Check the installed valve spring height with a ruler graduated in 1/32-inch increments (see illustration) or a dial caliper. If the heads were sent out for service work, the installed height should be correct (but don't automatically assume it is). The measurement is taken from the top of each spring seat or shim(s) to the top of the oil shield (or the bottom of the retainer/rotator, the two points are the same). If the height is greater than specified, shims can be added under the springs to correct it.
Caution: *Do not, under any circumstances, shim the springs to the point where the installed height is less than specified.*

9   Apply moly-base grease to the rocker arm faces and the pivot balls, then install the rocker arms and pivots on the cylinder head studs. Thread the nuts on three or four turns only.

---

14 Piston/connecting rod assembly - removal

Refer to illustrations 14.1, 14.3 and 14.5
Note: *Prior to removing the piston/connecting rod assemblies, remove the cylinder*

heads, the oil pan and the oil pump by referring to the appropriate Sections in Chapter 2, Part A.

1   Completely remove the ridge at the top of each cylinder with a ridge reaming tool (see illustration). Follow the manufacturer's instructions provided with the tool. Failure to remove the ridge before attempting to remove the piston/connecting rod assemblies will result in piston breakage.

2   After the cylinder ridges have been removed, turn the engine upside-down so the crankshaft is facing up.

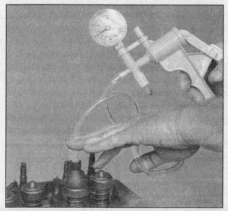

13.7 A special adapter and vacuum pump are required to check the O-ring valve stem seals for leaks

13.8 Be sure to check the valve spring installed height (the distance from the top of the seat/shims to the top of the shield or the bottom of the retainer)

14.1 A ridge reamer is required to remove the ridge from the top of each cylinder - do this before removing the pistons!

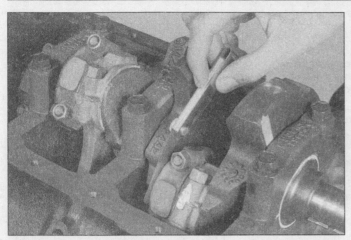

14.3 Check the connecting rod side clearance with a feeler gauge as shown

14.5 To prevent damage to the crankshaft journals and cylinder walls, slip sections of rubber or plastic hose over the rod bolts before removing the pistons

15.2 Check crankshaft endplay with a dial indicator . . .

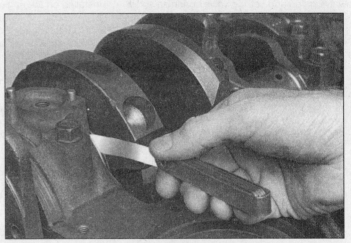

15.3 . . . or slip feeler gauges between the crankshaft and main bearing thrust surfaces - the endplay is equal to the feeler gauge thickness

3   Before the connecting rods are re-moved, check the endplay with feeler gauges. Slide them between the first connecting rod and the crankshaft throw until the play is removed (see illustration). The endplay is equal to the thickness of the feeler gauge(s). If the endplay exceeds the service limit, new connecting rods will be required. If new rods (or a new crankshaft) are installed, the endplay may fall under the specified minimum. If it does, the rods will have to be machined to restore it - consult an automotive machine shop for advice if necessary. Repeat the pro-cedure for the remaining connecting rods.

4   Check the connecting rods and caps for identification marks. If they aren't plainly marked, use a small center punch to make the appropriate number of indentations on each rod and cap.

5   Loosen each of the connecting rod cap nuts 1/2-turn at a time until they can be removed by hand. Remove the number one connecting rod cap and bearing insert. Do not drop the bearing insert out of the cap. Slip a short length of plastic or rubber hose over each connecting rod cap bolt to protect the crankshaft journal and cylinder wall when the piston is removed (see illustration). Push the connecting rod/piston assembly out through the top of the engine. Use a wooden hammer handle to push on the upper bearing insert in the connecting rod. If resistance is felt, double-check to make sure all of the ridge was removed from the cylinder.

6   Repeat the procedure for the remaining cylinders. After removal, reassemble the con-necting rod caps and bearing inserts in their respective connecting rods and install the cap nuts finger-tight. Leaving the old bearing inserts in place until reassembly will help pre-vent the connecting rod bearing surfaces from being accidentally nicked or gouged.

15   Crankshaft - removal

Refer to illustrations 15.2, 15.3, 15.4a and 15.4b

Note: The crankshaft can be removed only after the engine has been removed from the vehicle. It's assumed the flywheel or drive-plate, vibration damper, timing chain, oil pan, oil pump and piston/connecting rod assem-blies have already been removed.

1   Before the crankshaft is removed, check the endplay. Mount a dial indicator with the stem in-line with the crankshaft and touching one of the crank throws.

2   Push the crankshaft all the way to the rear and zero the dial indicator. Next, pry the crankshaft to the front as far as possible and check the reading on the dial indicator (see illustration). The distance it moves is the endplay. If it's greater than specified, check the crankshaft thrust surfaces for wear. If no wear is evident, new main bearings should correct the endplay.

3   If a dial indicator isn't available, feeler gauges can be used. Gently pry or push the crankshaft all the way to the front of the engine. Slip feeler gauges between the crankshaft and the front face of the thrust main bearing to determine the clearance (see illustration).

4   Check the main bearing caps to see if they're marked to indicate their locations.

15.4a Use a center punch or number stamping dies to mark the main bearing caps to ensure installation in their original locations on the block (make the punch marks near one of the bolt heads)

15.4b The arrow on the main bearing cap indicates the front of the engine

16.1 Pull the core plugs from the block with pliers

They should be numbered consecutively from the front of the engine to the rear. If they aren't, mark them with number stamping dies or a center punch **(see illustration)**. Main bearing caps generally have a cast-in arrow **(see illustration)**, which points to the front of the engine. Loosen each of the main bearing cap bolts 1/4-turn at a time each, until they can be removed by hand.

5   Gently tap the caps with a soft-face hammer, then separate them from the engine block. If necessary, use the bolts as levers to remove the caps. Try not to drop the bearing inserts if they come out with the caps.

6   Carefully lift the crankshaft out of the engine. It's a good idea to have an assistant available, since the crankshaft is quite heavy. With the bearing inserts in place in the engine block and main bearing caps, return the caps to their respective locations on the engine block and tighten the bolts finger-tight.

16   Engine block - cleaning

Refer to illustrations 16.1, 16.8 and 16.10
Note: *The core plugs (also known as freeze or soft plugs) may be difficult or impossible to retrieve if they're driven into the block coolant passages.*

1   Remove the soft plugs from the engine block. To do this, knock one side of the plugs into the block with a hammer and punch, then pull them out with pliers **(see illustration)**.

2   Using a gasket scraper, remove all traces of gasket material from the engine block. Be very careful not to nick or gouge the gasket sealing surfaces.

3   Remove the main bearing caps and separate the bearing inserts from the caps and the engine block. Tag the bearings, indicating which cylinder they were removed from and whether they were in the cap or the block, then set them aside.

4   Using a 1/4-inch drive breaker bar or ratchet, remove all of the threaded oil gallery

16.8 Clean and restore all threaded holes in the block - especially the main bearing cap and head bolt holes - with a tap (be sure to remove debris from the holes when you're done)

plugs from the rear of the block. Discard the plugs and use new ones when the engine is reassembled.

5   If the engine is extremely dirty it should be taken to an automotive machine shop to be steam cleaned or hot tanked.

6   After the block is returned, clean all oil holes and oil galleries one more time. Brushes specifically designed for this purpose are available at most auto parts stores. Flush the passages with warm water until the water runs clear, dry the block thoroughly and wipe all machined surfaces with a light, rust preventive oil. If you have access to compressed air, use it to speed the drying process and blow out all the oil holes and galleries.

7   If the block isn't extremely dirty or sludged up, you can do an adequate cleaning job with warm soapy water and a stiff brush. Take plenty of time and do a thorough job. Regardless of the cleaning method used, be sure to clean all oil holes and galleries very thoroughly, dry the block completely and coat all machined surfaces with light oil.

8   The threaded holes in the block must be clean to ensure accurate torque readings

16.10 A large socket on an extension can be used to drive the new core plugs into the bores

during reassembly. Run the proper size tap into each of the holes to remove any rust, corrosion, thread sealant or sludge and to restore damaged threads **(see illustration)**. If possible, use compressed air to clear the holes of debris produced by this operation. Now is a good time to clean the threads on the head bolts and the main bearing cap bolts as well.

9   Reinstall the main bearing caps and tighten the bolts finger-tight.

10   After coating the sealing surfaces of the new soft plugs with Permatex no. 1 sealant (or equivalent), install them in the engine block. Make sure they're driven in straight and seated properly or leakage could result. Special tools are available for this purpose, but equally good results can be obtained using a large socket, with an outside diameter that will just slip into the soft plug, and a hammer **(see illustration)**.

11   Apply non-hardening sealant (such as Permatex number 2 or Teflon tape) to the new oil gallery plugs and thread them into the holes at the rear of the block. Make sure they're tightened securely.

12   If the engine isn't going to be reassembled right away, cover it with a large plastic trash bag to keep it clean.

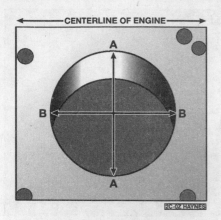

17.4a Measure the diameter of each cylinder at a right angle to the engine centerline (A), and parallel to engine centerline (B) - out-of-round is the difference between A and B; taper is the difference between A and B at the top of the cylinder and A and B at the bottom of the cylinder

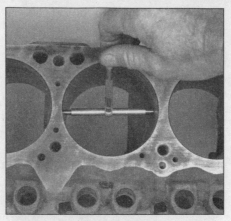

17.4b The ability to "feel" when the telescoping gauge is at the correct point will be developed over time, so work slowly and repeat the check until you're satisfied the bore measurement is accurate

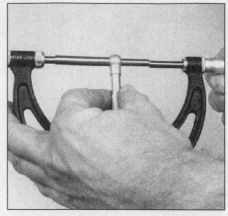

17.4c The gauge is then measured with a micrometer to determine the bore size

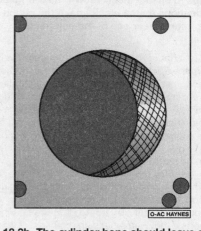

18.3b The cylinder hone should leave a smooth, crosshatch pattern with the lines intersecting at approximately a 60-degree angle

17   Engine block - inspection

Refer to illustrations 17.4a, 17.4b and 17.4c

1   Before the block is inspected, it should be cleaned as described in Section 14. Double-check to make sure the ridge at the top of each cylinder has been completely removed.

2   Visually check the block for cracks, rust and corrosion. Look for stripped threads in the threaded holes. It's also a good idea to have the block checked for hidden cracks by an automotive machine shop with the special equipment to do this type of work. If defects are found, have the block repaired, if possible, or replaced.

3   Check the cylinder bores for scuffing and scoring. Check the cylinders for taper and out-of-round conditions as follows:

4   Measure the diameter of each cylinder at the top (just under the ridge area), center and bottom of the cylinder bore, parallel to the crankshaft axis **(see illustrations)**. **Note:** *These measurements should not be made with the bare block mounted on an engine stand - the cylinders will be distorted and the measurements will be inaccurate.*

5   Next, measure each cylinder's diameter at the same three locations across the crankshaft axis. The taper of the cylinder is the difference between the bore diameter at the top of the cylinder and the diameter at the bottom.The out-of round specification of the cylinder bore is the difference between the parallel and perpendicular readings. Compare your results to those listed in this Chapter's Specifications. Repeat the procedure for the remaining pistons and cylinders.

6   If the cylinder walls are badly scuffed or scored, or if they're out-of-round or tapered beyond the limits given in the Specifications, have the engine block rebored and honed at an automotive machine shop. If a rebore is

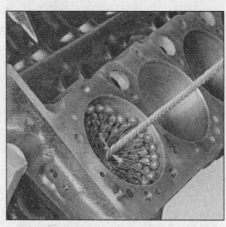

18.3a If this is the first time you've ever honed cylinders, you'll get better results with a "bottle brush" hone than you will with a traditional spring-loaded hone

done, oversize pistons and rings will be required.

7   If the cylinders are in reasonably good condition and not worn to the outside of the limits, and if the piston-to-cylinder clearances can be maintained properly, then they don't have to be rebored. Honing is all that's necessary (see Section 16).

18   Cylinder honing

Refer to illustrations 18.3a and 18.3b

1   Prior to engine reassembly, the cylinder bores must be honed so the new piston rings will seat correctly and provide the best possible combustion chamber seal. **Note:** *If you don't have the tools or don't want to tackle the honing operation, most automotive machine shops will do it for a reasonable fee.*

2   Before honing the cylinders, install the main bearing caps and tighten the bolts to the specified torque.

3   Two types of cylinder hones are com-

monly available - the flex hone or "bottle brush" type and the more traditional surfacing hone with spring-loaded stones. Both will do the job, but for the less experienced mechanic the "bottle brush" hone will probably be easier to use. You'll also need plenty of light oil or honing oil, some rags and an electric drill motor. Proceed as follows:

a) *Mount the hone in the drill motor, compress the stones and slip it into the first cylinder* **(see illustration)**.

b) *Lubricate the cylinder with plenty of oil, turn on the drill and move the hone up-and-down in the cylinder at a pace which will produce a fine crosshatch pattern on the cylinder walls. Ideally, the crosshatch lines should intersect at approximately a 60-degree angle* **(see illustration)**. *Be sure to use plenty of lubricant and don't take off any more material than absolutely necessary to produce the desired finish.* **Note:** *Piston ring manufacturers may specify a smaller crosshatch angle than the traditional 60-degrees - read and follow any instructions printed on the piston ring packages.*

19.4a The piston ring grooves can be cleaned with a special tool, as shown here, . . .

19.4b . . . or a piece of broken piston ring

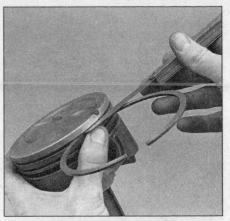

19.10 Check the ring side clearance with a feeler gauge at several points around the groove

c) *Do not withdraw the hone from the cylinder while it's running. Instead, shut off the drill and continue moving the hone up-and-down in the cylinder until it comes to a complete stop, then compress the stones and withdraw the hone. If you're using a "bottle brush" type hone, stop the drill motor, then turn the chuck in the normal direction of rotation while withdrawing the hone from the cylinder.*

d) *Wipe the oil out of the cylinder and repeat the procedure for the remaining cylinders.*

4   After the honing job is complete, chamfer the top edges of the cylinder bores with a small file so the rings won't catch when the pistons are installed. Be very careful not to nick the cylinder walls with the end of the file.

5   The entire engine block must be washed again very thoroughly with warm, soapy water to remove all traces of the abrasive grit produced during the honing operation. **Note:** *The bores can be considered clean when a white cloth - dampened with clean engine oil - used to wipe down the bores does not pick up any more honing residue, which will show up as gray areas on the cloth. Be sure to run a brush through all oil holes and galleries and flush them with running water.*

6   After rinsing, dry the block and apply a coat of light rust preventive oil to all machined surfaces. Wrap the block in a plastic trash bag to keep it clean and set it aside until reassembly.

19   Piston/connecting rod assembly - inspection

Refer to illustrations 19.4a, 19.4b, 19.10 and 19.11

1   Before the inspection process can be carried out, the piston/connecting rod assemblies must be cleaned and the original piston rings removed from the pistons. **Note:** *Always use new piston rings when the engine is reassembled.*

2   Using a piston ring installation tool, carefully remove the rings from the pistons. Be careful not to nick or gouge the pistons in the process.

3   Scrape all traces of carbon from the top (known as the crown) of the piston. A hand-held wire brush or a piece of fine emery cloth can be used once the majority of the deposits have been scraped away. Do not, under any circumstances, use a wire brush mounted in an electric drill to remove deposits from the pistons. The piston material is soft and will be eroded away by the wire brush.

4   Use a piston ring groove cleaning tool to remove carbon deposits from the ring grooves **(see illustration)**. If a tool isn't available, a piece broken off the old ring will do the job **(see illustration)**. Be very careful to remove only the carbon deposits - don't remove any metal and don't nick or scratch the sides of the ring grooves.

5   Once the deposits have been removed, clean the piston/rod assemblies with solvent and dry them with compressed air (if available). Make sure the oil return holes in the back sides of the ring grooves are clear.

6   If the pistons aren't damaged or worn excessively, and if the engine block isn't rebored, new pistons won't be necessary. Normal piston wear appears as even vertical wear on the piston thrust surfaces and slight looseness of the top ring in its groove. New piston rings, on the other hand, should always be used when an engine is rebuilt.

7   Carefully inspect each piston for cracks around the skirt, at the pin bosses and at the ring lands.

8   Look for scoring and scuffing on the thrust faces of the skirt, holes in the piston crown and burned areas at the edge of the crown. If the skirt is scored or scuffed, the engine may have been suffering from overheating and/or abnormal combustion, which caused excessively high operating temperatures. The cooling and lubrication systems should be checked thoroughly. A hole in the piston crown is an indication that abnormal combustion (preignition) was occurring. Burned areas at the edge of the piston crown are usually evidence of spark knock (detona-

tion). If any of the above problems exist, the causes must be corrected or the damage will occur again.

9   Corrosion of the piston, in the form of small pits, indicates that coolant is leaking into the combustion chamber and/or the crankcase. Again, the cause must be corrected or the problem may persist in the rebuilt engine.

10   Measure the piston ring side clearance by laying a new piston ring in each ring groove and slipping a feeler gauge in beside it **(see illustration)**. Check the clearance at three or four locations around each groove. Be sure to use the correct ring for each groove; they are different. If the side clearance is greater than specified, new pistons will have to be used.

11   Check the piston-to-bore clearance by measuring the bore (see Section 17) and the piston diameter. Make sure that the pistons and bores are correctly matched. Measure the piston across the skirt, at a 90-degree angle to and in-line with the piston pin **(see illustration)**. Subtract the piston diameter from the bore diameter to obtain the clear-

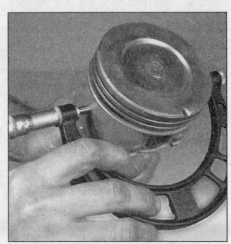

19.11 Measure the piston diameter at a 90-degree angle to the piston pin and in-line with it

20.1 Chamfer the oil holes to remove sharp edges that might gouge or scratch the new bearings

20.2 Clean the crankshaft oil passages with a wire or stiff plastic bristle brush and flush them out with solvent

20.4 Rubbing a penny lengthwise on each journal will give you a quick idea of its condition - if copper rubs off the penny and adheres to the crankshaft, the journals should be reground

ance. If it's greater than specified, the block will have to be rebored and new pistons and rings installed.

12   Check the piston-to-rod clearance by twisting the piston and rod in opposite directions. Any noticeable play indicates that there is excessive wear, which must be corrected. The piston/connecting rod assemblies should be taken to an automotive machine shop to have the pistons and rods rebored and new pins installed.

13   If the pistons must be removed from the connecting rods for any reason, they should be taken to an automotive machine shop. While they're there have the connecting rods checked for bend and twist, since automotive machine shops have special equipment for this purpose. **Note:** *Unless new pistons and/or connecting rods must be installed, do not disassemble the pistons and connecting rods.*

14   Check the connecting rods for cracks and other damage. Temporarily remove the rod caps, lift out the old bearing inserts, wipe the rod and cap bearing surfaces clean and inspect them for nicks, gouges and scratches. After checking the rods, replace

the old bearings, slip the caps into place and tighten the nuts finger-tight.

20 Crankshaft - inspection

Refer to illustrations 20.1, 20.2, 20.4, 20.5 and 20.6

1   Remove all burrs from the crankshaft oil holes with a stone, file or scraper **(see illustration).**

2   Clean the crankshaft with solvent and dry it with compressed air (if available). Be sure to clean the oil holes with a stiff brush **(see illustration)** and flush them with solvent. **Warning:** *Wear eye protection when using compressed air.*

3   Check the main and connecting rod bearing journals for uneven wear, scoring, pits and cracks. Check the rest of the crankshaft for cracks and other damage.

4   Rub a penny across each journal several times **(see illustration).** If a journal picks up copper from the penny, it's too rough and must be reground.

5   Check the rest of the crankshaft for cracks and other damage **(see illustration).** It should be magnafluxed to reveal hidden cracks - an automotive machine shop will handle the procedure.

6   Using a micrometer, measure the diameter of the main and connecting rod journals and compare the results to the Specifications **(see illustration).** By measuring the diameter at a number of points around each journal's circumference, you'll be able to determine whether or not the journal is out-of-round. Take the measurement at each end of the journal, near the crank throws, to determine if the journal is tapered.

7   If the crankshaft journals are damaged, tapered, out-of-round or worn beyond the limits given in the Specifications, have the crankshaft reground by an automotive machine shop. Be sure to use the correct size bearing inserts if the crankshaft is reconditioned.

8   Refer to Section 21 and examine the main and rod bearing inserts.

20.5 If the seals have worn grooves in the crankshaft journals, or if the seal journals are nicked or scratched, the new seal(s) will leak

20.6 Measure the diameter of each crankshaft journal at several points to detect taper and out-of-round conditions

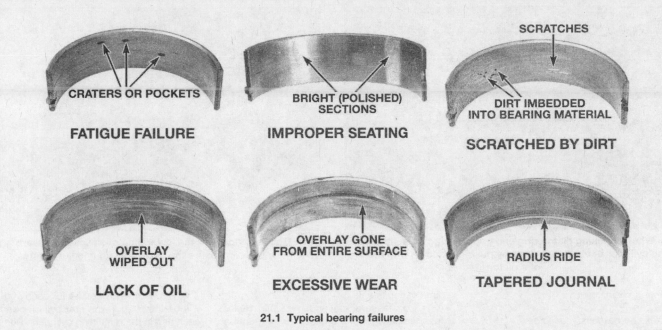

21.1 Typical bearing failures

21 Main and connecting rod bearings - inspection

Refer to illustration 21.1

1   Even though the main and connecting rod bearings should be replaced with new ones during the engine overhaul, the old bearings should be retained for close examination, as they may reveal valuable information about the condition of the engine **(see illustration)**.

2   Bearing failure occurs because of lack of lubrication, the presence of dirt or other foreign particles, overloading the engine and corrosion. Regardless of the cause of bearing failure, it must be corrected before the engine is reassembled to prevent it from happening again.

3   When examining the bearings, remove them from the engine block, the main bearing caps, the connecting rods and the rod caps and lay them out on a clean surface in the same general position as their location in the engine. This will enable you to match any bearing problems with the corresponding crankshaft journal.

4   Dirt and other foreign particles get into the engine in a variety of ways. If may be left in the engine during assembly, or it may pass through filters or the PCV system. It may get into the oil, and from there into the bearings. Metal chips from machining operations and normal engine wear are often present. Abrasives are sometimes left in engine components after reconditioning, especially when parts aren't thoroughly cleaned using the proper cleaning methods. Whatever the source, these foreign objects often end up embedded in the soft bearing material and are easily recognized. Large particles will not embed in the bearing and will score or gouge the bearing and journal. The best prevention for this cause of bearing failure is to clean all parts thoroughly and keep everything spotlessly clean during engine reassembly. Frequent and regular engine oil and filter changes are also recommended.

5   Lack of lubrication (or lubrication breakdown) has a number of interrelated causes. Excessive heat (which thins the oil), overloading (which squeezes the oil from the bearing face) and oil leakage or throw off (from excessive bearing clearances, worn oil pump or high engine speeds) all contribute to lubrication breakdown. Blocked oil passages, which usually are the result of misaligned oil holes in a bearing shell, will also oil starve a bearing and destroy it. When lack of lubrication is the cause of bearing failure, the bearing material is wiped or extruded from the steel backing of the bearing. Temperatures may increase to the point where the steel backing turns blue from overheating.

6   Driving habits can have a definite effect on bearing life. Full throttle, low speed operation in too high a gear (lugging the engine) puts very high loads on bearings, which tends to squeeze out the oil film. These loads cause the bearings to flex, which produces fine cracks in the bearing face (fatigue failure). Eventually the bearing material will loosen in pieces and tear away from the steel backing. Short trip driving leads to corrosion of bearings because insufficient engine heat is produced to drive off the condensed water and corrosive gases. These products collect in the engine oil, forming acid and sludge. As the oil is carried to the engine bearings, the acid attacks and corrodes the bearing material.

7   Incorrect bearing installation during engine assembly will lead to bearing failure as well. Tight fitting bearings leave insufficient bearing oil clearance and will result in oil starvation. Dirt or foreign particles trapped behind a bearing insert result in high spots on the bearing which lead to failure.

22 Engine overhaul - reassembly sequence

1   Before beginning engine reassembly, make sure you have all the necessary new parts, gaskets and seals as well as the following items on hand:

Common hand tools
1/2-inch drive torque wrench
Piston ring installation tool
Piston ring compressor
Short lengths of rubber or plastic hose to fit over connecting rod bolts
Plastigage
Feeler gauges
A fine-tooth file
New engine oil
Engine assembly lube or moly-base grease
RTV sealant (safe for use with oxygen sensors)
Anaerobic-type gasket sealant
Thread locking compound

2   To save time and avoid problems, engine reassembly must be done in the following general order:

New camshaft bearings (must be done by an automotive machine shop)
Piston rings
Crankshaft and main bearings
Piston/connecting rod assemblies
Oil pump and pick-up
Camshaft and lifters
Cylinder heads, pushrods and rocker arms
Timing chain and sprockets

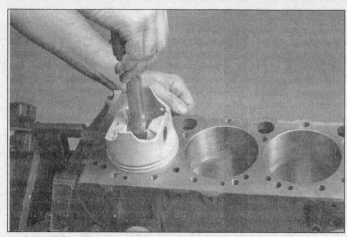

23.3 When checking piston ring end gap, the ring must be square in the cylinder bore - this is done by pushing it down with the top of a piston

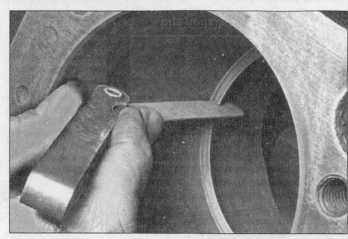

23.4 Once the ring is at the lower limit of travel and square in the cylinder, measure the end gap with a feeler gauge

Timing chain cover
Oil pan
Intake and exhaust manifolds
Rocker arm covers
Flywheel/driveplate

23 Piston rings - installation

Refer to illustrations 23.3, 23.4, 23.5, 23.9a, 23.9b and 23.12

1   Before installing the new piston rings, the ring end gaps must be checked. It's assumed the piston ring side clearance has been checked and verified correct (see Section 19).

2   Lay out the piston/connecting rod assemblies and the new ring sets so the ring sets will be matched with the same piston and cylinder during the end gap measurement and engine assembly.

3   Insert the top (number one) ring into the first cylinder and square it up with the cylinder walls by pushing it in with the top of the piston **(see illustration)**. The ring should be near the bottom of the cylinder, at the lower limit of ring travel.

4   To measure the end gap, slip feeler gauges between the ends of the ring until a gauge equal to the gap width is found **(see illustration)**. The feeler gauge should slide between the ring ends with a slight amount of drag. Compare the measurement to the Specifications. If the gap is larger or smaller than specified, double-check to make sure you have the correct rings before proceeding.

5   If the gap is too small, it must be enlarged or the ring ends may come in contact with each other during engine operation, which can cause serious damage. The end gap can be increased by filing the ring ends very carefully with a fine file. Mount the file in a vise equipped with soft jaws, slip the ring over the file with the ends contacting the file face and slowly move the ring to remove material from the ends **(see illustration)**. When performing this operation, file only from the outside in.

6   Excess end gap is not critical unless it's greater than 0.040-inch. Again, double-check to make sure you have the correct rings for the engine.

7   Repeat the procedure for each ring that will be installed in the first cylinder and for each ring in the remaining cylinders. Remember to keep rings, pistons and cylinders matched up.

8   Once the ring end gaps have been checked/corrected, the rings can be installed on the pistons.

9   The oil control ring (lowest one on the piston) is installed first. It is composed of three separate components. Slip the spacer/expander into the groove **(see illustration)**. If an anti-rotation tang is used, make sure it's inserted into the drilled hole in the ring groove. Install the lower side rail. Do not use a piston ring installation tool on the oil ring side rails, as they may be damaged. Instead, place one end of the side rail into the groove between the spacer/expander and the ring land, hold it firmly in place and slide a finger around the piston while pushing the rail into the groove **(see illustration)**. Next, install the upper side rail in the same manner.

10   After the three oil ring components have been installed, check to make sure both the upper and lower side rails can be turned

23.5 If the end gap is too small, clamp a file in a vise and file the ring ends (from the outside in only) to enlarge the gap slightly

23.9a Install the three-piece oil control ring first, one part at a time, beginning with the spacer/expander, . . .

23.9b . . . followed by the side rails - DO NOT use a piston ring installation tool to install the oil ring side rails

23.12 Install the compression rings with a ring expander - the mark (arrow) must face up

24.10 Lay the Plastigage strips on the main bearing journals, parallel to the crankshaft centerline

smoothly in the ring groove.

11   The number two (middle) ring is installed next. It is stamped with a mark which must face up, toward the top of the piston. **Note:** *Always follow the instructions printed on the ring package or box - different manufacturers may require different approaches. Do not mix up the top and middle rings, as they have different cross sections.*

12   Use a piston ring installation tool and make sure the identification mark is facing the top of the piston, then slip the ring into the middle groove on the piston **(see illustration)**. Don't expand the ring any more than necessary to slide it over the piston.

13   Install the number one (top) ring in the same manner. Make sure the mark is facing up. Be careful not to confuse the number one and number two rings.

14   Repeat the procedure for the remaining pistons and rings.

24   Crankshaft - installation and main bearing oil clearance check

Refer to illustrations 24.10 and 24.14

1   Crankshaft installation is the first step in engine reassembly. It is assumed at this point that the engine block and crankshaft have been cleaned, inspected and repaired or reconditioned.

2   Position the engine with the bottom facing up.

3   Remove the main bearing cap bolts and lift out the caps. Lay them out in the proper order to ensure they are installed correctly.

4   If they're still in place, remove the old bearing inserts from the block and the main bearing caps. Wipe the main bearing surfaces of the block and caps with a clean, lint free cloth. They must be kept spotlessly clean.

Main bearing oil clearance check

Note: *Don't touch the faces of the new bearing inserts with your fingers. Oil and acids from your skin can etch the bearings.*

5   Clean the back sides of the new main bearing inserts and lay one bearing half in each main bearing saddle in the block. Lay the other bearing half from each bearing set in the corresponding main bearing cap. Make sure the tab on the bearing insert fits into the recess in the block or cap. Also, the oil holes in the block must line up with the oil holes in the bearing insert. Do not hammer the bearing into place and don't nick or gouge the bearing faces. No lubrication should be used at this time.

6   The flanged thrust bearing must be installed in the rear cap and saddle.

7   Clean the faces of the bearings in the block and the crankshaft main bearing journals with a clean, lint free cloth. Check or clean the oil holes in the crankshaft, as any dirt here can go only one way - straight through the new bearings.

8   Once you're certain the crankshaft is clean, carefully lay it in position (an assistant would be very helpful here) in the main bearings.

9   Before the crankshaft can be permanently installed, the main bearing oil clearance must be checked.

10   Trim several pieces of the appropriate size of Plastigage (they must be slightly shorter than the width of the main bearings) and place one piece on each crankshaft main bearing journal, parallel with the journal axis **(see illustration)**.

11   Clean the faces of the bearings in the caps and install the caps in their respective positions (do not mix them up) with the arrows pointing toward the front of the engine. Do not disturb the Plastigage.

12   Starting with the center main and working out toward the ends, tighten the main bearing cap bolts, in three steps, to the specified torque. Do not rotate the crankshaft at any time during this operation.

13   Remove the bolts and carefully lift off the main bearing caps. Keep them in order. Do not disturb the Plastigage or rotate the crankshaft. If any of the main bearing caps are difficult to remove, tap them gently from side-to-side with a soft-face hammer to loosen them.

14   Compare the width of the crushed Plastigage on each journal to the scale printed on the Plastigage container to obtain the main bearing oil clearance **(see illustration)**. Check the Specifications to make sure it's correct.

15   If the clearance is not as specified, the bearing inserts may be the wrong size (which means different ones will be required). Before deciding that different inserts are needed, make sure that no dirt or oil was between the bearing inserts and the caps or block when the clearance was measured. If the Plastigage was wider at one end than the other, the journal may be tapered (refer to Section 20).

16   Carefully scrape all traces of the Plastigage material off the main bearing journals and/or the bearing faces. Do not nick or scratch the bearing faces - use your fingernail or the edge of a credit card.

24.14 Compare the width of the crushed Plastigage to the scale on the envelope to determine the main bearing oil clearance (always take the measurement at the widest point of the Plastigage); be sure to use the correct scale - standard and metric ones are included

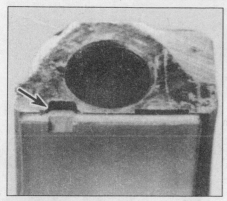

25.3 Make sure the bearing tang fits securely into the notch in the rod cap

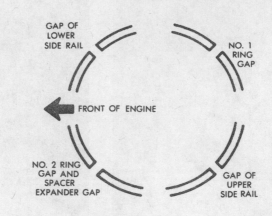

25.5 Ring end gap positions

Final crankshaft installation

17   Carefully lift the crankshaft out of the engine. Clean the bearing faces in the block, then apply a thin, uniform layer of clean moly-base grease or engine assembly lube to each of the bearing surfaces. Be sure to coat the thrust faces as well as the journal face of the rear bearing.

18   If you're working on a 1990 or earlier 7.4 liter (big block) engine, install the rear main oil seal halves in the engine block and rear main bearing cap (refer to Part A, Section 16, for main seal installation details).

19   Make sure the crankshaft journals are clean, then lay the crankshaft back in place in the block. Clean the faces of the bearings in the caps, then apply lubricant to them. Install the caps in their respective positions with the arrows pointing toward the front of the engine. Install the bolts.

20   Tighten all except the rear cap bolts (the one with the thrust bearing) to the specified torque. Work from the center out and approach the final torque in three steps. Tighten the rear cap bolts to 10-to-12 ft-lbs. Tap the ends of the crankshaft forward and backward with a lead or brass hammer to line up the main bearing and crankshaft thrust surfaces. Retighten all main bearing cap bolts to the specified torque, starting with the center main and working out toward the ends. On models with four bolt main bearing caps, tighten the inner bolts first, then the outer bolts, and be sure to note that different torque figures are supplied for the inner and outer bolts.

21   On manual transmission equipped models, install a new pilot bearing in the end of the crankshaft (see Chapter 8).

22   Rotate the crankshaft a number of times by hand to check for obvious binding.

23   Check the crankshaft endplay with a feeler gauge or a dial indicator as described in Section 15. The endplay should be correct if the crankshaft thrust faces aren't worn or damaged and new bearings have been installed.

24   If you're working on a V6, small block V8, or 1991 or later 7.4 liter engine, install the crankshaft rear oil seal and housing (refer to Part A, Section 16, for installation details).

25   Piston/connecting rod assembly - installation and rod bearing oil clearance check

Refer to illustrations 25.3, 25.5, 25.8, 25.9, 25.11 and 25.13

1   Before installing the piston/connecting rod assemblies, the cylinder walls must be perfectly clean, the top edge of each cylinder must be chamfered, and the crankshaft must be in place.

2   Remove the connecting rod cap from the end of the number one connecting rod. Remove the old bearing inserts and wipe the bearing surfaces of the connecting rod and cap with a clean, lint free cloth. They must be kept spotlessly clean.

Connecting rod bearing oil clearance check

Note: *Don't touch the faces of the new bearing inserts with your fingers. Oil and acids from your skin can etch the bearings.*

3   Clean the back side of the new upper bearing half, then lay it in place in the connecting rod. Make sure the tang on the bearing fits into the recess in the rod **(see illustration)**. Do not hammer the bearing insert into place and be very careful not to nick or gouge the bearing face. Do not lubricate the bearing at this time.

4   Clean the back side of the other bearing insert and install it in the rod cap. Again, make sure the tab on the bearing fits into the recess in the cap, and do not apply any lubricant. It is critically important that the mating surfaces of the bearing and connecting rod are perfectly clean and oil free when they're assembled.

5   Space the piston ring gaps around the piston **(see illustration)**, then slip a section of plastic or rubber hose over each connecting rod cap bolt.

6   Lubricate the piston and rings with clean engine oil and attach a piston ring compressor to the piston. Leave the skirt protruding about 1/4-inch to guide the piston into the cylinder. The rings must be compressed until they're flush with the piston.

7   Rotate the crankshaft until the number one connecting rod journal is at BDC (bottom dead center) and apply a coat of engine oil to the cylinder walls.

8   With the notch on top of the piston facing the front of the engine **(see illustration)**, gently insert the piston/connecting rod assembly into the number one cylinder bore and rest the bottom edge of the ring compressor on the engine block. Tap the top edge of the ring compressor to make sure it's contacting the block around its entire circumference.

9   Carefully tap on the top of the piston with the end of a wooden hammer handle while guiding the end of the connecting rod into place on the crankshaft journal **(see illustration)**. The piston rings may try to pop out of the ring compressor just before entering the cylinder bore, so keep some downward pressure on the ring compressor. Work slowly, and if any resistance is felt as the piston enters the cylinder, stop immediately. Find out what is hanging up and fix it before proceeding. Do not, for any reason, force the piston into the cylinder - you'll break a ring and/or the piston.

10   Once the piston/connecting rod assembly is installed, the connecting rod bearing oil clearance must be checked before the rod cap is permanently bolted in place.

11   Cut a piece of the appropriate size Plastigage slightly shorter than the width of the connecting rod bearing and lay it in place on the number one connecting rod journal, parallel with the journal axis **(see illustration)**.

12   Clean the connecting rod cap bearing face, remove the protective hoses from the connecting rod bolts and install the rod cap. Make sure the mating mark on the cap is on the same side as the mark on the connecting rod. Install the nuts and tighten them to the specified torque, working up to it in three steps. **Note:** *Use a thin-wall socket to avoid erroneous torque readings that can result if the socket becomes wedged between the rod cap and nut. Do not rotate the crankshaft at any time during this operation.*

13   Remove the rod cap, being very careful not to disturb the Plastigage. Compare the width of the crushed Plastigage to the scale

---

GAP OF LOWER SIDE RAIL

NO. 1 RING GAP

FRONT OF ENGINE

NO. 2 RING GAP AND SPACER EXPANDER GAP

GAP OF UPPER SIDE RAIL

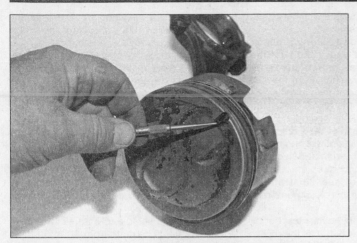

25.8 The notch or arrow on each piston must face the front end of the engine as the pistons are installed

25.9 Drive the piston gently into the cylinder bore with the end of a wooden or plastic hammer handle

printed on the Plastigage envelope to obtain the oil clearance **(see illustration)**. Compare it to the Specifications to make sure the clearance is correct. If the clearance is not as specified, the bearing inserts may be the wrong size (which means different ones will be required). Before deciding different inserts are needed, make sure no dirt or oil was between the bearing inserts and the connecting rod or cap when the clearance was measured. Also, recheck the journal diameter. If the Plastigage was wider at one end than the other, the journal may be tapered (refer to Section 20).

Final connecting rod installation

14   Carefully scrape all traces of the Plastigage material off the rod journal and/or bearing face. Be very careful not to scratch the bearing - use your fingernail or the edge of a credit card.

15   Make sure the bearing faces are perfectly clean, then apply a uniform layer of clean moly-base grease or engine assembly lube to both of them. You will have to push

the piston into the cylinder to expose the face of the bearing insert in the connecting rod - be sure to slip the protective hoses over the rod bolts first.

16   Slide the connecting rod back into place on the journal, remove the protective hoses from the rod cap bolts, install the rod cap and tighten the nuts to the specified torque. Again, work up to the torque in three steps.

17   Repeat the entire procedure for the remaining pistons/connecting rods.

18   The important points to remember are . . .

a) *Keep the back sides of the bearing inserts and the insides of the connecting rods and caps perfectly clean when assembling them.*

b) *Make sure you have the correct piston assembly for each cylinder.*

c) *The notch on the piston must face the front of the engine.*

d) *Lubricate the cylinder walls with clean oil.*

e) *Lubricate the bearing faces when installing the rod caps after the oil clearance has been checked.*

19   After all the piston/connecting rod

assemblies have been properly installed, rotate the crankshaft a number of times by hand to check for any obvious binding.

20   As a final step, the connecting rod endplay must be checked. Refer to Section 14 for this procedure. Compare the measured endplay to the Specifications to make sure it's correct. If it was correct before disassembly and the original crankshaft and rods were reinstalled, it should still be right. If new rods or a new crankshaft were installed, the endplay may be too small. If so, the rods will have to be removed and taken to an automotive machine shop for resizing.

26   Pre-oiling the engine after overhaul

Refer to illustrations 26.3, 26.5 and 26.6

1   After an overhaul it's a good idea to pre-oil the engine before it's installed in the vehicle and started for the first time. Pre-oiling will reveal any problems with the lubrication system at a time when corrections can be

25.11 Lay the Plastigage strips on each rod bearing journal, parallel to the crankshaft centerline

25.13 Measure the width of the crushed Plastigage with the scale on the envelope to determine the rod bearing oil clearance (be sure to use the correct scale - standard and metric ones are included)

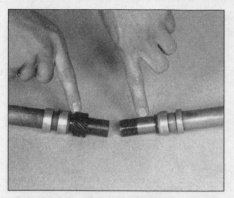

26.3 The pre-oil distributor (right) has the gear ground off and the advance weights removed

made easily and will prevent major engine damage. It will also allow the internal engine parts to be lubricated thoroughly in the normal fashion without the heavy loads associated with combustion placed on them.

2   The engine should be completely assembled with the exception of the distributor and rocker arm covers. The oil filter and oil pressure sending unit must be in place and the specified amount of oil must be in the crankcase (see Chapter 1).

3   A modified Chevrolet distributor will be needed for this procedure - a salvage yard should be able to supply one for a reasonable price. In order to function as a pre-oil tool, the distributor must have the gear on the lower end of the shaft ground off **(see illustration)**.

and, if equipped, the advance weights on the upper end of the shaft removed.

4   Install the pre-oil distributor in place of the original distributor and make sure the lower end of the shaft mates with the upper end of the oil pump driveshaft. Turn the distributor shaft until they're aligned and the distributor body seats on the block. Install the distributor hold-down clamp and bolt.

5   Mount the upper end of the shaft in the chuck of an electric drill and use the drill to turn the pre-oil distributor shaft, which will drive the oil pump and circulate the oil throughout the engine **(see illustration)**. **Note:** *The drill must turn in a clockwise direction.*

6   It may take two or three minutes, but oil should soon start to flow out of all the rocker arm holes, indicating that the oil pump is working properly **(see illustration)**. Let the oil circulate for several seconds, then shut off the drill.

7   Remove the pre-oil distributor, then install the rocker arm covers. The distributor should be installed after the engine is installed in the vehicle (see Chapter 5), so plug the hole with a clean cloth.

27   Initial start-up and break-in after overhaul

1   Once the engine has been installed in the vehicle, double-check the engine oil and coolant levels.

2   With the spark plugs out of the engine

and the ignition disabled by disconnecting the primary wires to the coil, crank the engine until oil pressure registers on the gauge.

3   Install the spark plugs, hook up the plug wires and reconnect the wires to the coil.

4   Start the engine. It may take a few moments for the gasoline to reach the fuel injection unit, but the engine should start without a great deal of effort.

5   After the engine starts, it should be allowed to warm up to normal operating temperature. While the engine is warming up, make a thorough check for oil and coolant leaks.

6   Shut the engine off and recheck the engine oil and coolant levels.

7   Drive the vehicle to an area with minimum traffic, accelerate from 30 to 50 mph, then allow the vehicle to slow to 30 mph with the throttle closed. Repeat the procedure 10 or 12 times. This will load the piston rings and cause them to seat properly against the cylinder walls. Check again for oil and coolant leaks.

8   Drive the vehicle gently for the first 500 miles (no sustained high speeds) and keep a constant check on the oil level. It isn't unusual for an engine to use oil during the break-in period.

9   At approximately 500 to 600 miles, change the oil and filter.

10   For the next few hundred miles, drive the vehicle normally. Do not pamper it or abuse it.

11   After 2000 miles, change the oil and filter again and consider the engine fully broken in.

26.5 An electric drill connected to the modified distributor shaft drives the oil pump - make sure it turns clockwise as viewed from above

26.6 Oil, assembly lube or grease will begin to flow out of the rocker arm holes if the oil pump and lubrication system are functioning properly

Chapter 3
Cooling, heating and air conditioning systems

Contents

Specifications

General

Radiator cap rating	15 psi
Thermostat rating	195-degrees F (91-degrees C)
Coolant capacity	See Chapter 1

Torque specifications

	Ft-lbs
Fan-to-pulley nuts	18
Thermostat cover bolts	
7.4 liter V8 engine	30
All others	20
Water pump mounting bolts	30

Component location

Typical 5.0/5.7 liter V8 engine cooling, heating and air conditioning system

1	Radiator cap	5	Water pump	8	Coolant reservoir
2	Air conditioning compressor	6	Thermostat	9	Air conditioning accumulator
3	Fan shroud and radiator	7	Heater and evaporator assembly	10	Air conditioning pressure switch
4	Upper radiator hose				

1   General information

The cooling system consists of an aluminum cross-flow radiator, a thermostat and a crankshaft pulley-driven water pump.
The radiator cooling fan is mounted on the front of the water pump and incorporates a fluid drive fan clutch, saving horsepower and reducing noise. A fan shroud is mounted on the rear of the radiator.

The system is pressurized by a spring-loaded radiator cap, which increases the boiling point of the coolant. If the coolant temperature goes above this increased boiling point, the extra pressure in the system forces the radiator cap valve off its seat and exposes the overflow pipe. The overflow pipe leads to a coolant recovery system. This consists of a plastic reservoir in which the coolant which normally escapes due to expansion is retained. When the engine cools, the excess coolant is drawn back into the radiator, maintaining the system at full capacity. This is a continuous process and provided the level in the reservoir is correctly maintained, it is not necessary to add coolant

to the radiator.

Coolant in the right side of the radiator circulates up the lower radiator hose to the water pump, where it is forced through the water passages in the cylinder block. The coolant then travels up into the cylinder head, circulates around the combustion chambers and valve seats, travels out of the cylinder head past the open thermostat into the upper radiator hose and back into the radiator.

When the engine is cold the thermostat restricts the circulation of coolant to the engine. The thermostat is located in the front of the intake manifold. When the minimum operating temperature is reached, the thermostat begins to open, allowing coolant to return to the radiator.

Automatic transmission-equipped models have a cooler element incorporated into the radiator to cool the transmission fluid.

The heating system works by directing air through the heater core mounted in the dash and then to the interior of the vehicle by a system of ducts. Temperature is controlled by mixing heated air with fresh air, using a system of flapper doors in the ducts, and a heater motor.

Air conditioning is an optional accessory, consisting of an evaporator core located under the dash, a condenser in front of the radiator, an accumulator in the engine compartment and a belt-driven compressor mounted at the front of the engine.

2   Antifreeze - general information

Refer to illustration 2.2
Warning: *Do not allow antifreeze to come in contact with your skin or painted surfaces of the vehicle. Rinse off spills immediately with plenty of water. NEVER leave antifreeze lying around in an open container or in a puddle in the driveway or on the garage floor. Children and pets are attracted by it's sweet smell. Antifreeze is fatal if ingested.*

The cooling system should be filled with a water/ethylene glycol based antifreeze solution which will prevent freezing down to at least -20-degrees F (even lower in cold climates). It also provides protection against corrosion and increases the coolant boiling point.

On 1988 through 1995 vehicles, the

2.2 1996 and later models use a special coolant that is good for five years or 150,000 miles

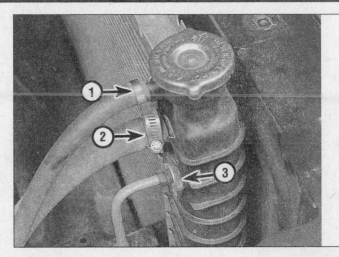

3.2 Disconnect all the hoses and lines from the radiator

1 Overflow hose
2 Heater hose
3 Transmission cooler line (lower line not visible in this photo)

coolant should be changed every 30,000 miles or every two years, whichever comes first. On 1996 and later models, the factory installed a special coolant (Dex-cool) which is good for 150,000 miles or five years, whichever comes first. Vehicles equipped with Dex-cool coolant will have a sticker indicating so attached to the coolant recovery reservoir **(see illustration)**.

Before adding antifreeze to the system, check all hose connections. Antifreeze can leak through very minute openings.

The exact mixture of antifreeze to water which you should use depends on the relative weather conditions. The mixture should contain at least 50 percent antifreeze, but should never contain more than 70 percent antifreeze.

3 Radiator - removal and installation

Refer to illustrations 3.2, 3.4, 3.5a, 3.5b and 3.6

Warning: *The engine must be completely cool when this procedure is performed.*

Removal

Note: *Late model vehicles use spring type radiator hose clamps. If you decide to reuse them, make sure that the hose is installed on a connection that is clean and dry. The connection should be scraped down to bare metal if it has been painted or otherwise coated. Don't try to reuse these clamps on aftermarket hoses. Replace them with conventional worm drive type clamps.*

1   Disconnect the negative cable from the battery.

2   Drain the cooling system as described in Chapter 1, then disconnect the overflow, heater and upper and lower radiator hoses from the radiator **(see illustration)**.

3   If equipped with an automatic transmission, remove the transmission cooler lines from the side of the radiator - be careful not to twist the lines or damage the fittings. It is a good idea to use a flare nut wrench rather than an open end wrench. Plug the ends of the disconnected lines to prevent leakage and stop dirt from entering the system. Have a drip pan ready to catch any spills.

4   If equipped with an engine oil cooler, disconnect the lines on the opposite side of the radiator, as described in the previous

3.4 Most models have engine oil cooler lines (arrow) attached to the side tank

step **(see illustrations)**.

5   Unbolt and remove the fan shroud **(see illustration)**. It's only necessary to remove the upper portion for many service operations.

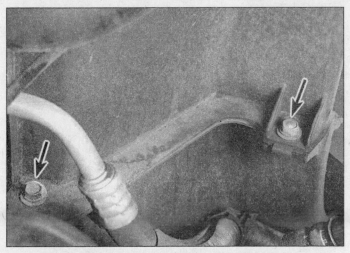

3.5a Typical fan shroud center mounting screws

3.5b Typical fan shroud upper mounting screws

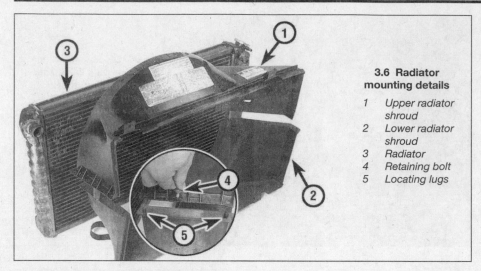

3.6 Radiator mounting details

1   Upper radiator shroud
2   Lower radiator shroud
3   Radiator
4   Retaining bolt
5   Locating lugs

6   Remove the radiator mounting brackets (if equipped) and lift the radiator from the engine compartment **(see illustration)**. Take care not to contact the fan blades.

7   Prior to installation of the radiator, replace any damaged hose clamps and radiator hoses.

Installation

8   Radiator installation is the reverse of removal. When installing the radiator, make sure that the radiator seats properly in the lower saddles and that the upper brackets secure, but do not compress, the radiator core.

9   After installation, check the engine oil and automatic transmission fluid levels.

4   Thermostat - check and replacement

Refer to illustrations 4.8 and 4.9
Warning: *The engine must be completely cool when this procedure is performed.*
Note: *Don't drive the vehicle without a ther-*

mostat! The computer will stay in open loop and emissions and fuel economy will suffer.

Check

1   Before condemning the thermostat, check the coolant level, drivebelt tension, drivebelt tension and temperature gauge (or light) operation.

2   If the engine takes a long time to warm up, the thermostat is probably stuck open. Replace the thermostat.

3   If the engine runs hot, check the temperature of the upper radiator hose. If the hose isn't hot, the thermostat is probably stuck shut. Replace the thermostat.

4   If the upper radiator hose is hot, it means the coolant is circulating and the thermostat is open. Refer to the troubleshooting section for the cause of overheating.

5   If an engine has been overheated, you may find damage such as leaking head gaskets, scuffed pistons and warped or cracked cylinder heads.

Replacement

6   Drain coolant (about three quarts) from the radiator, until the coolant level is below

the thermostat housing (See Chapter 1).

7   Disconnect the upper radiator hose from the thermostat housing cover, which is located at the forward end of the intake manifold.

8   Remove the nuts/bolts and lift the cover off **(see illustration)**. It may be necessary to move the belt tensioner bracket aside and tap the cover with a soft-face hammer to break the gasket seal.

9   Note how it's installed, then remove the thermostat **(see illustration)**.

10   Use a scraper or putty knife to remove all traces of old gasket material and sealant from the mating surfaces. Make sure no gasket material falls into the coolant passages; it's a good idea to stuff a rag in the passage. Clean the mating surfaces with lacquer thinner or acetone.

11   Apply a thin layer of RTV sealant to the gasket mating surfaces of the housing and cover, then install the new thermostat in the engine. Make sure the correct end faces up - the spring is directed down into the housing/manifold.

12   Position a new gasket on the housing and make sure the gasket holes line up with the bolt holes in the housing.

13   Carefully position the cover on the housing and install the bolts. Tighten them to the specified torque - do not overtighten them or the cover may be distorted.

14   Reattach the radiator hose to the cover and tighten the clamp - now may be a good time to check and replace the hoses and clamps (see Chapter 1).

15   Refer to Chapter 1 and refill the system, then run the engine and check carefully for leaks.

5   Cooling fan and fan clutch - removal and installation

Refer to illustrations 5.3a and 5.3b
1   The cooling fan should be replaced if the blades become damaged or bent. The fluid drive fan clutch is disengaged when the engine is cold, or at high engine speeds, when the silicone fluid inside the clutch is contained in the reservoir section by centrifugal action. Symptoms of failure of the fan clutch are continuous noisy operation, looseness leading to vibration and evidence of silicone fluid leaks.

2   Disconnect the negative cable from the battery. Remove the upper fan shroud (see Section 3).

3   On 1996 and later V6 and small block V8 engines, use a large spanner wrench to remove the fan clutch from the water pump hub. On all others, loosen the fan clutch-to-hub nuts **(see illustrations)**.

4   Remove the drivebelt (see Chapter 1).

5   Remove the fan assembly from the water pump.

6   The fan clutch can be unbolted from the fan blade assembly for replacement.

7   Installation is the reverse of removal.

4.8 Remove the nuts/bolts (arrows) and lift off the cover (the shape of the cover varies)

4.9 Lift out the thermostat - note the location of the spring

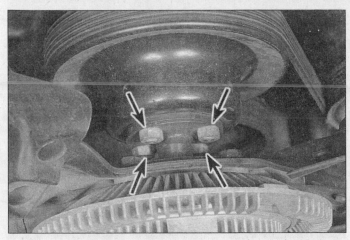

5.3a Loosen/tighten the fan mounting nuts (arrows) with the drivebelt in place

5.3b On 1996 and later V6 and small block V8 models, the fan is threaded to the water pump hub by a large nut. A special tool or a large adjustable wrench will be needed remove it

6 Water pump - check

Refer to illustrations 6.3 and 6.5

1   Water pump failure can cause overheating and serious damage to the engine. There are three ways to check the operation of the water pump while it is installed on the engine. If any one of the three following quick checks indicates water pump problems, it should be replaced immediately.

2   Start the engine and warm it up to normal operating temperature. Squeeze the upper radiator hose. If the water pump is working properly, you should feel a pressure surge as the hose is released.

3   A seal protects the water pump impeller shaft bearing from contamination by engine coolant. If this seal fails, a weep hole in the water pump snout will leak coolant **(see illustration)** (an inspection mirror can be used to look at the underside of the pump if the hole isn't on top). If the weep hole is leaking, shaft bearing failure will follow. Replace the water pump immediately.

4   Besides contamination by coolant after a seal failure, the water pump impeller shaft bearing can also be prematurely worn out by

an improperly tensioned drivebelt. When the bearing wears out, it emits a high pitched squealing sound. If such a noise is coming from the water pump during engine operation, the shaft bearing has failed - replace the water pump immediately. Note: Do not confuse belt noise with bearing noise.

5   To identify excessive bearing wear before the bearing actually fails, grasp the water pump pulley and try to force it up-and-down or from side-to-side **(see illustration)**. If the pulley can be moved either horizontally or vertically, the bearing is nearing the end of its service life. Replace the water pump.

7 Water pump - removal and installation

Refer to illustrations 7.6, 7.7a and 7.7b

Removal

1   Disconnect the negative cable from the battery.
2   Drain the coolant (see Chapter 1).
3   Loosen the fan pulley nuts/bolts and then remove the drivebelt (see Chapter 1).
4   Loosen the hose clamps for the lower

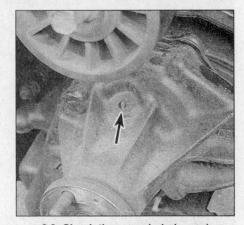

6.3 Check the weep hole (arrow) for leakage

radiator hose and disconnect the hose from the water pump. On 7.4L V8 models, disconnect the coolant by-pass hose from the water pump.

5   Remove the fan assembly (see Section 5) and water pump pulley.

6   On some models the compressor, alternator or power steering brackets may attach to the water pump **(see illustration)**. Where

6.5 Check the pump for loose or rough bearings

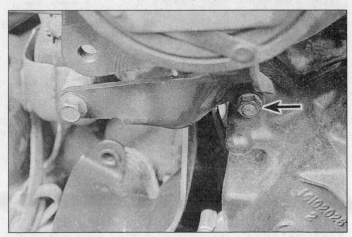

7.6 Remove all brackets (arrow) that attach to the water pump

7.7a Remove the four nuts/bolts (arrows) and detach the pump

7.7b Grasp the water pump and rock it back-and-forth to break
the gasket seal

necessary, loosen the components so that the brackets can be moved aside and the water pump bolts removed.

7   Remove the mounting bolts from the water pump and detach it from the block **(see illustration)**. It may be necessary to grasp the pump securely and rock it back-and-forth to break the gasket seal **(see illustration)**.

Installation

8   Clean the sealing surfaces on both the block and the water pump. Wipe the mating surfaces with a rag saturated with lacquer thinner or acetone.

9   Apply a thin layer of RTV sealant to the block mounting surfaces and install new water pump gaskets.

10   Apply a thin layer of RTV sealant to the water pump mounting surfaces.

11   Place the water pump in position and install the bolts and studs finger-tight. Work carefully so the gaskets don't slip out of position. Remember to replace any mounting brackets secured by the water pump mounting bolts. Tighten the bolts to the torque listed in this Chapter's specifications.

12   Install the water pump pulley and fan assembly and tighten the pulley nuts by hand.

13   Install the lower radiator hose, heater hose and hose clamps. Tighten the hose clamps securely.

14   Install the drivebelt (see Chapter 1) and tighten the fan mounting nuts securely.

15   Add coolant to the specified level (see Chapter 1).

16   Connect the cable to the negative terminal of the battery.

17   Start the engine and check the water pump and hoses for leaks.

8   Coolant reservoir - removal and installation

Refer to illustration 8.2

1   Remove the coolant overflow hose from

the reservoir.

2   Remove the screws and detach the reservoir **(see illustration)**.

3   Prior to installation make sure the reservoir is clean and free of debris which could be drawn into the radiator (wash it with soap and water if necessary).

4   Installation is the reverse of removal.

9   Heater - general information

The heater circulates engine coolant through a small radiator (heater core) in the cab. Air is drawn in through an opening in the cowl, then blown (by the blower motor) through the heater core to pick up heat. The heated air is blended with varying amounts of unheated air to regulate the temperature. The heated air is then blown into the cab. Various doors in the heater control the flow of air to the floor and through the instrument louvers and defroster outlets.

10   Heater blower assembly - removal and installation

Front heater (all models)

Refer to illustrations 10.3, 10.4a, 10.4b and 10.5

1   The heater assembly is attached to the dash panel on the right side of the vehicle. The air inlet assembly and coolant hoses are located on the engine side of the firewall, while the heater core, blower assembly and air distributor duct are on the passenger's side.

2   Disconnect the negative cable from the battery.

3   Disconnect the blower wiring and hose **(see illustration)**.

4   It may be necessary to remove the glove box and the right side kick panel. On 1995 and earlier models, disconnect the ECM wiring connectors. Remove the bolt from the

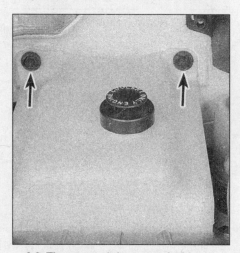

8.2 The reservoir is secured with two
screws (arrows)

right side of the instrument panel. Pull the corner of the instrument panel out for sufficient clearance, remove the blower mounting screws and withdraw the motor and fan **(see illustrations)**.

5   On 1988 through 1991 models, the fan can be removed from the motor shaft after the nut has been unscrewed **(see illustration)**.

6   Installation is the reverse of removal.

7   On 1992 and later models, to remove the blower fan, perform the following:

a) *Using wire cutters, remove 1/2-inch of the plastic tip at the end of the motor shaft.*

b) *Use a small puller to draw the fan off the motor shaft. Alternatively, use a drill press or arbor press with the proper supports to press the motor off the fan. Note: Do not put pressure on the blower motor, only the motor shaft.*

c) *The fan should be reinstalled by pressing it onto the motor shaft. Leave 0.22 inch of clearance between the fan and the motor mount plate.*

10.3 Remove the hose, the wire connector and then the mounting screws (arrows)

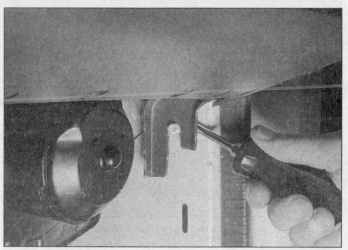

10.4a If necessary for clearance, remove the retaining clip and pry the lower dash mounting bracket over the stud . . .

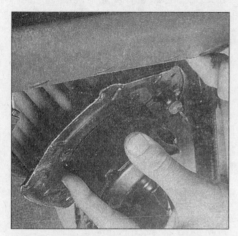

10.4b . . . then pull out on the dash and lower the blower assembly

Rear auxiliary heater (Suburban models)

8   Disconnect the negative cable from the battery.
9   Remove the right-hand rear quarter

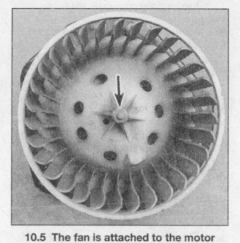

10.5 The fan is attached to the motor shaft by a nut (arrow)

inside trim panel.
10   Disconnect the blower motor wiring.
11   Remove the blower motor mounting screws and withdraw the blower motor from the fan module.
12   Installation is the reverse of removal.

11 Heater controls - removal and installation

Warning: *If equipped with an airbag, disable the airbag system before working in the vicinity of the steering wheel, instrument panel or any airbag system component. Failure to do so could cause accidental deployment of the airbag resulting in personal injury (see Chapter 12).*

Front heater

1988 through 1994 models
Refer to illustrations 11.3 and 11.4
1   Disconnect the negative cable from the battery.
2   Remove the radio for access to the heater controls (see Chapter 12).
3   Remove the four heater control mounting screws (see illustration).
4   Reach behind the unit and unplug the electrical connector (see illustration).
5   Label and detach the control cables, if equipped. Withdraw the control assembly

11.3 Remove the mounting screws (arrows) and pull the control assembly out far enough to disconnect the electrical connections

11.4 Unplug the electrical connector

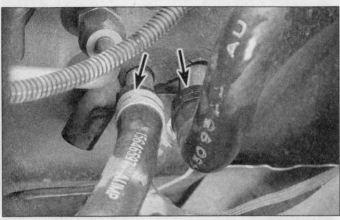

12.3 Use a pair of pliers to remove heater hose clamps (arrows)

12.10 Lower the heater housing to the floor and remove from the truck

through the opening in the dash.

6   Installation is the reverse of removal.

1995 and later models

7   Disconnect the negative cable from the battery.

8   Remove the instrument cluster trim panel (see Chapter 12).

9   Using a small screwdriver, release the retainers and pull the control panel out of the instrument panel **(see illustration)**.

10   Disconnect the electrical connectors.

11   Installation is the reverse of removal.

Rear auxiliary heater (Suburban models)

12   Disconnect the negative cable from the battery.

13   Remove the overhead console single mounting front screw. Pull the overhead console forward to release the rear mounting tabs from the headliner and remove the console.

14   Disconnect the electrical connector.

15   Using a small screwdriver, pry the front auxiliary control panel from the front console.

16   To remove the rear auxiliary control panel, remove the bezel, then pry the control panel from the headliner. Disconnect the electrical connector.

17   Installation is the reverse of removal.

---

12 Heater housing and core - removal and installation

Warning: *If equipped with an airbag, disable the airbag system before working in the vicinity of the steering wheel, instrument panel or any airbag system component. Failure to do so could cause accidental deployment of the airbag resulting in personal injury (see Chapter 12).*

Front heater

1988 through 1994 models

Refer to illustrations 12.3, 12.10 and 12.12

1   Disconnect the negative cable at the battery.

2   Remove the coolant reservoir (see Section 8).

3   Place a drain pan under the heater core, disconnect the coolant hoses from the core **(see illustration)** and plug them or fasten the ends up as high as possible so the coolant does not run out. Allow the coolant in the heater core to drain into the container.

4   Remove the mounting screws/nuts from the heater housing in the engine compartment.

5   Remove the glovebox liner and door.

6   Label and disconnect the heater controls.

7   Disconnect and remove the computer (ECM) and mounting bracket (see Chapter 6).

8   Remove the radio antenna cable (if equipped) at the mast for access.

9   Remove the kick panel and detach the right lower corner of the dash panel. Pull the heater assembly to the rear for access and disconnect the wiring harness.

10   Remove the screws/nuts retaining the heater housing inside the cab **(see illustration)**.

11   Remove the heater housing from the vehicle.

12   Detach the core restraining straps and remove the core **(see illustration)**.

13   Installation is the reverse of removal.

12.12 Remove the heater core retaining bolt and strap (arrows)

1995 and later models

14   Disconnect the negative battery cable.

15   Drain the engine coolant. Refer to Chapter 1.

16   Disconnect the wiring connectors at the heater blower motor.

17   Remove the center duct from under the instrument panel.

18   Remove the kick panel from the right side.

19   Remove the cover from the blower motor.

20   Remove the motor from the blower assembly. Refer to Section 9.

21   Disconnect the steering column. Allow it to drop slightly.

22   Remove the instrument panel bolts and roll the instrument panel as a unit upwards.

23   Remove the coolant recovery reservoir from the engine compartment.

24   Disconnect the heater hoses from the firewall connections.

25   Remove the screw under the cowl near the evaporator pipe. Hold the heater case to the cowl while doing this.

26   Remove the four screws and two nuts on the engine side that retain the heater case to the cowl.

27   Remove the heater case from under the instrument panel.

28   Remove the seven screws retaining the cover to the case and remove the cover.

29   Remove the heater core.

30   Installation is the reverse of removal. It is easiest to have someone assist you when installing the heater case.

Rear auxiliary heater (Suburban models)

Warning: *If the vehicle is equipped with the optional secondary air conditioning system, have the air conditioning system discharged by a dealer service department or service station before beginning this procedure.*

Note: *If the vehicle is equipped with the optional secondary air conditioning system, the rear air conditioning evaporator is mounted in the rear heater housing along with the heater core and fan assembly.*

13.9 Feel the accumulator outlet and evaporator inlet with the air conditioning running to check the refrigerant charge

31 Disconnect the negative cable from the battery.
32 Remove the right-hand rear quarter inside trim panel.
33 Remove the right-hand rear wheel opening liner.
34 Working under the right-hand rear of the vehicle, place a drain pan under the heater core fittings, disconnect the coolant hoses from the core and plug them so the coolant does not run out. Allow the coolant in the heater core to drain into the container.
35 Disconnect the blower motor wiring.
36 Remove the drain valve.
37 Remove the heater housing mounting bolts and nuts and remove the housing assembly.
38 Remove the clips/nuts and separate the housing, then remove the heater core.
39 Installation is the reverse of removal.

13 Air conditioning system - check and maintenance

Refer to illustration 13.9
Warning: *The air conditioning system is under high pressure. Do NOT loosen any fittings or remove any components until after the system has been discharged. Air conditioning refrigerant should be properly discharged into an EPA-approved container at a dealership service department or an air conditioning repair facility. Always wear eye protection when disconnecting air conditioning system fittings.*
Caution: *The air conditioning system on 1995 and later models uses the non- ozone depleting refrigerant, referred to as R-134a. The R-134a refrigerant and its lubricating oil are not compatible with the R-12 system and under no circumstances should the two different types of refrigerant and lubricating oil be intermixed. If mixed, it could result in costly compressor failure due to improper lubrication.*
Note: *Some Suburban models are equipped with an optional secondary air conditioning*

system at the rear. This optional rear system has an additional evaporator located in the rear heater housing along with various hoses and pipes to carry refrigerant to and from the rear evaporator.

Check

1 The following maintenance steps should be performed on a regular basis to ensure that the air conditioner continues to operate at peak efficiency.
 a) *Check the tension of the drivebelt and adjust if necessary (see Chapter 1).*
 b) *Check the condition of the hoses. Look for cracks, hardening and deterioration.* **Warning:** *Do not replace A/C hoses until the system has been discharged (see* **Warning** *above).*
 c) *Check the fins of the condenser for leaves, bugs and other foreign material. A soft brush and compressed air can be used to remove them.*
 d) *Check the wire harness for correct routing, broken wires, damaged insulation, etc. Make sure the harness connections are clean and tight.*
 e) *Maintain the correct refrigerant charge.*
2 The system should be run for about 10 minutes at least once a month. This is particularly important during the winter months because long-term non-use can cause hardening of the internal seals.
3 Because of the complexity of the air conditioning system and the special equipment required to effectively work on it, accurate troubleshooting of the system should be left to a professional mechanic. One probable cause for poor cooling that can be determined by the home mechanic is low refrigerant charge. Should the system lose its cooling ability, the following procedure will help you pinpoint the cause.
4 Warm the engine to normal operating temperature.
5 The hood and doors should be open.
6 Set the control mode selector lever to the Norm position.
7 Set the temperature selector lever to the Cold position.

14.2a Unplug the electrical connector (arrow)

8 Set the blower control selector knob to the Hi position.
9 With the compressor engaged, feel the evaporator inlet pipe between the orifice and the evaporator and put your other hand on the surface of the accumulator outlet **(see illustration)**.
10 If both surfaces feel about the same temperature and if both feel a little cooler than the ambient temperature, the freon level is probably okay. The problem is elsewhere.
11 If the inlet pipe has frost accumulation or feels cooler than the accumulator surface, the refrigerant charge is low. Recharging the air conditioning system should be left to a dealer service department or an automotive air conditioning repair shop. Note: Because of recent Federal regulations proposed by the Environmental Protection Agency, 14-ounce cans of refrigerant are no longer available to the home mechanic. Expensive bulk refrigerant drums may still be available, but special tools and procedures are necessary to recharge using these drums (see the *Haynes Automotive Heating and Air Conditioning Manual*).

14 Air conditioning compressor - removal and installation

Refer to illustrations 14.2a, 14.2b and 14.4
Warning: *The air conditioning system is under high pressure. Do NOT loosen any fittings or remove any components until after the system has been discharged. Air conditioning refrigerant should be properly discharged into an EPA-approved container at a dealership service department or an air conditioning repair facility. Always wear eye protection when disconnecting air conditioning system fittings.*

Removal

1 Disconnect the negative cable from the battery.
2 Disconnect the wire harness from the air conditioning compressor and remove the line fitting bolt from the back side of the compressor **(see illustrations)**.

14.2b The refrigerant lines are retained to the compressor by a single bolt

14.4 Typical compressor mounting details

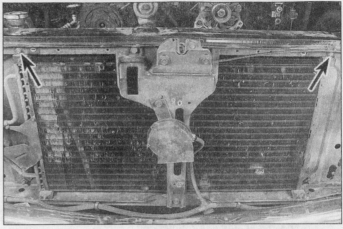

15.5 Remove the condenser mounting brackets (arrows)

3   Remove the drivebelt (refer to Chapter 1).

4   Remove the compressor-to-bracket bolts **(see illustration)** and nuts and lift the compressor from the engine compartment.

Installation

5   Place the compressor in position on the bracket and install the nuts and bolts finger-tight. Once all the compressor mounting nuts and bolts are installed, tighten them securely.

6   Install the drivebelt (see Chapter 1).

7   Connect the wire harness to the compressor. Install the line fitting bolt to the compressor, using new O-rings lubricated with clean refrigeration oil, and tighten it securely.

8   Connect the cable to the negative terminal of the battery.

9   Take the vehicle to a dealer service department or service station and have the system evacuated and recharged.

---

15 Air conditioning condenser - removal and installation

Refer to illustration 15.5

Warning: *The air conditioning system is under high pressure. Do NOT loosen any fittings or remove any components until after the system has been discharged. Air conditioning refrigerant should be properly discharged into an EPA-approved container at a dealership service department or an air conditioning repair facility. Always wear eye protection when disconnecting air conditioning system fittings.*

1   Disconnect the negative cable from the battery.

2   Remove the grille assembly (see Chapter 11).

3   Remove the hood latch and vertical support.

4   Disconnect the refrigerant line fittings. Be sure to use a back-up wrench to prevent damage to the fittings.

5   Remove the condenser mounting brackets **(see illustration)**.

6   Lift the condenser from the vehicle.

7   Installation is the reverse of removal.

8   Have the system evacuated, recharged and leak tested by the shop that discharged it.

---

16 Air conditioning accumulator - removal and installation

Refer to illustration 16.3

Warning: *The air conditioning system is under high pressure. Do NOT loosen any fittings or remove any components until after the system has been discharged. Air conditioning refrigerant should be properly discharged into an EPA-approved container at a dealership service department or an air conditioning repair facility. Always wear eye protection when disconnecting air conditioning system fittings.*

Removal

1   Disconnect the negative cable from the battery.

2   Disconnect the accumulator inlet and outlet lines. Cap or plug the open lines immediately.

3   Remove the accumulator mounting bolts and detach the accumulator assembly **(see illustration)**.

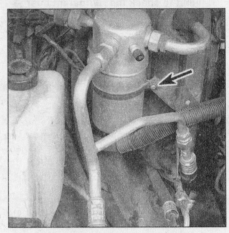

16.3 Remove the accumulator bracket bolts

Installation

4   Check the amount of oil in the old accumulator and add this amount plus the following amount of fresh refrigerant oil to the new accumulator:

a) *1988 through 1994 models: plus 2 ounces of 525 viscosity refrigerant oil.*

b) *1995 models: plus 3.5 ounces of polyalkaline glycol (PAG) refrigerant oil.*

5   Place the new accumulator into position, install the mounting bolts and tighten them securely.

6   Install the inlet and outlet lines, using clean 525 viscosity refrigerant oil on the new O-rings.

7   Connect the cable to the negative terminal of the battery.

8   Have the system evacuated and recharged by a dealer service department or service station.

Chapter 4
Fuel and exhaust systems

Contents

Specifications

Fuel pressure

1988 through 1995 models
V6 and small block V8 engines ... 9 to 13 psi
7.4L V8 engine ... 26 to 32 psi
1996 and later models
V6 and small block V8 engines ... 60 to 66 psi
7.4L V8 engine ... 56 to 62 psi

Fuel injector resistance

TBI systems ... 1.16 to 1.36 ohms
Central SFI systems ... 1.37 to 1.77 ohms
MPFI systems ... 11.4 to 12.6 ohms

Torque specifications

Ft-lbs (unless otherwise indicated)

TBI components
Throttle body mounting nuts ... 12
Fuel inlet nut ... 30
Fuel outlet nut ... 21
Central SFI components
Fuel meter bolts ... 88 in-lb
Inlet pipe nuts ... 22
Fuel line bracket bolt ... 53 in-lbs
Fuel pipe retainer nuts ... 27 in-lbs
MPFI components
Fuel rail bolts ... 89 in-lbs
Fuel pipe nuts ... 20
Fuel tank strap nuts ... 33

Component location - TBI Systems

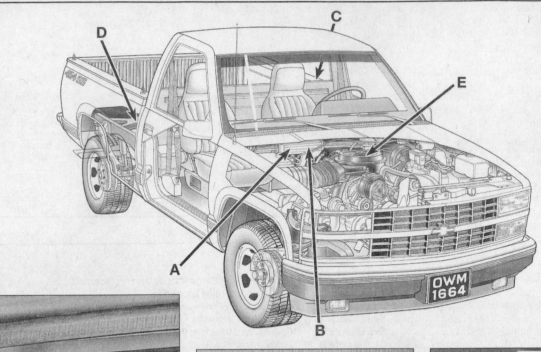

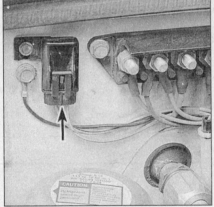

A - The fuel pump fuse and fuse holder are typically located in the engine compartment on the passengers side fire wall under the relay cover

B - The fuel pump relay is typically located in the engine compartment on the passengers side fire wall under the relay cover

C - The fuel filter is typically located in the rear of the truck on the driver's side frame rail

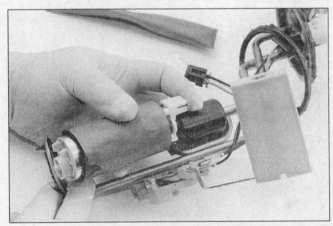

D - The fuel pump is located in the fuel tank

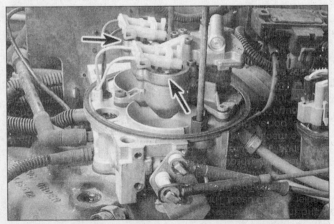

E - The fuel injectors are located under the air cleaner in the throttle body (arrows) (TBI models)

1 General information

Warning: *Gasoline is extremely flammable, so take extra precautions when you work on any part of the fuel system. Don't smoke or allow open flames or bare light bulbs near the work area, and don't work in a garage where a natural gas-type appliance (such as a water heater or a clothes dryer) is present. Since gasoline is carcinogenic, wear latex gloves when there's a possibility of being exposed to fuel, and, if you spill any fuel on your skin, rinse it off immediately with soap and water. Mop up any spills immediately and do not store fuel-soaked rags where they could ignite. The fuel system is under constant pressure, so, if any fuel lines are to be disconnected, the fuel pressure in the system must be relieved first. When you perform any kind of work on the fuel system, wear safety glasses and have a Class B type fire extinguisher on hand.*

Fuel system

The fuel system consists of a fuel tank, an electric fuel pump, a fuel pump relay, fuel lines and the fuel injection system. All 1995 and earlier models use a Throttle Body Injection (TBI) system. The throttle body system utilizes two injectors, mounted in a carburetor-like housing (throttle body). Fuel is sprayed under pressure into a conventional-type intake manifold where it is delivered to the intake ports. Big block 7.4L engines (1988 through 1995) are equipped with a heavy duty fuel pump to increase fuel pressure to the TBI unit. **Note:** *1997 through 2000 models are equipped with a fuel pump/fuel level sending unit module that is serviced as a complete unit.*

1996 and later V6, 5.0L and 5.7L V8 models use a Central Sequential Fuel Injection (Central SFI) system and 1996 and later 7.4L V8 models use a Multi-Port Sequential Fuel Injection system (MPFI).

On the Central SFI system, the throttle body is located on top of the upper intake manifold. The centrally located fuel meter body is mounted in the space between the upper and lower manifolds. The injector unit consists of six (V6 models) or eight (V8 models) fuel injectors connected by hoses to poppet nozzles at each cylinder.

The MPFI system used on 1996 and later 7.4L engines uses a plastic fuel rail assembly mounted to the lower intake manifold. Fuel flows through the fuel rail to the eight injectors that are attached to the fuel rail. A fuel pressure regulator, which is also attached to the fuel rail, regulates fuel pressure in the rail by returning some of the fuel directly to the fuel tank when lower pressure is desired (such as at idle or cruise). A Schraeder-valve-type test port allows a fuel pressure gauge to be connected directly to the fuel rail for diagnosis. The throttle body is mounted on the upper intake manifold.

On all models, the injectors are essentially electrical solenoids. Fuel is delivered to each injector at a constant pressure level determined by a fuel pressure regulator and excess fuel is returned to the fuel tank. A signal from the PCM opens the injector, allowing fuel to spray into the throttle body or intake port. The amount of time the injector is held open determines the air/fuel mixture ratio.

Fuel is circulated from the fuel tank to the fuel injection system, and back to the fuel tank, through a pair of metal lines running along the under side of the vehicle. An electric fuel pump is attached to the fuel level sending unit inside the fuel tank. To reduce the likelihood of vapor lock, a vapor return system routes all vapors and hot fuel back to the fuel tank through a separate return line.

Exhaust system

The exhaust system includes an exhaust manifold equipped with an oxygen sensor, a catalytic converter, an exhaust pipe and a muffler.

The catalytic converter is an emission control device added to the exhaust system to reduce pollutants. Refer to Chapter 6 for more information regarding the catalytic converter.

2 Fuel pressure relief procedure

Warning: *See the* **Warning** *in Section 1.*
Note: *After the fuel pressure has been relieved, it's a good idea to lay a shop towel over any fuel connection to be disassembled to absorb the residual fuel that may leak out when servicing the fuel system.*

1   Before servicing any fuel system component, you must relieve the fuel pressure to minimize the risk of fire and personal injury.
2   Remove the fuel filler cap – this will relieve any pressure built up in the tank.
3   Disconnect the cable from the negative battery terminal. **Caution:** *On models equipped with the Theftlock audio system, be sure the lockout feature is turned off before performing any procedure which requires disconnecting the battery (see the front of this manual).*
4   Throttle Body Injection models (1988 through 1995) have an internal constant bleed feature which relieves the fuel system pressure when the engine is off. No further steps are required.
5   On Central SFI and MPFI engines (1996 through 2000), locate the test port on the fuel inlet line or fuel rail (see Section 3). Remove the cap and connect a fuel pressure gauge, equipped with a bleed-off valve and drain tube, to the test port. Relieve the fuel pressure by bleeding the fuel through the bleed-off valve and into an approved fuel container.
6   Place shop towels around the fuel fitting to be disconnected to absorb any residual fuel that may spill out.
7   After servicing is complete, reconnect the negative battery cable.

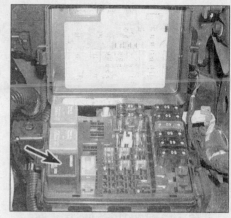

3.3 Location of the fuel pump relay (V8 Central SFI model shown)

3 Fuel pump/fuel pressure - check

Warning: *See the* **Warning** *in Section 1.*

Preliminary check

Refer to illustration 3.3

1   If you suspect insufficient fuel delivery, first inspect all fuel lines to ensure that the problem is not simply a leak in a line.
2   Set the parking brake and have an assistant turn the ignition switch to the ON position while you listen to the fuel pump (inside the fuel tank). You should hear a "whirring" sound, lasting for approximately two seconds, indicating the fuel pump is operating. If the fuel pump is operating, proceed to the pressure check.
3   If there is no sound, turn the ignition key Off and remove the cover from the underhood electrical center. Locate the fuel pump relay. The fuel pump relay is located on the passenger's side firewall under the relay cover in the engine compartment on 1988 through 1995 models or with the fuses and relays in the convenience center in the engine compartment on 1996 through 2000 models **(see illustration)**. Check for battery voltage to the relay using the wiring schematics at the end of Chapter 12. Also, test the relay (see Chapter 12).
4   If the fuses and relay are good, check the fuel pump relay control circuit from the relay to the ECM/PCM. If the circuit is good, have the ECM/PCM diagnosed by a dealer service department or other qualified repair shop.
5   If power is present at the fuel pump connector and the fuel pump does not operate when connected, replace the fuel pump.

Pressure check

Refer to illustrations 3.7a, 3.7b and 3.7c
Note 1: *In order to perform the fuel pressure test, you will need a fuel pressure gauge capable of measuring high fuel pressure. The fuel gauge must be equipped with the proper fitting required to attach it to the test port. To test the fuel pressure regulator, a fuel shut off valve must be installed in the fuel return line with the necessary adapters.*

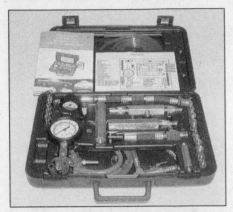

3.7a This aftermarket fuel pressure testing kit contains all the necessary fittings and adapters, along with the fuel pressure gauge, to test most automotive fuel systems

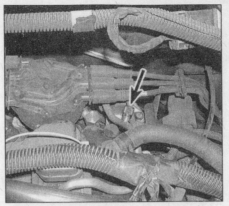

3.7b Fuel pressure test port location on V6 Central SFI models

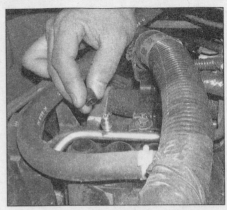

3.7c Fuel pressure test port location on V8 Central SFI models

Note 2: *Some models are equipped with an oil pressure/fuel pump switch. If the oil pressure drops below the specified oil pressure level, the oil pressure switch will act as a fuel pressure cut-off device. Be sure to check the oil pressure switch (Chapter 2) and circuit (Chapter 12 wiring diagrams) in the event of a difficult problem diagnosing the fuel pump circuit.*

6   Relieve the fuel pressure (see Section 2).
7   Install a fuel pressure gauge.
   a) On TBI systems, install a T-fitting between the TBI unit and the inlet fuel line and attach a fuel pressure gauge
   b) On Central SFI and MPFI systems, remove the cap from the fuel pressure test port and attach a fuel pressure gauge **(see illustrations)**.
8   Turn the ignition key On (engine not running); the fuel pump should run for approximately two seconds then shut off. Note the pressure indicated on the gauge and compare your reading with the pressure listed in this Chapter's Specifications. Cycle the ignition key On and Off several times, if necessary, to obtain the highest reading.
9   If the fuel pressure is lower than specified, turn the ignition key Off and relieve the fuel system pressure. Install a fuel shut-off valve in the fuel return line and close the valve. **Caution:** *Do not pinch the flexible fuel line shut or damage to the fuel line may occur.* Turn the ignition key On and note the fuel pressure. **Caution:** *Do not allow the fuel pressure to rise above 75 psi or damage to the fuel pressure regulator may occur.* If the fuel pressure is now above the specified pressure, replace the fuel pressure regulator. If the fuel pressure is lower than specified, check the fuel lines and the fuel filter for restrictions. If no restriction is found, remove the fuel pump (see Section 7) and check the fuel strainer for restrictions, check the fuel flex pipe for leaks and check the fuel pump wiring for high resistance. If no problems are found, replace the fuel pump.
10   If the fuel pressure recorded in Step 8 is higher than specified, check the fuel return line for restrictions. If no restrictions are

found, replace the fuel pressure regulator.
11   If the fuel pressure is within specifications, start the engine. **Warning:** *Make sure the fuel pressure gauge hose is positioned away from the engine drivebelt before starting the engine.* With the engine running, the fuel pressure should be 3 to 10 psi below the pressure recorded in Step 8. If it isn't, remove the vacuum hose from the fuel pressure regulator (except TBI models) and verify there is 12 to 14 in-Hg of vacuum present at the hose. If vacuum is not present at the hose, check the hose for a restriction or a broken hose. If vacuum is present, reconnect the hose to the fuel pressure regulator. If the fuel pressure regulator does not decrease the fuel pressure with vacuum applied, replace the fuel pressure regulator. **Note:** *On TBI systems, the fuel pressure regulator cannot be accessed without some disassembly. Therefore the fuel pressure regulator vacuum check cannot be performed.*
12   Turn the engine off and monitor the fuel pressure for five minutes. The fuel pressure should not drop more than 5 psi within five minutes. If it does, there is a leak in the fuel line, a fuel injector is leaking or the fuel pump module check valve is defective. To determine if the fuel injectors are leaking, cycle the ignition key On and Off several times to obtain the highest fuel pressure reading, then immediately shut-off both the fuel supply and return lines. If the pressure drops below 5 psi within five minutes, a fuel injector (or injectors) is leaking (or the fuel line or fuel rail may be leaking, but such a leak would be very apparent). If the fuel injectors hold pressure, the main fuel line is leaking or the fuel pump is defective.

4   Fuel lines and fittings - repair and replacement

Refer to illustrations 4.2, 4.10, 4.11a, 4.11b, 4.11c and 4.11d
Warning: *See the* **Warning** *in Section 1.*
1   Always relieve the fuel pressure before servicing fuel lines or fittings (see Section 2).
2   Metal fuel supply and vapor lines extend from the fuel tank to the engine compartment. The lines are secured to the underbody

or frame with plastic retainers **(see illustration)**. Flexible hose connects the metal lines to the fuel tank, fuel filter and fuel rail. Fuel lines must be occasionally inspected for leaks or damage.
3   In the event of any fuel line damage, metal lines may be repaired with steel tubing of the same diameter, provided the correct fittings are used. Flexible lines, on the other hand, must be replaced with factory replacement parts; others may fail from the high pressures of this system. Never repair a damaged section of steel line with rubber hose and hose clamps.
4   If evidence of contamination is found in the system or fuel filter during disassembly, the line should be disconnected and blown out. Check the fuel strainer on the fuel pump module for damage and deterioration.
5   Don't route fuel line or hose within four inches of any part of the exhaust system or within ten inches of the catalytic converter. Fuel line must never be allowed to chafe against the engine, body or frame. A minimum of 1/4-inch clearance must be maintained around a fuel line.
6   When replacing a fuel line, remove all fasteners attaching the fuel line to the vehicle body.
7   Because fuel lines used on fuel-injected vehicles are under high pressure, they require special consideration.

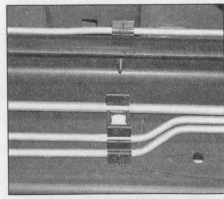

4.2 The metal fuel lines are secured to the underbody with a plastic retainer

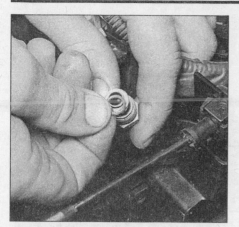

4.10 Always replace fuel line O-rings

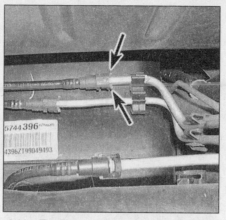

4.11a To disconnect a plastic collar two-tab type fitting, squeeze the two tabs together and pull the lines apart

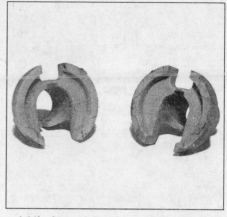

4.11b A special tool (available at most auto parts stores) is required to disconnect the metal collar type fitting

Steel tubing

8   If replacement of a steel fuel line or emission line is called for, use steel tubing meeting the manufacturers specification.

9   Don't use copper or aluminum tubing to replace steel tubing. These materials cannot withstand normal vehicle vibration.

10   Some fuel lines have threaded fittings with O-rings (see illustration). Any time the fittings are loosened to service or replace components:

a) Use a flare-nut wrench on the fitting nut and a backup wrench on the stationary portion of the fitting while loosening and tightening the fittings.

b) Check all O-rings for cuts, cracks and deterioration. Replace any that appear hardened, worn or damaged.

c) If the lines are replaced, always use original equipment parts, or parts that meet the original equipment standards.

Flexible hose

11   There are various methods of disconnecting the fittings, depending upon the type of quick-connect fitting installed on the fuel line (see illustrations). Clean any debris from around the fitting. Disconnect the fitting and carefully remove the fuel line from the vehicle. **Caution:** *The quick-connect fittings are not serviced separately. Do not attempt to repair these types of fuel lines in the event the fitting or line becomes damaged. Replace the entire fuel line as an assembly.*

12   Installation is the reverse of removal with the following additions:

a) *Clean the quick-connect fittings with a lint-free cloth and apply clean engine oil the fittings.*

b) *After connecting a quick-connect fitting, check the integrity of the connection by attempting to pull the lines apart.*

c) *Use new O-rings at the threaded fittings (if equipped).*

d) *Cycle the ignition key On and Off several times and check for leaks at the fitting, before starting the engine.*

5   Fuel tank - removal and installation

Refer to illustrations 5.6, 5.9 and 5.10
Warning: *See the* **Warning** *in Section 1.*

Note: *If necessary, clean the fuel tank and areas surrounding the fuel lines and hoses to prevent contaminating the fuel system.*

1   Remove the fuel tank filler cap to relieve fuel tank pressure.

2   Relieve the fuel system pressure (see Section 2).

3   Disconnect the cable from the negative battery terminal. **Caution:** *On models equipped with the Theftlock audio system, be sure the lockout feature is turned off before performing any procedure which requires disconnecting the battery (see the front of this manual).*

4   Using a siphoning kit (available at most auto parts stores), siphon the fuel into an approved gasoline container. **Warning:** *Do not start the siphoning action by mouth!*

5   Raise the vehicle and support it securely on jackstands.

6   Disconnect the clamp from the fuel filler pipe near the fuel tank and separate the filler pipe (see illustration).

7   Disconnect the fuel pump harness connectors from the pump, if accessible.

8   Remove the fuel tank shield (if equipped) from the bottom of the fuel tank.

4.11c To disconnect a metal collar type fitting, remove the safety tether (arrow) from the fitting . . .

4.11d . . . place the tool over the fuel line, insert it squarely into the fitting and pull the lines apart (the tool is not required to connect the lines)

5.6 Loosen the hose clamps and disconnect the fuel filler and vent hoses (arrows) from the fuel tank

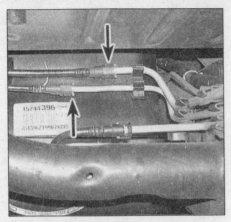

5.9 Disconnect the fuel supply and return lines (arrows)

Note: *Some models are equipped with an off-road fuel tank shield that covers the fuel tank straps while others are equipped with fuel tank shields installed between the straps and the tank.*

9   Disconnect the fuel supply and return lines (see Section 4) **(see illustration)**.
10   Position a transmission jack under the fuel tank and support the tank. Remove the fuel tank strap bolts and remove the straps **(see illustration)**.
11   On 1997 and later models, lower the tank slightly and disconnect the electrical connectors from the fuel pump module.
12   Lower the jack and remove the tank from the vehicle.
13   Installation is the reverse of removal.

6   Fuel tank cleaning and repair - general information

1   Cleaning and repair of the fuel tank (due to fuel contamination) should be performed by a professional with the proper training to carry out this critical and potentially danger-ous work. Even after cleaning and flushing, explosive fumes may remain inside the fuel tank.
2   If the fuel tank is removed from the vehi-cle, it should not be placed in an area where sparks or open flames could ignite the fumes coming out of the tank. Be especially careful inside a garage where a natural gas-type appliance is located.

7   Fuel pump - removal and installation

Warning: *See the* **Warning** *in Section 1.*
Note: *On later model vehicles equipped with dual fuel tanks, a balance pump is used to connect the two tanks. This pump operates at about 7 psi and fills the front tank as needed from the rear. It is located on the left frame rail.*

1   Disconnect the cable from the negative battery terminal **Caution:** *On models*

5.10 Remove the fuel tank retaining strap bolts (arrows)

equipped with the Theftlock audio system, be sure the lockout feature is turned off before performing any procedure which requires dis-connecting the battery (see the front of this manual).
2   Relieve the fuel pressure (see Section 2) and remove the fuel tank (see Section 5).

1988 through 1996 models

Refer to illustration 7.4

3   The fuel pump/sending unit assembly is located inside the fuel tank. It's held in place by a cam lockring mechanism.
4   To unlock the fuel pump/sending unit assembly, turn the lockring counterclockwise with a hammer and a brass punch **(see illus-tration)**. **Warning:** *DO NOT use a steel punch to knock the lockring loose. A spark could cause an explosion.*
5   Carefully extract the fuel pump/sending unit assembly from the tank. **Caution:** *The fuel level float and sending unit are delicate. Don't bump them into the lockring during removal or the accuracy of the sending unit may be affected.*
6   Check the condition of the seal around the mouth of the lockring mechanism. If it's dried out, cracked or deteriorated, replace it.
7   Inspect the strainer on the lower end of the fuel pump. If it's dirty, remove it, clean it with solvent and blow it out with compressed air. If it's too dirty to be cleaned, replace it.

7.4 Use a brass punch to tap the lock ring counterclockwise until the tabs align with the recessed areas of the fuel tank

8   If you have to separate the fuel pump and sending unit, pull the fuel pump into the rubber connector and slide the pump away from the bottom support. Care should be taken to prevent damage to the rubber insu-lator and fuel strainer during removal. After the pump clears the bottom support, pull it out of the rubber connector for removal.
9   Insert the fuel pump/sending unit assembly into the fuel tank. Turn the lockring clockwise until the locking cam is fully engaged by the retaining tangs.
10   The remainder of installation is the reverse of removal.

1997 through 2000 models

Refer to illustrations 7.11, 7.12 and 7.13

11   Disconnect the fuel lines and electrical connectors from the fuel pump module **(see illustration)**.
12   While prying the locking tab out, rotate the fuel pump module retaining ring counter-clockwise until it's loose **(see illustration)**.
13   Remove the fuel pump module from the tank **(see illustration)**. Angle the assembly slightly to avoid damaging the fuel level send-ing unit float. **Warning:** *Some fuel may remain in the module reservoir and spill as the module is removed. Have several shop towels ready and a drain pan nearby to place the module in.*
14   The electric fuel pump is not serviced

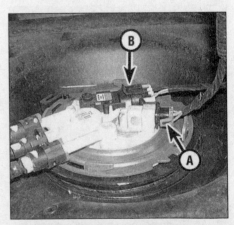

7.11 Lower the fuel tank and disconnect the fuel pump/fuel level sending unit (A) and fuel tank pressure sensor (B) electrical connectors from the fuel pump module

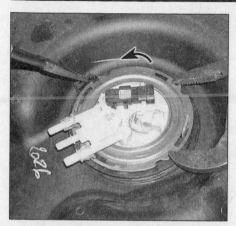

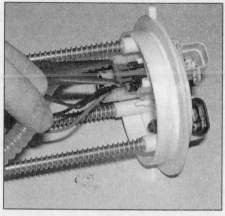

7.12 Release the locking tab and loosen the fuel pump module retaining ring by rotating it counterclockwise

7.13 Carefully remove the fuel pump module from the tank and drain the fuel from the reservoir

8.11 Disconnect the fuel pump/fuel level sending unit electrical connector from the fuel pump module

separately. In the event of failure, the complete assembly must be replaced. Transfer the fuel pressure sensor and fuel level sending unit to the new fuel pump module assembly, if necessary (see Section 8).

15   Clean the fuel tank sealing surface and install a new seal on the fuel pump module.

16   Install the fuel pump module, aligning the fuel line fittings with the fuel lines.

17   Press the fuel pump module down until seated and install the retaining ring. Make sure the retaining ring is fully seated and the locking tab is engaged with the slot.

8   Fuel level sending unit - check and replacement

Warning: *See the **Warning** in Section 1.*

Check

1   Remove the fuel tank and the fuel level sending unit (1988 through 1996) or the fuel pump module (1997 through 2000) (see Sections 5 and 7).

2   Connect the probes of an ohmmeter to the fuel level sensor terminals of the fuel pump electrical connector. Refer to the wiring

diagrams at the end of Chapter 12 for the appropriate terminals.

3   Position the float in the down (empty) position and note the reading on the ohmmeter.

4   Move the float up to the full position while watching the meter.

5   If the fuel level sending unit resistance does not change smoothly as the float travels from empty to full, replace the fuel level sending unit assembly.

Replacement

1988 through 1996 models

6   Remove the fuel tank and the fuel pump/fuel level sending unit (see Sections 5 and 7).

7   Remove the sending unit harness connector.

8   Remove the sending unit mounting screws. Separate the sending unit from the frame of the fuel pump/sending unit assembly.

9   Installation is the reverse of removal.

1997 through 2000 models

Refer to illustrations 8.11, 8.12 and 8.13

10   Remove the fuel tank and the fuel pump

module (see Sections 5 and 7).

11   Disconnect the fuel level sending unit electrical connector from the module cover **(see illustration)**.

12   Remove the sending unit retaining clip **(see illustration)**.

13   Pinch the tabs together and slide the fuel level sending unit off the module **(see illustration)**. Note the routing of the wiring for installation.

14   Installation is the reverse of removal.

9   Air filter housing - removal and installation

Note: *TBI systems are equipped with the conventional style air cleaner housing mounted directly on top of the throttle body. Refer to Chapter 1 for additional illustrations.*
Refer to illustrations 9.2, 9.3, 9.4 and 9.5

1   Disconnect the electrical connector from the mass airflow sensor.

2   Disconnect the hold down clips **(see illustration)** and remove the air filter housing cover.

3   Grasp the air filter and twist while pulling

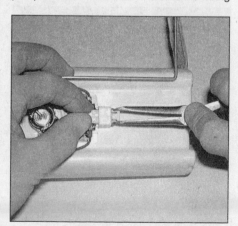

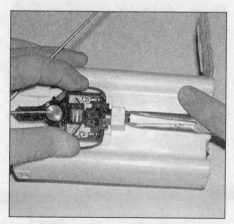

8.12 Remove the sending unit retaining clip

8.13 Pinch the tabs together and remove the fuel level sending unit from module

9.2 Release the hold down clips (arrows) (central SFI model shown)

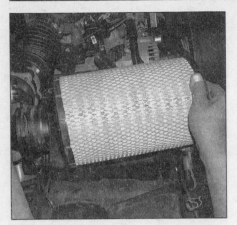

9.3 Twist air filter off housing duct while holding air filter housing

9.4 The bolt is accessed from the fenderwell area

9.5 On Central SFI V6 models, remove the wing nut (arrow) and tilt the resonator forward to detach the clip from the throttle body

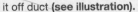

it off duct (see illustration).

4   Remove the bolt from the fenderwell area directly under air filter housing (see illustration).

5   Depress the tabs on the locking clip under the air filter housing to release the assembly. Pivot the air filter housing and separate it from duct.

6   Installation is the reverse of removal.

10 Accelerator cable - replacement

Refer to illustrations 10.4, 10.5 and 10.6

1   Disconnect the cable from the negative battery terminal. Caution: On models equipped with the Theftlock audio system, be sure the lockout feature is turned off before performing any procedure which requires disconnecting the battery (see the front of this manual).

2   Access the throttle body:

a) On TBI systems, remove the air filter assembly from the TBI unit

b) On Central SFI and MPFI systems, remove the air intake duct and resonator from the throttle body (see Section 9).

3   Detach the cruise control cable from the

throttle lever, if equipped.

4   Rotate the throttle lever and separate the accelerator cable end from the throttle lever (see illustration).

5   Depress the locking tabs on the cable housing and push the cable housing through the bracket. Detach the cable from the cable routing retainers (see illustration).

6   Remove the trim panel from under the dash and detach the cable from the accelerator pedal (see illustration).

7   Depress the locking tabs on the cable housing and push the cable through the firewall and into the engine compartment.

8   Remove the cable from the engine compartment.

9   Installation is the reverse of removal.

11 Fuel injection systems - general information

Electronic fuel injection provides optimum fuel/air mixture ratios at all stages of combustion and offers better throttle response characteristics than carburetion. It also enables the engine to run at the leanest possible fuel/air mixture ratio, greatly reduc-

ing the exhaust gas emissions.

The fuel injection systems consist of three sub-systems: air intake, engine control and fuel delivery. The system uses an Electronic Control Module (1988 through 1995) or a Powertrain Control Module (PCM) (1996 through 2000) along with the sensors (coolant temperature sensor (ECT), throttle position sensor (TPS), manifold absolute pressure sensor (MAP), oxygen sensor (O2), etc) to determine the proper air/fuel ratio under all operating conditions.

The fuel injection system and the engine control system is closely linked in function and design. For additional information, refer to Chapter 6.

Throttle Body Injection (TBI) systems

All 1995 and earlier models use a Throttle Body Injection (TBI) system. All TBI models employ a twin-injector throttle body injection (TBI) unit known as the Model 220. The TBI system is controlled by an Electronic Control Module (ECM), which monitors engine performance and adjusts the fuel/air

10.4 Rotate the throttle lever and pass the cable through the slot in the throttle lever

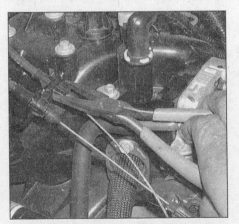

10.5 Depress the locking tabs and remove the cable from the bracket

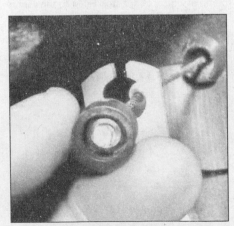

10.6 Pull the accelerator cable retainer out of the pedal and slide the cable through the slot

12.7 On MPFI models, use a stethoscope to determine if the injectors are working properly - they should make a steady clicking sound that rises and falls with engine speed changes

12.8 Measure the resistance of each injector across the two terminals of the injector (MPFI model shown)

mixture accordingly during all engine operating conditions. Models with the big block 7.4L engine are equipped with a heavy duty fuel pump that allows increased fuel pressure to the TBI unit for heavy load applications. Excess fuel is returned to the fuel tank by a separate fuel return line.

Central Sequential Fuel Injection (Central SFI) systems

1996 and later V6, 5.0L and 5.7L V8 models use a Central Sequential Fuel Injection (Central SFI) system. The Central SFI fuel meter body and injector assembly is housed between the upper and lower intake manifolds. It is controlled by the Powertrain Control Module (PCM). The Central SFI unit consists of six (V6 models) or eight (V8 models) fuel injectors which supply fuel through the individual hoses to the poppet valves located at each cylinder port. The throttle body is located on top of the upper intake manifold.

Multi Port Fuel Injection (MPFI) systems

1996 and later 7.4L V8 models use a Multi-Port Sequential Fuel Injection system (MPFI). Multi Port Fuel Injection (MPFI) systems are equipped with a throttle body that is mounted on the side of the upper intake manifold. A plastic fuel rail and eight fuel injectors are mounted in the lower intake manifold. The injectors are solenoid-actuated pintle types consisting of a solenoid, plunger, needle valve and housing. When current is applied to the solenoid coil, the needle valve raises and pressurized fuel sprays out the nozzle. The injection quantity is determined by the length of time the valve is open (the length of time during which current is supplied to the solenoid coils).

Air intake system

The air intake system consists of the air filter, the air intake ducts, the throttle body and the intake manifold. Central SFI and

MPFI models are equipped with an upper and a lower intake manifold.

When the engine is idling, the air/fuel ratio is controlled by the idle air control system, which consists of the on-board computer and the idle air control valve. This idle air control regulates the amount of airflow past the throttle plate and into the intake manifold, thus increasing or decreasing the engine idle speed. The on-board computer receives information from the sensors (vehicle speed, coolant temperature, air conditioning, power steering mode etc.) and adjusts the idle according to the demands of the engine and driver. Refer to Chapter 6 for information on the idle air control valve.

Emissions and engine control system

The emissions and engine control system is described in detail in Chapter 6.

Fuel delivery system

The fuel delivery system consists of these components: the fuel pump, the fuel pressure regulator, the fuel meter body (Central SFI) or fuel rail (MPFI) and the fuel injectors.

The fuel pump is an electric type. Fuel is drawn through an inlet screen into the pump, flows through the one-way valve, passes through the fuel filter and is delivered to the fuel meter body/fuel rail and injectors. The pressure regulator maintains a constant fuel pressure to the injectors. Excess fuel is routed back to the fuel tank through the fuel pressure regulator.

The fuel pump relay is located on the passenger's side firewall under the relay cover in the engine compartment on 1988 through 1995 models or with the fuses and relays in the convenience center in the engine compartment on 1996 through 2000 models. The ECM/PCM controls the relay by supplying battery voltage to the relay coil. When energized, the fuel pump relay connects battery voltage to the fuel pump.

12 Fuel injection system - check

Refer to illustrations 12.7, 12.8 and 12.10
Note: *The following procedure is based on the assumption that the fuel pressure is adequate (see Section 3).*

1   Check all electrical connectors that are related to the system. Check the ground wire connections for tightness. Loose connectors and poor grounds can cause many problems that resemble more serious malfunctions.

2   Check to see that the battery is fully charged, as the control unit and sensors depend on an accurate supply voltage in order to properly meter the fuel.

3   Check the air filter element - a dirty or partially blocked filter will severely impede performance and economy (see Chapter 1).

4   Check the related fuses. If a blown fuse is found, replace it and see if it blows again. If it does, search for a wire shorted to ground in the harness.

5   Check the air intake duct from the air filter housing to the throttle body for leaks, which will result in an excessively lean mixture. Also check the condition of all vacuum hoses connected to the intake manifold and/or throttle body.

6   Remove the air intake duct from the throttle body and check for dirt, carbon or other residue build-up on the throttle bore and throttle plate. If it's dirty, clean it with carburetor cleaner spray, a toothbrush and a shop towel. **Caution:** *Do not use a solvent containing Methyl Ethyl Ketone or damage to the throttle body may occur.*

7   On MPFI systems, start the engine and place an automotive stethoscope against each injector, one at a time, and listen for a clicking sound, indicating operation **(see illustration)**. If you don't have a stethoscope, place the tip of a screwdriver against the injector and listen through the handle.

8   On TBI and MPFI systems, disconnect the injector(s) electrical connector(s) and measure the resistance of each injector **(see illustration)**. Compare the measurements

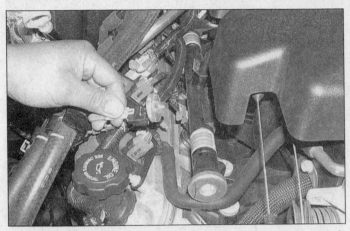

12.10 Install the "noid" light (available at most auto parts stores) into each injector electrical connector and confirm that it blinks when the engine is cranking

13.8 When disconnecting the fuel feed and return lines, be sure to use a back-up wrench to prevent damage to the lines

with the resistance values listed in this Chapter's Specifications. **Note:** *On Central SFI models, disconnect the fuel injector harness main connector at the fuel meter body and perform the tests there. Refer to the wiring diagrams at the end of Chapter 12 for additional information.*

9   Turn the ignition key On and check for battery voltage to the injector(s) at the injector harness connectors. If battery voltage is not present, check the fuel injector fuse and related wiring (see Chapter 12).

10   On TBI and MPFI models, install an injector test light ("noid" light) into each injector electrical connector, one at a time **(see illustration)**. Crank the engine over. Confirm that the light flashes evenly on each connector. This tests the ECM/PCM control of the injectors. If the light does not flash, have the ECM/PCM checked at a dealer service department or other properly equipped repair facility. **Note:** *On Central SFI models, disconnect the fuel injector harness main connector at the fuel meter body and perform the tests there. Refer to the wiring diagrams at the end of Chapter 12 for additional information.*

11   The remainder of the engine control system checks can be found in Chapter 6.

13   Throttle Body Injection (TBI) unit - component replacement

Warning: *See the* **Warning** *in Section 1.*
Note: *Because of its relative simplicity, the throttle body assembly doesn't have to be removed from the intake manifold or disassembled for component replacement. However, for the sake of clarity, the following procedures are shown with the TBI assembly removed from the vehicle.*

1   Relieve the fuel system pressure (see Section 2).

2   Disconnect the cable from the negative battery terminal. **Caution:** *On models equipped with the Theftlock audio system, be sure the lockout feature is turned off before performing any procedure which requires disconnecting the battery (see the front of this manual).*

Throttle body unit

Refer to illustrations 13.8 and 13.9
Note: *The fuel injectors, pressure regulator, throttle position sensor and idle air control valve can be replaced without removing the throttle body assembly.*

3   Remove the air cleaner housing.

4   Unplug the electrical connectors from the idle air control valve, throttle position sensor and fuel injectors.

5   Remove the wiring harness and insulating grommet from the throttle body.

6   Remove the throttle linkage and return spring, transmission control and cruise control cables (if applicable).

7   Using pieces of numbered tape, mark all of the vacuum hoses to the throttle body and disconnect them.

8   Disconnect the fuel inlet and return lines. Use a back-up wrench on the inlet and return fitting nuts to prevent damage to the throttle body and fuel lines **(see illustration)**. Remove the fuel line nut O-rings and discard them.

9   Remove the TBI assembly mounting bolts and lift the unit off the intake manifold **(see illustration)**. Stuff a rag into the intake manifold opening and carefully scrape all traces of old gasket material off the intake manifold and throttle body mating surfaces. Scrape carefully so you don't damage the delicate aluminum surfaces.

10   Installation is the reverse of the removal procedure.

11   Be sure to install a new throttle body-to-intake manifold gasket and new fuel line O-rings

12   Tighten the mounting bolts to the torque listed in the beginning of this chapter.

13   Turn the ignition switch On, without starting the engine, and check for fuel leaks.

14   Check to see if the accelerator pedal is free by depressing it to the floor and releasing it (with the ignition switch off).

Component replacement

15   Remove the air cleaner housing assembly, adapter and gaskets (see Chapter 1).

Fuel meter cover/fuel pressure regulator assembly

Refer to illustrations 13.17, 13.18 and 13.19
Note: *The fuel pressure regulator is housed in the fuel meter cover. Whether you are replacing the meter cover or the regulator itself, the entire assembly must be replaced. The regu-*

13.9 To detach the throttle body from the intake manifold, remove the bolts (arrows)

13.17 Unscrew the five cover
retaining screws

13.18 Carefully peel away the old outlet passage and cover
gaskets with a razor blade

13.19 DO NOT remove the four pressure
regulator screws (arrows) from the fuel
meter cover

13.28 To remove an
injector, slip the tip of a
standard screwdriver
under the lip of the lug on
top of the injector and,
using another screwdriver
as a fulcrum, carefully pry
the injector up and out

lator must not be removed from the cover.
16   Unplug the electrical connectors to the
fuel injectors.
17   Remove the cover screws (see illustration) and detach the fuel meter cover.
18   Remove the fuel meter outlet passage
gasket, cover gasket and pressure regulator
seal. Carefully remove old gasket material
that's stuck with a razor blade (see illustration). Caution: *Do not attempt to reuse either
of the gaskets.*
19   Inspect the cover for dirt, foreign material and casting warpage. If it's dirty, clean it
with a shop rag soaked in solvent. Do not
immerse the fuel meter cover in solvent - it
could damage the pressure regulator
diaphragm and gasket. Warning: *Do not
remove the four screws (see illustration)
securing the pressure regulator to the fuel
meter cover. The regulator contains a large
spring under compression which, if accidentally released, could cause injury. Disassembly might also result in a fuel leak between the
diaphragm and the regulator housing. The
new fuel meter cover assembly will include a
new pressure regulator.*
20   Install the new pressure regulator seal,

fuel meter outlet passage gasket and cover
gasket.
21   Install the fuel meter cover assembly
using Loctite 262 or equivalent on the
screws. Note: *The short screws go next to
the injectors.*
22   Attach the electrical connectors to both
injectors.
23   Attach the cable to the negative terminal
of the battery.
24   With the engine off and the ignition on,
check for leaks around the gasket and fuel
line couplings.
25   Install the air cleaner, adapter and gaskets.

Fuel injector assembly

*Refer to illustrations 13.28, 13.33, 13.34,
13.35, 13.36 and 13.37*
26   To unplug the electrical connectors from
the fuel injectors, squeeze the plastic tabs
and pull straight up.
27   Remove the fuel meter cover/pressure
regulator assembly. Note: *Do not remove the
fuel meter cover assembly gasket - leave it in
place to protect the casting from damage
during injector removal.*
28   Use a screwdriver and fulcrum (see
illustration) to pry out the injector.
29   Remove the upper (larger) and lower
(smaller) O-rings and filter from the injector.

30   Remove the steel back-up washer from
the top of the injector cavity.
31   Inspect the fuel injector filter for dirt and
contamination. If present, check for the presence of dirt in the fuel lines and fuel tank.
32   Be sure to replace the fuel injector with
an identical part. Injectors from other models
can fit in the Model 220 TBI assembly but are
calibrated for different flow rates.
33   Slide the new filter into place on the
nozzle of the injector (see illustration).
34   Lubricate the new lower (smaller) O-ring

13.33 Slide the new filter onto the nozzle
of the fuel injector

13.34 Lubricate the lower O-ring with transmission fluid, then place it on the shoulder in the bottom of the injector cavity

13.35 Place the steel back-up washer on the shoulder near the top of the injector cavity

13.36 Lubricate the upper O-ring with transmission fluid, then install it on top of the steel washer

13.37 Make sure the lug is aligned with the groove in the bottom of the fuel injector cavity

13.49 Remove the fuel inlet and outlet nuts from the fuel meter body

with automatic transmission fluid and place it on the small shoulder at the bottom of the fuel injector cavity in the fuel meter body **(see illustration)**.

35   Install the steel back-up washer in the injector cavity **(see illustration)**.

36   Lubricate the new upper (larger) O-ring with automatic transmission fluid and install it on top of the steel back-up washer **(see illustration)**. **Note:** *The back-up washer and large O-ring must be installed before the injector. If they aren't, improper seating of the large O-ring could cause fuel leakage.*

37   To install the injector, align the raised lug on the injector base with the groove in the fuel meter body cavity **(see illustration)**. Push down on the injector until it's fully seated in the fuel meter body. **Note:** *The electrical terminals should be parallel with the throttle shaft.*

38   Install the fuel meter cover assembly and gasket.

39   Attach the cable to the negative terminal of the battery.

40   With the engine off and the ignition on, check for fuel leaks.

41   Attach the electrical connectors to the fuel injectors.

42   Install the air cleaner housing assembly, adapter and gaskets.

Throttle Position Sensor (TPS)

43   For information on the TPS, see Chapter 6.

Idle Air Control (IAC) valve

44   For information on the IAC valve, see Chapter 6.

Fuel meter body assembly

Refer to illustrations 13.49 and 13.51

45   Unplug the electrical connectors from the fuel injectors.

46   Remove the fuel meter cover/pressure regulator assembly, fuel meter cover gasket, fuel meter outlet gasket and pressure regulator seal.

47   Remove the fuel injectors.

48   Unscrew the fuel inlet and return line threaded fittings, detach the lines and remove the O-rings.

49   Remove the fuel inlet and outlet nuts and gaskets from the fuel meter body assembly **(see illustration)**. Note the locations of the

nuts to ensure proper reassembly. The inlet nut has a larger passage than the outlet nut.

50   Remove the gasket from the inner end of each fuel nut.

51   Remove the fuel meter body-to-throttle body screws and detach the fuel meter body from the throttle body **(see illustration)**.

13.51 Once the fuel inlet and outlet nuts are off, pull the fuel meter body straight up to separate it from the throttle body

14.3 Remove the retaining clip and disconnect the electrical connector from the fuel meter body (V6 model shown)

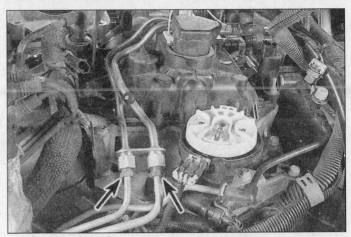

14.4a Disconnect the fuel supply and return lines from the fittings (arrows) (V6 model shown)

14.4b Remove the fuel line nuts and retainers (arrows) and remove the fuel lines from the fuel meter body (V6 model shown)

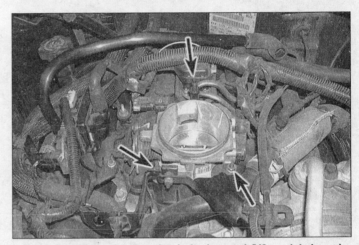

14.10 Throttle body mounting bolts (arrows) (V6 model shown)

52   Install the new throttle body-to-fuel meter body gasket. Match the cut-out portions in the gasket with the openings in the throttle body.

53   Install the fuel meter body on the throttle body. Coat the fuel meter body-to-throttle body screws with thread locking compound before installing them.

54   Install the fuel inlet and outlet nuts, with new gaskets, in the fuel meter body and tighten the nuts to the specified torque. Install the fuel inlet and return line threaded fittings with new O-rings. Use a back-up wrench to prevent the nuts from turning.

55   Install the fuel injectors.

56   Install the fuel meter cover/pressure regulator assembly.

57   Attach the cable to the negative terminal of the battery.

58   Attach the electrical connectors to the fuel injectors.

59   With the engine off and the ignition on, check for leaks around the fuel meter body, the gasket and around the fuel line nuts and threaded fittings.

60   Install the air cleaner housing assembly, adapters and gaskets.

14   Fuel meter body (Central SFI) – component replacement

Warning: *See the* **Warning** *in Section 1.*
Note: *When replacing components of the fuel meter body/injector assembly, refer to the identification numbers on the fuel meter body and injectors. Fuel injectors are calibrated with different flow rates and must not be interchanged with injectors from a different application.*

1   Relieve the fuel system pressure (see Section 2).

2   Disconnect the cable from the negative battery terminal. **Caution:** *On models equipped with the Theftlock audio system, be sure the lockout feature is turned off before performing any procedure which requires disconnecting the battery (see the front of this manual).*

Component replacement

Refer to illustrations 14.3, 14.4a and 14.4b

3   Remove the retaining clip and disconnect the electrical connector from the fuel meter body **(see illustration)**.

4   Disconnect the fuel supply and return lines from the fittings at the rear of the engine **(see illustration)**. Remove the bracket bolt. Loosen the nuts attaching the fuel lines to the fuel meter body and remove the lines **(see illustration)**.

Throttle body

Refer to illustrations 14.10

5   On V8 models, partially drain the cooling system (see Chapter 1).

6   Remove the air intake duct and the resonator (see Section 9).

7   Label and detach the electrical connectors and vacuum hoses from the throttle body.

8   Detach the accelerator cable and bracket from the throttle body (see Section 10).

9   On V8 models, remove the coolant hoses from the throttle body.

10   Remove the mounting bolts **(see illustration)** and separate the throttle body from the air intake plenum.

Upper intake manifold and fuel meter body

Refer to illustrations 14.11, 14.12, 14.13a, 14.13b, 14.14 and 14.15

11   Remove the ignition coil/module assem-

14.11 Upper intake manifold bolt locations (arrows) (upper intake manifold removed for clarity) (V6 model shown)

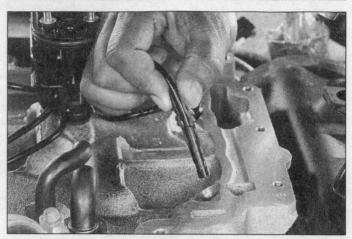

14.12 Squeeze the tabs and pull the poppet nozzle out of the intake manifold

14.13a Using two tools (arrows), pry the locking tabs away from the fuel meter body . . .

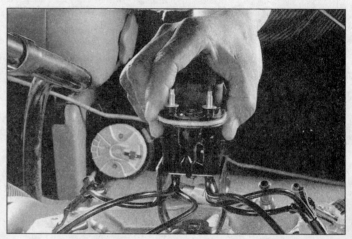

14.13b . . and remove the fuel meter body along with the fuel lines and poppet nozzles from the intake manifold

bly (see Chapter 5). Remove the EVAP purge valve (see Chapter 6). Remove the remaining mounting bolts and carefully remove the upper intake manifold **(see illustration)**.

12   Detach the poppet nozzles by squeezing the tabs together and pulling the nozzle straight out of the intake manifold **(see illus-**

tration). **Note:** *Apply a numbered tag to each nozzle or line with the corresponding cylinder number.*

13   Pry the bracket locking tabs away from the fuel meter body and pull the assembly off the bracket **(see illustrations)**. Place the assembly on a clean work bench.

14   Remove the fuel injector hold-down plate nuts and remove the plate from the fuel meter body **(see illustration)**.

15   While pulling down on the injector tube fitting, push the injector out of the fuel meter body with a dull screwdriver **(see illustration)**. Be careful not to damage the electrical

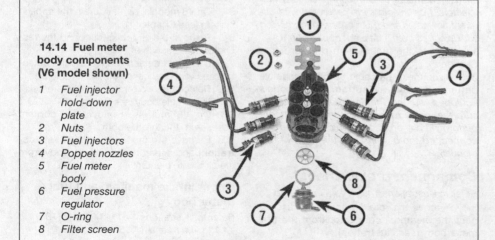

14.14 Fuel meter body components (V6 model shown)

1   Fuel injector hold-down plate
2   Nuts
3   Fuel injectors
4   Poppet nozzles
5   Fuel meter body
6   Fuel pressure regulator
7   O-ring
8   Filter screen

14.15 To remove an injector from the fuel meter body, pull on the tube fitting while pushing the injector out

14.17 Remove the fuel pressure regulator retaining clip (V6 model shown)

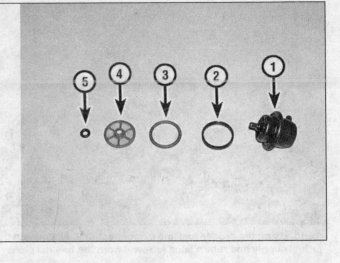

14.18 Fuel pressure regulator components

1 *Fuel pressure regulator*
2 *Back-up ring*
3 *Large O-ring*
4 *Filter disc*
5 *Small O-ring*

terminals. **Caution:** *Do not attempt to remove the fuel line or poppet nozzle from the injector. They are serviced as a complete assembly.*

Fuel pressure regulator

Refer to illustrations 14.17 and 14.18

16 Remove the upper intake manifold for access to the fuel meter body.

17 Remove the pressure regulator retaining clip and detach the fuel pressure regulator **(see illustration)**.

18 Be sure to replace all O-ring seals, lubricating them with a light film of engine oil **(see illustration)**. **Note:** *The small O-ring may remain in the fuel meter body or fuel rail.*

19 Check the filter disc for contamination and clean or replace it as necessary.

20 The remainder of installation is the reverse of removal.

Component installation

21 Replace the injector O-rings. Apply a light coat of clean engine oil to the O-rings and press the injector into the fuel meter body until seated. Make sure the electrical terminals are properly aligned and the fuel tubes and nozzles are properly routed.

22 Install the injector hold-down plate and nuts.

23 Install the fuel meter body onto the intake manifold bracket. Install the poppet nozzles into the intake manifold, snapping them into place. Gently pull up on the fuel tube to ensure the nozzles are properly seated.

24 Inspect the fuel meter body and upper intake manifold seals for damage. Install new seals, if necessary. Install the upper intake manifold. Apply thread locking compound to the upper intake manifold bolts and tighten the bolts to the torque listed in Chapter 2A Specifications. Install the EVAP purge valve and ignition module assembly.

25 Inspect the fuel line O-rings and retainers for damage. Replace the O-rings and retainers, if necessary. Install the fuel lines onto the fuel meter body. Apply thread locking compound to the fuel line bracket bolt and install the bracket.

26 Inspect the throttle body seal for damage. Replace the seal, if necessary and install the throttle body.

27 The remainder of installation is the reverse of removal.

28 After the fuel meter body/injector assembly installation is complete, turn the ignition switch to On, but don't operate the starter (this activates the fuel pump for about two seconds, which builds up fuel pressure in the fuel lines and the fuel meter body). Cycle the ignition On and Off several times, then check the fuel lines and fuel meter body for fuel leakage.

15 Fuel rail and injectors (MPFI) – component replacement

Warning: *See the* **Warning** *in Section 1.*

Caution: *All open fittings, lines and holes must be capped or plugged to prevent dirt from entering the system when any components are removed.*

Note: *When replacing components of the fuel rail and injector assembly, refer to the identification numbers on the injectors. Fuel injectors are calibrated with different flow rates and must not be interchanged with injectors from a different application.*

1 Relieve the fuel system pressure (see Section 2).

2 Disconnect the cable from the negative battery terminal. **Caution:** *On models equipped with the Theftlock audio system, be sure the lockout feature is turned off before performing any procedure which requires disconnecting the battery (see the front of this manual).*

Component replacement

Throttle body

Refer to illustration 15.7

3 Remove the air inlet duct.

4 Remove the wiring connectors from the Idle Air Control (IAC) valve and Throttle Position Sensor (TPS).

5 Detach the accelerator cable and cruise control cable (if equipped) from the throttle body (see Section 10).

6 Remove the accelerator cable bracket.

7 Remove the throttle body bolts and the throttle body **(see illustration)**.

8 Carefully clean the gasket surfaces and install a new gasket. Use aerosol carburetor cleaner and a rag to remove carbon deposits from the bore of the throttle body.

9 Installation is the reverse of removal.

10 Check the accelerator pedal for binding or sticking before starting the engine.

15.7 Throttle body mounting nuts (arrows) (7.4L V8 models)

15.13 Using the proper fuel line disconnect tool, disconnect the fuel supply and return lines (arrows) from the fuel rail pipes

15.15 Pull the retainer up, push in on the tab and disconnect the electrical connector from the fuel injector

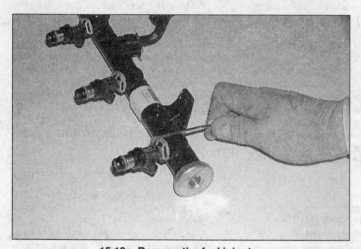

15.19a Remove the fuel injector retaining clip . . .

15.19b . . . and pry the injector out the fuel rail with a forked tool

Fuel rail assembly

Refer to illustrations 15.13, 15.15, 15.19a and 15.19b

11   Remove the distributor (see Chapter 5).

12   Remove the upper intake manifold (see Chapter 2A).

13   Disconnect the fuel supply and return lines **(see illustration)** from the fuel rail (see Section 4).

14   Remove the fuel line bracket bolt and detach the fuel line from the bracket.

15   Disconnect the fuel injector wiring harness from each injector and set the harness aside **(see illustration)**.

16   Remove all five fuel rail retaining bolts.

17   Disconnect the vacuum line at the fuel pressure regulator.

18   Carefully lift the fuel rail up and detach the injectors from the intake manifold ports.

19   To remove the injectors from the fuel rail, remove the injector retaining clip and pull the injector from the fuel rail **(see illustrations)**. Discard the injector retaining clips and install new ones on reassembly.

20   Remove the O-rings from the injectors and discard them. Save the back-up O-rings

and use them on reassembly.

21   Lubricate each O-ring with clean engine oil and install them onto the injectors. Make sure the back-up O-rings are installed first.

22   Install the injectors onto the fuel rail and retain them with a new retaining clip.

23   Install the complete fuel rail assembly onto the manifold. Make sure that the injector electrical connectors face outward.

24   The rest of the installation is the reverse of removal. Install new O-rings on the fuel lines. Refer to Chapter 2A Specifications for the upper intake manifold torque specifications.

Fuel pressure regulator

Refer to illustration 15.28

25   Remove the ignition coil (see Chapter 5).

26   Remove the upper intake manifold (see Chapter 2A).

27   Detach the vacuum line from the fuel pressure regulator.

28   Remove the snap-ring retaining the fuel pressure regulator to the fuel rail **(see illustration)**

29   Place a rag under the regulator to col-

lect the fuel spillage, then twist and pull it out of the fuel rail. Note the locations of the various O-rings and remove them from the regulator.

30   Install new O-rings onto the regulator. Make sure they're in the correct order.

31   Insert the regulator into the fuel rail and

15.28 Remove the fuel pressure regulator retaining clip

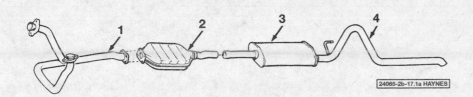

16.1a Exploded view of a typical exhaust system

1   Exhaust crossover pipe
2   Catalytic converter

3   Muffler
4   Exhaust pipe

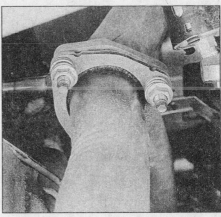

16.1b The exhaust pipe is connected to the exhaust manifold with three spring-loaded nuts

16.1c Here's a typical exhaust system hanger - they should be inspected for cracks and replaced if deteriorated

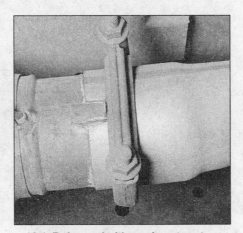

16.4 Before unbolting exhaust system components such as this exhaust pipe clamp, apply penetrating oil to the fastener threads

install the snap ring. Make sure the snap-ring is fully engaged in the groove. Pull on the regulator to verify the installation.

32 The remainder of installation is the reverse of removal. Turn the ignition On and check for fuel leaks.

16 Exhaust system servicing - general information

Refer to illustrations 16.1a, 16.1b, 16.1c and 16.4
Warning: *Inspection and repair of exhaust system components should be done only after it has cooled completely. Also, when working under the vehicle, make sure it's securely supported on jackstands.*

1   The exhaust system consists of the exhaust manifolds, the catalytic converter, the muffler, the tailpipe and all connecting pipes, brackets, hangers and clamps **(see illustrations)**. The exhaust system is attached to the body with mounting brackets and rubber hangers **(see illustration)**. If any of the parts are improperly installed, excessive noise and vibration will be transmitted to the body.

2   Conduct regular inspections of the exhaust system to keep it safe and quiet. Look for any damaged or bent parts, open seams, holes, loose connections, excessive corrosion or other defects which could allow exhaust fumes to enter the vehicle. Deteriorated exhaust system components should not be repaired; they should be replaced with new parts.

3   If the exhaust system components are extremely corroded or rusted together, welding equipment will probably be required to remove them. The convenient way to accomplish this is to have a muffler repair shop remove the corroded sections with a cutting torch. If, however, you want to save money by doing it yourself (and you don't have a welding outfit with a cutting torch), simply cut off the old components with a hacksaw. If you have compressed air, special pneumatic cutting chisels can also be used. If you do decide to tackle the job at home, be sure to wear safety goggles to protect your eyes from metal chips and work gloves to protect your hands.

4   Here are some simple guidelines to follow when repairing the exhaust system:

a) *Work from the back to the front when removing exhaust system components.*
b) *Apply penetrating oil to the exhaust system component fasteners to make them easier to remove* **(see illustration)**.
c) *Use new gaskets, hangers and clamps when installing exhaust systems components.*
d) *Apply anti-seize compound to the threads of all exhaust system fasteners during reassembly.*
e) *Be sure to allow sufficient clearance between newly installed parts and all points on the underbody to avoid overheating the floor pan and possibly damaging the interior carpet and insulation. Pay particularly close attention to the catalytic converter and heat shield.*

Notes

Chapter 5
Engine electrical systems

Contents

Specifications

General

Battery voltage	
Engine off	12.0 to 13.2 volts
Engine running	13.5 to 14.7 volts

Torque specifications

	Ft-lbs
Alternator mounting bolts	
V6 engine	
Front mounting bolts	37
Rear bracket bolt	18
V8 engines	37
Distributor hold-down bolt	18
Starter mounting bolts	
V6 engine	32
V8 engines	37

Component location

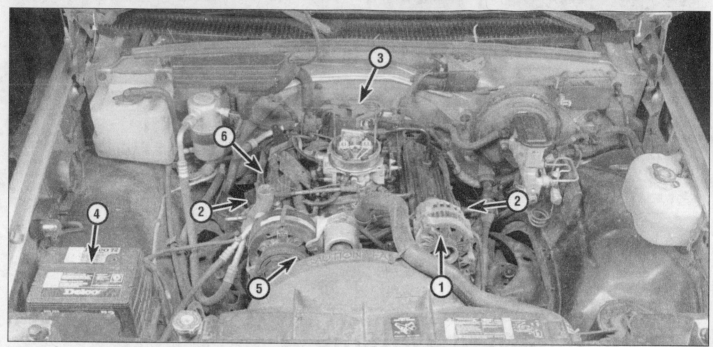

1.1a Typical 5.0/5.7L V8 engine electrical system (1988 through 1995 models)

1 Alternator
2 Spark plugs
3 Distributor, ignition coil and module

4 Battery and battery cables
5 Drivebelt(s)

6 Starter motor and starter solenoid
   (lower part of engine at transmission
   bellhousing)

1.1b Typical 5.0/5.7L V8 engine electrical system (1996 through 2000 models)

1 Alternator
2 Spark plugs
3 Distributor

4 Battery and battery cables
5 Drivebelt(s)

6 Starter motor and starter solenoid
   (lower part of engine at transmission
   bellhousing)

1 General information and precautions

General information

Refer to illustrations 1.1a and 1.1b

The engine electrical systems include all ignition, charging and starting components **(see illustrations)**. Because of their engine-related functions, these components are discussed separately from body electrical devices such as the lights, the instruments, etc. (which are included in Chapter 12).

The ignition system consists of the ignition switch, the battery, the coil, the primary (low tension) and secondary (high tension) circuits, the distributor and the spark plugs.

1988 through 1995 models use the conventional High Energy Ignition (HEI) system, whereas 1996 and later models (equipped with the Central SFI system) use the Enhanced Distributor Ignition (EDI) system. The conventional distributor system (1995 and earlier) uses a typical distributor containing a pick-up coil and a module. The distributor on the Enhanced Ignition system houses only the camshaft position sensor and the rotor. The other normal functions of the distributor are handled by a crankshaft position sensor and a computer which triggers the coil. Neither distributor utilizes centrifugal or vacuum advance mechanisms. The ignition timing is controlled by the computer.

The computer monitors information inputs from the various sensors to compute the most desirable spark timing. All ignition systems use a knock sensor which signals the computer to retard timing in the event detonation or preignition is detected. The coil is separately mounted on all models. On Enhanced Ignition models it is driven by the ignition control driver module which is mounted next to it.

Precautions

Always observe the following precautions when working on the electrical system:

a) *Be extremely careful when servicing engine electrical components. They are easily damaged if checked, connected or handled improperly.*

b) *Never leave the ignition switched on for long periods of time when the engine is not running.*

c) *Never disconnect the battery cables while the engine is running.*

d) *Maintain correct polarity when connecting battery cables from another vehicle during jump starting - see the "Booster battery (jump) starting" section at the front of this manual.*

e) *Always disconnect the negative battery cable before working on the electrical system.*

It's also a good idea to review the safety-related information regarding the engine electrical systems located in the *"Safety first!"* section at the front of this manual, before beginning any operation included in this Chapter.

Battery disconnection

Caution: *On models equipped with the Theft-lock audio system, be sure the lockout feature is turned off before performing any procedure which requires disconnecting the battery (see the front of this manual).*

Several systems on the vehicle require battery power to be available at all times, either to ensure their continued operation (such as the clock) or to maintain control unit memories (such as that in the engine management system's computer [ECM/PCM]) which would be wiped out if the battery were to be disconnected. Therefore, whenever the battery is to be disconnected, first note the following to ensure that there are no unforeseen consequences of this action:

a) *First, on any vehicle with power door locks, it is a wise precaution to remove the key from the ignition and to keep it with you, so that it does not get locked inside if the power door locks should engage accidentally when the battery is reconnected!*

b) *The engine management system's ECM/PCM will lose the information stored in its memory when the battery is disconnected. This includes idling and operating values, and any fault codes detected (see Chapter 6). Whenever the battery is disconnected, the information relating to idle speed control and other operating values will have to be re-programmed into the unit's memory. The ECM/PCM does this by itself, but until then, there may be surging, hesitation, erratic idle and a generally inferior level of performance. To allow the ECM/PCM to relearn these values, start the engine and run it as close to idle speed as possible until it reaches its normal operating temperature, then run it for approximately two minutes at 1200 rpm. Next, drive the vehicle as far as necessary - approximately 5 miles of varied driving conditions is usually sufficient - to complete the relearning process.*

Devices known as "memory-savers" can be used to avoid some of the above problems. Precise details vary according to the device used. Typically, it is plugged into the cigarette lighter, and is connected by its own wires to a spare battery; the vehicle's own battery is then disconnected from the electrical system, leaving the "memory-saver" to pass sufficient current to maintain audio unit security codes and ECM/PCM memory values, and also to run permanently live circuits such as the clock, all the while isolating the battery in the event of a short-circuit occurring while work is carried out. **Warning:** *Some of these devices allow a considerable amount of current to pass, which can mean that many of the vehicle's systems are still operational when the main battery is disconnected. If a "memory-saver" is used, ensure*

that the circuit concerned is actually "dead" before carrying out any work on it!

2 Battery - emergency jump starting

Refer to the Booster battery (jump) starting procedure at the front of this manual.

3 Battery - check and replacement

Warning: *Hydrogen gas is produced by the battery, so keep open flames and lighted cigarettes away from it at all times. Always wear eye protection when working around a battery. Rinse off spilled electrolyte immediately with large amounts of water.*

Check

Refer to illustrations 3.2 and 3.3

1   The battery's surface charge must be removed before accurate voltage measurements can be made. Turn On the high beams for ten seconds, then turn them Off, let the vehicle stand for two minutes. Remove the battery from the vehicle (see Steps 4 through 10).

2   Check the battery state of charge. Visually inspect the indicator eye on the top of the battery, if the indicator eye is clear, charge the battery as described in Chapter 1. Next perform an open voltage circuit test using a digital voltmeter **(see illustration)**. With the engine and all accessories Off, connect the negative probe of the voltmeter to the negative terminal of the battery and the positive probe to the positive terminal of the battery. The battery voltage should be 12.4 volts or more. If the battery is less than the specified voltage, charge the battery before proceeding to the next test. Do not proceed with the battery load test unless the battery charge is correct.

3   Perform a battery load test. An accurate check of the battery condition can only be

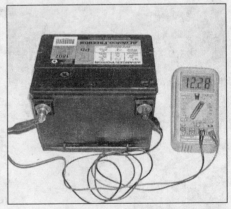

3.2 To test the open circuit voltage of the battery, connect a voltmeter to the battery - a fully charged battery should measure at least 12.4 volts (depending on outside air temperature)

3.3 Connect a battery load tester to the battery and check the battery condition under load following the tool manufacturer's instructions

3.6 Before removing the battery, remove the fender brace (A) (if equipped), then remove the battery retainer (B) and lift out the battery (late model shown)

performed with a load tester (available at most auto parts stores). This test evaluates the ability of the battery to operate the starter and other accessories during periods of heavy amperage draw (load). Install a special battery load testing tool onto the terminals **(see illustration)**. Load test the battery according to the tool manufacturer's instructions. This tool utilizes a carbon pile to increase the load demand (amperage draw) on the battery. Maintain the load on the battery for 15 seconds or less and observe that the battery voltage does not drop below 9.6 volts. If the battery condition is weak or defective, the tool will indicate this condition immediately. **Note:** *Cold temperatures will cause the minimum voltage requirements to drop slightly. Follow the chart given in the tool manufacturer's instructions to compensate for cold climates. Minimum load voltage for freezing temperatures (32 degrees F) should be approximately 9.1 volts.*

Replacement

Refer to illustrations 3.6 and 3.8

4   Disconnect the cable from the negative battery terminal. **Caution:** *On models*

equipped with the Theftlock audio system, be sure the lockout feature is turned off before performing any procedure which requires disconnecting the battery (see the front of this manual).

5   Disconnect the positive battery cable.

6   Remove the battery retainer bolt and retainer **(see illustration)**.

7   Remove the battery and place it on a workbench. Remove the battery insulator. **Note:** *Battery handling tools are available at most auto parts stores for a reasonable price. They make it easier to remove and carry the battery.*

8   While the battery is removed, inspect the tray, retainer brackets and related fasteners for corrosion or damage **(see illustration)**.

9   If corrosion is evident, remove the battery tray and use a baking soda/water solution to clean the corroded area to prevent further oxidation. Repaint the area as necessary using rust resistant paint.

10   Clean and service the battery and cables (see Chapter 1).

11   If you are replacing the battery, make sure you purchase one that is identical to

yours, with the same dimensions, amperage rating, cold cranking amps rating, etc. Make sure it is fully charged prior to installation in the vehicle.

12   Installation is the reverse of removal. Connect the positive cable first and the negative cable last.

13   After connecting the cables to the battery, apply a light coating of petroleum jelly or grease to the connections to help prevent corrosion.

4   Battery cables - replacement

Refer to illustrations 4.4a and 4.4b

Caution: *On models equipped with the Theftlock audio system, be sure the lockout feature is turned off before performing any procedure which requires disconnecting the battery (see the front of this manual).*

1   Periodically inspect the entire length of each battery cable for damage, cracked or burned insulation and corrosion. Poor battery cable connections can cause starting problems and decreased engine performance.

2   Check the cable-to-terminal connections at the ends of the cables for cracks, loose wire strands and corrosion. The presence of white, fluffy deposits under the insulation at the cable terminal connection is a sign that the cable is corroded and should be replaced. Check the terminals for distortion, missing mounting bolts and corrosion.

3   When removing the cables, always disconnect the negative cable first and hook it up last or the battery may be shorted by the tool used to loosen the cable clamps. Even if only the positive cable is being replaced, be sure to disconnect the negative cable first (see Chapter 1 for further information regarding battery cable maintenance).

4   Disconnect the old cables from the battery, then disconnect them at the opposite end. Detach the cables from the starter solenoid, underhood electrical center and ground terminals, as necessary **(see illustrations)**. Note the routing of each cable to

3.8 Inspect the tray, retainer brackets and related fasteners for corrosion or damage - if necessary, remove the bolts (arrows) and the battery tray (late model shown)

4.4a One branch of the positive cable is connected to the underhood electrical center

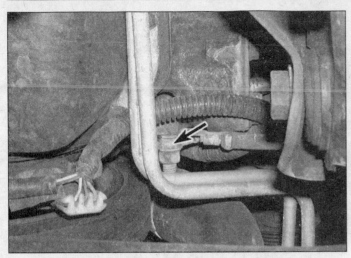

4.4b The negative battery cable is bolted to the engine block (arrow)

6.4 To use a calibrated ignition tester, simply disconnect a spark plug wire, hook the wire to the tester, clip the tester to a convenient ground and operate the starter - if there's enough power to fire the plug, sparks will be visible between the electrode tip and the tester body

ensure correct installation.

5   If you are replacing either or both of the battery cables, take them with you when buying new cables. It is vitally important that you replace the cables with identical parts. Cables have characteristics that make them easy to identify: positive cables are usually red and larger in cross-section; ground cables are usually black and smaller in cross-section.

6   Clean the threads of the starter solenoid or ground connection with a wire brush to remove rust and corrosion. Apply a light coat of battery terminal corrosion inhibitor or petroleum jelly to the threads to prevent future corrosion.

7   Attach the cable to the terminal and tighten the mounting nut/bolt securely.

8   Before connecting a new cable to the battery, make sure that it reaches the battery without having to be stretched.

---

5   Ignition system – general information

Warning: *Because of the very high voltage generated by the ignition system, extreme care should be taken whenever an operation involving ignition components is performed. This not only includes the distributor, coil(s), module and spark plug wires, but related items that are connected to the systems as well, such as the plug connections, tachometer and testing equipment.*

1988 through 1995 models (OBD-I) are equipped with the High Energy Ignition (HEI) system. 1996 through 2000 models (OBD-II) are equipped with the Enhanced Distributor Ignition (EDI) system.

High Energy Ignition (HEI) system

OBD I engines (1988 through 1995) use a special HEI distributor that is mounted at the front of the engine. HEI distributors covered by this manual are equipped with a pick-up coil and module. The ignition coil is mounted separate from the distributor. All spark timing changes are carried out by the ECM which monitors data from various engine sensors, computes the desired spark timing and signals the distributor to change the timing accordingly. No vacuum or mechanical advance is used.

Enhanced Distributor Ignition (EDI) system

OBD II engines (1996 and later) are equipped with an Enhanced Distributor Ignition (EDI) system. The EDI ignition system consists of the camshaft sensor (distributor housing), cap and rotor, distributor drive shaft, an ignition module, an ignition coil/coil driver, knock sensors, primary and secondary wiring, spark plugs and the necessary control circuits (wiring harness) for the entire system. This ignition system is enhanced to operate in the close tolerances of the OBD II system. The PCM monitors the information from various engine sensors and computes the correct spark timing via a direct line from the computer to the coil driver (IC).

The camshaft sensor detects camshaft position and sends this information to the computer (PCM). The sole purpose of the camshaft sensor is to provide the PCM with the information for any misfire trouble codes. In the event of failure or damage, the camshaft sensor is not directly involved with vehicle driveability.

---

6   Ignition system - check

Refer to illustrations 6.4, 6.12, 6.13, 6.17a, 6.17b and 6.18

Warning 1: *Because of the high voltage gen-erated by the ignition system, extreme care should be taken whenever an operation is performed involving ignition components. This not only includes the ignition coil, but related components and test equipment.*

Warning 2: *The following procedure requires the engine to be cranked during testing, make sure the meter leads, loose clothing, long hair, etc. are away from the moving parts of the engine (drivebelt, cooling fan, etc.) before cranking the engine.*

General checks

1   Before proceeding with the ignition system, check the following items:

a) *Make sure the battery cable clamps, where they connect to the battery, are clean and tight.*

b) *Test the condition of the battery (see Section 3). If it does not pass all the tests, replace it with a new battery.*

c) *Check the ignition coil and ignition control module external wiring and connections.*

d) *Check the related fuses inside the underhood electrical center (see Chapter 12). If they're burned, determine the cause and repair the circuit.*

2   If the engine turns over but won't start or has a severe misfire, make sure there is sufficient secondary ignition voltage to fire the spark plugs.

3   Disable the fuel system by removing the fuel pump relay (see Chapter 4).

4   Disconnect a spark plug wire from one of the spark plugs and attach a calibrated ignition system tester (available at most auto parts stores) to the spark plug boot. Connect the clip on the tester to a bolt or metal bracket on the engine **(see illustration)**. Crank the engine and watch the end of the tester to see if bright blue, well-defined sparks occur (weak spark or intermittent spark is the same as no spark).

5   If spark occurs, sufficient voltage is reaching the plug to fire it. Repeat the check

at the remaining spark plug wires to verify that the distributor cap, rotor, spark plug wires, ignition coil(s) and control systems are functioning properly. If the ignition system is operating properly the problem lies elsewhere; i.e. a mechanical or fuel system problem. However, the spark plugs may be fouled, so remove and check them as described in Chapter 1.

6   If no spark occurs at one or more wires, remove the suspected spark plug wire from the ignition coil and check the terminals at both ends for damage. Connect an ohmmeter to the ends of the spark plug wire and check the wire for an open or high resistance. If the spark plug wire resistance is greater than 30 K-ohms, replace the wire.

7   If the engine won't start due to no spark or misfires severely, proceed with the ignition system check according to engine type as follows: **Warning:** *The following tests require the engine to be cranked. Keep all loose clothing, hair, etc. away from the drivebelt and engine cooling fan as the starter is operated or seriously injury may result.*

1988 through 1995 models

8   Disconnect the ignition coil wire from the distributor cap, connect the calibrated ignition tester to the coil wire, crank the engine and check for spark. If adequate sparks occur at the coil wire, remove the distributor cap and check the distributor cap and rotor as described in Chapter 1. Replace the defective parts as necessary. Crank the engine while watching the distributor rotor. If the rotor does not turn, the distributor gear is stripped or the distributor shaft, timing chain/gears or camshaft are broken or damaged.

9   If no spark occurs at the coil wire, use an ohmmeter to check the resistance of the coil wire. Coil wire resistance should be approximately 1,000 ohms per inch. Replace the coil wire if defective.

10   Disconnect the two-terminal electrical connector from the ignition control module at the distributor. Turn the ignition key On and check for battery voltage at the pink or white wire terminal (refer to the wiring diagrams at the end of Chapter 12). If battery voltage is not available at the ignition coil and/or ignition module, check the circuits from the ignition switch to the coil or module (don't forget to check the fuses first).

11   Reconnect the two-terminal electrical connector onto the ignition module and with the ignition key ON (engine not running), check for voltage at the TACH terminal. The TACH terminal is taped back in the harness near the distributor. If there is less than 10 volts available, check the TACH circuit from the distributor. This test, checks for a shorted module or a grounded circuit from the ignition coil to the module. The distributor module should be turned off, so normal voltage should be about 12 volts. If the module is turned ON, the voltage will be low, but above one volt. This could cause the ignition coil to

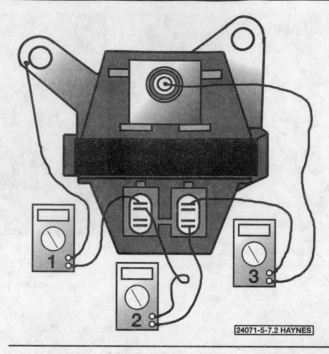

6.12 To check the ignition coil, use an ohmmeter to perform the following checks

1   *On the high scale, the ohmmeter should read infinity*

2   *On the low scale, the ohmmeter should read very low or zero*

3   *On the high scale, the ohmmeter should not read infinity*

fail from excessive heat.

12   Using an ohmmeter, check the primary and secondary resistance of the ignition coil **(see illustration)**. Replace the ignition coil if defective.

13   Using an ohmmeter, check the pick-up coil resistance at the ignition module connector. This test will require the distributor cap removed and the harness connector removed from the module **(see illustration)**. Pick-up coil resistance should range between 500 to 1,500 ohms. Flex the harness and observe the resistance. If the resistance values fluctuate, there is a damaged pick-up coil harness. Replace the pick-up coil assembly if any of the tests fail (see Section 8).

14   If all the above ignition system component checks are correct, then test the ignition module. A HEI module tester can determine if the module is defective. If the special test equipment is not available, have the module tested by a qualified automotive repair facility.

1996 through 2000 models

15   Disconnect the ignition coil wire from the distributor cap, connect the calibrated ignition tester to the coil wire, crank the engine and check for spark. If adequate sparks occur at the coil wire, remove the distributor cap and check the distributor cap and rotor as described in Chapter 1. Replace the defective parts as necessary. Crank the engine while watching the distributor rotor. If the rotor does not turn, the distributor gear is stripped or the distributor shaft, timing chain/gears or camshaft are broken or damaged.

16   If no spark occurs at the coil wire, use an ohmmeter to check the resistance of the coil wire. Coil wire resistance should be approximately 1,000 ohms per inch. Replace the coil wire if defective.

17   Disconnect the electrical connector from the ignition coil and from the ignition control module. Turn the ignition key On and check for battery voltage at the pink wire ter-

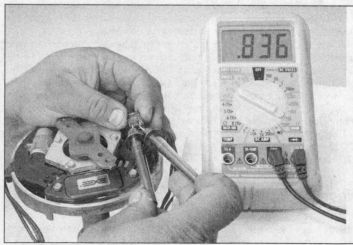

6.13 To test the pick-up coil, first connect an ohmmeter between the indicated terminal and ground, then connect it between both terminals

minal of each harness connector **(see illustrations)**. Also check for continuity to battery ground at the black wire terminal of the ignition module harness connector. If battery voltage is not available at the ignition coil and/or ignition module, check the circuits from the underhood electrical center to the coil or module (don't forget to check the fuses first).

18   Using an ohmmeter, check the primary and secondary resistance of the ignition coil **(see illustration)**. Replace the ignition coil if defective.

19   If the previous checks are correct, check the trigger signal from the ignition control module. Reconnect the electrical connector to the ignition control module. Attach the lead of a test light to the positive battery terminal and touch the probe of the test light to the white/black wire terminal at the ignition coil connector. Crank the engine. The test light should blink with the engine cranking if a trigger signal is present. If a trigger signal is not present, disconnect the electrical connector from the ignition control module and connect the positive probe of a voltmeter to the white wire terminal of the harness connector. Connect the negative lead to a good engine ground point and set the meter on the AC volts scale. Crank the engine. Approximately 1.0 to 4.0 volts should be indicated, if not, check the crankshaft position sensor (see Chapter 6). If the crankshaft position sensor is good, check the related circuits for continuity. If the circuits are good, have the PCM checked by a dealer service department or other qualified repair shop. **Note:** *Refer to the wiring diagrams at the end of Chapter 12 for wire color identification for testing and additional information on the circuits.*

20   If the 1.0 to 4.0 volts ignition control signal was present at the ignition control module connector, but no trigger signal was present at the ignition coil connector, check the white/black wire for continuity between the ignition module connector and the ignition coil connector. If the circuit is good, replace the ignition control module.

7   Ignition module - replacement

1   Disconnect the cable from the negative battery terminal. **Caution:** *On models equipped with the Theftlock audio system, be sure the lockout feature is turned off before performing any procedure which requires disconnecting the battery (see the front of this manual).*

2   Access the distributor:
a) *On TBI systems, remove the air filter assembly from the TBI unit*
b) *On Central SFI and MPFI systems, remove the air intake duct and resonator from the throttle body (see Chapter 4).*

1988 through 1995 models
Refer to illustrations 7.5 and 7.7
Note: *It's not necessary to remove the dis-*

6.17a Ignition coil harness connector terminal identification

1   *12-volt supply*
2   *Not used*
3   *Coil driver (from ignition control module)*

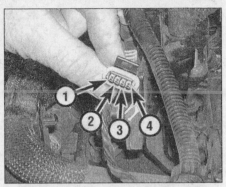

6.17b Ignition control module harness connector terminal identification

1   *Ignition coil driver*
2   *Ground*
3   *Ignition timing control (from PCM)*
4   *12-volt supply*

tributor from the engine to replace the ignition module.

3   Remove the distributor cap and wires as an assembly and position them out of the way (see Chapter 1).

4   Remove the rotor.

5   Carefully detach the wires from the module terminals **(see illustration)**. **Caution:** *Do not pull on the wires or the connectors may be damaged.*

6   Remove the screws and lift out the

module. **Note:** *The module can only be tested with special equipment. If you suspect it's malfunctioning, have it checked by a qualified automotive repair facility.*

7   Installation is the reverse of removal. Be sure to apply the silicone dielectric grease supplied with the new module to the bottom of the ignition module **(see illustration)** - DO NOT use any other type of grease! If the grease isn't used, the module will overheat and destroy itself.

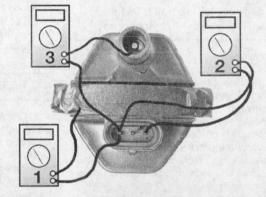

6.18 To check the ignition coil, use an ohmmeter to perform the following three checks

1   *The ohmmeter should read infinity*
2   *The ohmmeter should read approximately 0.1 ohm*
3   *The ohmmeter should read from 5,000 to 25,000 ohms*

7.5 Unplug both electrical connectors from the module

7.7 Apply silicone lubricant to the bottom of the ignition module (see arrow) - the lubricant dissipates heat and prevents the module from overheating

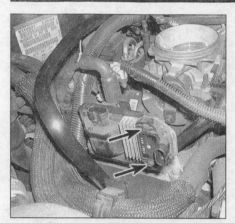

7.10 Ignition control module mounting screws (1996 and later models) (arrows)

8.4 Before removing the pick-up coil, unplug the lead from the ignition module

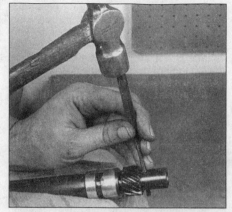

8.6a To remove the pick-up coil, mount the distributor shaft in a vise equipped with soft jaws and, using a pin punch and hammer, knock out the roll pin

1996 through 2000 models

Refer to illustration 7.10

8   The ignition control module can be removed without removing the coil bracket from the engine.

9   Disconnect the electrical connector from the ignition control module.

10   Remove the mounting screws and remove the ignition control module from the bracket **(see illustration).**

11   Installation is the reverse of removal.

---

8   Ignition pick-up coil (1995 and earlier models) - replacement

---

Refer to illustrations 8.4, 8.6a, 8.6b, 8.6c and 8.7

1   Disconnect the cable from the negative battery terminal. **Caution:** *On models equipped with the Theftlock audio system, be sure the lockout feature is turned off before performing any procedure which requires disconnecting the battery (see the front of this manual).*

2   Remove the distributor cap and rotor (see Chapter 1).

3   Remove the distributor from the engine (Section 10).

4   Detach the pick-up coil leads from the module **(see illustration).**

5   Mark the distributor shaft and gear so they can be reassembled in the same relationship.

6   Carefully mount the distributor in a vise equipped with soft jaws and, using a hammer and punch, remove the roll pin from the distributor shaft and gear **(see illustrations).** Pull out the distributor shaft **(see illustration).**

7   To detach the pick-up coil, remove the retaining clip **(see illustration).**

8   Lift the pick-up coil assembly straight up and detach it from the distributor.

9   Installation is the reverse of removal.

---

9   Ignition coil - replacement

---

1   Disconnect the cable from the negative battery terminal. **Caution:** *On models equipped with the Theftlock audio system, be sure the lockout feature is turned off before performing any procedure which requires disconnecting the battery (see the front of this manual).*

1988 through 1995 models

2   If not already done, detach the coil high tension lead and the primary wire connector.

3   Remove the mounting fasteners and separate the coil from the engine.

4   Installation is the reverse of removal

1996 through 2000 models

Refer to illustration 9.6

5   Disconnect the electrical connectors from the ignition coil and ignition control module. Detach the coil wire from the ignition coil high-tension terminal.

6   Remove the ignition coil/module bracket mounting bolts and remove the assembly from the engine **(see illustration).** Remove the ignition control module from the bracket.

7   Place the assembly on a workbench. Using the appropriate size drill, drill out the center of the rivets retaining the coil to the bracket. Use a drift punch to punch out the rivets and remove the coil from the bracket.

8   Attach the ignition coil to the bracket using new screws. **Note:** *Screws are provided with a new ignition coil.* Attach the ignition module to the bracket.

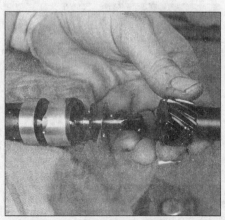

8.6b Remove the driven gear and spacer washers or springs from the end of the shaft - be sure to note their installed order

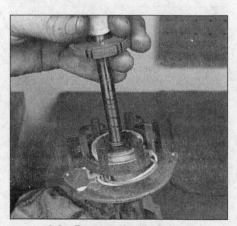

8.6c Remove the shaft from the distributor

8.7 To detach the pick-up coil from the distributor, remove the retaining clip

9.6 Remove the ignition coil/module bracket mounting bolts (arrows) (V6 models shown)

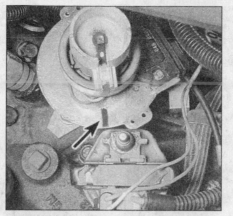

10.6a Make a mark on the distributor housing (arrow) to show where the rotor is pointing (HEI distributor shown)

10.6b Apply a paint mark on the edge of the distributor body directly below the rotor tip and in line with it (EDI distributor shown)

9   Install the assembly on the engine and connect the electrical connectors and coil wire.

10   Distributor - removal and installation

Removal

Refer to illustrations 10.6a, 10.6b and 10.7

1   Disconnect the cable from the negative battery terminal. **Caution:** *On models equipped with the Theftlock audio system, be sure the lockout feature is turned off before performing any procedure which requires disconnecting the battery (see the front of this manual).*

2   Remove the air intake duct and resonator assembly from the throttle body (see Chapter 4).

3   Position the engine with the number one cylinder at TDC on the compression stroke (see Chapter 2A).

4   Disconnect the electrical connector from the distributor.

5   Disconnect the coil wire from the distributor cap. Label and detach the spark plug

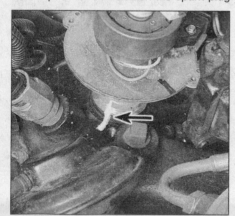

10.7 Mark the position of the distributor base in relation to the engine (arrow) before loosening the distributor hold-down clamp

wires from the spark plugs. Detach the spark plug wire retainers from the studs and brackets. Loosen the distributor cap mounting screws, remove the cap from the distributor and position the cap (with the spark plug wires attached) aside.

6   The distributor rotor should be pointing at the alignment mark; if necessary apply a paint mark on the edge of the distributor body directly below the rotor tip and in line with it **(see illustrations)**.

7   Mark the position of the distributor base to the engine to ensure the distributor can be re-installed in exactly the same position as originally installed **(see illustration)**.

8   Remove the distributor hold-down bolt and pull out the distributor. Remove and discard the O-ring.

Installation

9   If the crankshaft has been moved while the distributor is out, the number one piston must be repositioned at TDC. This can be done by feeling for compression pressure at the number one spark plug hole as the crankshaft is rotated. Once compression is felt, continue rotating the crankshaft until the mark on the crankshaft damper is aligned with the TDC mark on the timing indicator (see Chapter 2A).

10   Install a new O-ring on the distributor housing.

11   Position the rotor.

   a) On 1988 through 1995 models, turn the rotor slightly off-set 10 to 15 degrees before installing the distributor. This will allow the helical gears to mess with the camshaft as the distributor is slowly lowered into the engine block.

   b) On 1996 through 2000 models, turn the rotor until it points approximately 42-degrees counterclockwise from the mark made in Step 6. **Note:** *Make sure the oil pump drive gear is properly aligned with the tab on the distributor shaft. If necessary use a long screwdriver to turn the oil pump drive shaft.*

12   Insert the distributor into the engine block. As the distributor gear engages the

camshaft, the rotor will rotate clockwise and when fully seated, the rotor must align with the mark made in Step 6. Rotate the distributor base until the marks made in Step 7 align. **Caution:** *The distributor must be installed the same position as originally installed. Make sure the spark plug wire terminals are perpendicular to the engine centerline and the rotor remains aligned with the alignment mark. If the distributor is installed incorrectly, the engine will run poorly, the SERVICE ENGINE SOON light will illuminate and a diagnostic trouble code will set (see Chapter 6).*

13   Install the distributor hold-down clamp and tighten the bolt to the torque listed in this Chapter's Specifications.

14   The remainder of installation is the reverse of removal.

11   Charging system - general information and precautions

The main components of the charging system are alternator (with an integral voltage regulator), the battery and the wiring connecting the components. The components work together to supply electrical power for the electrical system and maintain the battery in a charged condition. The alternator is driven by the drivebelt at the front of the engine.

There are two types of alternators used on these models. They are the SI type or the CS type. Both types have a conventional pulley and fan.

To determine which type of alternator is installed on your vehicle, look at the fasteners employed to attach the two halves of the alternator housing. All CS models use rivets or special bolts instead of screws. For all intents and purposes, CS types should be considered non-serviceable and, if defective, should be exchanged as cores for new or rebuilt units.

The purpose of the voltage regulator is to limit the alternator voltage output to a preset value. This prevents power surges and

12.2 To measure battery voltage, attach the voltmeter leads to the battery terminals (engine OFF) - to measure charging voltage, start the engine

13.4a Alternator mounting details (typical big block V8 engine)

circuit overloads during peak voltage output. On all models with which this manual is concerned, the voltage regulator is integral with the alternator.

The charging system doesn't ordinarily require periodic maintenance. However, the drivebelt, battery and wires and connections should be inspected at the intervals outlined in Chapter 1.

The instrument panel warning light should come on when the ignition key is turned to START, then go off immediately after the engine has started. If the warning light stays on or comes on when the engine is running, a charging system problem has occurred (see Section 9).

Be very careful when making electrical circuit connections to a vehicle equipped with an alternator and note the following:

a) *When reconnecting wires to the alternator from the battery, be sure to note the polarity.*

b) *Before using arc welding equipment to repair any part of the vehicle, disconnect the wires from the alternator and the battery terminals.* **Caution:** *On models equipped with the Theftlock audio system, be sure the lockout feature is turned off before performing any procedure which requires disconnecting the battery (see the front of this manual).*

c) *Never start the engine with a battery charger connected.*

d) *Always disconnect both battery leads before using a battery charger.*

e) *The alternator is turned by an engine drivebelt which could cause serious injury if your hands, hair or clothes become entangled in it with the engine running.*

f) *Because the alternator is connected directly to the battery, it could arc or cause a fire if overloaded or shorted out.*

g) *Wrap a plastic bag over the alternator and secure it with rubber bands before steam cleaning the engine.*

12 Charging system - check

Refer to illustration 12.2
Note: *1996 and later models are equipped with an On-Board Diagnostic (OBD) II system that is useful for detecting charging system problems. Refer to Chapter 6 for the list of diagnostic codes and procedures for obtaining the codes.*

1   If a malfunction occurs in the charging circuit, do not immediately assume that the alternator is causing the problem. First check the following items:

a) *The battery cables where they connect to the battery. Make sure the connections are clean and tight.*

b) *The battery electrolyte specific gravity (by observing the charge indicator on the battery). If it is low, charge the battery.*

c) *Check the external alternator wiring and connections.*

d) *Check the drivebelt condition and tension (see Chapter 1).*

e) *Check the alternator mounting bolts for tightness.*

f) *Run the engine and check the alternator for abnormal noise.*

2   Connect a voltmeter to the positive and negative battery terminals **(see illustration)**. Check the battery voltage with the engine off. It should be approximately 12.4 to 12.6 volts, if the battery is fully charged.

3   Start the engine and check the battery voltage again. It should now be greater than the voltage recorded in Step 2, but not more than 14.7 volts.

4   If the indicated voltage reading is less or more than the specified charging voltage, have the charging system checked at a dealer service department or other properly equipped repair facility. **Note:** *Many auto parts stores will bench test an alternator off the vehicle. Refer to your local auto parts store regarding their policy, many will perform this service free of charge.*

13.4b Alternator mounting details (typical V6 and small block V8 engines)

13 Alternator - removal and installation

Refer to illustrations 13.4a and 13.4b
1   Disconnect the cable from the negative battery terminal. **Caution:** *On models equipped with the Theftlock audio system, be sure the lockout feature is turned off before performing any procedure which requires disconnecting the battery (see the front of this manual).*

2   Detach the wires from the alternator.

3   Remove the alternator drivebelt (see Chapter 1).

4   Remove the mounting bolts and separate the alternator from the engine **(see illustrations)**.

5   If you're replacing the alternator, take the old one with you when purchasing the replacement. Make sure the new/rebuilt unit looks identical to the old one. Look at the terminals - they should be the same in number, size and location as the terminals on the old alternator. Finally, look at the identification numbers stamped into the housing or printed

14.2 Mark the drive end frame and rectifier end frame assemblies with a scribe or permanent felt-tip pen before separating the two halves of the alternator

14.3a With the through-bolts removed, carefully separate the end frame assemblies

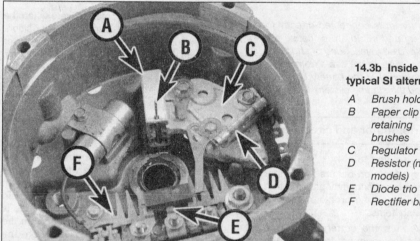

14.3b Inside the typical SI alternator

A Brush holder
B Paper clip retaining brushes
C Regulator
D Resistor (not all models)
E Diode trio
F Rectifier bridge

14 Alternator brushes and regulator - replacement

Refer to illustrations 14.2, 14.3a, 14.3b, 14.4, 14.5, 14.6, 14.7 and 14.10
Note: *The following procedure applies only to early-model SI type alternators. Later-model alternators do not have separately replaceable parts.*

1   Remove the alternator from the vehicle (Section 13).
2   Scribe or paint marks on the front and rear end frame housings of the alternator to facilitate reassembly **(see illustration)**.
3   Remove the four through-bolts holding the front and rear end frames together, then separate the drive end frame from the rectifier end frame **(see illustrations)**.
4   Remove the bolts holding the stator to the rear end frame and separate the stator from the end frame **(see illustration)**.
5   Remove the nuts attaching the diode trio to the rectifier bridge and remove the trio **(see illustration)**.
6   Remove the screws attaching the resistor (not used on all models), regulator and brush holder to the end frame and remove the brush holder **(see illustration)**.

on a tag attached to the housing. Make sure the numbers are the same on both alternators.
6   Many new/rebuilt alternators DO NOT have a pulley installed, so you may have to switch the pulley from the old unit to the new/rebuilt one. When buying an alternator, find out the shop's policy regarding pulleys -

some shops will perform this service free of charge.
7   Installation is the reverse of removal.
8   After the alternator is installed, check the drivebelt tension (see Chapter 1).
9   Check the charging voltage to verify proper operation of the alternator (see Section 11).

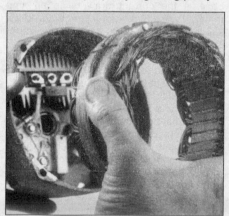

14.4 After removing the bolts holding the stator assembly to the end frame, detach the stator

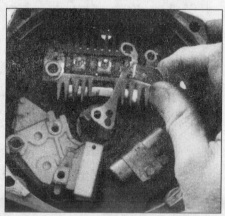

14.5 Remove the nuts attaching the diode trio to the rectifier bridge

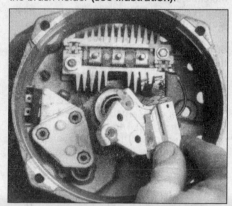

14.6 After removing the screws that attach the regulator, brush holder and the resistor (if equipped) to the end frame, detach the brush holder

14.7 Slip the brush retainer off the brush holder and remove the brushes

14.10 To hold the brushes in place during reassembly, insert a paper clip through the hole in the end frame nearest the rotor shaft

7   Remove the brushes from the brush holder by slipping the brush retainer off the brush holder **(see illustration)**.

8   Remove the springs from the brush holder.

9   Installation is the reverse of the removal procedure, noting the following:

10   When installing the brushes in the brush holder, install the brush closest to the end frame first. Slip the paper clip through the rear of the end frame to hold the brush, then insert the second brush and push the paper clip in to hold both brushes while reassembly is completed **(see illustration)**. The paper clip should not be removed until the front and rear end frames have been bolted together.

15 Starting system - general information and precautions

The starter motor assembly is a permanent magnet, planetary gear drive starter motor. The starter motor assembly is serviced as a complete unit. If any component of the starter motor fails, including the solenoid, the entire assembly must be replaced.

The sole function of the starting system is to turn over the engine quickly enough to allow it to start. The starting system consists of the battery, starter motor assembly and the wiring connecting the components.

When the ignition key is turned to the START position, the starter solenoid is actuated through the starter control circuit. The starter solenoid then connects the battery to the starter motor. The battery supplies the electrical energy to the starter motor, which does the actual work of cranking the engine.

Always observe the following precautions when working on the starting system:

a) *Excessive cranking of the starter motor can overheat it and cause serious damage. Never operate the starter motor for more than 15 seconds at a time without pausing to allow it to cool for at least two minutes.*

b) *The starter is connected directly to the battery and could arc or cause a fire if mishandled, overloaded or shorted.*

c) *Always detach the cable from the negative terminal of the battery before working on the starting system.*

16 Starter motor and circuit - check

Refer to illustration 16.4

1   If a malfunction occurs in the starting circuit, do not immediately assume that the starter is causing the problem. First, check the following items:

a) *Make sure the battery cable clamps, where they connect to the battery, are clean and tight.*

b) *Check the condition of the battery cables (see Section 4). Replace any defective battery cables with new parts.*

c) *Test the condition of the battery (see Section 3). If it does not pass all the tests, replace it with a new battery.*

d) *Check the starter motor wiring and connections.*

e) *Check the starter motor mounting bolts for tightness.*

f) *Check the related fuses in the engine compartment fuse box (see Chapter 12). If they're blown, determine the cause and repair the circuit.*

g) *Check the ignition switch circuit for correct operation (see Chapter 12).*

h) *Check the starter relay (located in the underhood electrical center) for proper operation (see Chapter 12).*

i) *Check the operation of the clutch start switch (manual transmission) or the Park/Neutral position switch (automatic transmission) (see Chapter 8 or 7B). These systems must operate correctly to provide battery voltage to the starter relay. Also, refer to the wiring diagrams at the end of Chapter 12 for additional information.*

2   If the starter does not activate when the ignition switch is turned to the start position, check for battery voltage to the starter solenoid. This will determine if the solenoid is receiving the correct voltage from the starter relay. Install a 12-volt test light or a voltmeter to the starter solenoid terminal (purple wire). While an assistant turns the ignition switch to the start position, observe the test light or voltmeter. The test light should shine brightly or battery voltage should be indicated on the voltmeter. If voltage is not available to the starter solenoid, refer to the wiring diagrams in Chapter 12 and check the fuses, ignition switch, starter relay and related wiring in series with the starting system. If voltage is available but there is no movement from the starter motor, remove the starter from the engine (see Section 17) and bench test the starter (see Step 4).

3   If the starter turns over slowly, check the starter cranking voltage and the current draw from the battery. This test must be performed with the starter assembly on the engine. Crank the engine over (for 10 seconds or less) and observe the battery voltage. It should not drop below 8.5 volts. Also, observe the current draw using an amp meter. Typically a starter amperage draw should not exceed 350 amps. If the starter motor amperage draw is excessive, have it tested by a dealer service department or other qualified repair shop. There are several conditions that may affect the starter cranking potential. The battery must be in good condition and the battery cold-cranking rating must not be under-rated for the particular application. Be sure to check the battery specifications carefully. The battery terminals and cables must be clean and not corroded. Also, in cases of extreme cold temperatures, make sure the battery and/or engine block is warmed before performing the tests.

4   If the starter is receiving voltage but does not activate, remove and check the starter motor assembly on the bench. Most likely the starter motor or solenoid is defec-

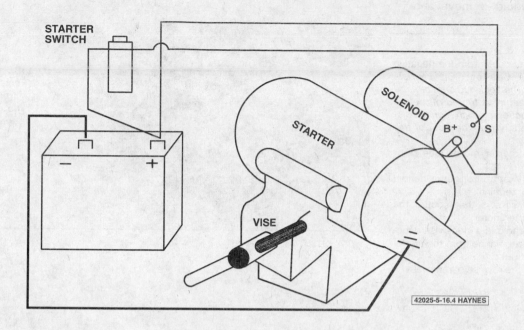

16.4 Starter motor bench testing details

tive. In some rare cases, the engine may be seized so be sure to try and rotate the crankshaft pulley (see Chapter 2A or 2B) before proceeding. With the starter assembly mounted in a vise on the bench, install one jumper cable from the positive terminal of a test battery to the B+ terminal on the starter. Install another jumper cable from the negative terminal of the battery to the body of the starter **(see illustration)**. Install a starter switch and apply battery voltage to the solenoid S terminal (for 10 seconds or less) and observe the solenoid plunger, shift lever and overrunning clutch extend and rotate the pinion drive. If the pinion drive extends but

does not rotate, the solenoid is operating but the starter motor is defective. If there is no movement but the solenoid clicks, the solenoid and/or the starter motor is defective. If the solenoid plunger extends and rotates the pinion drive, the starter assembly is operating properly.

17 Starter motor - removal and installation

Refer to illustrations 17.4 and 17.5

1   Disconnect the cable from the negative battery terminal. **Caution:** *On models*

equipped with the Theftlock audio system, be sure the lockout feature is turned off before performing any procedure which requires disconnecting the battery (see the front of this manual).

2   Remove the starter motor shield, if equipped.

3   Raise the vehicle and support it securely on jackstands.

4   Clearly label, then disconnect the wires from the terminals on the starter motor and solenoid **(see illustration)**.

5   Remove the mounting bolts and detach the starter **(see illustration)**.

6   Installation is the reverse of removal.

17.4 There are three terminals on the end of a typical starter solenoid

1   *Battery terminal*
2   *Switch terminal (S)*
3   *Motor terminal (M)*

17.5 Typical starter motor installation details

18 Starter solenoid - removal and installation

Refer to illustration 18.5

1   Disconnect the cable from the negative battery terminal. **Caution:** *On models equipped with the Theftlock audio system, be sure the lockout feature is turned off before performing any procedure which requires disconnecting the battery (see the front of this manual).*

2   Remove the starter motor (see Section 17).

3   Disconnect the strap from the solenoid to the starter motor terminal.

4   Remove the screws that secure the solenoid to the starter motor.

5   Twist the solenoid in a clockwise direction to disengage the flange from the starter body **(see illustration).**

6   Installation is the reverse of removal.

18.5 To remove the solenoid housing from the starter motor, remove the screws and turn it clockwise

Chapter 6
Emissions control systems

Contents

Component location - TBI system

1.1a Typical emissions control locations - 5.0/5.7 liter V8 engines

1 Fuel injectors (arrows)
2 Single wire timing connector bypass
3 Exhaust oxygen sensor
4 Coolant temperature switch
5 Harness ground (ECM/PCM)
6 Coolant temperature sensor (ECM/PCM)
7 Positive Crankcase Ventilation (PCV) valve
8 Throttle Position Sensor (TPS)
9 Idle Air Control (IAC) valve
10 Exhaust Gas Recirculation (EGR) valve (arrow)
11 Manifold Absolute Pressure (MAP) sensor
12 SERVICE ENGINE SOON light
13 Vehicle Emission Control Information (VECI) label
14 Fuel vapor canister

1   Fuel injectors (arrows)

2   Single wire timing connector bypass

3   Exhaust oxygen sensor

4   Coolant temperature switch

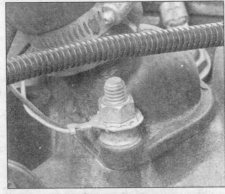

5   Harness ground (ECM/PCM)

6   Coolant temperature sensor (ECM/PCM)

7   Positive Crankcase Ventilation (PCV) valve

8   Throttle Position Sensor (TPS)

9   Idle Air Control valve (IAC)

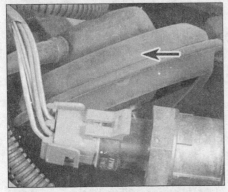

10   Exhaust Gas Recirculation (EGR) valve (arrow)

11   Manifold Absolute Pressure (MAP) sensor

12   SERVICE ENGINE SOON light

13 Vehicle Emission Control Information (VECI) label

14 Fuel vapor canister

Component location - Central SFI system

1.1b Typical engine component layout Central SFI models (5.7L engine shown)

1	IAT sensor	6	Electrical convenience center
2	MAF sensor	7	Powertrain control module (PCM)
3	MAP sensor (in intake manifold)	8	VECI label
4	IAC valve	9	Linear EGR valve
5	Air intake resonator	10	ECT sensor

1 General information

Refer to illustrations 1.1a, 1.1b and 1.6

To prevent pollution of the atmosphere from incompletely burned and evaporating gases, and to maintain good driveability and fuel economy, a number of emission control systems are incorporated (see illustrations). They include the:

Electronic engine control system
Positive Crankcase Ventilation (PCV) system
Exhaust Gas Recirculation (EGR) system
Evaporative (EVAP) emission control system

Secondary air injection (AIR) system
Thermostatic air cleaner (1988 through 1995 models)
Catalytic converter

All of these systems are linked, directly or indirectly, to the emission control system.

The Sections in this Chapter include general descriptions, checking procedures

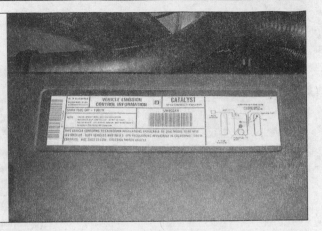

1.6 The Vehicle Emission Control Information (VECI) label is located in the engine compartment and contains information on the emission devices on your vehicle, vacuum line routing, etc.

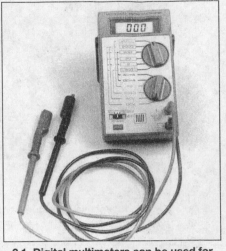

2.1 Digital multimeters can be used for testing all types of circuits; because of their high impedance, they are much more accurate than analog meters for measuring millivolts in low-voltage computer circuits

within the scope of the home mechanic and component replacement procedures (when possible) for each of the systems listed above.

Before assuming an emissions control system is malfunctioning, check the fuel and ignition systems carefully. The diagnosis of some emission control devices requires specialized tools, equipment and training. If checking and servicing become too difficult, or if a procedure is beyond your ability, consult a dealer service department. Remember, the most frequent cause of emissions problems is simply a loose or broken vacuum hose or wire, so always check the hose and wiring connections first.

This doesn't mean, however, that emission control systems are particularly difficult to maintain and repair. You can quickly and easily perform many checks and do most of the regular maintenance at home with common tune-up and hand tools. **Note:** *Because of a federally mandated extended warranty which covers the emission control system components, check with a dealer about warranty coverage before working on any emissions-related systems. Once the warranty has expired, you may wish to perform some of the component checks and/or replacement procedures in this Chapter to save money.*

Pay close attention to any special precautions outlined in this Chapter. It should be noted that the illustrations of the various systems may not exactly match the system

installed on your vehicle because of changes made by the manufacturer during production or from year-to-year.

A Vehicle Emissions Control Information label is located in the engine compartment **(see illustration)**. This label contains important emissions specifications and adjustment information, as well as a vacuum hose schematic with emissions components identified. When servicing the engine or emissions systems, the VECI label in your particular vehicle should be checked for up-to-date information.

2   On Board Diagnostic (OBD) system and trouble codes

Diagnostic tool information

Refer to illustrations 2.1 and 2.2

1   A digital multimeter is necessary for checking fuel injection and emission related components **(see illustration)**. A digital volt-ohmmeter is preferred over the older style analog multimeter for several reasons. The analog multimeter cannot display the volts-ohms or amps measurement in hundredths and thousandths increments. When working with electronic circuits which are often very low voltage, this accurate reading is most important. Another good reason for the digital multimeter is the high impedance circuit. The digital multimeter is equipped with a high

resistance internal circuitry (10 million ohms). Because a voltmeter is hooked up in parallel with the circuit when testing, it is vital that none of the voltage being measured should be allowed to travel the parallel path set up by the meter itself. This dilemma does not show itself when measuring larger amounts of voltage (9 to 12 volt circuits) but if you are measuring a low voltage circuit such as the oxygen sensor signal voltage, a fraction of a volt may be a significant amount when diagnosing a problem. However, there are several exceptions where using an analog voltmeter may be necessary to test certain sensors.

2   Hand-held scanners are the most powerful and versatile tools for analyzing engine management systems used on later model vehicles **(see illustration)**. Each brand scan tool must be examined carefully to match the year, make and model of the vehicle you are working on. Often interchangeable cartridges are available to access the particular manufacturer (Ford, GM, Chrysler, etc.). Some manufacturers will specify by continent (Asia, Europe, USA, etc.).

3   With the arrival of the Federally mandated emission control system (OBD-II), a specially designed scanner has been developed. Several tool manufacturers have released OBD-II scan tools for the home mechanic. Ask the parts salesman at a local auto parts store for additional information concerning availability and cost.

On-Board Diagnostic system general description

4   The On Board Diagnostic (OBD) system consists of an Electronic Control Module (ECM) and information sensors which monitor various functions of the engine and send data back to the ECM. **Note:** *1996 and later OBD-II systems refer to the on-board computer as the Powertrain Control Module (PCM).*

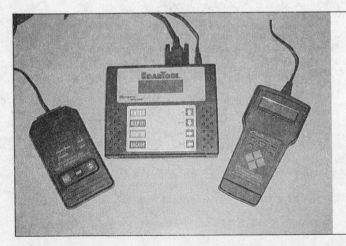

2.2 Scanners like the Actron Scantool and the AutoXray XP240 are powerful diagnostic aids - programmed with comprehensive diagnostic information, they can tell you just about anything you want to know about your engine management system

5   The OBD system is analogous to the central nervous system in the human body: The sensors (nerve endings) constantly relay information to the ECM (brain), which processes the data and, if necessary, sends out a command to change the operating parameters of the engine (body).

6   Here's a specific example of how one portion of this system operates: An oxygen sensor, located in the exhaust manifold, constantly monitors the oxygen content of the exhaust gas. If the percentage of oxygen in the exhaust gas is incorrect, indicating a too rich or too lean condition, an electrical signal is sent to the ECM. The ECM takes this information, processes it and then sends a command to the fuel injection system, telling it to change the air/fuel mixture. This happens in a fraction of a second and it goes on continuously when the engine is running. The end result is an air/fuel mixture ratio which is constantly maintained at a predetermined ratio, regardless of driving conditions.

1988 through 1995 models

7   One might think that a system which uses an on-board computer and electrical sensors would be difficult to diagnose. This is not necessarily the case. The Computer Command Control (CCC) system has a built-in diagnostic feature which indicates a problem by flashing a SERVICE ENGINE SOON light on the instrument panel. When this light comes on during normal vehicle operation, a fault in one of the information sensor circuits or the ECM itself has been detected. More importantly, the source of the malfunction is stored in the ECM's memory. These early electronic fuel and emission control systems are referred to as the On-Board Diagnostic (OBD-I) systems.

8   To retrieve this information from the ECM memory, you must use a short jumper wire to ground a diagnostic terminal. This terminal is part of a wiring connector known as the Assembly Line Data Link (ALDL) **(see illustration 2.33)**. The ALDL is located underneath the dashboard, on the left hand side.

1996 through 2000 models

9   This advanced electronically controlled fuel and emissions system (OBD-II) is linked with many other related engine management systems. It consists mainly of sensors, output actuators and a Powertrain Control Module (PCM). Completing the system are various other components which respond to commands from the PCM. **Note:** *1996 and later OBD-II systems refer to the on-board computer as the Powertrain Control Module (PCM).*

10   These later models require a Scan tool for code retrieval. However, many of the information sensor checks and replacement procedures on the OBD-I system, do apply to the OBD II system. Refer to the troubleshooting tips in the beginning of this manual to gain some insight to the most likely causes to a problem.

Information sensors

11   **Camshaft Position (CMP) sensor** – On 1996 and later models, the camshaft position sensor provides information on camshaft position. The PCM uses this information, along with the crankshaft position sensor information, to control fuel injection synchronization. The camshaft position sensor is located inside the distributor.

12   **Crankshaft Position (CKP) sensor** – On 1996 and later models, the crankshaft position sensor senses crankshaft position (TDC) during each engine revolution. The PCM uses this information to control ignition timing and fuel injection synchronization.

13   **Engine Coolant Temperature (ECT) sensor** - The engine coolant temperature sensor senses engine coolant temperature. The ECM/PCM uses this information to control fuel injection duration and ignition timing.

14   **Intake Air Temperature (IAT) sensor** - The intake air temperature senses the temperature of the air entering the intake manifold. The ECM/PCM uses this information to control fuel injection duration.

15   **Knock Sensor (KS)** - The knock sensor is a piezoelectric element that detects the sound of engine detonation, or "pinging". The ECM/PCM uses the input signal from the knock sensor to recognize detonation and retard spark advance to avoid engine damage.

16   **Manifold Absolute Pressure (MAP) sensor** - The manifold absolute pressure monitors intake manifold pressure and ambient barometric pressure. The ECM/PCM uses this input signal to determine engine load and adjusts fuel injection duration accordingly.

17   **Mass Airflow (MAF) sensor** – On 1996 and later models, the mass airflow sensor measures the amount of air passing through the sensor body and ultimately entering the engine. The PCM uses this information to control fuel delivery.

18   **Oxygen (O2) sensor** - The oxygen sensors generate a voltage signal that varies with the varying oxygen content of the exhaust gas. The ECM/PCM uses this information to determine if the fuel system is running rich or lean and make adjustments accordingly.

19   **Throttle Position Sensor (TPS)** - The throttle position sensor senses throttle movement and position. This signal enables the ECM/PCM to determine when the throttle is closed, in a cruise position, or wide open. The ECM/PCM uses this information to control fuel delivery and ignition timing.

20   **Vehicle Speed Sensor (VSS)** - The vehicle speed sensor provides information to the ECM/PCM to indicate vehicle speed.

21   **Miscellaneous PCM inputs** - In addition to the various sensors, the PCM on 1996 and later models, monitors various switches and circuits to determine vehicle operating conditions. The switches and circuits include:

a) *Air conditioning system*
b) *Battery voltage*
c) *Brake On/Off switch*
d) *Cruise control system*
e) *EGR valve position*
f) *Engine oil level and pressure*
g) *EVAP system*
h) *Fuel level and fuel tank pressure*
i) *Ignition switch*
j) *Park/neutral position switch*
k) *Sensor signal and ground circuits*
l) *Transmission controls*

Output actuators

22   **Air conditioning clutch relay** – On 1996 and later models, the PCM controls the operation of the air conditioning compressor clutch with the air conditioning clutch relay.

23   **Service Engine Soon light** - The ECM/PCM will illuminate the Service Engine Soon light if a malfunction in the electronic engine control system occurs.

24   **Cruise control module** – On 1996 and later models, the cruise control system operation is controlled by the PCM.

25   **Engine cooling fan relay** – On 1996 and later models, the engine cooling fan is controlled by the PCM according to information received from the engine coolant temperature sensor.

26   **Linear EGR valve** – On 1996 and later models, the electronic EGR valve is controlled by the PCM. Ideal EGR flow is determined by the PCM and the EGR valve pintle position is adjusted accordingly.

27   **EVAP canister purge and vent valve solenoids** – On 1996 and later models, the evaporative emission canister purge and vent valve solenoids are operated by the PCM to purge the fuel vapor canister and route fuel vapor to the intake manifold for combustion.

28   **Secondary Air Injection (AIR) pump and vacuum valve/solenoid** – On 1999 and 2000 models, the PCM operates the secondary air injection pump and opens the vacuum valve to inject fresh air into the exhaust stream, lower emission levels under certain operating conditions.

29   **Fuel injectors** - The ECM/PCM opens the fuel injectors individually in firing order sequence. The ECM/PCM also controls the time the injector is held open (pulse width). The pulse width of the injector (measured in milliseconds) determines the amount of fuel delivered. For more information on the fuel delivery system and the fuel injectors, including injector replacement, refer to Chapter 4.

30   **Fuel pump relay** - The fuel pump relay is activated by the ECM/PCM with the ignition switch in the Start or Run position. When the ignition switch is turned on, the relay is activated to supply initial line pressure to the system. For more information on fuel pump check and replacement, refer to Chapter 4.

31   **Idle Air Control valve (IAC)** - The idle air control valve controls the amount of air allowed to bypass the throttle plate when the throttle valve is closed or at idle position. The more air allowed to bypass the throttle plate, the higher the idle speed. The idle air control valve opening and the resulting idle speed is controlled by the ECM/PCM.

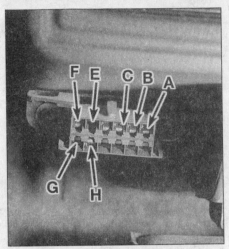

2.33 Assembly Line Data Link (ALDL) terminal identification (1995 and earlier models)

A   Ground
B   Diagnostic test terminal
C   A.I.R. (if used)
E   Serial data
F   T.C.C. (if used)
G   Fuel pump (CK)
H   Brake sense speed input (CK)

32   Ignition control module – On 1996 and later models, the PCM controls ignition timing through the ignition control module depending on engine operation conditions. The ignition control module is mounted externally to the distributor. Refer to Chapter 5 for more information on the ignition control module.

Obtaining trouble codes

1988 through 1995 models

Refer to illustration 2.33

33   To retrieve this information from the PCM on 1988 through 1995 models (which are OBD I models) you must use a short jumper wire to ground a diagnostic terminal. The terminal is part of an electrical connector called the Assembly Line Data Link (ALDL) **(see illustration)**. The ALDL is located under the dashboard, just below the instrument panel and to the left of the center console. To use the ALDL, remove the plastic cover (if equipped). With the electrical connector exposed to view, push one end of the jumper wire into the diagnostic TEST terminal and the other end into the GROUND terminal.

34   Turn the ignition to the ON position. **Caution:** *Do not start the engine with the TEST terminal grounded.* The "SERVICE ENGINE SOON" light should flash Trouble Code 12, indicating that the diagnostic system is working. Code 12 will consist of one flash, followed by a short pause, then two more flashes in quick succession. After a longer pause, the code will repeat itself two more times. If no other codes have been stored, Code 12 will continue to repeat itself until the jumper wire is disconnected. If addi-

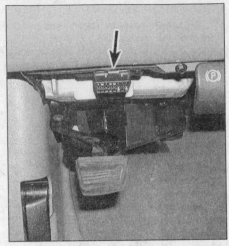

2.37 The diagnostic connector (arrow) is located under the instrument panel (1996 and later models)

tional Trouble Codes have been stored, they will follow Code 12. Again, each Trouble Code will flash three times before moving on.

35   Once the code(s) have been noted, use the Trouble Code Identification information which follows to locate the source of the fault. **Note:** *Whenever the battery cable is disconnected, all stored Trouble Codes in the PCM are erased. Be aware of this before you disconnect the battery.*

36   There are additional codes that relate only to models equipped the 4L60-E or 4L80-E electronic controlled transmission. These codes represent internal transmission problems that should be left to a dealer service department or an automotive or transmission repair shop. These codes are as follows: 37, 38, 39, 52, 53 and 58 through 87.

1996 through 2000 models

Note: *The diagnostic trouble codes on all OBD-II models can only be extracted from the Powertrain Control Module (PCM) using a specialized scan tool. Have the vehicle diagnosed by a dealer service department or other qualified automotive repair facility if the proper scan tool is not available.*

Refer to illustration 2.37

37   To retrieve this information from 1996 and later models (OBD II), a SCAN tool must be connected to the diagnostic connector **(see illustration)**. The SCAN tool is a hand-held digital computer scanner that interfaces with the on-board computer. The SCAN tool is a very powerful tool; it not only reads the trouble codes but also displays the actual operating conditions of the sensors and actuators. SCAN tools are necessary to accurately diagnose a modern computerized fuel injected engine. SCAN tools are available from automotive parts stores and specialty tool companies.

38   It should be noted that the self-diagnosis feature built into this system does not detect all possible faults. If you suspect a problem with the On Board Diagnostic (OBD-

II) system, but the SERVICE ENGINE SOON light has not come on and no trouble codes have been stored, take the vehicle to a dealer service department or other qualified repair shop for diagnosis.

39   Furthermore, when diagnosing an engine performance, fuel economy or exhaust emissions problem (which is not accompanied by a SERVICE ENGINE SOON light) do not automatically assume the fault lies in this system. Perform all standard troubleshooting procedures, as indicated elsewhere in this manual, before turning to the On Board Diagnostic (OBD-II) system.

40   Finally, since this is an electronic system, you should have a basic knowledge of automotive electronics before attempting any diagnosis. Damage to the PCM, Programmable Read Only Memory (PROM) calibration unit or related components can easily occur if care is not exercised.

Clearing diagnostic trouble codes

41   After the system has been repaired, the codes must be cleared from the ECM (OBD-I) or PCM (OBD-II) memory. The codes can be cleared by disconnecting battery power from the ECM/PCM for a minimum of thirty seconds. Battery power can be disconnected from the ECM/PCM by disconnecting the power connector (fusible link) near the positive battery terminal (if equipped), removing the IGN fuse or by disconnecting the negative battery cable from the battery. The preferred method for clearing diagnostic codes on an OBD-II model is by using a scan tool. **Caution:** *On models equipped with the Theftlock audio system, be sure the lockout feature is turned off before performing any procedure which requires disconnecting the battery (see the front of this manual).*

42   Always clear the codes from the ECM/PCM before starting the engine after a new electronic emission control component is installed onto the engine. The ECM/PCM stores the operating parameters of each sensor. The ECM/PCM may set a trouble code if a new sensor is allowed to operate before the parameters from the old sensor have been erased.

Diagnostic trouble code identification

43   The accompanying list of diagnostic trouble codes is a compilation of all the codes that may be encountered using a generic scan tool. Additional trouble codes may be obtainable with the use of the manufacturer specific scan tool. Not all codes pertain to all models and not all codes will illuminate the Service Engine Soon light when set. **Caution:** *To prevent damage to the ECM/PCM, the ignition switch must be OFF when disconnecting or connecting power to the ECM/PCM.* **Note:** *Disconnecting the negative battery terminal will erase any radio preset codes that have been stored.*

OBD-I trouble code chart

Trouble Code	Circuit or system	Probable cause
	Note: *Not all codes apply to all models.*	
12	Diagnostic	This code will flash whenever the diagnostic terminal is grounded with the ignition turned On and the engine not running. If additional trouble codes are stored in the ECM they will appear after this code has flashed three times.
13	Oxygen sensor circuit	Check the wiring and connectors from the oxygen sensor. Replace oxygen sensor (see Section 5).*
14	Coolant sensor circuit	If the engine is experiencing overheating problems, the problem must be rectified (high temperature indicated) before continuing (see Chapters 1 and 3). Check all wiring and connectors associated with the sensor. Replace the coolant sensor (see Section 4).*
15	Coolant sensor circuit	See above. Also, check the thermostat for proper operation (low temperature indicated).
16	VSS buffer	Code 16 will set if the ECM detects a signal loss from the Vehicle Speed Sensor buffer.
21	TPS circuit (signal voltage high)	Check for sticking or misadjusted TPS. Check all wiring and connections at the TPS and at the ECM. Replace TPS*.
22	TPS circuit (signal voltage low)	See above.
24	Vehicle Speed Sensor (VSS)	A fault in this circuit should be indicated only while the vehicle is in motion. Disregard code 24 if set when drive wheels are not turning. Check connections at the ECM.
32	Exhaust Gas Recirculation (EGR) failure	Check the vacuum source and all vacuum lines. Check the system electrical connectors at the ECM and EGR valve. Replace the EGR valve or ECM as necessary (see Section 8).*
33	Manifold Absolute Pressure (MAP) signal voltage high	Check vacuum hose(s) from MAP sensor. Check electrical sensor or circuit connections at the ECM. Replace MAP sensor (see Section 4).*
34	Manifold Absolute Pressure (MAP) signal voltage low	Check vacuum hose(s) from MAP sensor. Check electrical sensor or circuit connections at the ECM. Replace MAP sensor (see Section 4).*
35	Idle Air Control	Code 35 will set if the ECM detects an idle speed above or below the desired idle speed. Replace the IAC.*
36	Idle speed control actuator	Code 36 will set if the ECM detects an open or short circuit in the idle speed control actuator solenoid circuit.
42	Ignition Control Circuit	Check the wiring and connectors between the ignition module and the ECM. Check the ignition module (see Chapter 5). Replace the ECM.*
43	Electronic Spark Control	ESC module is not receiving a knock signal from the knock sensor. Check the knock (ESC) system sensor (see Section 4) or the ESC module. Have the module checked by a dealer service department.
44	Lean exhaust	Check the wiring and connectors from the oxygen sensor to the ECM. Check the ECM ground terminal. Check the fuel pressure (Chapter 4). Replace the oxygen sensor (see Section 5).*
45	Rich exhaust	Check the evaporative charcoal canister and its components for the presence of fuel. Check for fuel or contaminated oil. Check the fuel pressure regulator. Check for a leaking fuel injector. Check for a sticking EGR valve. Replace the oxygen sensor (see Section 5).*
51	PROM (MEMCAL)	Faulty or incorrect PROM (MEMCAL). Diagnosis should be performed by a dealer service department or other qualified repair shop.
53	System voltage high	Code 53 will set if the voltage at the ECM is greater than 17.1-volts. Check the charging system (see Chapter 5).
54	Fuel pump relay low voltage	Check the fuel pump relay and circuit for shorts or damage (see Chapter 4).
55	ECM failure	Check the ECM power and ground circuits. If OK, replace the ECM.*
	Note: *The following codes apply to 1994 and later models only.*	
28	Transmission range pressure switch	Code 28 will set if the ECM detects an open in one of the transmission pressure switch circuits.
37	Brake switch	Code 37 will set if the ECM detects the brake switch stuck ON.
38	Brake switch	Code 37 will set if the ECM detects the brake switch stuck OFF.
39	Torque converter	Code 39 will set if the ECM detects the torque converter clutch solenoid stuck OFF.clutch solenoid
52	System voltage high	Code 52 will set if the ECM detects ignition feed voltage greater than 16-volts for 90 minutes.

OBD-I trouble code chart (continued)

Trouble Code	Circuit or system	Probable cause

Note: *The following codes apply to 1994 and later models only.*

53	System voltage high	Code 53 will set if the ECM detects ignition feed voltage greater than 19.5-volts for 2 seconds.
58	Transmission fluid temperature sensor	Code 58 will set if the ECM detects high transmission fluid temperature (above 300-degrees F).
59	Transmission fluid temperature sensor	Code 59 will set if the ECM detects low transmission fluid temperature (below -40-degrees F).
66	3-2 shift control solenoid	Code 66 will set if the ECM detects an open or short circuit in the 3-2 solenoid circuit.
67	Torque converter clutch solenoid	Code 67 will set if the ECM detects an open or short circuit in the torque converter clutch solenoid circuit.
68	Transmission slipping	Code 68 will set if the ECM detects a difference in the engine speed and the transmission input speed.
69	Torque converter clutch solenoid	Code 69 will set if the ECM detects the torque converter clutch solenoid stuck ON.
72	Vehicle Speed Sensor	Code 72 will set if the ECM detects a transmission output speed signal loss.
73	Pressure control solenoid	Code 73 will set if the ECM detects a fault in the pressure control solenoid circuit.
74	Transmission input speed sensor	Code 74 will set if the ECM detects a fault in the transmission input speed sensor circuit.
75	System voltage low	Code 75 will set if the ECM detects low ignition feed voltage.
79	Transmission fluid temperature high	Code 79 will set if the ECM detects transmission fluid temperature greater than 295-degrees F for 30 minutes.
81	2-3 shift solenoid	Code 81 will set if the ECM detects an open or short circuit in the 2-3 shift solenoid circuit.
82	1-2 shift solenoid	Code 82 will set if the ECM detects an open or short circuit in the 1-2 shift solenoid circuit.
83	Torque converter clutch	Code 83 will set if the ECM detects an open or short circuit in the TCC solenoid circuit.
85	Transmission gear	Code 85 will set if the ECM detects the calculated transmission ratio different than the known ratio error ratio in any gear. The ECM uses this information to detect shift solenoid problems.
86	Transmission gear ratio error	Code 86 will set if the ECM detects the calculated transmission ratio lower than the known ratio in first or second gear. The ECM uses this information to detect shift solenoid problems.
87	Transmission gear ratio error	Code 87 will set if the ECM detects the calculated transmission ratio higher than the known ratio in third or fourth gear. The ECM uses this information to detect shift solenoid problems.

Component replacement may not cure the problem in all cases. For this reason, you may want to seek professional advice before purchasing replacement parts.

OBD II trouble code chart*

Code	Code Identification
P0101	Mass air flow (MAF) sensor circuit, range or performance problem
P0102	Mass air flow (MAF) sensor circuit, low input
P0103	Mass air flow (MAF) sensor circuit, high input
P0106	Manifold absolute pressure (MAP) sensor circuit, range or performance problem
P0107	Manifold absolute pressure (MAP) sensor circuit, low input
P0108	Manifold absolute pressure (MAP) sensor circuit, high input
P0112	Intake air temperature (IAT) circuit, low input
P0113	Intake air temperature (IAT) circuit, high input
P0117	Engine coolant temperature (ECT) circuit, low input
P0118	Engine coolant temperature (ECT) circuit, high input
P0121	Throttle position sensor (TPS) circuit, range or performance problem
P0122	Throttle position sensor (TPS) circuit, low input
P0123	Throttle position sensor (TPS) circuit, high input
P0125	Insufficient coolant temperature for closed loop fuel control

Code	Code Identification
P0131	Oxygen sensor circuit, low voltage (pre-converter sensor, left bank)
P0132	Oxygen sensor circuit, high voltage (pre-converter sensor, left bank)
P0133	Oxygen sensor circuit, slow response (pre-converter sensor, left bank)
P0134	Oxygen sensor circuit - no activity detected (pre-converter sensor, left bank)
P0135	Oxygen sensor heater circuit malfunction (pre-converter sensor, left bank)
P0137	Oxygen sensor circuit, low voltage (post-converter sensor, left bank)
P0138	Oxygen sensor circuit, high voltage (post-converter sensor, left bank)
P0140	Oxygen sensor circuit - no activity detected (post-converter sensor, left bank)
P0141	Oxygen sensor heater circuit malfunction (post-converter sensor, left bank)
P0143	Oxygen sensor circuit, low voltage (#2 post-converter sensor, left bank)
P0144	Oxygen sensor circuit, high voltage (#2 post-converter sensor, left bank)
P0146	Oxygen sensor circuit - no activity detected (#2 post-converter sensor, left bank)
P0147	Oxygen sensor heater circuit malfunction (#2 post-converter sensor, left bank)
P0151	Oxygen sensor circuit, low voltage (pre-converter sensor, right bank)
P0152	Oxygen sensor circuit, high voltage (pre-converter sensor, right bank)
P0153	Oxygen sensor circuit, slow response (pre-converter sensor, right bank)
P0154	Oxygen sensor circuit - no activity detected (pre-converter sensor, right bank)
P0155	Oxygen sensor heater circuit malfunction (pre-converter sensor, right bank)
P0157	Oxygen sensor circuit, low voltage (post-converter sensor, right bank)
P0158	Oxygen sensor circuit, high voltage (post-converter sensor, right bank)
P0160	Oxygen sensor circuit - no activity detected (post-converter sensor, right bank)
P0161	Oxygen sensor heater circuit malfunction (post-converter sensor, right bank)
P0171	System too lean, left bank
P0172	System too rich, left bank
P0174	System too lean, right bank
P0175	System too rich, right bank
P0300	Engine misfire detected
P0301	Cylinder number 1 misfire detected
P0302	Cylinder number 2 misfire detected
P0303	Cylinder number 3 misfire detected
P0304	Cylinder number 4 misfire detected
P0305	Cylinder number 5 misfire detected
P0306	Cylinder number 6 misfire detected
P0307	Cylinder number 7 misfire detected
P0308	Cylinder number 8 misfire detected
P0325	Knock sensor circuit malfunction
P0327	Knock sensor circuit, low output
P0336	Crankshaft position sensor circuit, range or performance problem
P0337	Crankshaft position sensor, low output
P0338	Crankshaft position sensor, high output
P0339	Crankshaft position sensor, circuit intermittent
P0340	Camshaft position sensor circuit
P0341	Camshaft position sensor circuit, range or performance problem
P0401	Exhaust gas recirculation, insufficient flow detected
P0404	Exhaust gas recirculation circuit, range or performance problem
P0405	Exhaust gas recirculation sensor circuit low
P0410	Secondary air injection system
P0418	Secondary air injection pump relay control circuit
P0420	Catalyst system efficiency below threshold, left bank
P0430	Catalyst system efficiency below threshold, right bank
P0440	Evaporative emission control system malfunction
P0441	Evaporative emission control system, purge control circuit malfunction
P0442	Evaporative emission control system, small leak detected
P0446	Evaporative emission control system, vent system performance
P0452	Evaporative emission control system, pressure sensor low input
P0453	Evaporative emission control system, pressure sensor high input
P0461	Fuel level sensor circuit, range or performance problem

OBD II trouble code chart*

Code	Code Identification
P0462	Fuel level sensor circuit, low input
P0463	Fuel level sensor circuit, high input
P0500	Vehicle speed sensor circuit
P0506	Idle control system, rpm lower than expected
P0507	Idle control system, rpm higher than expected
P0601	Powertrain Control Module, memory error
P0602	Powertrain Control module, programming error
P0603	Powertrain Control Module, memory reset error
P0604	Powertrain Control Module, memory error (RAM)
P0605	Powertrain Control Module, memory error (ROM)
P1106	Manifold absolute pressure sensor circuit intermittent high voltage
P1107	Manifold absolute pressure sensor circuit intermittent low voltage
P1111	Intake air temperature sensor circuit intermittent high voltage
P1112	Intake air temperature sensor circuit intermittent low voltage
P1114	Engine coolant temperature sensor circuit intermittent low voltage
P1115	Engine coolant temperature sensor circuit intermittent high voltage
P1121	Throttle position sensor circuit intermittent high voltage
P1122	Throttle position sensor circuit intermittent low voltage
P1133	Oxygen sensor insufficient switching (pre-converter sensor, left bank)
P1134	Oxygen sensor transition time ratio (pre-converter sensor, left bank)
P1153	Oxygen sensor insufficient switching (pre-converter sensor, right bank)
P1154	Oxygen sensor transition time ratio (pre-converter sensor, right bank)
P1345	Crankshaft position sensor/Camshaft position sensor correlation
P1351	Ignition control circuit high voltage
P1361	Ignition control circuit low voltage
P1380	Electronic brake control module rough road sensing error
P1381	No serial data from electronic brake control module
P1404	EGR valve closed pintle position
P1415	Secondary air injection system malfunction, left bank
P1416	Secondary air injection system malfunction, right bank
P1441	EVAP system flow during non-purge
P1508	Idle speed too low
P1509	Idle speed too high
P1621	PCM memory performance
P1626	Serial data communication failure with vehicle theft deterrent controller (no password)
P1631	Theft deterrent password incorrect

*Not all codes apply to all models

---

3   Electronic Control Module (ECM)/PROM/CALPAK - removal and installation

Caution: *The ignition key must always be turned OFF whenever you disconnect or connect power to the ECM/PCM or it can be internally damaged. This means during battery jumping, cable replacement, disconnecting the battery cables, etc. In addition, never touch the connector pins or the soldered parts on the circuit board of the ECM/PCM. The static electricity on your body can damage components.*

Caution: *Avoid static electricity damage to the ECM/PCM by grounding yourself to the body of the vehicle before touching the ECM/PCM and using a special anti-static pad to store the computer on, once it is removed.*

Note 1: *1996 and later OBD-II systems refer to the on-board computer as the Powertrain Control Module (PCM).*

Note 2: *On 1996 and later OBD-II systems, anytime the PCM is replaced with a new unit, the PCM must be reprogrammed by a dealership service department with special equipment. A crankshaft position sensor variation relearn procedure and a vehicle anti-theft system password relearn procedure must be performed, as well. The following procedure pertains to removal and installation of the original PCM only. If the PCM must be replaced with a new unit, take the vehicle to a dealership service department.*

1988 through 1995 models

ECM

Refer to illustration 3.5

1   If you are replacing the ECM, check the service number on the new and old ECM to verify that they are the same.

2   The Electronic Control Module (ECM) is located under the right hand side of the instrument panel.

3   Disconnect the cable from the negative battery terminal. **Caution:** *On models equipped with the Theftlock audio system, be sure the lockout feature is turned off before performing any procedure which requires disconnecting the battery (see the front of this manual).*

4   Remove the glove box to gain access to the ECM.

5   Remove the retaining bolts **(see illustration)** and carefully slide the ECM out far enough to unplug the electrical connectors.

6   Unplug both electrical connectors from the ECM. **Caution:** *The ignition switch must be turned off when pulling out or plugging in*

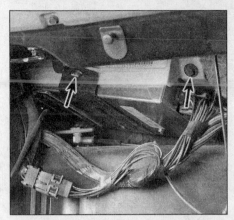

3.5 Remove the ECM retaining bolts (arrows) and carefully slide the ECM out

3.8 The CALPAK (top) and PROM (bottom) inside an ECM

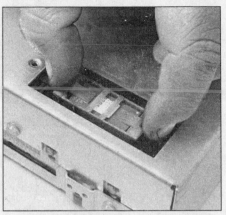

3.12 Grasp the PROM carrier at the ends and gently rock it until the PROM is disconnected

the connectors to prevent damage to the ECM.

7   Installation is the reverse of removal.

PROM

Refer to illustration 3.8

8   To allow one model of ECM to be used for many different vehicles, a device called a PROM (Programmable Read Only Memory) is used **(see illustration)**. The PROM is located inside the ECM and contains information on the vehicle's weight, engine, transmission, axle ratio, etc. One ECM part number can be used by many GM vehicles but the PROM is very specific and must be used only in the vehicle for which it was designed. For this reason, it's essential to check the latest parts book and Service Bulletin information for the correct part number when replacing a PROM. An ECM purchased at a dealer doesn't come with a PROM. The PROM from the old ECM must be carefully removed and installed in the new ECM.

CALPAK

9   A device known as a CALPAK **(see illustration 3.8)** is used to allow fuel delivery if other parts of the ECM are damaged. The CALPAK has an access door in the ECM and

replacement is the same as described for the PROM.

PROM/CALPAK replacement

Refer to illustrations 3.12, 3.13 and 3.14

10   If you are replacing the PROM, check to make sure that the service numbers match on both the old and new PROM.

11   Remove the PROM/CALPAK access cover.

12   Grasp the PROM carrier at the narrow ends **(see illustration)**. Gently rock the carrier from end-to-end. The PROM carrier and PROM should lift off the PROM socket easily.

13   Note the reference end of the PROM carrier **(see illustration)** before setting it aside.

14   Position the PROM carrier assembly squarely over the PROM socket with the small notched end of the carrier aligned with the small tang in the socket at the pin 1 end. Press on the PROM carrier until it seats firmly in the socket **(see illustration)**.

15   If the PROM is new, make sure the notch in the PROM is matched to the small notch in the carrier **(see illustration 3.13)**. **Caution:** *If the PROM is installed backwards and the ignition switch is turned on, the PROM will be destroyed.*

16   Attach the access cover to the ECM and tighten the screw(s).

17   Install the ECM.

18   Start the engine and enter the diagnostic mode (see Section 2). If no trouble codes occur, the PROM is correctly installed.

19   If Trouble Code 51 occurs, or if the SERVICE ENGINE SOON light comes on and remains on, the PROM isn't seated, is installed backwards, has bent pins or is defective.

20   If the PROM isn't seated, pressing firmly on both ends of the carrier should correct the problem.

21   If the pins have been bent, remove the PROM, straighten the pins and reinstall it. **Note:** *Do not touch the pins with your hands or damage to the PROM could occur. If the bent pins break or crack when you attempt to straighten them, discard the PROM and replace it with a new one.*

1996 through 2000 models

Refer to illustration 3.22

22   1996 through 2000 models are equipped with a Powertrain Control Module (PCM). The PCM is located under the hood, mounted to the left inner fender **(see illustration)**.

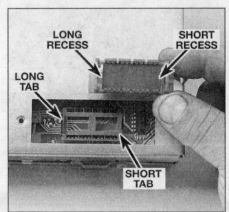

3.13 On later models, the notch in the PROM carrier is matched up with the small tang on the socket

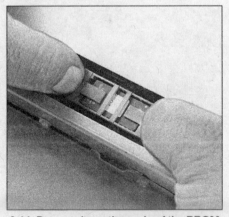

3.14 Press only on the ends of the PROM carrier - pressure on the center could result in bent or broken pins or damage to the PROM

3.22 The PCM is located on the top of the left inner fender on 1996 and later models

4.2a Throttle Position Sensor (TPS) location (V6 Central SFI model shown)

4.2b The Throttle Position Sensor (TPS) (arrow) is secured to the side of the TBI by two Torx screws (V8 TBI model shown)

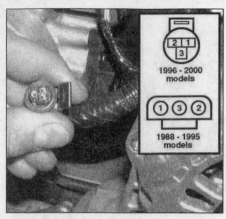

4.3 Disconnect the electrical connector from the TPS and check the voltage supply and ground circuits from the PCM at the harness connector

1   5-volt supply
2   Sensor ground
3   Throttle position sensor signal

23   The PCM can be removed and replaced easily by simply transferring the Knock Sensor PROM to the replacement PCM. The new PCM, however, will have to be programmed before it will operate. This requires a scan tool and dealer information, therefore this procedure must be performed by a dealer service department.

24   The PCM has the ability to learn the individual driving characteristics of the vehicle. If the battery is disconnected, the memory will be lost and the computer will have to relearn. This can affect driveability adversely during the first few miles of driving. To accomplish the relearning process, simply drive the truck normally for about ten miles.

---

4   Throttle Position Sensor (TPS) - check and replacement

1   The Throttle Position Sensor (TPS) is a variable potentiometer connected to the end of the throttle shaft on the throttle body. By monitoring the output voltage from the TPS, the ECM/PCM can determine fuel delivery based on throttle valve angle (driver demand). A broken or loose TPS can cause intermittent bursts of fuel from the injectors and an unstable idle because the ECM/PCM thinks the throttle is moving.

Check

Refer to illustrations 4.2a, 4.2b, 4.3 and 4.4
Note 1: *The TPS on TBI systems in non-adjustable. The TPS and TBI unit must be replaced as a complete unit in the event of failure.*
Note 2: *Performing the following test will set a diagnostic trouble code and illuminate the Service Engine Soon light. Clear the diagnostic trouble code after performing the tests and making the necessary repairs (see Section 2).*

2   The Throttle Position Sensor (TPS) is located on the side of the throttle body **(see illustrations)**. Check the terminals in the connector and the wires leading to the sensor for

looseness and breaks. Repair as required.
3   Before checking the TPS, check the voltage supply and ground circuits from the ECM/PCM. Disconnect the electrical connector from the TPS and connect the positive lead of a voltmeter to the gray wire terminal (1) and the negative lead to the black wire terminal (2) at the harness connector **(see illustration)**. Turn the ignition key On - the voltage should read approximately 5.0 volts. If the voltage is incorrect, check the wiring from the TPS to the ECM/PCM. If the circuits are good, have the ECM/PCM checked at a dealer service department or other properly equipped repair facility.
4   To check the TPS operation, reconnect the connector to the TPS and using a suitable probe, backprobe the dark blue wire terminal (3) of the TPS connector **(see illustration)**. Connect the positive lead of a voltmeter to the probe and the negative lead to a good engine ground point. Turn the ignition key On (engine not running), with the throttle fully closed the voltage should read approximately 0.6 volts. Gradually open the throttle - the voltage should increase smoothly to approxi-

mately 4.5 volts at wide-open throttle. If the test results are incorrect, replace the TPS.

Replacement

Refer to illustration 4.7
5   Access the TPS.
a) On TBI systems, remove the air filter assembly from the TBI unit
b) On Central SFI and MPFI systems, remove the air intake duct and resonator from the throttle body (see Chapter 4).
6   Disconnect the electrical connector from the TPS.
7   Remove the TPS mounting screws and remove the TPS from the throttle body **(see illustration)**.
8   Install a new O-ring on the TPS. With the throttle in the closed position, align the TPS with the throttle shaft and install the TPS. Tighten the screws securely.
9   The remainder of installation is the reverse of removal.

4.4 To check the TPS, backprobe the dark blue wire terminal of the TPS connector with a voltmeter (V6 Central SFI model shown)

4.7 Remove the TPS mounting screws (arrows) (V8 model shown)

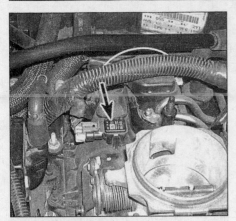

5.2a MAP sensor location (V6 Central
SFI models shown)

5.2b MAP sensor
mounting details (V8
TBI models shown)

A   Electrical
     connector
B   Vacuum hose
C   Mounting screws

5   Manifold Absolute Pressure (MAP) sensor - check and replacement

1   The Manifold Absolute Pressure (MAP) sensor monitors the intake manifold pressure changes resulting from changes in engine load and speed and converts the information into a voltage output. The ECM/PCM receives information as a varying voltage signal from closed throttle (high vacuum) to wide open throttle (low vacuum). The ECM/PCM uses the MAP sensor to control fuel delivery and ignition timing.

Check

Refer to illustrations 5.2a, 5.2b and 5.3
Note: *Performing the following test will set a diagnostic trouble code and illuminate the Service Engine Soon light. Clear the diagnostic trouble code after performing the tests and making the necessary repairs (see Section 2).*
2   The MAP sensor is located on the upper

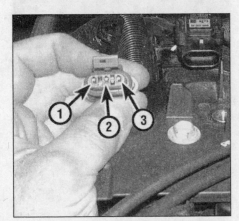

5.3 Disconnect the electrical connector
from the MAP sensor and check the
voltage supply and ground circuits from
the PCM at the harness connector

1   *Sensor ground*
2   *MAP sensor signal*
3   *5-volt supply*

intake manifold plenum **(see illustrations)**. Check the terminals in the connector and the wires leading to the sensor for looseness and breaks. Repair as required.
3   Before checking the MAP sensor, check the voltage supply and ground circuits from the ECM/PCM. Disconnect the electrical connector from the MAP sensor and connect the positive lead of a voltmeter to the gray wire terminal (3) (and the negative lead to the orange/black or black wire terminal (1) at the harness connector **(see illustration)**. Turn the ignition key On - the voltage should read approximately 5.0 volts. If the voltage is incorrect, check the wiring from the MAP sensor to the ECM/PCM. If the circuits are good, have the ECM/PCM checked at a dealer service department or other properly equipped repair facility.
4   To check the MAP sensor operation, reconnect the connector to the MAP sensor and using a suitable probe, backprobe the light green wire terminal (2) of the MAP sensor connector. Connect the positive lead of a voltmeter to the probe and the negative lead to a good engine ground point. Turn the ignition key On - with the engine not running the voltage should read 4.0 to 5.0 volts. Start the engine and allow it to idle - the voltage should decrease to approximately 0.5 to 2.0 volts. If the test results are incorrect, replace the MAP sensor.

Replacement

5   Access the MAP sensor.
     a) On TBI systems, remove the air cleaner assembly (see Chapter 4)
     b) On Central SFI systems, remove the intake air duct and resonator from the throttle body (see Chapter 4)
     c) On MPFI systems, remove the upper intake manifold from the engine (see Chapter 4)
6   Disconnect the electrical connector from the MAP sensor.
7   Remove the retaining bolts and withdraw the MAP sensor. Replace the MAP sensor seal in the upper intake manifold, if equipped.
8   Installation is the reverse of removal.

6   Mass Airflow (MAF) sensor - check and replacement

1   The MAF sensor measures the amount of air passing through the sensor body and ultimately entering the engine through the throttle body. The PCM uses this information to control fuel delivery - the more air entering the engine (acceleration), the more fuel required. **Note:** *Only 1996 through 2000 models are equipped with a MAF sensor.*

Check

Refer to illustrations 6.2 and 6.3
2   The Mass Airflow Sensor (MAF) is located on the air filter housing **(see illustration)**. A scan tool is necessary to check the output of the MAF sensor (see Section 2). The scan tool displays the sensor output in grams per second. With the engine idling at normal operating temperature, the display should read approximately 4.0 to 9.0 grams per second. When the engine is accelerated the values should rise quickly and remain steady at a steady engine speed.
3   Before checking the MAF sensor operation, check the voltage supply and ground circuits. Disconnect the electrical connector from the MAF sensor and connect the positive lead of a voltmeter to the pink wire termi-

6.2 The Mass Airflow (MAF) sensor is
attached to the air filter housing

6.3 Disconnect the electrical connector from the MAF sensor and check the voltage supply and ground circuits at the harness connector

1   *MAF sensor signal*
2   *MAF sensor ground*
3   *12-volt supply*

nal (4) at the negative lead to the black/white wire terminal (3) at the harness connector **(see illustration)**. Turn the ignition key ON - the voltage should read approximately 12.0 volts. If the voltage is incorrect, check the circuits from the MAP sensor to the power distribution center and engine ground point (don't forget to check the fuses first). If the power and ground circuits are good, check the MAF sensor operation with a scan tool. If the MAF sensor does not respond as described in Step 2, replace the MAF sensor.

Replacement

Refer to illustration 6.6
4   Disconnect the electrical connector from the MAF sensor.
5   Loosen the hose clamp securing the air intake duct to the MAF sensor and remove the duct.
6   Loosen the hose clamp retaining the MAF sensor to the air filter cover and remove the sensor **(see illustration)**. **Caution:** *Handle the MAF sensor with care. Damage to this sensor will affect the operation of the entire fuel injection system.*
7   Installation is the reverse of removal.

6.6 Loosen the hose clamps (arrows) and remove the Mass Airflow sensor

7   Intake Air Temperature (IAT) sensor - check and replacement

Refer to illustration 7.1
1   The Intake Air Temperature (IAT) sensor is a thermistor (a resistor which varies the value of its resistance in accordance with temperature changes) **(see illustration)**. The change in the resistance values will directly affect the voltage signal from the sensor to the PCM. As the sensor temperature INCREASES, the resistance values will DECREASE. As the sensor temperature DECREASES, the resistance values will INCREASE. **Note:** *Only 1996 through 2000 models are equipped with an IAT sensor.*

Check

Refer to illustration 7.3
Note: *Performing the following test will set a diagnostic trouble code and illuminate the Service Engine Soon light. Clear the diagnostic trouble code after performing the tests and making the necessary repairs (see Section 2).*
2   The Intake Air Temperature (IAT) sensor is mounted either in the air intake duct near the air cleaner or in the air cleaner. Check the terminals in the connector and the wires leading to the sensor for looseness and breaks. Repair as required.
3   Before checking the intake air temperature sensor, check the voltage supply and ground circuits from the PCM. Disconnect the electrical connector from the IAT sensor and connect the positive lead of a voltmeter to the tan wire terminal (1) and the negative lead to the black wire terminal (2) at the harness connector **(see illustration)**. Turn the ignition key ON - the voltage should read approximately 5 0 volts. If the voltage is incorrect, check the wiring from the sensor to the PCM. If the circuits are good, have the PCM checked at a dealer service department or other properly equipped repair facility.

Temperature (degrees-F)	Resistance (ohms)
212	176
194	240
176	332
158	458
140	668
122	972
112	1182
104	1458
95	1800
86	2238
76	2795
68	3520
58	4450
50	5670
40	7280
32	9420

7.1 Intake Air Temperature (IAT) sensor and Engine Coolant Temperature (ECT) sensor approximate temperature vs. resistance values

4   With the ignition switch OFF, disconnect the electrical connector from the IAT sensor. Using an ohmmeter, measure the resistance between the two Intake Air Temperature sensor terminals on the sensor while it is completely cold (50 to 80-degrees F) **(see illustration)**. Reconnect the electrical connector to the sensor, start the engine and warm it up until it reaches operating temperature (180 to 200-degrees F), disconnect the connector and check the resistance again. Compare your measurements to the resistance chart **(see illustration 7.1)**. If the sensor resistance test results are incorrect, replace the intake air temperature sensor. **Note:** *A more accurate check may be performed by removing the air intake duct and heating the sensor with a heat gun or hair dryer while you monitor the resistance of the sensor.*

Replacement

5   Disconnect the electrical connector from the sensor.
6   Carefully remove the sensor from the air intake duct or the air cleaner assembly.
7   Installation is the reverse of removal.

8   Engine Coolant Temperature (ECT) sensor - check and replacement

1   The Engine Coolant Temperature (ECT) sensor is a thermistor (a resistor which varies the value of its resistance in accordance with temperature changes). The change in the resistance values will directly affect the voltage signal from the sensor to the ECM/PCM. As the sensor temperature INCREASES, the resistance values will DECREASE. As the sensor temperature DECREASES, the resistance values will INCREASE.

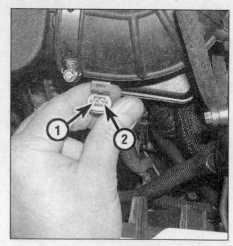

7.3 Disconnect the electrical connector from the intake air temperature sensor and check the voltage supply and ground circuits from the PCM at the harness connector

1   *IAT sensor signal*
2   *Sensor ground*

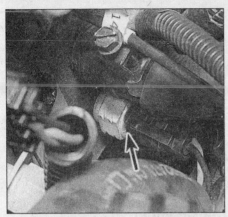

8.2 A typical engine coolant temperature sensor (arrow) (V8 TBI model shown)

Check

Refer to illustrations 8.2 and 8.3

Note: *Performing the following test will set a diagnostic trouble code and illuminate the Service Engine Soon light. Clear the diagnostic trouble code after performing the tests and making the necessary repairs (see Section 2).*

2   The engine coolant temperature sensor threads into a coolant passage at the front of the engine near the thermostat housing **(see illustration)**. Check the terminals in the connector and the wires leading to the sensor for looseness and breaks. Repair as required.

3   Before checking the engine coolant temperature sensor, check the voltage supply and ground circuits from the ECM/PCM. Disconnect the electrical connector from the engine coolant temperature sensor and connect a voltmeter to the two terminals of the harness connector **(see illustration)**. Turn the ignition key On - the voltage should read approximately 5.0 volts. If the voltage is incorrect, check the wiring from the engine coolant temperature sensor to the

ECM/PCM. If the circuits are good, have the ECM/PCM checked at a dealer service department or other properly equipped repair facility.

4   With the ignition switch OFF, disconnect the electrical connector from the engine coolant temperature sensor. Using an ohmmeter, measure the resistance between the two terminals on the sensor while it is completely cold (50 to 80-degrees F). Reconnect the electrical connector to the sensor, start the engine and warm it up until it reaches operating temperature (180 to 200-degrees F), disconnect the connector and check the resistance again. Compare your measurements to the resistance chart **(see illustration 7.1)**. If the sensor resistance test results are incorrect, replace the engine coolant temperature sensor. **Note:** *A more accurate check may be performed by removing the sensor and suspending the tip of the sensor in a container of water. Heat the water on the stove while you monitor the resistance of the sensor.*

Replacement

Warning: *Wait until the engine is completely cool before beginning this procedure.*

5   Drain the cooling system (see Chapter 1).

6   Disconnect the electrical connector from the sensor and carefully unscrew the sensor.

7   Before installing the new sensor, wrap the threads with Teflon sealing tape to prevent leakage and thread corrosion.

8   Installation is the reverse of removal.

9 Crankshaft Position (CKP) sensor - check and replacement

1   The Crankshaft Position (CKP) sensor provides the PCM with a crankshaft position signal. The PCM uses the signal to determine

the spark sequence (firing order) for each cylinder. The PCM also uses the signal to precisely control ignition timing and calculate engine speed (RPM). The signal is used by the Onboard Diagnostic system for misfire detection. The crankshaft position sensor is triggered by slots cut into a reluctor ring on the crankshaft. The sensor tip is positioned approximately 0.050 inch from the reluctor ring. As the notches pass the sensor the magnetic field is altered, producing a pulsating voltage. The ignition system will not operate if the PCM does not receive a crankshaft position sensor input. **Note:** *Only 1996 through 2000 models are equipped with a crankshaft position sensor.*

Check

Refer to illustrations 9.2 and 9.3

Note: *Performing the following test will set a diagnostic trouble code and illuminate the Service Engine Soon light. Clear the diagnostic trouble code after performing the tests and making the necessary repairs (see Section 2).*

2   The crankshaft position sensor is located on the engine front cover **(see illustration)**. Check the terminals in the connector and the wires leading to the sensor for looseness and breaks. Repair as required.

3   Before checking the crankshaft position sensor, check the voltage supply from the underhood electrical center. Disconnect the electrical connector and connect the positive lead of a voltmeter to the pink wire terminal **(see illustration)**. Connect the negative lead of the voltmeter to a good engine ground point. Turn the ignition key On - the voltage should read approximately 12.0 volts. If the voltage is incorrect, check the wiring from the crankshaft position sensor harness connector to the underhood electrical center and repair as necessary. **Note:** *Refer to the wiring diagrams at the end of Chapter 12 for more information on the circuits.*

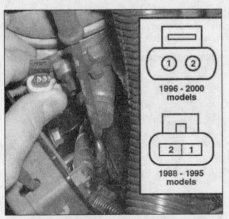

8.3 Disconnect the electrical connector from the Engine Coolant Temperature sensor and check the voltage supply and ground circuits from the PCM at the harness connector

1   *ECT sensor signal*
2   *Sensor ground*

9.2 Crankshaft Position (CKP) sensor location

9.3 Disconnect the Crankshaft Position sensor electrical connector (arrow) and check the voltage supply at the harness side of the connector

1   *12-volt supply*
2   *Sensor ground*
3   *Sensor signal*

4   To check the crankshaft position sensor operation, reconnect the connector to the crankshaft position sensor and using a suitable probe, backprobe the yellow wire terminal (3) of the crankshaft position sensor connector. Connect the positive lead of a voltmeter to the probe and the negative lead to a good engine ground point. Set the meter to the AC volts scale. Crank the engine, the meter should indicate approximately 5.0 volts AC with the engine cranking. If a CKP sensor signal is not present, replace the crankshaft position sensor.

Replacement

Note: *Anytime a crankshaft position sensor is disturbed, A Crankshaft Position Sensor Variation Learning Procedure should be performed or a false misfire diagnostic trouble code may be set. If after replacing the sensor, a false diagnostic trouble codes is set, take the vehicle to a dealership service department for the procedure.*

5   Disconnect the cable from the negative battery terminal. **Caution:** *On models equipped with the Theftlock audio system, be sure the lockout feature is turned off before performing any procedure which requires disconnecting the battery (see the front of this manual).*

6   Raise the vehicle and support it securely on jackstands.

7   Remove the skid plate, if equipped.

8   Disconnect the electrical connector from the sensor.

9   Remove the crankshaft position sensor mounting bolt and remove the sensor.

10   Installation is the reverse of removal.

---

10 Camshaft Position (CMP) sensor - check and replacement

1   The camshaft position sensor is very similar in operation to the crankshaft position sensor, but it produces a signal pulse only once every two crankshaft revolutions, corresponding to cylinder number one Top Dead Center. The camshaft position sensor, in conjunction with the crankshaft position sensor,

10.2 Camshaft position sensor location (V6 Central SFI model shown)

determines the timing for the fuel injection on each cylinder. **Note:** *Only 1996 through 2000 models are equipped with a camshaft position sensor.*

Check

Refer to illustrations 10.2 and 10.3

Note: *Performing the following test will set a diagnostic trouble code and illuminate the Service Engine Soon light. Clear the diagnostic trouble code after performing the tests and making the necessary repairs (see Section 2).*

2   The camshaft position sensor is located in the distributor **(see illustration)**. Check the terminals in the connector and the wires leading to the sensor for looseness and breaks. Repair as required.

3   Before checking the camshaft position sensor, check the voltage supply from the underhood electrical center. Disconnect the electrical connector and connect the positive lead of a voltmeter to the pink wire terminal (1) **(see illustration)**. Connect the negative lead of the voltmeter to a good engine ground point. Turn the ignition key On - the voltage should read approximately 12.0 volts. If the voltage is incorrect, check the wiring from the camshaft position sensor harness connector to the underhood electrical center and repair as necessary. **Note:** *Refer to the*

wiring diagrams at the end of Chapter 12 for more information on the circuits.

4   To check the camshaft position sensor operation, reconnect the connector to the camshaft position sensor and using a suitable probe, backprobe the brown/white wire terminal (2) of the camshaft position sensor connector. Connect the positive lead of a voltmeter to the probe and the negative lead to a good engine ground point. Set the meter to the AC volts scale. Crank the engine, the meter should indicate approximately 5.0 volts AC with the engine cranking. If a CMP sensor signal is not present, replace the camshaft position sensor.

Replacement

Refer to illustration 10.8

5   Disconnect the cable from the negative battery terminal. **Caution:** *On models equipped with the Theftlock audio system, be sure the lockout feature is turned off before performing any procedure which requires disconnecting the battery (see the front of this manual).*

6   Remove the distributor cap and rotor (see Chapter 1).

7   Disconnect the electrical connector from the camshaft position sensor.

8   Using a breaker bar and socket on the crankshaft pulley bolt, rotate the engine until the square slot in the reluctor aligns with the camshaft position sensor **(see illustration)**.

9   Remove the camshaft position sensor mounting screws and remove the sensor from the distributor.

10   Installation is the reverse of removal. Apply thread locking compound to the camshaft position sensor, rotor and distributor cap screws before installing them.

---

11 Oxygen sensor - check and replacement

Refer to illustrations 11.1a and 11.1b

1   An oxygen sensor measures the oxygen remaining in the exhaust gas after the com-

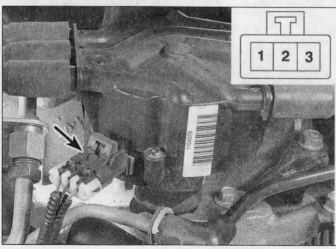

10.8 To remove the camshaft position sensor, rotate the crankshaft until the square slot in the reluctor (arrow) aligns with the camshaft position sensor

10.3 Disconnect the electrical connector from the camshaft position sensor and check the voltage supply and ground circuits at the harness connector

1   *12-volt supply*
2   *Sensor signal*
3   *Sensor ground*

11.1a The oxygen sensor is located in the exhaust system, under the vehicle, on most models

11.1b The post-converter oxygen sensor is located in the exhaust pipe after the catalytic converter (OBD-II system shown)

11.6 Backprobe the oxygen sensor signal wire at the electrical connector for testing

bustion process. The leftover oxygen in the exhaust reacts with the elements inside the oxygen sensor to produce a voltage output that varies from 0.1 volt (high oxygen, lean mixture) to 0.9 volt (low oxygen, rich mixture). Early models (1988 through 1995) are equipped with a single wire O2 sensor mounted in the exhaust pipe after the exhaust manifold **(see illustration)**. Late models (1996 through 2000) are equipped with four oxygen sensors; two pre-converter oxygen sensors and two post-converter oxygen sensors **(see illustration)**. The pre-converter oxygen sensor is mounted in the exhaust system before the catalytic converter. The PCM monitors the varying voltage signal from the pre-converter oxygen sensor continuously to determine the required fuel injector pulse width, controlling the engine air/fuel ratio. A mixture ratio of 14.7 parts air to 1 part fuel is the ideal ratio for gasoline fuel to minimize exhaust emissions, as well as the best combination of fuel economy and engine performance. Based on oxygen sensor signals, the ECM/PCM tries to maintain this air/fuel ratio of 14.7:1 at all times.

2   Also on late model O2 sensors, the post-converter oxygen sensor (mounted in the exhaust system after the catalytic converter) has no effect on PCM control of the air/fuel ratio. However, the post-converter sensor is identical to the pre-converter sensor and operates in the same way. The PCM uses the post-converter signal to monitor the efficiency of the catalytic converter. A post-converter oxygen sensor will produce a slower fluctuating voltage signal that reflects the lower oxygen content in the post-catalyst exhaust.

3   An oxygen sensor produces no voltage when it is below its normal operating temperature of about 600-degrees F. During this warm-up period, the ECM/PCM operates in an open-loop fuel control mode. It does not use the oxygen sensor signal as a feedback indication of residual oxygen in the exhaust. Instead, the ECM/PCM controls fuel metering based on the inputs of other sensors and its own programs. All oxygen sensors are

equipped with a heating element, powered by fused ignition voltage, to heat the oxygen sensor to operating range as quickly as possible.

4   Proper operation of an oxygen sensor depends on four conditions:

 a) *Electrical - The low voltages generated by the sensor require good, clean connections which should be checked whenever a sensor problem is suspected or indicated.*

 b) *Outside air supply - The sensor needs air circulation to the internal portion of the sensor. Whenever the sensor is installed, make sure the air passages are not restricted.*

 c) *Proper operating temperature - The ECM/PCM will not react to the sensor signal until the sensor reaches approximately 600-degrees F. This factor must be considered when evaluating the performance of the sensor.*

 d) *Unleaded fuel - Unleaded fuel is essential for proper operation of the sensor.*

5   The ECM/PCM can detect several different oxygen sensor problems and set diagnostic trouble codes to indicate the specific fault (see Section 2). When an oxygen sensor fault occurs, the ECM/PCM will disregard the oxygen sensor signal voltage and revert to open-loop fuel control as described previously.

Check

Refer to illustration 11.6

Caution: *The oxygen sensor is very sensitive to excessive circuit loads and circuit damage of any kind. For safest testing, disconnect the oxygen sensor connector, install jumper wires between the two connectors and connect your voltmeter to the jumper wires. If jumper wires aren't available, carefully backprobe the wires in the connector shell with suitable probes (such as T-pins). Do not puncture the oxygen sensor wires or try to backprobe the sensor itself. Use only a digital voltmeter to test an oxygen sensor.*

Note: *Performing the following test will set a diagnostic trouble code and illuminate the*

Service Engine Soon light. Clear the diagnostic trouble code after performing the tests and making the necessary repairs (see Section 2).

6   Connect your voltmeter positive (+) lead to the purple or purple/white wire and connect the negative (-) lead to the tan or tan/white wire at the oxygen sensor connector (see illustration). Turn the ignition ON but do not start the engine. The meter should read approximately 400 to 450 millivolts (0.40 to 0.45 volt). If it doesn't, trace and repair the circuit from the sensor to the ECM/PCM. Note: On single wire O2 sensors, connect the negative lead (-) of the voltmeter to an engine ground point. The oxygen sensor signal voltage readings should be the same on a single wire O2 sensor (early) as a four-wire O2 sensor on late models. Refer to the wiring diagrams at the end of Chapter 12 for additional information on the oxygen sensor circuits.

7   Start the engine and let it warm up to normal operating temperature; again check the oxygen sensor signal voltage.

 a) *Voltage from an pre-converter sensor should range from 100 to 900 millivolts (0.1 to 0.9 volt) and switch actively between high and low readings.*

 b) *Voltage from a post-converter sensor should also read between 100 to 900 millivolts (0.1 to 0.9 volt) but it should not switch actively. The post-converter oxygen sensor voltage may stay toward the center of its range (about 400 millivolts) or stay for relatively longer periods of time at the upper or lower limits of the range.*

8   On late models (1996 through 2000), check the battery voltage supply and ground circuits to the oxygen sensor heater. Disconnect the electrical connector and connect the voltmeter negative (-) lead to the black wire terminal and the positive (+) lead to the pink wire terminal of the sensor connector. Turn the ignition ON (engine not running); the meter should read approximately 12 volts. If battery voltage is not present, check the power and ground circuits to the sensor (don't forget to check the fuses first).

11.13 A special slotted socket, allowing clearance for the wiring harness, may be required for oxygen sensor removal (the tool is available at most auto parts stores)

12.2a The knock sensor (arrow) is located on the right side of the engine block (early model shown)

12.2b The knock sensor is threaded into the transmission mounting flange portion of the engine block below the oil pressure sending unit (late model V6 engine shown)

9   Also on late models (1996 through 2000), allow the oxygen sensor to cool and check the resistance of the oxygen sensor heater. With the connector disconnected, connect an ohmmeter to the two oxygen sensor heater terminals of the connector (oxygen sensor side). The oxygen sensor pigtail is generally not color coded, but the heater wires are usually the white wires. The oxygen sensor heater resistance should be 3.0 to 14.0 ohms. If an open circuit or excessive resistance is indicated, replace the oxygen sensor. **Note:** *If the tests indicate that a sensor is good, and not the cause of a driveability problem or diagnostic trouble code, check the wiring harness and connectors between the sensor and the ECM/PCM for an open or short circuit. If no problems are found, have the vehicle checked by a dealer service department or other qualified repair shop.*

Replacement

Refer to illustration 11.13
10   The exhaust pipe contracts when cool, and the oxygen sensor may be hard to loosen when the engine is cold. To make sensor removal easier, start and run the engine for a minute or two; then shut it off. Be careful not to burn yourself during the following procedure. Also observe these guidelines when replacing an oxygen sensor.

a) *The sensor has a permanently attached pigtail and electrical connector which should not be removed from the sensor. Damage or removal of the pigtail or electrical connector can harm operation of the sensor.*
b) *Keep grease, dirt and other contaminants away from the electrical connector and the louvered end of the sensor.*
c) *Do not use cleaning solvents of any kind on the oxygen sensor.*
d) *Do not drop or roughly handle the sensor.*

11   If replacing the post-converter oxygen sensor, raise the vehicle and place it securely on jackstands.
12   Disconnect the electrical connector from the sensor.

13   Using a suitable wrench or specialized oxygen sensor socket, unscrew the sensor from the exhaust pipe **(see illustration)**.
14   Anti-seize compound must be used on the threads of the sensor to aid future removal. The threads of most new sensors will be coated with this compound. If not, be sure to apply anti-seize compound before installing the sensor.
15   Install the sensor and tighten it securely.
16   Reconnect the electrical connector to the sensor and lower the vehicle.

12   Knock sensor and module - check and replacement

1   The knock sensor detects abnormal vibration (spark knock or pinging) in the engine. The knock control system is designed to reduce spark knock during periods of heavy detonation. This allows the engine to use maximum spark advance to improve driveability. Knock sensors produce AC output voltage which increases with the severity of the knock. The signal is fed into the ECM/PCM and the timing is retarded to compensate for the severe detonation. Early models are equipped with a separate knock sensor module mounted near the throttle body. Late models are equipped with a replaceable knock sensor module in the PCM.

Check

Refer to illustrations 12.2a and 12.2b
2   Depending on the year and engine application, the knock sensor is located on the rear of the engine block in the back of the cylinder head or the side of the cylinder head below the exhaust manifolds **(see illustrations)**.
3   Disconnect the electrical connector from the knock sensor. The knock sensor contains an internal 100K-ohm resistor. Using an ohmmeter, measure the resistance between the terminal on the knock sensor and the engine block. The resistance should be approximately 1.5K to 10K (1988 through 1995) or 90K to 110K-ohms (1996 through

2000) - if the resistance is not as specified, replace the knock sensor.
4   To check the sensor operation, reconnect the connector to the sensor. Backprobe the wire terminal at the electrical connector using a suitable probe. Connect the positive lead of a voltmeter to the probe and the negative lead to a good engine ground point. Set the voltmeter on the AC volts scale. Start the engine and check for an AC voltage signal from the knock sensor. The AC voltage should increase as the engine speed increases. If a voltage signal is not present, replace the knock sensor.

Replacement

Warning: *The engine must be completely cool before beginning this procedure.*
5   Disconnect the cable from the negative battery terminal. **Caution:** *On models equipped with the Theftlock audio system, be sure the lockout feature is turned off before performing any procedure which requires disconnecting the battery (see the front of this manual).*

Knock sensor

6   Remove the distributor, if necessary (see Chapter 5).
7   Remove the oil pressure sending unit, if necessary.
8   Disconnect the electrical connector and remove the knock sensor from the engine block.
9   Installation is the reverse of removal. Be sure to install the distributor in exactly the same position as originally installed (see Chapter 5).

Electronic Spark Control (ESC) module (1988 through 1995 models)

Refer to illustration 12.11
Note: *1995 and earlier models use a separate ESC module mounted near the throttle body.*
10   Disconnect the cable from the negative battery terminal. **Caution:** *On models equipped with the Theftlock audio system, be sure the lockout feature is turned off before performing any procedure which requires dis-*

12.11 To detach the ESC module, unplug the electrical connector (B) and remove the mounting screws (A)

12.16 Remove the screws and the cover to access the knock sensor module

12.17 Pinch the tabs together and pull the knock sensor module straight up

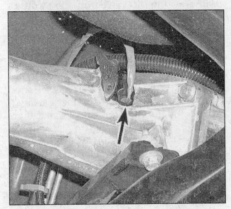

13.2 Vehicle speed sensor location

14.2 IAC valve location - V6 Central SFI model shown

connecting the battery (see the front of this manual).
11 Locate the module near the throttle body (see illustration).
12 Detach the electrical connector from the module.
13 Remove the mounting screws and detach the module.
14 Installation is the reverse of removal.

Knock sensor module (1996 through 2000 models)
Refer to illustrations 12.16 and 12.17
Note: The knock sensor module may be replaced in the original PCM. If a new PCM is being installed, it must be programmed at a dealer service department (see Section 3).
15 Remove the PCM (see Section 3).
16 Remove the knock sensor module cover (see illustration).
17 Carefully pinch the retaining tabs and pull the knock sensor straight up (see illustration).
18 To install the knock sensor module, align the tabs on the module with the notches on the socket.
19 Press down on the ends of the knock sensor module until the module is seated in the socket and the retaining tabs click into place.
20 Install the knock sensor module cover.
21 Install the PCM.

13 Vehicle Speed Sensor (VSS) - check and replacement

1 The Vehicle Speed Sensor (VSS) is a permanent magnet generator mounted on the transmission. The sensor is triggered by a toothed rotor on the transmission output shaft. As the output shaft rotates, the sensor produces an AC voltage, the frequency of which is proportional to vehicle speed. The ECM/PCM uses the sensor input signal for several different engine and transmission control functions. The VSS signal also drives the speedometer on the instrument panel. A defective VSS can cause various driveability and transmission problems.

Check
Refer to illustration 13.2
2 Raise the vehicle and support it securely on jackstands. Locate the vehicle speed sensor (see illustration). Check the terminals in the connector and the wires leading to the sensor for looseness and breaks. Repair as required.
3 To check the VSS operation, backprobe the two wire terminals of the VSS connector using suitable probes. Connect a voltmeter to the probes and set the meter on the AC volts scale. Turn the ignition key On (engine not running). Block one rear tire so it will not turn and rotate the other rear tire by hand while watching the voltmeter. Note: If the vehicle is equipped with a limited-slip differential, it is not necessary to block one of the drive wheels. The sensor should produce a minimum of 0.5 volts and the voltage should increase as the transmission output shaft rotates faster.
4 Turn the ignition key Off and disconnect the electrical connector from the sensor. Using an ohmmeter, measure the resistance across the two terminals of the sensor. The sensor resistance should be approximately 1,000 to 3,000 ohms at 68-degrees F. If the test results are incorrect, replace the vehicle speed sensor.

Replacement
5 Raise the vehicle and support it securely

on jackstands.
6 Disconnect the electrical connector from the VSS.
7 Remove mounting bolt and withdraw the VSS from the transmission case.
8 Replace the sensor O-ring.
9 Installation is the reverse of removal.

14 Idle Air Control (IAC) valve - check and replacement

1 The idle speed is controlled by the Idle Air Control (IAC) valve. The IAC valve regulates the air bypassing the throttle plate by moving the pintle in or out of the air passage. The IAC valve is controlled by the ECM/PCM, adjusting the idle speed depending upon the running conditions of the engine (air conditioning system, power steering, cold and warm running etc.). The engine idle speed is not adjustable on these models.

Check
Refer to illustrations 14.2 and 14.4
Note: Performing the following test will set a diagnostic trouble code and illuminate the Service Engine Soon light. Clear the diagnostic trouble code after performing the tests and making the necessary repairs (see Section 2).
2 The Idle Air Control (IAC) valve is located on the throttle body (see illustration). A scan tool is required for complete

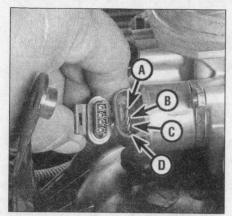

14.4 IAC valve terminal identification

A and B   IAC coil no. 1
C and D   IAC coil no. 2

14.7 Remove the screws (arrows) and withdraw the IAC valve from the throttle body (V6 Central SFI model shown)

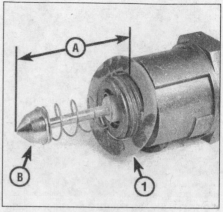

14.9 Typical IAC valve

1   O-ring
A   Pintle extension distance
B   Pintle diameter

15.2a PCV valve location - V6 Central SFI models shown

testing of the IAC valve and circuits. However, there are several tests the home mechanic can perform on the IAC system to verify operation but they are limited and are useful only in the case of definite IAC valve failure.

3   When the engine is started cold, the IAC valve should vary the idle as the engine begins to warm-up. Allow the engine to warm-up, then place a load on the engine by placing the transmission in gear (automatic), turning the air conditioning on and/or operating the power steering. The idle should remain steady or increase slightly. If the engine stumbles or stalls, or if there are obvious signs that the IAC valve is not working, stop the engine and continue testing.

4   Disconnect the electrical connector from the IAC valve. Using an ohmmeter, measure the resistance across terminals A and B of the IAC valve, then measure the resistance across terminals C and D **(see illustration)** - the resistance should be about the same on both sets (approximately 40 to 80 ohms). If one or both checks indicate an open circuit, replace the IAC valve.

5   If the IAC valve is good, have the ECM/PCM diagnosed by a dealer service department or other qualified repair shop.

Replacement

Refer to illustrations 14.7 and 14.9

6   Access the IAC valve.

a) *On TBI systems, remove the air filter assembly from the TBI unit*
b) *On Central SFI and MPFI systems, remove the air intake duct and resonator from the throttle body (see Chapter 4).*

7   Disconnect the electrical connector from the IAC valve. Remove the IAC valve:

a) *On early models (1988 through 1995), unscrew the IAC valve from the TBI unit*
b) *On late models (1996 through 2000), remove the two mounting screws from the valve and withdraw it from the throttle body (see illustration).*

8   Inspect the IAC valve pintle and the air passage and valve seat in the throttle body

for heavy carbon deposits. Clean the IAC valve with aerosol carburetor cleaner, a shop towel and a soft brush, if necessary. Do not submerge the IAC valve in any liquid cleaner. If the air passage requires further cleaning, remove the throttle body and clean it thoroughly.

9   If installing a new IAC valve, measure the distance from the tip of the IAC valve pintle to the mounting flange **(see illustration)**. If the distance is greater than 1-1/8 inch, press the pintle in by hand, as necessary. **Caution:** *Do not attempt to press the pintle in on a used IAC valve. The force required to move a pintle shaft with carbon build-up may damage the valve.*

10   Install a new O-ring and lubricate it with clean engine oil.

11   Install the IAC valve and tighten the screw(s) securely. Connect the electrical connector.

12   Cycle the ignition key On for ten seconds, then Off for ten seconds to reset the valve. Start the engine, allow it to idle for five minutes, turn the engine off for thirty seconds, then start the engine again and check the idle operation.

15   Crankcase ventilation system

Refer to illustrations 15.2a and 15.2b

1   When the engine is running, a certain amount of the gasses produced during combustion escape past the piston rings into the crankcase as blow-by gasses. The crankcase ventilation system is designed to reduce the resulting hydrocarbon emissions (HC) by routing the gasses and vapors from the crankcase into the intake manifold and combustion chambers, where they are consumed during engine operation.

2   All models use a Positive Crankcase Ventilation (PCV) system. The main component of the Positive Crankcase Ventilation (PCV) system is the PCV valve **(see illustration)**. Fresh air flows from the air intake duct through a vent tube into the engine. Crankcase vapors are drawn from the

crankcase by the PCV valve. To maintain idle quality and good driveability, the PCV valve restricts the flow when the intake manifold vacuum is high. When intake manifold vacuum is lower, maximum vapor flow is allowed through the valve **(see illustration)**.

3   Checking and replacement of the PCV valve is covered in Chapter 1.

16   Exhaust Gas Recirculation (EGR) system

Refer to illustration 16.2

1   The Exhaust Gas Recirculation (EGR) system is used to lower NOx (oxides of nitrogen) emission levels caused by high combustion temperatures. The EGR valve recirculates a small amount of exhaust gases into the intake manifold. The additional mixture lowers the temperature of combustion thereby reducing the formation of NOx compounds.

2   The EGR system on early models (1988 through 1995) consists of an EGR valve **(see illustration)**, an EGR solenoid valve and the engine's Electronic Control Module (ECM). Under certain operating conditions, such as

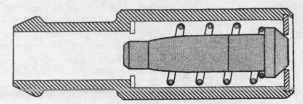

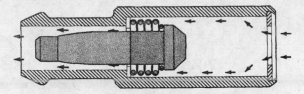

Engine Off or Engine Backfire—No Vapor Flow

High Intake Manifold Vacuum—Minimal Vapor Flow

15.2b Typical PCV valve operation

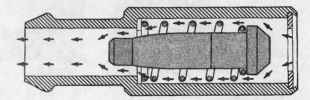

Moderate Intake Manifold Vacuum—Maximum Vapor Flow

16.2 The EGR valve is located on the intake manifold near the throttle body (early model shown)

16.9 Typical EGR solenoid valve

A   *Electrical connector*
B   *Intake manifold side vacuum hose*

16.16 Typical mounting location of a linear EGR valve

highway cruising, the ECM sends an electrical signal to the EGR solenoid valve, causing it to open and allow intake manifold vacuum to the EGR valve. When it receives this vacuum signal, the EGR valve opens, allowing exhaust gasses to flow into the intake manifold. **Note:** *1995 4.3L California models and all 1995 7.4L models are equipped with an electronic EGR valve.*

3   The EGR system on late models (1996 through 2000) consists of an electronic EGR valve and the PCM. The PCM controls the EGR flow rate by energizing the EGR valve solenoid coil, opening or closing the EGR passage in small increments. The PCM monitors the EGR valve pintle position with an EGR position sensor built into the EGR valve. This system allows for precise control of EGR flow, achieving optimum EGR flow depending on engine operating conditions.

Check

1988 through 1995 models

4   The most common driveability problem associated with a malfunctioning EGR system is an engine that runs extremely rough at idle speed and smoothes out when speed is increased. This problem can be caused by an EGR valve or EGR solenoid valve stuck in the open position, a misrouted vacuum hose (allowing vacuum to the EGR valve at idle) or a malfunctioning ECM. Because of its complexity and interrelationship to other systems

on the vehicle, the ECM should be checked by a dealer service department.

5   Inspect the vacuum hoses between the intake manifold, the EGR solenoid valve and the EGR valve. Look for cracking, hardening, general deterioration and misrouting (refer to the vacuum hose routing diagram on the emissions label). Replace any hoses that are in questionable condition.

6   Start the engine and allow it to idle. Disconnect the vacuum hose from the EGR valve and connect a hand vacuum pump.

7   Apply vacuum with the pump. The engine should run roughly or stall. If the idle does not change or changes very little, replace the EGR valve.

EGR solenoid valve (vehicles under 8500 GVW)

Refer to illustration 16.9

8   Turn the ignition off.

9   Disconnect the vacuum hose on the intake manifold side of the EGR solenoid valve and hook up a hand vacuum pump **(see illustration)**.

10   Apply vacuum with the pump. The valve

should hold vacuum. If it doesn't, replace the valve.

11   Due to the interrelationship with the ECM, any further checks should be left to a dealer service department or other qualified repair shop.

EGR solenoid valve (vehicles over 8500 GVW)

12   Turn the ignition ON (engine not running).

13   Disconnect the vacuum hose on the intake manifold side of the EGR solenoid and hook up a hand vacuum pump.

14   Apply vacuum with the pump. The EGR valve should not move. If the EGR valve moved, disconnect the electrical connector and repeat the test. If the EGR valve moved, replace the solenoid valve.

15   Due to the interrelationship with the ECM, any further checks should be left to a dealer service department or a qualified auto repair shop.

1996 through 2000 models

Refer to illustrations 16.16 and 16.17

16   The EGR valve is located at the front of the intake manifold **(see illustration)**. A scan

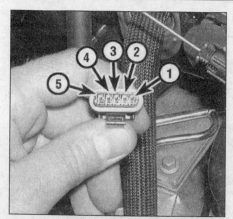

16.17 EGR valve harness connector terminal identification

1   EGR valve ground
2   Pintle position sensor ground
3   Pintle position sensor signal
4   Pintle position sensor 5-volt supply
5   EGR valve power

tool is required for complete testing of the EGR valve, control system and circuits. However, there are several tests the home mechanic can perform on the system to verify operation but they are limited and are useful only in the case of definite system failure.

17   Check the voltage supply and ground circuits to the EGR valve position sensor. Disconnect the electrical connector from the EGR valve. Connect the positive lead of a voltmeter to terminal no. 4 (gray wire) of the EGR valve electrical connector (harness side) **(see illustration)**. Connect the negative lead to terminal no. 2 (black or white wire). Turn the ignition key On - approximately 5.0 volts should be indicated on the meter. If the 5.0 volt supply voltage is not present, check the circuits from the PCM to the EGR valve. If the circuits are good, have the PCM diagnosed by a dealer service department or other qualified repair shop.

18   To check the EGR valve, use an ohmmeter to check the continuity of the EGR valve position sensor and the EGR solenoid coil. Check for continuity across terminals 2 and 4 (EGR sensor) and across terminals 1 and 5 (EGR solenoid coil) **(see illustration)**. If either check reveals an open circuit, replace the EGR valve.

Replacement
EGR valve

19   Access the EGR valve.

a) *On TBI systems, remove the air filter assembly from the TBI unit*
b) *On Central SFI and MPFI systems, remove the air intake duct and resonator from the throttle body (see Chapter 4).*

20   Disconnect the electrical connector from the EGR valve, if equipped.
21   Remove the EGR valve mounting bolts. Remove the EGR valve and gaskets. Discard the gaskets.
22   Using a gasket scraper, clean the EGR

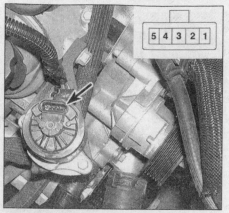

16.18 EGR valve terminal identification

valve gasket surfaces.
23   Installation is the reverse of removal.

EGR pipe

24   Remove the EGR pipe bracket bolt.
25   Loosen the fittings at each end of the pipe and remove the pipe.
26   Install the pipe and start the fittings, but do not fully tighten them. Loosely install the bracket bolt.
27   Align the pipe with the adapters and tighten the exhaust manifold fitting, followed by the intake manifold fitting. Tighten the bracket bolt.

17   Evaporative emissions control system

1   The fuel evaporative emissions control (EVAP) system absorbs fuel vapors from the fuel tank and, during engine operation, releases them into the engine intake system where they mix with the incoming air/fuel mixture. The main components of the evaporative emissions system are the canister (filled with activated charcoal to absorb fuel vapors), the purge valve, the vent valve, the fuel tank pressure sensor, the fuel tank and the vapor and purge lines. The EVAP system components vary slightly with different years and applications.
2   After passing through a check valve, fuel tank vapor is carried through the vapor hose to the charcoal canister. The activated charcoal in the canister absorbs and stores the vapors. When a programmed set of conditions are met (engine running, warmed to a pre-set temperature, etc.), the ECM/PCM opens the purge valve and the vent valve. Fuel vapors from the canister are then drawn through the purge hose by intake manifold vacuum into the intake manifold and combustion chamber where they are consumed during normal engine operation.
3   The ECM/PCM regulates the rate of vapor flow from the canister to the intake manifold by controlling the duty cycle of the EVAP purge valve control solenoid. During cold running conditions and hot start time

delay, the ECM/PCM does not energize the solenoid. After the engine has warmed up to the correct operating temperature, the ECM/PCM purges the vapors into the intake manifold according to the running conditions of the engine. The ECM/PCM will cycle (ON then OFF) the purge valve control solenoid about 5 to 10 times per second. The flow rate will be controlled by the pulse width, or length of time, the solenoid is allowed to be energized. **Note:** *Early systems are equipped with a purge control valve mounted on the top of the charcoal canister that is operated by engine vacuum.*
4   Models equipped with the OBD-II system (1996 through 2000) can perform a self-diagnostic check when the engine is started cold. When the programmed conditions are met, the PCM opens the EVAP canister purge valve, leaving the vent valve closed. This action allows the engine to draw a vacuum on the entire EVAP system. Once the proper vacuum level is reached, the PCM closes the purge valve, sealing the system. The PCM then monitors the fuel tank pressure sensor voltage and sets a diagnostic code if a leak is detected.
5   OBD-II models are also equipped with a fuel tank pressure sensor. The fuel tank pressure sensor operation is similar to the MAP sensor. The PCM supplies a 5-volt reference voltage and ground circuit to the sensor. The sensor returns a signal voltage to the PCM which varies according to the air pressure inside the fuel tank. When the air pressure inside the tank is equal to the outside air pressure (as with the fuel filler cap removed), the sensor output voltage is approximately 1.5 volts. With 14 in-Hg vacuum inside the tank the sensor output voltage is 4.5 volts.

Check

Note: *The evaporative control system, like all emission control systems, is protected by a Federally-mandated warranty (5 years or 50,000 miles at the time this manual was written). The EVAP system probably won't fail during the service life of the vehicle; however, if it does, the hoses or charcoal canister are usually to blame.*
6   Always check the hoses first. A disconnected, damaged or missing hose is the most likely cause of a malfunctioning EVAP system. Refer to the Vacuum Hose Routing Diagram (attached to the radiator support) to determine whether the hoses are correctly routed and attached. Repair any damaged hoses or replace any missing hoses as necessary.
7   On early models equipped without electronic purge controls, inspect the charcoal canister, purge control valve and the vacuum hoses for cracks, damage, misrouted hoses or component failures.
8   On late models equipped with electronic purge controls, check the related fuses and wiring to the purge and vent valves. Refer to the wiring diagrams at the end of Chapter 12, if necessary. The purge and vent valves are normally closed - no vapors will pass through the ports. When the PCM energizes the

17.10a The charcoal canister is located to the left of the radiator (early model shown)

17.10b Remove the EVAP canister bracket mounting bolt (arrow) (late model shown)

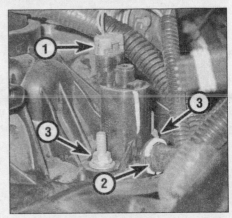

17.14 Details of the EVAP canister purge solenoid (5.0L V8 shown)

1 *Electrical connector*
2 *EVAP purge hose*
3 *Mounting nuts*

solenoid (by completing the circuit to ground), the valve opens and vapors flow through. A scan tool is required to thoroughly check the system. If the above checks fail to identify the problem area, have the system diagnosed by a dealer service department or other qualified repair shop.

Component replacement

9 All late model EVAP system hoses are equipped with quick-connect fittings. Before disconnecting a fitting, clean around the fitting and twist the fitting back-and-forth to loosen the seal. To disconnect a large hose fitting, squeeze the retainer tabs together and pull the fitting off the pipe. To disconnect a small hose fitting, push the locking tab in and pull the fitting off the pipe.

EVAP canister

Refer to illustrations 17.10a and 17.10b
10 The EVAP canister is located in several different locations according to year and application **(see illustrations)**.
11 On late models, raise the vehicle and support it securely on jackstands.
12 Disconnect the hoses from the canister (see Step 9). Remove the bracket mounting bolt and remove the canister.
13 Installation is the reverse of removal.

Purge valve

Refer to illustration 17.14
14 The purge valve is mounted on the charcoal canister on early models or on the intake manifold on late models **(see illustration)**.
15 On late models, disconnect the electrical connector. Depress the locking tab and remove the hose from the purge valve (see Step 9).
16 Remove the mounting nuts/bolt. If equipped, remove the wiring harness retainer from the mounting stud. Remove the purge valve.
17 Installation is the reverse of removal.

Vent valve (1996 through 2000 models)

18 The vent valve is mounted on a bracket near the fuel tank.
19 Raise the vehicle and support it securely on jackstands.
20 Disconnect the electrical connector. Remove the hose from the vent valve (see Step 9).
21 Release the retainers and remove the vent valve from the bracket.
22 Installation is the reverse of removal.

Fuel tank pressure sensor (1996 through 2000 models)

Refer to illustration 17.26
23 The fuel tank pressure sensor is located on the fuel pump module.
24 Remove the fuel tank (see Chapter 4).
25 Disconnect the electrical connector from the fuel tank pressure sensor.
26 Release the retaining clip and remove the sensor from the top of the fuel pump module **(see illustration)**.
27 Installation is the reverse of removal.

18 Secondary Air Injection (AIR) system

Refer to illustrations 18.1 and 18.2
1 Some models are equipped with a secondary air injection (AIR) system. The secondary air injection system is used to reduce tailpipe emissions on initial engine start-up. Early systems (1988 through 1998) rely mostly on mechanical components while late systems (1999 and 2000) are equipped with several electronic components. The secondary air injection (AIR) system on early models use a mechanical air pump to force the air into the exhaust stream. An Electric Air Control (EAC) valve, controlled by the vehicle's electronic control module (ECM) directs the air to the correct location, depending on engine temperature and driving conditions. During certain situations, such as deceleration, the air is diverted to the air cleaner to prevent backfiring from too much oxygen in the exhaust stream. One-way check valves **(see illustration)** are also used in the system's air lines to prevent exhaust gases from being forced back through the system. The system components include an engine driven air pump, electric air control valve, air flow and control hoses and check valves. **Note:** *Some late model 7.4L engines are equipped with the mechanical air pump and components similar to the early systems.*

17.26 Pry the retaining clips out (arrows) and withdraw the fuel tank pressure sensor from the fuel pump module

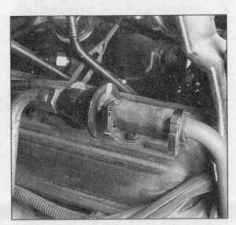

18.1 Typical secondary air management system check valve (early model shown)

18.2 Secondary air injection component locations (late model shown)

1   Air pump
2   Vacuum valve/solenoid
3   Air pump/solenoid relay
4   Air shut-off valve

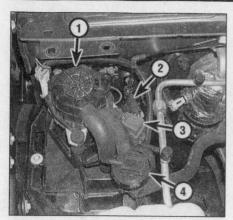

18.6 Using hose clamp pliers, squeeze the clamp tangs together, slide the clamp down the hose and remove the hose from the check valve

18.10 The filter can be pulled out of the air pump with needle-nose pliers

2   The secondary air injection (AIR) system on late models use an electric motor/pump assembly, relay, vacuum valve/solenoid, air shut-off valve, check valves and tubing to inject fresh air directly into the exhaust manifolds **(see illustration)**. The fresh air (oxygen) reacts with the exhaust gas in the catalytic converter to reduce HC and CO levels. The air pump and solenoid are controlled by the PCM through the AIR relay. During initial start-up, the PCM energizes the AIR relay, the relay supplies battery voltage to the air pump and the vacuum valve/solenoid, engine vacuum is applied to the air shut-off valve which opens and allows air to flow through the tubing into the exhaust manifolds. The PCM will operate the air pump until closed loop operation is reached (or four minutes, maximum). During normal operation, the check valves prevent exhaust backflow into the system.

Check

Refer to illustration 18.6

3   Check the air pump hoses and the vacuum hoses. Repair any damaged hoses or replace any missing hoses as necessary. Check the vacuum source to the vacuum valve/solenoid. Intake manifold vacuum should be present with the engine running.
4   To check the mechanical pump on early models, allow the engine to reach normal operating temperature and run it at about 1,500 rpm. Locate the hose running from the air pump and squeeze to check for pulsations. Have an assistant increase the engine speed and check for a parallel increase in air flow. If an increase is noted, the pump is functioning properly. If not, there is a fault in the pump.
5   To check the electronic air pump on late models, check the related fuses, the relay and the wiring to the air pump and vacuum valve/solenoid. Refer to Chapter 12 for the wiring diagrams, if necessary. On late mod-

els, the vacuum valve/solenoid is normally closed - no vacuum is applied to the air shut-off valve. When the PCM energizes the relay (by completing the circuit to ground), the air pump operates, the vacuum valve opens, vacuum is applied to the air shut-off valve, the shut-off valve opens and air flows through the tubing into the exhaust manifolds. A scan tool is required to thoroughly check the system. If the above checks fail to identify the problem area, have the system diagnosed by a dealer service department or other qualified repair shop.
6   Each check valve can be inspected after removing it from the hose **(see illustration)**. Make sure the engine is completely cool before attempting this. Try to blow through the check valve from both ends. Air should pass through it only in the direction of normal air flow. If it is stuck either open or closed, the valve should be replaced.

Component replacement

1988 through 1998 models

Air pump pulley (mechanical type) and filter

Refer to illustration 18.10

7   Push on the drivebelt to keep the pulley from turning, then loosen the pulley bolts.
8   Remove the drivebelt (see Chapter 1).
9   Remove the mounting bolts and lift off the pulley.
10   If the fan-like filter must be removed, grasp it firmly with a pair of needle-nose pliers **(see illustration)** and pull it from the pump. **Note:** *Do not insert a screwdriver between the filter and pump housing as the edge of the housing could be damaged. The filter will usually be distorted when pulled off. Be sure no fragments fall into the air intake hose.*
11   The new filter is installed by placing it in position on the pump, placing the pulley over it and tightening the pulley bolts evenly to draw the filter into the pump. Do not attempt to install a filter by pressing or hammering it into place. **Note:** *It is normal for the new filter to have an interference fit with the pump*

housing and, upon initial operation, it may squeal until worn in.
12   Install the drivebelt and, while compressing the belt, tighten the pulley bolts securely.
13   Install the drivebelt (see Chapter 1).

Hoses and tubes

14   To replace a tube or hose, always note how it is routed first, either with a sketch or with numbered pieces of tape.
15   Remove the defective hose or tube and replace it with a new one of the same material and size and tighten all connections.

Check valve

16   Disconnect the pump outlet hose at the check valve.
17   Unscrew the check valve from the pipe assembly. Be careful not to bend or twist the assembly.
18   Install a new valve after making sure that it is a duplicate of the part removed, then tighten all connections.

Electronic air control valve

19   Disconnect the cable from the negative battery terminal. **Caution:** *On models equipped with the Theftlock audio system, be sure the lockout feature is turned off before performing any procedure which requires disconnecting the battery (see the front of this manual).*
20   Disconnect the vacuum signal line from the valve. Disconnect the air hoses and electrical connectors.
21   Remove the mounting bolts and lift the valve off the adapter or bracket.
22   Installation is the reverse of the removal procedure.

Air pump

Refer to illustration 18.24

23   Remove the pulley and the drivebelt.
24   Remove the pump mounting bolts and separate the pump from the engine **(see illustration)**.
25   Detach the pump hose.
26   Installation is the reverse of removal. **Note:** *Do not tighten the pump mounting bolts until all components are installed.*

18.24 Typical air pump mounting details - 7.4 liter V8 engine

18.44 Remove the mounting nuts (arrows) and remove the check valve and pipe assembly

1999 and 2000 models

Air pump (electronic type)

27 Remove the bolts and the fender-to-cowl brace.

28 Disconnect the electrical connector from the air pump motor. Detach the hoses from the air pump.

29 Detach the air pump from the rubber mounting posts and remove the air pump assembly.

30 Installation is the reverse of removal.

Vacuum valve/solenoid

31 Disconnect the electrical connector from the valve/solenoid.

32 Label and disconnect the vacuum hoses from the valve/solenoid.

33 Remove the mounting screw and remove the vacuum valve/solenoid.

34 Installation is the reverse of removal.

Air shut-off valve

35 Detach the vacuum hose from the shut-off valve.

36 Detach the clamp from the assembly base.

37 Loosen the hose clamp and detach the air outlet hose from the shut-off valve.

38 Detach the shut-off valve from the air inlet hose and remove the valve.

39 Installation is the reverse of removal.

Air pump/solenoid relay

40 Disconnect the electrical connector from the relay.

41 Release the retaining tab and remove the relay from the bracket.

42 Installation is the reverse of removal.

Check valve and pipe

Warning: *The engine must be completely cool before beginning this procedure or serious burns may result.*

Refer to illustration 18.44

43 Loosen the clamp and remove the air hose from the check valve **(see illustration 18.6)**.

44 Remove the mounting bolts/nuts and remove the check valve and pipe assembly **(see illustration)**.

45 To remove the check valve from the pipe, clamp the large nut on the pipe in a vise and remove the check valve with an open-end wrench.

46 Clean the carbon deposits from the pipe flange and the exhaust manifold mounting surface. Remove the carbon deposits from the hole in the manifold, if necessary.

47 Install the check valve on the pipe and install the assembly onto the exhaust manifold with a new gasket. Tighten the fasteners securely.

48 The remainder of installation is the reverse of removal.

19 Thermostatic air cleaner (1988 through 1995 models)

General description

1 The thermostatic air cleaner regulates the temperature of the incoming air to the Throttle Body Injection unit. The air regulating damper is controlled by means of a self-contained, wax-pellet actuated assembly mounted in the air cleaner housing. When the incoming air is cold, the wax material sealed in the actuator is in a solid state and the damper closes off the cold air inlet. This causes all incoming air to be heated by the exhaust manifold. As the incoming air warms, the wax material expands by changing to liquid state which forces out a piston to reposition the damper allowing a cold and hot air mix or all cold air to enter the engine.

Checking

Note: *Make sure the engine is cold before beginning this check.*

2 Apply the parking brake and block the wheels.

3 Remove the air cleaner assembly. The damper door should be closed to the outside air.

4 Reinstall the air cleaner assembly and be sure the heat stove tube is connected at the air cleaner snorkel and the exhaust manifold.

5 Start the engine. Watch the damper door in the air cleaner snorkel. As the air warms up, the damper door should open slowly to the outside air.

6 If the air cleaner fails to operate as described, be sure the damper is not binding or sticking. Make sure it's not rusted in an open or closed position by attempting to move it by hand. If it's rusted, it can usually be freed by cleaning and oiling the hinge. If it fails to work properly after servicing, replace the air cleaner assembly.

20 Catalytic converter

Note: *Because of a Federally mandated warranty which covers emissions-related components such as the catalytic converter, check with a dealer service department before replacing the converter at your own expense.*

1 The catalytic converter is an emission control device added to the exhaust system to reduce pollutants from the exhaust gas stream. A three-way (reduction) catalyst design is used. The catalytic coating on the three-way catalyst contains platinum and rhodium, which lowers the levels of oxides of nitrogen (NOx) as well as hydrocarbons (HC) and carbon monoxide (CO).

2 The test equipment for a catalytic converter is expensive and highly sophisticated. If you suspect that the converter on your vehicle is malfunctioning, take it to a dealer or authorized emissions inspection facility for diagnosis and repair.

Check

3 Whenever the vehicle is raised for servicing of underbody components, check the converter for leaks, corrosion, dents and other damage. Check the flange bolts that attach the front and rear ends of the con-

verter to the exhaust system. If damage is discovered, the converter should be replaced.

4   A catalytic converter may become plugged. The easiest way to check for a restricted converter is to use a vacuum gauge to diagnose the effect of a blocked exhaust on intake vacuum.

a) *Connect a vacuum gauge to an intake manifold vacuum source.*

b) *Warm the engine to operating temperature, place the transmission in Park and apply the parking brake.*

c) *Note and record the vacuum reading at idle.*

d) *Open the throttle until the engine speed is about 2000 rpm.*

e) *Release the throttle quickly and record the vacuum reading.*

f) *Perform the test three more times, recording the reading after each test.*

g) *If the reading after the fourth test is more than one in-Hg lower than the reading recorded at idle, the catalytic converter, muffler or exhaust pipes may be plugged or restricted.*

20.7 Catalytic converter locations

Replacement

Refer to illustration 19.7

Note: *Refer to the exhaust system servicing section in Chapter 4 for additional information.*

5   Raise the vehicle and support it securely on jackstands.

6   Disconnect the electrical connectors from the oxygen sensors.

7   Remove the catalytic converter-to- exhaust pipe flange bolts and separate the exhaust pipe from the catalytic converter **(see illustration)**. Support the exhaust pipe.

8   Remove the bolts and detach the catalytic converter header pipe from the exhaust manifold (see Chapter 2A or 2B). Remove the catalytic converter and pipe assembly.

9   Clean the carbon deposits from the mounting flanges and install new gaskets.

10   Installation is the reverse of removal.

Chapter 7 Part A
Manual transmission

Contents

Specifications

Transmission lubricant type .... See Chapter 1

Torque specifications — Ft-lbs

Rear bearing retainer-to-transmission bolts (RPO M20)
Upper 20
Lower.. 30
U-joint flange-to-output shaft nut
Heavy-duty four-speed (RPO M20)................................. 100
Heavy-duty five-speed (RPO MT8, MW3)......................... 300
Transmission-to-engine bolts (five-speed and
normal-duty four-speed) 37
Transmission-to-clutch housing bolts (heavy-duty transmission)........... 74

1 General information

Vehicles covered by this manual are equipped with either a four or five-speed manual or a three or four-speed automatic transmission. Information on the manual transmission is included in this Part of Chapter 7. Information on the automatic transmission can be found in Part B of this Chapter. You'll also find certain procedures common to both automatic and manual transmissions - such as oil seal replacement - here in Part A. Information on the transfer case used on 4WD models is in Part C.

Most manual transmissions are normal-duty five-speed (RPO MG5) or four-speed (RPO MCO) types. Both of these transmissions have aluminum cases. Some models are equipped with heavy-duty four-speed (RPO M20) or five-speed (RPO MT8, MW3) transmissions, which you can identify by their cast iron cases.

Depending on the expense involved in having a transmission overhauled, it may be a better idea to consider replacing it with either a new or rebuilt one. Your local dealer or transmission shop should be able to supply information concerning cost, availability and exchange policy. Regardless of how you decide to remedy a transmission problem, you can still save a lot of money by removing and installing the unit yourself.

2   Shift lever - removal and installation

Removal

1   If the vehicle is equipped with 4WD, remove the transfer case shift lever boot (see Chapter 7, Part C).
2   Remove the screws and slide the boot, along with the cover plate or retainer, up slightly on the shift lever.
3   To remove the lever on a vehicle equipped with a heavy-duty (cast iron case) four-speed, push the lever cap down and turn the lever counterclockwise.
4   To remove the lever on a vehicle equipped with a normal-duty (aluminum case) four-speed or a five-speed, loosen the jam nut and unscrew the lever.

Installation

5   To install the shift lever on a heavy-duty four-speed, place the lever in position, slightly counterclockwise of its normal position. Push down on the cap and turn the lever clockwise, to its normal position.
6   To install the shift lever on a normal-duty four-speed or a five-speed, screw the lever on and tighten the jam nut.
7   Make sure the shift pattern on the knob is in correct alignment.
8   The remainder of installation is the reverse of removal.

3   Transmission - removal and installation

Removal

1   Disconnect the negative cable from the battery.
2   Remove the shift lever (see Section 2).
3   Raise the vehicle and support it securely on jackstands.
4   Drain the transmission lubricant (see Chapter 1).
5   Remove the driveshaft(s) (Chapter 8). Use a plastic bag to cover the end of the transmission to prevent fluid loss and contamination.
6   If the vehicle is equipped with 4WD, remove the transfer case (see Chapter 7, Part C).
7   Remove any parking brake assembly components that are in the way (see Chapter 9).
8   Remove the exhaust system components as necessary for clearance (see Chapter 4).
9   Unplug all wire harness connectors from the transmission.
10   On 1995 and earlier models, detach the clutch release cylinder and secure it aside. On 1996 and later models, detach the hydraulic line from the release cylinder using the special tool (see Chapter 8). Cap the open line and secure it aside.

11   If the transmission is a normal-duty (aluminum case) type, remove the inspection cover.
12   Note the position of all wiring harness clips attached to the transmission, then detach them.
13   Support the engine. This can be done from above with an engine hoist, or by placing a jack (with a block of wood as an insulator) under the engine oil pan. The engine should remain supported at all times while the transmission is out of the vehicle.
14   Support the transmission with a jack - preferably a special jack made for this purpose. Safety chains will help steady the transmission on the jack.
15   Remove the nuts from the crossmember bolts. Raise the transmission slightly and remove the crossmember.
16   On models equipped with a heavy-duty (cast iron case) transmission, remove the bolts and spring washers securing the transmission to the clutch housing. On models equipped with a normal-duty transmission, remove the transmission-to-engine bolts.
17   Make a final check that all wires have been disconnected from the transmission and then move the transmission and jack toward the rear of the vehicle until the transmission input shaft is clear of the clutch or clutch housing. Keep the transmission level as this is done.
18   Once the input shaft is clear, lower the transmission and remove it from under the vehicle. **Caution:** *Do not depress the clutch pedal while the transmission is out of the vehicle.*
19   Inspect the clutch components (on models equipped with a heavy-duty transmission, you'll have to remove the clutch housing first). In most cases, new clutch components should be routinely installed if the transmission is removed (see Chapter 8).

Installation

20   Install the clutch components, if they were removed (Chapter 8).
21   On models equipped with a heavy-duty four-speed, attach the clutch housing, if it was removed, and tighten the bolts to the torque specified in Chapter 8.
22   With the transmission secured to the jack, raise it into position behind the engine or clutch housing and then carefully slide it forward, engaging the input shaft with the clutch plate hub. Do not use excessive force to install the transmission - if the input shaft won't slide into place, readjust the angle of the transmission so it's level and/or turn the input shaft so the splines engage properly with the clutch.
23   Once the transmission is flush with the clutch housing or engine, install the transmission-to-engine or clutch housing bolts. Tighten the bolts to the specified torque.
24   Install the crossmember and transmission mount. Tighten all nuts and bolts securely.
25   Remove the jacks supporting the transmission and the engine.

26   Install the various components removed previously. Refer to Chapter 7, Part C, for installation of the transfer case (if equipped), Chapter 8 for the installation of the driveshaft(s) and Chapter 4 for information regarding the exhaust system components.
27   Make a final check to verify all wires and hoses have been reconnected and the transmission has been filled with lubricant to the proper level (see Chapter 1). Lower the vehicle.
28   Install the shift lever (see Section 2).
29   Connect the negative battery cable. Road test the vehicle and check for leaks.

4   Transmission overhaul - general information

Overhauling a manual transmission is a difficult job for the do-it-yourselfer. It involves the disassembly and reassembly of many small parts. Numerous clearances must be precisely measured and, if necessary, changed with select fit spacers and snaprings. As a result, if transmission problems arise, it can be removed and installed by a competent do-it-yourselfer, but overhaul should be left to a transmission repair shop. Rebuilt transmissions may be available - check with your dealer parts department and auto parts stores. At any rate, the time and money involved in an overhaul is almost sure to exceed the cost of a rebuilt unit.

Nevertheless, it's not impossible for an inexperienced mechanic to rebuild a transmission if the special tools are available and the job is done in a deliberate step-by-step manner so nothing is overlooked.

The tools necessary for an overhaul include internal and external snap-ring pliers, a bearing puller, a slide hammer, a set of pin punches, a dial indicator and possibly a hydraulic press. In addition, a large, sturdy workbench and a vise or transmission stand will be required.

During disassembly of the transmission, make careful notes of how each piece comes off, where it fits in relation to other pieces and what holds it in place. This will make it much easier to get the transmission back together.

Before taking the transmission apart for repair, it will help if you have some idea what area of the transmission is malfunctioning.

Certain problems can be closely tied to specific areas in the transmission, which can make component examination and replacement easier. Refer to the Troubleshooting section at the front of this manual for information regarding possible sources of trouble.

5   Oil seal - replacement

Refer to illustrations 5.1, 5.5 and 5.7
Note: *This procedure applies to both manual and automatic transmissions.*

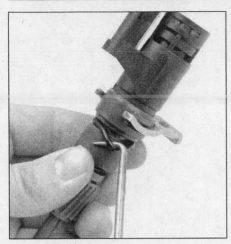

5.1 To replace the speed sensor O-ring, pull it off with a hooked removal tool, as shown here

1   Oil leaks frequently occur due to wear of the extension housing oil seal and bushing (if equipped), and/or the speedometer drive gear oil seal and O-ring **(see illustration)**. Replacement of these seals is relatively easy, since the repairs can usually be performed without removing the transmission from the vehicle.

2   The extension housing oil seal is located at the extreme rear of the transmission, where the driveshaft is attached. If leakage at the seal is suspected, raise the vehicle and support it securely on jackstands. If the seal is leaking, transmission lubricant will be built up on the front of the driveshaft and may be dripping from the rear of the transmission.

3   Remove the driveshaft (see Chapter 8).

All manual transmissions except heavy-duty four-speed (RPO M20) and all automatic transmissions

4   Using a soft-face hammer, carefully tap the dust shield (if equipped) to the rear and remove it from the transmission. Be careful not to distort it. On cast iron case (heavy duty) five-speed manual transmissions, remove the nut and U-joint flange.

5   Using a screwdriver or pry bar, carefully pry the oil seal and bushing (if equipped) out of the rear of the transmission **(see illustration)**. Do not damage the splines on the transmission output shaft.

6   If the oil seal and bushing cannot be removed with a screwdriver or pry bar, a special oil seal removal tool (available at auto parts stores) will be required.

7   Using a large section of pipe or a very large deep socket as a drift, install the new oil seal **(see illustration)**. Drive it into the bore squarely and make sure it's completely seated. Install a new bushing using the same method.

8   Reinstall the U-joint flange and nut (if equipped) and tighten the nut to the torque listed in this Chapter's Specifications. Reinstall the dust shield (if equipped) by carefully tapping it into place.

RPO M20 (cast iron case) manual transmission

9   Disconnect the parking brake (see Chapter 9).

10   Unplug the electrical connector from the bearing retainer.

11   Remove the nut and U-joint flange.

12   Disconnect the transmission mount (see Section 6), then raise the transmission and support it with a jack.

13   Remove the bearing retainer bolts and the retainer.

14   Remove the bearing retainer gasket and scrape away any old gasket material.

15   Pry out the old seal with a screwdriver or seal remover.

16   Coat the outside of the new seal with locking compound.

17   With the bearing retainer lying flat on a workbench, carefully tap the new seal into place with a hammer and large socket.

18   The remainder of installation is the reverse of removal.

All transmissions

19   Lubricate the splines of the transmission output shaft and the outside of the driveshaft sleeve yoke with light-weight grease, then install the driveshaft. Be careful not to damage the lip of the new seal.

5.5 Pry out the old extension housing seal with a large screwdriver or, if that won't work, a seal removal tool

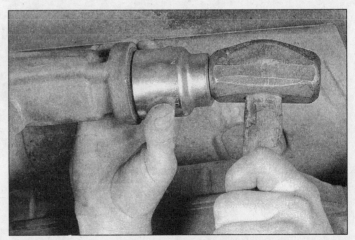

5.7 To install a new extension housing seal, tap it into place with a large socket and hammer

Notes

Chapter 7 Part B
Automatic transmission

Contents

Specifications

General
Transmission fluid type... See Chapter 1

Torque specifications
	Ft-lbs
Shift lever nut	17
Driveplate-to-torque converter bolt	
4L60	62
3L80/4L80	35

1 General information

The vehicles equipped with an automatic transmission have either a three-speed (3L80/3L80-HD) or a four-speed (4L60, 4L60-E or 4L80-E) unit. The four-speed units are equipped with a lock-up torque converter - known as a Torque Converter Clutch (or TCC). The clutch provides a direct connection between the engine and the drive wheels for improved efficiency and fuel economy. Beginning in 1991, an electronically-controlled automatic transmission, the Hydra-matic 4L80-E, was installed in some vehicles. Diagnosis and repair of this transmission must be done by a dealer service department or a repair shop.

The 4L60-E and 4L80-E electronic controlled transmissions are not equipped with the Throttle Valve (TV) cable assembly. The transmission functions normally controlled by the TV cable are controlled electronically.

Due to the complexity of the clutches and the hydraulic control system, and because of the special tools and expertise required to perform an automatic transmission overhaul, it should not be attempted by the home mechanic. Therefore, the proce-dures in this Chapter are limited to general diagnosis, routine maintenance, adjustment and transmission removal and installation.

If the transmission requires major repair work, it should be left to a dealer service department or an automotive or transmission repair shop. You can, however, remove and install the transmission yourself and save the expense, even if the repair work is done by a transmission specialist. You can also check and adjust the shift linkage, the throttle valve (TV) cable and the neutral start switch. **Caution:** *Never tow a disabled vehicle with an automatic transmission at speeds greater than 30 mph or distances over 50 miles.*

2 Diagnosis - general

Note: *Automatic transmission malfunctions may be caused by five general conditions: poor engine performance, improper adjust-ments, hydraulic malfunctions, mechanical malfunctions or malfunctions in the computer or its signal network. Diagnosis of these prob-lems should always begin with a check of the easily repaired items: fluid level and condition (Chapter 1), shift linkage adjustment and throt-tle linkage adjustment. Next, perform a road test to determine if the problem has been cor-rected or if more diagnosis is necessary. If the problem persists after the preliminary tests and corrections are completed, additional diagnosis should be done by a dealer service department or transmission repair shop. Refer to the Troubleshooting Section at the front of this manual for information on symptoms of transmission problems.*

Preliminary checks

1 Drive the vehicle to warm the transmis-sion to normal operating temperature.
2 Check the fluid level as described in Chapter 1:
a) *If the fluid level is unusually low, add enough fluid to bring the level within the designated area of the dipstick, then check for external leaks (see below).*
b) *If the fluid level is abnormally high, drain off the excess, then check the drained fluid for contamination by coolant. The presence of engine coolant in the auto-matic transmission fluid indicates that a failure has occurred in the internal radia-tor walls that separate the coolant from the transmission fluid (see Chapter 3).*

3.2 Remove the bolt (arrow) from the swivel, then detach the rod and swivel from the steering column

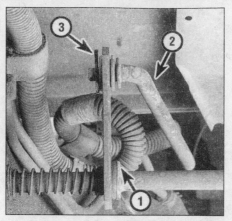
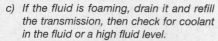

3.3 Remove the spring clip (3) and pull the equalizer rod (2) from the shift lever (1)

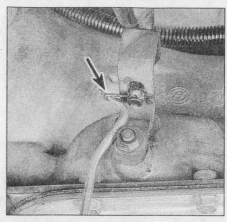

3.4 Remove the spring clip from the equalizer rod and detach the rod from the transmission shift lever

c) *If the fluid is foaming, drain it and refill the transmission, then check for coolant in the fluid or a high fluid level.*

3   Check the engine idle speed. **Note:** *If the engine is malfunctioning, do not proceed with the preliminary checks until it has been repaired and runs normally.*

4   Check the throttle valve cable for freedom of movement. Adjust it if necessary (see Section 4). **Note:** *The throttle cable may function properly when the engine is shut off and cold, but it may malfunction once the engine is hot. Check it cold and at normal engine operating temperature.*

5   Inspect the shift control linkage (Section 5). Make sure it's properly adjusted and the linkage operates smoothly.

Fluid leak diagnosis

6   Most fluid leaks are easy to locate visually. Repair usually consists of replacing a seal or gasket. If a leak is difficult to find, the following procedure may help.

7   Identify the fluid. Make sure it's transmission fluid and not engine oil or brake fluid (automatic transmission fluid is a deep red color).

8   Try to pinpoint the source of the leak. Drive the vehicle several miles, then park it over a large sheet of cardboard. After a minute or two, you should be able to locate the leak by determining the source of the fluid dripping onto the cardboard.

9   Make a careful visual inspection of the suspected component and the area immediately around it. Pay particular attention to gasket mating surfaces. A mirror is often helpful for finding leaks in areas that are hard to see.

10   If the leak still cannot be found, clean the suspected area thoroughly with a degreaser or solvent, then dry it.

11   Drive the vehicle for several miles at normal operating temperature and varying speeds. After driving the vehicle, visually inspect the suspected component again.

12   Once the leak has been located, the cause must be determined before it can be

properly repaired. If a gasket is replaced but the sealing flange is bent, the new gasket will not stop the leak. The bent flange must be straightened.

13   Before attempting to repair a leak, check to make sure the following conditions are corrected or they may cause another leak. **Note:** *Some of the following conditions cannot be fixed without highly specialized tools and expertise. Such problems must be referred to a transmission repair shop or a dealer service department.*

Gasket leaks

14   Check the pan periodically. Make sure the bolts are tight, no bolts are missing, the gasket is in good condition and the pan is flat (dents in the pan may indicate damage to the valve body inside).

15   If the pan gasket is leaking, the fluid level or the fluid pressure may be too high, the vent may be plugged, the pan bolts may be too tight, the pan sealing flange may be warped, the sealing surface of the transmission housing may be damaged, the gasket may be damaged or the transmission casting may be cracked or porous. If sealant instead of gasket material has been used to form a seal between the pan and the transmission housing, it may be the wrong sealant.

Seal leaks

16   If a transmission seal is leaking, the fluid level or pressure may be too high, the vent may be plugged, the seal bore may be damaged, the seal itself may be damaged or improperly installed, the surface of the shaft protruding through the seal may be damaged or a loose bearing may be causing excessive shaft movement.

17   Make sure the dipstick tube seal is in good condition and the tube is properly seated. Periodically check the area around the speedometer gear or sensor for leakage. If transmission fluid is evident, check the O-ring for damage.

Case leaks

18   If the case itself appears to be leaking,

the casting is porous and will have to be repaired or replaced.

19   Make sure the oil cooler hose fittings are tight and in good condition.

Fluid comes out vent pipe or fill tube

20   If this condition occurs, the transmission is overfilled, there is coolant in the fluid, the case is porous, the dipstick is incorrect, the vent is plugged or the drain back holes are plugged.

---

3   Shift linkage (1988 through 1994 models) - removal, installation and adjustment

---

Refer to illustrations 3.2, 3.3 and 3.4

Removal

1   Apply the parking brake.

2   Remove the screw and washer from the swivel and detach the shift linkage rod and the swivel from the steering column **(see illustration)**.

3   Remove the spring clip and detach the shift linkage rod from the equalizer lever **(see illustration)**. Don't lose the bearing and insulator.

4   Remove the spring clip and detach the equalizer rod **(see illustration)**.

5   Clean the metal parts with solvent and the rubber or nylon parts with soapy water. Wipe all parts with a clean, dry cloth.

Installation

6   Installation is the reverse of removal, but be sure to use new spring clips. After reassembling the shift linkage, adjust it (see below).

Adjustment

7   Apply the parking brake.

8   Loosen the swivel screw **(see illustration 3.2)**.

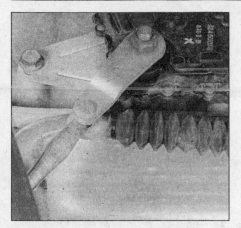

4.5 Pry the cable end from the transmission control lever stud

4.7 Carefully pry the horseshoe retainer from the shift cable

4.10 Disconnect the shift cable from the shift lever

9   Put the column selector lever in the N position (put the lever into the Neutral gate - don't rely on the indicator to find the neutral position).
10   Move the transmission shift lever (A in **illustration 3.3**) to its forward position, then back to the second detent.
11   Hold the shift linkage rod tightly in the swivel and tighten the shift lever nut to the specified torque.
12   Put the steering column shift lever in the P (Park) position.
13   Check the adjustment. The shift lever must go into all positions and the engine must start only in the P or N positions. If necessary, readjust the shift linkage and the park/neutral switch (see Section 6) until your adjustment meets both these criteria.
14   If the needle doesn't line up with the numbers/letters on the shift indicator when the shift linkage is adjusted properly, alter the position of the needle by changing the position of the indicator cable clip on the steering column shroud.

---

4   Shift cable (1995 and later models) - removal, installation and adjustment

Refer to illustrations 4.5, 4.7 and 4.10

Removal

1   Detach the cable from the negative terminal of the battery.
2   Apply the parking brake.
3   Block the rear wheels so the vehicle will not roll in either direction, then shift the transmission into the Neutral position.
4   On models so equipped, remove the transfer case shield (see Chapter 7C).
5   Pry the cable end from the transmission control lever stud **(see illustration)**.
6   Remove the cable from the transmission oil pan clip.
7   Remove the horseshoe retainer from the shift cable **(see illustration)**.
8   Squeeze the cable retainer while pulling the cable toward the back of the vehicle and

disconnect the cable.
9   Remove the steering column trim filler panel.
10   Pry the shift cable from the shift lever **(see illustration)**.
11   Squeeze the cable retainer while pulling the cable toward the front of the vehicle and disconnect the cable from the steering column bracket.
12   Remove the cowl trim panel and the door sill trim plate, then remove the seat.
13   Remove the cable from the floor clip and grommet.
14   Lift up the driver's side of the carpet and remove the grommet and cable from the vehicle.

Installation

15   Installation is the reverse of removal, but be sure not to handle the rubber boot as it will be damaged, leading to future cable failure.

Adjustment

16   Apply the parking brake.
17   Remove the retaining clip from the transmission rear support bracket.
18   Separate the body-core adjuster from the range selector pin.
19   Place the transmission shift selector shaft into the Neutral position.
20   Place the transmission shift lever on the steering column into the Neutral position.
21   Remove the horseshoe retainer from the shift cable **(see illustration 4.7)**.
22   Remove the cable from the transmission oil pan clip.
23   Install the cable back onto the transmission oil pan clip.
24   Install the horseshoe retainer onto the shift cable.
25   Make sure the transmission shift lever on the steering column and the shift selector shaft are still in the Neutral position. Reposition if necessary.
26   Place, then snap, the body-core adjustment onto the transmission selector shaft. Ensure the spring loaded body-core adjustment moves freely.
27   Push the locking tab into the body-core until it snaps. If necessary, wiggle the body-

core while pushing in the locking tab.
28   Insert the horseshoe retainer into the shift cable.
29   Check the adjustment. The shift lever must go into all positions and the engine must start only in the P or N positions only. If necessary, readjust the shift cable and the park/neutral switch (see Section 6) until your adjustment meets both these criteria.

---

5   Throttle valve (TV) cable (4L60/700R-4) - replacement and adjustment

Refer to illustrations 5.3, 5.4 and 5.7
1   The throttle valve (TV) cable used on these transmissions should not
be thought of as a "downshift" cable. The TV cable controls line pressure, shift feel, shift points, detent downshifts and part throttle downshifts. The function of the cable is similar to the combined functions of a detent cable and a vacuum modulator.

Replacement

2   Remove the air cleaner (see Chapter 5).
3   Detach the cable terminal (end) from the throttle lever **(see illustration)**.

5.3 Detach the throttle valve (TV) cable from the throttle lever by pulling it forward, off the mounting lug

5.4 Pinch the locking tangs of the TV cable housing with a pair of pliers and push the housing through the bracket

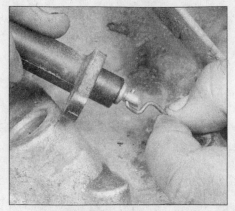

5.7 Remove the cable from the transmission link

6.1 The park/neutral switch is located on the lower end of the steering column, near the firewall (1994 and earlier models)

4   Compress the locking tangs on the cable housing and detach the housing from the bracket **(see illustration)**.
5   Remove the routing clips or straps.
6   Trace the cable to the transmission. Remove the bolt and the flat washer.
7   Pull up on the cable cover at the transmission until the cable is visible, then disconnect the cable from the transmission link **(see illustration)**.
8   Remove the seal.
9   Installation is the reverse of removal. Be sure to tighten the bolt securely. When you're finished reattaching the TV cable assembly, adjust it (see below).

Adjustment

10   With the engine off, depress and hold down the metal re-adjust tab at the engine end of the TV cable.
11   Move the slider until it stops against the fitting.
12   Release the re-adjust tab.
13   Rotate the throttle lever to its full travel position.
14   The slider must move (ratchet) toward the lever when the lever is rotated to its full travel position.
15   Make sure the cable moves freely. The cable may appear to function properly with the engine stopped and cold. Recheck it after the engine is hot.
16   Road test the vehicle.

---

6   Park/neutral switch - adjustment and replacement

1994 and earlier models

Adjustment

Refer to illustration 6.1

1   Place the shift lever in the Neutral (N) position. Move the switch housing **(see illustration)** all the way toward the Low (L) gear position (to the right).
2   Move the shift lever to the Park (P) position. The main housing and housing back

should ratchet, providing proper switch adjustment.

Replacement

3   Place the shift lever in Neutral.
4   Unplug the electrical connectors.
5   Spread the tangs on the housing and pull the switch up.
6   Align the actuator on the switch with the hole in the shift tube.
7   Position the rear portion of the switch (connector side) to fit into the cutout in the lower jacket.
8   Push down on the front of the switch to engage the two tangs.
9   Move the shift lever to Park - the switch is adjusted.
10   Plug in the electrical connectors.

1995 and later models

Refer to illustration 6.14

Replacement and adjustment

11   Firmly apply the parking brake, and place the shift lever in Neutral.
12   Pry the shift cable from the transmission shift lever ball-stud (see Section 4).
13   Remove the nut retaining the shift lever to the shaft and remove the lever.
14   Disconnect the electrical connector from the park/neutral switch, remove the mounting bolts and slide the switch off the shaft **(see illustration)**. Lightly file the end of

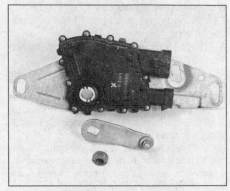

6.14 Typical park/neutral switch (1995 and later models)

the shaft to remove any burrs, if necessary.
15   To install the switch (transmission shaft still in Neutral), line up the flats on the switch with the flats on the shaft and lower the switch onto the shaft. Install the bolts.
16   The alignment of the switch is made by moving the switch one way or the other. A special tool is available that makes this easier, but it isn't absolutely necessary. If you are reinstalling the original switch, the bolts will have made a scratched circle on the mounting bosses. If you bolt it down with the bolts aligned exactly over these circles, the switch will be positioned correctly. If you are installing a new switch, the replacement switch will probably be equipped with a plastic pin that locks it into the Neutral position. Just bolt it down. When you attach the shift lever and cable and move the selector through its range, the pin will shear off and the switch will be perfectly adjusted.
17   Install the shift lever and shift cable.
18   Verify the engine will start in Park and Neutral and not in any other gear.
19   If the switch does not operate properly, loosen the mounting bolts and rotate it slightly until it does.

---

7   Transmission mount - check and replacement

Refer to illustration 7.1

Check

1   Insert a large screwdriver or pry bar into the space between the transmission and the crossmember and try to pry the transmission up slightly **(see illustration)**.
2   The transmission should not move away from the insulator much. If there is any separation of the rubber, the mount is worn out.

Replacement

3   To replace the mount, remove the nut attaching the insulator to the crossmember and the bolts attaching the insulator to the transmission.
4   Raise the transmission slightly with a

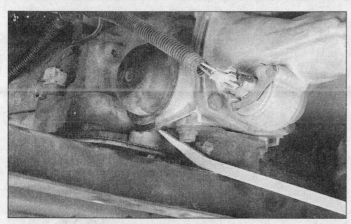

7.1 To check the rear transmission mount for wear, place a large screwdriver or pry bar between the crossmember and one of the mounting bolts and try to pry up on the transmission - it shouldn't move much

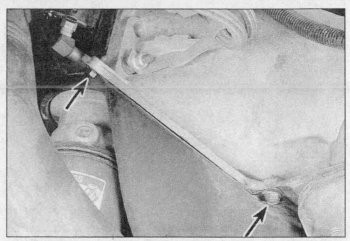

8.4 To detach the torque converter cover, remove the four bolts - the two shown on this side (arrow) and two on the other side

jack and remove the insulator.
5   Installation is the reverse of the removal procedure. Be sure to tighten the nuts/bolts securely.

8   Automatic transmission - removal and installation

Refer to illustrations 8.4, 8.5, 8.9, 8.17, 8.18, 8.20 and 8.21

Removal

1   Disconnect the negative cable from the battery.
2   Raise the vehicle and support it securely on jackstands.
3   Drain the transmission fluid (see Chapter 1), then reinstall the pan.
4   Remove the torque converter cover **(see illustration)**.
5   Mark the torque converter and the driveplate with a scribe or chalk so they can be installed in the same position **(see illustration)**.
6   Remove the driveplate-to-torque converter bolts. Turn the crankshaft (in a clockwise direction only, viewed from the front) for access to each bolt.
7   Remove the starter motor (see Chapter 5).
8   Remove the driveshaft (see Chapter 8); if the vehicle is equipped with 4WD, remove the front driveshaft also (see Chapter 8).
9   Unplug the vehicle speed sensor **(see illustration)**.
10   Unplug all wire harness connectors from the transmission.
11   If the vehicle is equipped with a 3L80/3L80-HD (400/475), disconnect the vacuum hose from the modulator (right side of the transmission).
12   Remove any exhaust components which will interfere with transmission removal (see Chapter 4).
13   If the vehicle is equipped with a 4L60 (700R-4), disconnect the TV cable from the transmission (see Section 5).

8.5 To ensure proper reassembly, mark the relationship between the driveplate and the torque converter

14   Disconnect the shift linkage or cable (see Section 3 or 4).
15   Support the engine with a jack. Use a block of wood under the oil pan to spread the load.
16   Support the transmission with a jack - preferably a jack made for this purpose.

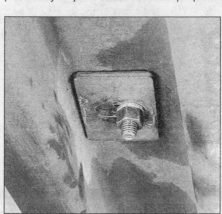

8.17 Remove the nut from the transmission mount-to-crossmember stud

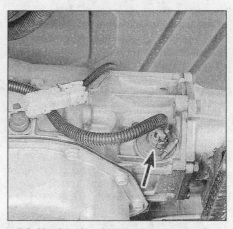

8.9 Unplug the electrical connector for the vehicle speed sensor (and any other connectors on the transmission)

Safety chains will help steady the transmission on the jack.
17   Remove the rear transmission mount-to-crossmember nut **(see illustration)**.
18   Remove the four (two per side) crossmember-to-frame nuts and bolts **(see illustration)**.

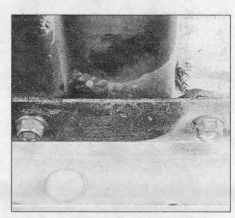

8.18 Remove the bolts and nuts from each end of the crossmember

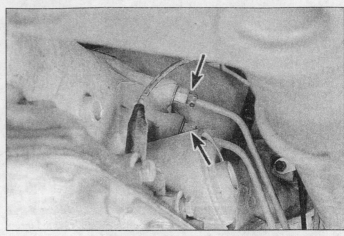

8.20 Remove the transmission bellhousing-to-engine bolts (arrows) - note that the upper right bolt also secures the transmission dipstick tube bracket

8.21 After lowering the transmission, disconnect the transmission oil cooler lines (arrows) and plug them to prevent loss of fluid

19   Raise the transmission enough to allow removal of the crossmember.

20   Remove the transmission-to-engine bolts **(see illustration)**.

21   Lower the transmission slightly and disconnect and plug the transmission fluid cooler lines **(see illustration)**. On 1995 and earlier models, use a flare-nut wrench to unthread the fitting nut. On 1996 and later models, the transmission cooler lines are equipped with quick-connect fittings. Disconnect the fitting as follows:

a)   *Grasp the plastic cap and pull it out of the fitting. Slide it back over the cooler line approximately two inches.*

b)   *Using a small hooked tool, pull out on one of the open ends of the retaining clip, rotate the clip out of the fitting and remove it completely.*

c)   *Pull the cooler line straight out of the fitting.*

22   Remove the transmission dipstick tube.

23   Move the transmission to the rear to disengage it from the engine block dowel pins and make sure the torque converter is detached from the driveplate. Secure the torque converter to the transmission so it won't fall out during removal.

Installation

24   Prior to installation, make sure the torque converter hub is securely engaged in the pump. On 1996 and later models, install

NEW quick-connector fitting E-clips into the transmission cooler line fittings as follows:

a)   *Hook one end of the E-clip into the slot in the transmission fitting.*

b)   *Rotate the E-clip around the fitting, squeeze the other end of the E-clip in and snap it into the slot in the fitting.*

c)   *Make sure all three "ears" are visible inside the fitting and the clip moves freely in the slots.*

d)   *Repeat the procedure for the other fitting.*

25   With the transmission secured to the jack, raise the transmission into position. Be sure to keep it level so the torque converter doesn't slide out. Connect the transmission fluid cooler lines. On 1996 and later models, connect the quick-connect fitting as follows:

a)   *Press the cooler line straight into the fitting until you hear or feel the E-clip snap around the cooler line.*

b)   *Look at the fitting and make sure the yellow band on the cooler line is not visible outside the fitting.*

c)   *Slide the plastic cap up the cooler line and snap it into the fitting.*

d)   *Pull out sharply on the cooler line to verify a good connection.*

e)   *If the plastic cap or E-clip will not seat properly, disconnect the fitting and install NEW parts as required.*

26   Turn the torque converter until the marks on the converter and driveplate are

aligned.

27   Move the transmission forward carefully until the dowel pins engage with the holes in the bellhousing.

28   Install the transmission housing-to-engine bolts. Tighten them securely.

29   Install the driveplate-to-torque converter bolts and tighten them to the specified torque.

30   Install the crossmember and lower the mount stud into its hole. Tighten the bolts and nuts securely.

31   Remove the jacks supporting the transmission and the engine.

32   Install the dipstick tube.

33   Install the starter motor (see Chapter 5).

34   Connect the vacuum hose(s) (if equipped).

35   Connect the shift and TV linkage or cable.

36   Plug in the transmission wire harness connectors.

37   Install the torque converter cover.

38   Install the driveshaft(s).

39   Connect the speedometer cable.

40   Adjust the shift linkage or cable.

41   Install any exhaust system components that were removed or disconnected.

42   Lower the vehicle.

43   Fill the transmission with the specified fluid (Chapter 1), run the engine and check for fluid leaks.

Chapter 7 Part C
Transfer case

Contents

Specifications

Torque specifications

	Ft-lbs
Transfer case output shaft yoke nut	
New Process/New Venture models	110
Borg Warner models	
Front	165
Rear	125
Input bearing retainer bolts	14
Shift lever nut	20
Transfer case-to-transmission bolts	33
Pump housing bolts	30
Rear extension housing-to-pump retainer bolts	23
Poppet screw	23
Speedometer sensor	23
Indicator light switch	17

1   General information

Four-wheel drive (4WD) models are equipped with a transfer case mounted on the rear of the transmission. Drive is transmitted from the engine, through the transmission and the transfer case to the front and rear axles by driveshafts.

Most models use the New Process 241 or New Venture NV241 transfer case. Heavy duty one-ton models and models with dual rear wheels use the Borg Warner 1370, 4401 or 4470. The New Venture NV243 is an electronically shifted transfer case used on 1996 and 1997 models and is very similar to the New Venture 241. The shifting operation of the NV243 is quite complex and is outside the scope of this manual. **Note:** A *metal tag riveted to the transfer case and identifies the model number and the reduction ratio.*

2   Shift linkage - check and adjustment

Refer to illustration 2.3

1   Place the shift lever in the 4-HIGH position.

2   Raise the vehicle and support it securely

2.3 Disconnect the linkage rod from the console shift lever (upper arrow; lower arrow points to the transfer case shift lever)

on jackstands.

3   Disconnect the linkage rod from the console shift lever **(see illustration)**.

4   Shift the transfer case into the 4-HIGH position (transfer case shift lever in full forward detent).

5   Adjust the swivel to align with the hole in

3.1 Remove the shift lever knob (arrow)

the console shift lever.

6   Lower the vehicle.

3   Shift lever - replacement

Refer to illustrations 3.1, 3.2 and 3.3

1   Remove the shift knobs from the shift levers **(see illustration)**.

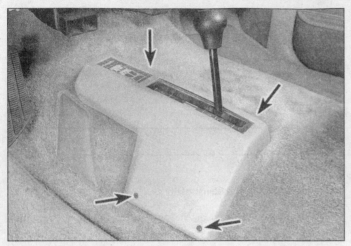

3.2 Remove the console retaining screws (arrows)

3.3 Remove the shift lever plate retaining bolts (arrows)

2   Remove the console screws and the console. Disconnect the indicator light harness from the console **(see illustration)**.
3   Remove the shift lever plate bolts **(see illustration)**.
4   Raise the vehicle and support it securely on jackstands.
5   Disconnect the rod from the shift lever **(see illustration 2.3)**.
6   Remove the shift lever.
7   Installation is the reverse of removal.

---

4   Seal replacement

Refer to illustration 4.3
Note: *This procedure applies to both the front output shaft and rear extension housing seals.*
1   Raise the vehicle and support it securely on jackstands.
2   Remove the driveshaft (front or rear, as applicable) (see Chapter 8).
3   Remove the nut and flat washers (not used at the rear on some models) **(see illustration)**.

4   Remove the driveshaft yoke or flange (if equipped).
5   Remove the shield (if used).
6   Pry out the seal with a screwdriver. Don't damage the seal bore.
7   Lubricate the new seal lips with ATF or petroleum jelly.
8   Drive the seal into place with a large socket. The outside diameter of the socket should be slightly smaller than the outside diameter of the seal.
9   The remainder of installation is the reverse of removal. Be sure to tighten the nut to the specified torque.

---

5   Transfer case - removal and installation

Refer to illustration 5.13

Removal

1   Disconnect the negative cable from the battery.
2   Raise the vehicle and support it securely on jackstands.

3   Remove the skid plate (if equipped).
4   Drain the transfer case lubricant (see Chapter 1).
5   Remove the front driveshaft (see Chapter 8).
6   Remove the left strut rod.
7   Remove the rear driveshaft (see Chapter 8).
8   Unplug all electrical connectors from the transfer case.
9   Disconnect the shift linkage.
10   Remove the exhaust system, if necessary, for clearance (see Chapter 4).
11   Support the transmission with a jack or jackstand. The transmission should remain supported at all times while the transfer case is out of the vehicle.
12   Support the transfer case with a jack - preferably a special jack made for this purpose. Safety chains will help steady the transfer case on the jack.
13   Remove the bolts securing the transmission to the transfer case **(see illustration)**. Don't lose the lock washers.
14   Make a final check that all wires and hoses have been disconnected from the transfer case, then move the transfer case

4.3 Hold the flange from turning with a chain wrench (or a flange holding tool) and loosen the retaining nut

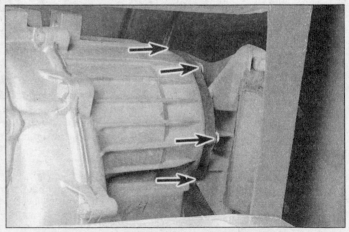

5.13 Remove the six transfer case to transmission mounting bolts - four of six bolts shown (arrows)

and jack toward the rear of the vehicle until the transfer case is clear of the transmission. Keep the transfer case level as this is done. Once the input shaft is clear, lower the transfer case and remove it from under the vehicle.

Installation

15 Installation is the reverse of removal. Be sure to tighten the transfer case-to-transmission bolts to the specified torque.

6 Transfer case - overhaul

Note: *This procedure applies to the New Process model 241 transfer case only.*
1   Remove the transfer case (see Section 5).
2   Clean the transfer case with solvent and a stiff brush.

External components

3   Remove the front output flange nut, the washer, the rubber sealing washer and the front output flange from the front output shaft.
4   Remove the indicator light switch and the O-ring seal.
5   Remove the speedometer sensor and seal.
6   Remove the poppet screw, O-ring seal, poppet spring and poppet plunger.

Mainshaft extension and oil pump housing

7   Remove the bolts and detach the rear extension housing.
8   Remove the bearing retainer snap-ring from the mainshaft.
9   Remove the pump retainer housing bolts.
10 Remove the pump retainer housing from the rear case half.
11 Remove the retainer snap-ring, speedometer tone wheel and retainer snap-ring from the mainshaft.
12 Remove the case bolts from the case halves. Note that the two longer case bolts go into the doweled case holes.
13 Insert screwdrivers into the slots cast into the case ends and pry the case halves apart. **Caution:** *Don't attempt to wedge the case halves apart anywhere else along their mating surfaces. Also, be careful not to damage the oil pump (located in the rear case half) while removing the rear case half.*
14 Remove the oil pump, the pick-up tube, the O-ring and the pump pick-up filter from the rear case half.
15 Remove the fork shift spring.
16 Remove the retainer snap-ring from the front output shaft.
17 Remove the mainshaft, the chain and the driven sprocket from the front case half as a unit. The mode shift fork and shift rail will be removed with the mainshaft.
18 Remove the retainer snap-ring from the

mainshaft.
19 Remove the synchronizer assembly. Remove the drive sprocket from the mainshaft.
20 Remove the range shift fork and the range shift hub. Remove the sector with shaft and the planetary carrier. It's necessary to rotate the sector with shaft to obtain clearance when removing the range fork.
21 Remove the shift lever nut, washer, shift lever, plastic washer and O-ring seal from the front case half.
22 Remove the input bearing retainer bolts and input bearing retainer from the front case half.
23 Remove the bearing retainer snap-ring.
24 Remove the planetary carrier and the input gear from the annuls gear with a soft-faced hammer.
25 Remove the retainer ring snap-ring from the input gear.
26 Remove the input bearing from the input gear with a bearing remover tool. Remove the carrier lock ring and the thrust washer.
27 Remove the drive sprocket bearing from the drive sprocket with needle bearing remover tool and slide hammer.
28 Remove the needle bearings from the input gear with the same tools.
29 Remove the snap-ring from the front output bearing retainer ring.
30 Remove the front output shaft seal from the front case half.
31 Remove the front output bearing from the front case half with a bearing driver.
32 Remove the seal from the mainshaft extension housing.
33 Remove the seal from the input bearing retainer.
34 Remove the front output rear bearing from the rear case half. Insert a needle bearing remover behind the needle bearings. Using a slide hammer, remove the bearing from the case.
35 Remove the mainshaft bearing from the oil pump retainer.
36 Remove the magnet from the front case half.
37 Scribe the location of the synchronizer hub and sleeve to aid in reassembly.
38 Remove the main drive synchronizer stop ring from the synchronizer sleeve.
39 Remove the spring retainer from the synchronizer sleeve.
40 Remove the synchronizer hub from the synchronizer.
41 Remove the oil pump screws from the oil pump.
42 Remove the inner gears.

Cleaning and inspection

43 Remove all old lubricant and dirt from the parts. Clean the bearings, shafts, sprockets and chain, and the oil feed ports and channels in each
case half. Apply compressed air to each oil feed port and channel to remove any obstructions or cleaning solvent residue. Clean all mating and sealing surfaces.
44 Inspect the bearings and thrust washers

for wear, spalling, brinnelling or corrosion.
45 Inspect the gear teeth for excessive wear or damage, spalling, cracks or corrosion.
46 Inspect the splines for excessive wear, spalling, cracks, twist or corrosion.
47 Inspect the shaft splines for excessive wear, spalling, cracks, distortion or corrosion.
48 Inspect the retainer rings for excessive wear, distortion or damage.
49 Inspect the case halves for damaged or warped mating surfaces, cracks, porosity or damaged threaded holes.
50 Inspect the synchronizer stop ring for cracks, chips, spalling or excessive wear.
51 Inspect the synchronizer hub and sleeve for cracks, chips, spalling or excessive wear.
52 Inspect the pads on the mode fork and the range fork for wear and distortion.
53 Inspect the oil pump gears and case halves for wear, spalling, cracks and damage. Replace the oil pump assembly as a unit if wear is evident.
54 Inspect the input gear, planetary carrier and range shift hub tooth for excessive wear.

Bearing and seal replacement

55 Drive the needle bearing assembly into the drive sprocket with drive gear needle bearing installer and a driver handle. Drive the bearing into the driven sprocket so that it's flush on the synchronizer side.
56 Drive the needle bearing into the rear case half with an input gear bearing installer (needle bearing) and a driver handle. The bearing must be flush with the boss on the case housing.
57 Install the front output bearing in the front case half with an output shaft bearing installer. Install the bearing snap-ring retainer.
58 Install the front output bearing in the pump retainer housing with the same tool.
59 Install the mainshaft pilot bearing in the input gear with an input gear bearing installer (needle bearing) and driver handle.
60 Install the thrust washer.
61 Install the carrier lock ring.
62 Install the retainer.
63 Install the input bearing in the input gear with an input gear bearing installer (needle bearing).
64 Install the retainer snap-ring in the input gear.
65 Install the input bearing retainer seal in the input bearing retainer.
66 Install the front output shaft seal in the front case half.
67 Install the magnet in the front case half.

Internal components

68 Assemble the synchronizer hub, the synchronizer sleeve and the three struts. Make sure the mark you scribed prior to disassembly is now aligned.
69 Install the spring retainer in the synchronizer sleeve.
70 Assemble the main drive synchronizer stop ring and the synchronizer sleeve.
71 Install the drive sprocket to the main-

shaft.

72   Install the planetary input gear assembly into the annulus gear with a soft-faced hammer.

73   Install the retainer snap-ring in the input bearing.

74   Apply RTV sealant to the input bearing retainer mating surfaces. Apply a thread locking compound to the bearing retainer bolts. Install the input bearing retainer to the front case half and tighten the bolts to the specified torque.

75   Install the sector with shaft into the front case half.

76   Install the shift lever O-ring, plastic washer, shift lever, washer and nut to the front case half. Tighten the nut to the specified torque.

77   Install the range shift hub and the range shift fork into the front case half (you'll have to rotate the sector to align the range shift fork).

78   Install the synchronizer assembly, mode shift fork and rail into the front case half.

79   Install the front output shaft to the front case half.

80   Install the mainshaft, drive sprocket, driven sprocket and chain as an assembly.

81   Install the retainer snap-ring on the front output shaft.

82   Install the fork shift spring on the mode shift rail.

83   Install the oil pump pick-up tube, oil tube connector and pump pick-up screen into the rear case.

84   Install the oil tube O-ring onto the oil pump pick-up tube. **Caution:** *If you damage the O-ring during assembly, it could result in pump failure.*

85   Attach the oil pump to the oil pump pick-up tube. Apply RTV sealer to the case mating surfaces.

86   Install the rear case over the mainshaft and onto the front case half. Be careful not to damage the oil pump while installing the rear case half.

87   Apply a thread locking compound to the case bolt threads and install the case bolts into the case halves. Remember: The two longer case bolts and washers go into the doweled case holes. Tighten the case bolts to the specified torque.

88   Apply a thread locking compound to the pump housing bolt threads and install the pump retainer housing and pump housing bolts to the rear case half. Tighten the case housing bolts to the specified torque.

89   Install the input bearing retainer snap-ring to the mainshaft.

90   Install a retainer snap-ring, the speedometer tone wheel and another retainer snap-ring to the mainshaft.

91   Apply a thread locking compound to the extension housing bolts, apply RTV sealer to the mating surfaces and install the rear extension housing and extension housing bolts to the pump retainer housing. Tighten the bolts to the specified torque.

92   Install the selection plunger, poppet spring, O-ring seal and poppet screw to the front case half. Tighten the poppet screw to the specified torque.

93   Install the speedometer sensor and O-ring to the pump retainer housing. Tighten the sensor to the specified torque.

94   Install the indicator light switch and O-ring to the front case housing. Tighten the switch to the specified torque.

95   Install the front output flange, rubber sealing washer, washer and flange nut. Tighten the nut to the specified torque.

Chapter 8
Clutch and driveline

Contents

Specifications

General

Clutch fluid type	See Chapter 1
Clutch disc lining thickness (minimum)	1/16 in

Torque specifications

Ft-lbs (unless otherwise indicated)

Clutch

Pressure plate-to-flywheel bolts	
5/16-inch bolts	12 to 18
3/8-inch bolts	22 to 32
Release lever ball stud	25
Bellhousing-to-engine bolts (heavy-duty [cast iron case] transmissions only)	55
Master cylinder mounting nuts	156 in-lbs
Release cylinder mounting bolts	
1995 and earlier	156 in-lbs
1996 and later	72 in-lbs

Driveshaft

Strap bolts

One-half/three-quarter ton vehicles	15
One-ton vehicles	27
Center support bearing nuts	25

Rear axle

Brake backing plate bolts	
With 8-1/2 inch differential ring gear	35
With 9-1/2 inch differential ring gear	105
Axleshaft-to-hub bolts (full-floating axle)	115
Pinion shaft lock screw	25

Front driveaxle (4WD models)

Hub nut	
1994 and earlier	173
1995	180
1996 and later	165
Mounting flange bolts	59

1   General information

The Sections in this Chapter deal with the components from the rear of the engine to the rear wheels (except for the transmission and transfer case, which are dealt with in Chapter 7) and forward to the front wheels on four-wheel drive (4WD) models. In this Chapter, the components are grouped into three categories: Clutch, driveshaft(s) and axle(s). Separate Sections within this Chapter cover checks and repair procedures for components in each of these three groups.

Since nearly all these procedures involve working under the vehicle, make sure it's safely supported on sturdy jackstands or a hoist where the vehicle can be safely raised and lowered.

2   Clutch - description and check

Refer to illustration 2.1

1   All vehicles with a manual transmission have a single dry plate, diaphragm spring-type clutch **(see illustration)**. The clutch disc has a splined hub which allows it to slide along the splines of the transmission input shaft. The clutch and pressure plate are held in contact by spring pressure exerted by the diaphragm in the pressure plate.

2   The clutch release system is operated by hydraulic pressure. The hydraulic release system consists of the clutch pedal, a master cylinder and fluid reservoir, the hydraulic line, a release (or slave) cylinder which actuates the clutch release lever and the clutch release (or throw out) bearing.

3   When pressure is applied to the clutch pedal to release the clutch, hydraulic pressure is exerted against the outer end of the clutch release lever. As the lever pivots the shaft fingers push against the release bearing. The bearing pushes against the fingers of the diaphragm spring of the pressure plate assembly, which in turn releases the clutch plate.

4   Terminology can be a problem when discussing the clutch components because common names are in some cases different from those used by the manufacturer. For example, the driven plate is also called the clutch plate or disc, the clutch release bearing is sometimes called a throw out bearing, the release cylinder is sometimes called the slave cylinder.

5   Other than to replace components with obvious damage, some preliminary checks should be performed to diagnose clutch problems.

a) *The first check should be of the fluid level in the clutch master cylinder. If the fluid level is low, add fluid as necessary and inspect the hydraulic system for leaks. If the master cylinder reservoir is dry, bleed the system as described in Section 8 and recheck the clutch operation.*

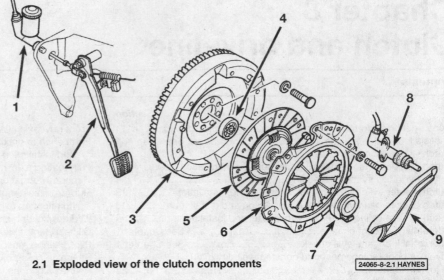

2.1 Exploded view of the clutch components   `24065-8-2.1 HAYNES`

1	Clutch master cylinder	4	Pilot bearing	7	Clutch release bearing
2	Clutch pedal	5	Clutch disc	8	Clutch slave cylinder
3	Flywheel	6	Clutch cover	9	Clutch release lever

b) *To check "clutch spin-down time," run the engine at normal idle speed with the transmission in Neutral (clutch pedal up - engaged). Disengage the clutch (pedal down), wait several seconds and shift the transmission into Reverse. No grinding noise should be heard. A grinding noise would most likely indicate a bad pressure plate or clutch disc.*

c) *To check for complete clutch release, run the engine (with the parking brake applied to prevent vehicle movement) and hold the clutch pedal approximately 1/2-inch from the floor. Shift the transmission between 1st gear and Reverse several times. If the shift is rough, component failure is indicated. Check the release cylinder pushrod travel. With the clutch pedal depressed completely, the release cylinder pushrod should extend substantially. If it doesn't, check the fluid level in the clutch master cylinder.*

d) *Visually inspect the pivot bushing at the top of the clutch pedal to make sure there's no binding or excessive play.*

e) *Crawl under the vehicle and make sure the clutch release lever is securely attached to the ball stud.*

3   Clutch master cylinder - removal, overhaul and installation

Note 1: *The overhaul procedure applies to 1992 and earlier models only. 1993 and later model master cylinders are not rebuildable. A new assembly must be installed. On 1993 through 1995 models, a complete master cylinder, release cylinder and hydraulic line assembly (pre-filled and bled at the factory) must be installed.*

Note 2: *Before beginning this procedure,* contact local parts stores and dealer service departments concerning the purchase of a rebuild kit or a new master cylinder. Availability and cost of the necessary parts may dictate whether the cylinder is rebuilt or replaced with a new one. If you decide to rebuild the cylinder, inspect the bore as described in Step 12 before purchasing parts.

Removal

Refer to illustration 3.2

1   Disconnect the negative cable from the battery.

2   Working under the dash, remove the steering column covers and the lower left air conditioning duct (if equipped), then disconnect the pushrod from the top of the clutch pedal. It's held in place with a spring clip **(see illustration)**.

3   On 1988 through 1992 models, remove the hydraulic line from the master cylinder. On 1993 through 1995 models, detach the release cylinder from the transmission. On 1996 and later models, remove the hydraulic line from the release cylinder at the access hole in the side of the bellhousing. It will be necessary to use a special tool available at auto parts stores to disconnect the quick release connection on 1996 and later models.

4   On 1988 through 1992 models, remove the two nuts that secure the master cylinder to the firewall and remove the master cylinder. **Caution:** *Don't allow brake fluid to come in contact with the paint - it will damage the finish.* On 1993 through 1995 models, remove the two nuts and the brackets retaining the tubing to the firewall. Remove the master cylinder, release cylinder and tubing as an assembly. On 1996 and later models, twist the master cylinder 45 degrees clockwise and pull it from the firewall. Remove the master cylinder with the tubing attached.

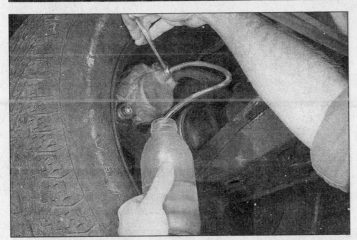

15.8 When bleeding the brakes, a clear piece of tubing is attached to the bleeder screw fitting and submerged in brake fluid - air bubbles can be easily seen in the tube and container (when no more bubbles appear, the air has been purged from the caliper or wheel cylinder)

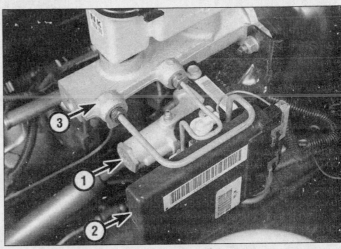

16.4a RWAL system components

1   Isolation/dump valve   3   Master cylinder
2   Control module

wheel lock-to-lock during inspection.

11   Bleed the brake system as described in Section 15.

Metal brake lines

12   When replacing brake lines, be sure to use the correct parts. Don't use copper tubing for any brake system components. Purchase steel brake lines from a dealer parts department or auto parts store.

13   Prefabricated brake line, with the tube ends already flared and fittings installed, is available at auto parts stores and dealer parts departments. These lines are also bent to the proper shapes.

14   When installing the new line make sure it's well supported in the brackets and has plenty of clearance between moving or hot components.

15   After installation, check the master cylinder fluid level and add fluid as necessary. Bleed the brake system as outlined in the next Section and test the brakes carefully before placing the vehicle into normal operation.

15 Brake system bleeding

Refer to illustration 15.8

Warning: *Wear eye protection when bleeding the brake system. If the fluid comes in contact with your eyes, immediately rinse them with water and seek medical attention.*

Note: *Bleeding the brake system is necessary to remove any air that's trapped in the system when it's opened during removal and installation of a hose, line, caliper, wheel cylinder or master cylinder.*

1   It will probably be necessary to bleed the system at all four brakes if air has entered the system due to low fluid level, or if the brake lines have been disconnected at the master cylinder.

2   If a brake line was disconnected only at a wheel, then only that caliper or wheel cylinder must be bled.

3   If a brake line is disconnected at a fitting located between the master cylinder and any of the brakes, that part of the system served by the disconnected line must be bled.

4   Remove any residual vacuum (or hydraulic pressure) from the brake power booster by applying the brake several times with the engine off.

5   Remove the master cylinder reservoir cover and fill the reservoir with brake fluid. Reinstall the cover. **Note:** *Check the fluid level often during the bleeding operation and add fluid as necessary to prevent the fluid level from falling low enough to allow air bubbles into the master cylinder.*

6   Have an assistant on hand, as well as a supply of new brake fluid, an empty clear plastic container, a length of 3/16-inch plastic, rubber or vinyl tubing to fit over the bleeder valve and a wrench to open and close the bleeder valve.

7   Beginning at the right rear wheel, loosen the bleeder screw slightly, then tighten it to a point where it's snug but can still be loosened quickly and easily.

8   Place one end of the tubing over the bleeder screw fitting and submerge the other end in brake fluid in the container **(see illustration)**.

9   Have the assistant pump the brakes a few times to get pressure in the system, then hold the pedal firmly depressed.

10   While the pedal is held depressed, open the bleeder screw just enough to allow a flow of fluid to leave the valve. Watch for air bubbles to exit the submerged end of the tube. When the fluid flow slows after a couple of seconds, tighten the screw and have your assistant release the pedal.

11   Repeat Steps 9 and 10 until no more air is seen leaving the tube, then tighten the bleeder screw and proceed to the left rear

wheel, the right front wheel and the left front wheel, in that order, and perform the same procedure. Be sure to check the fluid in the master cylinder reservoir frequently.

12   Never use old brake fluid. It contains moisture which can boil during periods of heavy braking, rendering the brakes useless.

13   Refill the master cylinder with fluid at the end of the operation.

14   Check the operation of the brakes. The pedal should feel solid when depressed, with no sponginess. If necessary, repeat the entire process. **Warning:** *Do not operate the vehicle if you are in doubt about the effectiveness of the brake system.*

16 Anti-lock brake system - general information

Refer to illustrations 16.4a and 16.4b

Description

The Anti-lock brake system is designed to maintain vehicle maneuverability, directional stability and optimum deceleration under severe braking conditions on most road surfaces. It does so by monitoring the rotational speed of the wheels and controlling the brake line pressure during braking. This prevents the wheels from locking up prematurely.

Two types of systems are used: Rear Wheel Anti-Lock (RWAL) and Four Wheel Anti-Lock (4WAL). RWAL only controls lockup on the rear wheels, whereas 4WAL prevents lockup on all four wheels.

Actuator assembly

The actuator assembly includes the master cylinder and a control valve which consists of a dump valve and an isolation valve. The valve operates by changing the brake fluid pressure in response to signals from the control unit.

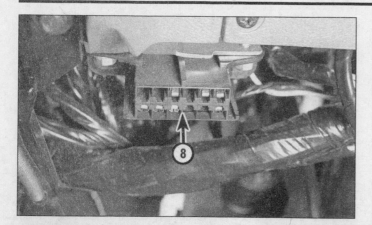

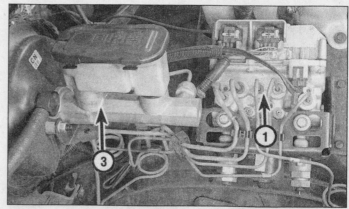

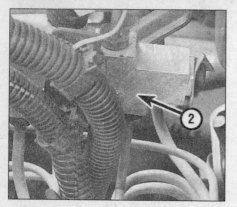

16.4b Four-wheel anti-lock (4WAL) brake system and related components

1   4WAL EHCU valve
2   Combination valve
3   Master cylinder
4   Brake pedal switch
5   Parking brake switch
6   Wheel speed sensors
7   Warning lights
8   Assembly line diagnostic link (ALDL)

Control unit

The control unit for the anti-lock brakes is called the Electro-Hydraulic Control Unit (EHCU) on 4WAL systems and Control Module on RWAL systems. The unit is mounted in the engine compartment below the master cylinder and is the "brain" for the system (see illustrations). The function of the control unit is to accept and process information received from the speed sensor(s) and brake light switch to control the hydraulic line pressure, avoiding wheel lockup. The control unit also constantly monitors the system, even under normal driving conditions, to find faults within the system.

If a problem develops within the system, the BRAKE (RWAL system) or ANTI-LOCK (4WAL system) warning light will glow on the dashboard. A diagnostic code will also be stored, which, when retrieved by a service technician, will indicate the problem area or component.

Speed sensor

On 4WAL systems, each wheel has a speed sensor. On RWAL systems, a rear wheel speed sensor is located in the transmission extension housing on 2WD models and in the transfer case on 4WD models. The speed sensor(s) sends a signal to the control unit indicating wheel rotational speed.
Brake light switch

The brake light switch signals the control unit when the driver steps on the brake pedal. Without this signal the anti-lock system won't activate.

Diagnosis and repair

If the BRAKE or ANTI-LOCK warning light on the dashboard comes on and stays on, make sure the parking brake is released and there's no problem with the brake hydraulic system. If neither of these is the cause, the anti-lock system is probably malfunctioning. Although special test procedures are necessary to properly diagnose the system, the home mechanic can perform a few preliminary checks before taking the vehicle to a dealer service department.

a) Make sure the brakes, calipers and wheel cylinders are in good condition.
b) Check the electrical connectors at the control unit.
c) Check the fuses.
d) Follow the wiring harness to the speed sensor(s) and brake light switch and make sure all connections are secure and the wiring isn't damaged.

If the above preliminary checks don't rectify the problem, the vehicle should be diagnosed by a dealer service department.

Chapter 10
Suspension and steering systems

Contents

Specifications

Torque specifications

Front suspension

2WD models

	Ft-lbs
Upper control arm-to-frame nuts	
1990 and earlier	88
1991 and later	140
Lower control arm-to-frame nuts	
1990 and earlier	96
1991 and later	121
Balljoint-to-upper control arm bolts	
C15/C25	17
C35	
All except 1991	52
1991 and later	17
Lower balljoint-to-knuckle nut	90
Upper balljoint-to-knuckle nut	
1990 and earlier	90
1991	70
1992	84
1993 and later	74

Torque specifications

Ft-lbs

Front suspension

4WD models

Upper control arm-to-frame nut
- 1990 and earlier 88
- 1991 and later 140

Lower control arm-to-frame nuts
- 1992 and earlier 96
- 1993 and later 121

Balljoint-to-control arm bolts
- K15/K25 17
- K35 52

Lower balljoint-to-knuckle nut
- 1991 and earlier 94
- 1992 and later 84

Upper balljoint-to-knuckle nut
- 1990 and earlier 94
- 1991 70
- 1992 84
- 1993 and later 94

Driveaxle nut-to-hub and bearing
- 1994 and earlier 173
- 1995 180
- 1996 and later 165

Hub and bearing assembly-to-steering knuckle
- 1991 and earlier 66
- 1992 and later 133

Rear suspension

Leaf spring-to-bracket nuts
- 1991 and earlier 81
- 1992 89
- 1993 through 1995 92
- 1996 and later 70

Leaf spring-to-shackle nuts
- 1995 and earlier 81
- 1996 and later 70

Shackle-to-bracket nuts
- 1995 and earlier 81
- 1996 and later 70

U-bolt nuts
- Models with 7.4 liter (big block) engine and/or dual rear wheels 109
- All others 81

Steering

Pitman arm-to-steering gear 184
Pitman arm-to-relay rod 40
Idler arm-to-relay rod 40
Idler arm-to-frame
- 1992 and earlier 78
- 1993 through 1995 59
- 1996 and later 73

Relay rod-to-tie-rod 40
Tie-rod-to-steering arm
- 1996 and earlier 40
- 1997 and later 46

Steering wheel nut 30
Steering damper-to-relay rod 46
Steering damper-to-frame bracket 30
Adjuster tube clamp nut 14
Steering column mounting nuts 22
Steering column shaft-to-intermediate shaft pinch bolt/nut 46
Steering gear-to-frame bolts
- Power steering
  - Through 1990 69
  - 1991 and later 100
- Manual steering 100

Flexible coupling clamp bolt 30

1.1 Steering and front suspension components (2WD model)

1	Stabilizer bar	6	Lower balljoint	11	Inner tie-rod
2	Coil spring and shock absorber	7	Lower control arm	12	Tie-rod adjuster tube
3	Steering gear	8	Lower shock mounting nuts and bolts	13	Outer tie-rod
4	Upper control arm	9	Pitman arm	14	Idler arm
5	Steering knuckle	10	Relay rod		

1 General information

Refer to illustrations 1.1, 1.2 and 1.3

The steering linkage **(see illustration)** consists of a Pitman arm, idler arm, relay rod, two adjustable tie-rods and a steering damper (not on all models). When the steering wheel is turned, the gear rotates the Pitman arm which forces the relay rod to one side. The tie-rods, which are connected to the relay rod by ball studs, transfer steering force to the wheels. The tie-rods are adjustable and are used for toe-in adjustments. The relay rod is supported by the Pitman arm and idler arm. The idler arm pivots on a support attached to the frame rail. The steering damper is attached to the frame end relay arm.

The front suspension is fully independent. Each wheel is connected to the frame by a steering knuckle, upper and lower ball joints and upper and lower control arms. Coil springs and shock absorbers are used on 2WD models; 4WD models use shocks and torsion bars **(see illustration)**. The coil springs are mounted between the spring pockets on the frame and the lower control

1.2 Typical front suspension components (4WD models)

1	Stabilizer bar	4	Outer tie rod end	6	Upper control arm ball joint
2	Lower control arm	5	Shock absorber	7	Stabilizer bar link
3	Front drive axle				

1.3 Rear suspension components

| 1 | Shock absorbers | 2 | Leaf springs | 3 | U-bolt anchor plates |

arms. The shocks are attached to the lower control arms by bolts and nuts; the upper end of each shock is attached to a bracket on the frame.

The rear suspension **(see illustration)** consists of a pair of multi-leaf springs and two shock absorbers. The rear axle assembly is attached to the leaf springs by U-bolts. The front ends of the springs are attached to the frame at the front hangers, through rubber bushings. The rear ends of the springs are attached to the frame by shackles which allow the springs to alter their length when the vehicle is in operation.

Frequently, when working on the suspension or steering system components, you may come across fasteners which seem impossible to loosen. These fasteners on the underside of the vehicle are continually subjected to water, road grime, mud, etc., and can become rusted or "frozen," making them extremely difficult to remove. In order to unscrew these stubborn fasteners without damaging them (or other components), be sure to use lots of penetrating oil and allow it to soak in for a while. Using a wire brush to clean exposed threads will also ease removal of the nut or bolt and prevent damage to the threads. Sometimes a sharp blow with a hammer and punch is effective in breaking the bond between a nut and bolt threads, but care must be taken to prevent the punch from slipping off the fastener and ruining the

threads. Heating the stuck fastener and surrounding area with a torch sometimes helps too, but isn't recommended because of the obvious dangers associated with fire. Long breaker bars and extension, or "cheater," pipes will increase leverage, but never use an extension pipe on a ratchet - the ratcheting mechanism could be damaged. Sometimes, turning the nut or bolt in the tightening (clockwise) direction first will help to break it loose. Fasteners that require drastic measures to unscrew should always be replaced with new ones.

Since most of the procedures that are dealt with in this Chapter involve jacking up the vehicle and working underneath it, a good pair of jackstands will be needed. A hydraulic floor jack is the preferred type of jack to lift the vehicle, and it can also be used to support certain components during various operations. **Warning:** *Never, under any circumstances, rely on a jack to support the vehicle while working on it. Also, whenever any of the suspension or steering fasteners are loosened or removed they must be inspected and, if necessary, replaced with new ones of the same part number or of original equipment quality and design. Torque specifications must be followed for proper reassembly and component retention. Never attempt to heat or straighten any suspension or steering components. Instead, replace bent or damaged parts with new ones.*

2   Shock absorber (front) - removal and installation

2WD models

Refer to illustrations 2.1 and 2.4

1   Using a backup wrench on the stem, remove the upper shock mounting nut **(see illustration)**.
2   Remove the retainer and grommet.
3   Raise the vehicle and support it securely

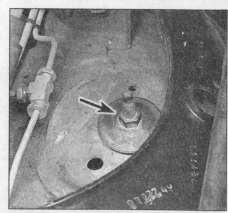

2.1 The shock absorber upper mounting nut (arrow) is located on the frame, right between the two control arm pivot bolts (2WD models)

2.4 The lower mounting bolts (arrows) are located on the under side of the control arm (2WD models)

2.8 Remove the shock absorber mounting nuts and bolts (arrows) and remove the shock absorber (4WD shown)

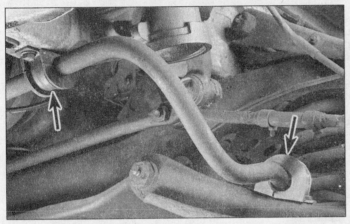

3.2a Stabilizer bar mounting details (2WD models)

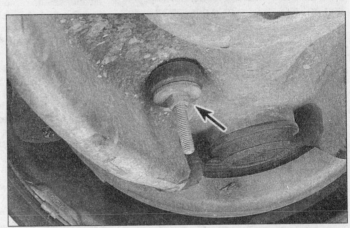

3.2b The nut for the stabilizer bar link bolt (arrow) is located on the under side of the control arm (2WD models)

on jackstands.

4   Working from underneath the vehicle, remove the two bolts which attach the lower end of the shock absorber to the lower control arm **(see illustration)** and pull the shock out from below.

5   Remove the lower grommet and retainer from the stem.

6   Installation is the reverse of removal. Be sure to tighten the upper mounting nut and the lower mounting bolts securely.

4WD models

Refer to illustration 2.8

7   Raise the vehicle and support it securely on jackstands.

8   Remove the shock lower mounting nut, washer and bolt **(see illustration)**. Note the direction in which the bolt points.

9   Collapse the shock absorber.

10   Remove the upper shock mounting nut, washer and bolt. Again, note the direction in which the bolt points.

11   Remove the shock absorber.

12   Installation is the reverse of removal. Be sure to install the bolts so that they're pointing in the same direction as they were prior to removal. Tighten all fasteners securely.

3   Stabilizer bar - removal and installation

Refer to illustrations 3.2a, 3.2b, 3.2c and 3.3

1   Raise the vehicle and support it securely on jackstands.

2   Remove the nuts from the link bolts and remove the link bolts **(see illustrations)**. **Note:** *Be sure to keep the parts for the left and right sides separate.*

3   Remove the stabilizer bar bracket bolts **(see illustration)**.

4   Remove the stabilizer bar.

5   Remove the rubber bushings.

6   Inspect all parts for wear and damage.

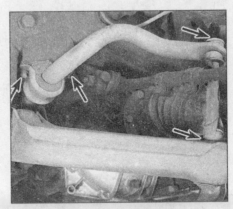

3.2c Remove the stabilizer bar link mounting nut and bolt (arrows) (4WD shown)

3.3 Remove the stabilizer bar bracket bolts (arrows) (2WD models)

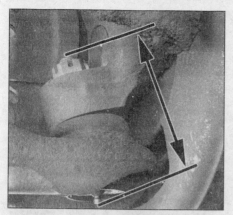

4.4a To determine balljoint wear on models with grease fittings, measure between the points shown

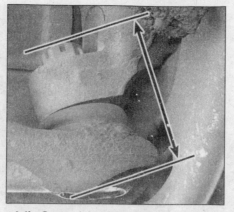

4.4b On models without grease fittings, measure between the points shown to check for balljoint wear

4.11 A special tool is required to push the balljoints out of the steering knuckle (an alternative tool, shown here, can be fabricated from a large bolt, nut, washer and socket)

7 When you install the rubber bushings on the stabilizer bar, be sure to position them so the slits face toward the front of the vehicle.

8 Installation is otherwise the reverse of removal. Be sure to tighten all fasteners securely.

4   Balljoints - check and replacement

Check

Upper balljoint

1 Loosen the wheel lug nuts, raise the front of the vehicle and support it securely on jackstands. Apply the parking brake. Remove the wheel.

2 Place a floor jack under the lower control arm and raise it slightly. Using a large screwdriver or pry bar, pry up on the upper control arm and watch for movement at the balljoint. Any movement indicates a worn balljoint. Now grasp the steering knuckle and attempt to move the top of it in-and-out - if any play is felt, the balljoint will have to be replaced.

Lower balljoint

Refer to illustrations 4.4a and 4.4b

3 Raise the vehicle, support it securely on

jackstands and remove the wheels.

4 Support the weight of the suspension with a jack. Measure the distance between the tip of the balljoint stud and the tip of the grease fitting below the balljoint (A) (if equipped with a grease fitting) or between the lower surface of the control arm and the top of the balljoint (B) **(see illustrations)**.

5 Lower the jack to allow the suspension to hang free and repeat the measurement.

6 If the difference between the two measurements exceeds 3/32-inch, the balljoint is worn and must be replaced with a new one.

Replacement

7 Raise the vehicle, support it securely on jackstands and remove the front wheel.

2WD models (upper balljoint)

Refer to illustrations 4.11, 4.12a, 4.12b and 4.12c

8 Remove the brake caliper and hang it out of the way (Chapter 9).

9 Remove the cotter key from the balljoint and back off the nut two turns.

10 Place a jack or jackstand under the lower control arm. **Note:** *The jack or jackstand must remain under the control arm during removal and installation of the balljoint to hold the spring and control arm in position.*

11 Separate the balljoint from the steering knuckle using a balljoint separator to press the balljoint out of the steering knuckle **(see illustration). Note:** *The use of a "picklefork" type balljoint separator may tear the balljoint boot.*

12 To remove the upper balljoint from the control arm, drill out the rivets **(see illustrations)**, remove the balljoint and clean the control arm. Install the new upper balljoint against the mating surface of the control arm and secure it with the supplied nuts and bolts **(see illustration)**.

2WD models (lower balljoint)

13 Remove the control arm (see Section 8) and take it to an automotive machine shop to have the balljoint pressed out and a new one pressed in.

2WD models (upper or lower balljoint)

14 Inspect the tapered holes in the steering knuckle, removing any accumulated dirt. If out-of-roundness, deformation or other damage is noted, the knuckle must be replaced with a new one (see Section 5).

15 Reconnect the balljoints to the steering

4.12a Drill completely through the upper balljoint rivets with a drill bit

4.12b Tap the rivets out with a punch

4.12c You don't need to rivet the new upper balljoint - install it with the nuts and bolts included in the kit

knuckle and tighten the nuts to the specified torque.

16 If the cotter key does not line up with the opening in the castellated nut, tighten (never loosen) the nut just enough to allow installation of the cotter pin.

17 Install the grease fittings and lubricate the new balljoints (Chap-ter 1).

18 Install the wheels and lower the vehicle.

19 The front end alignment should be checked by a dealer or alignment shop.

4WD models

20 The procedure for replacing an upper balljoint on a 4WD model is similar to that described above for 2WD models. The procedure for replacing a lower balljoint follows.

21 Raise the vehicle and support it securely on jackstands.

22 Remove the wheel.

23 Remove the front splash shield bolts. Pivot the shield out of the way to gain access to the tie-rod end.

24 Disconnect the tie-rod from the relay rod (see Sections 15 and 17).

25 Remove the driveaxle (see Chapter 8).

26 Center punch the bottom of each rivet.

27 Using a 1/8-inch drill bit, drill a guide hole 1/2-inch deep into the rivet heads.

28 Using a 5/16-inch drill bit, drill the rivet heads off. Drill a hole two-thirds the length of the rivet shank, using the same drill.

29 Knock the rivets out with a hammer and punch.

30 Remove the balljoint stud cotter pin.

31 Support the lower control arm with floor jack.

32 Loosen the balljoint nut a couple of turns.

33 Back off the torsion bar adjusting arm bolt to reduce the tension on the bar. Don't remove the bolt completely (see Section 8).

34 Separate the knuckle from the balljoint with a two-jaw puller or a "picklefork".

35 Remove the nut and separate the balljoint from the lower control arm.

36 Install the new balljoint to the control arm. Install the nuts and bolts and tighten

them to the specified torque.

37 Raise the lower control arm with a floor jack and insert the balljoint stud into the steering knuckle. Lower the jack until the balljoint stud seats in the hole, then install the nut and tighten it to the specified torque. Install a new cotter pin and bend the ends of the pin against the nut.

38 Load the torsion bar (see Section 11).

39 Install the driveaxle assembly (see Chapter 8).

40 Connect the inner tie-rod end to the relay rod, install the tie-rod end nut and tighten it to the specified torque.

41 Install the front splash shield and tighten the splash shield bolts securely.

42 Install the wheel and lug nuts.

43 Lower the vehicle.

44 Tighten the wheel lug nuts to the torque specified in the Chapter 1 Specifications.

---

5 Steering knuckle (2WD models) - removal and installation

1 Raise the front of the vehicle and support it securely on jackstands. Apply the parking brake.

2 Support the lower control arm with a jack so the coil spring is compressed to its normal ride height. **Warning:** *The jack must remain in this position throughout the entire procedure.*

3 Remove the wheel.

4 Remove the brake caliper (see Chapter 9) and the brake disc/hub assembly (see Chapter 1, Front wheel bearing check, repack and adjustment).

5 Remove the disc splash shield, if equipped.

6 Disconnect the tie-rod end from the knuckle (see Section 15).

7 Disconnect the balljoints from the steering knuckle (see Section 4).

8 Remove the steering knuckle.

9 Installation is the reverse of removal. Adjust the front wheel bearings (see Chap-

ter 1) and have the front wheel alignment checked by a dealer service department or alignment shop.

---

6 Coil spring (2WD models) - removal and installation

Removal

Refer to illustrations 6.5 and 6.7

1 Loosen the front wheel lug nuts, raise the vehicle and place it securely on jackstands. Remove the wheel.

2 Remove the shock absorber (see Section 2).

3 Remove the stabilizer bar link bolt (see Section 3).

4 Disconnect the outer tie-rod end from the steering knuckle (see Section 15).

5 Install a suitable internal type spring compressor in accordance with the tool manufacturer's instructions **(see illustration)**. Compress the spring enough to relieve all pressure from the spring seats (but don't compress it any more than necessary, or it could be ruined). When you can wiggle the spring, it's compressed enough. (You can buy a suitable spring compressor at most auto parts stores or rent one from a tool rental yard.)

6 Support the lower control arm with a floor jack.

7 Remove the control arm pivot bolts and nuts **(see illustration)**.

8 Pull the lower control arm down and to the rear, then guide the compressed coil spring out.

9 If the coil spring is being replaced, carefully unscrew the spring compressor.

Installation

10 Inspect the upper and lower spring insulators. If either insulator is cracked or excessively worn, replace it. Inspect the coil spring for chips in the corrosion protection coating. If the coating has been chipped or damaged,

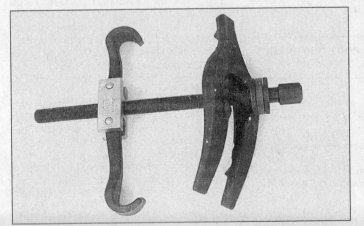

6.5 A typical aftermarket internal type spring compressor: The hooked arms grip the upper coils of the spring, the plate is inserted between the lower coils, and when the nut on the threaded rod is turned, the spring is compressed

6.7 With the spring safely compressed, support the lower control arm with a floor jack, then remove the pivot bolts and nuts (arrow indicates front pivot bolt)

replace the spring.

11   If the coil spring is being replaced, install the spring compressor and compress the spring.

12   With the lower spring insulator in place, position the spring on the lower control arm with the flat end of the spring facing up and the tapered end facing down. Make sure the tapered end seats on the lower control arm with the lower end of the spring seated in the lowest part of the spring seat. The end of the spring must cover all or part of one of the drain holes in the lower control arm, but the other hole must not be covered.

13   Put the floor jack under the lower control arm and raise the arm into position in the frame. Install the control arm pivot bolts and nuts. Tighten the nuts until they're snug but don't torque them yet.

14   Remove the spring compressor.

15   Reattach the outer tie-rod end to the steering knuckle (see Section 15).

16   Reattach the stabilizer bar link to the lower control arm (see Section 3).

17   Install the shock absorber (see Section 2).

18   Position the floor jack under the lower control arm balljoint and raise the arm to simulate normal ride height. Tighten the lower control arm pivot bolt nuts to the torque listed in this Chapter's Specifications.

19   Install the wheel, remove the jackstands and lower the vehicle. Tighten the wheel lug nuts to the torque listed in the Chapter 1 Specifications.

---

7   Upper control arm - removal and installation

Refer to illustration 7.6

Note: *This procedure applies to both 2WD and 4WD models.*

Removal

1   Loosen the wheel lug nuts, raise the front of the vehicle and support it securely on jackstands. Apply the parking brake. Remove the wheel.

2   Position a floor jack, with a wood block on the jack head (to act as a cushion), under the lower control arm in the area between the spring seat and the balljoint. Raise the jack slightly to take the spring pressure off the upper control arm. **Warning:** *The jack must remain in this position throughout the entire procedure.*

3   Remove the air cleaner extension, if necessary.

4   Disconnect the brake hose bracket from the upper control arm.

5   Disconnect the upper balljoint from the steering knuckle (Section 4).

6   If the vehicle has been retrofitted with an alignment kit, mark the positions of the adjuster cams to the frame so they can be returned to their original settings on installation. Remove the upper control arm pivot bolts and nuts **(see illustration)**. Remove the control arm.

7   Inspect the pivot bolt bushings for wear.

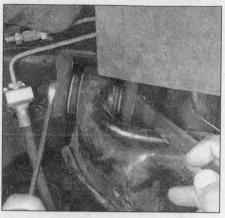

7.6 Remove the upper control arm pivot bolts - make sure the pivot bolts are installed with the heads facing each other

Replace them if necessary. **Note:** *The bushings on some models are welded in place and can't be removed. If they're worn, you'll have to replace the control arm. On other models, a hydraulic press may be required to accomplish removal and installation of the bushings, in which case you'll have to take the control arm to a dealer service department or other repair shop to have this done for you.*

Installation

8   Position the arm in the frame brackets and install the bolts and nuts. They must be installed with their heads towards the inside, facing each other, as shown in **illustration 7.6**. Don't tighten the nuts completely at this time. If an alignment kit has been installed, line up the previously applied matchmarks.

9   Attach the balljoint to the steering knuckle (see Section 4).

10   Connect the brake hose bracket to the upper control arm.

11   Install the wheel and lug nuts, then lower the vehicle. Tighten the lug nuts to the torque listed in the Chapter 1 Specifications.

12   Tighten the pivot bolt nuts to the torque listed in this Chapter's Specifications.

13   Install the air cleaner extension, if it was removed.

---

8   Lower control arm - removal and installation

2WD models

Removal

1   Loosen the wheel lug nuts, raise the vehicle and support it securely on jackstands. Remove the wheel.

2   Remove the coil spring (see Section 6).

3   Disconnect the lower balljoint (see Section 4).

4   Take the control arm to a dealer or properly equipped shop to have the balljoint and bushings replaced, if necessary.

Installation

5   Installation is the reverse of removal.

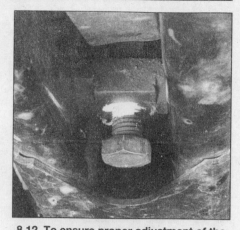

8.12 To ensure proper adjustment of the torsion bar upon reassembly, count the number of threads showing on the torsion bar adjuster bolt and mark the relationship of the bolt to the torsion bar adjuster nut as insurance

Make sure the pivot bolts are installed from the front **(see illustration 6.6)**, and don't tighten them until the vehicle is at normal ride height. Tighten all nuts to their specified torque, and if a new balljoint has been installed, lubricate it on completion.

4WD models

Refer to illustrations 8.12, 8.17 and 8.18

Removal

6   Loosen the wheel lug nuts, raise the vehicle and support it securely on jackstands. Remove the wheel.

7   Remove the front splash shield for access to the front end components.

8   Disconnect the stabilizer bar from the lower control arm (Section 3).

9   Remove the shock absorber (see Section 2).

10   Disconnect the inner tie-rod end from the relay rod (see Section 15).

11   Remove the driveaxle (see Chapter 8).

12   Follow the torsion bar back to the crossmember. Count the number of threads showing on the torsion bar adjuster bolt, and also mark the bolt to the torsion bar adjuster nut.

13   Loosen the torsion bar adjusting bolt as much as possible, without removing the bolt completely. This will reduce the tension on the bar.

14   Support the lower control arm with a floor jack. The jack head should be positioned as near to the balljoint as possible, and still allow access to the balljoint stud nut.

15   Disconnect the steering knuckle from the lower balljoint (see Section 4). Lift the knuckle and hub assembly up, then place a block of wood between the upper control arm and the frame to support the assembly out of the way.

16   Mark the relationship of the torsion bar - to-lower control arm, then SLOWLY lower the jack until the pressure from the torsion bar is completely released.

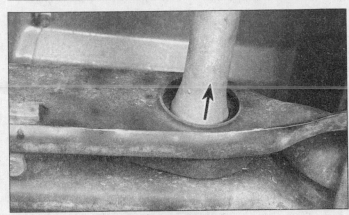

8.17 Slide the torsion bar forward (arrow)

8.18 Remove the lower control arm pivot bolts (arrow)

17   Slide the torsion bar forward, out of the adjuster arm **(see illustration)**.
18   Remove the lower control arm pivot bolts, nuts and washers **(see illustration)**. Remove the lower control arm and torsion bar as a unit.
19   Mark the front of the torsion bar with a piece of tape to insure correct installation, then separate the bar from the arm.
20   Check the bushings for damage or wear. Some models have welded-in bushings that can't be replaced. If this is the case, replace the control arm. Other models have replaceable bushings, but a press and special adapters are required to remove and install them. Take the control arm to dealer service department or other repair shop to have the bushings replaced for you.

Installation

21   Insert the torsion bar into its hole in the lower control arm. Raise the arm and bar up into position, inserting the rear end of the bar into the hole in the crossmember (it may be necessary to slide the bar forward in the control arm a little bit). Position the lower control arm in the frame brackets, inserting the front portion first.
22   Install the control arm pivot bolts. They must be inserted from front-to-rear **(see illustration 8.18)**. Install the washers and nuts, but don't tighten them completely at this time.
23   Slide the torsion bar back into the adjusting arm.
24   Carefully raise the lower control arm with the floor jack until the balljoint stud can be inserted into the hole in the steering knuckle. Install the balljoint stud nut, tighten it to the torque listed in this Chapter's Specifications, then install a new cotter pin.
25   Tighten the torsion bar adjusting nut until the distance between the crossmember and the end of the adjusting arm is the same as it was before removal.
26   Install the driveaxle.
27   Connect the inner tie-rod to the relay rod.
28   Install the shock absorber.
29   Connect the stabilizer bar to the lower control arm.
30   Install the wheel and lug nuts. Lower the

vehicle and tighten the lug nuts to the torque listed in the Chapter 1 Specifications.
31   Tighten the lower control arm pivot bolts to the torque listed in this Chapter's Specifications.
32   Install the splash shield.
33   Measure the vehicle's ride height on each side, from equal points on the frame to the ground. If the side that has been worked on is higher or lower than the other side, turn the torsion bar adjusting screw accordingly until the vehicle sits level. This may take a few tries, and it's important to roll the vehicle back and forth and jounce the front end between adjustments, to settle the suspension and get an accurate reading.

9   Steering knuckle (4WD models) - removal and installation

Removal

1   Remove the hub cover and loosen the driveaxle/hub nut about 1/4-turn.
2   Loosen the wheel lug nuts, raise the front of the vehicle and support it securely on jackstands. Apply the parking brake. Remove the wheel.
3   Disconnect the tie-rod end from the steering knuckle (see Sec-tion 15). Unbolt the brake caliper and hang it out of the way with a piece of wire (see Chapter 9). Remove the brake disc.
4   Remove the driveaxle/hub nut.
5   Support the lower control arm with a floor jack and detach the steering knuckle from the lower balljoint (see Section 4). **Warning:** The jack must remain in this position throughout the entire procedure.
6   Support the steering knuckle and separate it from the upper balljoint (see Section 4).
7   Using a puller, push the driveaxle out of the hub while withdrawing the steering knuckle and hub assembly.
8   If it's necessary to remove the hub, remove the three bolts and separate it from the knuckle.
9   Inspect the seal on the rear side of the knuckle. If it's damaged or shows signs of deterioration, pry it out with a large screw-

driver or pry bar. Install a new seal by driving it in with a socket that has an outside diameter slightly smaller than the seal.

Installation

10   Installation is the reverse of the removal procedure. Be sure to lubricate the driveaxle splines with multi-purpose grease, and tighten all of the fasteners to the specified torque.

10   Hub and bearing assembly (4WD models) - replacement

Refer to illustration 10.5
Note: *The hub and bearing assembly is a sealed unit and isn't serviceable. If it's defective, it must be replaced.*
1   Remove the hub cover and loosen the driveaxle/hub nut about a quarter of a turn.
2   Loosen the wheel lug nuts, raise the vehicle and support it securely on jackstands. Remove the wheel.
3   Unbolt the brake caliper and hang it out of the way with a piece of wire (see Chapter 9). Remove the brake disc.
4   Remove the driveaxle/hub nut.
5   Remove the hub assembly-to-steering knuckle bolts **(see illustrations)**. **Note:** *Some models have three bolts, others have four.*

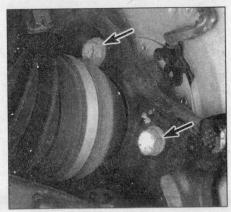

10.5a To detach the hub and bearing assembly from the steering knuckle, remove these bolts (arrows) . . .

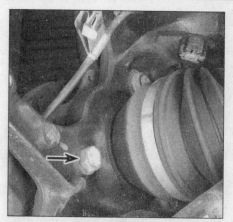

10.5b . . . and this bolt (arrow) (upper bolt is the same upper bolt shown in the previous photo)

12.2 To replace a rear shock absorber, remove the nuts and bolts (arrows) from the frame bracket . . .

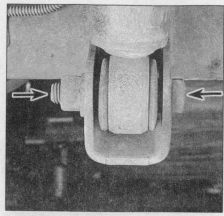

12.3 . . . then remove the nut, bolt and washer (arrow) from the axle bracket

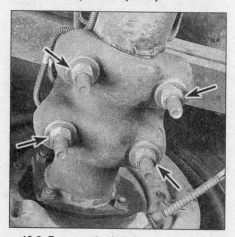

13.2 Remove the U-bolt nuts (arrows)

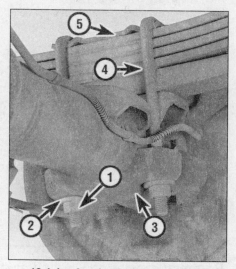

13.4 Leaf spring installation detail

1   Nut
2   Washer
3   Anchor plate
4   U-bolt
5   Spacer

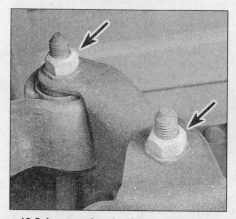

13.5 Loosen the shackle-to-spring nut (upper arrow), then remove the shackle-to-rear bracket nut, bolt and washers (lower arrow)

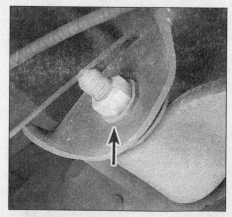

13.7 Remove the nut, bolt and washer (arrow) from the front bracket

Tap the hub assembly from side-to-side to break it loose from the steering knuckle. Using a puller, pull the hub assembly off the end of the driveaxle. Wrap the end of the driveaxle with a rag to prevent damaging it.
6   Installation is the reverse of the removal procedure. Be sure to lubricate the driveaxle splines with multi-purpose grease, and tighten all of the fasteners to the specified torque.

11 Torsion bar (4WD models) - removal and installation

Refer to Section 8 - torsion bar removal and installation is part of the lower control arm removal and installation procedure.

12 Shock absorber (rear) - removal and installation

Refer to illustrations 12.2 and 12.3
1   Raise the rear of the vehicle and support securely on jackstands. Block the front wheels so the vehicle doesn't roll off the stands.

2   Remove the shock absorber upper mounting nuts and bolts from the frame bracket **(see illustration)**.
3   Remove the lower mounting nut, washer and bolt from the axle bracket **(see illustration)**.
4   Remove the shock absorber.
5   Installation is the reverse of removal. Make sure you install the nuts and bolts facing in the proper direction.

13 Leaf spring/shackle - removal and installation

Refer to illustrations 13.2, 13.4, 13.5, 13.7 and 13.9
1   Raise the rear of the vehicle and support it securely on jackstands. Block the front wheels to keep the vehicle from rolling off the stands. Support the axle with a floor jack and

raise it slightly to relieve the tension on the leaf springs.
2   Remove the U-bolt nuts and washers **(see illustration)**.
3   Remove the anchor plate.
4   Remove the U-bolts and spacer **(see illustration)**.
5   Loosen the shackle-to-spring nut **(see illustration)**.

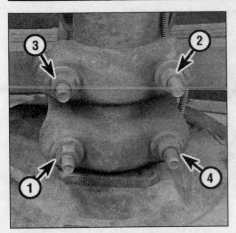

13.9 Be sure to follow the recommended tightening sequence when reassembling the U-bolts

6   Remove the shackle-to-rear bracket nut, washers and bolt.

7   Remove the spring-to-front bracket nut, washers and bolt **(see illustration)**.

8   Remove the spring assembly from the vehicle.

9   Installation is the reverse of removal. Tighten the U-bolt nuts in a diagonal sequence **(see illustration)**. Tighten all the fasteners to the torque listed in this Chapter's Specifications.

14 Steering wheel - removal and installation

Refer to illustrations 14.4a, 14.4b, 14.5, 14.7 and 14.8

Warning: *Anytime you are working in the vicinity of airbag wiring or components, disable the SIR (airbag) system (see Chapter 12).*

1   Disconnect both cables from the battery (see Chapter 5). **Caution:** *On models equipped with a Delco Loc II anti-theft audio system, be sure the lockout feature is turned off before performing any procedure which requires disconnecting the battery.*

2   On 1994 and earlier models, simply pry off the horn cap.

3   On airbag-equipped models, refer to Chapter 12 and disable the airbag system.

4   On 1995 models, turn the steering wheel 90-degrees to gain access to the holes in the backside (the side facing the dash) of the steering wheel. Insert a thin hard tool such as a ball-point pen or a scribe into the hole for each of the four spring-loaded fasteners **(see illustrations)**. Push in firmly against the head of each fastener with the tool and pull on the airbag module simultaneously with the other hand.

5   On 1996 and later models, turn the steering wheel 90-degrees to gain access to the holes in the backside (the side facing the dash) of the steering wheel. Insert a screwdriver into the hole for each of the four spring clips **(see illustration)** and push the spring aside to release the pin. There are four pins

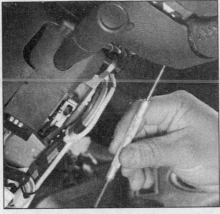

14.4a To detach the airbag module from the steering wheel on 1995 models, rotate the wheel 90-degrees, insert a hard and thin object - such as a scribe - and push in firmly against each of the four ball-lock fasteners to unlock the airbag module from the wheel

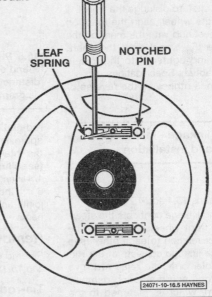

14.5 To detach the airbag module from the steering wheel on 1996 models, rotate the wheel 90-degrees, insert a screwdriver into each of the four holes in the backside of the steering wheel and pry each leaf spring aside to release it from its notched pin (there are four of them)

LEAF SPRING   NOTCHED PIN

24071-10-16.5 HAYNES

and four springs.

6   On airbag-equipped models, unplug the yellow electrical connector from the module and set the module aside, with the airbag side of the module facing UP. **Warning:** *Carry the airbag module with the trim side facing*

14.4b Unplug the yellow electrical connector from the back of the airbag module; the arrows point at the four ball-lock type fasteners used on 1995 models

away from your body, and set it aside in an isolated area with the trim side facing up.

7   Remove the steering wheel retaining nut and mark the position of the steering wheel to the shaft, if marks don't already exist or don't line up **(see illustration)**.

14.7 Mark the relationship of the steering wheel to the steering shaft before removing the wheel

14.8 Remove the steering wheel with a steering wheel puller - do not hammer on the steering shaft

15.1 Steering linkage components (2WD model shown, 4WD similar)

1 Pitman arm
2 Idler arm
3 Relay rod
4 Adjustable tie-rod

8   Use a puller to detach the steering wheel from the shaft **(see illustration)**. Don't hammer on the shaft to dislodge the wheel.
9   To install the wheel, align the mark on the steering wheel hub with the mark on the shaft and slide the wheel onto the shaft. Install the nut and tighten it to the torque listed in this Chapter's Specifications.
10   Installation is otherwise the reverse of removal.

15 Steering linkage - inspection, removal and installation

Inspection

Refer to illustrations 15.1 and 15.5

1   The steering linkage connects the steering gear to the front wheels and keeps the wheels in proper relation to each other **(see illustration)**. The linkage consists of the Pitman arm, the idler arm, the relay rod, two adjustable tie-rods and a steering damper. The Pitman arm, which is fastened to the steering gear shaft, moves the relay rod back-and-forth. The relay rod is supported on the other end by a frame-mounted idler arm. The back-and-forth motion of the relay rod is transmitted to the steering knuckles through a pair of tie-rod assemblies. Each tie-rod is made up of an inner and outer tie-rod end, a threaded adjuster tube and two clamps.
2   Set the wheels in the straight ahead position and lock the steering wheel.
3   Raise one side of the vehicle until the tire is approximately 1-inch off the ground.
4   Mount a dial indicator with the needle resting on the outside edge of the wheel. Grasp the front and rear of the tire and using light pressure, wiggle the wheel back-and-forth and note the dial indicator reading. The gauge reading should be less than 0.108-inch. If the play in the steering system is more than specified, inspect each steering linkage pivot point and ball stud for looseness and replace parts if necessary.
5   Raise the vehicle and support it on jackstands. Push up, then pull down on the relay

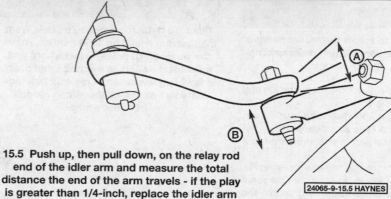

15.5 Push up, then pull down, on the relay rod end of the idler arm and measure the total distance the end of the arm travels - if the play is greater than 1/4-inch, replace the idler arm

24065-9-15.5 HAYNES

rod end of the idler arm, exerting a force of approximately 25 pounds each way. Measure the total distance the end of the arm travels **(see illustration)**. If the play is greater than 1/4-inch, replace the idler arm.
6   Check for torn ball stud boots, frozen joints and bent or damaged linkage components.

Removal and installation

Refer to illustrations 15.8, 15.9, 15.11, 15.13 and 15.15

Tie-rod

7   Loosen the wheel lug nuts, raise the vehicle and support it securely on jackstands.

Apply the parking brake. Remove the wheel.
8   Remove the cotter pin and loosen, but do not remove, the castellated nut from the ball stud **(see illustration)**.
9   Using a two jaw puller, separate the tie-rod end from the steering knuckle **(see illustration)**. Remove the castellated nut and pull the tie-rod end from the knuckle.
10   Remove the nut securing the inner tie-rod end to the relay rod. Separate the inner tie-rod end from the relay rod (see Step 9).
11   If the inner or outer tie-rod end must be replaced, measure the distance from the end of the adjuster tube to the center of the ball stud and record it **(see illustration)**. Loosen the adjuster tube clamp and unscrew the tie-

15.8 Remove the cotter pin and loosen - but don't remove - the castellated nut on the ball stud

15.9 Use a two-jaw puller to separate the tie-rod end from the steering knuckle, then remove the castellated nut and pull the tie-rod end out of the knuckle

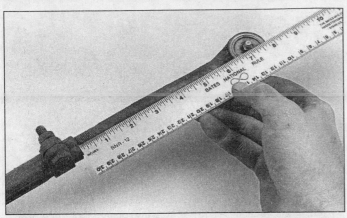

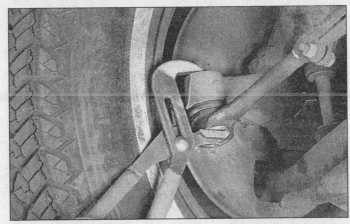

15.11 Measure the distance from the end of the adjuster tube to the center of the ball stud and record the measurement before loosening the adjuster tube clamp and unscrewing the tie-rod end

15.13 If the ball stud spins when you try to tighten the nut, force it into the tapered hole with a large pair of pliers

15.15 Note these guidelines when installing the tie-rod ends

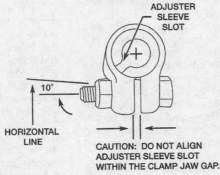

HORIZONTAL LINE

10°

ADJUSTER SLEEVE SLOT

CAUTION: DO NOT ALIGN ADJUSTER SLEEVE SLOT WITHIN THE CLAMP JAW GAP.

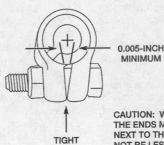

0.005-INCH MINIMUM

TIGHT

CAUTION: WHEN THE CLAMP IS TIGHT, THE ENDS MAY TOUCH BUT THE GAP NEXT TO THE ADJUSTER SLEEVE MUST NOT BE LESS THAN 0.005-INCH.

24065-9-15.15 HAYNES

rod end.

12   Lubricate the threaded portion of the tie-rod end with chassis grease. Screw the new tie-rod end into the adjuster tube and adjust the distance from the tube to the ball stud to the previously measured dimension. The number of threads showing on the inner and outer tie-rod ends should be equal within three threads. Don't tighten the clamp yet.

13   To install the tie-rod, connect the outer tie-rod end to the steering knuckle and install the castellated nut. Tighten the nut to the specified torque and install a new cotter pin. If the ball stud spins when attempting to tighten the nut, force it into the tapered hole with a large pair of pliers (see illustration). If necessary, tighten the nut slightly to align a slot in the nut with the hole in the ball stud.

14   Insert the inner tie-rod end ball stud into the relay rod until it's seated. Install the nut and tighten it to the specified torque.

15   Tighten the clamp nuts. The center of the bolt should be nearly horizontal and the adjuster tube slot must not line up with the gap in the clamps (see illustrations).

16   Install the wheel and lug nuts, lower the vehicle and tighten the lug nuts to the torque listed in the Chapter 1 Specifications. Drive the vehicle to an alignment shop to have the front end alignment checked and, if necessary, adjusted.

Idler arm

17   Raise the vehicle and support it securely on jackstands. Apply the parking brake.

18   Loosen but do not remove the idler arm-to-relay rod nut.

19   Separate the idler arm from the relay rod with a two jaw puller (see illustration 15.9). Remove the nut.

20   Remove the idler arm-to-frame bolts (see illustration 15.1).

21   To install the idler arm, position it on the frame and install the bolts, tightening them to the specified torque.

22   Insert the idler arm ball stud into the relay rod and install the nut. Tighten the nut to the specified torque. If the ball stud spins when attempting to tighten the nut, force it into the tapered hole with a large pair of pliers (see illustration 15.13).

Relay rod

23   Raise the vehicle and support it securely on jackstands. Apply the parking brake.

24   Separate the two inner tie-rod ends from the relay rod.

25   Separate the relay rod from the Pitman arm.

26   Separate the relay rod from the idler arm.

27   Installation is the reverse of the removal procedure. If the ball studs spin when attempting to tighten the nuts, force them into the tapered holes with a large pair of pliers (see illustration 15.13). Be sure to tighten all of the nuts to the specified torque.

Pitman arm

28   Raise the vehicle and support it securely on jackstands.

29   Remove the relay rod nut from the Pitman arm ball stud. Discard the nut - don't reuse it.

30   Using a puller, separate the relay rod from the Pitman arm ball stud.

31   Mark the Pitman arm and the steering gear shaft to ensure proper alignment at reassembly time.

32   Remove the Pitman arm nut and washer.

33   Remove the Pitman arm with a Pitman arm puller or a two-jaw puller.

34   Inspect the ball stud threads for damage. Inspect the ball stud seals for excessive wear. Clean the threads on the ball stud.

35   Installation is the reverse of removal. Make sure the marks you made on the Pitman arm and Pitman shaft are aligned. **Note:** *If a clamp type Pitman arm is used, spread the arm just enough, with a wedge, to slip the arm onto the Pitman shaft. Don't spread the arm more than necessary to slip it over the shaft with hand pressure. Do not hammer the arm onto the shaft or you may damage the steering gear.*

Steering damper

Refer to illustration 15.39

36   Inspect the steering damper for fluid leakage. A slight film of fluid near the shaft

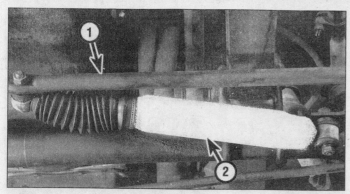

15.39 Steering damper assembly mounting details (4WD models)

1	*Steering relay rod*	2	*Steering damper*

16.2 If the vehicle has power steering, disconnect the power steering hose fittings (arrows)

seal is normal, but if there's excessive fluid present and it's obviously coming from the steering damper, replace the damper.

37   Inspect the steering damper bushing for excessive wear. If it's in bad shape, replace the damper.

38   To test the damper itself, disconnect it from the frame or axle end (see next step). Using as much travel as possible, extend and compress the damper. The resistance should be smooth and constant for each stroke. If any binding or unusual noises are present, replace the damper.

39   Remove the damper ballstud-to-relay rod cotter pin, then remove the nut **(see illustration)**. Separate the damper from the relay rod.

40   Remove the steering damper mounting bolt and nut, then remove the damper.

41   Installation is the reverse of removal. Tighten all the fasteners securely.

16   Steering gear - removal and installation

Refer to illustrations 16.2 and 16.3

Warning 1: *If equipped with an airbag, disable the airbag system before working in the vicinity of the steering wheel, instrument panel or any airbag system component. Failure to do so could cause accidental deployment of the airbag resulting in personal injury (see Chapter 12).*

Warning 2: *On models equipped with an airbag, DO NOT allow the steering column shaft to rotate with the steering gear removed or damage to the airbag system could occur. As a method of preventing the shaft from turning, wrap the seat belt around the rim of the steering wheel and buckle the belt in place.*

Removal

1   Raise the front of the vehicle and support it securely on jackstands. Apply the parking brake.

2   Place a drain pan under the steering gear (power steering only).

Disconnect the hose fittings **(see illustration)** and cap the ends to prevent excessive fluid loss and contamination.

3   If the vehicle has power steering, slide the plastic shield up the intermediate shaft far enough to clear the universal joint. Mark the relationship of the intermediate shaft lower universal joint to the steering gear input shaft. Remove the intermediate shaft lower pinch bolt **(see illustration)**. If the vehicle has manual steering, slide the plastic shield up the intermediate shaft, remove the adapter nut and washer, remove the adapter and unscrew the flexible coupling pinch bolt.

4   Mark the relationship of the Pitman arm to the shaft so it can be installed in the same position. Remove the Pitman arm nut and washer.

5   Remove the Pitman arm from the shaft with a two-jaw puller.

6   Support the steering gear and remove the mounting bolts. Lower the unit, separate the intermediate shaft from the steering gear input shaft and remove the steering gear from the vehicle. **Warning:** *On models equipped with an airbag, DO NOT allow the steering column shaft to rotate with the steering gear removed or damage to the airbag system could occur. As a method of preventing the shaft from turning, wrap the seat belt around the rim of the steering wheel and buckle the belt in place.*

Installation

7   Raise the steering gear into position and connect the intermediate shaft, aligning the marks.

8   Install the mounting bolts and washers and tighten them to the specified torque.

9   Slide the Pitman arm onto the shaft. Make sure the marks are aligned. Install the washer and nut and tighten the nut to the specified torque.

10   Install the lower intermediate shaft pinch bolt and tighten it to the specified torque. If the vehicle has manual steering, install the adapter, nut and washer. On all models, slide the plastic shield back down, over the universal joint/flexible coupling.

11   Connect the power steering hose fittings to the steering gear and fill the power steering pump reservoir with the recommended fluid (see Chapter 1).

12   Lower the vehicle and bleed the steering system (see Section 18).

17   Power steering pump - removal and installation

Refer to illustrations 17.3, 17.4, 17.5 and 17.8

Removal

1   Disconnect the cable from the negative

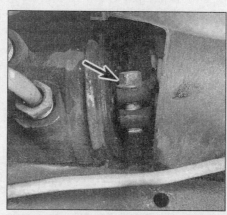

16.3 Remove the intermediate shaft-to-steering gear pinch bolt

17.3 A special puller is required to remove the power steering pump pulley

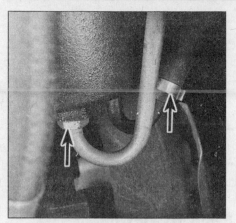

17.4 Disconnect the pressure and return hoses (arrows) from the power steering pump

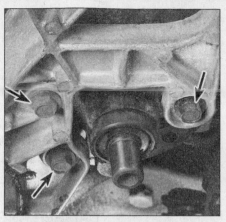

17.5 Remove the power steering pump mounting bolts (arrows)

17.8 A long bolt with the same thread pitch as the internal threads of the power steering pump shaft, a nut, washer and socket that's the same diameter as the pulley hub can be used to install the pulley on the shaft

terminal of the battery.

2   Remove the serpentine drivebelt (see Chapter 1).

3   Using a special power steering pump pulley remover, remove the pulley from the pump **(see illustration)**.

4   Position a drain pan under the power steering pump. Disconnect the pressure and return hoses from the backside of the pump **(see illustration)**. Plug the hoses to prevent contaminants from entering.

5   Remove the pump mounting fasteners **(see illustration)** and lift the pump from the vehicle, taking care not to spill fluid on the painted surfaces.

Installation

6   Position the pump in the mounting bracket and install the bolts and nut. Tighten the fasteners securely.

7   Connect the hoses to the pump. Tighten the fittings securely.

8   Press the pulley onto the shaft using a special pulley installer tool. An alternative tool can be fabricated from a long bolt, nut, washer and a socket of the same diameter as the pulley hub **(see illustration)**. Push the pulley onto the shaft until the front of the hub is flush with the shaft, but no further.

9   Install the drivebelt.

10   Fill the power steering reservoir with the recommended fluid (see Chapter 1) and bleed the system following the procedure described in the next Section.

18 Power steering system - bleeding

1   Following any operation in which the power steering fluid lines have
been disconnected, the power steering system must be bled to remove all air and obtain proper steering performance.

2   With the front wheels in the straight ahead position, check the power steering fluid level and, if low, add fluid until it reaches the Cold mark on the dipstick.

3   Start the engine and allow it to run at

fast idle. Recheck the fluid level and add more if necessary to reach the Cold mark on the dipstick.

4   Bleed the system by turning the wheels from side-to-side, without hitting the stops. This will work the air out of the system. Keep the reservoir full of fluid as this is done.

5   When the air is worked out of the system, return the wheels to the straight ahead position and leave the vehicle running for several more minutes before shutting it off.

6   Road test the vehicle to be sure the steering system is functioning normally and noise free.

7   Recheck the fluid level to be sure it's up to the Hot mark on the dipstick while the engine is at normal operating temperature. Add fluid if necessary (see Chapter 1).

19 Wheels and tires - general information

Refer to illustration 19.1

All vehicles covered by this manual are equipped with metric-size fiberglass or steel belted radial tires **(see illustration)**. Use of other size or type of tires may affect the ride and handling of the vehicle. Don't mix different types of tires, such as radials and bias belted, on the same vehicle as handling may be seriously affected. It's recommended that tires be replaced in pairs on the same axle, but if only one tire is being replaced, be sure

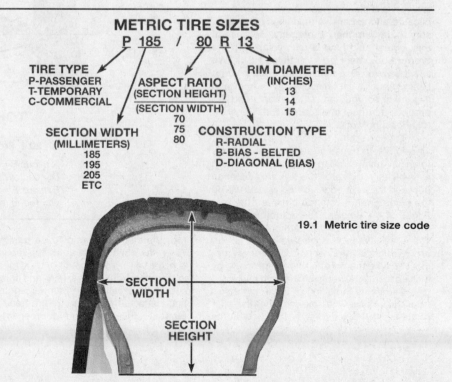

19.1 Metric tire size code

it's the same size, structure and tread design as the other.

Because tire pressure has a substantial effect on handling and wear, the pressure on all tires should be checked at least once a month or before any extended trips (see Chapter 1).

Wheels must be replaced if they're bent, dented, leak air, have elongated bolt holes, are heavily rusted, out of vertical symmetry or if the lug nuts won't stay tight. Wheel repairs that use welding or peening are not recommended.

Tire and wheel balance is important to the overall handling, braking and performance of the vehicle. Unbalanced wheels can adversely affect handling and ride characteristics as well as tire life. Whenever a tire is installed on a wheel, the tire and wheel should be balanced by a shop with the proper equipment.

---

20   Front end alignment - general information

Refer to illustration 20.1

A front end alignment refers to the adjustments made to the front wheels so they're in proper angular relationship to the suspension and the ground. Front wheels that are out of proper alignment not only affect steering control, but also increase tire wear. The only adjustment possible on these vehicles, as they come from the factory, is toe-in. Camber and caster can be adjusted **(see illustration)**, but only after an adjustment kit, available at GM dealers, is installed.

Getting the proper front wheel alignment is a very exacting process, one in which complicated and expensive machines are necessary to perform the job properly. Because of this, you should have a technician with the proper equipment perform these tasks. We will, however, use this space to give you a basic idea of what is involved with front end alignment so you can better understand the process and deal intelligently with the shop that does the work.

Toe-in is the turning in of the front wheels. The purpose of a toe specification is to ensure parallel rolling of the front wheels. In a vehicle with zero toe-in, the distance between the front edges of the wheels will be the same as the distance between the rear edges of the wheels. The actual amount of toe-in is normally only a fraction of an inch. Toe-in adjustment is controlled by the tie-rod end position on the inner tie-rod. Incorrect toe-in will cause the tires to wear improperly by making them scrub against the road surface.

Camber is the tilting of the front wheels from the vertical when viewed from the front of the vehicle. When the wheels tilt out at the

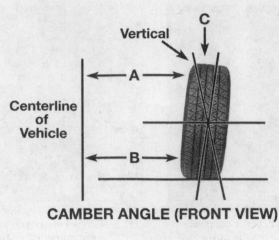

CAMBER ANGLE (FRONT VIEW)

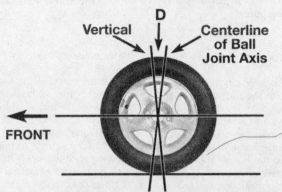

CASTER ANGLE (SIDE VIEW)

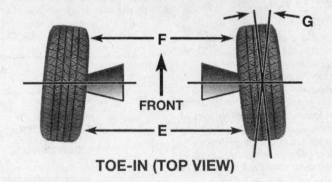

TOE-IN (TOP VIEW)

20.1 Front end alignment details

A minus B = C
D = caster (measured in degrees)
E minus F = toe-in (measured in inches)
G = toe-in (expressed in degrees)

---

top, the camber is said to be positive (+). When the wheels tilt in at the top the camber is negative (-). The amount of tilt is measured in degrees from the vertical and this measurement is called the camber angle. This angle affects the amount of tire tread which contacts the road and compensates for

changes in the suspension geometry when the vehicle is cornering or travelling over an undulating surface.

Caster is the tilting of the top of the front steering axis from the vertical. A tilt toward the rear is positive caster and a tilt toward the front is negative caster.

Chapter 11 Body

Contents

1 General information

The vehicles covered in this manual have a separate frame and body. As with other parts of the vehicle, proper maintenance of body components plays an important part in preserving the vehicle's market value. It's far less costly to handle small problems before they grow into larger ones. Information in this Chapter will tell you all you need to know to keep seals sealing, body panels aligned and general appearance up to par.

Major body components which are particularly vulnerable to accident damage can be unbolted and repaired or replaced. Among these parts are the body moldings, bumpers, fenders, hood, doors and all glass.

Only general body maintenance practices and body panel repair procedures within the scope of the do-it-yourselfer are included in this Chapter.

2 Body - maintenance

1 The condition of your vehicle's body is very important, because the resale value depends a great deal on it. It's much more difficult to repair a neglected or damaged body than it is to repair mechanical components. The hidden areas of the body, such as the wheel wells, the frame and the engine compartment, are equally important, although they don't require as frequent attention as the rest of the body.

2 Once a year, or every 12,000 miles, it's a good idea to have the underside of the body steam cleaned. All traces of dirt and oil will be removed and the area can then be inspected carefully for rust, damaged brake lines, frayed electrical wires, damaged cables and other problems. The front suspension com-

ponents should be greased after completion of this job.

3   At the same time, clean the engine and the engine compartment with a steam cleaner or water soluble degreaser.

4   The wheel wells should be given close attention, since undercoating can peel away and stones and dirt thrown up by the tires can cause the paint to chip and flake, allowing rust to set in. If rust is found, clean down to the bare metal and apply an anti-rust paint.

5   The body should be washed about once a week. Wet the vehicle thoroughly to soften the dirt, then wash it down with a soft sponge and plenty of clean soapy water. If the surplus dirt isn't washed off very carefully, it can wear down the paint.

6   Spots of tar or asphalt thrown up from the road should be removed with a cloth soaked in solvent.

7   Once every six months, wax the body and chrome trim. If a chrome cleaner is used to remove rust from any of the vehicle's plated parts, remember that the cleaner also removes part of the chrome, so use it sparingly.

3   Upholstery and carpets - maintenance

1   Every three months remove the carpets or mats and clean the interior of the vehicle (more frequently if necessary). Vacuum the upholstery and carpets to remove loose dirt and dust.

2   Vinyl upholstery can be cleaned with a sponge dampened with soapy water. It's a good idea to treat vinyl upholstery with a rubber and vinyl protectant to slow deterioration.

4   Vinyl trim - maintenance

Don't clean vinyl trim with detergents, caustic soap or petroleum-based cleaners. Plain soap and water works just fine, with a soft brush to clean dirt that may be ingrained. Wash the vinyl as frequently as the rest of the vehicle.

After cleaning, application of a high quality rubber and vinyl protectant will help prevent oxidation and cracks. The protectant can also be applied to weatherstripping, vacuum lines and rubber hoses, which often fail as a result of chemical degradation, and to the tires.

5   Body repair - minor damage

See photo sequence

Repair of scratches

1   If the scratch is superficial and does not penetrate to the metal of the body, repair is very simple. Lightly rub the scratched area with a fine rubbing compound to remove loose paint and built up wax. Rinse the area with clean water.

2   Apply touch-up paint to the scratch, using a small brush. Continue to apply thin layers of paint until the surface of the paint in the scratch is level with the surrounding paint. Allow the new paint at least two weeks to harden, then blend it into the surrounding paint by rubbing with a very fine rubbing compound. Finally, apply a coat of wax to the scratch area.

3   If the scratch has penetrated the paint and exposed the metal of the body, causing the metal to rust, a different repair technique is required. Remove all loose rust from the bottom of the scratch with a pocket knife, then apply rust inhibiting paint to prevent the formation of rust in the future. Using a rubber or nylon applicator, coat the scratched area with glaze-type filler. If required, the filler can be mixed with thinner to provide a very thin paste, which is ideal for filling narrow scratches. Before the glaze filler in the scratch hardens, wrap a piece of smooth cotton cloth around the tip of a finger. Dip the cloth in thinner and then quickly wipe it along the surface of the scratch. This will ensure that the surface of the filler is slightly hollow. The scratch can now be painted over as described earlier in this section.

Repair of dents

4   When repairing dents, the first job is to pull the dent out until the affected area is as close as possible to its original shape. There is no point in trying to restore the original shape completely as the metal in the damaged area will have stretched on impact and cannot be restored to its original contours. It's better to bring the level of the dent up to a point which is about 1/8-inch below the level of the surrounding metal. In cases where the dent is very shallow, it isn't worth trying to pull it out at all.

5   If the back side of the dent is accessible, it can be hammered out gently from behind using a soft-face hammer. While doing this, hold a block of wood firmly against the opposite side of the metal to absorb the hammer blows and prevent the metal from being stretched.

6   If the dent is in a section of the body which has double layers, or some other factor makes it inaccessible from behind, a different technique is required. Drill several small holes through the metal inside the damaged area, particularly in the deeper sections. Screw long, self tapping screws into the holes just enough for them to get a good grip in the metal. Now the dent can be pulled out by pulling on the protruding heads of the screws with locking pliers.

7   The next stage of repair is the removal of paint from the damaged area and from an inch or so of the surrounding metal. This is easily done with a wire brush or sanding disk in a drill motor, although it can be done just as effectively by hand with sandpaper. To complete the preparation for filling, score the surface of the bare metal with a screwdriver or the tang of a file or drill small holes in the affected area. This will provide a good grip for the filler material. To complete the repair, see the Section on filling and painting.

Repair of rust holes or gashes

8   Remove all paint from the affected area and from an inch or so of the surrounding metal using a sanding disk or wire brush mounted in a drill motor. If these are not available, a few sheets of sandpaper will do the job just as effectively.

9   With the paint removed, you will be able to determine the severity of the corrosion and decide whether to replace the whole panel, if possible, or repair the affected area. New body panels are not as expensive as most people think and it's often quicker to install a new panel than to repair large areas of rust.

10   Remove all trim pieces from the affected area except those which will act as a guide to the original shape of the damaged body, such as headlight shells, etc. Using metal snips or a hacksaw blade, remove all loose metal and any other metal that is badly affected by rust. Hammer the edges of the hole inward to create a slight depression for the filler material.

11   Wire brush the affected area to remove the powdery rust from the surface of the metal. If the back of the rusted area is accessible, treat it with rust-inhibiting paint.

12   Before filling is done, block the hole in some way. This can be done with sheet metal riveted or screwed into place, or by stuffing the hole with wire mesh.

13   Once the hole is blocked off, the affected area can be filled and painted. See the following subsection on filling and painting.

Filling and painting

14   Many types of body fillers are available, but generally speaking, body repair kits which contain filler paste and a tube of resin hardener are best for this type of repair work. A wide, flexible plastic or nylon applicator will be necessary for imparting a smooth and contoured finish to the surface of the filler material. Mix up a small amount of filler on a clean piece of wood or cardboard (use the hardener sparingly). Follow the manufacturer's instructions on the package, otherwise the filler will set incorrectly.

15   Using the applicator, apply the filler paste to the prepared area. Draw the applicator across the surface of the filler to achieve the desired contour and to level the filler surface. As soon as a contour that approximates the original one is achieved, stop working the paste. If you continue, the paste will begin to stick to the applicator. Continue to add thin layers of paste at 20-minute intervals until the level of the filler is just above the surrounding metal.

16   Once the filler has hardened, the excess can be removed with a body file. From then on, progressively finer grades of sandpaper

should be used, starting with a 180-grit paper and finishing with 600-grit wet-or-dry paper. Always wrap the sandpaper around a flat rubber or wooden block, otherwise the surface of the filler won't be completely flat. During the sanding of the filler surface, the wet-or-dry paper should be periodically rinsed in water. This will ensure that a very smooth finish is produced in the final stage.

17   At this point, the repair area should be surrounded by a ring of bare metal, which in turn should be encircled by the finely feathered edge of good paint. Rinse the repair area with clean water until all of the dust produced by the sanding operation is gone.

18   Spray the entire area with a light coat of primer. This will reveal any imperfections in the surface of the filler. Repair the imperfections with fresh filler paste or glaze filler and once more smooth the surface with sandpaper. Repeat this spray-and-repair procedure until you are satisfied that the surface of the filler and the feathered edge of the paint are perfect. Rinse the area with clean water and allow it to dry completely.

19   The repair area is now ready for painting. Spray painting must be carried out in a warm, dry, windless and dust free atmosphere. These conditions can be created if you have access to a large indoor work area, but if you are forced to work in the open, you will have to pick the day very carefully. If you are working indoors, dousing the floor in the work area with water will help settle the dust which would otherwise be in the air. If the repair area is confined to one body panel, mask off the surrounding panels. This will help minimize the effects of a slight mismatch in paint color. Trim pieces such as chrome strips, door handles, etc., will also need to be masked off or removed. Use masking tape and several thicknesses of newspaper for the masking operations.

20   Before spraying, shake the paint can thoroughly, then spray a test area until the spray painting technique is mastered. Cover the repair area with a thick coat of primer. The thickness should be built up using several thin layers of primer rather than one thick one. Using 600-grit wet-or-dry sandpaper, rub down the surface of the primer until it's very smooth. While doing this, the work area should be thoroughly rinsed with water and the wet-or-dry sandpaper periodically rinsed as well. Allow the primer to dry before spraying additional coats.

21   Spray on the top coat, again building up the thickness by using several thin layers of paint. Begin spraying in the center of the repair area and then, using a circular motion, work out until the whole repair area and about two inches of the surrounding original paint is covered. Remove all masking material 10 to 15 minutes after spraying on the final coat of paint. Allow the new paint at least two weeks to harden, then use a very fine rubbing compound to blend the edges of the new paint into the existing paint. Finally, apply a coat of wax.

6   Body repair - major damage

1   Major damage must be repaired by an auto body shop specifically equipped to repair major damage. These shops have the specialized equipment required to do the job properly.

2   If the damage is extensive, the body must be checked for proper alignment or the vehicle's handling characteristics may be adversely affected and other components may wear at an accelerated rate.

3   Due to the fact that all of the major body components (hood, fenders, etc.) are separate and replaceable units, any seriously damaged components should be replaced rather than repaired. Sometimes the components can be found in a wrecking yard that specializes in used vehicle components, often at considerable savings over the cost of new parts.

7   Hinges and locks - maintenance

Once every 3000 miles, or every three months, the hinges and latch assemblies on the doors, hood and tailgate should be given a few drops of light oil or lock lubricant. The door latch strikers should also be lubricated with a thin coat of grease to reduce wear and ensure free movement. Lubricate the door locks with spray-on graphite lubricant.

8   Windshield and fixed glass - replacement

Replacement of the windshield and fixed glass requires the use of special fast-setting adhesive/caulk materials and some specialized tools and techniques. These operations should be left to a dealer service department or a shop specializing in glass work.

9   Hood - removal, installation and adjustment

Note: *The hood is heavy and somewhat awkward to remove and install - at least two people should perform this procedure.*

Removal and installation
Refer to illustration 9.2

1   Use blankets or pads to cover the cowl area of the body and the fenders. This will protect the body and paint as the hood is lifted off.

2   Use a scribe or permanent felt-tip pen to make alignment marks around the bolt heads. This will ensure proper alignment during installation **(see illustration)**.

3   Disconnect any cables or wire harnesses which will interfere with removal.

4   Have an assistant support the weight of

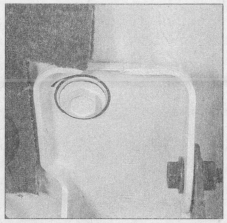

9.2 Use a scribe or permanent felt-tip pen to make alignment marks around the hood bolt heads

the hood. Remove the hinge-to-hood nuts or bolts.

5   Lift off the hood.

6   Installation is the reverse of removal.

Adjustment

7   Fore-and-aft and side-to-side adjustment of the hood is done by moving the hood in relation to the hinge plate after loosening the bolts or nuts.

8   Scribe a line around the entire hinge plate so you can judge the amount of movement.

9   Loosen the bolts or nuts and move the hood into correct alignment. Move it only a little at a time. Tighten the hinge bolts or nuts and carefully lower the hood to check the alignment.

10   If necessary after installation, the entire hood latch assembly can be adjusted up-and-down as well as from side-to-side on the radiator support so the hood closes securely and is flush with the fenders. To do this, scribe a line around the hood latch and mounting bolts to provide a reference point. Then loosen the bolts and reposition the latch assembly as necessary. Following adjustment, retighten the mounting bolts.

11   Finally, adjust the hood bumpers on the radiator support so the hood, when closed, is flush with the fenders.

12   The hood latch assembly, as well as the hinges, should be periodically lubricated with white lithium-base grease to prevent sticking and wear.

10   Door trim panel - removal and installation

1994 and earlier models
Refer to illustrations 10.2a, 10.2b, 10.3 and 10.6

1   Lower the window all the way down and disconnect the negative cable from the battery.

These photos illustrate a method of repairing simple dents. They are intended to supplement *Body repair - minor damage* in this Chapter and should not be used as the sole instructions for body repair on these vehicles.

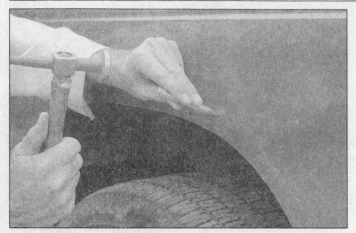

1   If you can't access the backside of the body panel to hammer out the dent, pull it out with a slide-hammer-type dent puller. In the deepest portion of the dent or along the crease line, drill or punch hole(s) at least one inch apart . . .

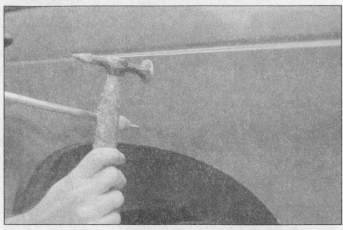

2   . . . then screw the slide-hammer into the hole and operate it. Tap with a hammer near the edge of the dent to help 'pop' the metal back to its original shape. When you're finished, the dent area should be close to its original contour and about 1/8-inch below the surface of the surrounding metal

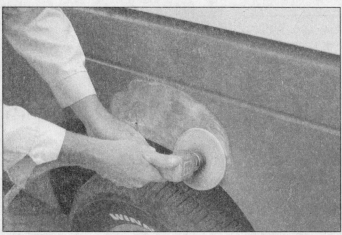

3   Using coarse-grit sandpaper, remove the paint down to the bare metal. Hand sanding works fine, but the disc sander shown here makes the job faster. Use finer (about 320-grit) sandpaper to feather-edge the paint at least one inch around the dent area

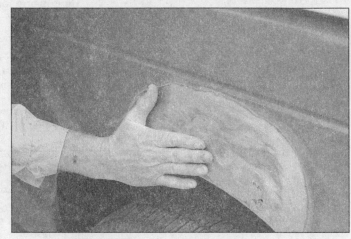

4   When the paint is removed, touch will probably be more helpful than sight for telling if the metal is straight. Hammer down the high spots or raise the low spots as necessary. Clean the repair area with wax/silicone remover

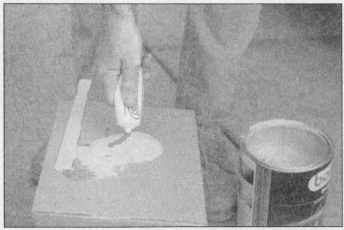

5   Following label instructions, mix up a batch of plastic filler and hardener. The ratio of filler to hardener is critical, and, if you mix it incorrectly, it will either not cure properly or cure too quickly (you won't have time to file and sand it into shape)

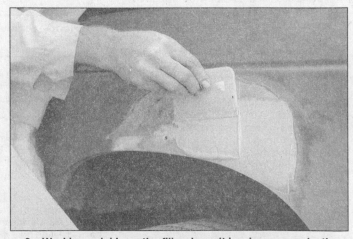

6   Working quickly so the filler doesn't harden, use a plastic applicator to press the body filler firmly into the metal, assuring it bonds completely. Work the filler until it matches the original contour and is slightly above the surrounding metal

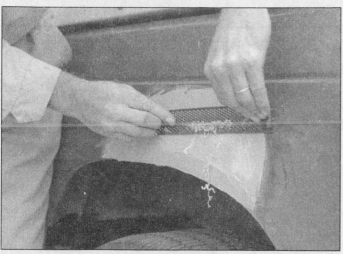

7 Let the filler harden until you can just dent it with your fingernail. Use a body file or Surform tool (shown here) to rough-shape the filler

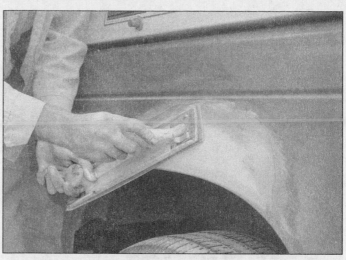

8 Use coarse-grit sandpaper and a sanding board or block to work the filler down until it's smooth and even. Work down to finer grits of sandpaper - always using a board or block - ending up with 360 or 400 grit

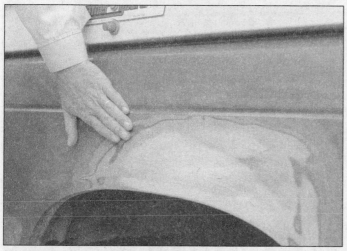

9 You shouldn't be able to feel any ridge at the transition from the filler to the bare metal or from the bare metal to the old paint. As soon as the repair is flat and uniform, remove the dust and mask off the adjacent panels or trim pieces

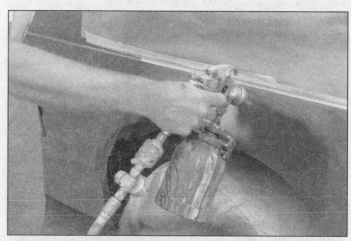

10 Apply several layers of primer to the area. Don't spray the primer on too heavy, so it sags or runs, and make sure each coat is dry before you spray on the next one. A professional-type spray gun is being used here, but aerosol spray primer is available inexpensively from auto parts stores

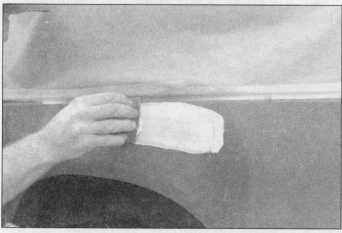

11 The primer will help reveal imperfections or scratches. Fill these with glazing compound. Follow the label instructions and sand it with 360 or 400-grit sandpaper until it's smooth. Repeat the glazing, sanding and respraying until the primer reveals a perfectly smooth surface

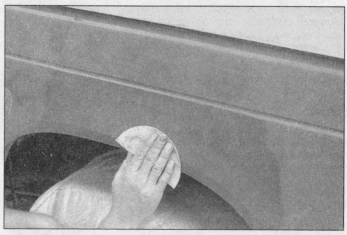

12 Finish sand the primer with very fine sandpaper (400 or 600-grit) to remove the primer overspray. Clean the area with water and allow it to dry. Use a tack rag to remove any dust, then apply the finish coat. Don't attempt to rub out or wax the repair area until the paint has dried completely (at least two weeks)

10.2a Using a small screwdriver, pry off the cover on each side of the pull strap and remove the screw underneath it

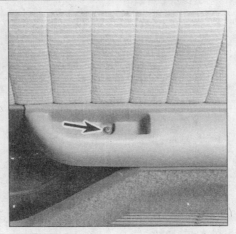

10.2b Remove the door panel retaining screw(s) located in the arm rest (arrow)

10.3 Using a small screwdriver, carefully pry off the control switch panel

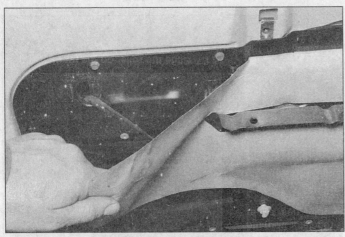

10.6 Be very careful when pulling the watershield off - don't tear or distort it

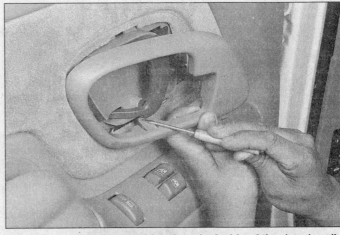

10.10 Slide a small screwdriver into the inside of the door handle bezel and release the tabs

2   Remove the door pull or armrest retaining screws (see illustrations).

3   On manual window regulator equipped models, remove the window crank. On power regulator models, pry out the control switch assembly and unplug it (see illustration).

4   Insert a putty knife or large screwdriver between the trim panel and the door and disengage the retaining clips. Work around the outer edge until the panel is free.

5   Once all of the clips are disengaged, detach the trim panel and remove it from the vehicle.

6   For access to the inner door, carefully peel back the plastic watershield (see illustration).

7   Prior to installation of the door panel, be sure to reinstall any clips in the panel which may have come out during the removal procedure and remain in the door itself.

8   Place the panel in position in the door, press the door panel into place until the clips are seated and install the armrest/door pullscrews. Install the manual regulator window crank or control switch assembly.

1995 and later models

Refer to illustrations 10.10, 10.12, 10.13a, 10.13b and 10.16

9   Disconnect the negative battery cable.

10   Remove the inside door handle bezel by carefully prying out the clips while pulling out the bezel (see illustration).

11   Remove the widow regulator handle, if equipped with manual windows.

12   Remove the two screws and the inner door pull (see illustration).

13   Remove the power accessory switch mounting panel by carefully prying it from the door panel (see illustrations). The panel must slide rearward as it is removed in order

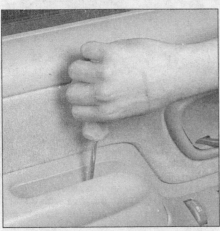

10.12 Remove the screws securing the pull handle

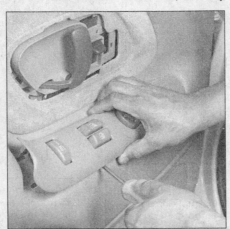

10.13a Carefully pry off the control panel assembly with a wide blade screwdriver

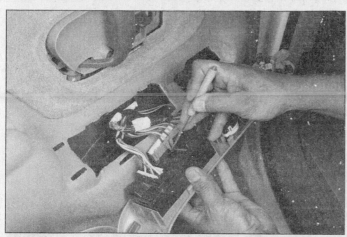

10.13b Disconnect the wiring connectors from the switches

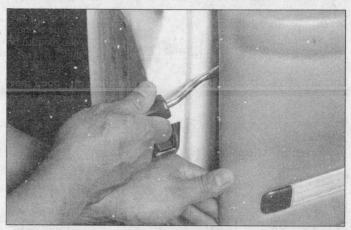

10.16 Carefully pry the door panel retaining clips off with a special door panel removal tool - be careful not to scratch the paint

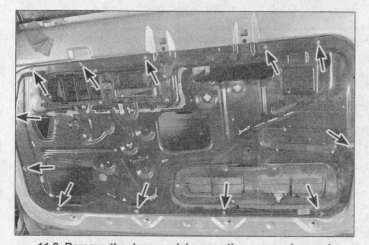

11.3 Remove the door module mounting screws (arrows)

11.5 Remove the two glass run channel bolts and pull the channel away from the glass (arrows)

to disengage the front clip. Disconnect the wiring. The small speaker can be disconnected by rotating the connector.

14   Remove the upper trim panel, if used, by prying it from the door.

15   Carefully pry off the armrest screw covers and remove the screws and cover.

16   Pry out the door panel retaining clips with a trim panel clip removal tool (available at most auto parts stores) or an equivalent tool **(see illustration)**.

17   Installation is the reverse of removal.

11   Door window glass and regulator - removal and installation

Refer to illustrations 11.3, 11.5 and 11.7

1   Lower the glass completely.

2   Remove the door trim panel and the watershield (see Section 10).

3   Remove the retaining screws, pull the door module back and disconnect the door lock and handle rods **(see illustration)**.

4   Remove the electrical connector, if equipped.

5   Remove the two glass run channel bolts

(see illustration) and move the run channel away from the glass.

6   Tilt the door module and window glass assembly and lower it out the bottom of the door.

7   Bend the tab down on the window run channel to slide the door glass from the regulator assembly **(see illustration)**.

8   For access to the power regulator components, drill out the rivets from the inside handle housing. On reassembly, use sheet metal screws in place of the rivets.

9   Drill out the rivets from the regulator assembly and separate the regulator from the door module. On reassembly, use sheet metal screws in place of the rivets.

10   Prior to installation, lubricate the window regulator mechanism with chassis grease. Installation of the glass and regulator is the reverse of removal.

12   Side latched window (extended cab models) - removal and installation

1   Open the window and block it in the

open position.

2   Drill out and remove the latch and hinge-retaining rivets. On reassembly, use sheet-metal screws.

3   Remove the window assembly.

4   Installation is the reverse of removal.

11.7 Slide the roller on the regulator arm out of the glass channel

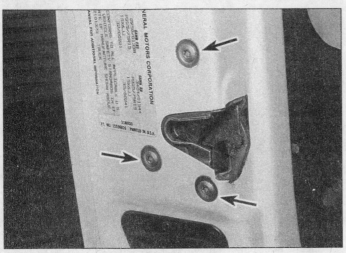

14.4 To remove the latch, unscrew the three mounting bolts (arrows)

14.7 To remove the door handle housing, drill out the mounting rivets (arrows) - during installation, use sheet metal screws in place of the rivets

13   End gate window (Sport-utility models) - removal and installation

1   Disconnect the rear gate window defogger wires attached to the strut assemblies.
2   On the lower end of the strut assembly, insert a small screwdriver between the ball and the strut ball socket and release the ball from the strut ball socket.
3   Support the end gate window and repeat for the other side.
4   Remove the hinge pin retainers and hinge pins.
5   Remove the end gate assembly.
6   Installation is the reverse of removal.

14   Door latch, lock cylinder and handle - removal and installation

Door latch

Refer to illustration 14.4

1   Remove the door trim panel (see Section 10).
2   Remove the screws from the door module **(see illustration 11.3)** and tilt it out at the top.
3   Detach the rods from the latch assembly.
4   Remove the latch mounting screws and pull the latch assembly out from inside the door **(see illustration)**.
5   Installation is the reverse of removal.

Inside door handle

Refer to illustration 14.7

6   Remove the door trim panel and the watershield (see Section 10).
7   Drill out the rivets from the inside handle housing and pull it out **(see illustration)**.
8   Detach the control rods from the handle.
9   Installation is the reverse of removal. Use sheet metal screws in place of the rivets.

Door lock cylinder and outside door handle

Refer to illustration 14.13

10   Remove the door trim panel and water deflector (see Section 10).
11   Remove the door module and window glass assembly (Section 11).
12   Detach the control rods from the handle and the lock cylinder.
13   Remove the handle mounting screws **(see illustration)**.
14   Remove the lock cylinder from the handle housing.
15   Remove the handle.
16   Installation is the reverse of removal.

15   Side and cargo door - removal and installation

Refer to illustrations 15.5a and 15.5b

1   Detach the negative cable from the battery.
2   Remove the door trim panel (see Section 10). Disconnect any wire harness con-

nectors and push them through the door opening so they won't interfere with door removal.
3   Place a jack or jackstand under the door or have an assistant on hand to support it when the hinge pins are removed. **Note:** *If a jack or jackstand is used, place a rag between it and the door to protect the door's painted surfaces.*
4   On side doors only, compress and remove the hinge spring using tool J-36604 or equivalent. **Warning:** *The spring may fly off the tool during removal. To prevent personal injury, cover the spring with a heavy rag before removing it.*
5   On side doors only, remove the hinge pin retainers. On all doors, drive out the pins and carefully lift off the door **(see illustrations)**. **Note:** *The cargo door hinges are not equipped with hinge pin retainers.*
6   If the door does not close properly after installation, the door latch striker can be adjusted both up-and-down and sideways to provide positive engagement with the latch mechanism. This is done by loosening the door striker bolt and moving the striker as necessary.

14.13 Door handle mounting bolts

15.5a Typical upper door hinge and pin

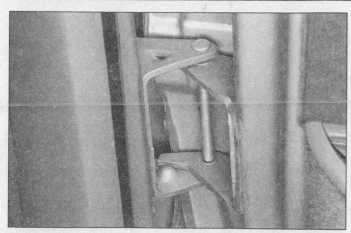

15.5b Typical lower door hinge and pin

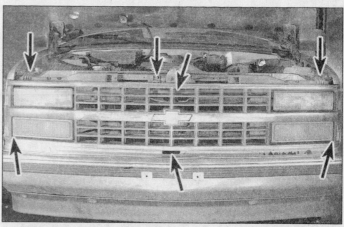

16.2a Remove the grill mounting screws (arrows) - the lower outer screws are behind the parking/turn signal lights

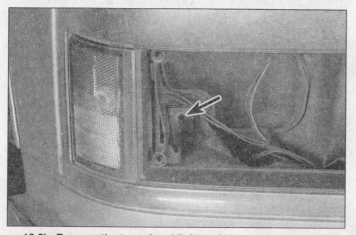

16.2b Remove the turn signal light and then remove the grill retaining screws (arrow) - passenger side shown

17.2 Remove the cable clip from the engine compartment (arrow)

16   Radiator grille - removal and installation

Refer to illustration 16.2a and 16.2b

1   On 1994 and earlier models, remove the parking light assemblies (see Chapter 12).
2   Remove the grille retaining screws (see illustrations).
3   Move the grille forward about 1/2-inch, then lift it up and out.
4   Installation is the reverse of removal.

17   Hood release cable - removal and installation

Refer to illustration 17.2

1   Remove the two bolts from the upper left portion of the radiator grille.
2   Disconnect the cable from the latch release, disengage the two cable clips, unbolt the hand lever in the passenger compartment and pull the cable through the firewall into the passenger compartment (see illustration).
3   Installation is the reverse of removal.

18   Front fender - removal and installation

Refer to illustrations 18.4a, 18.4b and 18.4c

1   Remove the hood and hood hinge (see Section 9).
2   Loosen the wheel lug nuts, raise the front of the vehicle and support it securely on jackstands. Apply the parking brake. Remove the front wheel.
3   Disconnect the antenna (left fender only) and all electrical connectors and other components that would interfere with fender removal.
4   Remove the fender mounting bolts (see illustrations).

18.4a Remove the front fender mounting bolts (arrows) - front view . . .

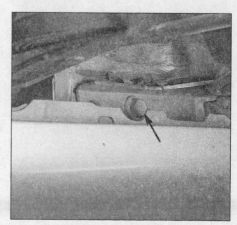

18.4b . . . top view from engine compartment . . .

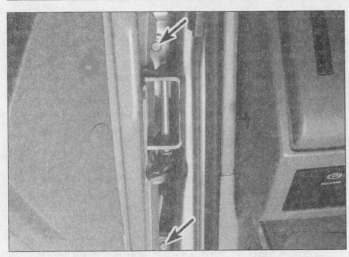

18.4c . . . rear view with the door open

19.2 Disengage the slot on the end of the support from the retaining dowel

5   Detach the fender. It's a good idea to have an assistant support the fender while it's being moved away from the vehicle to prevent damage to the surrounding body panels.

6   Installation is the reverse of removal. Tighten all fasteners securely.

19 Tailgate - removal and installation

Refer to illustration 19.2

Note: *The tailgate is heavy and somewhat awkward to remove and install - at least two people should perform this procedure.*

1   Lower the tailgate and pull the centers of the supports up.

2   Push each support forward to disengage the slot on the end of the support from the retaining dowel **(see illustration)**.

3   With the aid of an assistant, pull the right side of the tailgate rearward to disengage the hinge, then pull the tailgate to the right to disengage the left hinge.

4   Installation is the reverse of removal.

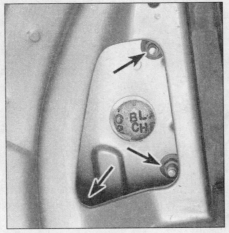

21.2 The outside mirror is retained by three nuts

20 End gate (Sport-utility models) - removal and installation

Note: *The end gate is heavy and somewhat awkward to remove and install - at least two people should perform this procedure.*

1   Remove the rear bumper and rear bumper filler panel.

2   Open the end gate.

3   Remove the left bolt.

4   Close the end gate and remove both retainers and the torque-rod-retaining bolts. Remove both retainers and torque rod.

5   Disconnect the rear gate release wires.

6   Open and support the end gate in the open position.

7   Disconnect both support-cable-retaining bolts from the end gate.

8   Remove the hinge pin retainers, drive out the pins and carefully lift off the end gate.

9   Installation is the reverse of removal.

21 Outside mirror - removal and installation

Refer to illustration 21.2

1   Remove the door trim panel (see Section 10).

2   Remove the mounting nuts **(see illustration)** and detach the mirror from the door.

3   Installation is the reverse of removal.

Chapter 12
Chassis electrical system

Contents

1   General information

Caution: *On models equipped with a Delco Loc II anti-theft audio system, be sure the lockout feature is turned off before performing any procedure which requires disconnecting the battery.*

The electrical system is a 12-volt, negative ground type. Power for the lights and all electrical accessories is supplied by a lead/acid-type battery which is charged by the alternator.

This Chapter covers repair and service procedures for the various electrical components not associated with the engine. Information on the battery, alternator, distributor and starter motor can be found in Chapter 5.

It should be noted that when portions of the electrical system are serviced, the negative battery cable should be disconnected from the battery to prevent electrical shorts and/or fires.

2   Electrical troubleshooting - general information

A typical electrical circuit consists of an electrical component, any switches, relays, motors, fuses, fusible links or circuit breakers related to that component and the wiring and connectors that link the component to both the battery and the chassis. To help you pinpoint an electrical circuit problem, wiring diagrams are included at the end of this book.

Before tackling any troublesome electrical circuit, first study the appropriate wiring diagrams to get a complete understanding of what makes up that individual circuit. Trouble spots, for instance, can often be narrowed down by noting if other components related to the circuit are operating properly. If several components or circuits fail at one time, chances are the problem is in a fuse or ground connection, because several circuits are often routed through the same fuse and ground connections.

Electrical problems usually stem from simple causes, such as loose or corroded connections, a blown fuse, a melted fusible link or a bad relay. Visually inspect the condition of all fuses, wires and connections in a problem circuit before troubleshooting it.

If testing instruments are going to be utilized, use the diagrams to plan ahead of time where you will make the necessary connections in order to accurately pinpoint the trouble spot.

The basic tools needed for electrical troubleshooting include a circuit tester or voltmeter (a 12-volt bulb with a set of test leads can also be used), a continuity tester, which includes a bulb, battery and set of test leads, and a jumper wire, preferably with a circuit breaker incorporated, which can be used to bypass electrical components. Before attempting to locate a problem with test instruments, use the wiring diagram(s) to decide where to make the connections.

Voltage checks

Voltage checks should be performed if a circuit is not functioning properly. Connect one lead of a circuit tester to either the negative battery terminal or a known good ground. Connect the other lead to a connector in the circuit being tested, preferably nearest to the battery or fuse. If the bulb of the tester lights, voltage is present, which means that the part of the circuit between the connector and the battery is problem free. Continue checking the rest of the circuit in the same fashion. When you reach a point at which no voltage is present, the problem lies between that point and the last test point with voltage. Most of the time the problem can be traced to a loose connection. **Note:** *Keep in mind that some circuits receive voltage only when the ignition key is in the Accessory or Run position.*

Finding a short

One method of finding shorts in a circuit is to remove the fuse and connect a test light or voltmeter in its place to the fuse terminals. There should be no voltage present in the circuit. Move the wiring harness from side-to-side while watching the test light. If the bulb goes on, there is a short to ground somewhere in that area, probably where the insulation has rubbed through. The same test can be performed on each component in the circuit, even a switch.

Ground check

Perform a ground test to check whether a component is properly grounded. Disconnect the battery and connect one lead of a selfpowered test light, known as a continuity tester, to a known good ground. Connect the other lead to the wire or ground connection being tested. If the bulb goes on, the ground is good. If the bulb does not go on, the ground is not good.

Continuity check

A continuity check is done to determine if there are any breaks in a circuit - if it is passing electricity properly. With the circuit off (no power in the circuit), a self-powered continuity tester can be used to check the circuit. Connect the test leads to both ends of the circuit (or to the "power" end and a good ground),

3.1 The fuse block is located under the instrument panel to the left of the steering column

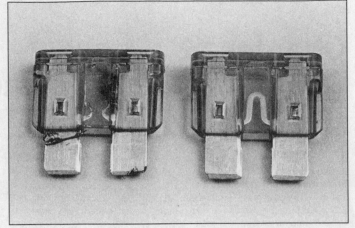

3.3 When a fuse blows, the element between the terminals melts - the fuse on the left is blown, the fuse on the right is good

and if the test light comes on the circuit is passing current properly. If the light doesn't come on, there is a break somewhere in the circuit. The same procedure can be used to test a switch, by connecting the continuity tester to the switch terminals. With the switch turned On, the test light should come on.

Finding an open circuit

When diagnosing for possible open circuits, it is often difficult to locate them by sight because oxidation or terminal misalignment are hidden by the connectors. Merely wiggling a connector on a sensor or in the wiring harness may correct the open circuit condition. Remember this when an open circuit is indicated when troubleshooting a circuit. Intermittent problems may also be caused by oxidized or loose connections.

Electrical troubleshooting is simple if you keep in mind that all electrical circuits are basically electricity running from the battery, through the wires, switches, relays, fuses and fusible links to each electrical component (light bulb, motor, etc.) and to ground, from which it is passed back to the battery. Any electrical problem is an interruption in the flow of electricity to and from the battery.

3   Fuses - general information

Refer to illustrations 3.1 and 3.3

The electrical circuits of the vehicle are protected by a combination of fuses, circuit breakers and fusible links. The fuse block is located under the instrument panel on the left side of the dashboard **(see illustration)**.

Each of the fuses is designed to protect a specific circuit, and the various circuits are identified on the fuse panel itself.

Miniaturized fuses are employed in the fuse block. These compact fuses, with blade terminal design, allow fingertip removal and replacement. If an electrical component fails, always check the fuse first. The best way to check the fuses is with a test light. Check for power at the exposed terminal tips of each

fuse. If power is present at one side of the fuse but not the other, the fuse is blown. A blown fuse can also be identified by visually inspecting it **(see illustration)**.

Be sure to replace blown fuses with the correct type. Fuses of different ratings are physically interchangeable, but only fuses of the proper rating should be used. Replacing a fuse with one of a higher or lower value than specified is not recommended. Each electrical circuit needs a specific amount of protection. The amperage value of each fuse is molded into the fuse body.

If the replacement fuse immediately fails, don't replace it again until the cause of the problem is isolated and corrected. In most cases, the cause will be a short circuit in the wiring caused by a broken or deteriorated wire.

4   Fusible links - general information

Refer to illustration 4.1
Caution: *On models equipped with a Delco Loc II anti-theft audio system, be sure the lockout feature is turned off before performing any procedure which requires disconnecting the battery.*

Some circuits are protected by fusible links **(see illustration)**. The links are used in circuits which are not ordinarily fused, such as the ignition circuit.

Although the fusible links appear to be a heavier gauge than the wire they are protecting, the appearance is due to the thick insulation. All fusible links are several wire gauges smaller than the wire they are designed to protect.

Fusible links cannot be repaired, but a new link of the same size wire can be put in its place. The procedure is as follows:

a) *Disconnect the negative cable from the battery.*
b) *Disconnect the fusible link from the wiring harness.*
c) *Cut the damaged fusible link out of the wiring just behind the connector.*
d) *Strip the insulation back approximately 1/2-inch.*
e) *Position the connector on the new fusible link and crimp it into place.*
f) *Use rosin core solder at each end of the new link to obtain a good solder joint.*
g) *Use plenty of electrical tape around the soldered joint. No wires should be exposed.*
h) *Connect the battery ground cable. Test the circuit for proper operation.*

4.1 On some models the fusible links are located in the engine compartment, under a cover on the firewall; on others they are located near the positive battery cable

6.4 Remove the turn signal flasher from the fuse panel (arrow)

6.9 Remove the hazard flasher from its fastener under the dash and then unplug the flasher unit from the connector (arrow)

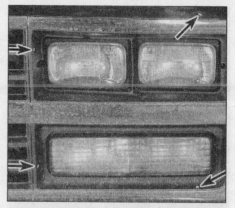

7.1 Headlight bezel screw locations (sealed beam) - four headlight system shown

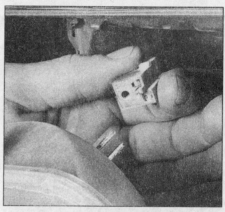

7.2 Pull the light forward and disconnect the plug from the rear (sealed beam)

5 Circuit breakers - general information

Circuit breakers protect components such as power windows, power door locks and headlights. Some circuit breakers are located in the fuse box.

On some models the circuit breaker resets itself automatically, so an electrical overload in a circuit breaker protected system will cause the circuit to fail momentarily, then come back on. If the circuit does not come back on, check it immediately. Once the condition is corrected, the circuit breaker will resume its normal function. Some circuit breakers must be reset manually.

6 Turn signal and hazard flashers - check and replacement

Refer to illustrations 6.4 and 6.9
Warning: *If equipped with an airbag, disable the airbag system before working in the vicinity of the steering wheel, instrument panel or any airbag system component. Failure to do so could cause accidental deployment of the airbag, resulting in personal injury (see Section 18).*
Caution: *On models equipped with a Delco Loc II anti-theft audio system, be sure the lockout feature is turned off before performing any procedure which requires disconnecting the battery.*

Turn signal flasher

1   The turn signal flasher, a small canister-shaped unit located in the convenience center under the dash, flashes the turn signals.
2   When the flasher unit is functioning properly, an audible click can be heard during its operation. If the turn signals fail on one side or the other and the flasher unit does not make its characteristic clicking sound, a faulty turn signal bulb is indicated.
3   If both turn signals fail to blink, the problem may be due to a blown fuse, a faulty flasher unit, a broken switch or a loose or

open connection. If a quick check of the fuse box indicates that the turn signal fuse has blown, check the wiring for a short before installing a new fuse.
4   To replace the flasher, simply pull it out of its electrical connector **(see illustration)**.
5   Make sure that the replacement unit is identical to the original. Compare the old one to the new one before installing it.
6   Installation is the reverse of removal.

Hazard flasher

7   The hazard flasher, a small canister-shaped unit located behind the main light switch behind the dash panel, flashes all four turn signals simultaneously when activated.
8   The hazard flasher is checked in a fashion similar to the turn signal flasher (see Steps 2 and 3).
9   To replace the hazard flasher, pull it from its connector under the dash and install a new one **(see illustration)**.
10   Make sure the replacement unit is identical to the one it replaces. Compare the old one to the new one before installing it.
11   Installation is the reverse of removal.

7 Headlights - removal and installation

Sealed beam

Refer to illustrations 7.1 and 7.2
1   Remove the bezel retaining screws, taking care not to disturb the adjustment screws **(see illustration)**.
2   Pull the sealed beam unit forward and disconnect the plug from the rear **(see illustration)**.
3   Installation is the reverse of removal. Make sure the number molded into the face of the lens is at the top.

Composite type

Refer to illustrations 7.6, 7.7a and 7.7b
Warning: *Halogen gas filled bulbs are under pressure and may shatter if the surface is scratched or the bulb is dropped. Wear eye*

protection and handle the bulbs carefully, grasping only the base whenever possible. Do not touch the surface of the bulb with your fingers because the oil from your skin will cause hotspots and the bulb will fail prematurely. If you do touch the bulb surface, clean it with rubbing alcohol.
4   Remove the grille (see Chapter 11).
5   Remove the four screws from the headlamp assembly.
6   Pull the headlamp assembly forward to access to the bulbs. Unplug the electrical connector **(see illustration)**.
7   Twist the bulb and lock ring counter-clockwise, and pull the bulb and holder assembly out of the headlamp assembly **(see illustrations)**.
8   Be sure to replace the high beam bulb assembly with another high beam assembly, and the low beam bulb assembly with another low beam assembly.
9   Installation is the reverse of removal.

8 Headlights - adjustment

Refer to illustrations 8.1a, 8.1b and 8.3
Note: *The headlights must be aimed correctly. If adjusted incorrectly they could blind the driver of an oncoming vehicle and cause a*

7.6 Unplug the headlight electrical connector (composite)

7.7a To remove the headlight bulb holder on composite-type lights, turn it counterclockwise . . .

7.7b . . . and pull it out of the headlight (don't try to pull the bulb out of the holder - they're sold as a single unit)

8.1a Headlight aiming screws - dual headlight

A   *Vertical adjusting screw*
B   *Horizontal adjusting screw*

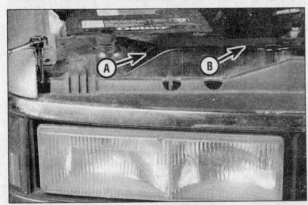

8.1b Headlight aiming screws - four headlights

A   *Vertical adjusting screw*
B   *Horizontal adjusting screw*

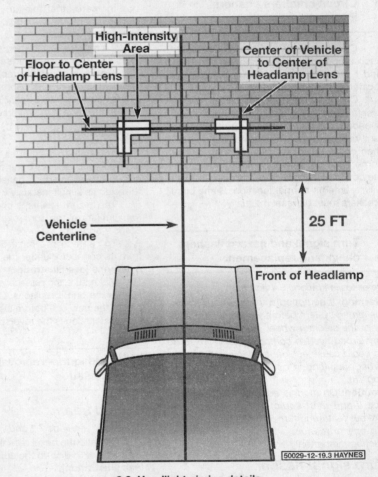

8.3 Headlight aiming details

serious accident or seriously reduce your ability to see the road. The headlights should be checked for proper aim every 12 months and any time a new headlight is installed or front end body work is performed. It should be emphasized that the following procedure is only an interim step which will provide temporary adjustment until the headlights can be adjusted by a properly equipped shop.

1   Headlights have two spring loaded adjusting screws, one for controlling up-and-down movement and one for controlling left-and-right movement **(see illustrations)**.
2   There are several methods of adjusting the headlights. The simplest method requires a blank wall 25 feet in front of the vehicle and a level floor.
3   Position masking tape vertically on the

wall in reference to the vehicle centerline and the centerlines of both headlights **(see illustration)**.
4   Position a horizontal tape line in reference to the centerline of all the headlights. **Note:** *It may be easier to position the tape on the wall with the vehicle parked only a few inches away.*
5   Adjustment should be made with the

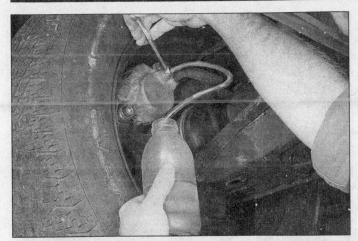

15.8 When bleeding the brakes, a clear piece of tubing is attached to the bleeder screw fitting and submerged in brake fluid - air bubbles can be easily seen in the tube and container (when no more bubbles appear, the air has been purged from the caliper or wheel cylinder)

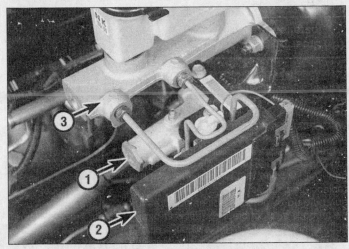

16.4a RWAL system components

1   Isolation/dump valve   3   Master cylinder
2   Control module

wheel lock-to-lock during inspection.
11   Bleed the brake system as described in Section 15.

Metal brake lines

12   When replacing brake lines, be sure to use the correct parts. Don't use copper tubing for any brake system components. Purchase steel brake lines from a dealer parts department or auto parts store.
13   Prefabricated brake line, with the tube ends already flared and fittings installed, is available at auto parts stores and dealer parts departments. These lines are also bent to the proper shapes.
14   When installing the new line make sure it's well supported in the brackets and has plenty of clearance between moving or hot components.
15   After installation, check the master cylinder fluid level and add fluid as necessary. Bleed the brake system as outlined in the next Section and test the brakes carefully before placing the vehicle into normal operation.

15   Brake system bleeding

Refer to illustration 15.8
Warning: *Wear eye protection when bleeding the brake system. If the fluid comes in contact with your eyes, immediately rinse them with water and seek medical attention.*
Note: *Bleeding the brake system is necessary to remove any air that's trapped in the system when it's opened during removal and installation of a hose, line, caliper, wheel cylinder or master cylinder.*
1   It will probably be necessary to bleed the system at all four brakes if air has entered the system due to low fluid level, or if the brake lines have been disconnected at the master cylinder.

2   If a brake line was disconnected only at a wheel, then only that caliper or wheel cylinder must be bled.
3   If a brake line is disconnected at a fitting located between the master cylinder and any of the brakes, that part of the system served by the disconnected line must be bled.
4   Remove any residual vacuum (or hydraulic pressure) from the brake power booster by applying the brake several times with the engine off.
5   Remove the master cylinder reservoir cover and fill the reservoir with brake fluid. Reinstall the cover. **Note:** *Check the fluid level often during the bleeding operation and add fluid as necessary to prevent the fluid level from falling low enough to allow air bubbles into the master cylinder.*
6   Have an assistant on hand, as well as a supply of new brake fluid, an empty clear plastic container, a length of 3/16-inch plastic, rubber or vinyl tubing to fit over the bleeder valve and a wrench to open and close the bleeder valve.
7   Beginning at the right rear wheel, loosen the bleeder screw slightly, then tighten it to a point where it's snug but can still be loosened quickly and easily.
8   Place one end of the tubing over the bleeder screw fitting and submerge the other end in brake fluid in the container (**see illustration**).
9   Have the assistant pump the brakes a few times to get pressure in the system, then hold the pedal firmly depressed.
10   While the pedal is held depressed, open the bleeder screw just enough to allow a flow of fluid to leave the valve. Watch for air bubbles to exit the submerged end of the tube. When the fluid flow slows after a couple of seconds, tighten the screw and have your assistant release the pedal.
11   Repeat Steps 9 and 10 until no more air is seen leaving the tube, then tighten the bleeder screw and proceed to the left rear

wheel, the right front wheel and the left front wheel, in that order, and perform the same procedure. Be sure to check the fluid in the master cylinder reservoir frequently.
12   Never use old brake fluid. It contains moisture which can boil during periods of heavy braking, rendering the brakes useless.
13   Refill the master cylinder with fluid at the end of the operation.
14   Check the operation of the brakes. The pedal should feel solid when depressed, with no sponginess. If necessary, repeat the entire process. **Warning:** *Do not operate the vehicle if you are in doubt about the effectiveness of the brake system.*

16   Anti-lock brake system - general information

Refer to illustrations 16.4a and 16.4b

Description

The Anti-lock brake system is designed to maintain vehicle maneuverability, directional stability and optimum deceleration under severe braking conditions on most road surfaces. It does so by monitoring the rotational speed of the wheels and controlling the brake line pressure during braking. This prevents the wheels from locking up prematurely.
Two types of systems are used: Rear Wheel Anti-Lock (RWAL) and Four Wheel Anti-Lock (4WAL). RWAL only controls lockup on the rear wheels, whereas 4WAL prevents lockup on all four wheels.

Actuator assembly
The actuator assembly includes the master cylinder and a control valve which consists of a dump valve and an isolation valve. The valve operates by changing the brake fluid pressure in response to signals from the control unit.

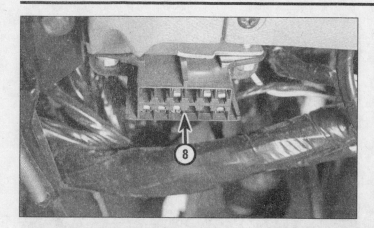

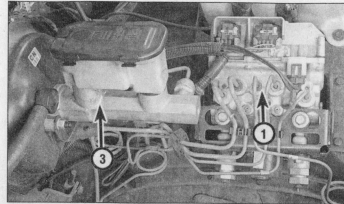

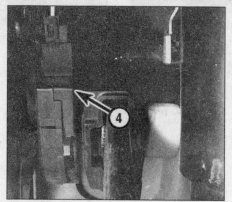

16.4b Four-wheel anti-lock (4WAL) brake system and related components

1   *4WAL EHCU valve*
2   *Combination valve*
3   *Master cylinder*
4   *Brake pedal switch*
5   *Parking brake switch*
6   *Wheel speed sensors*
7   *Warning lights*
8   *Assembly line diagnostic link (ALDL)*

Control unit

The control unit for the anti-lock brakes is called the Electro-Hydraulic Control Unit (EHCU) on 4WAL systems and Control Module on RWAL systems. The unit is mounted in the engine compartment below the master cylinder and is the "brain" for the system **(see illustrations)**. The function of the control unit is to accept and process information received from the speed sensor(s) and brake light switch to control the hydraulic line pressure, avoiding wheel lockup. The control unit also constantly monitors the system, even under normal driving conditions, to find faults within the system.

If a problem develops within the system, the BRAKE (RWAL system) or ANTI-LOCK (4WAL system) warning light will glow on the dashboard. A diagnostic code will also be stored, which, when retrieved by a service technician, will indicate the problem area or component.

Speed sensor

On 4WAL systems, each wheel has a speed sensor. On RWAL systems, a rear wheel speed sensor is located in the transmission extension housing on 2WD models and in the transfer case on 4WD models. The speed sensor(s) sends a signal to the control unit indicating wheel rotational speed.

Brake light switch

The brake light switch signals the control unit when the driver steps on the brake pedal. Without this signal the anti-lock system won't activate.

Diagnosis and repair

If the BRAKE or ANTI-LOCK warning light on the dashboard comes on and stays on, make sure the parking brake is released and there's no problem with the brake hydraulic system. If neither of these is the cause, the anti-lock system is probably malfunctioning. Although special test procedures are necessary to properly diagnose the system, the home mechanic can perform a few preliminary checks before taking the vehicle to a dealer service department.

a) *Make sure the brakes, calipers and wheel cylinders are in good condition.*
b) *Check the electrical connectors at the control unit.*
c) *Check the fuses.*
d) *Follow the wiring harness to the speed sensor(s) and brake light switch and make sure all connections are secure and the wiring isn't damaged.*

If the above preliminary checks don't rectify the problem, the vehicle should be diagnosed by a dealer service department.

Chapter 10
Suspension and steering systems

Contents

Specifications

Torque specifications

Front suspension

2WD models

	Ft-lbs
Upper control arm-to-frame nuts	
1990 and earlier	88
1991 and later	140
Lower control arm-to-frame nuts	
1990 and earlier	96
1991 and later	121
Balljoint-to-upper control arm bolts	
C15/C25	17
C35	
All except 1991	52
1991 and later	17
Lower balljoint-to-knuckle nut	90
Upper balljoint-to-knuckle nut	
1990 and earlier	90
1991	70
1992	84
1993 and later	74

Torque specifications

Front suspension

Ft-lbs

4WD models

Upper control arm-to-frame nut
- 1990 and earlier 88
- 1991 and later 140

Lower control arm-to-frame nuts
- 1992 and earlier 96
- 1993 and later 121

Balljoint-to-control arm bolts
- K15/K25 17
- K35 52

Lower balljoint-to-knuckle nut
- 1991 and earlier 94
- 1992 and later 84

Upper balljoint-to-knuckle nut
- 1990 and earlier 94
- 1991 70
- 1992 84
- 1993 and later 94

Driveaxle nut-to-hub and bearing
- 1994 and earlier 173
- 1995 180
- 1996 and later 165

Hub and bearing assembly-to-steering knuckle
- 1991 and earlier 66
- 1992 and later 133

Rear suspension

Leaf spring-to-bracket nuts
- 1991 and earlier 81
- 1992 89
- 1993 through 1995 92
- 1996 and later 70

Leaf spring-to-shackle nuts
- 1995 and earlier 81
- 1996 and later 70

Shackle-to-bracket nuts
- 1995 and earlier 81
- 1996 and later 70

U-bolt nuts
- Models with 7.4 liter (big block) engine and/or dual rear wheels 109
- All others 81

Steering

Pitman arm-to-steering gear 184
Pitman arm-to-relay rod 40
Idler arm-to-relay rod 40
Idler arm-to-frame
- 1992 and earlier 78
- 1993 through 1995 59
- 1996 and later 73
Relay rod-to-tie-rod 40
Tie-rod-to-steering arm
- 1996 and earlier 40
- 1997 and later 46
Steering wheel nut 30
Steering damper-to-relay rod 46
Steering damper-to-frame bracket 30
Adjuster tube clamp nut 14
Steering column mounting nuts 22
Steering column shaft-to-intermediate shaft pinch bolt/nut 46
Steering gear-to-frame bolts
- Power steering
  - Through 1990 69
  - 1991 and later 100
- Manual steering 100
Flexible coupling clamp bolt 30

1.1 Steering and front suspension components (2WD model)

1	Stabilizer bar	6	Lower balljoint
2	Coil spring and shock absorber	7	Lower control arm
3	Steering gear	8	Lower shock mounting nuts and bolts
4	Upper control arm	9	Pitman arm
5	Steering knuckle	10	Relay rod

11	Inner tie-rod
12	Tie-rod adjuster tube
13	Outer tie-rod
14	Idler arm

1   General information

Refer to illustrations 1.1, 1.2 and 1.3

The steering linkage **(see illustration)** consists of a Pitman arm, idler arm, relay rod, two adjustable tie-rods and a steering damper (not on all models). When the steering wheel is turned, the gear rotates the Pitman arm which forces the relay rod to one side. The tie-rods, which are connected to the relay rod by ball studs, transfer steering force to the wheels. The tie-rods are adjustable and are used for toe-in adjustments. The relay rod is supported by the Pitman arm and idler arm. The idler arm pivots on a support attached to the frame rail. The steering damper is attached to the frame end relay arm.

The front suspension is fully independent. Each wheel is connected to the frame by a steering knuckle, upper and lower ball joints and upper and lower control arms. Coil springs and shock absorbers are used on 2WD models; 4WD models use shocks and torsion bars **(see illustration)**. The coil springs are mounted between the spring pockets on the frame and the lower control

1.2 Typical front suspension components (4WD models)

1	Stabilizer bar	4	Outer tie rod end
2	Lower control arm	5	Shock absorber
3	Front drive axle		

6	Upper control arm ball joint
7	Stabilizer bar link

1.3 Rear suspension components

1   *Shock absorbers*   2   *Leaf springs*   3   *U-bolt anchor plates*

arms. The shocks are attached to the lower control arms by bolts and nuts; the upper end of each shock is attached to a bracket on the frame.

The rear suspension **(see illustration)** consists of a pair of multi-leaf springs and two shock absorbers. The rear axle assembly is attached to the leaf springs by U-bolts. The front ends of the springs are attached to the frame at the front hangers, through rubber bushings. The rear ends of the springs are attached to the frame by shackles which allow the springs to alter their length when the vehicle is in operation.

Frequently, when working on the suspension or steering system components, you may come across fasteners which seem impossible to loosen. These fasteners on the underside of the vehicle are continually subjected to water, road grime, mud, etc., and can become rusted or "frozen," making them extremely difficult to remove. In order to unscrew these stubborn fasteners without damaging them (or other components), be sure to use lots of penetrating oil and allow it to soak in for a while. Using a wire brush to clean exposed threads will also ease removal of the nut or bolt and prevent damage to the threads. Sometimes a sharp blow with a hammer and punch is effective in breaking the bond between a nut and bolt threads, but care must be taken to prevent the punch from slipping off the fastener and ruining the

threads. Heating the stuck fastener and surrounding area with a torch sometimes helps too, but isn't recommended because of the obvious dangers associated with fire. Long breaker bars and extension, or "cheater," pipes will increase leverage, but never use an extension pipe on a ratchet - the ratcheting mechanism could be damaged. Sometimes, turning the nut or bolt in the tightening (clockwise) direction first will help to break it loose. Fasteners that require drastic measures to unscrew should always be replaced with new ones.

Since most of the procedures that are dealt with in this Chapter involve jacking up the vehicle and working underneath it, a good pair of jackstands will be needed. A hydraulic floor jack is the preferred type of jack to lift the vehicle, and it can also be used to support certain components during various operations. **Warning:** *Never, under any circumstances, rely on a jack to support the vehicle while working on it. Also, whenever any of the suspension or steering fasteners are loosened or removed they must be inspected and, if necessary, replaced with new ones of the same part number or of original equipment quality and design. Torque specifications must be followed for proper reassembly and component retention. Never attempt to heat or straighten any suspension or steering components. Instead, replace bent or damaged parts with new ones.*

2   Shock absorber (front) - removal and installation

2WD models

Refer to illustrations 2.1 and 2.4

1   Using a backup wrench on the stem, remove the upper shock mounting nut **(see illustration)**.

2   Remove the retainer and grommet.

3   Raise the vehicle and support it securely

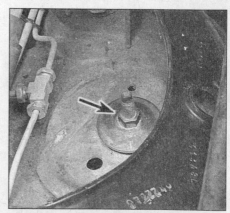

2.1 The shock absorber upper mounting nut (arrow) is located on the frame, right between the two control arm pivot bolts (2WD models)

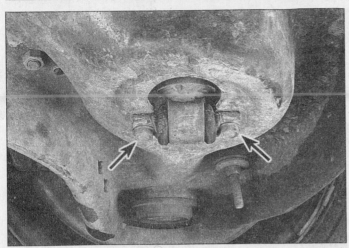

2.4 The lower mounting bolts (arrows) are located on the under side of the control arm (2WD models)

2.8 Remove the shock absorber mounting nuts and bolts (arrows) and remove the shock absorber (4WD shown)

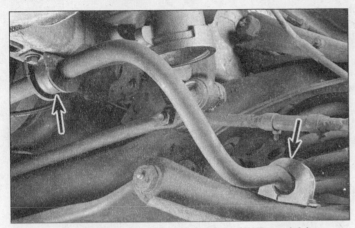

3.2a Stabilizer bar mounting details (2WD models)

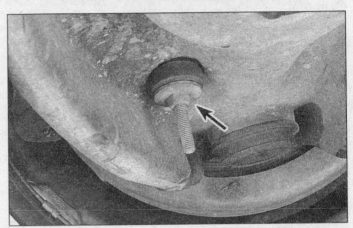

3.2b The nut for the stabilizer bar link bolt (arrow) is located on the under side of the control arm (2WD models)

on jackstands.

4   Working from underneath the vehicle, remove the two bolts which attach the lower end of the shock absorber to the lower control arm (see illustration) and pull the shock out from below.

5   Remove the lower grommet and retainer from the stem.

6   Installation is the reverse of removal. Be sure to tighten the upper mounting nut and the lower mounting bolts securely.

4WD models

Refer to illustration 2.8

7   Raise the vehicle and support it securely on jackstands.

8   Remove the shock lower mounting nut, washer and bolt (see illustration). Note the direction in which the bolt points.

9   Collapse the shock absorber.

10   Remove the upper shock mounting nut, washer and bolt. Again, note the direction in which the bolt points.

11   Remove the shock absorber.

12   Installation is the reverse of removal. Be sure to install the bolts so that they're pointing in the same direction as they were prior to removal. Tighten all fasteners securely.

3   Stabilizer bar - removal and installation

Refer to illustrations 3.2a, 3.2b, 3.2c and 3.3

1   Raise the vehicle and support it securely on jackstands.

2   Remove the nuts from the link bolts and remove the link bolts (see illustrations). **Note:** *Be sure to keep the parts for the left and right sides separate.*

3   Remove the stabilizer bar bracket bolts (see illustration).

4   Remove the stabilizer bar.

5   Remove the rubber bushings.

6   Inspect all parts for wear and damage.

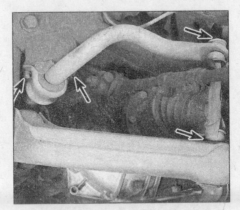

3.2c Remove the stabilizer bar link mounting nut and bolt (arrows) (4WD shown)

3.3 Remove the stabilizer bar bracket bolts (arrows) (2WD models)

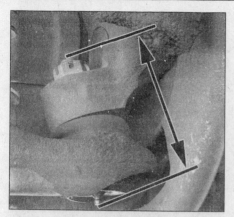

4.4a To determine balljoint wear on models with grease fittings, measure between the points shown

4.4b On models without grease fittings, measure between the points shown to check for balljoint wear

4.11 A special tool is required to push the balljoints out of the steering knuckle (an alternative tool, shown here, can be fabricated from a large bolt, nut, washer and socket)

7   When you install the rubber bushings on the stabilizer bar, be sure to position them so the slits face toward the front of the vehicle.

8   Installation is otherwise the reverse of removal. Be sure to tighten all fasteners securely.

---

4 Balljoints - check and replacement

Check

Upper balljoint

1   Loosen the wheel lug nuts, raise the front of the vehicle and support it securely on jackstands. Apply the parking brake. Remove the wheel.

2   Place a floor jack under the lower control arm and raise it slightly. Using a large screwdriver or pry bar, pry up on the upper control arm and watch for movement at the balljoint. Any movement indicates a worn balljoint. Now grasp the steering knuckle and attempt to move the top of it in-and-out - if any play is felt, the balljoint will have to be replaced.

Lower balljoint

Refer to illustrations 4.4a and 4.4b

3   Raise the vehicle, support it securely on

jackstands and remove the wheels.

4   Support the weight of the suspension with a jack. Measure the distance between the tip of the balljoint stud and the tip of the grease fitting below the balljoint (A) (if equipped with a grease fitting) or between the lower surface of the control arm and the top of the balljoint (B) **(see illustrations)**.

5   Lower the jack to allow the suspension to hang free and repeat the measurement.

6   If the difference between the two measurements exceeds 3/32-inch, the balljoint is worn and must be replaced with a new one.

Replacement

7   Raise the vehicle, support it securely on jackstands and remove the front wheel.

2WD models (upper balljoint)

Refer to illustrations 4.11, 4.12a, 4.12b and 4.12c

8   Remove the brake caliper and hang it out of the way (Chapter 9).

9   Remove the cotter key from the balljoint and back off the nut two turns.

10   Place a jack or jackstand under the lower control arm. **Note:** *The jack or jackstand must remain under the control arm during removal and installation of the balljoint to hold the spring and control arm in position.*

11   Separate the balljoint from the steering knuckle using a balljoint separator to press the balljoint out of the steering knuckle **(see illustration). Note:** *The use of a "picklefork" type balljoint separator may tear the balljoint boot.*

12   To remove the upper balljoint from the control arm, drill out the rivets **(see illustrations)**, remove the balljoint and clean the control arm. Install the new upper balljoint against the mating surface of the control arm and secure it with the supplied nuts and bolts **(see illustration)**.

2WD models (lower balljoint)

13   Remove the control arm (see Section 8) and take it to an automotive machine shop to have the balljoint pressed out and a new one pressed in.

2WD models (upper or lower balljoint)

14   Inspect the tapered holes in the steering knuckle, removing any accumulated dirt. If out-of-roundness, deformation or other damage is noted, the knuckle must be replaced with a new one (see Section 5).

15   Reconnect the balljoints to the steering

4.12a Drill completely through the upper balljoint rivets with a drill bit

4.12b Tap the rivets out with a punch

4.12c You don't need to rivet the new upper balljoint - install it with the nuts and bolts included in the kit

knuckle and tighten the nuts to the specified torque.

16   If the cotter key does not line up with the opening in the castellated nut, tighten (never loosen) the nut just enough to allow installation of the cotter pin.

17   Install the grease fittings and lubricate the new balljoints (Chapter 1).

18   Install the wheels and lower the vehicle.

19   The front end alignment should be checked by a dealer or alignment shop.

4WD models

20   The procedure for replacing an upper balljoint on a 4WD model is similar to that described above for 2WD models. The procedure for replacing a lower balljoint follows.

21   Raise the vehicle and support it securely on jackstands.

22   Remove the wheel.

23   Remove the front splash shield bolts. Pivot the shield out of the way to gain access to the tie-rod end.

24   Disconnect the tie-rod from the relay rod (see Sections 15 and 17).

25   Remove the driveaxle (see Chapter 8).

26   Center punch the bottom of each rivet.

27   Using a 1/8-inch drill bit, drill a guide hole 1/2-inch deep into the rivet heads.

28   Using a 5/16-inch drill bit, drill the rivet heads off. Drill a hole two-thirds the length of the rivet shank, using the same drill.

29   Knock the rivets out with a hammer and punch.

30   Remove the balljoint stud cotter pin.

31   Support the lower control arm with floor jack.

32   Loosen the balljoint nut a couple of turns.

33   Back off the torsion bar adjusting arm bolt to reduce the tension on the bar. Don't remove the bolt completely (see Section 8).

34   Separate the knuckle from the balljoint with a two-jaw puller or a "picklefork".

35   Remove the nut and separate the balljoint from the lower control arm.

36   Install the new balljoint to the control arm. Install the nuts and bolts and tighten

them to the specified torque.

37   Raise the lower control arm with a floor jack and insert the balljoint stud into the steering knuckle. Lower the jack until the balljoint stud seats in the hole, then install the nut and tighten it to the specified torque. Install a new cotter pin and bend the ends of the pin against the nut.

38   Load the torsion bar (see Section 11).

39   Install the driveaxle assembly (see Chapter 8).

40   Connect the inner tie-rod end to the relay rod, install the tie-rod end nut and tighten it to the specified torque.

41   Install the front splash shield and tighten the splash shield bolts securely.

42   Install the wheel and lug nuts.

43   Lower the vehicle.

44   Tighten the wheel lug nuts to the torque specified in the Chapter 1 Specifications.

5   Steering knuckle (2WD models) - removal and installation

1   Raise the front of the vehicle and support it securely on jackstands. Apply the parking brake.

2   Support the lower control arm with a jack so the coil spring is compressed to its normal ride height. **Warning:** *The jack must remain in this position throughout the entire procedure.*

3   Remove the wheel.

4   Remove the brake caliper (see Chapter 9) and the brake disc/hub assembly (see Chapter 1, Front wheel bearing check, repack and adjustment).

5   Remove the disc splash shield, if equipped.

6   Disconnect the tie-rod end from the knuckle (see Section 15).

7   Disconnect the balljoints from the steering knuckle (see Section 4).

8   Remove the steering knuckle.

9   Installation is the reverse of removal. Adjust the front wheel bearings (see Chap-

ter 1) and have the front wheel alignment checked by a dealer service department or alignment shop.

6   Coil spring (2WD models) - removal and installation

Removal

Refer to illustrations 6.5 and 6.7

1   Loosen the front wheel lug nuts, raise the vehicle and place it securely on jackstands. Remove the wheel.

2   Remove the shock absorber (see Section 2).

3   Remove the stabilizer bar link bolt (see Section 3).

4   Disconnect the outer tie-rod end from the steering knuckle (see Section 15).

5   Install a suitable internal type spring compressor in accordance with the tool manufacturer's instructions **(see illustration)**. Compress the spring enough to relieve all pressure from the spring seats (but don't compress it any more than necessary, or it could be ruined). When you can wiggle the spring, it's compressed enough. (You can buy a suitable spring compressor at most auto parts stores or rent one from a tool rental yard.)

6   Support the lower control arm with a floor jack.

7   Remove the control arm pivot bolts and nuts **(see illustration)**.

8   Pull the lower control arm down and to the rear, then guide the compressed coil spring out.

9   If the coil spring is being replaced, carefully unscrew the spring compressor.

Installation

10   Inspect the upper and lower spring insulators. If either insulator is cracked or excessively worn, replace it. Inspect the coil spring for chips in the corrosion protection coating. If the coating has been chipped or damaged,

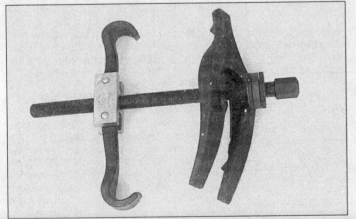

6.5 A typical aftermarket internal type spring compressor: The hooked arms grip the upper coils of the spring, the plate is inserted between the lower coils, and when the nut on the threaded rod is turned, the spring is compressed

6.7 With the spring safely compressed, support the lower control arm with a floor jack, then remove the pivot bolts and nuts (arrow indicates front pivot bolt)

replace the spring.

11   If the coil spring is being replaced, install the spring compressor and compress the spring.

12   With the lower spring insulator in place, position the spring on the lower control arm with the flat end of the spring facing up and the tapered end facing down. Make sure the tapered end seats on the lower control arm with the lower end of the spring seated in the lowest part of the spring seat. The end of the spring must cover all or part of one of the drain holes in the lower control arm, but the other hole must not be covered.

13   Put the floor jack under the lower control arm and raise the arm into position in the frame. Install the control arm pivot bolts and nuts. Tighten the nuts until they're snug but don't torque them yet.

14   Remove the spring compressor.

15   Reattach the outer tie-rod end to the steering knuckle (see Section 15).

16   Reattach the stabilizer bar link to the lower control arm (see Section 3).

17   Install the shock absorber (see Section 2).

18   Position the floor jack under the lower control arm balljoint and raise the arm to simulate normal ride height. Tighten the lower control arm pivot bolt nuts to the torque listed in this Chapter's Specifications.

19   Install the wheel, remove the jackstands and lower the vehicle. Tighten the wheel lug nuts to the torque listed in the Chapter 1 Specifications.

---

7   Upper control arm - removal and installation

Refer to illustration 7.6

Note: *This procedure applies to both 2WD and 4WD models.*

Removal

1   Loosen the wheel lug nuts, raise the front of the vehicle and support it securely on jackstands. Apply the parking brake. Remove the wheel.

2   Position a floor jack, with a wood block on the jack head (to act as a cushion), under the lower control arm in the area between the spring seat and the balljoint. Raise the jack slightly to take the spring pressure off the upper control arm. **Warning:** *The jack must remain in this position throughout the entire procedure.*

3   Remove the air cleaner extension, if necessary.

4   Disconnect the brake hose bracket from the upper control arm.

5   Disconnect the upper balljoint from the steering knuckle (Section 4).

6   If the vehicle has been retrofitted with an alignment kit, mark the positions of the adjuster cams to the frame so they can be returned to their original settings on installation. Remove the upper control arm pivot bolts and nuts **(see illustration)**. Remove the control arm.

7   Inspect the pivot bolt bushings for wear.

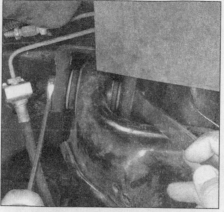

7.6   Remove the upper control arm pivot bolts - make sure the pivot bolts are installed with the heads facing each other

Replace them if necessary. **Note:** *The bushings on some models are welded in place and can't be removed. If they're worn, you'll have to replace the control arm. On other models, a hydraulic press may be required to accomplish removal and installation of the bushings, in which case you'll have to take the control arm to a dealer service department or other repair shop to have this done for you.*

Installation

8   Position the arm in the frame brackets and install the bolts and nuts. They must be installed with their heads towards the inside, facing each other, as shown in **illustration 7.6**. Don't tighten the nuts completely at this time. If an alignment kit has been installed, line up the previously applied matchmarks.

9   Attach the balljoint to the steering knuckle (see Section 4).

10   Connect the brake hose bracket to the upper control arm.

11   Install the wheel and lug nuts, then lower the vehicle. Tighten the lug nuts to the torque listed in the Chapter 1 Specifications.

12   Tighten the pivot bolt nuts to the torque listed in this Chapter's Specifications.

13   Install the air cleaner extension, if it was removed.

---

8   Lower control arm - removal and installation

2WD models

Removal

1   Loosen the wheel lug nuts, raise the vehicle and support it securely on jackstands. Remove the wheel.

2   Remove the coil spring (see Section 6).

3   Disconnect the lower balljoint (see Section 4).

4   Take the control arm to a dealer or properly equipped shop to have the balljoint and bushings replaced, if necessary.

Installation

5   Installation is the reverse of removal.

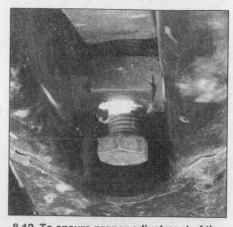

8.12   To ensure proper adjustment of the torsion bar upon reassembly, count the number of threads showing on the torsion bar adjuster bolt and mark the relationship of the bolt to the torsion bar adjuster nut as insurance

Make sure the pivot bolts are installed from the front **(see illustration 6.6)**, and don't tighten them until the vehicle is at normal ride height. Tighten all nuts to their specified torque, and if a new balljoint has been installed, lubricate it on completion.

4WD models

Refer to illustrations 8.12, 8.17 and 8.18

Removal

6   Loosen the wheel lug nuts, raise the vehicle and support it securely on jackstands. Remove the wheel.

7   Remove the front splash shield for access to the front end components.

8   Disconnect the stabilizer bar from the lower control arm (Section 3).

9   Remove the shock absorber (see Section 2).

10   Disconnect the inner tie-rod end from the relay rod (see Section 15).

11   Remove the driveaxle (see Chapter 8).

12   Follow the torsion bar back to the crossmember. Count the number of threads showing on the torsion bar adjuster bolt, and also mark the bolt to the torsion bar adjuster nut.

13   Loosen the torsion bar adjusting bolt as much as possible, without removing the bolt completely. This will reduce the tension on the bar.

14   Support the lower control arm with a floor jack. The jack head should be positioned as near to the balljoint as possible, and still allow access to the balljoint stud nut.

15   Disconnect the steering knuckle from the lower balljoint (see Section 4). Lift the knuckle and hub assembly up, then place a block of wood between the upper control arm and the frame to support the assembly out of the way.

16   Mark the relationship of the torsion bar-to-lower control arm, then SLOWLY lower the jack until the pressure from the torsion bar is completely released.

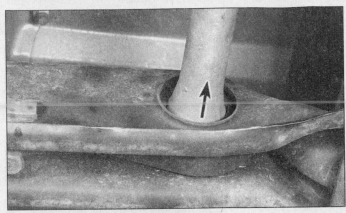

8.17 Slide the torsion bar forward (arrow)

8.18 Remove the lower control arm pivot bolts (arrow)

17 Slide the torsion bar forward, out of the adjuster arm **(see illustration)**.
18 Remove the lower control arm pivot bolts, nuts and washers **(see illustration)**. Remove the lower control arm and torsion bar as a unit.
19 Mark the front of the torsion bar with a piece of tape to insure correct installation, then separate the bar from the arm.
20 Check the bushings for damage or wear. Some models have welded-in bushings that can't be replaced. If this is the case, replace the control arm. Other models have replaceable bushings, but a press and special adapters are required to remove and install them. Take the control arm to dealer service department or other repair shop to have the bushings replaced for you.

Installation

21 Insert the torsion bar into its hole in the lower control arm. Raise the arm and bar up into position, inserting the rear end of the bar into the hole in the crossmember (it may be necessary to slide the bar forward in the control arm a little bit). Position the lower control arm in the frame brackets, inserting the front portion first.
22 Install the control arm pivot bolts. They must be inserted from front-to-rear **(see illustration 8.18)**. Install the washers and nuts, but don't tighten them completely at this time.
23 Slide the torsion bar back into the adjusting arm.
24 Carefully raise the lower control arm with the floor jack until the balljoint stud can be inserted into the hole in the steering knuckle. Install the balljoint stud nut, tighten it to the torque listed in this Chapter's Specifications, then install a new cotter pin.
25 Tighten the torsion bar adjusting nut until the distance between the crossmember and the end of the adjusting arm is the same as it was before removal.
26 Install the driveaxle.
27 Connect the inner tie-rod to the relay rod.
28 Install the shock absorber.
29 Connect the stabilizer bar to the lower control arm.
30 Install the wheel and lug nuts. Lower the

vehicle and tighten the lug nuts to the torque listed in the Chapter 1 Specifications.
31 Tighten the lower control arm pivot bolts to the torque listed in this Chapter's Specifications.
32 Install the splash shield.
33 Measure the vehicle's ride height on each side, from equal points on the frame to the ground. If the side that has been worked on is higher or lower than the other side, turn the torsion bar adjusting screw accordingly until the vehicle sits level. This may take a few tries, and it's important to roll the vehicle back and forth and jounce the front end between adjustments, to settle the suspension and get an accurate reading.

9 Steering knuckle (4WD models) - removal and installation

Removal

1 Remove the hub cover and loosen the driveaxle/hub nut about 1/4-turn.
2 Loosen the wheel lug nuts, raise the front of the vehicle and support it securely on jackstands. Apply the parking brake. Remove the wheel.
3 Disconnect the tie-rod end from the steering knuckle (see Section 15). Unbolt the brake caliper and hang it out of the way with a piece of wire (see Chapter 9). Remove the brake disc.
4 Remove the driveaxle/hub nut.
5 Support the lower control arm with a floor jack and detach the steering knuckle from the lower balljoint (see Section 4). **Warning:** *The jack must remain in this position throughout the entire procedure.*
6 Support the steering knuckle and separate it from the upper balljoint (see Section 4).
7 Using a puller, push the driveaxle out of the hub while withdrawing the steering knuckle and hub assembly.
8 If it's necessary to remove the hub, remove the three bolts and separate it from the knuckle.
9 Inspect the seal on the rear side of the knuckle. If it's damaged or shows signs of deterioration, pry it out with a large screw-

driver or pry bar. Install a new seal by driving it in with a socket that has an outside diameter slightly smaller than the seal.

Installation

10 Installation is the reverse of the removal procedure. Be sure to lubricate the driveaxle splines with multi-purpose grease, and tighten all of the fasteners to the specified torque.

10 Hub and bearing assembly (4WD models) - replacement

Refer to illustration 10.5
Note: *The hub and bearing assembly is a sealed unit and isn't serviceable. If it's defective, it must be replaced.*
1 Remove the hub cover and loosen the driveaxle/hub nut about a quarter of a turn.
2 Loosen the wheel lug nuts, raise the vehicle and support it securely on jackstands. Remove the wheel.
3 Unbolt the brake caliper and hang it out of the way with a piece of wire (see Chapter 9). Remove the brake disc.
4 Remove the driveaxle/hub nut.
5 Remove the hub assembly-to-steering knuckle bolts **(see illustrations)**. **Note:** *Some models have three bolts, others have four.*

10.5a To detach the hub and bearing assembly from the steering knuckle, remove these bolts (arrows) . . .

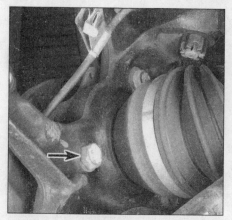

10.5b . . . and this bolt (arrow) (upper bolt is the same upper bolt shown in the previous photo)

12.2 To replace a rear shock absorber, remove the nuts and bolts (arrows) from the frame bracket . . .

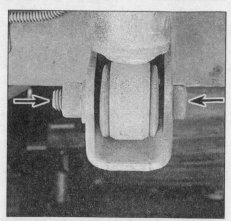

12.3 . . . then remove the nut, bolt and washer (arrow) from the axle bracket

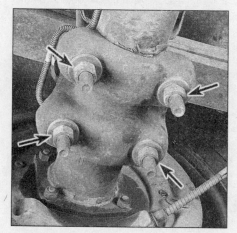

13.2 Remove the U-bolt nuts (arrows)

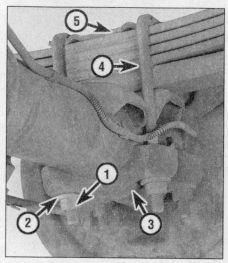

13.4 Leaf spring installation detail

1   *Nut*
2   *Washer*
3   *Anchor plate*
4   *U-bolt*
5   *Spacer*

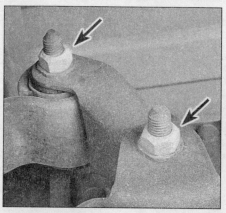

13.5 Loosen the shackle-to-spring nut (upper arrow), then remove the shackle-to-rear bracket nut, bolt and washers (lower arrow)

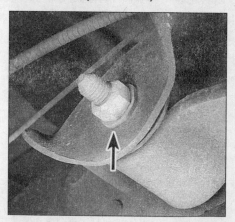

13.7 Remove the nut, bolt and washer (arrow) from the front bracket

Tap the hub assembly from side-to-side to break it loose from the steering knuckle. Using a puller, pull the hub assembly off the end of the driveaxle. Wrap the end of the driveaxle with a rag to prevent damaging it.
6   Installation is the reverse of the removal procedure. Be sure to lubricate the driveaxle splines with multi-purpose grease, and tighten all of the fasteners to the specified torque.

11   Torsion bar (4WD models) - removal and installation

Refer to Section 8 - torsion bar removal and installation is part of the lower control arm removal and installation procedure.

12   Shock absorber (rear) - removal and installation

Refer to illustrations 12.2 and 12.3
1   Raise the rear of the vehicle and support securely on jackstands. Block the front wheels so the vehicle doesn't roll off the stands.

2   Remove the shock absorber upper mounting nuts and bolts from the frame bracket **(see illustration)**.
3   Remove the lower mounting nut, washer and bolt from the axle bracket **(see illustration)**.
4   Remove the shock absorber.
5   Installation is the reverse of removal. Make sure you install the nuts and bolts facing in the proper direction.

13   Leaf spring/shackle - removal and installation

Refer to illustrations 13.2, 13.4, 13.5, 13.7 and 13.9
1   Raise the rear of the vehicle and support it securely on jackstands. Block the front wheels to keep the vehicle from rolling off the stands. Support the axle with a floor jack and

raise it slightly to relieve the tension on the leaf springs.
2   Remove the U-bolt nuts and washers **(see illustration)**.
3   Remove the anchor plate.
4   Remove the U-bolts and spacer **(see illustration)**.
5   Loosen the shackle-to-spring nut **(see illustration)**.

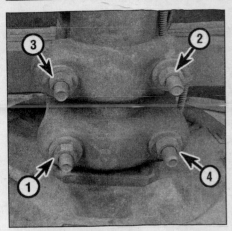

13.9 Be sure to follow the recommended tightening sequence when reassembling the U-bolts

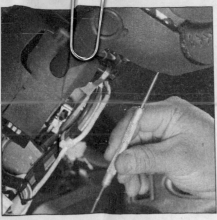

14.4a To detach the airbag module from the steering wheel on 1995 models, rotate the wheel 90-degrees, insert a hard and thin object - such as a scribe - and push in firmly against each of the four ball-lock fasteners to unlock the airbag module from the wheel

14.4b Unplug the yellow electrical connector from the back of the airbag module; the arrows point at the four ball-lock type fasteners used on 1995 models

6   Remove the shackle-to-rear bracket nut, washers and bolt.

7   Remove the spring-to-front bracket nut, washers and bolt **(see illustration)**.

8   Remove the spring assembly from the vehicle.

9   Installation is the reverse of removal. Tighten the U-bolt nuts in a diagonal sequence **(see illustration)**. Tighten all the fasteners to the torque listed in this Chapter's Specifications.

14 Steering wheel - removal and installation

Refer to illustrations 14.4a, 14.4b, 14.5, 14.7 and 14.8

Warning: *Anytime you are working in the vicinity of airbag wiring or components, disable the SIR (airbag) system (see Chapter 12).*

1   Disconnect both cables from the battery (see Chapter 5). **Caution:** *On models equipped with a Delco Loc II anti-theft audio system, be sure the lockout feature is turned off before performing any procedure which requires disconnecting the battery.*

2   On 1994 and earlier models, simply pry off the horn cap.

3   On airbag-equipped models, refer to Chapter 12 and disable the airbag system.

4   On 1995 models, turn the steering wheel 90-degrees to gain access to the holes in the backside (the side facing the dash) of the steering wheel. Insert a thin hard tool such as a ball-point pen or a scribe into the hole for each of the four spring-loaded fasteners **(see illustrations)**. Push in firmly against the head of each fastener with the tool and pull on the airbag module simultaneously with the other hand.

5   On 1996 and later models, turn the steering wheel 90-degrees to gain access to the holes in the backside (the side facing the dash) of the steering wheel. Insert a screwdriver into the hole for each of the four spring clips **(see illustration)** and push the spring aside to release the pin. There are four pins

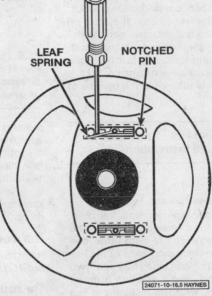

14.5 To detach the airbag module from the steering wheel on 1996 models, rotate the wheel 90-degrees, insert a screwdriver into each of the four holes in the backside of the steering wheel and pry each leaf spring aside to release it from its notched pin (there are four of them)

and four springs.

6   On airbag-equipped models, unplug the yellow electrical connector from the module and set the module aside, with the airbag side of the module facing UP. **Warning:** *Carry the airbag module with the trim side facing away from your body, and set it aside in an isolated area with the trim side facing up.*

7   Remove the steering wheel retaining nut and mark the position of the steering wheel to the shaft, if marks don't already exist or don't line up **(see illustration)**.

14.7 Mark the relationship of the steering wheel to the steering shaft before removing the wheel

14.8 Remove the steering wheel with a steering wheel puller - do not hammer on the steering shaft

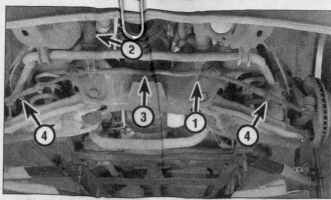

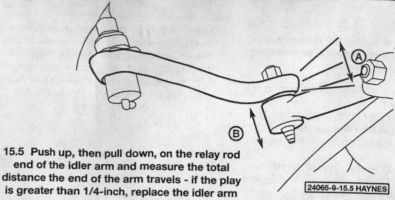

15.1 Steering linkage components (2WD model shown, 4WD similar)

1. *Pitman arm*
2. *Idler arm*
3. *Relay rod*
4. *Adjustable tie-rod*

15.5 Push up, then pull down, on the relay rod end of the idler arm and measure the total distance the end of the arm travels - if the play is greater than 1/4-inch, replace the idler arm

24065-9-15.5 HAYNES

8   Use a puller to detach the steering wheel from the shaft **(see illustration)**. Don't hammer on the shaft to dislodge the wheel.

9   To install the wheel, align the mark on the steering wheel hub with the mark on the shaft and slide the wheel onto the shaft. Install the nut and tighten it to the torque listed in this Chapter's Specifications.

10   Installation is otherwise the reverse of removal.

15   Steering linkage - inspection, removal and installation

Inspection

Refer to illustrations 15.1 and 15.5

1   The steering linkage connects the steering gear to the front wheels and keeps the wheels in proper relation to each other **(see illustration)**. The linkage consists of the Pitman arm, the idler arm, the relay rod, two adjustable tie-rods and a steering damper. The Pitman arm, which is fastened to the steering gear shaft, moves the relay rod back-and-forth. The relay rod is supported on the other end by a frame-mounted idler arm. The back-and-forth motion of the relay rod is transmitted to the steering knuckles through a pair of tie-rod assemblies. Each tie-rod is made up of an inner and outer tie-rod end, a threaded adjuster tube and two clamps.

2   Set the wheels in the straight ahead position and lock the steering wheel.

3   Raise one side of the vehicle until the tire is approximately 1-inch off the ground.

4   Mount a dial indicator with the needle resting on the outside edge of the wheel. Grasp the front and rear of the tire and using light pressure, wiggle the wheel back-and-forth and note the dial indicator reading. The gauge reading should be less than 0.108-inch. If the play in the steering system is more than specified, inspect each steering linkage pivot point and ball stud for looseness and replace parts if necessary.

5   Raise the vehicle and support it on jackstands. Push up, then pull down on the relay

rod end of the idler arm, exerting a force of approximately 25 pounds each way. Measure the total distance the end of the arm travels **(see illustration)**. If the play is greater than 1/4-inch, replace the idler arm.

6   Check for torn ball stud boots, frozen joints and bent or damaged linkage components.

Removal and installation

Refer to illustrations 15.8, 15.9, 15.11, 15.13 and 15.15

Tie-rod

7   Loosen the wheel lug nuts, raise the vehicle and support it securely on jackstands.

15.8 Remove the cotter pin and loosen - but don't remove - the castellated nut on the ball stud

Apply the parking brake. Remove the wheel.

8   Remove the cotter pin and loosen, but do not remove, the castellated nut from the ball stud **(see illustration)**.

9   Using a two jaw puller, separate the tie-rod end from the steering knuckle **(see illustration)**. Remove the castellated nut and pull the tie-rod end from the knuckle.

10   Remove the nut securing the inner tie-rod end to the relay rod. Separate the inner tie-rod end from the relay rod (see Step 9).

11   If the inner or outer tie-rod end must be replaced, measure the distance from the end of the adjuster tube to the center of the ball stud and record it **(see illustration)**. Loosen the adjuster tube clamp and unscrew the tie-

15.9 Use a two-jaw puller to separate the tie-rod end from the steering knuckle, then remove the castellated nut and pull the tie-rod end out of the knuckle

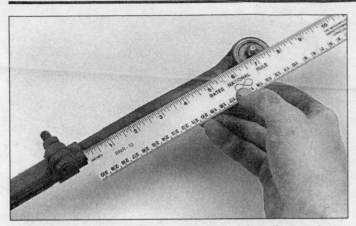

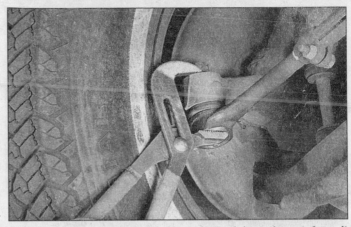

15.11 Measure the distance from the end of the adjuster tube to the center of the ball stud and record the measurement before loosening the adjuster tube clamp and unscrewing the tie-rod end

15.13 If the ball stud spins when you try to tighten the nut, force it into the tapered hole with a large pair of pliers

15.15 Note these guidelines when installing the tie-rod ends

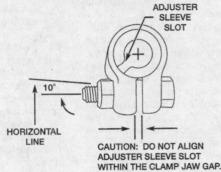

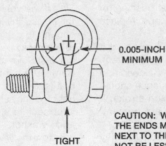

ADJUSTER SLEEVE SLOT

10°

HORIZONTAL LINE

CAUTION: DO NOT ALIGN ADJUSTER SLEEVE SLOT WITHIN THE CLAMP JAW GAP.

0.005-INCH MINIMUM

TIGHT

CAUTION: WHEN THE CLAMP IS TIGHT, THE ENDS MAY TOUCH BUT THE GAP NEXT TO THE ADJUSTER SLEEVE MUST NOT BE LESS THAN 0.005-INCH.

24065-9-15.15 HAYNES

rod end.

12   Lubricate the threaded portion of the tie-rod end with chassis grease. Screw the new tie-rod end into the adjuster tube and adjust the distance from the tube to the ball stud to the previously measured dimension. The number of threads showing on the inner and outer tie-rod ends should be equal within three threads. Don't tighten the clamp yet.

13   To install the tie-rod, connect the outer tie-rod end to the steering knuckle and install the castellated nut. Tighten the nut to the specified torque and install a new cotter pin. If the ball stud spins when attempting to tighten the nut, force it into the tapered hole with a large pair of pliers **(see illustration)**. If necessary, tighten the nut slightly to align a slot in the nut with the hole in the ball stud.

14   Insert the inner tie-rod end ball stud into the relay rod until it's seated. Install the nut and tighten it to the specified torque.

15   Tighten the clamp nuts. The center of the bolt should be nearly horizontal and the adjuster tube slot must not line up with the gap in the clamps **(see illustrations)**.

16   Install the wheel and lug nuts, lower the vehicle and tighten the lug nuts to the torque listed in the Chapter 1 Specifications. Drive the vehicle to an alignment shop to have the front end alignment checked and, if necessary, adjusted.

Idler arm

17   Raise the vehicle and support it securely

on jackstands. Apply the parking brake.

18   Loosen but do not remove the idler arm-to-relay rod nut.

19   Separate the idler arm from the relay rod with a two jaw puller **(see illustration 15.9)**. Remove the nut.

20   Remove the idler arm-to-frame bolts **(see illustration 15.1)**.

21   To install the idler arm, position it on the frame and install the bolts, tightening them to the specified torque.

22   Insert the idler arm ball stud into the relay rod and install the nut. Tighten the nut to the specified torque. If the ball stud spins when attempting to tighten the nut, force it into the tapered hole with a large pair of pliers **(see illustration 15.13)**.

Relay rod

23   Raise the vehicle and support it securely on jackstands. Apply the parking brake.

24   Separate the two inner tie-rod ends from the relay rod.

25   Separate the relay rod from the Pitman arm.

26   Separate the relay rod from the idler arm.

27   Installation is the reverse of the removal procedure. If the ball studs spin when attempting to tighten the nuts, force them into the tapered holes with a large pair of pliers **(see illustration 15.13)**. Be sure to tighten all of the nuts to the specified torque.

Pitman arm

28   Raise the vehicle and support it securely on jackstands.

29   Remove the relay rod nut from the Pitman arm ball stud. Discard the nut - don't reuse it.

30   Using a puller, separate the relay rod from the Pitman arm ball stud.

31   Mark the Pitman arm and the steering gear shaft to ensure proper alignment at reassembly time.

32   Remove the Pitman arm nut and washer.

33   Remove the Pitman arm with a Pitman arm puller or a two-jaw puller.

34   Inspect the ball stud threads for damage. Inspect the ball stud seals for excessive wear. Clean the threads on the ball stud.

35   Installation is the reverse of removal. Make sure the marks you made on the Pitman arm and Pitman shaft are aligned. **Note:** *If a clamp type Pitman arm is used, spread the arm just enough, with a wedge, to slip the arm onto the Pitman shaft. Don't spread the arm more than necessary to slip it over the shaft with hand pressure. Do not hammer the arm onto the shaft or you may damage the steering gear.*

Steering damper

Refer to illustration 15.39

36   Inspect the steering damper for fluid leakage. A slight film of fluid near the shaft

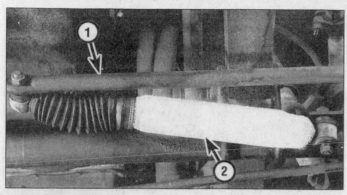

15.39 Steering damper assembly mounting details (4WD models)

1   Steering relay rod   2   Steering damper

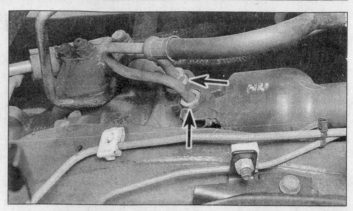

16.2 If the vehicle has power steering, disconnect the power steering hose fittings (arrows)

seal is normal, but if there's excessive fluid present and it's obviously coming from the steering damper, replace the damper.

37   Inspect the steering damper bushing for excessive wear. If it's in bad shape, replace the damper.

38   To test the damper itself, disconnect it from the frame or axle end (see next step). Using as much travel as possible, extend and compress the damper. The resistance should be smooth and constant for each stroke. If any binding or unusual noises are present, replace the damper.

39   Remove the damper ballstud-to-relay rod cotter pin, then remove the nut **(see illustration)**. Separate the damper from the relay rod.

40   Remove the steering damper mounting bolt and nut, then remove the damper.

41   Installation is the reverse of removal. Tighten all the fasteners securely.

16   Steering gear - removal and installation

Refer to illustrations 16.2 and 16.3

Warning 1: *If equipped with an airbag, disable the airbag system before working in the vicinity of the steering wheel, instrument panel or any airbag system component. Failure to do so could cause accidental deployment of the airbag resulting in personal injury (see Chapter 12).*

Warning 2: *On models equipped with an airbag, DO NOT allow the steering column shaft to rotate with the steering gear removed or damage to the airbag system could occur. As a method of preventing the shaft from turning, wrap the seat belt around the rim of the steering wheel and buckle the belt in place.*

Removal

1   Raise the front of the vehicle and support it securely on jackstands. Apply the parking brake.

2   Place a drain pan under the steering gear (power steering only).

Disconnect the hose fittings **(see illustration)** and cap the ends to prevent excessive fluid loss and contamination.

3   If the vehicle has power steering, slide the plastic shield up the intermediate shaft far enough to clear the universal joint. Mark the relationship of the intermediate shaft lower universal joint to the steering gear input shaft. Remove the intermediate shaft lower pinch bolt **(see illustration)**. If the vehicle has manual steering, slide the plastic shield up the intermediate shaft, remove the adapter nut and washer, remove the adapter and unscrew the flexible coupling pinch bolt.

4   Mark the relationship of the Pitman arm to the shaft so it can be installed in the same position. Remove the Pitman arm nut and washer.

5   Remove the Pitman arm from the shaft with a two-jaw puller.

6   Support the steering gear and remove the mounting bolts. Lower the unit, separate the intermediate shaft from the steering gear input shaft and remove the steering gear from the vehicle. **Warning:** *On models equipped with an airbag, DO NOT allow the steering column shaft to rotate with the steering gear removed or damage to the airbag system could occur. As a method of preventing the shaft from turning, wrap the seat belt around the rim of the steering wheel and buckle the belt in place.*

16.3 Remove the intermediate shaft-to-steering gear pinch bolt

Installation

7   Raise the steering gear into position and connect the intermediate shaft, aligning the marks.

8   Install the mounting bolts and washers and tighten them to the specified torque.

9   Slide the Pitman arm onto the shaft. Make sure the marks are aligned. Install the washer and nut and tighten the nut to the specified torque.

10   Install the lower intermediate shaft pinch bolt and tighten it to the specified torque. If the vehicle has manual steering, install the adapter, nut and washer. On all models, slide the plastic shield back down, over the universal joint/flexible coupling.

11   Connect the power steering hose fittings to the steering gear and fill the power steering pump reservoir with the recommended fluid (see Chapter 1).

12   Lower the vehicle and bleed the steering system (see Section 18).

17   Power steering pump - removal and installation

Refer to illustrations 17.3, 17.4, 17.5 and 17.8

Removal

1   Disconnect the cable from the negative

17.3 A special puller is required to remove the power steering pump pulley

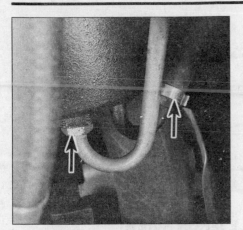

17.4 Disconnect the pressure and return hoses (arrows) from the power steering pump

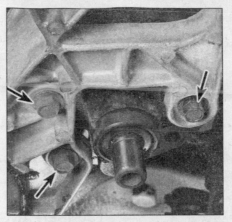

17.5 Remove the power steering pump mounting bolts (arrows)

17.8 A long bolt with the same thread pitch as the internal threads of the power steering pump shaft, a nut, washer and socket that's the same diameter as the pulley hub can be used to install the pulley on the shaft

terminal of the battery.

2   Remove the serpentine drivebelt (see Chapter 1).

3   Using a special power steering pump pulley remover, remove the pulley from the pump **(see illustration)**.

4   Position a drain pan under the power steering pump. Disconnect the pressure and return hoses from the backside of the pump **(see illustration)**. Plug the hoses to prevent contaminants from entering.

5   Remove the pump mounting fasteners **(see illustration)** and lift the pump from the vehicle, taking care not to spill fluid on the painted surfaces.

Installation

6   Position the pump in the mounting bracket and install the bolts and nut. Tighten the fasteners securely.

7   Connect the hoses to the pump. Tighten the fittings securely.

8   Press the pulley onto the shaft using a special pulley installer tool. An alternative tool can be fabricated from a long bolt, nut, washer and a socket of the same diameter as the pulley hub **(see illustration)**. Push the pulley onto the shaft until the front of the hub is flush with the shaft, but no further.

9   Install the drivebelt.

10   Fill the power steering reservoir with the recommended fluid (see Chapter 1) and bleed the system following the procedure described in the next Section.

18   Power steering system - bleeding

1   Following any operation in which the power steering fluid lines have
been disconnected, the power steering system must be bled to remove all air and obtain proper steering performance.

2   With the front wheels in the straight ahead position, check the power steering fluid level and, if low, add fluid until it reaches the Cold mark on the dipstick.

3   Start the engine and allow it to run at

fast idle. Recheck the fluid level and add more if necessary to reach the Cold mark on the dipstick.

4   Bleed the system by turning the wheels from side-to-side, without hitting the stops. This will work the air out of the system. Keep the reservoir full of fluid as this is done.

5   When the air is worked out of the system, return the wheels to the straight ahead position and leave the vehicle running for several more minutes before shutting it off.

6   Road test the vehicle to be sure the steering system is functioning normally and noise free.

7   Recheck the fluid level to be sure it's up to the Hot mark on the dipstick while the engine is at normal operating temperature. Add fluid if necessary (see Chapter 1).

19   Wheels and tires - general information

Refer to illustration 19.1

All vehicles covered by this manual are equipped with metric-size fiberglass or steel belted radial tires **(see illustration)**. Use of other size or type of tires may affect the ride and handling of the vehicle. Don't mix different types of tires, such as radials and bias belted, on the same vehicle as handling may be seriously affected. It's recommended that tires be replaced in pairs on the same axle, but if only one tire is being replaced, be sure

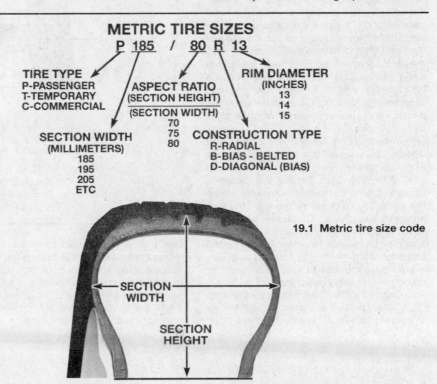

METRIC TIRE SIZES

P 185 / 80 R 13

TIRE TYPE
P-PASSENGER
T-TEMPORARY
C-COMMERCIAL

ASPECT RATIO
(SECTION HEIGHT)
(SECTION WIDTH)
70
75
80

RIM DIAMETER
(INCHES)
13
14
15

SECTION WIDTH
(MILLIMETERS)
185
195
205
ETC

CONSTRUCTION TYPE
R-RADIAL
B-BIAS - BELTED
D-DIAGONAL (BIAS)

SECTION WIDTH

SECTION HEIGHT

19.1 Metric tire size code

it's the same size, structure and tread design as the other.

Because tire pressure has a substantial effect on handling and wear, the pressure on all tires should be checked at least once a month or before any extended trips (see Chapter 1).

Wheels must be replaced if they're bent, dented, leak air, have elongated bolt holes, are heavily rusted, out of vertical symmetry or if the lug nuts won't stay tight. Wheel repairs that use welding or peening are not recommended.

Tire and wheel balance is important to the overall handling, braking and performance of the vehicle. Unbalanced wheels can adversely affect handling and ride characteristics as well as tire life. Whenever a tire is installed on a wheel, the tire and wheel should be balanced by a shop with the proper equipment.

20 Front end alignment - general information

Refer to illustration 20.1

A front end alignment refers to the adjustments made to the front wheels so they're in proper angular relationship to the suspension and the ground. Front wheels that are out of proper alignment not only affect steering control, but also increase tire wear. The only adjustment possible on these vehicles, as they come from the factory, is toe-in. Camber and caster can be adjusted **(see illustration)**, but only after an adjustment kit, available at GM dealers, is installed.

Getting the proper front wheel alignment is a very exacting process, one in which complicated and expensive machines are necessary to perform the job properly. Because of this, you should have a technician with the proper equipment perform these tasks. We will, however, use this space to give you a basic idea of what is involved with front end alignment so you can better understand the process and deal intelligently with the shop that does the work.

Toe-in is the turning in of the front wheels. The purpose of a toe specification is to ensure parallel rolling of the front wheels. In a vehicle with zero toe-in, the distance between the front edges of the wheels will be the same as the distance between the rear edges of the wheels. The actual amount of toe-in is normally only a fraction of an inch. Toe-in adjustment is controlled by the tie-rod end position on the inner tie-rod. Incorrect toe-in will cause the tires to wear improperly by making them scrub against the road surface.

Camber is the tilting of the front wheels from the vertical when viewed from the front of the vehicle. When the wheels tilt out at the

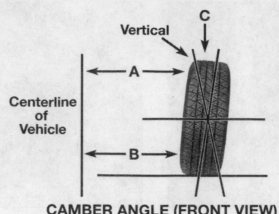

CAMBER ANGLE (FRONT VIEW)

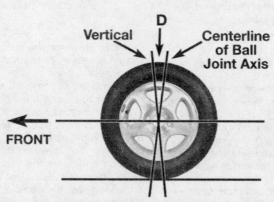

CASTER ANGLE (SIDE VIEW)

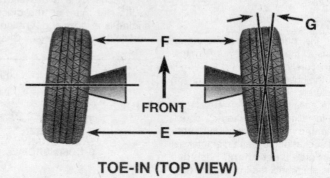

TOE-IN (TOP VIEW)

20.1 Front end alignment details

A minus B = C
D = caster (measured in degrees)
E minus F = toe-in (measured in inches)
G = toe-in (expressed in degrees)

top, the camber is said to be positive (+). When the wheels tilt in at the top the camber is negative (-). The amount of tilt is measured in degrees from the vertical and this measurement is called the camber angle. This angle affects the amount of tire tread which contacts the road and compensates for

changes in the suspension geometry when the vehicle is cornering or travelling over an undulating surface.

Caster is the tilting of the top of the front steering axis from the vertical. A tilt toward the rear is positive caster and a tilt toward the front is negative caster.

Chapter 11 Body

Contents

1 General information

The vehicles covered in this manual have a separate frame and body. As with other parts of the vehicle, proper maintenance of body components plays an important part in preserving the vehicle's market value. It's far less costly to handle small problems before they grow into larger ones. Information in this Chapter will tell you all you need to know to keep seals sealing, body panels aligned and general appearance up to par.

Major body components which are particularly vulnerable to accident damage can be unbolted and repaired or replaced. Among these parts are the body moldings, bumpers, fenders, hood, doors and all glass.

Only general body maintenance practices and body panel repair procedures within the scope of the do-it-yourselfer are included in this Chapter.

2 Body - maintenance

1   The condition of your vehicle's body is very important, because the resale value depends a great deal on it. It's much more difficult to repair a neglected or damaged body than it is to repair mechanical components. The hidden areas of the body, such as the wheel wells, the frame and the engine compartment, are equally important, although they don't require as frequent attention as the rest of the body.

2   Once a year, or every 12,000 miles, it's a good idea to have the underside of the body steam cleaned. All traces of dirt and oil will be removed and the area can then be inspected carefully for rust, damaged brake lines, frayed electrical wires, damaged cables and other problems. The front suspension com-

ponents should be greased after completion of this job.

3   At the same time, clean the engine and the engine compartment with a steam cleaner or water soluble degreaser.

4   The wheel wells should be given close attention, since undercoating can peel away and stones and dirt thrown up by the tires can cause the paint to chip and flake, allowing rust to set in. If rust is found, clean down to the bare metal and apply an anti-rust paint.

5   The body should be washed about once a week. Wet the vehicle thoroughly to soften the dirt, then wash it down with a soft sponge and plenty of clean soapy water. If the surplus dirt isn't washed off very carefully, it can wear down the paint.

6   Spots of tar or asphalt thrown up from the road should be removed with a cloth soaked in solvent.

7   Once every six months, wax the body and chrome trim. If a chrome cleaner is used to remove rust from any of the vehicle's plated parts, remember that the cleaner also removes part of the chrome, so use it sparingly.

---

3   Upholstery and carpets - maintenance

---

1   Every three months remove the carpets or mats and clean the interior of the vehicle (more frequently if necessary). Vacuum the upholstery and carpets to remove loose dirt and dust.

2   Vinyl upholstery can be cleaned with a sponge dampened with soapy water. It's a good idea to treat vinyl upholstery with a rubber and vinyl protectant to slow deterioration.

---

4   Vinyl trim - maintenance

Don't clean vinyl trim with detergents, caustic soap or petroleum-based cleaners. Plain soap and water works just fine, with a soft brush to clean dirt that may be ingrained. Wash the vinyl as frequently as the rest of the vehicle.

After cleaning, application of a high quality rubber and vinyl protectant will help prevent oxidation and cracks. The protectant can also be applied to weatherstripping, vacuum lines and rubber hoses, which often fail as a result of chemical degradation, and to the tires.

---

5   Body repair - minor damage

See photo sequence

Repair of scratches

1   If the scratch is superficial and does not penetrate to the metal of the body, repair is very simple. Lightly rub the scratched area with a fine rubbing compound to remove loose paint and built up wax. Rinse the area with clean water.

2   Apply touch-up paint to the scratch, using a small brush. Continue to apply thin layers of paint until the surface of the paint in the scratch is level with the surrounding paint. Allow the new paint at least two weeks to harden, then blend it into the surrounding paint by rubbing with a very fine rubbing compound. Finally, apply a coat of wax to the scratch area.

3   If the scratch has penetrated the paint and exposed the metal of the body, causing the metal to rust, a different repair technique is required. Remove all loose rust from the bottom of the scratch with a pocket knife, then apply rust inhibiting paint to prevent the formation of rust in the future. Using a rubber or nylon applicator, coat the scratched area with glaze-type filler. If required, the filler can be mixed with thinner to provide a very thin paste, which is ideal for filling narrow scratches. Before the glaze filler in the scratch hardens, wrap a piece of smooth cotton cloth around the tip of a finger. Dip the cloth in thinner and then quickly wipe it along the surface of the scratch. This will ensure that the surface of the filler is slightly hollow. The scratch can now be painted over as described earlier in this section.

Repair of dents

4   When repairing dents, the first job is to pull the dent out until the affected area is as close as possible to its original shape. There is no point in trying to restore the original shape completely as the metal in the damaged area will have stretched on impact and cannot be restored to its original contours. It's better to bring the level of the dent up to a point which is about 1/8-inch below the level of the surrounding metal. In cases where the dent is very shallow, it isn't worth trying to pull it out at all.

5   If the back side of the dent is accessible, it can be hammered out gently from behind using a soft-face hammer. While doing this, hold a block of wood firmly against the opposite side of the metal to absorb the hammer blows and prevent the metal from being stretched.

6   If the dent is in a section of the body which has double layers, or some other factor makes it inaccessible from behind, a different technique is required. Drill several small holes through the metal inside the damaged area, particularly in the deeper sections. Screw long, self tapping screws into the holes just enough for them to get a good grip in the metal. Now the dent can be pulled out by pulling on the protruding heads of the screws with locking pliers.

7   The next stage of repair is the removal of paint from the damaged area and from an inch or so of the surrounding metal. This is easily done with a wire brush or sanding disk in a drill motor, although it can be done just as effectively by hand with sandpaper. To complete the preparation for filling, score the surface of the bare metal with a screwdriver or the tang of a file or drill small holes in the affected area. This will provide a good grip for the filler material. To complete the repair, see the Section on filling and painting.

Repair of rust holes or gashes

8   Remove all paint from the affected area and from an inch or so of the surrounding metal using a sanding disk or wire brush mounted in a drill motor. If these are not available, a few sheets of sandpaper will do the job just as effectively.

9   With the paint removed, you will be able to determine the severity of the corrosion and decide whether to replace the whole panel, if possible, or repair the affected area. New body panels are not as expensive as most people think and it's often quicker to install a new panel than to repair large areas of rust.

10   Remove all trim pieces from the affected area except those which will act as a guide to the original shape of the damaged body, such as headlight shells, etc. Using metal snips or a hacksaw blade, remove all loose metal and any other metal that is badly affected by rust. Hammer the edges of the hole inward to create a slight depression for the filler material.

11   Wire brush the affected area to remove the powdery rust from the surface of the metal. If the back of the rusted area is accessible, treat it with rust-inhibiting paint.

12   Before filling is done, block the hole in some way. This can be done with sheet metal riveted or screwed into place, or by stuffing the hole with wire mesh.

13   Once the hole is blocked off, the affected area can be filled and painted. See the following subsection on filling and painting.

Filling and painting

14   Many types of body fillers are available, but generally speaking, body repair kits which contain filler paste and a tube of resin hardener are best for this type of repair work. A wide, flexible plastic or nylon applicator will be necessary for imparting a smooth and contoured finish to the surface of the filler material. Mix up a small amount of filler on a clean piece of wood or cardboard (use the hardener sparingly). Follow the manufacturer's instructions on the package, otherwise the filler will set incorrectly.

15   Using the applicator, apply the filler paste to the prepared area. Draw the applicator across the surface of the filler to achieve the desired contour and to level the filler surface. As soon as a contour that approximates the original one is achieved, stop working the paste. If you continue, the paste will begin to stick to the applicator. Continue to add thin layers of paste at 20-minute intervals until the level of the filler is just above the surrounding metal.

16   Once the filler has hardened, the excess can be removed with a body file. From then on, progressively finer grades of sandpaper

should be used, starting with a 180-grit paper and finishing with 600-grit wet-or-dry paper. Always wrap the sandpaper around a flat rubber or wooden block, otherwise the surface of the filler won't be completely flat. During the sanding of the filler surface, the wet-or-dry paper should be periodically rinsed in water. This will ensure that a very smooth finish is produced in the final stage.

17   At this point, the repair area should be surrounded by a ring of bare metal, which in turn should be encircled by the finely feathered edge of good paint. Rinse the repair area with clean water until all of the dust produced by the sanding operation is gone.

18   Spray the entire area with a light coat of primer. This will reveal any imperfections in the surface of the filler. Repair the imperfections with fresh filler paste or glaze filler and once more smooth the surface with sandpaper. Repeat this spray-and-repair procedure until you are satisfied that the surface of the filler and the feathered edge of the paint are perfect. Rinse the area with clean water and allow it to dry completely.

19   The repair area is now ready for painting. Spray painting must be carried out in a warm, dry, windless and dust free atmosphere. These conditions can be created if you have access to a large indoor work area, but if you are forced to work in the open, you will have to pick the day very carefully. If you are working indoors, dousing the floor in the work area with water will help settle the dust which would otherwise be in the air. If the repair area is confined to one body panel, mask off the surrounding panels. This will help minimize the effects of a slight mismatch in paint color. Trim pieces such as chrome strips, door handles, etc., will also need to be masked off or removed. Use masking tape and several thicknesses of newspaper for the masking operations.

20   Before spraying, shake the paint can thoroughly, then spray a test area until the spray painting technique is mastered. Cover the repair area with a thick coat of primer. The thickness should be built up using several thin layers of primer rather than one thick one. Using 600-grit wet-or-dry sandpaper, rub down the surface of the primer until it's very smooth. While doing this, the work area should be thoroughly rinsed with water and the wet-or-dry sandpaper periodically rinsed as well. Allow the primer to dry before spraying additional coats.

21   Spray on the top coat, again building up the thickness by using several thin layers of paint. Begin spraying in the center of the repair area and then, using a circular motion, work out until the whole repair area and about two inches of the surrounding original paint is covered. Remove all masking material 10 to 15 minutes after spraying on the final coat of paint. Allow the new paint at least two weeks to harden, then use a very fine rubbing compound to blend the edges of the new paint into the existing paint. Finally, apply a coat of wax.

6   Body repair - major damage

1   Major damage must be repaired by an auto body shop specifically equipped to repair major damage. These shops have the specialized equipment required to do the job properly.

2   If the damage is extensive, the body must be checked for proper alignment or the vehicle's handling characteristics may be adversely affected and other components may wear at an accelerated rate.

3   Due to the fact that all of the major body components (hood, fenders, etc.) are separate and replaceable units, any seriously damaged components should be replaced rather than repaired. Sometimes the components can be found in a wrecking yard that specializes in used vehicle components, often at considerable savings over the cost of new parts.

7   Hinges and locks - maintenance

Once every 3000 miles, or every three months, the hinges and latch assemblies on the doors, hood and tailgate should be given a few drops of light oil or lock lubricant. The door latch strikers should also be lubricated with a thin coat of grease to reduce wear and ensure free movement. Lubricate the door locks with spray-on graphite lubricant.

8   Windshield and fixed glass - replacement

Replacement of the windshield and fixed glass requires the use of special fast-setting adhesive/caulk materials and some specialized tools and techniques. These operations should be left to a dealer service department or a shop specializing in glass work.

9   Hood - removal, installation and adjustment

Note: *The hood is heavy and somewhat awkward to remove and install - at least two people should perform this procedure.*

Removal and installation
Refer to illustration 9.2

1   Use blankets or pads to cover the cowl area of the body and the fenders. This will protect the body and paint as the hood is lifted off.

2   Use a scribe or permanent felt-tip pen to make alignment marks around the bolt heads. This will ensure proper alignment during installation **(see illustration)**.

3   Disconnect any cables or wire harnesses which will interfere with removal.

4   Have an assistant support the weight of

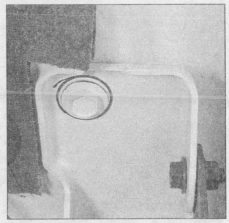

9.2 Use a scribe or permanent felt-tip pen to make alignment marks around the hood bolt heads

the hood. Remove the hinge-to-hood nuts or bolts.

5   Lift off the hood.

6   Installation is the reverse of removal.

Adjustment

7   Fore-and-aft and side-to-side adjustment of the hood is done by moving the hood in relation to the hinge plate after loosening the bolts or nuts.

8   Scribe a line around the entire hinge plate so you can judge the amount of movement.

9   Loosen the bolts or nuts and move the hood into correct alignment. Move it only a little at a time. Tighten the hinge bolts or nuts and carefully lower the hood to check the alignment.

10   If necessary after installation, the entire hood latch assembly can be adjusted up-and-down as well as from side-to-side on the radiator support so the hood closes securely and is flush with the fenders. To do this, scribe a line around the hood latch and mounting bolts to provide a reference point. Then loosen the bolts and reposition the latch assembly as necessary. Following adjustment, retighten the mounting bolts.

11   Finally, adjust the hood bumpers on the radiator support so the hood, when closed, is flush with the fenders.

12   The hood latch assembly, as well as the hinges, should be periodically lubricated with white lithium-base grease to prevent sticking and wear.

10   Door trim panel - removal and installation

1994 and earlier models
Refer to illustrations 10.2a, 10.2b, 10.3 and 10.6

1   Lower the window all the way down and disconnect the negative cable from the battery.

These photos illustrate a method of repairing simple dents. They are intended to supplement *Body repair - minor damage* in this Chapter and should not be used as the sole instructions for body repair on these vehicles.

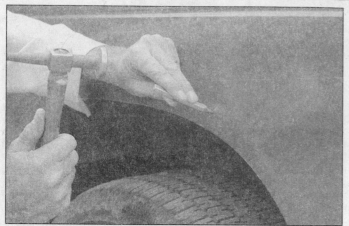

1   If you can't access the backside of the body panel to hammer out the dent, pull it out with a slide-hammer-type dent puller. In the deepest portion of the dent or along the crease line, drill or punch hole(s) at least one inch apart . . .

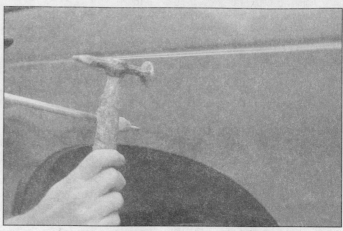

2   . . . then screw the slide-hammer into the hole and operate it. Tap with a hammer near the edge of the dent to help 'pop' the metal back to its original shape. When you're finished, the dent area should be close to its original contour and about 1/8-inch below the surface of the surrounding metal

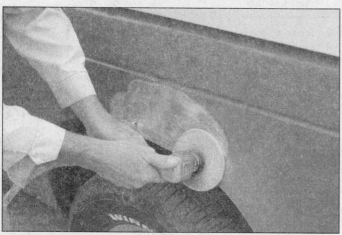

3   Using coarse-grit sandpaper, remove the paint down to the bare metal. Hand sanding works fine, but the disc sander shown here makes the job faster. Use finer (about 320-grit) sandpaper to feather-edge the paint at least one inch around the dent area

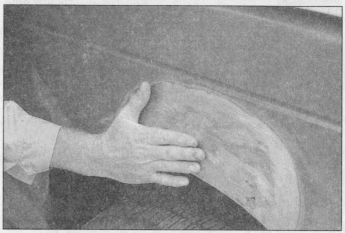

4   When the paint is removed, touch will probably be more helpful than sight for telling if the metal is straight. Hammer down the high spots or raise the low spots as necessary. Clean the repair area with wax/silicone remover

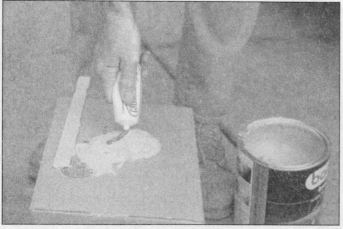

5   Following label instructions, mix up a batch of plastic filler and hardener. The ratio of filler to hardener is critical, and, if you mix it incorrectly, it will either not cure properly or cure too quickly (you won't have time to file and sand it into shape)

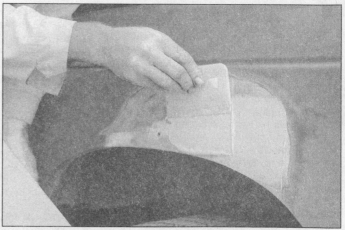

6   Working quickly so the filler doesn't harden, use a plastic applicator to press the body filler firmly into the metal, assuring it bonds completely. Work the filler until it matches the original contour and is slightly above the surrounding metal

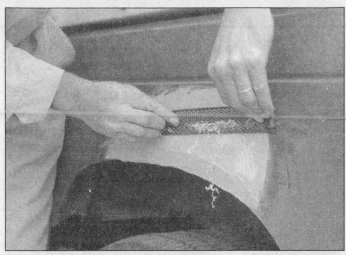

7　Let the filler harden until you can just dent it with your fingernail. Use a body file or Surform tool (shown here) to rough-shape the filler

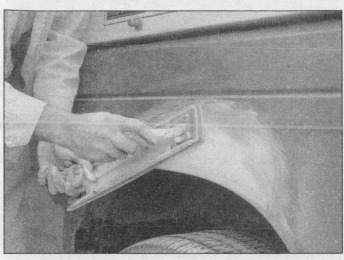

8　Use coarse-grit sandpaper and a sanding board or block to work the filler down until it's smooth and even. Work down to finer grits of sandpaper - always using a board or block - ending up with 360 or 400 grit

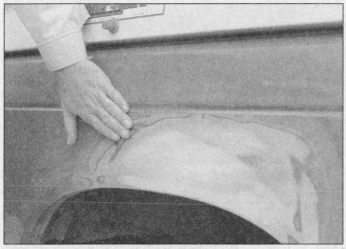

9　You shouldn't be able to feel any ridge at the transition from the filler to the bare metal or from the bare metal to the old paint. As soon as the repair is flat and uniform, remove the dust and mask off the adjacent panels or trim pieces

10　Apply several layers of primer to the area. Don't spray the primer on too heavy, so it sags or runs, and make sure each coat is dry before you spray on the next one. A professional-type spray gun is being used here, but aerosol spray primer is available inexpensively from auto parts stores

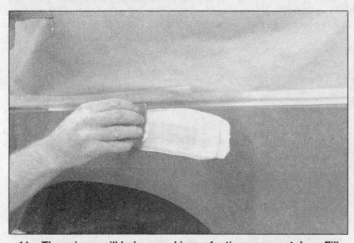

11　The primer will help reveal imperfections or scratches. Fill these with glazing compound. Follow the label instructions and sand it with 360 or 400-grit sandpaper until it's smooth. Repeat the glazing, sanding and respraying until the primer reveals a perfectly smooth surface

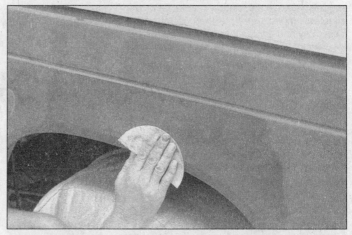

12　Finish sand the primer with very fine sandpaper (400 or 600-grit) to remove the primer overspray. Clean the area with water and allow it to dry. Use a tack rag to remove any dust, then apply the finish coat. Don't attempt to rub out or wax the repair area until the paint has dried completely (at least two weeks)

10.2a Using a small screwdriver, pry off the cover on each side of the pull strap and remove the screw underneath it

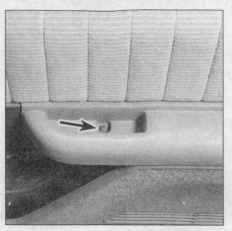

10.2b Remove the door panel retaining screw(s) located in the arm rest (arrow)

10.3 Using a small screwdriver, carefully pry off the control switch panel

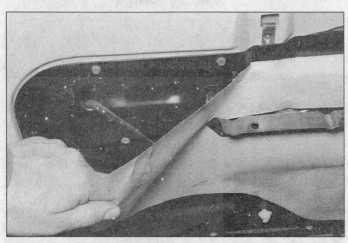

10.6 Be very careful when pulling the watershield off - don't tear or distort it

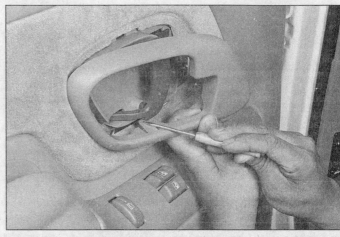

10.10 Slide a small screwdriver into the inside of the door handle bezel and release the tabs

2   Remove the door pull or armrest retaining screws **(see illustrations)**.

3   On manual window regulator equipped models, remove the window crank. On power regulator models, pry out the control switch assembly and unplug it **(see illustration)**.

4   Insert a putty knife or large screwdriver between the trim panel and the door and disengage the retaining clips. Work around the outer edge until the panel is free.

5   Once all of the clips are disengaged, detach the trim panel and remove it from the vehicle.

6   For access to the inner door, carefully peel back the plastic watershield **(see illustration)**.

7   Prior to installation of the door panel, be sure to reinstall any clips in the panel which may have come out during the removal procedure and remain in the door itself.

8   Place the panel in position in the door, press the door panel into place until the clips are seated and install the armrest/door pullscrews. Install the manual regulator window crank or control switch assembly.

1995 and later models

Refer to illustrations 10.10, 10.12, 10.13a, 10.13b and 10.16

9   Disconnect the negative battery cable.

10   Remove the inside door handle bezel by carefully prying out the clips while pulling out the bezel **(see illustration)**.

11   Remove the widow regulator handle, if equipped with manual windows.

12   Remove the two screws and the inner door pull **(see illustration)**.

13   Remove the power accessory switch mounting panel by carefully prying it from the door panel **(see illustrations)**. The panel must slide rearward as it is removed in order

10.12 Remove the screws securing the pull handle

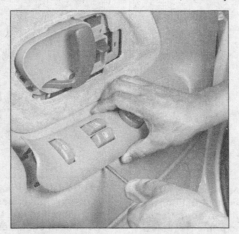

10.13a Carefully pry off the control panel assembly with a wide blade screwdriver

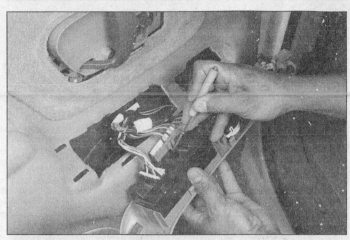

10.13b Disconnect the wiring connectors from the switches

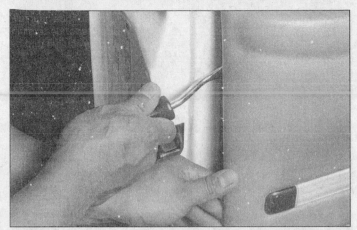

10.16 Carefully pry the door panel retaining clips off with a special door panel removal tool - be careful not to scratch the paint

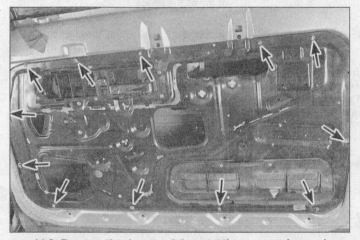

11.3 Remove the door module mounting screws (arrows)

11.5 Remove the two glass run channel bolts and pull the channel away from the glass (arrows)

to disengage the front clip. Disconnect the wiring. The small speaker can be disconnected by rotating the connector.

14   Remove the upper trim panel, if used, by prying it from the door.

15   Carefully pry off the armrest screw covers and remove the screws and cover.

16   Pry out the door panel retaining clips with a trim panel clip removal tool (available at most auto parts stores) or an equivalent tool **(see illustration)**.

17   Installation is the reverse of removal.

11   Door window glass and regulator - removal and installation

Refer to illustrations 11.3, 11.5 and 11.7

1   Lower the glass completely.

2   Remove the door trim panel and the watershield (see Section 10).

3   Remove the retaining screws, pull the door module back and disconnect the door lock and handle rods **(see illustration)**.

4   Remove the electrical connector, if equipped.

5   Remove the two glass run channel bolts

(see illustration) and move the run channel away from the glass.

6   Tilt the door module and window glass assembly and lower it out the bottom of the door.

7   Bend the tab down on the window run channel to slide the door glass from the regulator assembly **(see illustration)**.

8   For access to the power regulator components, drill out the rivets from the inside handle housing. On reassembly, use sheet metal screws in place of the rivets.

9   Drill out the rivets from the regulator assembly and separate the regulator from the door module. On reassembly, use sheet metal screws in place of the rivets.

10   Prior to installation, lubricate the window regulator mechanism with chassis grease. Installation of the glass and regulator is the reverse of removal.

12   Side latched window (extended cab models) - removal and installation

1   Open the window and block it in the

open position.

2   Drill out and remove the latch and hinge-retaining rivets. On reassembly, use sheet-metal screws.

3   Remove the window assembly.

4   Installation is the reverse of removal.

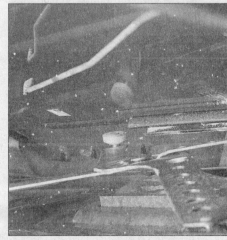

11.7 Slide the roller on the regulator arm out of the glass channel

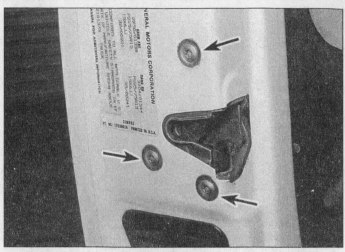

14.4 To remove the latch, unscrew the three mounting bolts (arrows)

14.7 To remove the door handle housing, drill out the mounting rivets (arrows) - during installation, use sheet metal screws in place of the rivets

13 End gate window (Sport-utility models) - removal and installation

1   Disconnect the rear gate window defogger wires attached to the strut assemblies.
2   On the lower end of the strut assembly, insert a small screwdriver between the ball and the strut ball socket and release the ball from the strut ball socket.
3   Support the end gate window and repeat for the other side.
4   Remove the hinge pin retainers and hinge pins.
5   Remove the end gate assembly.
6   Installation is the reverse of removal.

14 Door latch, lock cylinder and handle - removal and installation

Door latch

Refer to illustration 14.4
1   Remove the door trim panel (see Section 10).
2   Remove the screws from the door module **(see illustration 11.3)** and tilt it out at the top.
3   Detach the rods from the latch assembly.
4   Remove the latch mounting screws and pull the latch assembly out from inside the door **(see illustration)**.
5   Installation is the reverse of removal.

Inside door handle

Refer to illustration 14.7
6   Remove the door trim panel and the watershield (see Section 10).
7   Drill out the rivets from the inside handle housing and pull it out **(see illustration)**.
8   Detach the control rods from the handle.
9   Installation is the reverse of removal. Use sheet metal screws in place of the rivets.

Door lock cylinder and outside door handle

Refer to illustration 14.13
10   Remove the door trim panel and water deflector (see Section 10).
11   Remove the door module and window glass assembly (Section 11).
12   Detach the control rods from the handle and the lock cylinder.
13   Remove the handle mounting screws **(see illustration)**.
14   Remove the lock cylinder from the handle housing.
15   Remove the handle.
16   Installation is the reverse of removal.

15 Side and cargo door - removal and installation

Refer to illustrations 15.5a and 15.5b
1   Detach the negative cable from the battery.
2   Remove the door trim panel (see Section 10). Disconnect any wire harness con-

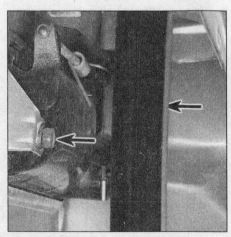

14.13 Door handle mounting bolts

nectors and push them through the door opening so they won't interfere with door removal.
3   Place a jack or jackstand under the door or have an assistant on hand to support it when the hinge pins are removed. **Note:** *If a jack or jackstand is used, place a rag between it and the door to protect the door's painted surfaces.*
4   On side doors only, compress and remove the hinge spring using tool J-36604 or equivalent. **Warning:** *The spring may fly off the tool during removal. To prevent personal injury, cover the spring with a heavy rag before removing it.*
5   On side doors only, remove the hinge pin retainers. On all doors, drive out the pins and carefully lift off the door **(see illustrations)**. **Note:** *The cargo door hinges are not equipped with hinge pin retainers.*
6   If the door does not close properly after installation, the door latch striker can be adjusted both up-and-down and sideways to provide positive engagement with the latch mechanism. This is done by loosening the door striker bolt and moving the striker as necessary.

15.5a Typical upper door hinge and pin

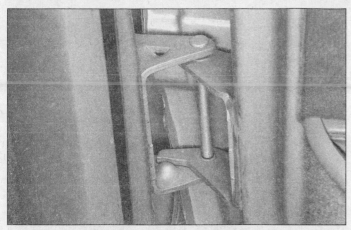

15.5b Typical lower door hinge and pin

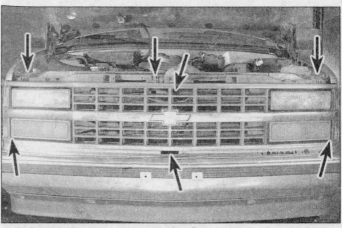

16.2a Remove the grill mounting screws (arrows) - the lower outer screws are behind the parking/turn signal lights

16.2b Remove the turn signal light and then remove the grill retaining screws (arrow) - passenger side shown

17.2 Remove the cable clip from the engine compartment (arrow)

16 Radiator grille - removal and installation

Refer to illustration 16.2a and 16.2b

1   On 1994 and earlier models, remove the parking light assemblies (see Chapter 12).
2   Remove the grille retaining screws **(see illustrations)**.
3   Move the grille forward about 1/2-inch, then lift it up and out.
4   Installation is the reverse of removal.

17 Hood release cable - removal and installation

Refer to illustration 17.2

1   Remove the two bolts from the upper left portion of the radiator grille.
2   Disconnect the cable from the latch release, disengage the two cable clips, unbolt the hand lever in the passenger compartment and pull the cable through the firewall into the passenger compartment **(see illustration)**.
3   Installation is the reverse of removal.

18 Front fender - removal and installation

Refer to illustrations 18.4a, 18.4b and 18.4c

1   Remove the hood and hood hinge (see Section 9).
2   Loosen the wheel lug nuts, raise the

front of the vehicle and support it securely on jackstands. Apply the parking brake. Remove the front wheel.
3   Disconnect the antenna (left fender only) and all electrical connectors and other components that would interfere with fender removal.
4   Remove the fender mounting bolts **(see illustrations)**.

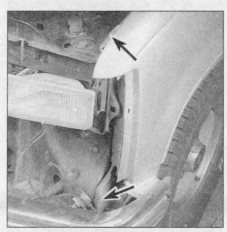

18.4a Remove the front fender mounting bolts (arrows) - front view . . .

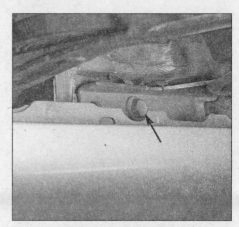

18.4b . . . top view from engine compartment . . .

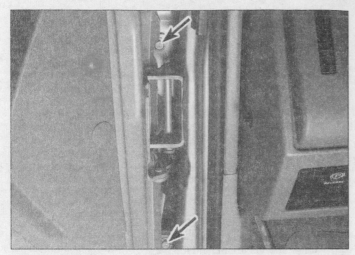

18.4c . . . rear view with the door open

19.2 Disengage the slot on the end of the support from the retaining dowel

5   Detach the fender. It's a good idea to have an assistant support the fender while it's being moved away from the vehicle to prevent damage to the surrounding body panels.
6   Installation is the reverse of removal. Tighten all fasteners securely.

19   Tailgate - removal and installation

Refer to illustration 19.2
Note: *The tailgate is heavy and somewhat awkward to remove and install - at least two people should perform this procedure.*
1   Lower the tailgate and pull the centers of the supports up.
2   Push each support forward to disengage the slot on the end of the support from the retaining dowel **(see illustration)**.
3   With the aid of an assistant, pull the right side of the tailgate rearward to disengage the hinge, then pull the tailgate to the right to disengage the left hinge.
4   Installation is the reverse of removal.

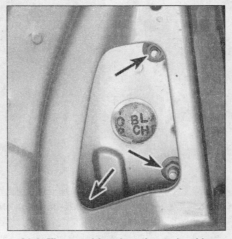

21.2 The outside mirror is retained by three nuts

20   End gate (Sport-utility models) - removal and installation

Note: *The end gate is heavy and somewhat awkward to remove and install - at least two*

people should perform this procedure.
1   Remove the rear bumper and rear bumper filler panel.
2   Open the end gate.
3   Remove the left bolt.
4   Close the end gate and remove both retainers and the torque-rod-retaining bolts. Remove both retainers and torque rod.
5   Disconnect the rear gate release wires.
6   Open and support the end gate in the open position.
7   Disconnect both support-cable-retaining bolts from the end gate.
8   Remove the hinge pin retainers, drive out the pins and carefully lift off the end gate.
9   Installation is the reverse of removal.

21   Outside mirror - removal and installation

Refer to illustration 21.2
1   Remove the door trim panel (see Section 10).
2   Remove the mounting nuts **(see illustration)** and detach the mirror from the door.
3   Installation is the reverse of removal.

Chapter 12
Chassis electrical system

Contents

1 General information

Caution: *On models equipped with a Delco Loc II anti-theft audio system, be sure the lockout feature is turned off before performing any procedure which requires disconnecting the battery.*

The electrical system is a 12-volt, negative ground type. Power for the lights and all electrical accessories is supplied by a lead/acid-type battery which is charged by the alternator.

This Chapter covers repair and service procedures for the various electrical components not associated with the engine. Information on the battery, alternator, distributor and starter motor can be found in Chapter 5.

It should be noted that when portions of the electrical system are serviced, the negative battery cable should be disconnected from the battery to prevent electrical shorts and/or fires.

2 Electrical troubleshooting - general information

A typical electrical circuit consists of an electrical component, any switches, relays, motors, fuses, fusible links or circuit breakers related to that component and the wiring and connectors that link the component to both the battery and the chassis. To help you pinpoint an electrical circuit problem, wiring diagrams are included at the end of this book.

Before tackling any troublesome electrical circuit, first study the appropriate wiring diagrams to get a complete understanding of what makes up that individual circuit. Trouble spots, for instance, can often be narrowed down by noting if other components related to the circuit are operating properly. If several components or circuits fail at one time, chances are the problem is in a fuse or ground connection, because several circuits are often routed through the same fuse and ground connections.

Electrical problems usually stem from simple causes, such as loose or corroded connections, a blown fuse, a melted fusible link or a bad relay. Visually inspect the condition of all fuses, wires and connections in a problem circuit before troubleshooting it.

If testing instruments are going to be utilized, use the diagrams to plan ahead of time where you will make the necessary connections in order to accurately pinpoint the trouble spot.

The basic tools needed for electrical troubleshooting include a circuit tester or voltmeter (a 12-volt bulb with a set of test leads can also be used), a continuity tester, which includes a bulb, battery and set of test leads, and a jumper wire, preferably with a circuit breaker incorporated, which can be used to bypass electrical components. Before attempting to locate a problem with test instruments, use the wiring diagram(s) to decide where to make the connections.

Voltage checks

Voltage checks should be performed if a circuit is not functioning properly. Connect one lead of a circuit tester to either the negative battery terminal or a known good ground. Connect the other lead to a connector in the circuit being tested, preferably nearest to the battery or fuse. If the bulb of the tester lights, voltage is present, which means that the part of the circuit between the connector and the battery is problem free. Continue checking the rest of the circuit in the same fashion. When you reach a point at which no voltage is present, the problem lies between that point and the last test point with voltage. Most of the time the problem can be traced to a loose connection. **Note:** *Keep in mind that some circuits receive voltage only when the ignition key is in the Accessory or Run position.*

Finding a short

One method of finding shorts in a circuit is to remove the fuse and connect a test light or voltmeter in its place to the fuse terminals. There should be no voltage present in the circuit. Move the wiring harness from side-to-side while watching the test light. If the bulb goes on, there is a short to ground somewhere in that area, probably where the insulation has rubbed through. The same test can be performed on each component in the circuit, even a switch.

Ground check

Perform a ground test to check whether a component is properly grounded. Disconnect the battery and connect one lead of a selfpowered test light, known as a continuity tester, to a known good ground. Connect the other lead to the wire or ground connection being tested. If the bulb goes on, the ground is good. If the bulb does not go on, the ground is not good.

Continuity check

A continuity check is done to determine if there are any breaks in a circuit - if it is passing electricity properly. With the circuit off (no power in the circuit), a self-powered continuity tester can be used to check the circuit. Connect the test leads to both ends of the circuit (or to the "power" end and a good ground),

3.1 The fuse block is located under the instrument panel to the left of the steering column

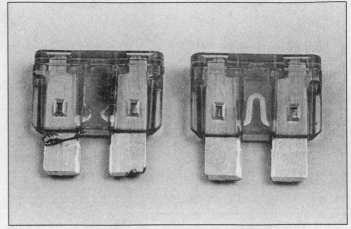

3.3 When a fuse blows, the element between the terminals melts - the fuse on the left is blown, the fuse on the right is good

and if the test light comes on the circuit is passing current properly. If the light doesn't come on, there is a break somewhere in the circuit. The same procedure can be used to test a switch, by connecting the continuity tester to the switch terminals. With the switch turned On, the test light should come on.

Finding an open circuit

When diagnosing for possible open circuits, it is often difficult to locate them by sight because oxidation or terminal misalignment are hidden by the connectors. Merely wiggling a connector on a sensor or in the wiring harness may correct the open circuit condition. Remember this when an open circuit is indicated when troubleshooting a circuit. Intermittent problems may also be caused by oxidized or loose connections.

Electrical troubleshooting is simple if you keep in mind that all electrical circuits are basically electricity running from the battery, through the wires, switches, relays, fuses and fusible links to each electrical component (light bulb, motor, etc.) and to ground, from which it is passed back to the battery. Any electrical problem is an interruption in the flow of electricity to and from the battery.

3   Fuses - general information

Refer to illustrations 3.1 and 3.3

The electrical circuits of the vehicle are protected by a combination of fuses, circuit breakers and fusible links. The fuse block is located under the instrument panel on the left side of the dashboard **(see illustration)**.

Each of the fuses is designed to protect a specific circuit, and the various circuits are identified on the fuse panel itself.

Miniaturized fuses are employed in the fuse block. These compact fuses, with blade terminal design, allow fingertip removal and replacement. If an electrical component fails, always check the fuse first. The best way to check the fuses is with a test light. Check for power at the exposed terminal tips of each

fuse. If power is present at one side of the fuse but not the other, the fuse is blown. A blown fuse can also be identified by visually inspecting it **(see illustration)**.

Be sure to replace blown fuses with the correct type. Fuses of different ratings are physically interchangeable, but only fuses of the proper rating should be used. Replacing a fuse with one of a higher or lower value than specified is not recommended. Each electrical circuit needs a specific amount of protection. The amperage value of each fuse is molded into the fuse body.

If the replacement fuse immediately fails, don't replace it again until the cause of the problem is isolated and corrected. In most cases, the cause will be a short circuit in the wiring caused by a broken or deteriorated wire.

4   Fusible links - general information

Refer to illustration 4.1
Caution: *On models equipped with a Delco Loc II anti-theft audio system, be sure the lockout feature is turned off before performing any procedure which requires disconnecting the battery.*

Some circuits are protected by fusible links **(see illustration)**. The links are used in circuits which are not ordinarily fused, such as the ignition circuit.

Although the fusible links appear to be a heavier gauge than the wire they are protecting, the appearance is due to the thick insulation. All fusible links are several wire gauges smaller than the wire they are designed to protect.

Fusible links cannot be repaired, but a new link of the same size wire can be put in its place. The procedure is as follows:

a) *Disconnect the negative cable from the battery.*
b) *Disconnect the fusible link from the wiring harness.*
c) *Cut the damaged fusible link out of the wiring just behind the connector.*
d) *Strip the insulation back approximately 1/2-inch.*
e) *Position the connector on the new fusible link and crimp it into place.*
f) *Use rosin core solder at each end of the new link to obtain a good solder joint.*
g) *Use plenty of electrical tape around the soldered joint. No wires should be exposed.*
h) *Connect the battery ground cable. Test the circuit for proper operation.*

4.1 On some models the fusible links are located in the engine compartment, under a cover on the firewall; on others they are located near the positive battery cable

6.4 Remove the turn signal flasher from the fuse panel (arrow)

6.9 Remove the hazard flasher from its fastener under the dash and then unplug the flasher unit from the connector (arrow)

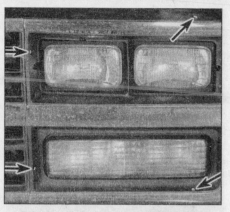

7.1 Headlight bezel screw locations (sealed beam) - four headlight system shown

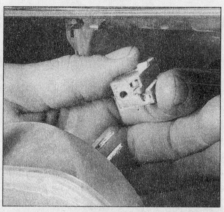

7.2 Pull the light forward and disconnect the plug from the rear (sealed beam)

5 Circuit breakers - general information

Circuit breakers protect components such as power windows, power door locks and headlights. Some circuit breakers are located in the fuse box.

On some models the circuit breaker resets itself automatically, so an electrical overload in a circuit breaker protected system will cause the circuit to fail momentarily, then come back on. If the circuit does not come back on, check it immediately. Once the condition is corrected, the circuit breaker will resume its normal function. Some circuit breakers must be reset manually.

6 Turn signal and hazard flashers - check and replacement

Refer to illustrations 6.4 and 6.9
Warning: *If equipped with an airbag, disable the airbag system before working in the vicinity of the steering wheel, instrument panel or any airbag system component. Failure to do so could cause accidental deployment of the airbag, resulting in personal injury (see Section 18).*
Caution: *On models equipped with a Delco Loc II anti-theft audio system, be sure the lockout feature is turned off before performing any procedure which requires disconnecting the battery.*

Turn signal flasher

1   The turn signal flasher, a small canister-shaped unit located in the convenience center under the dash, flashes the turn signals.
2   When the flasher unit is functioning properly, an audible click can be heard during its operation. If the turn signals fail on one side or the other and the flasher unit does not make its characteristic clicking sound, a faulty turn signal bulb is indicated.
3   If both turn signals fail to blink, the problem may be due to a blown fuse, a faulty flasher unit, a broken switch or a loose or

open connection. If a quick check of the fuse box indicates that the turn signal fuse has blown, check the wiring for a short before installing a new fuse.
4   To replace the flasher, simply pull it out of its electrical connector **(see illustration)**.
5   Make sure that the replacement unit is identical to the original. Compare the old one to the new one before installing it.
6   Installation is the reverse of removal.

Hazard flasher

7   The hazard flasher, a small canister-shaped unit located behind the main light switch behind the dash panel, flashes all four turn signals simultaneously when activated.
8   The hazard flasher is checked in a fashion similar to the turn signal flasher (see Steps 2 and 3).
9   To replace the hazard flasher, pull it from its connector under the dash and install a new one **(see illustration)**.
10   Make sure the replacement unit is identical to the one it replaces. Compare the old one to the new one before installing it.
11   Installation is the reverse of removal.

7 Headlights - removal and installation

Sealed beam

Refer to illustrations 7.1 and 7.2
1   Remove the bezel retaining screws, taking care not to disturb the adjustment screws **(see illustration)**.
2   Pull the sealed beam unit forward and disconnect the plug from the rear **(see illustration)**.
3   Installation is the reverse of removal. Make sure the number molded into the face of the lens is at the top.

Composite type

Refer to illustrations 7.6, 7.7a and 7.7b
Warning: *Halogen gas filled bulbs are under pressure and may shatter if the surface is scratched or the bulb is dropped. Wear eye*

protection and handle the bulbs carefully, grasping only the base whenever possible. Do not touch the surface of the bulb with your fingers because the oil from your skin will cause hotspots and the bulb will fail prematurely. If you do touch the bulb surface, clean it with rubbing alcohol.
4   Remove the grille (see Chapter 11).
5   Remove the four screws from the headlamp assembly.
6   Pull the headlamp assembly forward to access to the bulbs. Unplug the electrical connector **(see illustration)**.
7   Twist the bulb and lock ring counter-clockwise, and pull the bulb and holder assembly out of the headlamp assembly **(see illustrations)**.
8   Be sure to replace the high beam bulb assembly with another high beam assembly, and the low beam bulb assembly with another low beam assembly.
9   Installation is the reverse of removal.

8 Headlights - adjustment

Refer to illustrations 8.1a, 8.1b and 8.3
Note: *The headlights must be aimed correctly. If adjusted incorrectly they could blind the driver of an oncoming vehicle and cause a*

7.6 Unplug the headlight electrical
connector (composite)

7.7a To remove the headlight bulb holder
on composite-type lights, turn
it counterclockwise . . .

7.7b . . . and pull it out of the headlight
(don't try to pull the bulb out of the holder
- they're sold as a single unit)

8.1a Headlight aiming screws - dual headlight

    A   Vertical adjusting screw
    B   Horizontal adjusting screw

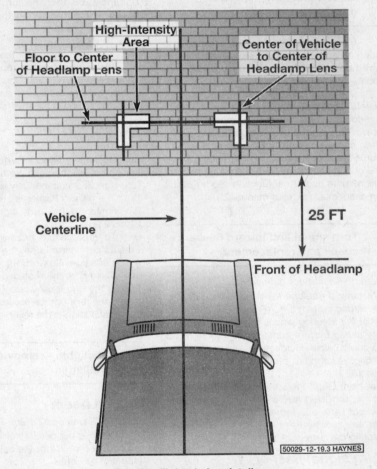

8.3 Headlight aiming details

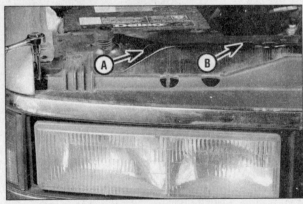

8.1b Headlight aiming screws - four headlights

    A   Vertical adjusting screw
    B   Horizontal adjusting screw

serious accident or seriously reduce your ability to see the road. The headlights should be checked for proper aim every 12 months and any time a new headlight is installed or front end body work is performed. It should be emphasized that the following procedure is only an interim step which will provide temporary adjustment until the headlights can be adjusted by a properly equipped shop.

1   Headlights have two spring loaded adjusting screws, one for controlling up-and-down movement and one for controlling left-and-right movement **(see illustrations)**.

2   There are several methods of adjusting the headlights. The simplest method requires a blank wall 25 feet in front of the vehicle and a level floor.

3   Position masking tape vertically on the wall in reference to the vehicle centerline and the centerlines of both headlights **(see illustration)**.

4   Position a horizontal tape line in reference to the centerline of all the headlights. **Note:** *It may be easier to position the tape on the wall with the vehicle parked only a few inches away.*

5   Adjustment should be made with the

9.1 Remove the tail lamp assembly mounting screws and remove the assembly

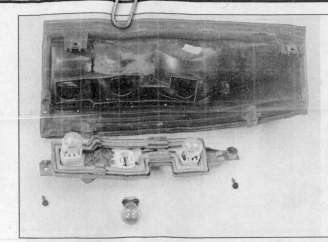

9.3 After removing the screws, pull the bulb carrier back - to remove a bulb, push it in and turn it counterclockwise, then pull it out

10.2 Remove the instrument cluster trim panel retaining screws (arrows)

vehicle sitting level, the gas tank half-full and no unusually heavy load in the vehicle.

6   Starting with the low beam adjustment, position the high intensity zone so it is two inches below the horizontal line and two inches to the right of the headlight vertical line. Adjustment is made by turning the top adjusting screw clockwise to raise the beam and counterclockwise to lower the beam. The adjusting screw on the side should be used in the same manner to move the beam left or right.

7   With the high beams on, the high intensity zone should be vertically centered with the exact center just below the horizontal line. **Note:** *It may not be possible to position the headlight aim exactly for both high and low beams. If a compromise must be made, keep in mind that the low beams are the most used and have the greatest effect on driver safety.*

8   Have the headlights adjusted by a dealer service department or service station at the earliest opportunity.

9   Bulb replacement

Refer to illustrations 9.1 and 9.3

1   The lenses of many lights are held in place by screws, which makes it a simple procedure to gain access to the bulbs **(see illustration)**.

2   On some lights the lenses are held in place by clips. The lenses can be removed either by unsnapping them or by using a small screwdriver to pry them off.

3   Several types of bulbs are used. Some are removed by pushing in and turning them counterclockwise. Others can simply be unclipped from the terminals or pulled straight out of the socket **(see illustration)**.

4   To replace the center high-mount brake light, remove the lens retaining screws and lens. Remove the bulb assembly retaining screws and disconnect the electrical connector from the bulb assembly. Remove the bulb assembly.

5   To replace the overhead console bulb,

push upward on the lamp assembly and turn to the left. Lower the lamp assembly and remove the bulb and base from the back of the lamp assembly. Pull the bulb straight out of base.

6   To gain access to the instrument panel bulbs, the instrument panel will have to be removed first.

10   Switches - removal and installation

Warning: *If equipped with an airbag, disable the airbag system before working in the vicinity of the steering wheel, instrument panel or any airbag system component. Failure to do so could cause accidental deployment of the airbag, resulting in personal injury (see Section 18).*

Caution: *On models equipped with a Delco Loc II anti-theft audio system, be sure the lockout feature is turned off before performing any procedure which requires disconnecting the battery.*

1988 through 1994 models

1   Disconnect the negative cable at the battery.

Headlight switch

Refer to illustrations 10.2 and 10.4

2   Remove the instrument cluster trim

panel retaining screws **(see illustration)**.

3   Carefully remove the electrical connectors directly behind the light switch and remove the panel.

4   Remove the light switch retaining screws and lift the switch from the instrument cluster trim panel **(see illustration)**.

5   Install the switch by reversing the removal procedure. Make sure that the grounding ring is installed on the switch.

10.4 Remove the headlight switch retaining screws and detach the switch from the backside of the trim panel

10.7 Remove the bolts (arrows) and the two retaining nuts on the steering column support (arrows)

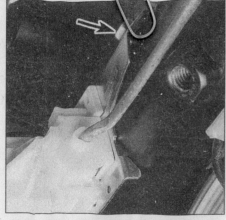

10.9 Remove the upper bolt (arrow) and the inner bolt (behind the switch) to remove the headlight dimmer switch

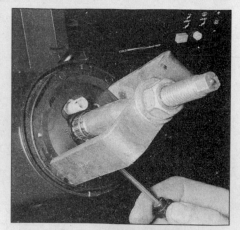

10.12 Depress the locking plate and remove the retaining clip with a small screwdriver

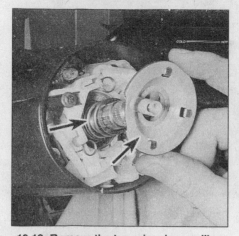

10.13 Remove the turn signal cancelling cam and spring (arrows)

10.15 Remove the screws that retain the turn signal switch and lever

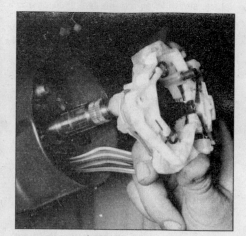

10.17 Pull the wiring loom through the steering column

Headlight dimmer switch

Refer to illustrations 10.7 and 10.9

6   The headlight dimmer switch is connected to the turn signal switch with an actuating rod and it is located on the lower section of the steering column.

7   Remove the steering column support bracket bolts and nuts and lower the steering column (**see illustration**).

8   Disconnect the dimmer switch electrical connector.

9   Remove the bolts that retain the dimmer switch to the steering column (**see illustration**).

Park/Neutral switch/back-up light switch (automatic transmission)

10   Refer to Chapter 7B for the removal procedure.

Windshield wiper/washer switch

Refer to illustrations 10.12, 10.13, 10.15, 10.17, 10.18, 10.19 and 10.21

11   Remove the steering wheel (see Chapter 10, Section 14).

12   Compress the locking plate with a special tool and simultaneously remove the clip that retains the locking plate to the steering

column (**see illustration**). Remove the locking plate.

13   Remove the turn signal cancelling cam and spring (**see illustration**).

14   Remove the hazard warning button from the steering column.

15   Remove the turn signal switch retaining screws (**see illustration**). **Note:** *Be sure to remember the location of the turn signal lever for purposes of correct installation.*

16   Disconnect the turn signal electrical connector located near the bottom of the steering column.

17   Remove the steering column wire loom cover in order to slide the turn signal switch wiring through the steering column. Pull the turn signal switch assembly up and out (**see illustration**).

18   Use a paper clip and depress the retaining spring on the ignition key warning buzzer switch (**see illustration**) and remove the ignition key warning buzzer switch from the turn signal switch housing.

19   Remove the Torx head bolts that attach the turn signal switch housing to the steering column (**see illustration**) and remove the housing from the column.

20   Disconnect the handle from the wind-

shield wiper switch by pulling the handle directly out. Carefully wiggle the handle as you pull to avoid jarring or breaking the mechanism.

21   Drive the pin through the backside of the switch housing (**see illustration**) and remove the windshield wiper switch from the housing.

22   Installation is the reverse of removal.

Ignition switch

Refer to illustration 10.27

23   Disconnect the negative cable at the battery.

24   Place the ignition switch in the Lock position. If the key lock cylinder has been removed, pull the actuating rod up until a definite stop can be felt and then move down one detent.

25   Lower and support the steering column (see illustration 10.7).

26   Remove the ignition switch retaining screws and lift the switch out of the steering column jacket.

27   Prior to installation, make sure the ignition switch is in the Lock position (**see illustration**).

28   Connect the actuating rod to the switch.

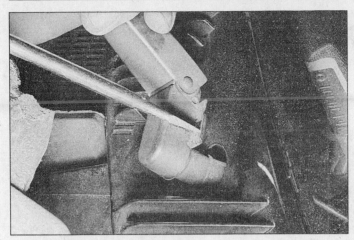

13.2 Flip the latch up, remove the nut and detach the wiper arm

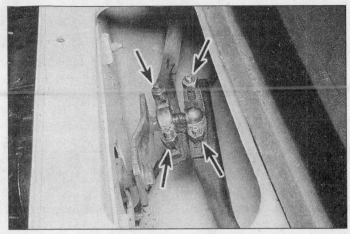

13.4 Disconnect the linkage from the wiper motor (arrows)

so could cause accidental deployment of the airbag resulting in personal injury (see Section 18).

10   Disconnect the negative cable at the battery.

11   Remove the cup holder from the instrument panel.

12   Unhook the 4 clips across the top and 3 across the bottom of the instrument cluster trim panel. Remove the trim panel.

13   Disconnect the electrical connectors for the headlight switch, dimmer control and accessory switches.

14   Remove the instrument cluster mounting screws and carefully pull the cluster out of the dash.

15   The instrument cluster and the housing must not be separated because of the danger of static electricity damaging the computer chips that are contained within the cluster (see illustration 12.8). If the instrument cluster must be replaced, take it to a dealer service department, exchange units may be available.

16   Installation is the reverse of removal.

13   Windshield wiper motor - removal and installation

Refer to illustrations 13.2, 13.4 and 13.5
Caution: *On models equipped with a Delco Loc II anti-theft audio system, be sure the lockout feature is turned off before performing any procedure which requires disconnecting the battery.*

1   Disconnect the negative cable at the battery.

2   Remove the windshield wiper arms **(see illustration)**.

3   Remove the cowl vent grille retaining screws and lift the grille up.

4   Disconnect the linkage from the wiper motor crank arm **(see illustration)**. *Note: Do not remove the nut and crank arm from the motor shaft.*

5   Remove the wiper motor mounting bolts **(see illustration)**.

6   Remove the wiper motor electrical con-

13.5 Remove the wiper motor mounting bolts (arrows)

nector and detach the motor from the mounting bracket.

7   Installation is the reverse of removal.

14   Rear window wiper motor - removal and installation

Caution: *On models equipped with a Delco Loc II anti-theft audio system, be sure the lockout feature is turned off before performing any procedure which requires disconnecting the battery.*

1   Disconnect the negative cable at the battery.

2   To remove the wiper arm, raise the blade off the rear glass. Insert a 0.125-inch drill bit, or metal rod, into the arm access hole to release the locking device and remove the arm. Remove the washer hose from the arm.

3   Remove the wiper motor cover retainers and cover.

4   Disconnect the wiper motor electrical connector.

5   Remove the wiper motor mounting bolt, washer, spacer and nut.

6   Remove the wiper motor and retainer from the rear glass.

7   Installation is the reverse of removal.

15   Radio and speakers - removal and installation

Caution: *On models equipped with a Delco Loc II anti-theft audio system, be sure the lockout feature is turned off before performing any procedure which requires disconnecting the battery.*

Radio receiver (1988 through 1994 models)

Refer to illustration 15.4

1   Disconnect the negative cable at the battery.

2   Remove the ashtray.

3   Remove the electrical connectors from the radio receiver.

4   Remove the radio support bracket and the radio receiver from the dash **(see illustration)**.

5   Installation is the reverse of removal.

Radio receiver (1995 and later models)

Warning: *If equipped with an airbag, disable the airbag system before working in the vicinity of the steering wheel, instrument panel or any airbag system component. Failure to do*

15.4 Remove the radio receiver retaining screws (arrows)

15.11 To remove the radio receiver, remove these screws (you'll have to remove the heater/air conditioner control head for access to the lower radio screw)

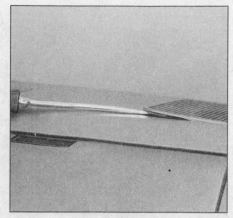

15.15 Use a screwdriver to pry up the speaker grille

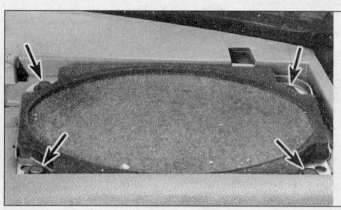

15.16 Remove the speaker retaining screws (arrows)

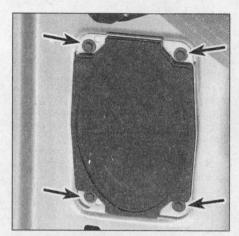

15.20 Remove the rear speaker mounting screws (arrow)

so could cause accidental deployment of the airbag resulting in personal injury (see Section 18).

6   Disconnect the negative cable at the battery.

7   Unhook the 4 clips across the top and 3 across the bottom of the instrument cluster trim panel. Remove the trim panel.

8   Using a small screwdriver, release the retainers and pull the radio unit out of the instrument panel.

9   Disconnect the electrical connectors and antenna lead from the radio unit.

10   Installation is the reverse of removal.

Control head (1988 through 1994 models)

Refer to illustration 15.11

11   Remove the trim bezel. Remove the heater/air conditioner control head and the screws that retain the radio control head to the dash **(see illustration)**.

12   Remove the electrical connectors and the antenna connector from the control head.

13   Remove the control head from the dash.

14   Installation is the reverse of removal.

Front speaker

Refer to illustrations 15.15 and 15.16

15   Use a dull screwdriver and carefully pry the speaker grille up **(see illustration)**.

16   Remove the screws that retain the speaker to the dash **(see illustration)**.

17   Raise the speaker and disconnect the wires.

18   Installation is the reverse of removal.

Rear speaker

Refer to illustration 15.20

19   Use a dull screwdriver and carefully pry the speaker grille out.

20   Remove the speaker mounting screws, **(see illustration)** detach the speaker then disconnect the speaker wires.

21   Installation is the reverse of removal.

---

16   Power door lock system - description and check

The power door lock system operates the door lock actuators mounted in each door. The system consists of the switches, actuators and associated wiring. Diagnosis can usually be limited to simple checks of the wiring connections and actuators for minor faults which can be easily repaired. These include:

a) *Check the system fuse and/or circuit breaker.*

b) *Check the switch wires for damage and loose connections. Check the switches for continuity.*

c) *Remove the door panel(s) and check the actuator wiring connections to see if they're loose or damaged. Inspect the actuator rods (if equipped) to make sure they aren't bent or damaged. Inspect the actuator wiring for damaged or loose connections. The actuator can be checked by applying battery power momentarily. A discernible click indicates that the solenoid is operating properly.*

---

17   Power window system - description and check

The power window system operates the electric motors mounted in the doors which lower and raise the windows. The system consists of the control switches, the motors (regulators), glass mechanisms and associated wiring. Diagnosis can usually be limited to simple checks of the wiring connections and motors for minor faults which can be easily repaired. These include:

18.3a There are two (discriminating) or crash sensors (arrow) at the front, plus . . .

18.3b . . . an arming sensor (arrow) mounted under the vehicle

a) *Inspect the power window actuating switches for broken wires and loose connections.*

b) *Check the power window fuse/and or circuit breaker.*

c) *Remove the door panel(s) and check the power window motor wires to see if they're loose or damaged. Inspect the glass mechanisms for damage which could cause binding.*

---

18 Airbag - general information

Caution: *On models equipped with a Delco Loc II anti-theft audio system, be sure the lockout feature is turned off before performing any procedure which requires disconnecting the battery.*

Description

1   These models are equipped with a Supplemental Inflatable Restraint (SIR) system, more commonly called an airbag. The SIR system is designed to protect the driver and passenger from serious injury in the event of a head-on or frontal collision.

2   The SIR system consists of an airbag in the center of the steering wheel (and on some later models, in the passenger's side of the instrument panel), three crash sensors mounted at the front and under the vehicle and the Diagnostic Energy Reserve Module (DERM) behind the center of the instrument panel (1995 and 1996 models) or the Sensing and Diagnostic Module (SDM) mounted under the driver's seat (1997 and 1998 models).

Sensors

Refer to illustrations 18.3a and 18.3b

3   The system has three sensors: two discriminating or crash sensors at the front of the vehicle mounted on the frame rails and an arming sensor located under the left side of the vehicle **(see illustrations).**

4   The front crash sensors are basically

pressure sensitive switches that complete an electrical circuit during an impact of sufficient G force. The arming sensor is calibrated to send voltage to the airbag module when it senses a dramatic drop in vehicle speed readying it for deployment. The electrical signal from the crash sensors is sent to the DERM, that then completes the circuit and inflates the airbag.

Diagnostic/Energy Reserve Module (DERM) or Sensing and Diagnostic Module (SDM)

5   The diagnostic module contains an on-board microprocessor which monitors the operation of the system. It checks this system every time the vehicle is started, causing the AIRBAG light to go on, then off seven times, if the system is operating properly. If there is a fault in the system, the light will go on and stay on and the airbag control module will store fault codes indicating the nature of the fault. If the AIRBAG light does go on and stay on, the vehicle should be taken to your dealer immediately for service.

Operation

6   For the airbag to deploy, an impact of sufficient G force must occur within 30-degrees of the vehicle centerline. When this condition occurs, the circuit to the airbag inflator is closed and the airbag inflates. If the battery is destroyed by the impact, or is too low to power the inflator, a back-up power unit inside the DERM or SDM supplies current to the airbag.

Self-diagnosis system

7   A self-diagnosis circuit in the module displays a light when the ignition switch is turned to the On position. If the system is operating normally, the light should go out after seven flashes. If the light doesn't come on, or doesn't go out after seven flashes, or if it comes on while you're driving the vehicle, there's a malfunction in the SIR system. Have it inspected and repaired as soon as possible. Do not attempt to troubleshoot or service

18.9 Remove the airbag fuse (refer to the fuse block cover to make sure it's the right one)

the SIR system yourself. Even a small mistake could cause the SIR system to malfunction when you need it.

Servicing components near the SIR system

8   Nevertheless, there are times when you need to remove the steering wheel, radio or service other components on or near the dashboard. At these times, you'll be working around components and wire harnesses for the SIR system. SIR wires are easy to identify: They're all covered with bright yellow conduit. Do not tamper with or use electrical test equipment on yellow wires. *ALWAYS DISABLE THE SIR SYSTEM BEFORE WORKING NEAR THE SIR SYSTEM COMPONENTS OR RELATED WIRING.*

Disabling the SIR system

Refer to illustrations 18.9 and 18.11
Warning: *Anytime you are working in the vicinity of airbag wiring or components, DISABLE THE SIR SYSTEM.*

9   Turn the steering wheel to the straight ahead position, place the ignition switch in Lock, remove the key, then remove the

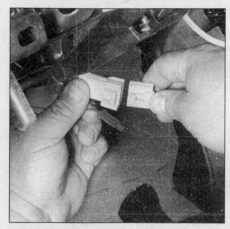

**18.10 The driver's side airbag Connector
Position Assurance (CPA) connector is
found at the steering column**

Color of wire insulation

BLK	Black	PPL	Purple
BRN	Brown	TR	Tracer
CHK	Check	YEL	Yellow
CR	Cross	WHT	White
GRN	Green	BLU	Blue
NAT	Natural	STR	Stripe
SGL	Single	PNK	Pink
ORN	Orange	DK	Dark
GRY	Gray	LT	Light

19.4 Wiring diagram color codes

airbag fuse from the fuse block **(see illustration)**.

10   Remove the knee bolster and sound insulator panel (see Chapter 11) below the instrument panel. To disable the driver's side airbag, unplug the yellow Connector Position Assurance (CPA) steering column harness connector at the base of the steering column **(see illustration)**. To disable the passenger's side airbag, unplug the CPA electrical connector to the right of the steering column, fastened to a bracket.

Enabling the SIR system

11   After you've disabled the airbag and performed the necessary service, plug in the steering column (driver's side) and passenger side Connector Position Assurance (CPA) connectors. Reinstall the knee bolster and sound insulator.

12   Install the airbag fuse.

19   Wiring diagrams - general information

Refer to illustration 19.4

Since it isn't possible to include all wiring diagrams for every year covered by this manual, the following diagrams are those that are typical and most commonly needed.

Prior to troubleshooting any circuits, check the fuses and circuit breakers (if equipped) to make sure they're in good condition. Make sure the battery is properly charged and check the cable connections (Chapter 1).

When checking a circuit, make sure that all connectors are clean, with no broken or loose terminals. When unplugging a connector, do not pull on the wires. Pull only on the connector housings themselves.

Refer to the accompanying table for the wire color codes applicable to the diagrams in this manual **(see illustration)**.

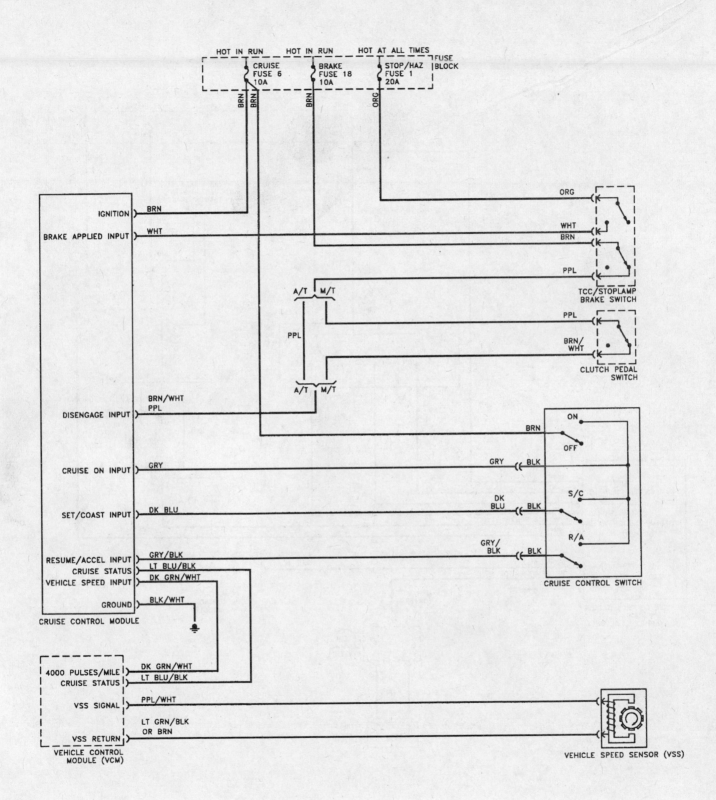

Typical 1996 and later cruise control system

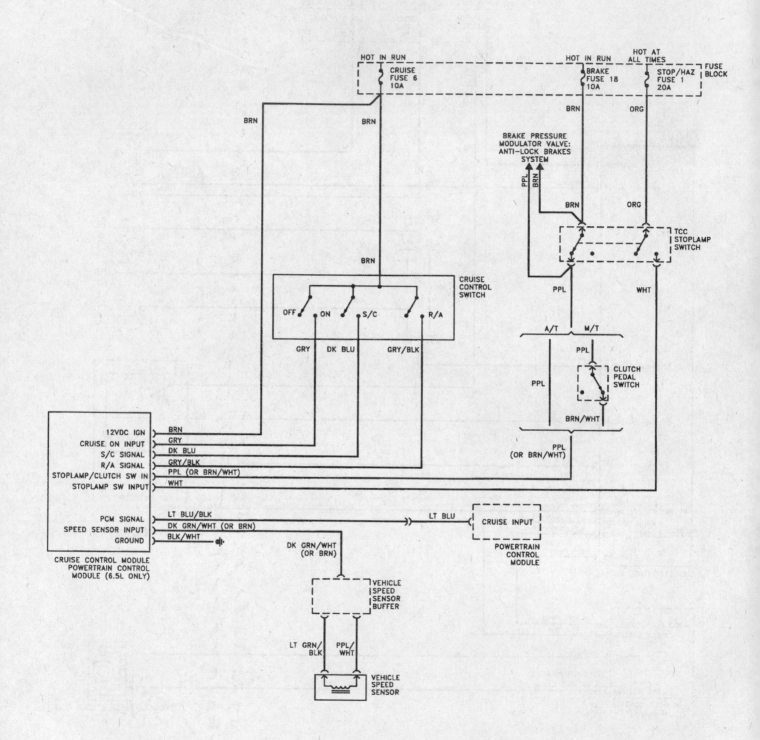

Typical 1994 and 1995 cruise control system

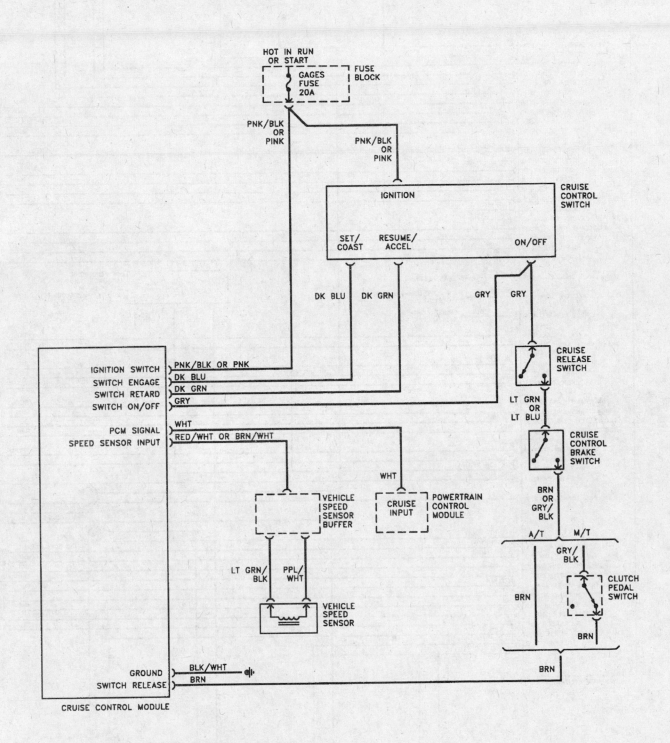

Typical 1993 and earlier cruise control system

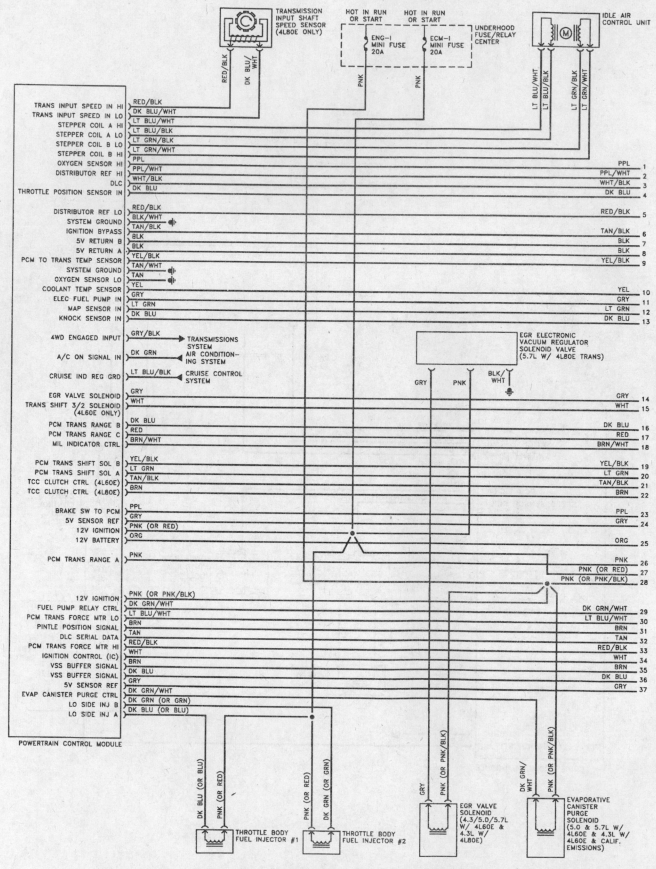

Typical 1988 through 1995 engine controls (1 of 3)

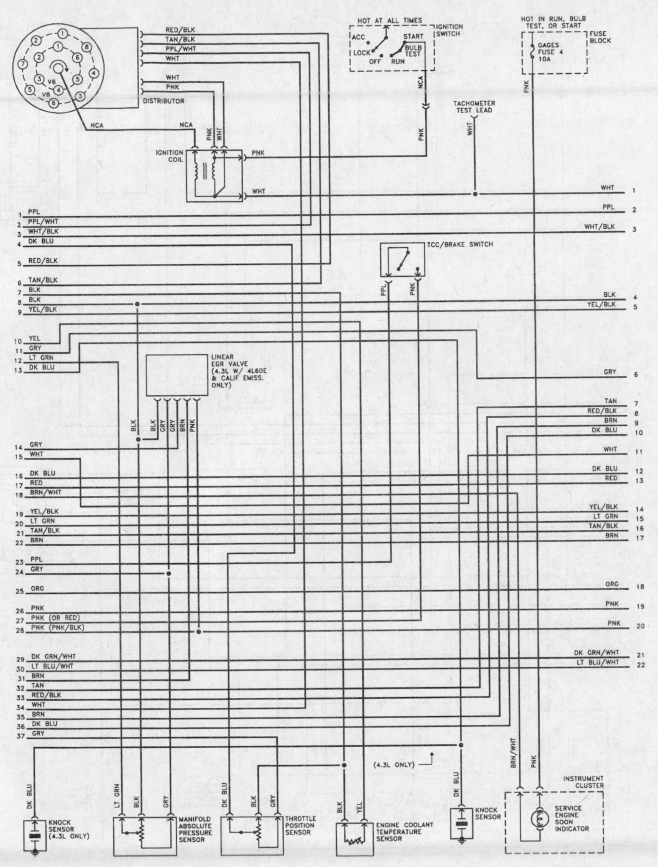

Typical 1988 through 1995 engine controls (2 of 3)

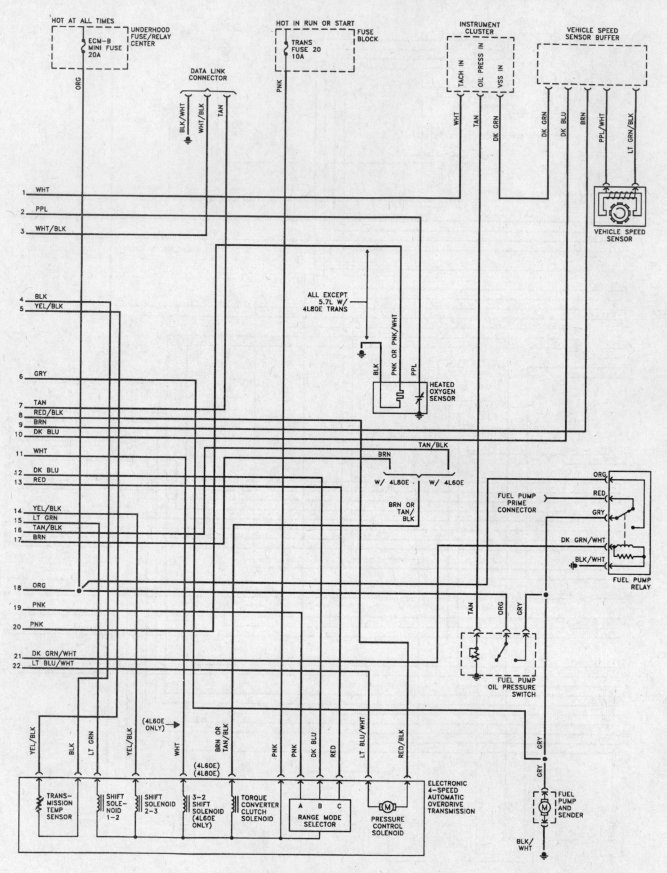

Typical 1988 through 1995 engine controls (3 of 3)

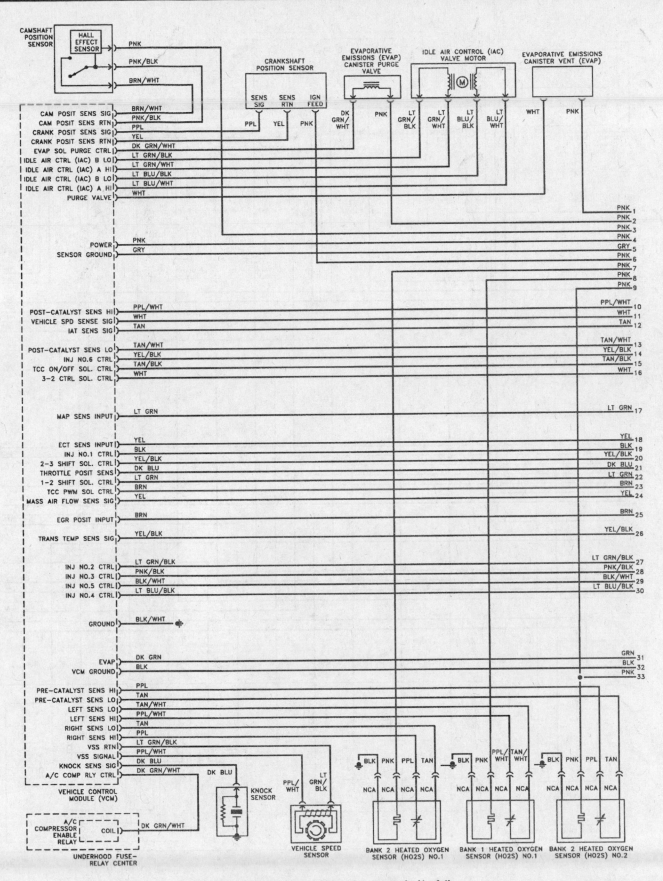

Typical 1996 and later 4.3L engine controls (1 of 4)

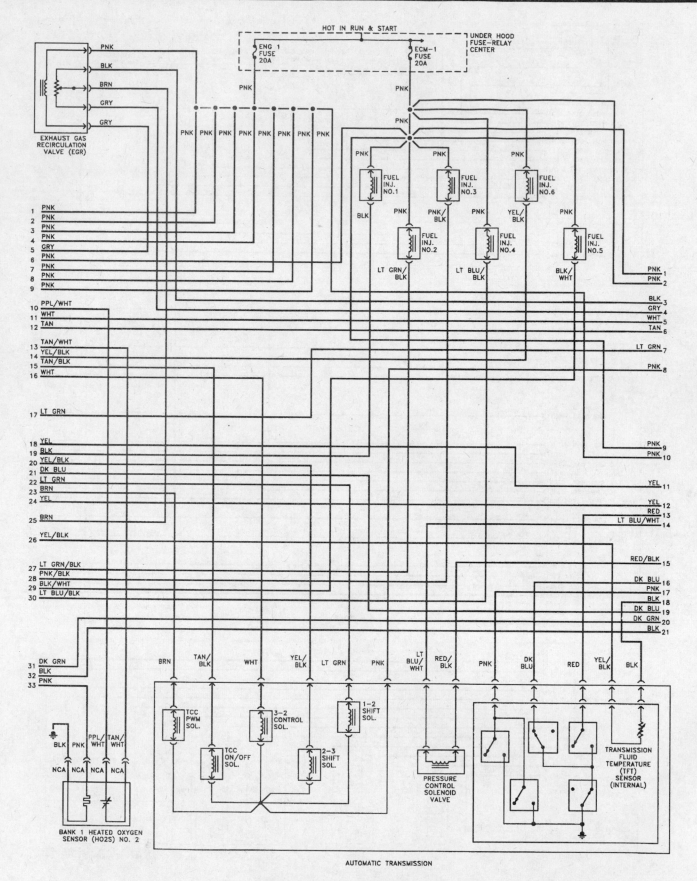

Typical 1996 and later 4.3L engine controls (2 of 4)

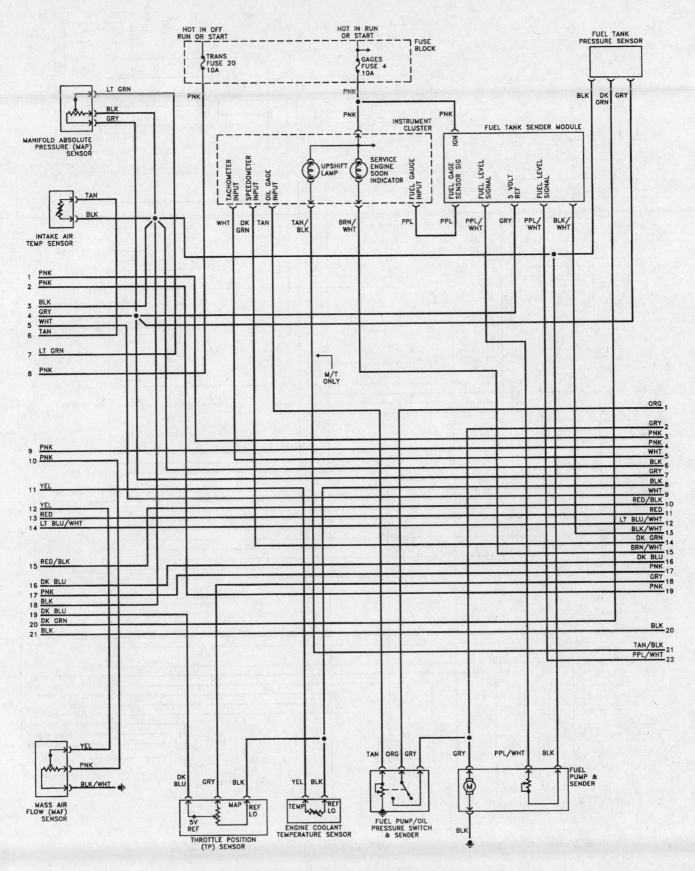

Typical 1996 and later 4.3L engine controls (3 of 4)

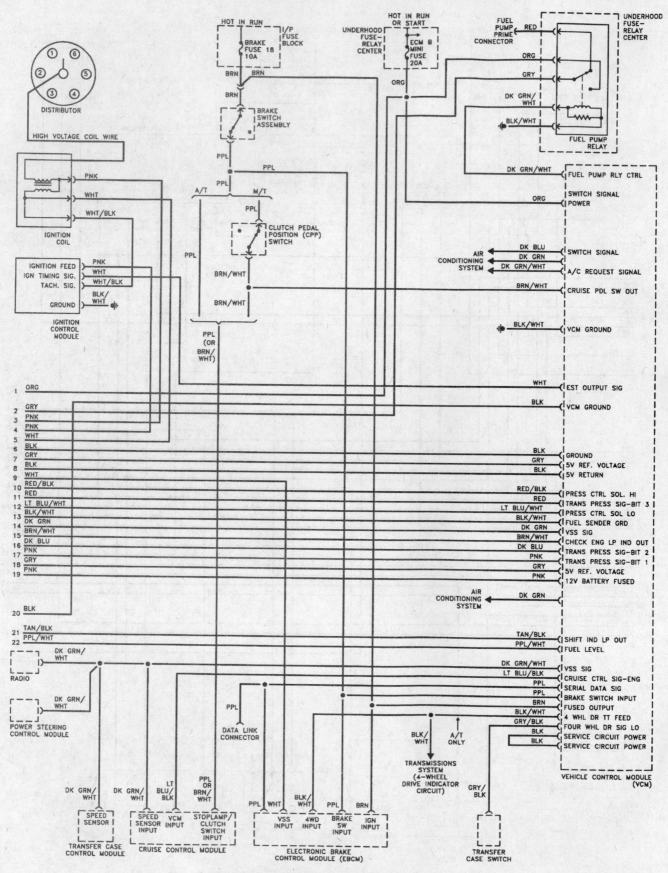

Typical 1996 and later 4.3L engine controls (4 of 4)

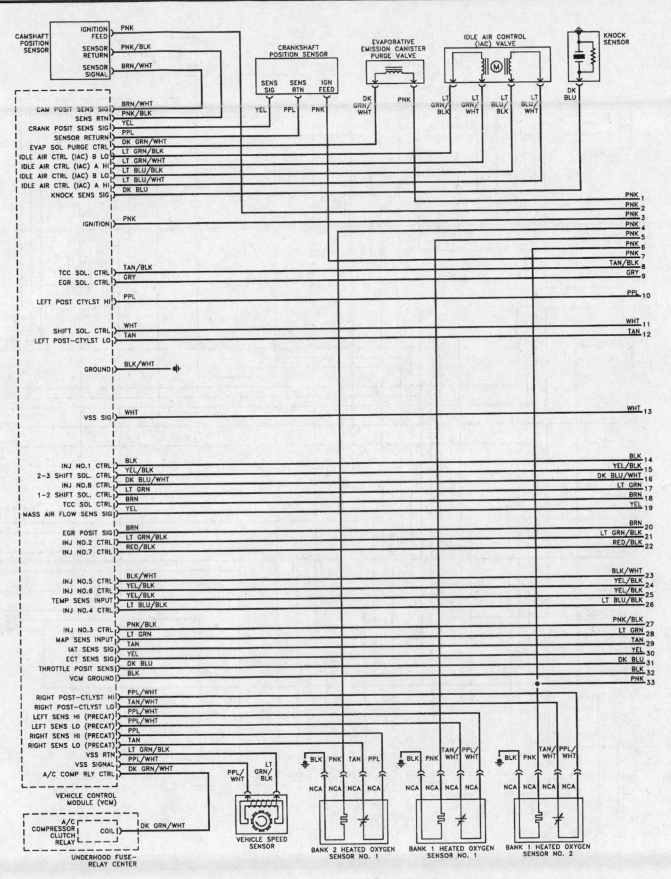

Typical 1996 and later 5.0L, 5.7L and 7.4L engine controls (1 of 4)

Chapter 12 Chassis electrical system

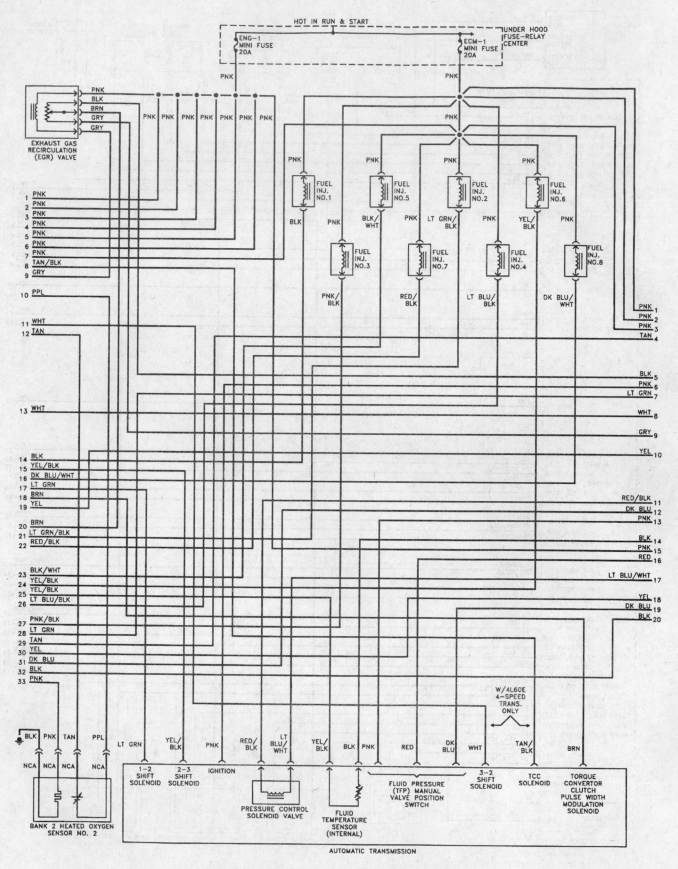

Typical 1996 and later 5.0L, 5.7L and 7.4L engine controls (2 of 4)

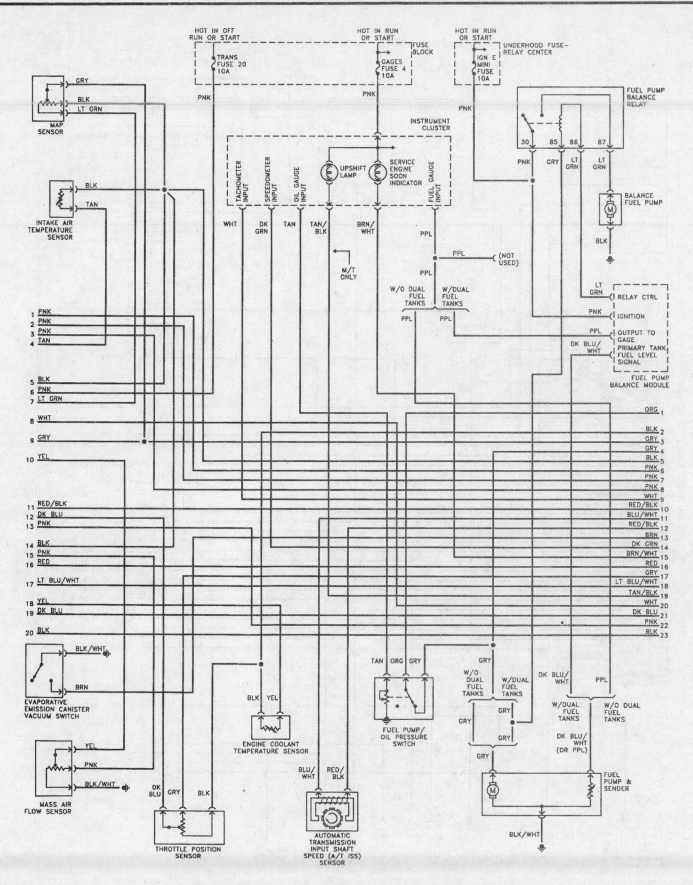

Typical 1996 and later 5.0L, 5.7L and 7.4L engine controls (3 of 4)

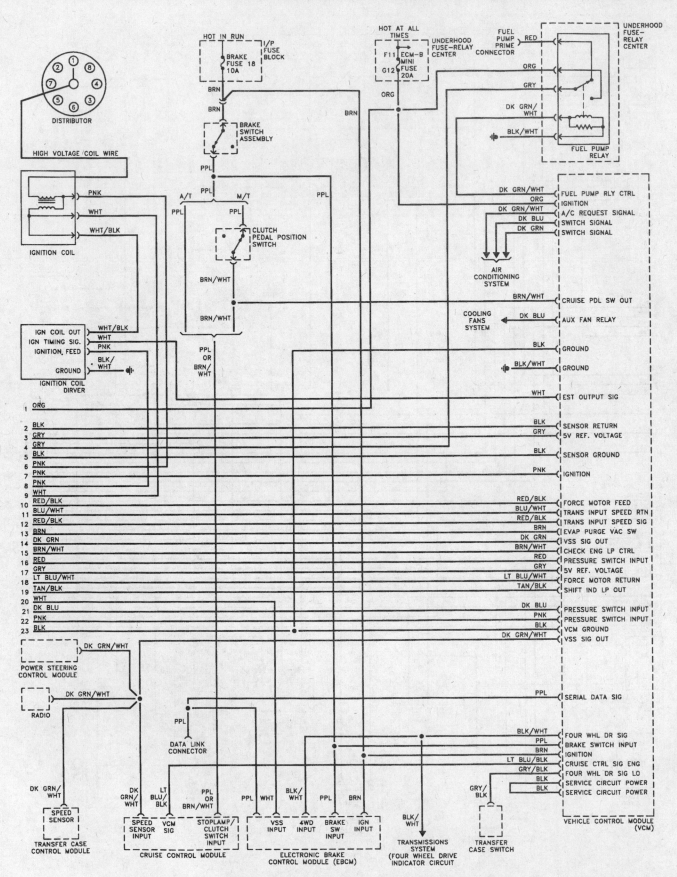

Typical 1996 and later 5.0L, 5.7L and 7.4L engine controls (4 of 4)

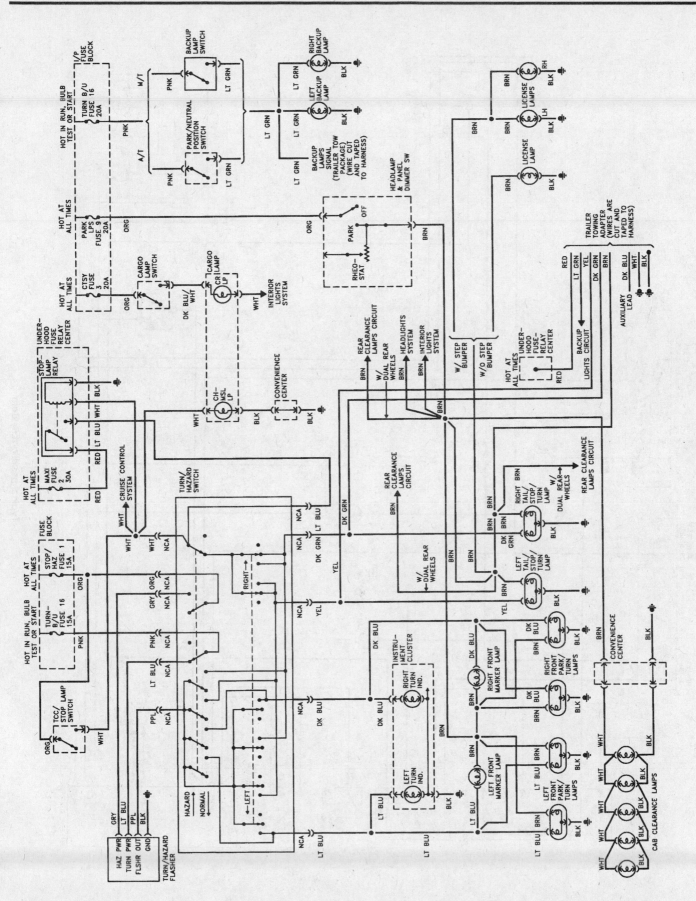

Typical exterior light system

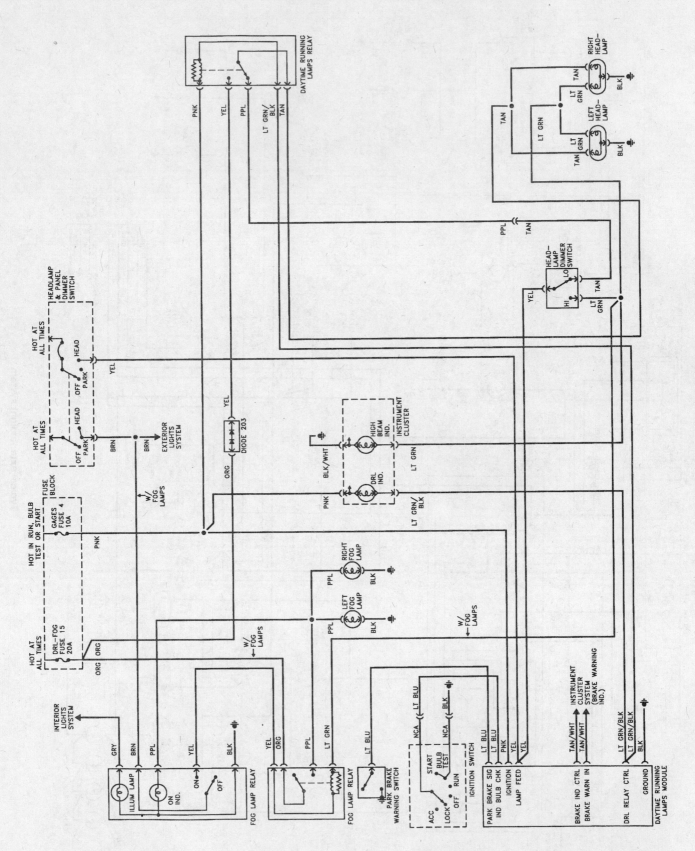

Typical headlight system

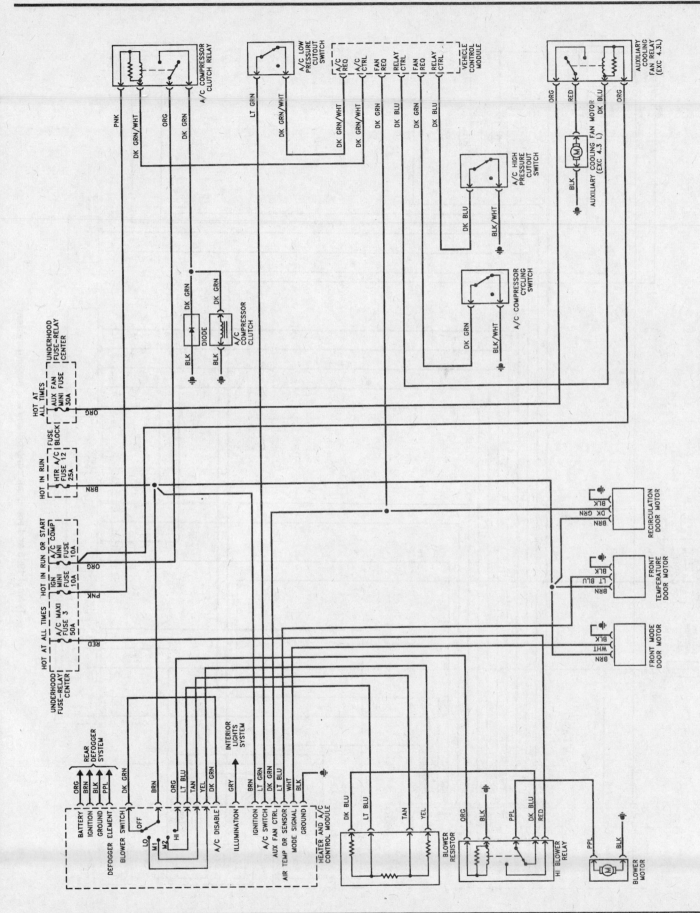

Typical 1994 and later air conditioning and heating system

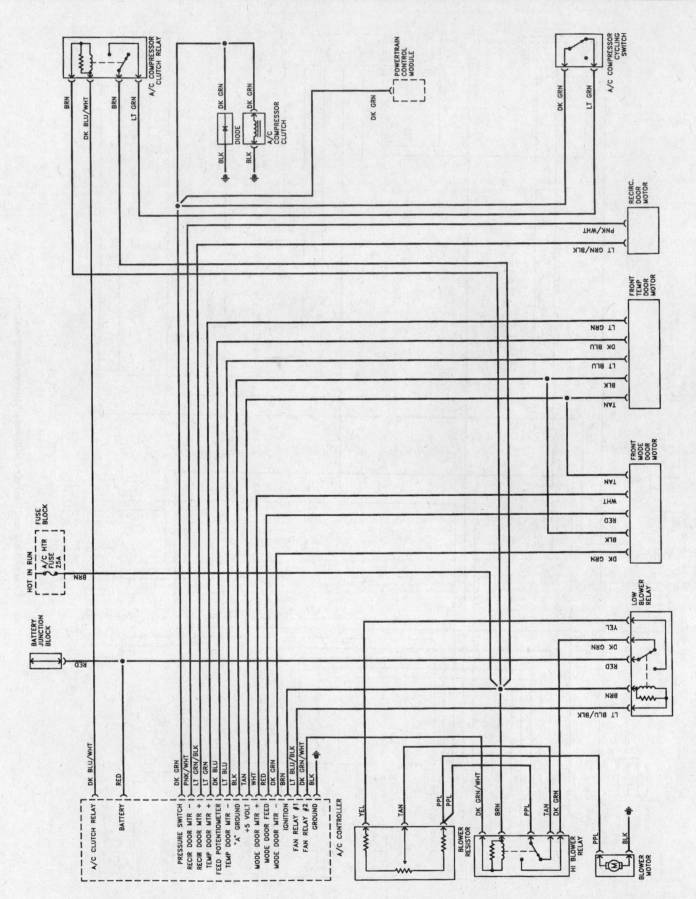

Typical 1995 and earlier air conditioning and heating system

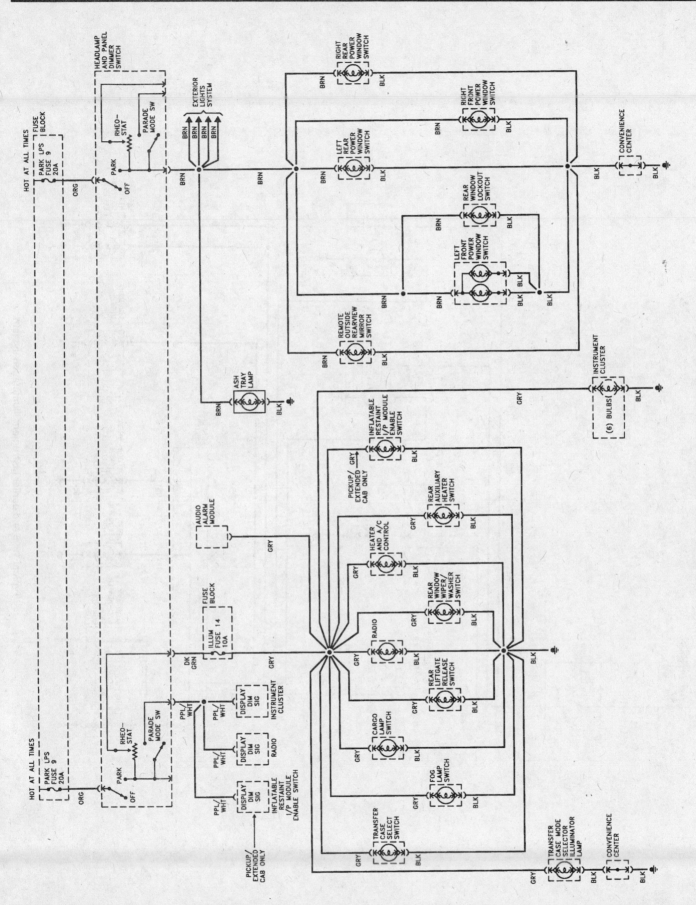

Typical 1996 and later instrument illumination system

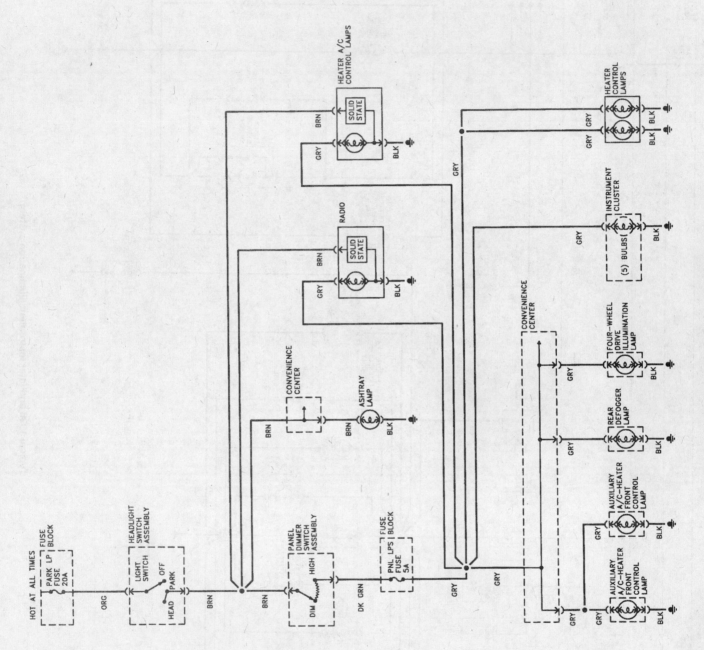

Typical 1995 and earlier instrument illumination system

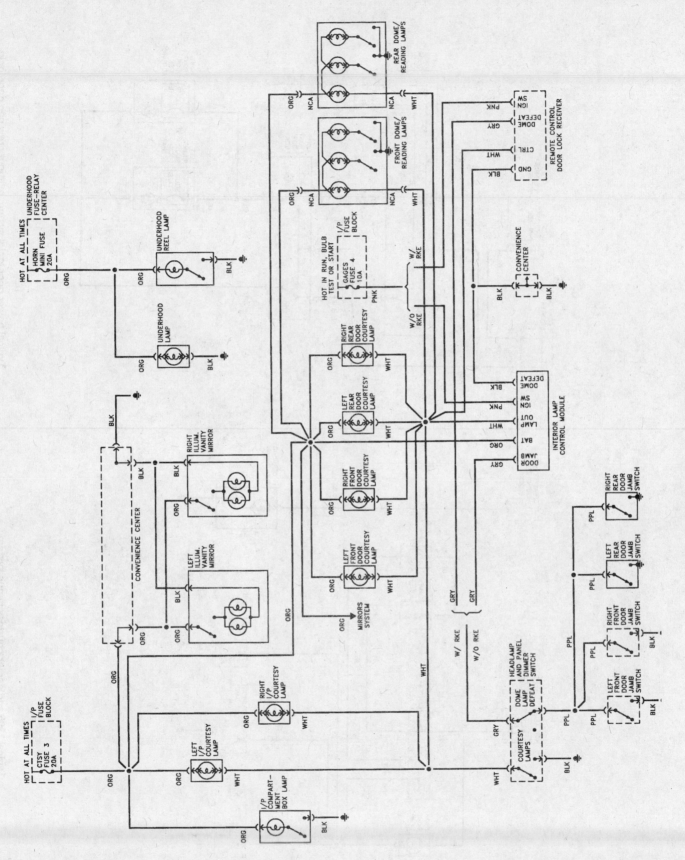

Typical 1996 and later courtesy lamps system

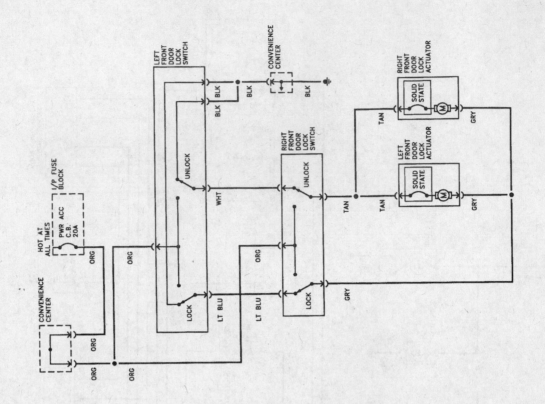

Typical power door locks system (without crew cab door lock)

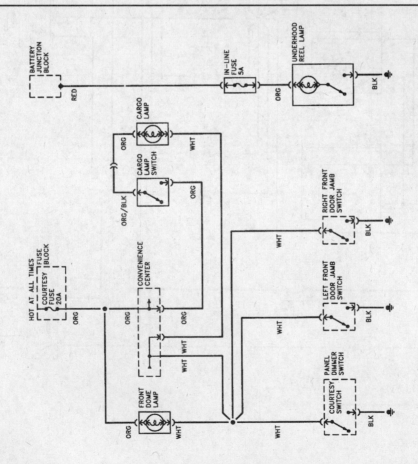

Typical 1995 and earlier courtesy lamps system

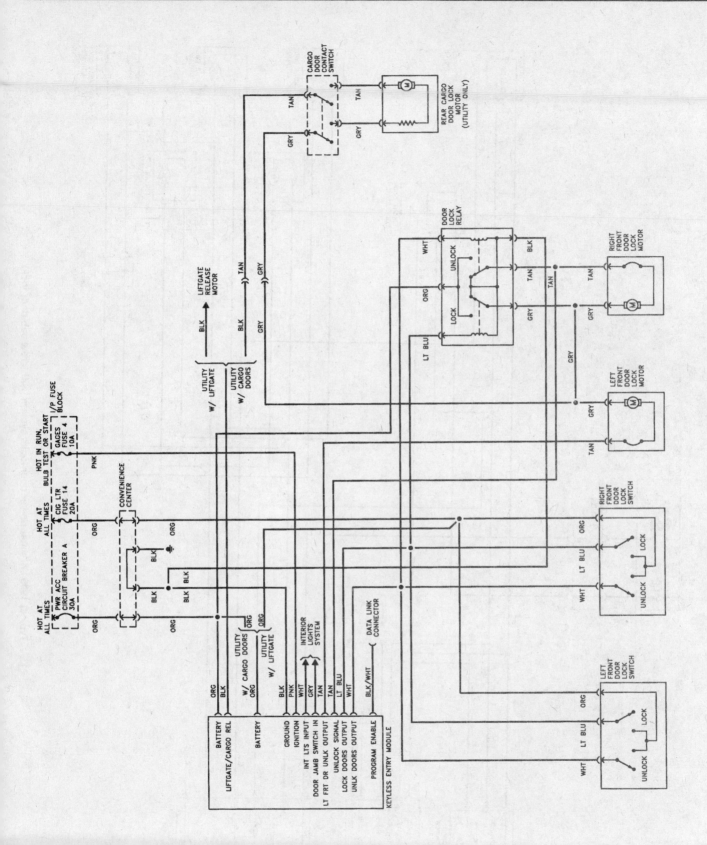

Typical 1995 and later power door locks system (without crew cab keyless entry)

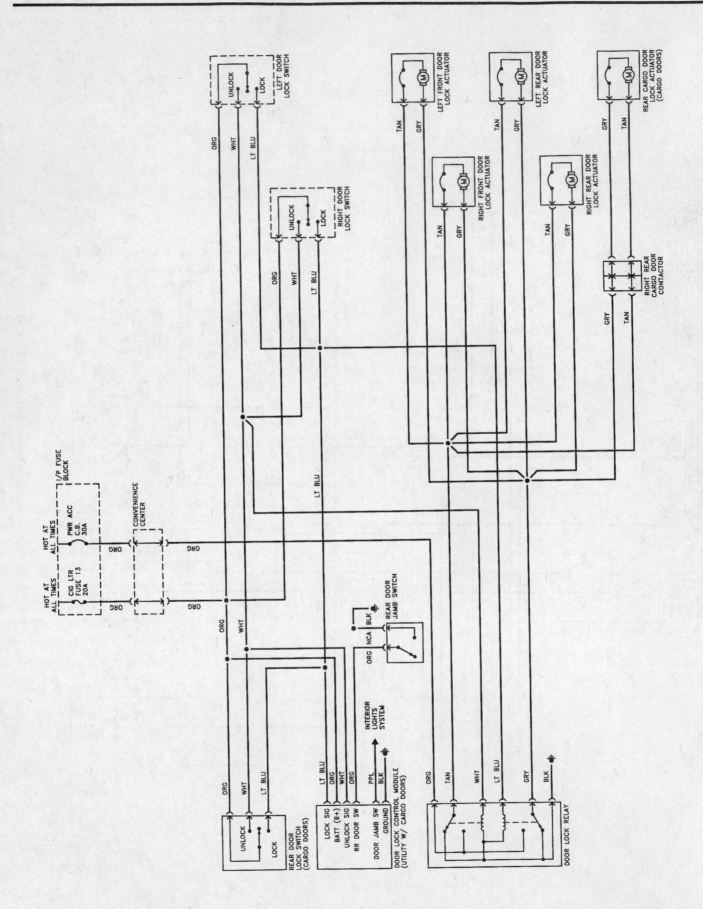

Typical 1990 and later power door locks system (with crew cab door lock)

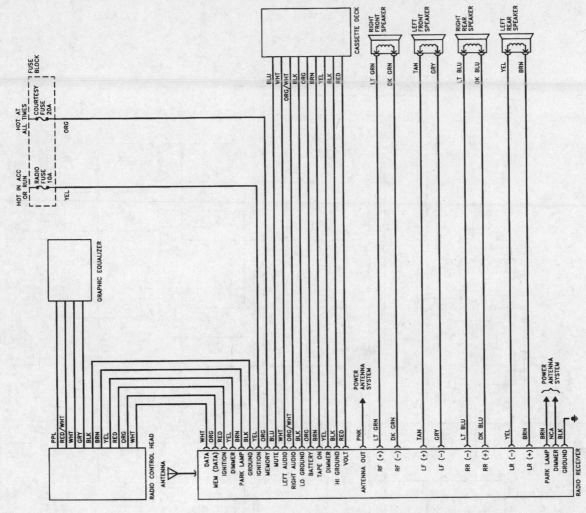

Typical audio system

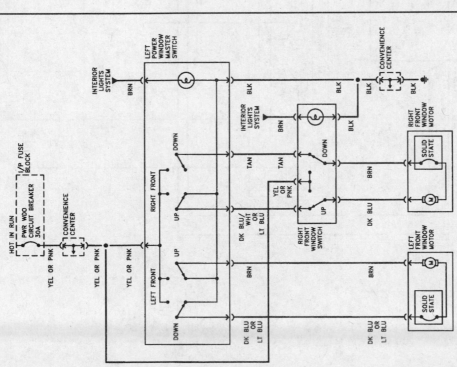

Typical 2 door power window system

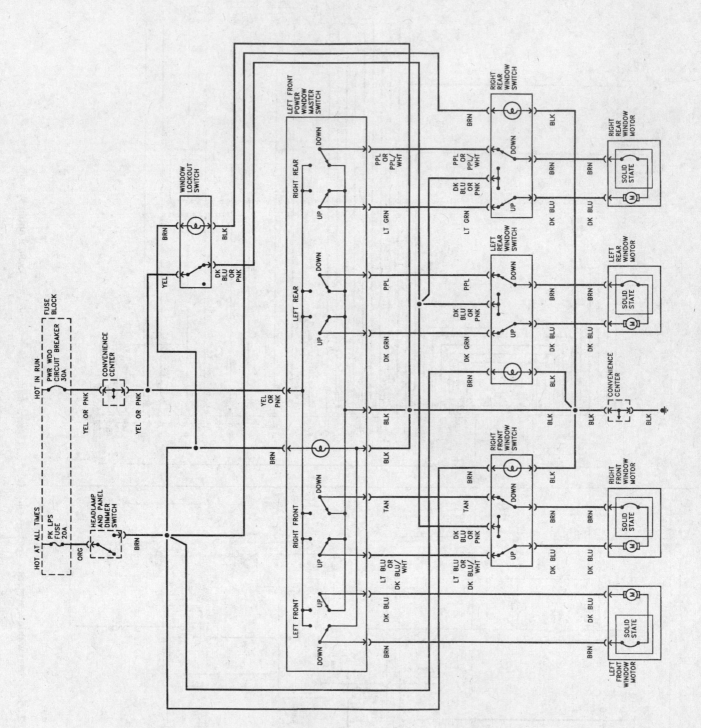

Typical 4 door power window system

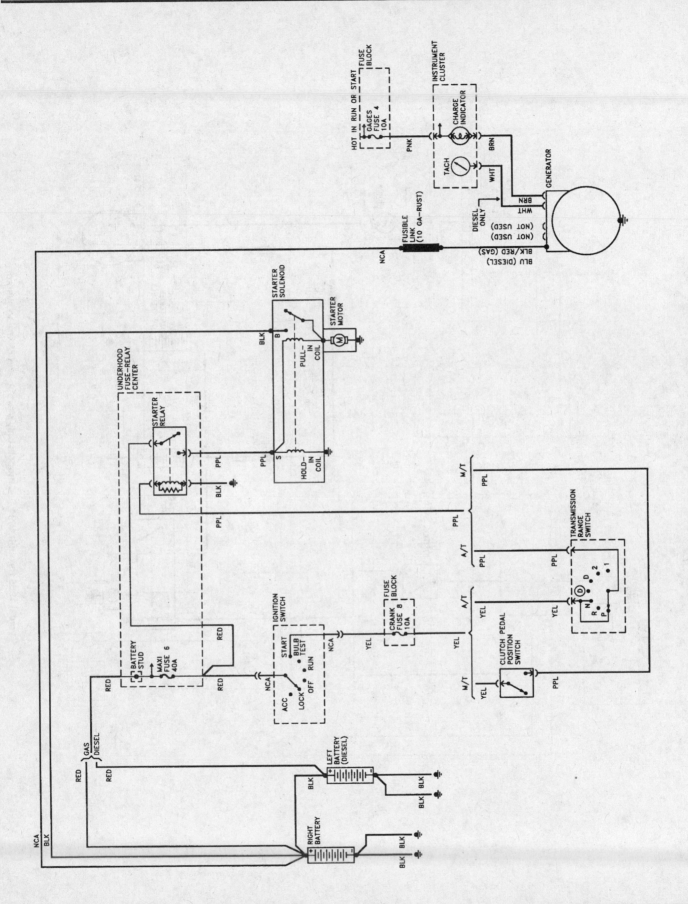

Typical 1988 and later C/K and Sierra models starting and charging system

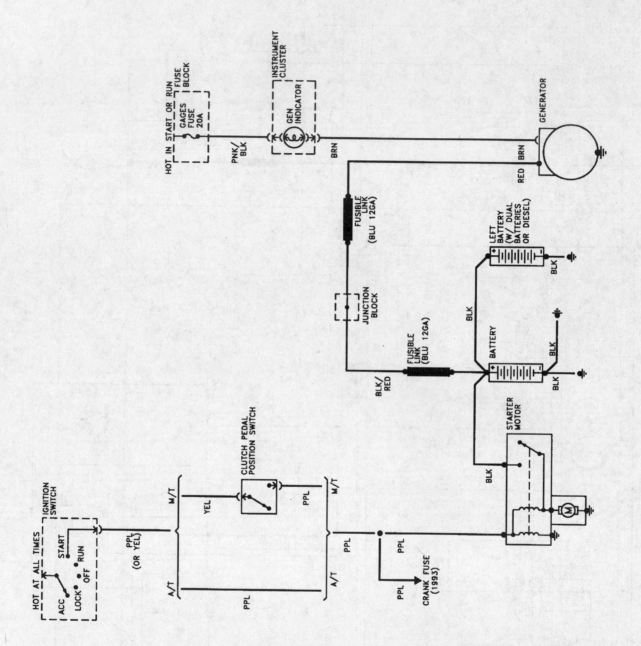

Typical 1988 through 1994 C/K models only starting and charging system

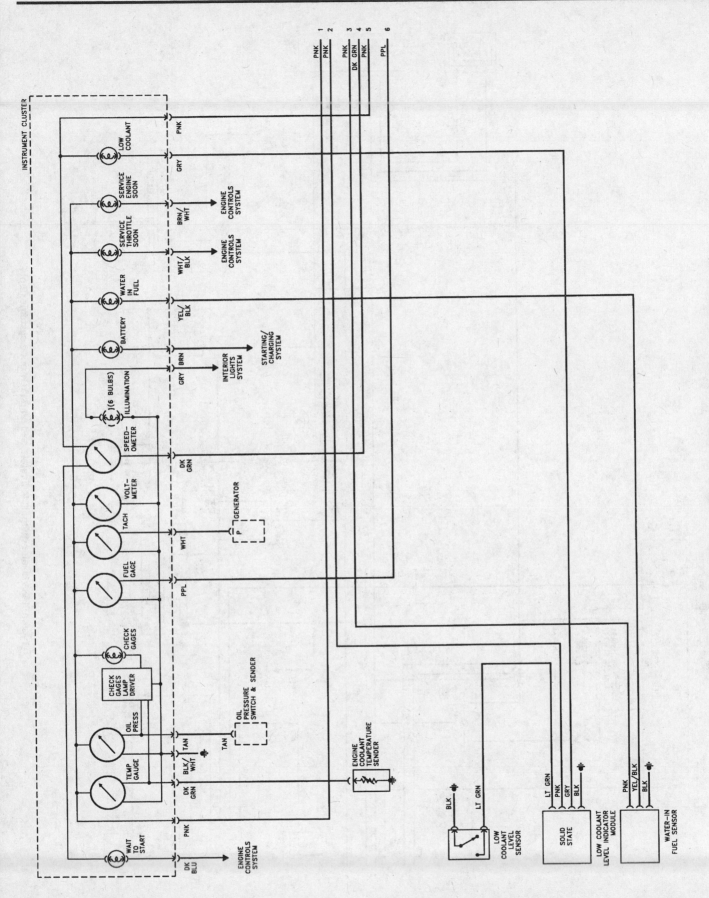

Typical 1995 and later gauges, indicators and engine warning systems (1 of 2)

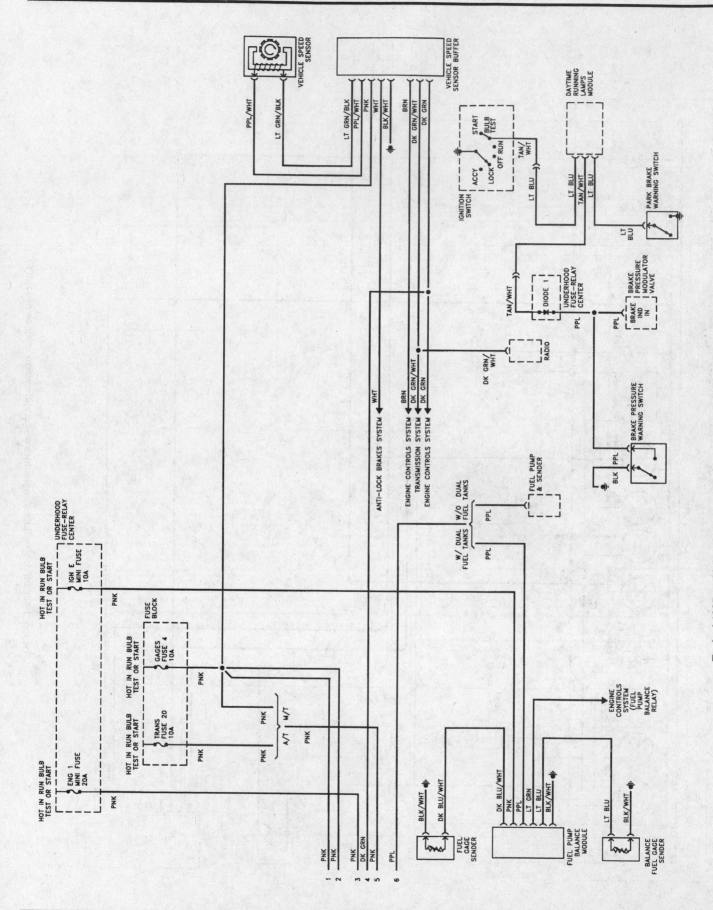

Typical 1995 and later gauges, indicators and engine warning systems (2 of 2)

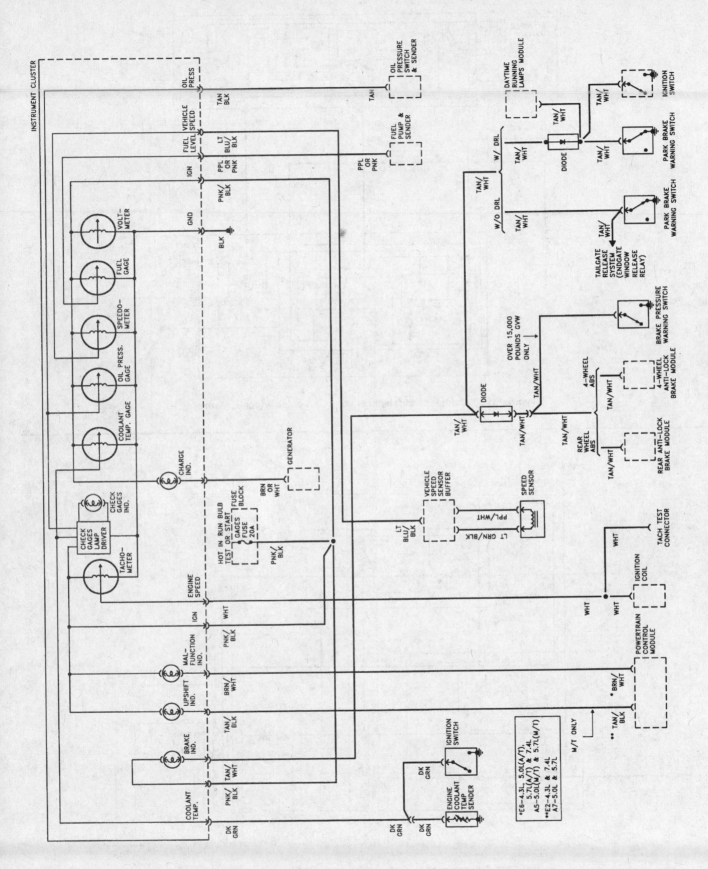

Typical 1988 through 1994 gauges, indicators and engine warning systems

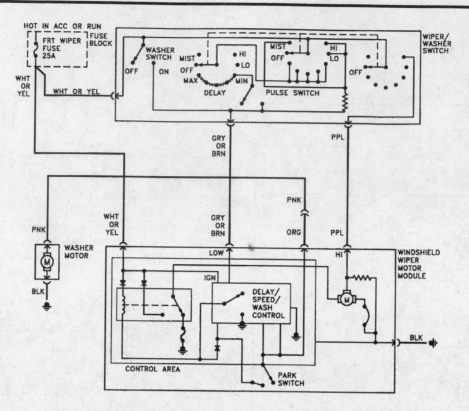

Typical 1988 and later windshield washer and pulse wiper system

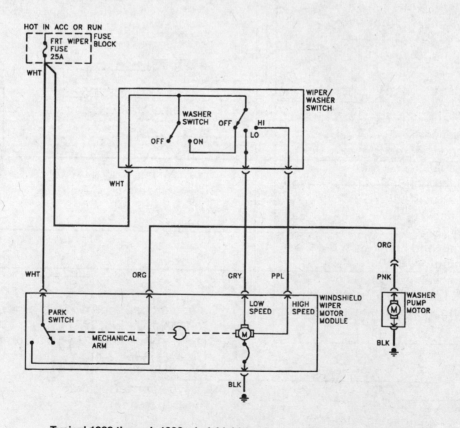

Typical 1988 through 1993 windshield washer and 2-speed wiper system

Index

O

Oil pan, removal and installation, 2A-17
Oil pressure sending unit location, 2B-6
Oil pump, removal and installation, 2A-17
Oil seal
    replacement, 7A-2
    semi-floating axle, replacement, 8-11
On Board Diagnostic (OBD) system and trouble
    codes, 6-4
Outside mirror, removal and installation, 11-10
Oxygen sensor, check and replacement, 6-16

P

Park/Neutral switch, 6-13, 7B-5
Parking brake
    adjustment, 9-17
    cables, removal and installation, 9-17
Pilot bearing, inspection and replacement, 8-6
Pinion oil seal, rear, replacement, 8-12
Piston rings, installation, 2B-20
Piston/connecting rod assembly
    inspection, 2B-17
    installation and rod bearing oil clearance check, 2B-21
    removal, 2B-13
Positive Crankcase Ventilation (PCV)
    system, 1-28, 6-16
Power door lock system, description and check, 12-10
Power steering
    fluid level check, 1-13
    pump, removal and installation, 10-14
    system, bleeding, 10-15
Power window system, description and check, 12-10
Pre-oiling the engine after overhaul, 2B-23

R

Radiator grille, removal and installation, 11-9
Radiator, removal and installation, 3-3
Rear axle
    assembly, removal and installation, 8-12
    bearing (semi-floating axle), replacement, 8-11
Rear pinion oil seal, replacement, 8-12
Repair operations possible with the engine in the
    vehicle, 2A-4
Rocker arm covers, removal and installation, 2A-4
Rocker arms and pushrods, removal, inspection and
    installation, 2A-5

S

Safety first, 0-20
Seal replacement, transfer case, 7C-2
Seat
    back latch check, 1-24
    belt check, 1-24
Secondary Air Injection (AIR) system, 6-23
Semi-floating rear axleshaft, removal and
    installation, 8-10
Sequential Fuel Injection systems-general
    information, 4-8
Shaft (front) and axle tube assembly (4WD models),
    removal and installation, 8-16
Shift cable (1995 and later models), removal,
    installation and adjustment, 7B-3
Shift lever, removal and installation
    manual transmission, 7A-2
    transfer case, 7C-1
Shift linkage
    automatic transmission, 1988 through
        1994 models, 7B-2
    transfer case, 7C-1
Shock absorber, removal and installation
    front, 10-4
    rear, 10-10
Side and cargo door, removal and installation, 11-8
Side latched window (extended cab models),
    removal and installation, 11-7
Spark plug
    replacement, 1-29
    wire check and replacement, 1-30
Stabilizer bar, removal and installation, 10-5
Starter motor
    and circuit, check, 5-12
    removal and installation, 5-13
Starter safety switch check, 1-23
Starter solenoid, removal and installation, 5-14
Starting system, general information and
    precautions, 5-12
Steering system
    gear, removal and installation, 10-14
    general information, 10-3
    knuckle removal and installation
        2WD models, 10-7
        4WD models, 10-9
    linkage, inspection, removal and installation, 10-12
    power steering
        pump, removal and installation, 10-14
        system, bleeding, 10-15
    wheel, removal and installation, 10-11
Suspension and steering systems, 10-1 through 10-16
    check, 1-18
    systems, general information, 10-3
    Switches, removal and installation, 12-5

T

Tailgate, removal and installation, 11-10
Thermostat, check and replacement, 3-4
Thermostatic air cleaner, 1-29, 6-25
Throttle body
    mounting bolt torque check, 1-23
    removal and installation, 4-9
Throttle Body Injection (TBI)
    system, 4-5
    unit, component replacement, 4-10
Throttle cable, removal and installation, 4-9
Throttle linkage inspection, 1-23
Throttle Position Sensor (TPS), check and
    replacement, 6-12
Throttle valve (TV) cable (4L60/700R-4), replacement
    and adjustment, 7B-3
Timing cover, chain and sprockets, removal and
    installation, 2A-12
Tire and tire pressure checks, 1-11
Tire rotation, 1-20
Tools, 0-11
Top Dead Center (TDC) for number one piston,
    locating, 2A-12
Torsion bar (4WD models), removal and
    installation, 10-10
Towing the vehicle, 0-16
Transfer case, 7C-1 through 7C-4
    general information, 7C-1
    lubricant level check (4WD models only), 1-19
    overhaul, 7C-3
    removal and installation, 7C-2
    seal replacement, 7C-2
    shift lever, replacement, 7C-1
    shift linkage, check and adjustment, 7C-1
Transmission
    automatic, 7B-1 through 7B-6
        diagnosis, general, 7B-1
        fluid and filter change, 1-23
        fluid level check, 1-12
        general information, 7B-1
        mount, check and replacement, 7B-4
        park/neutral switch, adjustment and
            replacement, 7B-4
        removal and installation, 7B-5
        shift cable (1995 and later models), removal,
            installation and adjustment, 7B-3
        shift linkage (1988 through 1994 models), removal,
            installation and adjustment, 7B-2
        Throttle valve (TV) cable (4L60/700R-4),
            replacement and adjustment, 7B-3
    manual, 7A-1 through 7A-4
        general information, 7A-1
        lubricant change, 1-25
        lubricant level check, 1-19

        oil seal, replacement, 7A-2
        overhaul, general information, 7A-2
        shift lever, removal and installation, 7A-2
        removal and installation, 7A-2
Trouble codes, 6-4
Troubleshooting, 0-21
Tune-up and routine maintenance, 1-1 through 1-32
Tune-up general information, 1-10
Turn signal and hazard flashers, check and
    replacement, 12-3

U

Underhood hose check and replacement, 1-15
Universal joints, removal, overhaul and installation,
    8-9
Upholstery and carpets, maintenance, 11-2
Upper control arm, removal and installation, 10-8

V

Vacuum power brake booster, removal and
    installation, 9-18
Valve
    servicing, 2B-12
    springs, retainers and seals, replacement, 2A-6
Vehicle identification numbers, 0-6
Vehicle Speed Sensor (VSS), check and
    replacement, 6-19
Vinyl trim, maintenance, 11-2

W

Water pump
    check, 3-5
    removal and installation, 3-5
Wheel
    bearing check (front), repack and adjustment (2WD
        models only), 1-26
    cylinder, removal, overhaul and installation, 9-14
Wheels and tires, general information, 10-15
Window
    end gate, removal and installation, 11-8
    power system, description and check, 12-10
    rear, wiper motor, removal and installation, 12-9
    side latched (extended cab models), removal and
        installation, 11-7
Windshield and fixed glass, replacement, 11-3
Windshield wiper motor, removal and installation, 12-9
Wiper blade inspection and replacement, 1-16
Wiring diagrams, general information, 12-12
Working facilities, 0-8

Haynes Automotive Manuals

NOTE: New manuals are added to this list on a periodic basis. If you do not see a listing for your vehicle, consult your local Haynes dealer for the latest product information.

ACURA
12020 **Integra** '86 thru '89 & **Legend** '86 thru '90
12021 **Integra** '90 thru '93 & **Legend** '91 thru '95

AMC
     Jeep CJ - *see JEEP (50020)*
14020 **Mid-size models** '70 thru '83
14025 **(Renault) Alliance & Encore** '83 thru '87

AUDI
15020 **4000** all models '80 thru '87
15025 **5000** all models '77 thru '83
15026 **5000** all models '84 thru '88

AUSTIN-HEALEY
     Sprite - *see MG Midget (66015)*

BMW
*18020 **3/5 Series** not including diesel or all-wheel drive models '82 thru '92
18021 **3-Series** incl. Z3 models '92 thru '98
18025 **320i** all 4 cyl models '75 thru '83
18050 **1500 thru 2002** except Turbo '59 thru '77

BUICK
*19010 **Buick Century** '97 thru '02
     Century (front-wheel drive) - *see GM (38005)*
*19020 **Buick, Oldsmobile & Pontiac Full-size** (Front-wheel drive) '85 thru '02
     Buick Electra, LeSabre and Park Avenue; **Oldsmobile** Delta 88 Royale, Ninety Eight and Regency; **Pontiac** Bonneville
19025 **Buick Oldsmobile & Pontiac Full-size** (Rear wheel drive)
     Buick Estate '70 thru '90, Electra '70 thru '84, LeSabre '70 thru '85, Limited '74 thru '79 **Oldsmobile** Custom Cruiser '70 thru '90, Delta 88 '70 thru '85, Ninety-eight '70 thru '84 **Pontiac** Bonneville '70 thru '81, Catalina '70 thru '81, Grandville '70 thru '75, Parisienne '83 thru '86
19030 **Mid-size Regal & Century** all rear-drive models with V6, V8 and Turbo '74 thru '87
     Regal - *see GENERAL MOTORS (38010)*
     Riviera - *see GENERAL MOTORS (38030)*
     Roadmaster - *see CHEVROLET (24046)*
     Skyhawk - *see GENERAL MOTORS (38015)*
     Skylark - *see GM (38020, 38025)*
     Somerset - *see GENERAL MOTORS (38025)*

CADILLAC
21030 **Cadillac Rear Wheel Drive** all gasoline models '70 thru '93
     Cimarron - *see GENERAL MOTORS (38015)*
     DeVille - *see GM (38031 & 38032)*
     Eldorado - *see GM (38030 & 38031)*
     Fleetwood - *see GM (38031)*
     Seville - *see GM (38030, 38031 & 38032)*

CHEVROLET
*24010 **Astro & GMC Safari Mini-vans** '85 thru '03
24015 **Camaro V8** all models '70 thru '81
24016 **Camaro** all models '82 thru '92
24017 **Camaro & Firebird** '93 thru '02
     Cavalier - *see GENERAL MOTORS (38016)*
     Celebrity - *see GENERAL MOTORS (38005)*
24020 **Chevelle, Malibu & El Camino** '69 thru '87
24024 **Chevette & Pontiac T1000** '76 thru '87
     Citation - *see GENERAL MOTORS (38020)*
24032 **Corsica/Beretta** all models '87 thru '96
24040 **Corvette** all V8 models '68 thru '82
24041 **Corvette** all models '84 thru '96
10305 **Chevrolet Engine Overhaul Manual**
24045 **Full-size Sedans** Caprice, Impala, Biscayne, Bel Air & Wagons '69 thru '90
24046 **Impala SS & Caprice and Buick Roadmaster** '91 thru '96
     Impala - *see LUMINA (24048)*
     Lumina '90 thru '94 - *see GM (38010)*
*24048 **Lumina & Monte Carlo** '95 thru '03
     Lumina APV - *see GM (38035)*
24050 **Luv Pick-up** all 2WD & 4WD '72 thru '82
     Malibu '97 thru '00 - *see GM (38026)*
24055 **Monte Carlo** all models '70 thru '88
     Monte Carlo '95 thru '01 - *see LUMINA (24048)*

24059 **Nova** all V8 models '69 thru '79
24060 **Nova and Geo Prizm** '85 thru '92
24064 **Pick-ups '67 thru '87** - Chevrolet & GMC, all V8 & in-line 6 cyl, 2WD & 4WD '67 thru '87; Suburbans, Blazers & Jimmys '67 thru '91
24065 **Pick-ups '88 thru '98** - Chevrolet & GMC, full-size pick-ups '88 thru '98, C/K Classic '99 & '00, Blazer & Jimmy '92 thru '94; Suburban '92 thru '99; Tahoe & Yukon '95 thru '99
*24066 **Pick-ups '99 thru '03** - Chevrolet Silverado & GMC Sierra full-size pick-ups '99 thru '02, Suburban/Tahoe/Yukon/Yukon XL '00 thru '02
24070 **S-10 & S-15 Pick-ups** '82 thru '93, Blazer & Jimmy '83 thru '94,
*24071 **S-10 & S-15 Pick-ups** '94 thru '01, **Blazer & Jimmy** '95 thru '01, **Hombre** '96 thru '01
*24072 **Chevrolet TrailBlazer & TrailBlazer EXT, GMC Envoy & Envoy XL, Oldsmobile Bravada** '02 and '03
24075 **Sprint** '85 thru '88 & **Geo Metro** '89 thru '01
24080 **Vans - Chevrolet & GMC** '68 thru '96

CHRYSLER
25015 **Chrysler Cirrus, Dodge Stratus, Plymouth Breeze** '95 thru '00
10310 **Chrysler Engine Overhaul Manual**
25020 **Full-size Front-Wheel Drive** '88 thru '93
     K-Cars - *see DODGE Aries (30008)*
     Laser - *see DODGE Daytona (30030)*
25025 **Chrysler LHS, Concorde, New Yorker, Dodge Intrepid, Eagle Vision,** '93 thru '97
*25026 **Chrysler LHS, Concorde, 300M, Dodge Intrepid,** '98 thru '03
25030 **Chrysler & Plymouth Mid-size** front wheel drive '82 thru '95
     Rear-wheel Drive - *see Dodge (30050)*
*25035 **PT Cruiser** all models '01 thru '03
*25040 **Chrysler Sebring, Dodge Avenger** '95 thru '02

DATSUN
28005 **200SX** all models '80 thru '83
28007 **B-210** all models '73 thru '78
28009 **210** all models '79 thru '82
28012 **240Z, 260Z & 280Z** Coupe '70 thru '78
28014 **280ZX** Coupe & 2+2 '79 thru '83
     300ZX - *see NISSAN (72010)*
28016 **310** all models '78 thru '82
28018 **510 & PL521 Pick-up** '68 thru '73
28020 **510** all models '78 thru '81
28022 **620 Series Pick-up** all models '73 thru '79
     720 Series Pick-up - *see NISSAN (72030)*
28025 **810/Maxima** all gasoline models, '77 thru '84

DODGE
     400 & 600 - *see CHRYSLER (25030)*
30008 **Aries & Plymouth Reliant** '81 thru '89
30010 **Caravan & Plymouth Voyager** '84 thru '95
*30011 **Caravan & Plymouth Voyager** '96 thru '02
30012 **Challenger/Plymouth Saporro** '78 thru '83
30016 **Colt & Plymouth Champ** '78 thru '87
30020 **Dakota Pick-ups** all models '87 thru '96
*30021 **Durango** '98 & '99, **Dakota** '97 thru '99
30025 **Dart, Demon, Plymouth Barracuda, Duster & Valiant** 6 cyl models '67 thru '76
30030 **Daytona & Chrysler Laser** '84 thru '89
     Intrepid - *see CHRYSLER (25025, 25026)*
*30034 **Neon** all models '95 thru '99
30035 **Omni & Plymouth Horizon** '78 thru '90
30040 **Pick-ups** all full-size models '74 thru '93
*30041 **Pick-ups** all full-size models '94 thru '01
30045 **Ram 50/D50 Pick-ups & Raider and Plymouth Arrow Pick-ups** '79 thru '93
30050 **Dodge/Plymouth/Chrysler** RWD '71 thru '89
30055 **Shadow & Plymouth Sundance** '87 thru '94
30060 **Spirit & Plymouth Acclaim** '89 thru '95
*30065 **Vans - Dodge & Plymouth** '71 thru '03

EAGLE
     Talon - *see MITSUBISHI (68030, 68031)*
     Vision - *see CHRYSLER (25025)*

FIAT
34010 **124 Sport Coupe & Spider** '68 thru '78
34025 **X1/9** all models '74 thru '80

FORD
10355 **Ford Automatic Transmission Overhaul**
36004 **Aerostar Mini-vans** all models '86 thru '97
36006 **Contour & Mercury Mystique** '95 thru '00
36008 **Courier Pick-up** all models '72 thru '82
*36012 **Crown Victoria & Mercury Grand Marquis** '88 thru '00
10320 **Ford Engine Overhaul Manual**
36016 **Escort/Mercury Lynx** all models '81 thru '90
36020 **Escort/Mercury Tracer** '91 thru '00
36022 **Ford Escape & Mazda Tribute** '01 thru '03
36024 **Explorer & Mazda Navajo** '91 thru '01
36025 **Ford Explorer & Mercury Mountaineer** '02 and '03
36028 **Fairmont & Mercury Zephyr** '78 thru '83
36030 **Festiva & Aspire** '88 thru '97
36032 **Fiesta** all models '77 thru '80
*36034 **Focus** all models '00 and '01
36036 **Ford & Mercury Full-size** '75 thru '87
36044 **Ford & Mercury Mid-size** '75 thru '86
36048 **Mustang V8** all models '64-1/2 thru '73
36049 **Mustang II** 4 cyl, V6 & V8 models '74 thru '78
36050 **Mustang & Mercury Capri** all models Mustang, '79 thru '93; Capri, '79 thru '86
*36051 **Mustang** all models '94 thru '03
36054 **Pick-ups & Bronco** '73 thru '79
36058 **Pick-ups & Bronco** '80 thru '96
*36059 **F-150 & Expedition** '97 thru '02, **F-250** '97 thru '99 & **Lincoln Navigator** '98 thru '02
*36060 **Super Duty Pick-ups, Excursion** '97 thru '02
36062 **Pinto & Mercury Bobcat** '75 thru '80
36066 **Probe** all models '89 thru '92
36070 **Ranger/Bronco II** gasoline models '83 thru '92
*36071 **Ranger** '93 thru '00 & **Mazda Pick-ups** '94 thru '00
36074 **Taurus & Mercury Sable** '86 thru '95
*36075 **Taurus & Mercury Sable** '96 thru '01
36078 **Tempo & Mercury Topaz** '84 thru '94
36082 **Thunderbird/Mercury Cougar** '83 thru '88
36086 **Thunderbird/Mercury Cougar** '89 and '97
36090 **Vans** all V8 Econoline models '69 thru '91
*36094 **Vans** full size '92 thru '01
*36097 **Windstar Mini-van** '95 thru '03

GENERAL MOTORS
10360 **GM Automatic Transmission Overhaul**
38005 **Buick Century, Chevrolet Celebrity, Oldsmobile Cutlass Ciera & Pontiac 6000** all models '82 thru '96
*38010 **Buick Regal, Chevrolet Lumina, Oldsmobile Cutlass Supreme & Pontiac Grand Prix** (FWD) '88 thru '02
38015 **Buick Skyhawk, Cadillac Cimarron, Chevrolet Cavalier, Oldsmobile Firenza & Pontiac J-2000 & Sunbird** '82 thru '94
*38016 **Chevrolet Cavalier & Pontiac Sunfire** '95 thru '04
38020 **Buick Skylark, Chevrolet Citation, Olds Omega, Pontiac Phoenix** '80 thru '85
38025 **Buick Skylark & Somerset, Oldsmobile Achieva & Calais and Pontiac Grand Am** all models '85 thru '98
*38026 **Chevrolet Malibu, Olds Alero & Cutlass, Pontiac Grand Am** '97 thru '00
38030 **Cadillac Eldorado** '71 thru '85, **Seville** '80 thru '85, **Oldsmobile Toronado** '71 thru '85, **Buick Riviera** '79 thru '85
*38031 **Cadillac Eldorado & Seville** '86 thru '91, **DeVille** '86 thru '93, **Fleetwood & Olds Toronado** '86 thru '92, **Buick Riviera** '86 thru '93
38032 **Cadillac DeVille** '94 thru '02 **& Seville** - '92 thru '02
38035 **Chevrolet Lumina APV, Olds Silhouette & Pontiac Trans Sport** all models '90 thru '96
*38036 **Chevrolet Venture, Olds Silhouette, Pontiac Trans Sport & Montana** '97 thru '01
     General Motors Full-size Rear-wheel Drive - *see BUICK (19025)*

GEO
     Metro - *see CHEVROLET Sprint (24075)*
     Prizm - '85 thru '92 see CHEVY (24060), '93 thru '02 see TOYOTA Corolla (92036)

(Continued on other side)

* Listings shown with an asterisk (*) indicate model coverage as of this printing. These titles will be periodically updated to include later model years - consult your Haynes dealer for more information.

Haynes North America, Inc., 861 Lawrence Drive, Newbury Park, CA 91320-1514 • (805) 498-6703

Haynes Automotive Manuals (continued)

40030 **Storm** all models '90 thru '93
Tracker - see SUZUKI Samurai (90010)

GMC
Vans & Pick-ups - see CHEVROLET

HONDA
42010 **Accord CVCC** all models '76 thru '83
42011 **Accord** all models '84 thru '89
42012 **Accord** all models '90 thru '93
42013 **Accord** all models '94 thru '97
*42014 **Accord** all models '98 thru '02
42020 **Civic 1200** all models '73 thru '79
42021 **Civic 1300 & 1500 CVCC** '80 thru '83
42022 **Civic 1500 CVCC** all models '75 thru '79
42023 **Civic** all models '84 thru '91
42024 **Civic & del Sol** '92 thru '95
*42025 **Civic** '96 thru '00, **CR-V** '97 thru '00, **Acura Integra** '94 thru '00
42026 **Civic** '01 thru '04, **CR-V** '02 thru '04
42040 **Prelude CVCC** all models '79 thru '89

HYUNDAI
*43010 **Elantra** all models '96 thru '01
43015 **Excel & Accent** all models '86 thru '98

ISUZU
Hombre - see CHEVROLET S-10 (24071)
*47017 **Rodeo** '91 thru '02; **Amigo** '89 thru '94 and '98 thru '02; **Honda Passport** '95 thru '02
47020 **Trooper & Pick-up** '81 thru '93

JAGUAR
49010 **XJ6** all 6 cyl models '68 thru '86
49011 **XJ6** all models '88 thru '94
49015 **XJ12 & XJS** all 12 cyl models '72 thru '85

JEEP
50010 **Cherokee, Comanche & Wagoneer Limited** all models '84 thru '01
50020 **CJ** all models '49 thru '86
*50025 **Grand Cherokee** all models '93 thru '04
50029 **Grand Wagoneer & Pick-up** '72 thru '91
Grand Wagoneer '84 thru '91, Cherokee & Wagoneer '72 thru '83, Pick-up '72 thru '88
*50030 **Wrangler** all models '87 thru '00
50035 **Liberty** '02 thru '04

LEXUS
ES 300 - see TOYOTA Camry (92007)

LINCOLN
Navigator - see FORD Pick-up (36059)
*59010 **Rear-Wheel Drive** all models '70 thru '01

MAZDA
61010 **GLC Hatchback** (rear-wheel drive) '77 thru '83
61011 **GLC** (front-wheel drive) '81 thru '85
61015 **323 & Protegé** '90 thru '00
*61016 **MX-5 Miata** '90 thru '97
61020 **MPV** all models '89 thru '94
Navajo - see Ford Explorer (36024)
61030 **Pick-ups** '72 thru '93
Pick-ups '94 thru '00 - see Ford Ranger (36071)
61035 **RX-7** all models '79 thru '85
61036 **RX-7** all models '86 thru '91
61040 **626** (rear-wheel drive) all models '79 thru '82
61041 **626/MX-6** (front-wheel drive) '83 thru '92
61042 **626** '93 thru '01, **MX-6/Ford Probe** '93 thru '97

MERCEDES-BENZ
63012 **123 Series Diesel** '76 thru '85
63015 **190 Series** four-cyl gas models, '84 thru '88
63020 **230/250/280** 6 cyl sohc models '68 thru '72
63025 **280 123 Series** gasoline models '77 thru '81
63030 **350 & 450** all models '71 thru '80

MERCURY
64200 **Villager & Nissan Quest** '93 thru '01
All other titles, see FORD Listing.

MG
66010 **MGB** Roadster & GT Coupe '62 thru '80
66015 **MG Midget, Austin Healey Sprite** '58 thru '80

MITSUBISHI
68020 **Cordia, Tredia, Galant, Precis & Mirage** '83 thru '93
68030 **Eclipse, Eagle Talon & Ply. Laser** '90 thru '94
*68031 **Eclipse** '95 thru '01, **Eagle Talon** '95 thru '98
68035 **Mitsubishi Galant** '94 thru '03
68040 **Pick-up** '83 thru '96 & **Montero** '83 thru '93

NISSAN
72010 **300ZX** all models including Turbo '84 thru '89
72015 **Altima** all models '93 thru '04
72020 **Maxima** all models '85 thru '92
*72021 **Maxima** all models '93 thru '01
72030 **Pick-ups** '80 thru '97 **Pathfinder** '87 thru '95
*72031 **Frontier Pick-up** '98 thru '01, **Xterra** '00 & '01, **Pathfinder** '96 thru '01
72040 **Pulsar** all models '83 thru '86
Quest - see MERCURY Villager (64200)
72050 **Sentra** all models '82 thru '94
72051 **Sentra & 200SX** all models '95 thru '99
72060 **Stanza** all models '82 thru '90

OLDSMOBILE
73015 **Cutlass** V6 & V8 gas models '74 thru '88
For other OLDSMOBILE titles, see BUICK, CHEVROLET or GENERAL MOTORS listing.

PLYMOUTH
For PLYMOUTH titles, see DODGE listing.

PONTIAC
79008 **Fiero** all models '84 thru '88
79018 **Firebird** V8 models except Turbo '70 thru '81
79019 **Firebird** all models '82 thru '92
79040 **Mid-size Rear-wheel Drive** '70 thru '87
For other PONTIAC titles, see BUICK, CHEVROLET or GENERAL MOTORS listing.

PORSCHE
80020 **911** except Turbo & Carrera 4 '65 thru '89
80025 **914** all 4 cyl models '69 thru '76
80030 **924** all models including Turbo '76 thru '82
80035 **944** all models including Turbo '83 thru '89

RENAULT
Alliance & Encore - see AMC (14020)

SAAB
*84010 **900** all models including Turbo '79 thru '88

SATURN
*87010 **Saturn** all models '91 thru '02
87020 **Saturn** all L-series models '00 thru '04

SUBARU
89002 **1100, 1300, 1400 & 1600** '71 thru '79
89003 **1600 & 1800** 2WD & 4WD '80 thru '94

SUZUKI
90010 **Samurai/Sidekick & Geo Tracker** '86 thru '01

TOYOTA
92005 **Camry** all models '83 thru '91
92006 **Camry** all models '92 thru '96
*92007 **Camry, Avalon, Solara, Lexus ES 300** '97 thru '01
92015 **Celica Rear Wheel Drive** '71 thru '85
92020 **Celica Front Wheel Drive** '86 thru '99
92025 **Celica Supra** all models '79 thru '92
92030 **Corolla** all models '75 thru '79
92032 **Corolla** all rear wheel drive models '80 thru '87
92035 **Corolla** all front wheel drive models '84 thru '92
92036 **Corolla & Geo Prizm** '93 thru '02
92040 **Corolla Tercel** all models '80 thru '82
92045 **Corona** all models '74 thru '82
92050 **Cressida** all models '78 thru '82
92055 **Land Cruiser** FJ40, 43, 45, 55 '68 thru '82
92056 **Land Cruiser** FJ60, 62, 80, FZJ80 '80 thru '96
92065 **MR2** all models '85 thru '87
92070 **Pick-up** all models '69 thru '78
92075 **Pick-up** all models '79 thru '95
*92076 **Tacoma** '95 thru '00, **4Runner** '96 thru '00, **& T100** '93 thru '98
*92078 **Tundra** '00 thru '02 & **Sequoia** '01 thru '02
92080 **Previa** all models '91 thru '95

*92082 **RAV4** all models '96 thru '02
92085 **Tercel** all models '87 thru '94

TRIUMPH
94007 **Spitfire** all models '62 thru '81
94010 **TR7** all models '75 thru '81

VW
96008 **Beetle & Karmann Ghia** '54 thru '79
*96009 **New Beetle** '98 thru '00
96016 **Rabbit, Jetta, Scirocco & Pick-up** gas models '74 thru '91 & Convertible '80 thru '92
96017 **Golf, GTI & Jetta** '93 thru '98 & **Cabrio** '95 thru '98
*96018 **Golf, GTI, Jetta & Cabrio** '99 thru '02
96020 **Rabbit, Jetta & Pick-up** diesel '77 thru '84
96023 **Passat** '98 thru '01, **Audi A4** '96 thru '01
96030 **Transporter 1600** all models '68 thru '79
96035 **Transporter 1700, 1800 & 2000** '72 thru '79
96040 **Type 3 1500 & 1600** all models '63 thru '73
96045 **Vanagon** all air-cooled models '80 thru '83

VOLVO
97010 **120, 130 Series & 1800 Sports** '61 thru '73
97015 **140 Series** all models '66 thru '74
97020 **240 Series** all models '76 thru '93
97040 **740 & 760 Series** all models '82 thru '88
97050 **850 Series** all models '93 thru '97

TECHBOOK MANUALS
10205 **Automotive Computer Codes**
10210 **Automotive Emissions Control Manual**
10215 **Fuel Injection Manual, 1978 thru 1985**
10220 **Fuel Injection Manual, 1986 thru 1999**
10225 **Holley Carburetor Manual**
10230 **Rochester Carburetor Manual**
10240 **Weber/Zenith/Stromberg/SU Carburetors**
10305 **Chevrolet Engine Overhaul Manual**
10310 **Chrysler Engine Overhaul Manual**
10320 **Ford Engine Overhaul Manual**
10330 **GM and Ford Diesel Engine Repair Manual**
10340 **Small Engine Repair Manual, 5 HP & Less**
10341 **Small Engine Repair Manual, 5.5 - 20 HP**
10345 **Suspension, Steering & Driveline Manual**
10355 **Ford Automatic Transmission Overhaul**
10360 **GM Automatic Transmission Overhaul**
10405 **Automotive Body Repair & Painting**
10410 **Automotive Brake Manual**
10411 **Automotive Anti-lock Brake (ABS) Systems**
10415 **Automotive Detailing Manual**
10420 **Automotive Eelectrical Manual**
10425 **Automotive Heating & Air Conditioning**
10430 **Automotive Reference Manual & Dictionary**
10435 **Automotive Tools Manual**
10440 **Used Car Buying Guide**
10445 **Welding Manual**
10450 **ATV Basics**

SPANISH MANUALS
98903 **Reparación de Carrocería & Pintura**
98905 **Códigos Automotrices de la Computadora**
98910 **Frenos Automotriz**
98915 **Inyección de Combustible 1986 al 1999**
99040 **Chevrolet & GMC Camionetas** '67 al '87 Incluye Suburban, Blazer & Jimmy '67 al '91
99041 **Chevrolet & GMC Camionetas** '88 al '98 Incluye Suburban '92 al '98, Blazer & Jimmy '92 al '94, Tahoe y Yukon '95 al '98
99042 **Chevrolet & GMC Camionetas Cerradas** '68 al '95
99055 **Dodge Caravan & Plymouth Voyager** '84 al '95
99075 **Ford Camionetas y Bronco** '80 al '94
99077 **Ford Camionetas Cerradas** '69 al '91
99088 **Ford Modelos de Tamaño Mediano** '75 al '86
99091 **Ford Taurus & Mercury Sable** '86 al '95
99095 **GM Modelos de Tamaño Grande** '70 al '90
99100 **GM Modelos de Tamaño Mediano** '70 al '88
99110 **Nissan Camioneta** '80 al '96, **Pathfinder** '87 al '95
99118 **Nissan Sentra** '82 al '94
99125 **Toyota Camionetas y 4Runner** '79 al '95

Over 100 Haynes motorcycle manuals also available